SCOTTISH LEAGUE PLAYERS' RECORDS

SCOTTISH FOOTBALL LEAGUE DIVISIONS A AND ONE
1946/47 to 1974/75

Published in Great Britain by Tony Brown,
4 Adrian Close, Beeston, Nottingham NG9 6FL.
Telephone 0115 973 6086. E-mail soccer@innotts.co.uk
First published 2004

*SoccerData is a specialist publisher of books on association football. Publications
include 'Definitive' club histories and season-by-season guides from 1888/89 to
the 1950s. Please write to the address above for a catalogue or visit the web site.*

Printed by the Book Factory

ISBN 1 899468 65 X

INTRODUCTION

This second volume of Scottish League Players' Records provides details of the career of every player that made an appearance in Division One (or Division "A") of the Scottish League between 1946/47 and 1974/75. Whenever possible we have included details of his career elsewhere, such as the Football League, abroad, or in the lower divisions of the Scottish League; however this information (especially with regard to the Scottish League Division Two) is not comprehensive and has been included only to give as complete a record as possible of each player's career.

Statistics for the First Division have been compiled by Richard Beal, with the remaining information collated by Steve Emms, using sources such as Rothmans Yearbooks, club histories and "who's who" books that have been published on Scottish clubs. Thanks are therefore due to the authors of these books, and also to Duncan Watt, Jim Stewart, Jim Jeffrey, Peter McLeish and Les Zammit, all of whom have provided additional information from their own records. My thanks also go to Derek Gray for his work on Scottish Premier Division records (which we published in 2002) and to Tony Brown for his advice and assistance in publishing the series.

Work on the third volume, covering the pre-war period from 1890 to 1939, is currently in progress. Information on this period of Scottish football is sadly very limited, and the authors would therefore be pleased to hear from any club historian who feels that he or she can assist with the project. All assistance will of course be acknowledged, and will help to ensure that the information in the book is as accurate as possible. Please write to the publisher or direct to me at 28 Briar Close, Evesham, WR11 4JQ.

Steve Emms
May 2004

KEY TO THE STATISTICS

The "Macs' will be found separately at the end of the list of players whose surnames begin with the letter "M". Under each player's name the first line gives (where known) their place and date of birth and similar information for their death. Details of international caps are also shown. Beneath this, the information is divided into six columns.

The first column lists the clubs played for, followed by a column showing the seasons spent at each club; an "L" or "T" against the season indicates that the player was either on loan or on trial at the club. This is followed by three columns giving the number of times the player appeared in the starting line-up, the number of appearances made as a substitute, and the number of goals scored. All figures relate to League games only.

The final columns shows which division or league the statistics relate to. "P" indicates the Premier division of the Scottish League, and "D1", "D2" and "D3" the other Scottish divisions. For a time after the Second World War the leagues were identified by letters (A, B and C) rather than by numbers, but we have used the divisional numbers throughout for ease of reference. "FL" indicates the English Football League or Premiership, "NA" the North American Soccer League, "NP" the Northern Professional Soccer League and "NL" to the Northern Premier League. No entry in this column indicates that the club was either non-league or foreign.

In some places an asterisk appears against a club's name. This indicates that although a player of the same name (or at least with the same initials) made the appearances listed, we have not been able to confirm that this is the same player. Again, correspondence will be welcome.

ABEL Gregor
b. Falkirk 9.4.1949
Falkirk
Bo'ness U   L

Club	Season	Apps	Sub	Gls	Div
Falkirk	69/70	23			D2
	70/71	29			D1
	71/72	18			D1
Clydebank	72/73	26	4		D2
	73/74	29	3		D2
	74/75	38			D2
	75/76	24			D2
	76/77	39			D1
	77/78	25	1		P
	78/79	37			D1
	79/80	9			D1
Alloa A	79/80	18			D2
	80/81	6	1		D2

ACKERMAN Alfred Arthur Eric
b. Daspoort, S Africa 5.1.1929
d. Dunnottar, S Africa 10.7.1988
Pretoria Municipal

Club	Season	Apps	Gls	Div
Clyde	47/48	2	1	D1
	48/49	10	7	D1
	49/50	21	12	D1
Hull C	50/51	34	21	FL
Norwich C	51/52	28	6	FL
	52/53	29	20	FL
	53/54	9	5	FL
Hull C	53/54	29	17	FL
	54/55	29	11	FL
Derby Co	54/55	7	2	FL
	55/56	19	15	FL
	56/57	10	4	FL
Carlisle U	56/57	28	20	FL
	57/58	46	35	FL
	58/59	23	7	FL
Millwall	58/59	14	7	FL
	59/60	37	18	FL
	60/61	30	10	FL
Dartford				

ADAIR Gerald William
b. Edinburgh 16.2.1955
West Bromwich A

Club	Season	Apps	Sub	Gls	Div
Hibernian	73/74	4			D1
	74/75				D1
Dunfermline A	75/76	19	1	1	D1
Meadowbank T	76/77	11	2	2	D2
	77/78	23	4	5	D2
	78/79	21		7	D2
Armadale Thistle					

ADAM James
b. Blantyre 13.5.1931
Blantyre Celtic

Club	Season	Apps	Gls	Div
Aldershot	50/51			FL
Spennymoor U	51/52			
	52/53			
Luton T	53/54	3		FL
	54/55	25	9	FL
	55/56	30	5	FL
	56/57	18	1	FL
	57/58	32	3	FL
	58/59	29	4	FL
Aston Villa	59/60	21	3	FL
	60/61	3		FL
Stoke C	61/62	22	7	FL
Falkirk	62/63	20	4	D1
	63/64	2		D1
South Melbourne Hellas				

ADAMS James

Club	Season	Apps	Div
Morton	69/70	1	D1

ADAMS Edward
Newtongrange Star

Club	Season	Apps	Div
Queen of the South	54/55	3	D1
	55/56		D1
	56/57		D1
Cowdenbeath	57/58		D2
Eyemouth U			

ADAMS George
b. Glasgow c1951
Petershill

Club	Season	Apps	Sub	Gls	Div
Aberdeen	69/70	1			D1
	70/71				
	71/72				
	72/73				
Partick T	73/74	1			D1
Stranraer	73/74	1			D2
Alloa A	73/74	4		4	D2
East Stirlingshire	74/75	27	6	2	D2
	75/76	20		4	D2

ADAMS Peter

Club	Season	Apps	Gls	Div
Third Lanark	50/51	21	1	D1
	51/52	4		D1

ADAMS Thomas
b. Glasgow 12.2.1916 d. ?.10.1984
Neilston V

Club	Season	Apps	Gls	Div
East Fife	35/36	33	14	D2
	36/37	30	11	D2
	37/38	30	8	D2
	38/39	32	16	D2
	46/47	23	3	D2
	47/48	28	5	D2
	48/49	14	5	D1
Forfar A	49/50	27	5	D2
	50/51			D2
	51/52			D2

ADAMSON Robert

Club	Season	Apps	Sub	Gls	Div
Dundee	60/61	8		1	D1
Raith R	61/62	24		6	D1
	62/63	27		8	D1
Morton	63/64	18		8	D2
	64/65	8		2	D1
St Mirren	65/66	33		13	D1
	66/67	23		2	D1
	67/68	29	2	16	D2
	68/69	28		7	D1
	69/70	8			D1
Arbroath	69/70	5			D2

ADDISON Derek
b. 8.7.1955
Lochee U

Club	Season	Apps	Sub	Gls	Div
Dundee U	73/74	4			D1
	74/75	6	1	1	D1
	75/76	3	1		P
	76/77	6		7	P
	77/78	18	2	3	P
	78/79	24	4	3	P
	79/80	13	4		P
	80/81	11	3	1	P
Heart of Midlothian	81/82	32		4	D1
St Johnstone	82/83	36		2	D1
	83/84	18	1		P
	84/85	13			D1
	85/86	30		1	D2
Brechin C	86/87	1			D1

ADDISON Eric
Berwick R
Falkirk

Club	Season	Apps	Gls	Div
Stirling A	60/61			D2
	61/62	3	1	D1
Montrose				

ADDISON Ian
Dundonald Bluebell

Club	Season	Apps	Div
East Fife	50/51	4	D1
Dunfermline A			
Berwick R			

ADIE John
b. Windygates 2.3.1930 d. 9.9.1994
Windygates Juveniles

Club	Season	Apps	Div
Heart of Midlothian	47/48		D1
	48/49	4	D1
	49/50		D1
	50/51	2	D1
	51/52	10	D1
	52/53	7	D1
	53/54	26	D1
	54/55	7	D1
East Fife	55/56	28	D1
	56/57	8	D1
	57/58	5	D1
Dundee U	58/59	5	D2

AGNEW James

Club	Season	Apps	Gls	Div
Clyde	46/47	2		D1
	47/48	3	1	D1

AHERN Brian
b. Glasgow 15.11.1952
St Lukes BG

Club	Season	Apps	Sub	Gls	Div
Clyde	71/72	13			D1
	72/73	34		9	D2
	73/74	31	2	2	D1
	74/75	33		1	D1
	75/76	25		1	D1
	76/77	30	1	12	D2
	77/78	39		6	D2
	78/79	38	1	8	D1
	79/80	34		2	D1
	80/81	39		12	D2
Ayr U	81/82	36	1	4	D1
	82/83	32	1	5	D1
Clyde	83/84	32	4	3	D1
	84/85	34	3	2	D1
	85/86	35		4	D1
	86/87	3	5	1	D1
Albion R	87/88	33			D2

AIKMAN Archibald Webster
b. Falkirk c1925 d. 19.2.1998
Heart of Midlothian

Club	Season	Apps	Gls	Div
St Mirren	46/47	21	9	D1
Falkirk	47/48	27	20	D1
	48/49	28	21	D1
Manchester C	49/50			FL
	50/51			FL
	51/52			FL
	52/53			FL
Falkirk	53/54	9	2	D1
	54/55			D1
Dundee U	54/55	11	6	D2
	55/56	30	8	D2
	56/57	14	3	D2

AIRD H

Club	Season	Apps	Div
Morton	50/51	1	D1
	51/52	1	D1

AIRD Kenneth
b. Glasgow 13.4.1947
Drumchapel Amateurs
Celtic

Club	Season	Apps	Sub	Gls	Div
St Mirren	65/66	17		1	D1
	66/67	19		2	D1
St Johnstone	67/68	30	1	7	D1
	68/69	32		8	D1
	69/70	32		5	D1
	70/71	24		2	D1
	71/72	30		6	D1
	72/73	12		4	D1
Heart of Midlothian	72/73	10			D1
	73/74	17	1	2	D1
	74/75	12		5	D1
	75/76	26	2	7	P
	76/77	13	3		P
Arbroath	77/78	1			D1

AIRD Peter
b. Glencraig 29.8.1921 d. Glenrothes 6.12.2000
Bowhill R

Club	Season	Apps	Goals	Div
Hibernian	46/47	26		D1
	47/48	9		D1
	48/49	7		D1
	49/50	2		D1
East Fife	50/51	12		D1
	51/52	19		D1
	52/53			D1
	53/54	2		D1
Caerphilly T				

AIRD William
b. Glencraig
Bowhill R

Club	Season	Apps	Goals	Div
Morton	46/47	25		D1
Queen of the South	47/48	24	5	D1
	48/49	29		D1
Elgin C	49/50			
Queen of the South	50/51			D2
	51/52	21		D1
Llanelly				

AIRLIE Seton Montgomery
b. Carmyle 22.3.1920
St Josephs Tollcross
St Mungo Juveniles
Greyfriars
Celtic
St Anthonys L
Motherwell T

Club	Season	Apps	Goals	Div
Celtic	46/47	6	3	D1
Cannes				
Worcester C				

AITCHISON Robert
b. Edinburgh 11.11.1943
Edinburgh Emmet
St Bernards
Newtongrange Star

Club	Season	Apps	Goals	Div
Heart of Midlothian	63/64			D1
	64/65			D1
	65/66	2		D1
	66/67	1		D1
East Fife	67/68	4		D2
Arniston R				
Bonnyrigg Rose				

AITKEN Andrew
Annbank U

Club	Season	Apps	Sub	Goals	Div
Ayr U	68/69				D2
	69/70	3	1		D1
	70/71	1			D1

AITKEN Andrew Fox Scott
b. Edinburgh 21.8.1934
Edinburgh Emmet
Cliftonville

Club	Season	Apps	Goals	Div
Hibernian	56/57	9	2	D1
	57/58	6	1	D1
	58/59	17	8	D1
	59/60	3		D1
West Bromwich A	59/60	16		FL
	60/61	6	2	FL
Falkirk	60/61	9	4	D2
	61/62			D1
Raith R	62/63	13	2	D1

AITKEN Andrew Irvine
d. Glasgow 8.6.2000
Shawfield Jnrs
Queen's Park
Third Lanark
Hamilton A

Club	Season	Apps	Goals	Div
Queen's Park	46/47	26	14	D1
	47/48	25	11	D1

AITKEN Charles
b. Gorebridge c1934
Arniston R

Club	Season	Apps	Goals	Div
Motherwell	49/50			D1
	50/51	4	2	D1
	51/52	3		D1
	52/53			D1
	53/54	2		D2
	54/55	27	8	D1
	55/56	28	5	D1
	56/57	33	4	D1
	57/58	34	2	D1
	58/59	33	2	D1
	59/60	31	1	D1
	60/61	13	2	D1
	61/62	31	3	D1
	62/63	26	4	D1
	63/64	23	1	D1
	64/65	11	2	D1
	65/66	14	2	D1

AITKEN David

Club	Season	Apps	Goals	Div
Aberdeen	53/54	2		D1

AITKEN Frederick
Valleyfield Colliery

Club	Season	Apps	Sub	Goals	Div
St Johnstone	66/67	12		2	D1
	67/68	18	1	4	D1
	68/69	30		11	D1
	69/70	31		3	D1
	70/71	15	3	3	D1
	71/72	26		5	D1
	72/73	24	2	5	D1
	73/74	16	1	1	D1
	74/75	2	2	1	D1
Eastern (Hong Kong)					
Alloa A	77/78	2			D1

AITKEN George Graham
b. Lochgelly 28.5.1925
d. Sunderland 22.1.2003 Caps: S - 8
Lochgelly St Andrews
Lochgelly Albert
Wolverhampton W T

Club	Season	Apps	Goals	Div
East Fife	46/47	25	1	D2
	47/48	19	1	D2
	48/49	22	2	D1
	49/50	27	1	D1
Third Lanark	50/51	9		D1
	51/52	11	1	D1
Sunderland	51/52	23		FL
	52/53	35	1	FL
	53/54	34	1	FL
	54/55	36	1	FL
	55/56	41		FL
	56/57	40		FL
	57/58	32		FL
	58/59	4		FL
Gateshead	58/59	14		FL
	59/60	44		FL

AITKEN John
Airdrieonians

Club	Season	Apps	Goals	Div
Ayr U	48/49			D2
	49/50	12	5	D2
Morton	50/51	1	1	D1

AITKEN Morris
b. Valleyfield 16.2.1944
Dundonald Bluebell

Club	Season	Apps	Goals	Div
East Fife	63/64	30	17	D2
	64/65	10	1	D2
	65/66	8	1	D2
Stirling A	65/66	1		D1
Alloa A	66/67	3		D2

AITKEN Robert
b. Markinch

Club	Season	Apps	Goals	Div
Falkirk	46/47	3		D1
	47/48	7	1	D1
Stirling A	48/49			D2
	49/50	1		D1
East Fife	49/50	3	2	D1
	50/51			D1
	51/52	1	1	D1
Brechin C	52/53			D3
	53/54			D3

AITKEN Robert

Club	Season	Apps	Goals	Div
Raith R	67/68	2		D1

AITKENHEAD Jack W
Stoneyburn U

Club	Season	Apps	Goals	Div
Motherwell	49/50	1		D1
	50/51	5		D1
	51/52	3		D1

AITKENHEAD John
b. Cambuslang c. 1924 d. 28.3.1987
Queen's Park

Club	Season	Apps	Goals	Div
Hibernian	46/47	14	6	D1
	47/48	4	1	D1
	48/49	4	3	D1
Motherwell	48/49	7	3	D1
	49/50	29	8	D1
	50/51	22	9	D1
	51/52	29	10	D1
	52/53	27	8	D1
	53/54	24	5	D2
	54/55	7		D1
	55/56	20	6	D1
	56/57	5	1	D1
Hamilton A	56/57	11	4	D2

ALEXANDER Douglas
Westrigg Bluebell

Club	Season	Apps	Goals	Div
Dundee	56/57	1		D1
	57/58	1		D1

ALEXANDER Robert
Kilmarnock Amateurs
Troon
Kilmarnock

Club	Season	Apps	Goals	Div
Hamilton A	64/65	17	9	D2
	65/66	15	3	D1

ALEXANDER Thomas

Club	Season	Apps	Goals	Div
Queen's Park	46/47	5	2	D1
	47/48	29	4	D1
Morton	48/49	10	1	D1
	49/50	26	13	D2
	50/51	17	5	D1
	51/52	18	4	D1

ALEXANDER Thomas

Club	Season	Apps	Sub	Goals	Div
Rangers	70/71	2			D1
	71/72				D1
	72/73				D1
Stranraer	73/74	10	2	2	D2

ALISON James
b. Peebles 11.10.1923

Club	Season	Apps	Goals	Div
Falkirk	46/47	21	4	D1
	47/48	23	2	D1
	48/49	22	4	D1
	49/50	7		D1
Manchester C	49/50	10		FL
	50/51	9		FL
	51/52			FL
Aldershot	52/53	30	6	FL
	53/54	37	1	FL
	54/55	45		FL
	55/56	35	1	FL
	56/57	24		FL
Weymouth				

ALLAN James

Club	Season	Apps		Goals	Div
Stenhousemuir	49/50	24		15	D2
	50/51				D2
	51/52				D2
	52/53	23		14	D2
Stirling A	53/54	6		2	D1
Dunfermline A	53/54	4		2	D2
	54/55				D2
Raith R	55/56	2			D1

ALLAN John
b. Stirling 22.3.1931
Comrie

Club	Season	Apps		Goals	Div
Dunfermline A	53/54	18		4	D2
	54/55				D2
Aberdeen	55/56	17		11	D1
	56/57	4		4	D1
Third Lanark	57/58	34		26	D1
	58/59	3		2	D1
Bradford PA	58/59	10		8	FL
	59/60	33		27	FL
	60/61	28		17	FL
Halifax T	606/1	10		1	FL

ALLAN Robert

Club	Season	Apps		Goals	Div
St Andrews U					
East Fife	57/58	10			D1
	58/59				D2
	59/60				D2
	60/61				D2

ALLAN Thomson Sandlands
b. Longridge 5.10.1946 Caps: S - 2
Holy Cross Academy
Edina Hearts

Club	Season	Apps		Goals	Div
Hibernian	63/64				D1
	64/65				D1
	65/66	12			D1
	66/67	30			D1
	67/68	14			D1
	68/69	13			D1
	69/70	1			D1
Dundee	72/73	29			D1
	73/74	33			D1
	74/75	34			D1
	75/76	36			P
	76/77	10			D1
	77/78	17			D1
	78/79				D1
Meadowbank T	L 78/79	2			D2
Heart of Midlothian	78/79	16			P
	79/80	8			D1
Falkirk	80/81	12			D1

ALLAN William

Club	Season	Apps		Goals	Div
Clyde	50/51	6			D1

ALLAN William

Club	Season	Apps		Goals	Div
Hibernian	50/51	1			D1

ALLAN William

Club	Season	Apps			Goals	Div
Bo'ness U						
Aberdeen	61/62	6			1	D1
	62/63	26				D1
	63/64	3				D1
St Mirren	63/64	25			4	D1
	64/65	1				D1
Falkirk	64/65	24			3	D1
Durban C						
Morton	67/68	31	1		14	D1
	68/69	27	1		2	D1
	69/70	8	2		3	D1
Cowdenbeath	70/71	6				D1
Durban C						
Alloa A						

ALLISON Kenneth
b. Edinburgh 6.1.1937

Club	Season	Apps		Goals	Div
Hibernian	58/59	5		4	D1
Dumbarton	59/60				D2
Cowdenbeath	60/61				D2
	61/62	32		15	D2
	62/63				D2
Darlington	63/64	30		15	FL
	64/65	36		20	FL
	65/66	8		4	FL
Lincoln C	65/66	12		7	FL
	66/67	29	1	6	FL
Rochester Lancers					

ALLISTER John Grandison
b. Edinburgh 30.6.1927
Tranent Jnrs

Club	Season	Apps		Goals	Div
Chelsea	49/50				FL
	50/51				FL
	51/52	3		1	FL
	52/53	1			FL
Aberdeen	52/53	25		2	D1
	53/54	26		5	D1
	54/55	21		4	D1
	55/56	22		1	D1
	56/57	20		6	D1
	57/58	3			D1
Chesterfield	58/59				FL
Deveronvale					

ALMOND Clifford

Club	Season	Apps		Goals	Div
Australia					
Stirling A	54/55	8			D1
Dundee					

ANCELL Robert Francis Dudgeon
b. Dumfries 16.6.1911
d. Monifieth 5.7.1987 Caps: S - 2
Mid Annandale

Club	Season	Apps		Goals	Div
St Mirren	30/31	28			D1
	31/32	31			D1
	32/33	26			D1
	33/34	33			D1
	34/35	38			D1
	35/36				D1
	36/37	2			D1
Newcastle U	36/37	26			FL
	37/38	29			FL
	38/39	42		1	FL
Dundee	46/47	24			D2
	47/48	27			D1
	48/49	7			D1
Aberdeen	48/49	15			D1
Dundee	49/50	6			D1
Berwick R	50/51				D3
	51/52				D3

ANDERSON Alexander
b. Linlithgow
Stenhousemuir

Club	Season	Apps		Goals	Div
Stirling A	49/50	11		3	D1
	50/51				D2
	51/52	28		11	D1
	52/53	29		14	D2
	53/54	9		1	D1
Stenhousemuir	53/54	17		9	D2
	54/55				D2
Dunfermline A	54/55				D2
	55/56	19		3	D1
	56/57	29		3	D1

ANDERSON Alexander
b. Craigneuk 22.6.1939 d. Hamilton ?.12.1997
Lesmahagow Jnrs

Club	Season	Apps		Goals	Div
Hamilton A	57/58	14		4	D2
	58/59	33		16	D2
Rangers	59/60	1			D1
	60/61				D1
	61/62				D1
Hamilton A	L 61/62	34			D2
Queen of the South	62/63	33		4	D1
Hamilton A	63/64	36		5	D2
	64/65	34		5	D2
	65/66	33		7	D1
Clyde	66/67	34		1	D1
	67/68	25	2	2	D1
	68/69	30		4	D1
	69/70	24	2	4	D1

ANDERSON Andrew
b. 7.8.1953
Sighthill Amateurs

Club	Season	Apps		Goals	Div
Partick T	71/72	2			D1
	72/73				D1
	73/74	14			D1
	74/75	31	1		D1
	75/76	20	2		D1
	76/77	10	2		P
	77/78	26	1	1	P
	78/79	18	2	1	P
	79/80	26			P
	80/81	21			P
	81/82	21			P

ANDERSON Arthur Alan Duncan
b. Edinburgh 21.12.1939

Club	Season	Apps		Goals	Div
Falkirk	59/60	1			D2
Millwall	59/60				FL
	60/61	31			FL
	61/62	43			FL
Scunthorpe U	62/63	6			FL
Heart of Midlothian	63/64	8			D1
	64/65	33			D1
	65/66	34		1	D1
	66/67	29		3	D1
	67/68	22	2	4	D1
	68/69	19	2	3	D1
	69/70	34		2	D1
	70/71	34		3	D1
	71/72	28		2	D1
	72/73	30		2	D1
	73/74	27			D1
	74/75	28			D1
	75/76	22		1	P

ANDERSON Christopher
b. Aberdeen 30.8.1925 d. 27.5.1986
Mugiemoss
Aberdeen

Club	Season	Apps		Goals	Div
Hartlepools U	L 46/47	2			FL
	47/48				FL
Aberdeen	48/49	7			D1
	49/50	29			D1
	50/51	20		1	D1
	51/52	11			D1
	52/53	4			D1
Arbroath	53/54	19		1	D2

ANDERSON David
b. ?.?.1948
Bonnyrigg Rose
Heart of Midlothian

Club	Season	Apps		Goals	Div
Dunfermline A	66/67	1			D1
Dumbarton	68/69				D2
	69/70	29			D2
Morton	70/71				
Hamilton A	70/71	10			D2

ANDERSON Desmond
b. Edinburgh 9.1.1938
Ayr U

Club	Season				Div
Hibernian	57/58	2			D1
Morton	58/59				D2
	59/60				D2
	60/61				D2
Millwall	61/62				FL
	62/63	21		1	FL
	63/64	23			FL

ANDERSON Edward
Kirkintilloch Rob Roy

Club	Season				Div
Clyde	69/70	22			D1
	70/71	18	1		D1
	71/72	19			D1
	72/73	36		1	D2
	73/74	23	1	1	D1
	74/75	23		1	D1
	75/76	25			D1
	76/77	35			D2
	77/78	36	2		D2
	78/79	38		1	D1
	79/80	17		1	D1

ANDERSON George
b. Port Glasgow 25.12.1953
Port Glasgow Jnrs

Club	Season				Div
Morton	69/70	2	3		D1
	70/71	23	1	1	D1
	71/72	33		1	D1
	72/73	30		2	D1
	73/74	26	1		D1
	74/75	25	1		D1
	75/76	9		1	D1
	76/77	35		2	D1
	77/78	37		9	D1
	78/79	12		1	P
	79/80	20	2	1	P
	80/81	4		1	P
Airdrieonians	80/81	19	1	1	P
	81/82	18			P
	82/83	28	1	2	D1
	83/84	27	3	1	D1
	84/85	13	3		D1
Morton	85/86	16	2	1	D1
	86/87	1			D1

ANDERSON Ian

Club	Season				Div
Morton	66/67	5		2	D2
	67/68	1	1		D1

ANDERSON Ian
b. Edinburgh 11.9.1954
Salvesen BC

Club	Season				Div
Dundee	72/73	5	1	1	D1
	73/74	4			D1
	74/75	13	1	2	D1
	75/76	2			P
St Johnstone	75/76	20		1	P
	76/77	30		8	D1
Tampa Bay Rowdies	77	11		2	NA
St Johnstone	77/78	10	1		D1
Dumbarton	78/79	1	1		D1
Houston Hurricanes	79	30		5	NA
	80	30		9	NA

ANDERSON James

Club	Season				Div
Falkirk	57/58	2			D1
St Johnstone	58/59	31		12	D2
	59/60	1			D2

ANDERSON James

Club	Season				Div
Aberdeen	62/63	1			D1
	63/64	3			D1

ANDERSON James
Forres Mechanics

Club	Season				Div
St Johnstone	65/66	6		3	D1
	66/67	2			D1
Elgin C					

ANDERSON John
Newarthill Hearts

Club	Season				Div
Motherwell	49/50	1			D1
Stirling A	50/51				D2
	51/52	5		2	D1
Hamilton A	51/52	20			D2

ANDERSON John Hugh Todd
b. Johnstone 11.1.1937
Johnstone Burgh

Club	Season				Div
Stoke C	57/58	4		1	FL
	58/59	6		1	FL
	59/60	4			FL
	60/61	10			FL
Morton	61/62				D2
	62/63				D2
Third Lanark	63/64	12		3	D1

ANDERSON John Lochart
b. Glasgow 5.4.1928
Glasgow Benburb

Club	Season				Div
Partick T	51/52	12			D1
	52/53				D1
Northampton T	53/54	14		5	FL
Exeter C	54/55	7			FL
Dundee	55/56	3		1	D1
Wrexham	56/57	44		18	FL
	57/58	38		5	FL
	58/59	16		4	FL
Rochdale	59/60	28		5	FL
Chester	60/61	17		2	FL
Wrexham	61/62	1			FL
Colwyn Bay U					

ANDERSON Norman
b. Salsburgh 4.8.1957

Club	Season				Div
Airdrieonians	74/75	3	6		D1
	75/76	9			D1
	76/77	8	1		D1
	77/78	10	5		D1
	78/79	26	2		D1
	79/80	36			D1
	80/81	30			P
	81/82	29		1	P
	82/83	22			D1
	83/84	19		2	D1
Ayr U	84/85	29		2	D1
	85/86	6			D1
Brechin C	85/86	13		1	D1
Queen of the South	86/87	31			D1
	87/88	2	2		D1
Stirling A	87/88	10			D2
Clyde	87/88	6			D1
	88/89	9			D1
Cumnock					

ANDERSON Oliver

Club	Season				Div
Celtic	37/38				D1
	38/39	11		3	D1
Alloa A	46/47				D2
Third Lanark	T 47/48				D1
Airdrieonians	47/48	7		1	D1
Falkirk	48/49	9		4	D1
Kilmarnock	T 50/51	1			D2

ANDERSON Robert
b. Aberdeen 21.1.1937

Club	Season				Div
Partick T	57/58	2			D1
	58/59	1		1	D1
Chesterfield	59/60	4			FL

ANDERSON Thomas
b. Kilmarnock
SS & E Athletic

Club	Season				Div
Motherwell	46/47				D1
	47/48	2			D1
	48/49				D1
Albion R	49/50	9		1	D2
	50/51				D2
	51/52				D2
Clyde	52/53	19			D1
	53/54	20			D1
	54/55	29			D1
	55/56	14			D1

ANDERSON Thomas
b. Dalry
Ardrossan Winton R

Club	Season				Div
St Mirren	52/53	19		4	D1
	53/54	16		1	D1
	54/55	10		2	D1
Falkirk	55/56	1			D1
Ayr U	56/57				D1

ANDERSON Thomas
b. Uddingston 24.3.1941
Strathclyde

Club	Season				Div
Stirling A	63/64	19		1	D2
	64/65	22			D2
	65/66	17			D1
Albion R	66/67	21		1	D2
East Stirlingshire	67/68	10			D2

ANDERSON Thomas Cowan
b. Haddington 24.9.1934
Heart of Midlothian

Club	Season				Div
Queen of the South	55/56	4		1	D1
	56/57	1			D1
Watford	56/57	19		5	FL
	57/58	33		7	FL
Bournemouth	58/59				
QPR	58/59	10		3	FL
Torquay U	59/60	9		4	FL
Stockport Co	60/61	45		11	FL
	61/62	15		6	FL
Doncaster R	61/62	16		3	FL
Wrexham	61/62	10		2	FL
	62/63	2		1	FL
S Melbourne Hellas	63				
Barrow	63/64	11		3	FL
S Melbourne Hellas	64				
Watford	64/65	20		2	FL
	65/66	1			FL
St Mirren	65/66	7			D1
Melbourne George Cr	66				
	67				
Orient	67/68	8	1		FL
Limerick					

ANDERSON Wallace

Club	Season				Div
Falkirk	49/50	10		2	D1
	50/51	3			D1

ANDERSON Walter

Club	Season				Div
St Mirren	50/51	5			D1
	51/52	2			D1
Stirling A					
Albion R	52/53	4			D2

ANDERSON William
b. Lochore 6.11.1926

Club	Season				Div
Hibernian	53/54	1			D1
Southend U	54/55	15		1	FL
	55/56	1			FL
Weymouth					

ANDREW William

Club	Season				Div
Falkirk	58/59	8			D1
	59/60	2			D2
Stirling A	60/61				D2

ANDREWS George
Banks o'Dee

Club	Season				Div
Stirling A	54/55	3			D1

ANDREWS James Patrick
b. Invergordon 1.2.1927

Club	Season	Apps	Sub	Goals	Div
Dundee	48/49	10		1	D1
	49/50	15		2	D1
	50/51	15		2	D1
	51/52				
West Ham U	51/52	23		2	FL
	52/53	23		5	FL
	53/54	31		6	FL
	54/55	21		6	FL
	55/56	16		2	FL
Leyton Orient	56/57	14		4	FL
	57/58	16		1	FL
	58/59	6			FL
QPR	59/60	46		10	FL
	60/61	32		6	FL
	61/62	4			FL

ANTON George McC
Whitletts Victoria

Club	Season	Apps	Sub	Goals	Div
Kilmarnock	58/59				D1
	59/60	1			D1
Stranraer	60/61				D2
	61/62	36			D2
	62/63				D2
	63/64				D2
	64/65				D2
	65/66				D2
Ayr U	66/67	12			D1
	67/68				D2
Stranraer	67/68				D2
Annbank U					

ARCHDEACON O

Club	Season	Apps	Sub	Goals	Div
St Mirren	55/56	1		1	D1
	56/57	2			D1

ARCHIBALD D

Club	Season	Apps	Sub	Goals	Div
Raith R	54/55	9		3	D1

ARCHIBALD E

Club	Season	Apps	Sub	Goals	Div
St Mirren	53/54	1			D1
	54/55	2		1	D1

ARCHIBALD James

Club	Season	Apps	Sub	Goals	Div
Dundee	49/50	3			D1
	50/51				D1
Third Lanark	51/52	3			D1

ARCHIBALD Steven
b. Glasgow 27.9.1956 Caps: S - 27
Crofoot U
Fernhill A

Club	Season	Apps	Sub	Goals	Div
Clyde	74/75	2		2	D1
	75/76	14	2	2	D1
	76/77	30	1	3	D2
Aberdeen	77/78	10		4	P
	78/79	30	2	13	P
	79/80	34		12	P
Tottenham H	80/81	40	1	20	FL
	81/82	26	1	6	FL
	82/83	31		11	FL
	83/84	31	1	21	FL
Barcelona	84/85				
	85/86				
	86/87				
	87/88				
Blackburn R	87/88	20		6	FL
Hibernian	88/89	31		13	P
	89/90	8	5	2	P
St Mirren	90/91	16		2	P
Reading	91/92	1			FL
Ayr U	91/92	1			D1
Clyde	91/92	4		2	D2
Fulham	92/93	2			FL
	93/94				FL
East Fife	94/95	12	1	1	D2
	95/96	29	2	6	D2
	96/97	5			D1

ARENTOFT Preben
b. Copenhagen 1.11.1942 Caps: Den - 9
Bronshoj BK

Club	Season	Apps	Sub	Goals	Div
Morton	65/66	20		3	D1
	66/67				D2
	67/68	32		2	D1
	68/69	17		2	D1
Newcastle U	68/69	10		2	FL
	69/70	22	4		FL
	70/71	14			FL
Blackburn R	71/72	12		2	FL
	72/73	45		1	FL
	73/74	37			FL
Helsingborg IF					

ARGUE James
b. c1949 d. ?.8.1993
Kilsyth R

Club	Season	Apps	Sub	Goals	Div
St Johnstone	68/69	1			D1
	69/70	4	3	1	D1
	70/71	27			D1
	71/72	20	1		D1
	72/73	31		1	D1
	73/74	31			D1
	74/75	26		1	D1

ARMSTRONG Douglas
b. Edinburgh 13.6.1925
North Merchiston BC
Edinburgh Ashton
Haddington A

Club	Season	Apps	Sub	Goals	Div
Heart of Midlothian	51/52	2			D1
	52/53	19			D1
	53/54	16		1	D1
	54/55	6			D1
Third Lanark					

ARMSTRONG Matthew
b. Newton Stewart 12.11.1911
Port Glasgow Jnrs
Celtic

Club	Season	Apps	Sub	Goals	Div
Aberdeen	31/32	9		2	D1
	32/33	7		3	D1
	33/34	12		14	D1
	34/35	36		31	D1
	35/36	30		30	D1
	36/37	36		24	D1
	37/38	34		19	D1
	38/39	27		13	D1
Queen of the South	46/47	27		13	D1
Elgin C					
Peterhead					

ARMSTRONG William
b. Carlisle 25.10.1949
Hawick Royal Albert

Club	Season	Apps	Sub	Goals	Div
Stirling A	68/69			4	D2
	69/70	32		5	D2
	70/71			7	D2
	71/72	21		9	D2
Morton	71/72	8		4	D1
	72/73	21	4	2	D1
Berwick R	73/74	30	3	2	D2
	74/75	12	8	2	D2

ARNISON Joseph William
b. Johannesburg 27.6.1924 d. ?.?.1996

Club	Season	Apps	Sub	Goals	Div
Rangers	46/47	7		1	D1
	47/48				D1
Luton T	48/49	30		17	FL
	49/50	13		2	FL
	50/51	1			FL
Berea Park					

ARROL John
Duntocher Hibs

Club	Season	Apps	Sub	Goals	Div
East Stirlingshire	63/64	18			D1
ES Clydebank	64/65	35			D2
Dundee	65/66	5			D1
	66/67	28			D1
	67/68	10			D1
	68/69	1			D1
Dunfermline A	69/70	11			D1
	70/71	20			D1
	71/72	23			D1
	72/73	36			D2
	73/74	12			D1
Partick T	74/75	15			D1
	75/76				D1
Clyde	76/77	14			D2
	77/78	39			D2
	78/79	37			D1
St Johnstone	79/80	10			D1

ARTHUR Robert
b. Port Glasgow 1.6.1945
Saltcoats V
Kilbirnie Ladeside

Club	Season	Apps	Sub	Goals	Div
Kilmarnock	66/67				D1
	67/68	25			D1
	68/69	6		1	D1
	69/70	1			D1
	70/71	4			D1
Morton	70/71	4			D1
Australia					
Largs Thistle					

ASHE Armour Donald
b. Paisley 14.10.1925 d. Accrington 15.6.1968
Dalry Thistle

Club	Season	Apps	Sub	Goals	Div
Aberdeen	49/50	1			D1
St Mirren	50/51	3			D1
	51/52	7			D1
	52/53	11			D1
Stockport Co	53/54	2			FL
Accrington S	53/54	29			FL
	54/55	45			FL
	55/56	44			FL
	56/57	38			FL
	57/58	6			FL
Gateshead	57/58	28		1	FL
	58/59	26			FL
Southport	59/60	14		2	FL
Horwich RMI					

ATKINSON John

Club	Season	Apps	Sub	Goals	Div
Morton	46/47	1			D1
Stirling A	47/48				D3

AULD Robert
b. Maryhill 23.3.1938 Caps: S - 3
Partick T BC
Panmure Thistle
Maryhill Harp

Club	Season	Apps	Sub	Goals	Div
Celtic	55/56				D1
Dumbarton	L 56/57				D2
Celtic	57/58	2			D1
	58/59	27		9	D1
	59/60	20		3	D1
	60/61	15		4	D1
Birmingham C	61/62	39		5	FL
	62/63	36		9	FL
	63/64	34		10	FL
	64/65	17		2	FL
Celtic	64/65	12		10	D1
	65/66	17		8	D1
	66/67	27		7	D1
	67/68	19	1	5	D1
	68/69	9	4	1	D1
	69/70	15	3	5	D1
	70/71	4		1	D1
Hibernian	71/72	8	3	3	D1

AUSTIN Alan

Club	Season	Apps	Sub	Goals	Div
Rangers	57/58	1			D1

AYRES S

Third Lanark	46/47	1		D1

AYTON James
b. Barrhead 15.10.1923 d. Leicester 25.8.1988
Neilston V

Third Lanark	46/47	26	3	D1
	47/48	13	2	D1
	48/49	4	2	D1
Leicester C	48/49	5	1	FL
	49/50	1		FL
	50/51	2		FL
Shrewsbury T	51/52	25	1	FL
Bedford T				

AZEVEDO Fernando
b. Brazil

St Mirren	65/66	1		D1

BACON J

Raith R	62/63	1		D1

BAIKIE Eric
Hutcheson Vale

Aberdeen	49/50	2		D1
	50/51	1		D1
Dunfermline A	51/52			D2
	52/53	18	1	D2
	53/54	30		D2
	54/55			D2
	55/56	11	1	D1
	56/57	1		D1
St Johnstone	57/58	21		D2
	58/59	6		D2

BAILLIE William Craig
b. Airdrie 6.7.1944
Kirkintilloch Rob Roy

Brighton & HA	61/62			FL
	62/63	4	1	FL
Cambridge U	63/64			
Motherwell	63/64	3	1	D1
	64/65	3	2	D1
Distillery				

BAILLIE Colin

Third Lanark	64/65	8		D1
	65/66	36		D2
	66/67	33	2	D2
Queen of the South	67/68	13	1	D2

BAILLIE Douglas
b. Drycross 27.1.1937
Douglas Water Thistle

Airdrieonians	53/54	5	3	D1
	54/55			D2
Swindon T	L 55/56	1		FL
Airdrieonians	55/56	4		D1
	56/57	14		D1
	57/58	25	2	D1
	58/59	23		D1
	59/60	26	8	D1
Rangers	60/61	5		D1
	61/62	16		D1
	62/63	6		D1
	63/64	4		D1
Third Lanark	64/65	19	3	D1
Falkirk	64/65	9	3	D1
	65/66	25		D1
	66/67	29	1	D1
	67/68	34	3	D1
	68/69	7		D1
Dunfermline A	68/69	1	3	D1
	69/70	18		D1

BAILLIE James
Cambridge U

Dunfermline A	73/74	5	2	D1
Berwick R	74/75	19	4 1	D2

BAILLIE Joseph
b. Glasgow 26.2.1929 d. Maryhill 23.3.1966
St Rochs

Celtic	46/47	1		D1
	47/48	5		D1
	48/49	7		D1
	49/50	24		D1
	50/51	28		D1
	51/52	30		D1
	52/53	12		D1
	53/54	1		D1
Wolverhampton W	54/55	1		FL
	55/56			FL
Bristol C	56/57	10		FL
Leicester C	57/58	21		FL
	58/59	37		FL
	59/60	17		FL
Bradford PA	60/61	7	1	FL

BAILLIE Malcolm

Third Lanark	46/47	1		D1
	47/48	4		D1
	48/49	1		D1
Morton	49/50	10	4	D2
St Johnstone	50/51	2		D2
Inverness Caley				
Stirling A	52/53			D2
Fleetwood				
Cowdenbeath	53/54	2		D2

BAILLIE Oliver
b. Kirkmuirhill
Kirkmuirhill
Larkhall Thistle

Kilmarnock	52/53			
	53/54	1		D2
	54/55	2		D1
	55/56			D1
	56/57			D1
	57/58			D1
Reading	L 57/58			FL
	58/59			FL
Kilmarnock	58/59			D1
	59/60			D1

BAIN Alexander Edward
b. Edinburgh 22.1.1936
Cockenzie Star

Motherwell	54/55	11	6	D1
	55/56	9	3	D1
	56/57	3	1	D1
Huddersfield T	57/58	19	8	FL
	58/59	10	3	FL
Chesterfield	59/60	18	9	FL
Falkirk	60/61	9	6	D2
Bournemouth	61/62	8	4	FL
Poole T				
Falkirk	62/63	9	5	D1

BAIN Ian

East Fife	47/48			D2
	48/49			D1
	49/50			D1
Stirling A	49/50	30	2	D2
	50/51			D2
	51/52	21		D1
	52/53	22		D2
	53/54	23	1	D1
	54/55	9		D1
Raith R	54/55	13	1	D1
	55/56	27	1	D1
	56/57	22	1	D1
	57/58	6		D1
Dunfermline A	58/59	21		D1
	59/60	2		D1

BAIN William Clark
b. Alloa 16.1.1924

Falkirk	46/47	4	1	D1
Dunfermline A	47/48			D2
	48/49			D2
	49/50	9	5	D2
Hartlepools U	50/51	2		FL
Dunfermline A				

BAINES Roy
b. Derby 7.2.1950
Woodpecker Bar
Roe Farm
Derby Co

Hibernian	68/69			D1
	69/70			D1
	70/71	23		D1
	71/72			D1
Morton	72/73	24		D1
	73/74	34		D1
	74/75	33		D1
	75/76	25		D1
	76/77	1		D1
Celtic	76/77	5		P
	77/78			P
	78/79	7		P
Morton	78/79	14		P
	79/80	36		P
	80/81	36		P
	81/82	36		P
	82/83	33		P
St Johnstone	83/84	26		P
	84/85	13		D1

BAIRD Archibald
b. Rutherglen
Strathclyde

Aberdeen	46/47	14	6	D1
	47/48	13	3	D1
	48/49	7	1	D1
	49/50	18	6	D1
	50/51	27	5	D1
	51/52	23	5	D1
	52/53	2		D1
St Johnstone	53/54	27	3	D2
	54/55	26		D2
	55/56	25		D2

BAIRD Douglas Francis Hogg
b. Falkirk 26.11.1935
Armadale Thistle

Partick T	55/56	12		D1
	56/57	16		D1
	57/58	32	1	D1
	58/59	31		D1
	59/60	33		D1
	60/61	1		D1
Nottingham F	60/61	4		FL
	61/62	13		FL
	62/63	15		FL
Plymouth A	63/64	28		FL
	64/65	20		FL
	65/66	38	1	FL
	66/67	38	1	FL
	67/68	23		FL
Hamilton A	68/69			D2
	69/70	1		D2
	70/71			D2

BAIRD Hugh
b. Bellshill 14.3.1930 Caps: S - 1
Dalry Thistle

Airdrieonians	51/52	5	1	D1
	52/53	12	10	D1
	53/54	23	10	D1
	54/55	30	34	D2
	55/56	33	26	D1
	56/57	31	30	D1
Leeds U	57/58	40	20	FL
	58/59	6	2	FL
Aberdeen	58/59	25	12	D1
	59/60	28	5	D1
	60/61	8		D1
	61/62	5	4	D1
Brechin C				
Deverondale				
Rothes				

BAIRD John

East Fife	46/47	5		D2
	47/48	1		D2
	48/49	1		D1

BAIRD Samuel
b. Denny 13.5.1930 Caps: S - 7
Rutherglen Glencairn

Club	Season	Apps	Sub	Goals	Div
Clyde	49/50	2			D1
	50/51	3		2	D1
	51/52				D2
	52/53	30		8	D1
	53/54	29		9	D1
Preston NE	54/55	15		2	FL
Rangers	55/56	33		14	D1
	56/57	32		9	D1
	57/58	31		8	D1
	58/59	6		4	D1
	59/60	19		4	D1
Hibernian	60/61	28		3	D1
	61/62	11		2	D1
Third Lanark	62/63	24		1	D1
Stirling A	63/64	12		1	D2

BAKER Gerard Austin
b. New York 11.4.1938 Caps: USA - 7
Larkhall Thistle

Club	Season	Apps	Sub	Goals	Div
Chelsea	55/56				
Motherwell	56/57	2		1	D1
	57/58	9		3	D1
St Mirren	58/59	21		19	D1
	59/60	33		21	D1
	60/61	9		2	D1
Manchester C	60/61	22		9	FL
	61/62	15		5	FL
Hibernian	61/62	21		10	D1
	62/63	28		13	D1
	63/64	10		4	D1
Ipswich T	63/64	20		15	FL
	64/65	36		16	FL
	65/66	38		11	FL
	66/67	30		13	FL
	67/68	11		3	FL
Coventry C	67/68	18	1	4	FL
	68/69	8	3	1	FL
	69/70	1			FL
Brentford	L 69/70	8		2	FL
Margate					
Nuneaton B					
Bedworth U					

BAKER James
Stevenston U

Club	Season	Apps	Sub	Goals	Div
Queen of the South	46/47	3		1	D1
	47/48	7		3	D1
	48/49	3		2	D1
Third Lanark	49/50	6			D1
Ayr U	50/51				D2

BAKER Joseph Henry
b. Liverpool 17.7.1940
d. Wishaw 6.10.2003 Caps: E - 8
Edinburgh Thistle
Coltness U
Armadale Thistle

Club	Season	Apps	Sub	Goals	Div
Chelsea	T				
Hibernian	57/58	25		14	D1
	58/59	26		25	D1
	59/60	33		42	D1
	60/61	33		21	D1
Torino	61/62				
Arsenal	62/63	39		29	FL
	63/64	39		26	FL
	64/65	42		25	FL
	65/66	24		13	FL
Nottingham F	65/66	14		5	FL
	66/67	35		5	FL
	67/68	39		16	FL
	68/69	30	1	4	FL
Sunderland	69/70	24	1	2	FL
	70/71	15	1	10	FL
Hibernian	70/71	11		8	D1
	71/72	10	1	4	D1
Raith R	72/73	24		25	D2
	73/74	25		9	D2

BALFOUR John
d. Dalmellington ?.7.1969
Ardeer Recreation

Club	Season	Apps	Sub	Goals	Div
Ayr U	65/66	7		2	D2
	66/67	1			D1
Craigmark Burntonians					

BALL Allan
b. Hetton-le-Hole 26.2.1943
Stanley U

Club	Season	Apps	Sub	Goals	Div
Queen of the South	63/64	19			D1
	64/65	36			D2
	65/66	36			D2
	66/67	38			D2
	67/68	36			D2
	68/69				D2
	69/70	36			D2
	70/71				D2
	71/72	36			D2
	72/73	18			D2
	73/74	36			D2
	74/75	38			D2
	75/76	24			D1
	76/77	38			D1
	77/78	39			D1
	78/79	16			D1
	79/80	19			D2
	80/81	20			D2
	81/82	29			D1
Gretna					

BALUNAS Matthew
b. Carfin
New Stevenston

Club	Season	Apps	Sub	Goals	Div
Third Lanark	46/47	24			D1
	47/48	19			D1
	48/49	30			D1
	49/50	30			D1
	50/51	30			D1
	51/52	25			D1
	52/53	29			D1

BANNAN Thomas Neilson
b. Darngavel 13.4.1930
Plains St Davids

Club	Season	Apps	Sub	Goals	Div
Airdrieonians	46/47				D2
	47/48				D1
	48/49				D2
	49/50	8		6	D2
	50/51	3		1	D1
Stirling A	L				
Wrexham	51/52	40		12	FL
	52/53	45		18	FL
	53/54	37		14	FL
	54/55	36		16	FL
Lincoln C	55/56	31		7	FL
	56/57	36		12	FL
Wrexham	57/58	28		8	FL
	58/59	40		15	FL
Barrow	59/60	32		11	FL
	60/61	13		4	FL

BARBOUR J

Club	Season	Apps	Sub	Goals	Div
Queen of the South	46/47	1			D1

BARCLAY J

Club	Season	Apps	Sub	Goals	Div
Airdrieonians	47/48	1			D1

BARCLAY J

Club	Season	Apps	Sub	Goals	Div
Falkirk	53/54	2			D1

BARCLAY Matthew

Club	Season	Apps	Sub	Goals	Div
Third Lanark	46/47	4			D1
	47/48	17			D1
	48/49	23			D1
	49/50	9		1	D1
Ayr U	50/51				D2

BARCLAY William
b. Larkhall 11.7.1924
Larkhall Thistle

Club	Season	Apps	Sub	Goals	Div
Motherwell	46/47	27		6	D1
	47/48	18			D1
	48/49	10			D1
Bury	48/49	12		1	FL
	49/50	5			FL
Clyde	49/50	17		7	D1
	50/51	11		1	D1
	51/52				D2
Third Lanark	52/53	7		1	D1
	53/54	13			D2
	54/55				D2
	55/56				D2
Hamilton A	L 55/56	3		1	D2
Montrose					

BARLOW Andrew

Club	Season	Apps	Sub	Goals	Div
Hamilton A	52/53	1			D2
	53/54	4			D1

BARNES Charles
Jubilee A

Club	Season	Apps	Sub	Goals	Div
Cowdenbeath	70/71	1			D1

BARRETT Thomas
b. Edinburgh
Shotts Bon Accord
Hibernian

Club	Season	Apps	Sub	Goals	Div
Hamilton A	L 53/54	10		1	D1
	54/55	27		2	D2
	55/56	18		1	D2
	56/57	2			D2
	57/58	4			D2

BARRIE William

Club	Season	Apps	Sub	Goals	Div
Falkirk	50/51	6			D1

BARRY Roy Alexander
b. Edinburgh 19.9.1942
Musselburgh A

Club	Season	Apps	Sub	Goals	Div
Heart of Midlothian	61/62	3			D1
	62/63	28		1	D1
	63/64	28			D1
	64/65	16		7	D1
	65/66	17			D1
	66/67	2			D1
Dunfermline A	66/67	28		5	D1
	67/68	32			D1
	68/69	31			D1
	69/70	3			D1
Coventry C	69/70	14	1		FL
	70/71	1			FL
	71/72	27		1	FL
	72/73	40		1	FL
Crystal Palace	73/74	31		1	FL
	74/75	10	1		FL
Hibernian	74/75	11			D1
	75/76				P
East Fife	76/77	12			D1

BARTRAM Andreas Per
b. Denmark 8.1.1944 Caps: Den - 1
OB Odense

Club	Season	Apps	Sub	Goals	Div
Morton	66/67	7		5	D2
	67/68	7	4	1	D1
	68/69	22	1	13	D1
Crystal Palace	69/70	8	2	2	FL
Morton	70/71	14	1	6	D1
OB Odense					

BATHGATE Sydney
b. Aberdeen 20.12.1919 d. ?.?.1962
Aberdeen Parkvale

Club	Season				Div
Chelsea	46/47	7			FL
	47/48	32			FL
	48/49	17			FL
	49/50	10			FL
	50/51	34			FL
	51/52	32			FL
	52/53	3			FL
Hamilton A	53/54	10			D1
Keith					

BATTON Andrew

Club	Season				Div
Morton	47/48	1			D1
	48/49	8			D1
	49/50	6			D2
	50/51	12			D1
	51/52	8			D1
	52/53	26			D2
Albion R	53/54	1			D2

BAULD Philip Spinelli
b. Glasgow 20.9.1929 d. ?.?.1994

Club	Season				Div
Clyde	52/53	1			D1
Plymouth A	53/54				FL
Aldershot	54/55	3			FL
Tonbridge					

BAULD William Russell Logan
b. Newcraighall 24.1.1928 d. 11.3.1977
Caps: S - 3
Niddrie Marehill
Edinburgh Waverley
Musselburgh A
Newtongrange Star

Club	Season				Div
Heart of Midlothian	46/47				D1
Edinburgh C	L 46/47				
Heart of Midlothian	47/48				D1
	48/49	24		17	D1
	49/50	29		30	D1
	50/51	30		15	D1
	51/52	29		13	D1
	52/53	23		10	D1
	53/54	21		10	D1
	54/55	25		21	D1
	55/56	20		15	D1
	56/57	24		12	D1
	57/58	9		5	D1
	58/59	20		15	D1
	59/60	17		10	D1
	60/61	11		3	D1
	61/62	10		6	D1

BAXTER James Curran
b. Hill o'Beath 29.9.1939
d. Glasgow 13.4.2001 Caps: S - 34
Halbeath Youth Club
Crossgates Primrose

Club	Season				Div
Raith R	57/58	3		1	D1
	58/59	26			D1
	59/60	32		2	D1
Rangers	60/61	27		1	D1
	61/62	29		2	D1
	62/63	32		4	D1
	63/64	26		4	D1
	64/65	22		6	D1
Sunderland	65/66	35		7	FL
	66/67	36		3	FL
	67/68	16			FL
Nottingham F	67/68	22		2	FL
	68/69	25	1	1	FL
Rangers	69/70	14		1	D1

BAXTER John

Club	Season				Div
Hibernian	57/58	33		2	D1
	58/59	12		1	D1
	59/60	30		7	D1
	60/61	24		5	D1
	61/62	27		1	D1
	62/63	10		3	D1
	63/64	24		2	D1
	64/65	28			D1
	65/66	20			D1
Falkirk	66/67	13	2		D1
Clydebank					

BAXTER Robert Denholm
b. Gilmerton 23.1.1911
d. Middleton St George 4.1991 Caps: S - 3
Tranent Jnrs
Musselburgh Bruntonians

Club	Season				Div
Middlesbrough	32/33	25		5	FL
	33/34	36		6	FL
	34/35	39		6	FL
	35/36	39		2	FL
	36/37	37			FL
	37/38	38			FL
	38/39	33			FL
Heart of Midlothian	46/47	25			D1
Leith A					

BAXTER Thomas
b. Airdrie
Lanark U

Club	Season				Div
Queen of the South	50/51				D2
	51/52				D1
	52/53	5			D1
	53/54				D1
	54/55	13		3	D1
	55/56	9			D1
	56/57				D1
	57/58	1			D1
St Mirren	57/58	4			D1

BEATH

Club	Season				Div
Raith R	56/57	2			D1
	57/58	1			D1

BEATON Alexander

Club	Season				Div
Dundee	49/50	2			D1
	50/51	2			D1

BEATON James
Carluke R

Club	Season				Div
Motherwell	67/68	4			D1

BEATON William
b. Kincardine 30.9.1935
Thornton Hibernian

Club	Season				Div
Dunfermline A	58/59	6			D1
Aston Villa	58/59	1			FL
Airdrieonians	59/60	10			D1
	60/61	3			D1
	61/62	2			D1

BEATTIE Alexander
b. Glasgow c1923 d. Glasgow 30.7.1957
Rangers

Club	Season				Div
Ayr U	46/47				D2
	47/48				D2
	48/49				D2
	49/50	29		10	D2
	50/51				D2
	51/52				D2
	52/53	9		3	D2
	53/54	17		4	D2
	54/55				D2
	55/56				D2
	56/57	18		4	D1

BEATTIE Francis Whitfield
b. St Ninians 17.10.1933
Bonnybridge Jnrs

Club	Season				Div
Kilmarnock	53/54				
	54/55	15		3	D1
	55/56	29		9	D1
	56/57	21		7	D1
	57/58	20		8	D1
	58/59	27			D1
	59/60	33		1	D1
	60/61	28			D1
	61/62	30		1	D1
	62/63	34		1	D1
	63/64	33		1	D1
	64/65	31		1	D1
	65/66	30			D1
	66/67	29		1	D1
	67/68	25			D1
	68/69	27	1		D1
	69/70	8			D1
	70/71				D1
	71/72	1			D1

BEATTIE Norman
Inverurie Loco

Club	Season				Div
Dundee	64/65	6			D1
	65/66	2			D1

BEATTIE Richard Scott
b. Glasgow 24.10.1936
d. Old Kilpatrick 15.8.1990
Lusset Juveniles
Duntocher Hibs

Club	Season				Div
Celtic	55/56	31			D1
	56/57	29			D1
	57/58	33			D1
	58/59	20			D1
Portsmouth	59/60	39			FL
	60/61	40			FL
	61/62	43			FL
Peterborough U	62/63	10			FL
St Mirren	62/63	14			D1
	63/64	20			D1
Brechin C	64/65				D2

BEATTIE William
b. Peebles 10.7.1950
Baillieston

Club	Season				Div
Clyde	69/70	23			D1
	70/71	28	2	3	D1
	71/72	13			D1
	72/73	9	2	3	D2
	73/74	12	1		D1
Durban U					
Germiston Callies					
Forfar A	79/80	7	3		D2
	80/81	2			D2

BECK Thorolfur
b. Iceland c1940 d. Iceland ?.12.1999
Caps: Ice - 20
KR Reykjavik

Club	Season				Div
St Mirren	61/62	19		9	D1
	62/63	22		10	D1
	63/64	31		6	D1
	64/65	8		2	D1
Rangers	64/65	9		1	D1
	65/66	2		1	D1
Rouen	66/67				
St Louis Stars	67	11		2	NP
KR Reykjavik					

BECKETT William
b. Dumbarton
Renfrew Jnrs

Club	Season				Div
Rangers	50/51	1			D1
	51/52				D1
	52/53				D1
	53/54				D1
	54/55				D1
Cowdenbeath	55/56				D2
	56/57				D2

BEECHAM Charles

Club	Season				Div
Stirling A	58/59	1			D1

BELL Alan

Club	Season				Div
St Mirren	65/66	2			D1
	66/67	9			D1

BELL Alexander Stewart
b. Auchinleck 13.3.1931

Club	Season				Div
Partick T	51/52	1			D1
	52/53	10			D1
	53/54	1			D1
Exeter C	54/55	16			FL
	55/56				FL
	56/57	6			FL
	57/58	18			FL
Grimsby T	58/59	8			FL

BELL Andrew
b. 14.7.1932
Victoria Thistle
Heart of Midlothian T
Arthurlie

Club	Season				Div
Celtic	51/52	13			D1
	52/53				D2
	53/54	6			D1
	54/55	7			D1
Airdrieonians	55/56	3			D1
St Johnstone	56/57	13			D2
Albion R	57/58				D2

BELL Brian
Kello R

Club	Season					Div
Ayr U	73/74	6	12	2		D1
	74/75	2	3			D1
	75/76		2			P

BELL John
Baillieston Jnrs

Club	Season			Div
St Johnstone	61/62	20	4	D1
	62/63	23	9	D2
	63/64	3	1	D1
Raith R	63/64	24	1	D2
	64/65	9	4	D2

BELL John Albert
b. Edinburgh 25.4.1936
Dalkeith Thistle

Club	Season			Div
Stirling A	58/59	4		D1
	59/60	10	1	D1
Swindon T	60/61	25	2	FL
	61/62	6		FL

BELL Robert
b. Glasgow 20.3.1935

Club	Season			Div
Partick T	54/55	3		D1
	55/56	4		D1
Plymouth A	55/56	2	1	FL
	56/57			FL
Partick T	57/58	9	1	D1
	58/59			D1
Carlisle U	59/60	1		FL
Partick T				

BELL Robert McDicker
b. Ayr 16.9.1934
Whitletts Victoria

Club	Season			Div
Falkirk	54/55			D1
	55/56	1		D1
Ayr U	55/56			D2
	56/57	15		D1
Watford	57/58	33	1	FL
	58/59	40	1	FL
	59/60	24		FL
	60/61	45		FL
	61/62	40		FL
	62/63	37		FL
	63/64	40		FL
	64/65	9		FL
Folkestone				
Wealdstone				
Rolls Royce				

BENNETT

Club	Season		Div
Raith R	58/59	2	D1

BENNETT Alan
b. 29.12.1954
Crystal Palace

Club	Season				Div
Morton	72/73				D1
Hamilton A.	73/74	2	4		D2
Anniesland Waverley					
Dumbarton	74/75	2	1		D1
	75/76	1	2		D1
East Stirlingshire	76/77	28	3	5	D2
	77/78	35	1	2	D2
	78/79	34	1	5	D2
	79/80	26	6	2	D2
	80/81	14	4		D1

BENNETT David S
b. Aberdeen
Sunnybank

Club	Season		Div
Aberdeen	60/61	31	D1
	61/62	21	D1
	62/63	22	D1
	63/64	5	D1
	64/65	21	D1
	65/66	11	D1
Inverness Caley			

BENNETT Reuben
b. Aberdeen 21.12.1913 d. ?.12.1989
Aberdeen EE

Club	Season		Div
Hull C	35/36	3	FL
Queen of the South	36/37	3	D1
	37/38		D1
	38/39		D1
Dundee	46/47	18	D2
	47/48		D2
	48/49	3	D1
Ayr U			

BENNETT William
b. Newburgh 5.7.1955
Letham BC

Club	Season				Div
Heart of Midlothian	74/75	1			D1
	75/76				P
Berwick R	76/77	29	2	5	D2
	77/78	35	2	3	D2
Forfar A	78/79	29		1	D2
	79/80	29	3	1	D2
	80/81	34		1	D2
	81/82	37		2	D2
	82/83	33		1	D2
	83/84	18			D2
	84/85	28	2		D1
	85/86	14	1		D1
	86/87	21	3		D1
	87/88	24	7		D1
	88/89	28	2	1	D1
	89/90	2			D1
Arbroath	89/90	26	1		D2
Cowdenbeath	90/91	19			D2
	91/92	3			D2

BENNISON Peter

Club	Season			Div
Third Lanark	61/62	1	1	D1
	62/63	1		D1

BENVIE William
Nairn Thistle
Lochore Welfare

Club	Season			Div
Stirling A	56/57			D2
	57/58			D2
	58/59	33	3	D1
	59/60	14		D1
Dunfermline A	59/60	12	4	D1
	60/61	4	1	D1
Raith R	60/61	10	2	D1
	61/62	17	3	D1
Cowdenbeath	62/63			D2
	63/64	25	2	D2
Berwick R	64/65	12	1	D2

BERG Mogens
b. Denmark 8.6.1944 Caps: Den - 8
B1909 Odense

Club	Season				Div
Dundee U	64/65	19		6	D1
	65/66				D1
	66/67	8	3	1	D1
	67/68	9	9	1	D1
B1909 Odense					

BERNARD John
Bo'ness U

Club	Season			Div
East Fife	68/69			D2
	69/70	6	2	D2
	70/71		1	D2
	71/72	9	5	D1
	72/73	15	1	D1

BERTELSEN Carl
b. Denmark 15.11.1937 Caps: Den - 20
Esbjerg
Hadersley

Club	Season			Div
Morton	64/65	25	10	D1
	65/66	15	6	D1
Dundee				
Kilmarnock	65/66	8	3	D1
	66/67	17	10	D1
Odense BK				

BERTOLINI John
b. Alloa 21.3.1934
Sauchie Thistle
Alva Albion R
Falkirk T

Club	Season			Div
Stirling A	51/52	8	2	D1
	52/53	11	2	D2
Workington	52/53	14	2	FL
	53/54	14	1	FL
	54/55	34	9	FL
	55/56	41	13	FL
	56/57	37	7	FL
	57/58	43	3	FL
Brighton & HA	58/59	30		FL
	59/60	42	3	FL
	60/61	42	2	FL
	61/62	42	1	FL
	62/63	46	2	FL
	63/64	30	4	FL
	64/65	24		FL
	65/66	2		FL
	66/67			FL

BEVERIDGE Ian
Blantyre Victoria

Club	Season		Div
East Fife	54/55	1	D1
	55/56		D1
	56/57		D1
Dumbarton *	57/58		D2

BICKERSTAFFE D

Club	Season		Div
St Mirren	52/53	1	D1
	53/54	2	D1

BINNING James
b. Blantyre
Arbroath

Club	Season			Div
Queen of the South	51/52	30		D1
	52/53	30		D1
	53/54	28		D1
	54/55	21	1	D1
	55/56	34		D1
	56/57	34		D1
	57/58	31		D1
	58/59	15		D1

BIRD Eric

Club	Season				Div
Airdrieonians	68/69	9	1	1	D1
	69/70	12		1	D1
	70/71	4	5		D1
Berwick R	71/72	14	4		D2

BIRSE William

Club	Season	Apps	Sub	Gls	Div
Dundee	55/56	2			D1
	56/57	16		6	D1
East Fife	57/58	7			D1

BLACK Alan Douglas
b. Glasgow 4.6.1943
Drumchapel Amateurs
Dumbarton
Clydebank

Club	Season	Apps	Sub	Gls	Div
Dumbarton	61/62	6		1	D2
	62/63				D2
	63/64	27		6	D2
Sunderland	64/65	2			FL
	65/66	2	3		FL
Norwich C	66/67	8	2		FL
	67/68	24			FL
	68/69	18		1	FL
	69/70	33			FL
	70/71	37			FL
	71/72	19		1	FL
	72/73	22		1	FL
	73/74	11			FL
Dumbarton	73/74	10			D1
	74/75				D1

BLACK Andrew
b. Galston 27.11.1931
Galston

Club	Season	Apps	Sub	Gls	Div
Kilmarnock	47/48				D2
	48/49	2			D2
	49/50	1			D2
	50/51				D2
	51/52				D2
	52/53				D2
	53/54				D2
East Fife	53/54				D1
	54/55	2			D1
Stranraer	55/56				D2
	56/57				D2
	57/58				D2
	58/59				D2
Newton Stewart					

BLACK Gordon
b. Linlithgow
Hibernian

Club	Season	Apps	Sub	Gls	Div
Falkirk	53/54	23			D1
	54/55	15			D1
Dundee	55/56	32			D1
	56/57	33		2	D1
	57/58	20		2	D1
St Johnstone	58/59	6		2	D2

BLACK James

Club	Season	Apps	Sub	Gls	Div
Airdrieonians	62/63	1			D1
	63/64	8			D1
	64/65	6			D1
	65/66	27			D2
	66/67	34			D1
	67/68	34			D1
	68/69	33			D1
Hibernian	69/70	33			D1
	70/71	29		1	D1
	71/72	31			D1
	72/73	34			D1
	73/74	24			D1
Airdrieonians	74/75	33		1	D1
	75/76	25			D1
	76/77	34		1	D1
	77/78	33		1	D1
	78/79	22		1	D1

BLACK John

Club	Season	Apps	Sub	Gls	Div
Third Lanark	46/47	5			D1
Airdrieonians	47/48	12			D1

BLACK Robert
b. Thornhill
Connell Park R

Club	Season	Apps	Sub	Gls	Div
East Fife	46/47				D2
	47/48				D2
	48/49	21		6	D1
	49/50	24		4	D1
	50/51	28		9	D1
	51/52	2		3	D1
Queen of the South	52/53	24		3	D1
	53/54	30		12	D1
	54/55	27		5	D1
	55/56	32		14	D1
	56/57	33		11	D1
	57/58	31		12	D1
	58/59	27		5	D1

BLACK Robert

Club	Season	Apps	Sub	Gls	Div
Airdrieonians	58/59	21		12	D1
	59/60	1			D1
?	60/61				
	61/62				
	62/63				
Third Lanark	63/64	1			D1
	64/65	11		1	D1

BLACK Robert
b. Lugar 2.12.1934 d. Cumnock 24.4.1984
Lugar Boswell

Club	Season	Apps	Sub	Gls	Div
Kilmarnock	52/53				D2
	53/54	4			D2
	54/55	1			D1
	55/56	8			D1
	56/57	25		8	D1
	57/58	26		10	D1
	58/59	34		13	D1
	59/60	33		14	D1
	60/61	23		8	D1
	61/62	22		9	D1
	62/63	33		15	D1
	63/64	7		2	D1
	64/65	9		6	D1
	65/66	9		3	D1
Ayr U	66/67	26		2	D1
	67/68	33		9	D2
Corby T	68/69				
	69/70				
Troon Jnrs					

BLACK W L

Club	Season	Apps	Sub	Gls	Div
Queen's Park	50/51	17		2	D2
	51/52	2			D2
	52/53	4		2	D2
	53/54	6		1	D2
	54/55	7		1	D2
	55/56	2			D2
	56/57				D1
	57/58	3			D1

BLACKLEY John Henderson
b. Polmont 12.5.1948 Caps: S - 7
Gairdoch U

Club	Season	Apps	Sub	Gls	Div
Hibernian	67/68	3		1	D1
	68/69	13			D1
	69/70	31			D1
	70/71	29		2	D1
	71/72	33		2	D1
	72/73	29			D1
	73/74	31		1	D1
	74/75	21		1	D1
	75/76	34		1	P
	76/77	31			P
	77/78	7			P
Newcastle U	77/78	18			FL
	78/79	28			FL
Preston NE	79/80	27			FL
	80/81	21		2	FL
	81/82	3			FL
Hamilton A	81/82	19			D1
	82/83	19			D1
Hibernian	83/84	16			P

BLACKWOOD Charles
b. Edinburgh
Bo'ness U

Club	Season	Apps	Sub	Gls	Div
Dunfermline A	55/56	1			D1

BLACKWOOD Robert Rankin
b. Edinburgh 20.8.1934 d. Edinburgh 25.6.1997
Milton House Amateurs
Merchiston Thistle
Kelty R

Club	Season	Apps	Sub	Gls	Div
Heart of Midlothian	50/51				D1
	51/52				D1
	52/53	14		2	D1
	53/54	4			D1
	54/55	3			D1
	55/56	5			D1
	56/57				D1
	57/58	23		4	D1
	58/59	16		4	D1
	59/60	28		12	D1
	60/61	26		11	D1
	61/62	17		2	D1
Ipswich T	62/63	19		4	FL
	63/64	28		7	FL
	64/65	15		1	FL
Colchester U	65/66	41		3	FL
	66/67	20			FL
	67/68	43	1	3	FL
Hawick Royal Albert					

BLAIN Alexander C
Tarff Rovers

Club	Season	Apps	Sub	Gls	Div
Stranraer	58/59				D2
	59/60				D2
	60/61				D2
	61/62				D2
Clyde	62/63	21			D1
	63/64	23			D2
	64/65				D1
	65/66	1			D1
Stirling A	66/67				D2
Stranraer	67/68	1	1		D2

BLAIR James

Club	Season	Apps	Sub	Gls	Div
Airdrieonians	58/59	8			D1

BLAIR Ian

Club	Season	Apps	Sub	Gls	Div
Clyde	62/63	8			D1
Motherwell	63/64	2			D1

BLAIR James
b. Calderbank 13.1.1947
Shotts Bon Accord

Club	Season	Apps	Sub	Gls	Div
St Mirren	67/68	26		21	D2
	68/69	24	4	7	D1
	69/70	32		15	D1
Hibernian	70/71	16	2	5	D1
St Mirren	70/71	8			D1
	71/72	35		19	D2
	72/73	7		1	D2
Norwich C	72/73	2	3		FL
	73/74	1			FL
KV Mechelen					

BLUES George
Caps: Aus - 4
Dundee

Club	Season	Apps	Sub	Gls	Div
Falkirk	60/61	11			D2
	61/62	2			D1
	62/63	7		2	D1
	63/64	2			D1
Berwick R	63/64	8			D2
Raith R	64/65	2		1	D2
Alloa A	64/65	7			D2
South Africa					
APIA					

BLYTH Edward

Club	Season	App	Gls	Div
Queen's Park	47/48	4	2	D1
St Mirren	48/49	1		D1
	49/50	20	2	D1
	50/51	11	2	D1
	51/52	25	2	D1
	52/53	17	6	D1
	53/54	18	4	D1

BOAG James
b. Blairhall 12.11.1937
Dunipace

Club	Season	App	Gls	Div
Falkirk	60/61	2		D2
	61/62	2		D1
Bath C				
Exeter C	62/63	2		FL
Bath C				

BODEN Alexander
b. Hardgate 13.8.1925
Duntochter St Marys BG
Celtic

Club	Season	App	Gls	Div
Cowdenbeath	L 46/47			D2
Celtic	47/48	2		D1
	48/49	27		D1
	49/50	27		D1
	50/51	10		D1
	51/52	12		D1
	52/53	15		D1
	53/54	2		D1
	54/55	9	2	D1
	55/56	17		D1
Ayr U	56/57	19	3	D1
	57/58			D2

BOEL Henning
b. Denmark 15.8.1945 Caps: Den - 15
Ikast

Club	Season	App	Gls	Div
Washington Whips	68	15		NA
Aberdeen	68/69	15		D1
	69/70	28		D1
	70/71	34	2	D1
	71/72	14		D1
	72/73	6	1	D1
	73/74	7		D1

BOGAN Robert

Club	Season	App	Gls	Div
Third Lanark	46/47	14		D1
	47/48	6	4	D1
	48/49	8	1	D1
Stirling A	49/50	4		D1
Stranraer				

BOGAN Thomas
b. Glasgow 18.5.1920 d. 23.9.1993
Strathclyde
Blantyre Celtic
Renfrew
Hibernian

Club	Season	App	Gls	Div
Celtic	46/47	10	1	D1
	47/48	23	4	D1
	48/49	1		D1
Preston NE	48/49	11		FL
Manchester U	49/50	18	4	FL
	50/51	11	3	FL
Aberdeen	50/51	1		D1
	51/52	3	1	D1
Southampton	51/52	4	1	FL
	52/53	4	1	FL
Blackburn R	53/54	1		FL
Macclesfield T				

BOGIE Malcolm Fisher McKenzie
b. Edinburgh 26.12.1939
Balgreen R

Club	Season	App	Gls	Div
Hibernian	58/59	2		D1
	59/60			D1
	60/61			D1
	61/62			D1
	62/63	1		D1
Grimsby T	63/64	1		FL
Aldershot	64/65	2	1	FL

BOLT Robert
b. Lochgelly 29.1.1912

Club	Season	App	Gls	Div
Heart of Midlothian	33/34	1		D1
	34/35			D1
Dunfermline A	34/35	21		D1
	35/36	33	2	D1
	36/37	38	2	D1
Falkirk	37/38	38	5	D1
	38/39	36	3	D1
Rangers				
Third Lanark	46/47	21		D1
Falkirk	46/47			D1
	47/48	21	2	D1
Inverness Caley				

BOLTON George
Petershill

Club	Season	App	Gls	Div
Clyde	50/51	12		D1

BOLTON John McCaig
b. Lesmahagow 26.10.1941

Club	Season	App	Gls	Div
Raith R	61/62	1		D1
	62/63	16		D1
Ipswich T	63/64	32		FL
	64/65	18		FL
	65/66	19	2	FL
Morton	66/67			D2
Raith R	67/68	12		D1
	68/69	33		D1
	69/70	23	1	D1
Dumbarton	70/71			D2
	71/72	29		D2
	72/73	27		D1

BOND James Ernest
b. Preston 4.5.1929

Club	Season	App	Gls	Div
Manchester U	50/51			FL
	51/52	19	4	FL
	52/53	1		FL
Carlisle U	52/53	28	2	FL
	53/54	35	4	FL
	54/55	29	3	FL
	55/56	29	4	FL
	56/57	33	5	FL
	57/58	31	3	FL
	58/59	9	2	FL
Queen of the South	58/59	1	1	D1

BONE James
b. Bridge of Allan 22.9.1949 Caps: S - 2
Bannockburn
Airth Castle R

Club	Season	App	Sub	Gls	Div
Partick T	68/69	30	1	13	D1
	69/70	30	1	14	D1
	70/71	21	1	14	D2
	71/72	22		10	D1
Norwich C	71/72	13		4	FL
	72/73	26		5	FL
Sheffield U	72/73	12		6	FL
	73/74	18	1	3	FL
Celtic	73/74	3	1		D1
	74/75	2	1	1	D1
Arbroath	74/75	14		5	D1
	75/76	26		13	D1
	76/77	39		15	D1
	77/78	18		8	D1
St Mirren	77/78	13		3	P
	78/79	33		7	P
Toronto Blizzard	79	25		3	NA
St Mirren	79/80	32		6	P
Toronto Blizzard	80	25		4	NA
St Mirren	80/81	26	1	7	P
	81/82	20	6	4	P
Hong Kong R	82/83				
Heart of Midlothian	83/84	34		7	P
	84/85	16	5	4	P
Arbroath	84/85	8	1	1	D2
	85/86	15		1	D2
	86/87	5		1	D2

BONER David
b. Queensferry 12.10.1941

Club	Season	App	Gls	Div
Everton	58/59			FL
	59/60			FL
Dundee U	60/61	7	2	D1
	61/62	14	2	D1
Raith R	62/63	7		D1
Mansfield T	63/64	12	1	FL

BONNAR John
b. West Calder 11.1.1924 d. Glasgow 14.1.2004
Polkemmet Jnrs

Club	Season	App	Gls	Div
Arbroath	46/47			D2
	47/48			D2
Celtic	48/49	9		D1
	49/50	13		D1
	50/51	19		D1
	51/52	16		D1
	52/53	13		D1
	53/54	20		D1
	54/55	22		D1
	55/56	3		D1
	56/57	4		D1
	57/58			
Dumbarton	58/59			
St Johnstone	59/60	5		D2

BONTHRONE James
b. Kinglassie
Kinglassie Colliery

Club	Season	App	Gls	Div
East Fife	47/48			D2
	48/49			D1
	49/50	8	3	D1
	50/51	19	5	D1
	51/52	25	10	D1
	52/53	25	8	D1
	53/54	30	7	D1
	54/55	26	3	D1
	55/56	34	16	D1
	56/57	31	22	D1
	57/58	24	10	D1
Dundee	57/58	7	3	D1
	58/59	13	4	D1
	59/60	10	8	D1
Stirling A	59/60	10	7	D1
	60/61			D2
	61/62	2		D1
Queen of the South	61/62			D2

BOOTH Ashley
Banks o'Dee

Club	Season	App	Gls	Div
St Johnstone	62/63	24		D2
	63/64	4		D1
	64/65	1		D1
East Fife	65/66	1		D2

BOOTH David
Baillieston

Club	Season	App	Sub	Gls	Div
Morton	70/71	7	2	1	D1
	71/72	6	1		D1
Stranraer	72/73	18	1	2	D2

BOOTH James

Club	Season	App	Gls	Div
Arbroath	68/69	32		D1
	69/70	7	1	D2

BOOTLAND Charles

Club	Season	App	Gls	Div
Dumbarton	46/47			D2
	47/48			D2
Notts Co	T 47/48			FL
Dumbarton	48/49			D2
Clyde	48/49	10	2	D1
	49/50	8	4	D1
Kilmarnock	50/51	13	3	D2
	51/52			D2
Dundee U	51/52			D2

BORLAND William
Glasgow U

Club	Season	App	Sub	Gls	Div
St Mirren	71/72	9	11	7	D2
	72/73	3			D2
Dumbarton	73/74	3	3	1	D1
Stranraer	74/75	23	8	2	D2

BORTHWICK Walter Ross
b. Edinburgh 4.4.1948

Club	Season	Apps	Sub	Gls	Div
Morton	65/66	2			D1
	66/67	4	2	4	D2
Brighton & HA	66/67	1			FL
Dundee U	T 67/68				
East Fife	67/68	21		8	D2
	68/69			8	D2
	69/70	34		4	D2
	70/71			4	D2
	71/72	17		4	D2
	72/73	29	1	4	D1
	73/74	23		1	D1
St Mirren	74/75	35		7	D2
	75/76	10	7	3	D1
	76/77	4	6	1	D1
St Johnstone	76/77	21	1	2	D1
St Mirren	77/78		1		P
Dunfermline A	77/78	26	1	4	D2
	78/79	25	4	2	D2
	79/80	24			D1
	80/81	2	1		D1

BOSTOCK William
b. Inverkeithing c1944 d. Dunfermline 7.7.1996
Jubilee Athletic

Club	Season	Apps	Sub	Gls	Div
Cowdenbeath	66/67	10		3	D2
	67/68	16	7	6	D2
	68/69			23	D2
	69/70	20	10	10	D2
	70/71	19	1	3	D1
	71/72	33		13	D2
	72/73	32		10	D2
	73/74	18		2	D2
Lochgelly Albert					

BOTHA Ray
b. South Africa

Club	Season	Apps	Sub	Gls	Div
Aberdeen	46/47	1			D1
	47/48				D1
	48/49				D1

BOURKE John Francis
b. Glasgow 31.12.1953
Dumbarton U

Club	Season	Apps	Sub	Gls	Div
Dumbarton	73/74	12	4	7	D1
	74/75	29	2	5	D1
	75/76	25		17	D1
	76/77	35		19	D1
Dundee U	77/78	25	1	5	P
	78/79				P
Kilmarnock	78/79	27		21	D1
	79/80	30	3	1	P
	80/81	28	1	5	P
	81/82	33	1	4	D1
	82/83	10	9	1	P
Dumbarton	82/83	7	1		D1
	83/84	34		13	D1
	84/85	24	2	4	P
	85/86	25	2	8	D1
	86/87	8	3	1	D1
Brechin C	86/87	13	1	5	D1
	87/88	6	8	2	D2
Kilmarnock	87/88	9		2	D1
	88/89	2			D1
Lesmahagow					

BOWIE Donald Shaw

Club	Season	Apps	Sub	Gls	Div
Dumbarton	63/64	31		8	D2
Stirling A	64/65	29		4	D2
	65/66	7		1	D1

BOWIE Ernest
Kilmarnock Amateurs

Club	Season	Apps	Sub	Gls	Div
Kilmarnock	53/54				D1
	54/55				D1
	55/56	1			D1
Clyde	56/57				D2
Brakpan U					

BOWIE Neil
Pollok

Club	Season	Apps	Sub	Gls	Div
East Fife	54/55				D1
	55/56	2			D1
	56/57	7			D1
	57/58	32			D1
	58/59				D2
Hamilton A	58/59	4			D2
Brechin C	59/60				D2
	60/61				D2
	61/62	24		1	D2

BOWMAN Andrew
b. Pittenweem 7.3.1934

Club	Season	Apps	Sub	Gls	Div
Chelsea	51/52				FL
	52/53				FL
	53/54	1			FL
	54/55				FL
Heart of Midlothian	55/56	2			D1
	56/57	3			D1
	57/58	18		2	D1
	58/59	7			D1
	59/60	24			D1
	60/61	16		1	D1
Newport Co	61/62	42		6	FL
	62/63	27		1	FL
Tonbridge					
USA					
Hamilton A	65/66	11			D1
Hawick Royal Albert	66/67				
Stenhousemuir	67/68	11	1		D2

BOYD Alfred
b. Dundee 22.10.1920 d. S Africa 3.7.1998
Maryfield R
North End Jnrs

Club	Season	Apps	Sub	Gls	Div
St Johnstone	46/47	9		2	D2
Dundee	46/47	6			D2
	47/48	30		1	D1
	48/49	29		2	D1
	49/50	29		5	D1
	50/51	28		6	D1
	51/52	26		1	D1
	52/53	22		3	D1

BOYD Andrew
b. Prestwick
Dumbarton

Club	Season	Apps	Sub	Gls	Div
Cowdenbeath	46/47				D2
	47/48				D2
	48/49				D2
Morton	49/50	13		6	D2
	50/51	8			D1

BOYD Archibald

Club	Season	Apps	Sub	Gls	Div
Clyde	59/60	9		3	D1
	60/61	4			D1

BOYD J Alan

Club	Season	Apps	Sub	Gls	Div
Queen's Park	46/47	9		1	D1
	47/48				D1
	48/49	26		4	D2
	49/50	18		2	D2
Aberdeen	50/51	10		3	D1
	51/52	16		5	D1
	52/53	12		5	D1
	53/54	3		1	D1
	54/55				D1
	55/56	13		5	D1
	56/57	8		2	D1
	57/58	7		1	D1
East Fife	58/59	25		3	D2

BOYD James
b. Hamilton 14.8.1956
Crystal Palace

Club	Season	Apps	Sub	Gls	Div
Clyde	74/75	4	1		D1
	75/76	11	2		D1
	76/77	34		1	D2
	77/78	38		2	D2
Motherwell	78/79	9	2		P
Clyde	79/80	19	2		D1
	80/81	7			D2

BOYD John
Irvine V

Club	Season	Apps	Sub	Gls	Div
Morton	58/59				D2
	59/60				D2
	60/61				D2
	61/62	34			D2
	62/63				D2
	63/64	33		1	D2
	64/65	26			D1
	65/66	23			D1
	66/67	13		1	D2
Clydebank	66/67				D2
	67/68	11		1	D2
Motherwell	67/68	2			D1

BOYD William
Ashfield Jnrs

Club	Season	Apps	Sub	Gls	Div
Rangers	50/51				D1
	51/52	2			D1
	52/53				D1
	53/54				D1
	54/55				D1
	55/56				D1
Hamilton A	56/57	9		1	D2

BOYD William

Club	Season	Apps	Sub	Gls	Div
Airdrieonians	63/64	9		4	D1
	64/65	1			D1

BOYLE

Club	Season	Apps	Sub	Gls	Div
Third Lanark	59/60	2		2	D1

BOYLE G

Club	Season	Apps	Sub	Gls	Div
Hibernian	53/54	4			D1
	54/55	1			D1
	55/56				D1
	56/57	1			D1
	57/58	4			D1
	58/59	1			D1

BOYLE Peter
Larkhall Thistle

Club	Season	Apps	Sub	Gls	Div
Clyde	72/73	30		14	D2
	73/74	29	3	6	D1
	74/75	21	4	7	D1
	75/76	22	2	5	D1
	76/77	4		4	D2

BRADFORD Lewis
b. Gresley 24.11.1916

Club	Season	Apps	Sub	Gls	Div
Preston NE	34/35				FL
	35/36				FL
	36/37				FL
	37/38				FL
	38/39				FL
Kilmarnock	46/47	5			D1
Bradford C	46/47	34		1	FL
	47/48	31			FL
	48/49	3			FL
Newport Co	48/49	24			FL
Trowbridge T					
Bath C					

BRADLEY James
b. Greenock 21.3.1927

Club	Season	Apps	Sub	Gls	Div
Third Lanark	50/51	7		2	D1
	51/52	2			D1
Shrewsbury T	52/53	1			FL

BRADLEY William
b. Glasgow 26.6.1937
Saltcoats V

Club	Season	Apps	Sub	Gls	Div
Ayr U	57/58				D2
	58/59				D2
	59/60				D1
	60/61	8			D1
	61/62	21		7	D2
	62/63				D2
Hartlepools U	63/64	38		5	FL
	64/65	43		10	FL

BRADY Thomas

Falkirk	46/47	2		1	D1

BRAND Ralph Laidlaw

b. Edinburgh 18.12.1936 Caps: S - 8

Slateford A					
Rangers					
Broxburn A	L 52/53				
	53/54				
Rangers	54/55	3		2	D1
	55/56				D1
	56/57				D1
	57/58	22		12	D1
	58/59	25		21	D1
	59/60	9		2	D1
	60/61	34		24	D1
	61/62	33		23	D1
	62/63	32		19	D1
	63/64	31		19	D1
	64/65	17		6	D1
Manchester C	65/66	17		2	FL
	66/67	3			FL
Sunderland	67/68	28		7	FL
	68/69	3			FL
Raith R	69/70	23		5	D1
Albion R	70/71				D2
Hamilton A	71/72	7		2	D2

BRANDER George Milne

b. Aberdeen 1.11.1929 d. ?.?.1995

Aberdeen EE					
Raith R	50/51	17		4	D1
	51/52	8		3	D1
Newcastle U	52/53	5		2	FL
Stirling A	53/54	7		2	D1
	54/55	15		1	D1
Arbroath					
Fraserburgh					
Huntly					
Elgin C					

BRANNIGAN T

Morton	72/73	1			D1

BRECHIN J

Dunfermline A	66/67	1			D1

BRECKENRIDGE D

Queen of the South	51/52	1			D1
	52/53				D1
	53/54				D1
	54/55	1			D1

BREEN David

b. Paisley

Chelsea					
Montrose	64/65	14			D2
Airdrieonians	65/66	1			D2
	66/67	6			D1
	67/68	6			D1
	68/69	3	2		D1

BREMNER Desmond George

b. Aberchirder 7.9.1952 Caps: S - 1

Banks o'Dee					
Deverondale					
Hibernian	72/73	11			D1
	73/74	21		2	D1
	74/75	30		2	D1
	75/76	32		3	P
	76/77	36		4	P
	77/78	33		2	P
	78/79	31		5	P
	79/80	5			P
Aston Villa	79/80	36		3	FL
	80/81	42		2	FL
	81/82	38		3	FL
	82/83	36	1		FL
	83/84	14	3		FL
	84/85	4		1	FL
Birmingham C	84/85	30			FL
	85/86	32			FL
	86/87	40		4	FL
	87/88	37			FL
	88/89	28	1	1	FL
Fulham	89/90				FL
Walsall	89/90	2	4		FL
Stafford R					

BREMNER Gordon

Arsenal					
Motherwell	46/47	25		8	D1
	47/48	28		1	D1
	48/49	25		7	D1
	49/50	20		1	D1
	50/51	1			D1

BREMNER T Hutton

b. c1913 d. ?.?.1969

Queen's Park	29/30	3			D1
	30/31	28		6	D1
	31/32	29		3	D1
	32/33	26		7	D1
	33/34	24		7	D1
	34/35	32		7	D1
Motherwell	35/36	32		9	D1
	36/37	23		4	D1
	37/38	31		10	D1
	38/39	33		12	D1
Stranraer					
Hamilton A	46/47	15		4	D1

BRICE Gordon Henry John

b. Bedford 4.5.1924

Bedford St Clements					
Luton T	46/47	13			FL
Wolverhampton W	47/48	12			FL
Reading	47/48	5			FL
	48/49	42			FL
	49/50	42		2	FL
	50/51	46		4	FL
	51/52	44		3	FL
	52/53	19			FL
Fulham	52/53	4			FL
	53/54	42			FL
	54/55	27		1	FL
	55/56	14			FL
Ayr U	56/57	20			D1
	57/58				D2

BRIGGS James

b. ?.?.1937

St Marys YC					
Dundee U	55/56	6			D2
	56/57	15			D2
	57/58	22			D2
	58/59	1			D2
	59/60	7		1	D2
	60/61	34		6	D1
	61/62	34			D1
	62/63	28			D1
	63/64	32		9	D1
	64/65	34		3	D1
	65/66	34		3	D1
	66/67	27	1	1	D1
	67/68	19		2	D1
	68/69	1	3		D1
	69/70	1			D1
Montrose	70/71				D2
Keith					

BRIGGS Wilson Waite

b. Gorebridge 15.5.1942

Arniston R					
Gorebridge Youths					
Musselburgh Windsor					
Aston Villa	61/62	1			FL
	62/63	1			FL
	63/64				FL
	64/65				FL
	65/66				FL
	66/67				FL
	67/68				FL
Falkirk	68/69		1		D1
Partick T	69/70				D1
East Fife	69/70	3			D2

BRIMS Donald

b. Auchendinny 8.1.1934

Arniston Thistle					
Motherwell	56/57	5			D1
	57/58	6			D1
Bradford PA	58/59	41		2	FL
	59/60	36		1	FL
Third Lanark	60/61	4			D1

BRISCOE James Edward

b. St Helens 23.4.1917

d. Northampton 17.4.1981

St Helens T					
Preston NE	36/37	5			FL
Heart of Midlothian	37/38	28		8	D1
	38/39	34		9	D1
	46/47	2			D1
Northampton T	46/47	13		1	FL
	47/48	23		11	FL
	48/49	17		5	FL
Nuneaton B					
Wolverton T					

BRISCOE R

Queen of the South	54/55	2			D1

BRODIE Eric

b. Rattray 8.11.1940

Blairgowrie Jnrs					
Forfar A	58/59				D2
	59/60				D2
	60/61				D2
	61/62	8		5	D2
Dundee U	61/62	9		1	D1
	62/63				D1
Shrewsbury T	63/64	34		2	FL
	64/65	41		4	FL
	65/66	44		6	FL
	66/67	39	1	6	FL
	67/68	23	10	6	FL
Chester	68/69	32	1	4	FL
	69/70	11			FL
Tranmere R	69/70	27			FL
	70/71	37	1	3	FL
	71/72	17	2		FL

BRODIE Eric

Methil Star

Club	Season	Apps		Gls	Div
Dundee U	62/63	8		3	D1
	63/64				D1
	64/65				D1
East Fife	65/66				D2
	66/67				D2
	67/68				D2

BRODIE Kenneth

Club	Season	Apps		Gls	Div
Partick T	54/55	3			D1
	55/56				D1
	56/57				D1
	57/58	2			D1

BROGAN Frank Anthony

b. Glasgow 3.8.1942
Dumfries St Josephs
St Mungos Academy
Celtic
St Rochs L

Club	Season	Apps		Gls	Div
Celtic	61/62	10		4	D1
	62/63	18		4	D1
	63/64	9		5	D1
Ipswich T	64/65	40		13	FL
	65/66	40		8	FL
	66/67	35		15	FL
	67/68	36		17	FL
	68/69	31	1	2	FL
	69/70	19	1	3	FL
	70/71				FL
Halifax T	71/72	3		2	FL
	72/73	22	2	4	FL

BROGAN James Andrew

b. Glasgow 5.6.1944 Caps: S - 4
Dumfries St Josephs
St Rochs

Club	Season	Apps		Gls	Div
Celtic	63/64	3			D1
	64/65	13		1	D1
	65/66	2			D1
	66/67		1		D1
	67/68	18	1	1	D1
	68/69	29		2	D1
	69/70	27	1	1	D1
	70/71	26			D1
	71/72	20	1	1	D1
	72/73	20			D1
	73/74	30			D1
	74/75	19	1		D1
Coventry C	75/76	28			FL
	76/77				FL
Ayr U	76/77	10			P
	77/78	3			P

BROOKS George

Club	Season	Apps		Gls	Div
Falkirk	46/47	14		8	D1

BROOKS James

Club	Season	Apps		Gls	Div
Clyde	53/54	3			D1

BROWN

Club	Season	Apps		Gls	Div
Clyde	71/72	2			D1

BROWN Alexander

b. Glasgow 15.8.1930

Club	Season	Apps		Gls	Div
Partick T	50/51	5			D1
	51/52	2			D1
	52/53				D1
	53/54				D1
	54/55	2			D1
	55/56				D1
	56/57	1			D1
Preston NE	57/58				FL
Carlisle U	58/59	45			FL
	5960	37			FL
	60/61	20			FL

BROWN Alexander

b. Fife
Lochgelly Albert

Club	Season	Apps		Gls	Div
Dundee U	58/59	18			D2
	59/60	34			D2
	60/61	7			D1
	61/62	16			D1
Morton					

BROWN Alexander Dewar

b. Grangemouth 24.3.1939
Broxburn A
Partick T
Broxburn A L

Club	Season	Apps		Gls	Div
Partick T	57/58	7		1	D1
	58/59	2			D1
	59/60	15			D1
	60/61	34			D1
	61/62	34			D1
	62/63	34		7	D1
	63/64	1			D1
Everton	64/65	28		5	FL
	65/66	14	2		FL
	66/67	15	5	1	FL
	67/68	12	13	1	FL
	68/69	40		1	FL
	69/70	31	5		FL
	70/71	6	8	1	FL
Shrewsbury T	71/72	21			FL
Southport	72/73	17	2		FL
Fleetwood					
Poulton					
Blackpool R					

BROWN Alistair D

b. Dumbarton 29.3.1957
Vale of Leven Jnrs

Club	Season	Apps		Gls	Div
Dumbarton	74/75	10	3		D1
	75/76	19		2	D1
	76/77	28	6	5	D1
	77/78	38	1	6	D1
	78/79	25	4	4	D1
	79/80	31	3	1	D1
	80/81	24		7	D1
	81/82	22	8	6	D1
	82/83	12	4	1	D1
Stirling A	83/84				D2
St Neots					

BROWN Allan Duncan

b. Kennaway 12.10.1926 Caps: S - 14
Kennaway Hearts

Club	Season	Apps		Gls	Div
East Fife	46/47				D2
	47/48				D2
	48/49	22		5	D1
	49/50	30		12	D1
Blackpool	50/51	16		3	FL
	51/52	37		14	FL
	53/53	29		15	FL
	53/54	27		11	FL
	54/55	19		6	FL
	55/56	18		6	FL
	56/57	17		13	FL
Luton T	56/57	16		5	FL
	57/58	33		12	FL
	58/59	39		20	FL
	59/60	39		7	FL
	60/61	24		7	FL
Portsmouth	60/61	9		2	FL
	61/62	44		3	FL
	62/63	16		3	FL
Wigan A	63/64	3		5	CC
	64/65	35		12	CC

BROWN Charles

b. Dumfries c1923
LMS Rovers

Club	Season	Apps		Gls	Div
Queen of the South	48/49	9		3	D1
	49/50	16		6	D1
	50/51				D2
	51/52	5		1	D1
	52/53	2			D1
Tarff Rovers					

BROWN Charles

Club	Season	Apps		Gls	Div
Clyde	57/58	2		1	D1

BROWN Charles

Club	Season	Apps		Gls	Div
Morton	72/73	7	1	2	D1
	73/74	2	6	1	D1
	74/75	4	6	1	D1
	75/76	15	4	1	D1
	76/77	35	1	9	D1
	77/78	28	1	3	D1
Ayr U	78/79	1	1		D1
Morton	79/80	9	2	1	P
Clyde	80/81	2	1		D2
East Stirlingshire	80/81	3			D1
Largs Thistle	81/82				
	82/83				
	83/84				
	84/85				
	85/86				
Partick T	86/87	1			D1

BROWN Craig

Rangers

Club	Season	Apps		Gls	Div
Dundee	61/62	9			D1
	62/63	4			D1
	63/64	1			D1
Falkirk	64/65	8			D1
	65/66	8			D1
	66/67	1			D1
Stranraer	67/68				D2

BROWN David

Fauldhouse U

Club	Season	Apps		Gls	Div
Stirling A	61/62	13			D1
	62/63				D2
	63/64	17		2	D2
Albion R	63/64				D2
	64/65	33			D2
	65/66				D2

BROWN George

Club	Season	Apps		Gls	Div
Airdrieonians	61/62	6			D1

BROWN George Donaldson

b. Airdrie 8.5.1928
Whifflett Rob Roy
Larkhall Thistle

Club	Season	Apps		Gls	Div
Kilmarnock	47/48				D2
	48/49	11		2	D2
	49/50	1			D2
St Mirren	49/50	2			D1
	50/51	2			D1
Airdrieonians	50/51	7			D1
Southport	50/51	1			FL
Stenhousemuir	50/51				D2
	51/52				D2
Falkirk	52/53	13		3	D1
Hamilton A	53/54	24		2	D1
Clyde	54/55	8		2	D1
	55/56	10		1	D1
Bradford PA	56/57	17		2	FL
Poole T					
Yiewsley					
Ilkeston T					

BROWN Hugh

b. Carmyle 7.12.1921 d. ?.7.1994 Caps: S - 3
Yoker A

Club	Season	Apps		Gls	Div
Partick T	46/47	30		3	D1
	47/48	23		4	D1
	48/49	11		1	D1
	49/50	10		4	D1
Torquay U	50/51	27			FL
	51/52	28			FL

BROWN Hugh Murdoch
b. Greenock 6.11.1940

Kilmarnock Amateurs					
Kilmarnock	58/59	12		1	D1
	59/60	1			D1
	60/61	31		6	D1
	61/62	18			D1
	62/63	29		3	D1
	63/64	31		5	D1
	64/65	1			D1
	65/66	1			D1
	66/67	3	1		D1
	67/68	1			D1
Dumbarton	68/69				D2

BROWN Ian

Lochee Renton					
Dundee U	67/68	1	3		D1

BROWN James
b. Cumnock 16.2.1924 d. ?.1.2002

Kello R					
Motherwell	46/47	18		16	D1
	47/48				D1
Chesterfield	48/49	5		2	FL
Bradford C	48/49	20		11	FL
Queen of the South	49/50	14		1	D1
Carlisle U	50/51	14		9	FL
	51/52	1			FL
Queen of the South					

BROWN James

Falkirk	49/50	18		3	D1
	50/51	15		5	D1
	51/52	28		14	D2
	52/53	19		4	D1
	53/54	1			D1
Aberdeen	53/54				D1
	54/55	3		1	D1
Stirling A	55/56				D1

BROWN James

Raith R	49/50	1			D1

BROWN James

Bathgate					
Motherwell	57/58	1			D1

BROWN James

Kilsyth R					
Stirling A	60/61				D2
	61/62	23			D1
	62/63				D2
	63/64	19			D2
Hartlepools U	63/64				FL

BROWN James

St Mirren	64/65	2			D1
Berwick R					

BROWN James
b. Edinburgh 11.8.1950

Salvesen BC					
Heart of Midlothian	68/69	1	1		D1
	69/70	20	1	3	D1
	70/71	33		4	D1
	71/72	34		4	D1
	72/73	31	1	2	D1
	73/74	25	3	2	D1
	74/75	18	2		D1
	75/76	33	1	3	P
	76/77	34		3	P
	77/78	15			D1
	78/79	22	4		P
Hibernian	79/80	11	2		P
	80/81	29	2	1	D1
Dunfermline A	81/82	13			D1

BROWN James

Ladybank V					
Dunfermline A	69/70	8			D1
	70/71	8			D1
	71/72	1			D1
	72/73	7			D2
	73/74	6			D1
Raith R	74/75	23	6		D2
	75/76	26		3	D2
	76/77	20		2	D1
	77/78	2			D2

BROWN James Robertson
b. Buckhaven 19.7.1925

Bayview YC					
Heart of Midlothian	46/47	30			D1
	47/48	27			D1
	48/49	30			D1
	49/50	24			D1
	50/51	27			D1
	51/52	29			D1
	52/53				D1
Southend U L	52/53				FL
Kilmarnock	53/54	30			D2
	54/55	30			D1
	55/56	33			D1
	56/57	31			D1
	57/58	31			D1
	58/59	33			D1
	59/60	33			D1
	60/61	10			D1
St Mirren	60/61	23			D1
	61/62	21			D1
East Fife	62/63	3			D2
Stranraer	62/63				D2
Falkirk	62/63	4			D1
Polish White Eagles					

BROWN John
b. Airdrie

Craigton A					
Queen of the South	46/47	2			D1
	47/48	24		5	D1
	48/49	23		4	D1
	49/50	22		4	D1
	50/51				D2
	51/52	10		4	D1
	52/53	11		3	D1
	53/54	23		15	D1
	54/55	20		6	D1
	55/56	1			D1
St Mirren	55/56	13		1	D1

BROWN John

Hibernian	52/53	1			D1

BROWN John

Dunfermline A	58/59	1			D1

BROWN John

Sunnybank					
Aberdeen	52/53				D1
	53/54	1			D1
	54/55				D1
	55/56				D1
	56/57	5		1	D1
Arbroath	57/58				D2
	58/59				D2
	59/60	28		2	D1
	60/61				D2
East Fife	61/62				D2
	62/63				D2

BROWN John

St Mirren	66/67	3			D1
Berwick R	67/68	17	1		D2
	68/69			2	D2
	69/70	24	1	1	D2
	70/71			1	D2
	71/72	31	2		D2
	72/73	18	3	1	D2

BROWN John Bell
b. Troon 21.2.1915 Caps: S - 1

Glenburn R					
Clyde					
Shawfield Jnrs					
Clyde	35/36	22			D1
	36/37	31			D1
	37/38	38			D1
	38/39	38			D1
Hibernian	46/47	1			D1
	47/48	11			D1
Dundee	47/48	10			D1
	48/49	4			D1
Kilmarnock	49/50	1			D2
	50/51				D2

BROWN John Michael
b. London ?.?.1934

Queen's Park	38/39	3			D1
	46/47				D1
	47/48	9			D1
	48/49				D2
	49/50				D2
	50/51				D2
	51/52				D2
	52/53				D2
Shrewsbury T	53/54	5		3	FL

BROWN John Thomas
b. Edinburgh 2.4.1935

Hibernian	53/54	2			D1
	54/55				D1
	55/56				D1
	56/57				D1
Third Lanark	57/58	34		1	D1
	58/59	33		1	D1
	59/60	19			D1
Tranmere R	60/61	18			FL
	61/62	15			FL
Hartlepools U	62/63	46		5	FL
	63/64	22		5	FL
Scarborough					

BROWN Kenneth

Penicuik A					
Raith R	69/70	5			D1

BROWN Kenneth

St Mirren	70/71	4	1		D1

BROWN Matthew

Eastern Star					
Stirling A	51/52	2			D1
	52/53				D2
Inverness Caley					

BROWN R

Third Lanark	52/53	13		1	D1

BROWN Robert
b. Dunipace 19.3.1923 Caps: S - 3

Queen's Park					
Rangers	46/47	30			D1
	47/48	30			D1
	48/49	30			D1
	49/50	30			D1
	50/51	30			D1
	51/52	29			D1
	52/53				D1
	53/54	21			D1
	54/55	8			D1
	55/56	3			D1
Falkirk	56/57	17			D1
	57/58	6			D1

BROWN Robert
b. Motherwell 2.12.1931
Polkemmet Jnrs

Club	Season	Apps	Sub	Goals	Div
Motherwell	51/52				
	52/53	2			D1
	53/54	1			D2
	54/55				D1
	55/56				D1
Workington	56/57	42			FL
	57/58	39			FL
	58/59	46		1	FL
	59/60	10			FL
	60/61	46		1	FL
	61/62	43			FL
	62/63	44			FL
	63/64	44			FL
	64/65	36			FL
	65/66	43			FL
	66/67	19			FL
	67/68	5		1	FL

BROWN Robert

Club	Season	Apps	Sub	Goals	Div
Airdrieonians	69/70	5		1	D1
	70/71			1	D1

BROWN Russell

Club	Season	Apps	Sub	Goals	Div
Partick T	67/68	1		1	D1

BROWN Stewart
Beith

Club	Season	Apps	Sub	Goals	Div
Motherwell	55/56	5			D1
	56/57	4			D1
	57/58	2			D1
	58/59	13			D1

BROWN Thomas
b. Ayr

Club	Season	Apps	Sub	Goals	Div
Airdrieonians	47/48	4		1	D1
	48/49				D2
	49/50	29			D2
	50/51	22			D1
	51/52	24			D1
	52/53	13			D1
	53/54	12			D1
Cowdenbeath					

BROWN Thomas McJ
Stewarton U
Dreghorn Jnrs

Club	Season	Apps	Sub	Goals	Div
Kilmarnock	58/59	1			D1
	59/60	3		1	D1
	60/61				D1
	61/62				D1
	62/63				D1
	63/64				D1
	64/65				D1
	65/66				D1
Queen of the South	66/67	22			D2
Newton Stewart					

BROWN William

Club	Season	Apps	Sub	Goals	Div
Airdrieonians	47/48	5			D1
	48/49				D2
	49/50	25		7	D2
	50/51	14		5	D1
	51/52	11		2	D1
	52/53	1		1	D1
	53/54	18		5	D1

BROWN William
b. Musselburgh
Hull C

Club	Season	Apps	Sub	Goals	Div
Motherwell	70/71				D1
	71/72	9		1	D1
	72/73				D1
Raith R	73/74	31	1	1	D2
	74/75	17		1	D2
	75/76	18		1	D2
	76/77	23		2	D1
	77/78		1		D2

BROWN William Dallas Fyfe
b. Arbroath 8.10.1931 Caps: S - 28
Arbroath Cliffburn
Carnoustie Juveniles
Carnoustie Panmure

Club	Season	Apps	Sub	Goals	Div
Dundee	49/50	10			D1
	50/51	11			D1
	51/52	16			D1
	52/53	8			D1
	53/54	20			D1
	54/55	28			D1
	55/56	30			D1
	56/57	31			D1
	57/58	31			D1
	58/59	30			D1
Tottenham H	59/60	40			FL
	60/61	41			FL
	61/62	35			FL
	62/63	40			FL
	63/64	27			FL
	64/65	19			FL
	65/66	20			FL
Northampton T	66/67	17			FL
Hamilton Steelers					
Toronto Falcons	67	16			NP

BROWN William Falconer
b. Larkhall 20.10.1922 d. 27.5.1978
Larkhall Thistle

Club	Season	Apps	Sub	Goals	Div
Preston NE	46/47	8			FL
	47/48	1			FL
	48/49	28			FL
	49/50	3			FL
Queen of the South	49/50	8			D1
Elgin C	50/51				
Grimsby T	51/52	46		1	FL
	52/53	32			FL
	53/54	34			FL
	54/55	36			FL
	55/56	43			FL
	56/57	42			FL
	57/58	32			FL

BROWN Wilson
b. Lanark
Lanark U

Club	Season	Apps	Sub	Goals	Div
Heart of Midlothian	52/53				D1
	53/54				D1
	54/55				D1
	55/56	1			D1
	56/57	19			D1
	57/58	3			D1
	58/59	3			D1
	59/60	1			D1
Queen of the South	60/61				D2
	61/62				D2
	62/63				D1
	63/64				D1
	64/65				D2
Hamilton A	65/66	6			D1

BROWNING J

Club	Season	Apps	Sub	Goals	Div
Partick T	50/51	1			D1

BROWNLEE Kenneth
Newtongrange Star

Club	Season	Apps	Sub	Goals	Div
Aberdeen	55/56	9			D1
	56/57	9			D1
	57/58	28		1	D1
	58/59	5			D1
	59/60	16		4	D1
	60/61	29		18	D1
	61/62	27		4	D1
	62/63	9		1	D1
Third Lanark	63/64	19		1	D1
St Johnstone	63/64	4			D1
Airdrieonians					
Boksburg					

BROWNLIE John

Club	Season	Apps	Sub	Goals	Div
Clyde	58/59	3		2	D1
	59/60	3			D1

BROWNLIE John
b. Caldercruix 11.3.1952 Caps: S - 7
Pumpherston Jnrs

Club	Season	Apps	Sub	Goals	Div
Hibernian	69/70	1			D1
	70/71	22		1	D1
	71/72	33		3	D1
	72/73	19			D1
	73/74	11			D1
	74/75	28		3	D1
	75/76	33		5	P
	76/77	36		3	P
	77/78	29			P
Newcastle U	78/79	34			FL
	79/80	38			FL
	80/81	14			FL
	81/82	38		2	FL
Middlesbrough	82/83	12			FL
	83/84				FL
Hartlepool U	84/85	19		1	FL
Vasalunds					
Berwick R	85/86	15			D2
Blyth Spartans					

BRUCE

Club	Season	Apps	Sub	Goals	Div
Raith R	56/57	1			D1

BRUCE A

Club	Season	Apps	Sub	Goals	Div
Hibernian	48/49	1			D1

BRUCE Dennis

Club	Season	Apps	Sub	Goals	Div
Arbroath	67/68	35		32	D2
	68/69	33		8	D1
	69/70	18	2	9	D2
	70/71	19			D2
	71/72	2	6	2	D2
Forfar A	71/72	9		1	D2
Huntly					
Keith					
Elgin C					

BRUCE John

Club	Season	Apps	Sub	Goals	Div
Dundee	47/48	4			D1
	48/49	2		1	D1
Aberdeen	49/50	2			D1
	50/51	1			D1

BRUCE William

Club	Season	Apps	Sub	Goals	Div
Raith R	46/47				D2
Aberdeen	47/48	1			D1
	48/49				D1
	49/50				D1
Hibernian	50/51	1			D1
	51/52	2			D1
Inverness Caley					

BRYANS Robert

Club	Season	Apps	Sub	Goals	Div
Stirling A	53/54	2			D1
	54/55	7			D1
Dunfermline A	55/56	7			D1

BRYCE Alexander
b. c1945
Strathclyde

Club	Season	Apps	Sub	Goals	Div
Third Lanark	61/62	5		2	D1
	62/63	22		2	D1
	63/64	5			D1
Clyde	64/65	29		5	D1
	65/66	29		7	D1
Dundee	66/67	22		6	D1
	67/68	12	1	2	D1
	68/69	24	2	7	D1
	69/70	27	1	2	D1
	70/71	14	2	3	D1
	71/72	4	1	2	D1
Falkirk	71/72	7		1	D1
Cowdenbeath	72/73	8		5	D2

BRYCELAND Thomas
b. Greenock 1.3.1939
Gourock Jnrs

St Mirren	55/56	1			D1
	56/57	6		4	D1
	57/58	13		5	D1
	58/59	25		11	D1
	59/60	28		16	D1
	60/61	26		9	D1
	61/62	4		1	D1
	62/63	2		1	D1
Norwich C	62/63	31		6	FL
	63/64	42		12	FL
	64/65	37		5	FL
	65/66	40		8	FL
	66/67	34	1	8	FL
	67/68	31		8	FL
	68/69	19		1	FL
	69/70	19		1	FL
Oldham A	69/70	1			FL
	70/71	45		10	FL
	71/72	20			FL
St Mirren	71/72	14		2	D2
	72/73				D2

BRYDEN John
Motherwell Jnrs

Motherwell	52/53	1		D1
	53/54	3		D2
	54/55			D1

BUCHAN George
b. Aberdeen 2.5.1950

Aberdeen	68/69	3	1		D1
	69/70	4		1	D1
	70/71	12		1	D1
	71/72	1		1	D1
	72/73	4		4	D1
Manchester U	73/74			3	FL
Bury	74/75	41	1	3	FL
	75/76	16	7	3	FL
Motherwell	L 75/76				P
Mossley					

BUCHAN Gordon
Stonehaven

Arbroath	72/73	14	1		D1
	73/74	4	4		D1
	74/75	12	4		D1
Elgin C					

BUCHAN Martin McLean
b. Aberdeen 6.3.1949 Caps: S - 34
Banks o'Dee

Aberdeen	66/67	4			D1
	67/68	24		2	D1
	68/69	24	3	2	D1
	69/70	19		2	D1
	70/71	34		2	D1
	71/72	25		1	D1
Manchester U	71/72	13		1	FL
	72/73	42			FL
	73/74	42			FL
	74/75	41			FL
	75/76	42			FL
	76/77	33			FL
	77/78	28		1	FL
	78/79	37		2	FL
	79/80	42			FL
	80/81	26			FL
	81/82	27			FL
	82/83	3			FL
Oldham A	83/84	24			FL
	84/85	4			FL

BUCHAN Robert
b. Kelty 1.6.1929
Bayview YC
Lochgelly Albert

Heart of Midlothian	48/49	1			D1
	49/50				D1
	50/51				D1
	51/52	1			D1
Cowdenbeath	52/53				D2
	53/54	21			D2
Raith R	54/55	11		3	D1
	55/56				D1
	56/57	6		1	D1

BUCHANAN Alexander
Valleyfield Colliery

Raith R	68/69		D1
	69/70	8	D1

BUCHANAN Archibald
b. ?.?.1929 d. ?1.1984

Hibernian	46/47	12		5	D1
	47/48	29		1	D1
	48/49	26			D1
	49/50	24		2	D1
	50/51	27		4	D1
	51/52	25		2	D1
	52/53	24			D1
	53/54	20		1	D1
	54/55	3			D1
	55/56	9			D1
	56/57	3		1	D1
St Mirren	56/57	9			D1
	57/58	34		1	D1
Cowdenbeath	58/59				D2
	59/60				D2

BUCHANAN Edward
b. Banknock
Shettleston

Aberdeen	67/68	3	1		1	D1
	68/69					D1
Berwick R	69/70	15	1			D2
	70/71				2	D2

BUCHANAN John
b. Bonnybridge 9.6.1928

Clyde	46/47	1			D1
Kilsyth R					
Clyde	49/50	3		1	D1
	50/51	26		8	D1
	51/52				D2
	52/53	23		16	D1
	53/54	30		16	D1
	54/55	20		13	D1
Derby Co	54/55	11		3	FL
	55/56	15		4	FL
	56/57	6		5	FL
Bradford PA	57/58	12		10	FL
	58/59	45		21	FL
	59/60	36		6	FL
	60/61	42		21	FL
	61/62	23		7	FL
	62/63	6		1	FL

BUCHANAN John
b. Edinburgh 3.1.1935
Edinburgh Waverley

Hibernian	54/55	2		1	D1
	55/56	1			D1
	56/57	3			D1
	57/58				D1
	58/59				D1
	59/60	2		1	D1
	60/61	6		3	D1
Raith R	60/61	8		1	D1
Newport Co	61/62	31		7	FL
Gala Fairydean					
Duns					
Hawick Royal Albert					

BUCKLEY Patrick McCabe
b. Leith 31.1.1925 Caps: S - 3
Bo'ness U

St Johnstone	48/49	28		21	D2
	49/50	16		14	D2
	50/51	25		8	D2
	51/52	30		20	D2
Aberdeen	52/53	27		9	D1
	53/54	29		17	D1
	54/55	28		17	D1
	55/56	9		6	D1
	56/57	13		9	D1
Inverness Caley					

BUCKLEY Patrick McCabe
b. Leith 12.9.1946

Third Lanark	62/63	4			D1
	63/64	21		2	D1
Wolverhampton W	64/65	15		3	FL
	65/66	6		2	FL
	66/67	2		1	FL
	67/68	5	1	2	FL
Sheffield U	67/68	5			FL
	68/69	4	1	2	FL
	69/70		4		FL
	70/71		1		FL
	71/72				FL
Rotherham U	72/73	1	2		FL

BUNTEN John A D
Hurlford U

Kilmarnock	50/51		D2
	51/52	1	D2
	52/53		D2
	53/54		D2
Rhyl	54/55		
Kilmarnock	55/56	1	D1
	56/57		D1

BURGESS W S

Queen's Park	47/48	4	2	D1

BURKE Thomas
b. Greenock 18.10.1939

Clyde	60/61	1		D1
	61/62			D2
	62/63	1		D1
Barnsley	62/63	1		FL

BURN Ramsay
Pollok Jnrs

Ayr U	58/59		D2
	59/60	32	D1
	60/61	34	D1
	61/62	28	D2

BURNETT A

Falkirk	48/49	4		D1

BURNS Andrew

Clyde	58/59	1		D1
	59/60	1		D1
	60/61			D1
Albion R	61/62	1		D2

BURNS David McCathie
b. Buckhaven 13.3.1934
Petershill

Kilmarnock	56/57	19		2	D1
	57/58	17		5	D1
	58/59	12		2	D1
	59/60	1			D1
St Johnstone	59/60	10		1	D2
	60/61	5		1	D1
Arbroath	61/62	7			D2
East Fife	61/62	16		4	D2

BURNS Ian
b. Aberdeen
Banks o'Dee

Club	Season	Apps	Sub	Gls	Div
Aberdeen	57/58	13		1	D1
	58/59	21			D1
	59/60	22			D1
	60/61	21		1	D1
	61/62	19			D1
	62/63				D1
	63/64	26			D1
	64/65	18			D1
	65/66	2			D1
	66/67				D1
Brechin C	67/68	15		2	D2
	68/69			1	D2
	69/70	20		2	D2
Deveronvale					

BURNS James Chalmers
Dunipace

Club	Season	Apps	Sub	Gls	Div
Cowdenbeath	62/63				D2
	63/64	30			D2
	64/65	36		4	D2
	65/66	36		7	D2
	66/67	38		10	D2
	67/68	25		3	D2
Clyde	67/68	10	1	2	D1
	68/69	34		6	D1
	69/70	34		2	D1
	70/71	34		3	D1
	71/72	34		2	D1
	72/73	34		3	D2
	73/74	34		1	D1
	74/75	27		1	D1
	75/76	26			D1
Stirling A	76/77	39			D2
	77/78	8	6		D1
	78/79	5	2		D1
	79/80	5	1		D1
	80/81				

BURNS John

Club	Season	Apps	Sub	Gls	Div
Clyde	73/74	6			D1
	74/75	19		9	D1
	75/76	18	2	1	D1

BURNS Ralph

Club	Season	Apps	Sub	Gls	Div
Dunfermline A	56/57	15			D1
	57/58				D2
	58/59	4		1	D1

BURNS Thomas
St Mungos
Springboig YM

Club	Season	Apps	Sub	Gls	Div
Motherwell	70/71				D1
	71/72	2			D1
	72/73				D1
	73/74				D1

BURNS Thomas
b. Glasgow 16.12.1956 Caps: S - 8
St Mungos Academy
St Marys BG
Eastercraigs Amateurs
Celtic BC
Celtic
Maryhill Jnrs L

Club	Season	Apps	Sub	Gls	Div
Celtic	73/74				
	74/75		1		D1
Harare CSC L					
Celtic	75/76	5			P
	76/77	13	9	1	P
	77/78	22	1	3	P
	78/79	28	1	3	P
	79/80	12		3	P
	80/81	32	1	4	P
	81/82	33		9	P
	82/83	17		7	P
Blackpool L	82/83				FL
Celtic	83/84	31	1	9	P
	84/85	25	2	7	P
	85/86	34		5	P
	86/87	14	3		P
	87/88	21	6	2	P
	88/89	30	2	2	P
	89/90	8	1		P
Kilmarnock	89/90	22		3	D2
	90/91	37		8	D1
	91/92	41		3	D1
	92/93	39		2	D1
	93/94	12			P

BURRELL Alexander
b. Edinburgh 25.5.1955
Royston BC

Club	Season	Apps	Sub	Gls	Div
Heart of Midlothian	74/75	2			D1
	75/76	6			P
	76/77	6	2		P
Falkirk	77/78	30			D2
	78/79	22			D2
	79/80	35	1	1	D2
	80/81	12			D1
	81/82	12			D1
Meadowbank T	81/82	10			D2
	82/83	15	3		D2
Newtongrange Star					

BURRELL Gerald
b. Belfast 6.9.1926

Club	Season	Apps	Sub	Gls	Div
St Mirren	47/48	29		9	D1
	48/49	28		13	D1
	49/50	21		4	D1
	50/51	3			D1
	51/52	9			D1
Dundee	51/52	12		2	D1
	52/53	14		4	D1
	53/54	5			D1
Huddersfield T	53/54	19		3	FL
	54/55	36		6	FL
	55/56	4			FL
Chesterfield	56/57	24		3	FL
	57/58	27		1	FL
Portadown					

BURROWS Frank
b. Larkhall 30.1.1944

Club	Season	Apps	Sub	Gls	Div
Raith R	62/63	15		1	D1
	63/64	32			D2
	64/65	29			D2
Scunthorpe U	65/66	19		1	FL
	66/67	41		1	FL
	67/68	46		2	FL
Swindon T	68/69	44		1	FL
	69/70	38		2	FL
	70/71	37		1	FL
	71/72	38		1	FL
	72/73	34			FL
	73/74	30			FL
Mansfield T L	73/74	6			FL
Swindon T	74/75	32	3	2	FL
	75/76	37	1	2	FL
	76/77	3			FL

BUSBY Andrew
b. Glasgow 8.12.1947

Club	Season	Apps	Sub	Gls	Div
Third Lanark	66/67	11		5	D2
Partick T	67/68	1			D1
Vale of Leven	68/69				
	69/70				
Airdrieonians	70/71	30		21	D1
	71/72	30	1	10	D1
	72/73	32		12	D1
Heart of Midlothian	73/74	27	1	12	D1
	74/75	30		11	D1
	75/76	32		8	P
	76/77	25	1	3	P
	77/78	36		15	D1
	78/79	25	1	6	P
Toronto Blizzard	79	23		2	NA
	80	28		6	NA
Morton	80/81	26		5	P
	81/82	20	5		P
Queen of the South	82/83	24	4	7	D2
	83/84	9	8	4	D2

BUSH Rodney
b. S Africa
East London

Club	Season	Apps	Sub	Gls	Div
Dundee U	73/74		1		D1

BUTLER James
Kinnoull

Club	Season	Apps	Sub	Gls	Div
Arbroath	72/73		1		D1
	73/74		1		D1

BYRNE Alexander
b. Greenock 4.6.1933
Gourock Jnrs
Royal Engineers
Cheltenham T L

Club	Season	Apps	Sub	Gls	Div
Celtic	54/55				D1
	55/56				D1
	56/57	5		3	D1
	57/58	13		9	D1
	58/59	5		1	D1
	59/60	14		4	D1
	60/61	16		4	D1
	61/62	8			D1
	62/63	9		1	D1
Morton	63/64	7		6	D2
Queen of the South	63/64	9		2	D1
Hellas					
Juventus (Aus)					
Hellas					

BYRNE John
b. Cambuslang 20.5.1939
Pollok Jnrs

Club	Season	Apps	Sub	Gls	Div
Hamilton A T	57/58	1			D2
Preston NE	58/59				FL
Queen of the South	59/60				D2
	60/61				D2
Tranmere R	61/62	27		4	FL
Hibernian	62/63	18		5	D1
	63/64	5			D1
Barnsley	63/64	27		9	FL
	64/65	41		4	FL
Peterborough U	65/66	36	1	19	FL
	66/67	46		6	FL
	67/68	24		3	FL
Northampton T	67/68	22		3	FL
	68/69	18		1	FL

CADDELL Alexander
Drumchapel Amateurs

Club	Season	Apps	Sub	Gls	Div
Partick T	66/67	1			D1

CADENHEAD Andrew
Sunnybank

Club	Season	Apps	Sub	Gls	Div
Aberdeen	59/60	9			D1
	60/61	8			D1
	61/62	22			D1
	62/63				D1
	63/64				D1
St Johnstone					
Nairn Co					

CAIRNEY Bernard
b. Salsburgh 16.10.1945
Thornliewood U
Leicester C
Celtic — T

Club	Season	Apps	Subs	Goals	Div
Motherwell	65/66	15		7	D1
	66/67	20			D1
	67/68	5		2	D1
Wigan A	68/69	36		6	NL
	69/70	20	3	2	NL

Northwich V
Whitburn
Shotts Bon Accord

CAIRNEY Charles
b. Blantyre 21.9.1926
Cambuslang R

Club	Season	Apps	Subs	Goals	Div
Celtic	49/50	1			D1
Leyton Orient	50/51	4			FL
Barry T	51/52				
	52/53				
Bristol R	53/54	9		1	FL
	54/55	5			FL
Headington U	55/56	2			SL
Worcester C	55/56				
	56/57				

East Stirlingshire

CAIRNEY Philip
b. Baillieston ?.10.1952

Club	Season	Apps	Subs	Goals	Div
Clyde	71/72	16			D1
	72/73	32			D2
	73/74	34			D1
	74/75	13			D1
	75/76	25			D1
	76/77	25			D2
East Stirlingshire	77/78	7			D2
	78/79	14			D2

CAIRNIE David
Benburb

Club	Season	Apps	Subs	Goals	Div
Falkirk	63/64	1			D1

CAIRNS Alexander
Millerston Thistle

Club	Season	Apps	Subs	Goals	Div
Kilmarnock	69/70				D1
	70/71	16	1		D1
	71/72	25	1		D1
	72/73	4	1		D1
Queen of the South	73/74	32		1	D2

CAIRNS Bernard
b. Clydebank
Duntocher Hibs

Club	Season	Apps	Subs	Goals	Div
Airdrieonians	50/51	26		1	D1
	51/52	26			D1
	52/53	29			D1
	53/54	27			D1

CAIRNS David
b. St Andrews
Bowhill YC
Rangers
Shrewsbury T

Club	Season	Apps	Subs	Goals	Div
Forfar A	69/70	11			D2
	70/71				D2
Cowdenbeath	70/71	14		1	D1
	71/72	35		2	D2
	72/73	34		1	D2
	73/74	29	4	1	D2
	74/75	26	1		D2
Raith R	74/75	9			D2
	75/76	8	1		D2
Berwick R	76/77	32		1	D2
Brechin C	77/78	14	1		D2
	78/79	23		4	D2

CAIRNS James
Dunipace Jnrs

Club	Season	Apps	Subs	Goals	Div
Hibernian	46/47	1			D1
	47/48	1			D1
	48/49	16		1	D1
	49/50	30			D1
	50/51	7			D1
Third Lanark	51/52	11			D1
	52/53	4			D1
St Johnstone	53/54	4			D2

CAIRNS Kevin William
b. Hoole 29.9.1937
Walmer Bridge
Blackburn R
Weymouth
Carshalton

Club	Season	Apps	Subs	Goals	Div
Dundee U	60/61	21			D1
	61/62	2			D1
Southport	62/63	43		1	FL
	63/64	39			FL
	64/65	46			FL
	65/66	23	2		FL
	66/67	39			FL
Wigan A	67/68	4			CC
	68/69	5			NL

Walmer Bridge

CAIRNS Robert
b. Glenboig c1930

Club	Season	Apps	Subs	Goals	Div
Third Lanark	49/50	2			D1
Ayr U	50/51				D2
	51/52				D2
	52/53	17		5	D2
	53/54	14		2	D2

CAIRNS Robert
b. 5.11.1952
Leven Royals

Club	Season	Apps	Subs	Goals	Div
East Fife	69/70	22	2		D2
	70/71			2	D2
	71/72	17			D1
	72/73	7	3		D1
	73/74				D1
Ayr U	74/75	5	3		D1
Berwick R	74/75	6	2		D2
	75/76	5	1		D2
	76/77	6			D2
East Fife	78/79	34		4	D2
	79/80	35		1	D2
	80/81	15			D2
	81/82	13	3		D2

CALDER John
Heart of Midlothian

Club	Season	Apps	Subs	Goals	Div
Falkirk	66/67	3			D1

Addington (SAf)

CALDOW Eric
b. Cumnock 14.5.1934 Caps: S - 40
Cumnock Academy
Glenpark Juveniles
Muirkirk Jnrs
Ayr U T 50/51
Muirkirk Jnrs

Club	Season	Apps	Subs	Goals	Div
Rangers	53/54	8		2	D1
	54/55	11			D1
	55/56	26			D1
	56/57	30			D1
	57/58	29			D1
	58/59	32		4	D1
	59/60	16		4	D1
	60/61	33		2	D1
	61/62	29		3	D1
	62/63	20			D1
	63/64	3			D1
	64/65	26		2	D1
	65/66	2			D1
	66/67	25		1	D1

Stirling A
Corby T

CALDWELL Alexander
b. Edinburgh 23.10.1954
Melbourne Thistle

Club	Season	Apps	Subs	Goals	Div
Dundee	73/74	9	1		D1
	74/75	19	1		D1
	75/76	18	3	2	P
	76/77	31	2	1	D1
	77/78	18	3		D1
	78/79	14	2	1	D1
	79/80	2			P
St Johnstone	80/81	39		1	D1
	81/82	21		2	D1
	82/83	36		2	D1
	83/84	25			P
	84/85	17		3	D1
Forfar A	84/85	4	1		D1

Lossiemouth
Elgin C
Inverness Clachnacuddin
Rothes
Inverness Clachnacuddin

CALDWELL David William
b. Clydebank 7.5.1932

Club	Season	Apps	Subs	Goals	Div
Aberdeen	53/54	27			D1
	54/55	5			D1
	55/56	27			D1
	56/57	33			D1
	57/58	26			D1
	58/59	8			D1
	59/60	6			D1
Rotherham U	60/61	1			FL
Morton	61/62	25			D2
Toronto C	62				
	63				
	64				
	65				

Fraserburgh

CALDWELL George
Glenafton A

Club	Season	Apps	Subs	Goals	Div
Airdrieonians	63/64	8			D1
	64/65	7			D1
	65/66	5			D2
	66/67	6			D1
	67/68	15	1		D1
	68/69	23	1		D1
	69/70	23			D1
	70/71	13	1		D1
	71/72	10		1	D1
	72/73	23	2		D1
St Mirren	73/74	11			D2
Alloa A	73/74	12			D2

CALDWELL John

Club	Season	Apps	Subs	Goals	Div
Third Lanark	58/59	22			D1
	59/60	18			D1
	60/61	14			D1
	61/62	4			D1

CALLACHAN Ralph
b. Edinburgh 29.4.1955

Club	Season	Apps	Subs	Goals	Div
Heart of Midlothian	73/74	1			D1
	74/75	27	1	5	D1
	75/76	34	1	2	P
	76/77	13		2	P
Newcastle U	77/78	9			FL
Hibernian	78/79	33		9	P
	79/80	26	4	2	P
	80/81	38		4	D1
	81/82	29		4	P
	82/83	27	1	1	P
	83/84	29	4	4	P
	84/85	22	1	1	P
	85/86	3	2	1	P
Morton	86/87	1			D1
Meadowbank T	86/87	26		2	D2
	87/88	26	5	1	D1
Berwick R	88/89	31		4	D2
	89/90	30	1	1	D2
	90/91	18	4		D2
	91/92	12	7		D2

CALLAGHAN Thomas
b. Cowdenbeath 6.12.1945
Lochore Welfare

Club	Season				Div
Dunfermline A	62/63	5			D1
	63/64	24		6	D1
	64/65	30		1	D1
	65/66	22		4	D1
	66/67	9		2	D1
	67/68	33		8	D1
	68/69	2	3		D1
Celtic	68/69	12	3	3	D1
	69/70	12	2	2	D1
	70/71	19		2	D1
	71/72	28	2	1	D1
	72/73	27		2	D1
	73/74	16	6	2	D1
	74/75	19	3	2	D1
	75/76	22			P
San Antonio Thunder	76	9			NA
Celtic	76/77		1		P
Clydebank ·	76/77	22		2	D1
	77/78	5	3		P
Galway R	78/79				

CALLAGHAN William Andrew
b. Glasgow 9.12.1941
East Stirlingshire

Club	Season				Div
Aberdeen	61/62	23		7	D1
	62/63	1		1	D1
Toronto C	63				
Dumbarton	63/64				D2
Barnsley	64/65	15			FL
	65/66				FL
Albion R	66/67	26	1	5	D2
Stranraer	67/68	27	1	1	D2

CALLAGHAN William Thomas
b. Cowdenbeath 12.2.1943 Caps: S - 2
Crossgates Primrose

Club	Season				Div
Dunfermline A	57/58				D2
	58/59				D2
	59/60				D2
	60/61				D2
	61/62	1			D1
	62/63	22			D1
	63/64	29		1	D1
	64/65	32		1	D1
	65/66	29			D1
	66/67	33			D1
	67/68	31		1	D1
	68/69	33		1	D1
	69/70	27			D1
	70/71	14	1		D1
	71/72	34			D1
Berwick R	72/73	18		1	D2
	73/74	25		3	D2
	74/75				D2
Cowdenbeath	75/76	6			D2

CALLAN C Brian
Queen's Park

Club	Season				Div
St Mirren	54/55	27		6	D1
	55/56	4			D1
	56/57	2			D1
Third Lanark	57/58	15		2	D1
Stirling A	58/59	14		4	D1
	59/60				D1
Clyde	60/61	1			D1

CALLAN John
Queen's Park

Club	Season		Div
Stirling A	55/56	1	D1

CAMERON Alexander Ramsey
b. Leith 3.10.1943
St Bernards A

Club	Season		Div
Hibernian	62/63	12	D1
	63/64	3	D1
Oldham A	64/65	15	FL

CAMERON Angus
Blantyre

Club	Season			Div
Third Lanark	47/48	5		D1
	48/49			D1
Cowdenbeath	49/50	30	4	D2
	50/51			D2
	51/52			D2
Morton				

CAMERON Hugh D
Pollok Jnrs

Club	Season				Div
Kilmarnock	72/73	7	1	1	D1
	73/74	1	2		D2
Ayr U	74/75	6		1	D1
	75/76	4	9		P
Stranraer	76/77	33	3	1	D2
	77/78	16	1	2	D2
Craigmark Bruntonians					

CAMERON Hugh Gibson
b. Blantyre 1.2.1927
Burnbank A

Club	Season			Div
Clyde	46/47	13	2	D1
	47/48			D1
Torquay U	48/49	36	4	FL
	49/50	40	5	FL
	50/51	44	8	FL
Newcastle U	51/52	2		FL
Bury	51/52	9	1	FL
	52/53	15		FL
	53/54	5		FL
Workington	53/54	26	4	FL
	54/55	27		FL
	55/56	1		FL
St Mirren	56/57	1		D1
	57/58			

CAMERON James
b. Glasgow 7.12.1946
Ashfield

Club	Season				Div
Dundee U	66/67	2			D1
	67/68	18	4		D1
	68/69	33			D1
	69/70	31			D1
	70/71	34			D1
	71/72	28		1	D1
	72/73	12			D1
Falkirk	73/74	29			D1
	74/75	15	3		D2
	75/76	22		1	D1
	76/77	34		1	D1
Montrose	77/78	28			D1
Forfar A	78/79	32			D2
	79/80	33	1		D2
	80/81	5	2		D2

CAMERON John

Club	Season		Div
Clyde	60/61	30	D1

CAMERON John Alexander
b. Greenock 29.11.1929
Gourock Jnrs

Club	Season		Div
Motherwell	54/55	5	D1
	55/56	1	D1
Bradford PA	56/57	3	FL

CAMERON Kenneth W
b. Perth 15.7.1942
Blairgowrie Jnrs

Club	Season				Div
Dundee	62/63	3		3	D1
	63/64	15		11	D1
	64/65	16		14	D1
	65/66	28		12	D1
	66/67	13	5	8	D1
Kilmarnock	67/68	27	1	11	D1
Dundee U	68/69	34		27	D1
	69/70	13	10	8	D1
	70/71	16		11	D1
	71/72	18	4	7	D1
	72/73	27	2	10	D1
	73/74	8	6	1	D1
Montrose	74/75	36		17	D2
	75/76	8		4	D1

CAMERON Robert
Balgonie Scotia

Club	Season				Div
Dunfermline A	73/74	27	2	7	D1
	74/75	8	7	4	D1
	75/76	4	1		D1
	76/77	1	2		D2

CAMERON Walter

Club	Season			Div
Arbroath	63/64	33		D2
	64/65	22	1	D2
	65/66	25		D2
	66/67	35		D2
	67/68	32		D2
	68/69	2		D1

CAMPBELL Alan

Club	Season		Div
Arbroath	74/75	3	D1

CAMPBELL Donald

Club	Season		Div
Raith R	54/55	1	D1

CAMPBELL George
Dunbar U

Club	Season			Div
Heart of Midlothian	55/56			D1
	56/57	3	2	D1

CAMPBELL George

Club	Season			Div
Aberdeen	74/75		1	D1
	75/76	2		P
	76/77	4	1	P
	77/78		1	P
South Melbourne				

CAMPBELL Ian
Partick T
Shettleston

Club	Season				Div
Morton	69/70	7			D1
	70/71	3	1		D1
Ayr U	71/72	8			D1
	72/73	2	2	1	D1
Hamilton A	73/74	24		1	D2
	74/75	37	1	1	D2
	75/76	26		1	D1
	76/77	28	5	2	D1
Falkirk	77/78	3	1		D2

CAMPBELL Ian
b. c1954
Lochore Welfare

Club	Season				Div
Dunfermline A	73/74	27	2	7	D1
	74/75	8	7	4	D1
Arbroath	75/76			1	D1
Cowdenbeath	76/77	19	9	3	D2
Brechin C	77/78	27	7	6	D2
	78/79	38	1	16	D2
	79/80	36		25	D2
	80/81	32	2	11	D2
	81/82	34	2	16	D2
	82/83	39		23	D2
	83/84	37		19	D1
	84/85	23	4	8	D1
Dunfermline A	84/85	5	3	1	D2
	85/86	24	9	15	D2
	86/87	2	7		D1

CAMPBELL J M

Club	Season		Div
Queen's Park	47/48	1	D1

CAMPBELL James

Club	Season	Apps		Gls	Div
Clyde	46/47	29			D1
	47/48	26		1	D1
	48/49	30			D1
	49/50	27		1	D1
	50/51	25		2	D1
	51/52				D2
	52/53	21		1	D1
	53/54	22		1	D1
Queen of the South	54/55	1			D1

CAMPBELL James

Airdrie BC

Club	Season	Apps		Gls	Div
Airdrieonians	72/73			1	D1

CAMPBELL John

Royal Albert

Club	Season	Apps		Gls	Div
Hamilton A	38/39				
	46/47	28			D1
Queen of the South	47/48	4			D1
Clyde	48/49				D1
Arbroath	49/50	24			D2
	50/51				D2
	51/52				D2
	52/53	2			D2

CAMPBELL John

Club	Season	Apps		Gls	Div
Hibernian	53/54	2			D1

CAMPBELL John
b. Alexandria 22.9.1934
Kirkintilloch Rob Roy

Club	Season	Apps		Gls	Div
Motherwell	55/56				D1
	56/57				D1
	57/58	3			D1
	58/59				D1
Chesterfield	59/60	1			FL

CAMPBELL John
b. 27.2.1946
Greengairs U

Club	Season	Apps		Gls	Div
Partick T	63/64	6			D1
	64/65	16			D1
	65/66	26			D1
	66/67	11	1		D1
	67/68	34			D1
	68/69	24			D1
	69/70	5			D1
	70/71	4			D2
	71/72	21			D1
	72/73	11			D1
	73/74	30			D1
	74/75	29			D1
	75/76	19	1		D1
	76/77	33	1		P
	77/78	24	7		P
	78/79	30	2		P
	79/80	33	2	1	P
	80/81	34	3		P
	81/82	2			P

CAMPBELL Richard Menzies
b. Dunfermline 22.11.1953
Beath High
Townhill U
Dundee U

Club	Season	Apps		Gls	Div
Cowdenbeath	71/72	1	2		D2
	72/73	23	4	3	D2
	73/74	22	3	8	D2
Dunfermline A	74/75	14	1		D1
Ross Co	75/76				
	76/77				
Brechin C	77/78	25	4		D2
	78/79	30	3	1	D2
	79/80	17	8	3	D2
	80/81	30	3	1	D2
	81/82	21	5	2	D2
	82/83	15	1		D2
East Stirlingshire	82/83	11	1		D2

CAMPBELL Robert
b. Edinburgh
Linlithgow Rose

Club	Season	Apps		Gls	Div
Falkirk	52/53	22		12	D1
	53/54	6		2	D1
	54/55	29		1	D1
	55/56	19		3	D1

CAMPBELL Robert
b. Forres 7.10.1936
Lossiemouth U
Lossiemouth

Club	Season	Apps		Gls	Div
Heart of Midlothian	53/54	2			D1
	54/55				D1
	55/56	1			D1
	56/57				D1
Cowdenbeath	57/58				D2
	58/59				D2
	59/60				D2

CAMPBELL Robert

Club	Season	Apps		Gls	Div
St Mirren	58/59	10		2	D1
	59/60	4			D1
	60/61	28			D1
	61/62	21		1	D1
	62/63	30			D1
	63/64	16		1	D1
Morton	63/64	26		18	D2
	64/65	5		1	D1
	65/66	12		4	D1

CAMPBELL Robert

Club	Season	Apps		Gls	Div
St Mirren	60/61	3			D1
	61/62	10		1	D1
	62/63	10			D1
	63/64				D1
	64/65	8			D1
Motherwell	65/66	31		4	D1
	66/67	34		18	D1
	67/68	32	1	7	D1
	68/69	36		6	D2
	69/70	27		1	D1
	70/71				D1
Stranraer	71/72	6			D2

CAMPBELL Robert Inglis
b. Glasgow 28.6.1922 Caps: S - 5

Club	Season	Apps		Gls	Div
Falkirk	46/47	15		6	D1
Chelsea	47/48	32		11	FL
	48/49	36		7	FL
	49/50	35		4	FL
	50/51	33		6	FL
	51/52	32		5	FL
	52/53	18		3	FL
	53/54	2			FL
Reading	54/55	38		6	FL
	55/56	20			FL
	56/57	23		5	FL
	57/58	13		1	FL

CAMPBELL Samuel

Club	Season	Apps		Gls	Div
Partick T	46/47	3		1	D1

CAMPBELL T

Club	Season	Apps		Gls	Div
Airdrieonians	51/52	1			D1
	52/53	10		2	D1

CAMPBELL Thomas McMillan
b. Glasgow 20.2.1935
Tollcross Clydesdale
Largs Thistle

Club	Season	Apps		Gls	Div
Kilmarnock	55/56				D1
	56/57	9			D1
	57/58				D1
Albion R	58/59				D2
	59/60				D2
Dundee U	59/60	7		9	D2
	60/61	12		5	D1
Tranmere R	61/62	1			FL
Stenhousemuir	62/63				D2
Albion R	63/64	22		13	D2

CAMPBELL William Bowie
b. Greenock 26.7.1920 d. 7.12.1994
Caps: S - 5
Greenock Bluebell

Club	Season	Apps		Gls	Div
Morton	46/47	12			D1
	47/48	25		1	D1
	48/49	18		4	D1

CAMPBELL William Gibson
b. Belfast 2.7.1944 Caps: NI - 6
Distillery

Club	Season	Apps		Gls	Div
Sunderland	64/65	3			FL
	65/66	2		4	FL
Dundee	66/67	24		4	D1
	67/68	32		9	D1
	68/69	28	1	6	D1
	69/70	18	1		D1
Motherwell	70/71	11	1	1	D1
	71/72	28	1	2	D1
	72/73	21	1	3	D1
	73/74	11	2		D1
Linfield	74/75				
	75/76				
Hamilton A	L 75/76				D1

CANAVAN James

Club	Season	Apps		Gls	Div
East Fife	46/47				D2
	47/48				D2
	48/49	1			D1
St Johnstone	49/50	6			D2
Gloucester C					

CANDLIN Maurice Hall
b. Jarrow 11.11.1921 d. ?.?.1992
Yoker A
Clydebank

Club	Season	Apps		Gls	Div
Partick T	47/48	13			D1
	48/49	3			D1
Stirling A	48/49				D2
Northampton T	49/50	39			FL
	50/51	30		1	FL
	51/52	42			FL
	52/53	28			FL
Shrewsbury T	53/54	35		1	FL
	54/55	34		1	FL
Wellingborough T					

CANNON Bernard
b. 4.5.1922
Buncrana Amateurs
Mile End A
Blantyre Celtic

Club	Season	Apps		Gls	Div
Celtic	46/47	3			D1
	47/48				D1
Derry C	48/49				
	49/50				
Alloa A					

CANT James

Arbroath LC

Club	Season	Apps		Gls	Div
Arbroath	63/64	1			D2
	64/65	5		3	D2
	65/66	27		8	D2
	66/67	37		16	D2
	67/68	12	2	1	D2
Arbroath	68/69	22	3		D1
	69/70	34		7	D2
	70/71			5	D2
	71/72	35		10	D2
	72/73	30		3	D1
	73/74	27	1	3	D1
	74/75	8	2		D1
Montrose	75/76	21	2	2	D1
	76/77	16			D1
Raith R	76/77	1	1		D1

CANT James
b. Edinburgh 24.9.1953
Peebles R

Club	Season	Apps		Gls	Div
Heart of Midlothian	72/73	1			D1
	73/74	26			D1
	74/75	8			D1
	75/76				P
	76/77	1	1		P
Canberra C					

CANTWELL John
b. 21.11.1923 d. 24.3.1989
Glenboig St Josephs
Third Lanark T

Club	Season				
Celtic	46/47	8		5	D1
Dumbarton	47/48				D2
	48/49				D2
	49/50	15		1	D2
Morton	50/51	2			D1
Stenhousemuir	51/52				D2

CARABINE James
b. Blantyre 23.11.1911 d. ?.12.1987
Caps: S - 3
Larkhall Thistle

Club	Season				
Third Lanark	31/32	14			D1
	32/33	31		1	D1
	33/34	27			D1
	34/35				D2
	35/36	35		1	D1
	36/37	37		1	D1
	37/38	34		1	D1
	38/39	30		5	D1
	46/47	8		1	D1

CARGILL Tommy
b. 15.12.1944
Dundee

Club	Season				
Arbroath	66/67	28		3	D2
	67/68	33			D2
	68/69	23			D1
	69/70	36		1	D2
	70/71				D2
	71/72	36		6	D2
	72/73	32		2	D1
	73/74	27		1	D1
	74/75	31		2	D1
	75/76	25		1	D1
	76/77	36		1	D1
	77/78	17		4	D1
	78/79	39		1	D1
	79/80	33	1		D1
	80/81	3			D2

CARLYLE Walter
b. Grangemouth 23.5.1938
Shettleston U
Rangers

Club	Season				
Dundee U	60/61	15		3	D1
	61/62	28		17	D1
	62/63	29		16	D1
	63/64	6		2	D1
Motherwell	63/64	15		4	D1
	64/65	11		3	D1
St Johnstone	65/66	1			D1
Queen of the South	65/66	5		6	D2
East Stirlingshire *	66/67	22	3	7	D2

CARMICHAEL Angus McD E

Club	Season		
Queen's Park	47/48	20	D1
	48/49	21	D2
	49/50	1	D2

CARMICHAEL George

Club	Season			
Dundee	53/54	10	3	D1
	54/55	11	3	D1
	55/56	1		D1
	56/57			D1
Third Lanark	57/58	1	1	D1

CARMICHAEL Willie

Club	Season			
Clyde	54/55	15	2	D1
	55/56	7		D1

CARR Andrew

Club	Season			
Clyde	50/51	7	1	D1
	51/52			D2
	52/53			D1
	53/54	4	2	D1

CARR J

Club	Season			
Raith R	55/56	4		D1
	56/57	4	2	D1

CARR Joseph
Bonnyrigg Rose
Kilsyth St Patricks
Dunipace Jnrs

Club	Season			
St Johnstone	53/54	24	9	D2
	54/55	14	2	D2
	55/56	36	15	D2
	56/57	13	3	D2
	57/58	28	10	D2
	58/59	35	8	D2
	59/60	24	9	D2
	60/61	7	2	D1
	61/62	1		D1

CARRIE Arthur
Arbroath

Club	Season			
Albion R	47/48			D2
	48/49	1	1	D1

CARRIE Robert

Club	Season		
Falkirk	47/48	3	D1
	48/49	5	D1
	49/50	7	D1

CARROLL Patrick
b. Bridge of Allan 23.10.1957
Sauchie BC

Club	Season				
Hibernian	74/75	4			D1
	75/76	1			P
	76/77	5	2		P
	77/78	2	4		P
	78/79	1			P
Raith R	79/80	25	2	4	D1
	80/81	12	9	1	D1
	81/82	7	6		D1
Falkirk	82/83	12			D1
Bo'ness U					

CARROLL Robert
b. 13.5.1938
Campsie Black Watch
Irvine Meadow

Club	Season			
Celtic	57/58			D1
	58/59			D1
	59/60	10	1	D1
	60/61	17	6	D1
	61/62	28	12	D1
	62/63	6	2	D1
St Mirren	62/63	9	3	D1
	63/64	25	7	D1
	64/65	21	9	D1
Dundee U	65/66	2		D1
	66/67			D1
Coleraine				
Queen of the South	67/68			D2
Irvine Meadow				

CARRUTHERS Eric
b. Edinburgh 2.2.1953
Salvesen BC

Club	Season				
Heart of Midlothian	69/70	2			D1
	70/71	10		2	D1
	71/72	8	2	2	D1
	72/73	24	3	5	D1
	73/74	1			D1
	74/75	5	2		D1
Derby Co	74/75				FL
	75/76				FL
	76/77		1		FL

CARSON Alexander

Club	Season		
Clyde	47/48	4	D1

CARSON Joseph
b. Helensburgh 24.11.1953
Vale of Leven

Club	Season				
Arbroath	73/74	9	1	1	D1
	74/75	28	1	1	D1
	75/76	22		3	D1
	76/77	31			D1
	77/78	30	5	3	D1
	78/79	32	2	2	D1
	79/80	18			D1
Motherwell	79/80	16		1	D1
	80/81	36		3	D1
	81/82	34		3	D1
	82/83	20		1	P
	83/84	20			P
Dumbarton	83/84	5			D1
Partick T	84/85	34		5	D1
	85/86	32			D1
	86/87	35		4	D1
Stranraer	87/88	20			D2
Dumbarton	87/88	2	1		D1

CARTMELL George

Club	Season		
Falkirk	55/56	3	D1

CASKIE James

Club	Season			
Rangers	46/47	13	3	D1
	47/48	12		D1
	48/49	1		D1

CATTENACH David
b. Falkirk 27.6.1946
Woodburn A

Club	Season				
Stirling A	62/63				D2
Celtic	63/64				D1
	64/65				D1
	65/66	1			D1
	66/67				D1
	67/68	4	2	1	D1
	68/69	1			D1
	69/70		1		D1
	70/71	4			D1
Falkirk	71/72	13			D1
	72/73	22	9	2	D1
	73/74	2			D1

CATTERSON Peter
Kilmarnock Amateurs
Annbank U

Club	Season			
Kilmarnock	55/56	5	3	D1
	56/57			D1
Third Lanark	57/58			D1
Duntocher Hibs				
Carluke R				
Portadown				
Derry C				

CAVEN John
b. Edinburgh 6.7.1934

Club	Season			
Kilmarnock	56/57	3	1	D1
Brentford	57/58	6	1	FL
	58/59	1		FL

CAVEN John Brown
b. Kirkintilloch 11.10.1936
Bellshill Academy

Club	Season			
Airdrieonians	56/57	2	1	D1
	57/58	23	13	D1
	58/59			D1
	59/60	5	3	D1
	60/61	34	18	D1
	61/62	19	8	D1
Brighton & HA	61/62	9		FL
	62/63	1		FL
Raith R	62/63	11	4	D1
Morton	63/64	27	15	D2
	64/65	14	4	D1
	65/66			
Stirling A	66/67	3		D1

CAVIN Thomas
b. Kilmaurs 24.11.1923
Crosshouse U
Hurlford U

Club	Season	Apps	Sub	Goals	Div
Kilmarnock	46/47	1			D1
	47/48	16		5	D2
East Stirlingshire	48/49				
Stranraer	49/50				
Glenluce					
Wigton & Bladnoch					
Newton Stewart					

CHALMERS James
b. Aberdeen

Club	Season	Apps	Sub	Goals	Div
Aberdeen	49/50	1			D1
Dunfermline A					

CHALMERS James C

Club	Season	Apps	Sub	Goals	Div
Queen's Park	52/53	1			D2
Dunfermline A	53/54	4		1	D2
	54/55				D2
	55/56	11			D1
	56/57				D1
Queen's Park	57/58	13		1	D1
	58/59	1			D2
	59/60				D2
	60/61	10			D2
	61/62	1			D2

CHALMERS James Nixon
Larkhall Thistle

Club	Season	Apps	Sub	Goals	Div
Stirling A	51/52	14		4	D1
	52/53	18		10	D2
	53/54	29		11	D1
	54/55	15		2	D1
Dundee	54/55	12		6	D1
	55/56	13		2	D1
	56/57	32		9	D1
	57/58	9		2	D1
Kilmarnock	57/58	6		2	D1
	58/59	2			D1

CHALMERS Stephen
b. Glasgow 26.12.1936 Caps: S - 5
Kirkintilloch Rob Roy
Newmarket T
Ashfield

Club	Season	Apps	Sub	Goals	Div
Celtic	58/59	1			D1
	59/60	17		14	D1
	60/61	32		20	D1
	61/62	31		12	D1
	62/63	27		10	D1
	63/64	34		28	D1
	64/65	23		12	D1
	65/66	22		14	D1
Glentoran	L 65/66				
Celtic	66/67	28	1	23	D1
	67/68	13	4	9	D1
	68/69	17	4	11	D1
	69/70	5		2	D1
	70/71	3	1	2	D1
Morton	71/72	28	1	7	D1
	72/73	3		1	D1
Partick T	72/73	18	3	5	D1
	73/74	20	2	1	D1
	74/75		1		D1

CHECKLEY Andrew
Vale of Leven

Club	Season	Apps	Sub	Goals	Div
Dumbarton	74/75	4		2	D1

CHISHOLM Kenneth McTaggart
b. Glasgow 12.4.1925
d. Chester le Street 30.4.1990
Queen's Park

Club	Season	Apps	Sub	Goals	Div
Partick T	46/47	25		11	D1
	47/48	9		2	D1
Leeds U	47/48	17		7	FL
	48/49	23		10	FL
Leicester C	48/49	17		4	FL
	49/50	25		13	FL
Coventry C	49/50	5			FL
	50/51	38		24	FL
	51/52	25		10	FL
Cardiff C	51/52	11		8	FL
	52/53	34		13	FL
	53/54	18		12	FL
Sunderland	53/54	17		6	FL
	54/55	37		18	FL
	55/56	24		9	FL
Workington	56/57	30		12	FL
Glentoran	57/58				
Spennymoor U					
Los Angeles					

CHRISTENSEN Gert
b. Denmark

Club	Season	Apps	Sub	Goals	Div
Morton	72/73	11		3	D1

CHRISTIE Frank
b. Scone 17.2.1927 d. Perth 12.9.1996
Scone Jnrs
St Johnstone YM
Forfar A

Club	Season	Apps	Sub	Goals	Div
Liverpool	49/50	4			FL
East Fife	50/51	12			D1
	51/52	21			D1
	52/53	30			D1
	53/54	27		2	D1
	54/55	19			D1
	55/56	28		2	D1
	56/57	33			D1
	57/58	34		1	D1
	58/59				D2
	59/60				D2

CHRISTIE George
b. Aberdeen
Banks o'Dee

Club	Season	Apps	Sub	Goals	Div
Dundee	50/51	13		2	D1
	51/52	24		5	D1
	52/53	13		1	D1
	53/54	24		3	D1
	54/55	22		5	D1
	55/56	31		6	D1
	56/57	32		6	D1
	57/58	25		3	D1
Third Lanark	58/59	8		1	D1

CHRISTIE James
Pollok Jnrs

Club	Season	Apps	Sub	Goals	Div
Ayr U	59/60				D1
	60/61	10		5	D1
Rangers	61/62	3		3	D1
Hakoah (Aus)					

CHRISTIE Norman
b. Invergordon

Club	Season	Apps	Sub	Goals	Div
Third Lanark	47/48	1			D1
	48/49	9		1	D1
	49/50	20			D1
Ayr U	50/51				D2
	51/52				D2
Stirling A	52/53	29			D2
	53/54				D1
	54/55	3			D1
Brechin C					

CHURCH Charles

Club	Season	Apps	Sub	Goals	Div
Queen's Park	47/48	1			D1
	48/49				D2
	49/50				D2
	50/51	7		2	D2
	51/52	19		2	D2
	52/53	25		6	D2
	53/54	29		4	D2
	54/55	1			D2
	55/56	27		17	D2
	56/57	20		4	D1
	57/58	23		3	D1
	58/59	17		5	D2
	59/60	25		13	D2
	60/61	16		1	D2

CHURCH G

Club	Season	Apps	Sub	Goals	Div
Queen's Park	54/55	2			D2
	55/56	2			D2
	56/57	1			D1

CLAPPERTON G

Club	Season	Apps	Sub	Goals	Div
Airdrieonians	47/48	2			D1

CLARK Alexander

Club	Season	Apps	Sub	Goals	Div
St Mirren	61/62	2			D1
	62/63				D1
	63/64	13			D1
	64/65	8			D1
	65/66	30			D1
	66/67	24		1	D1
	67/68	10	1	2	D2

CLARK Alexander
b. Lanark 28.10.1956
Airdrie BC

Club	Season	Apps	Sub	Goals	Div
Airdrieonians	74/75	1		2	D1
	75/76	18	2	7	D1
	76/77	27	5	8	D1
	77/78	37	1	7	D1
	78/79	38		23	D1
	79/80	37		22	D1
	80/81	36		10	P
	81/82	30		15	P
West Ham U	82/83	26		7	FL
Rangers	82/83	10		4	P
	83/84	27	3	9	P
	84/85	1			P
Heart of Midlothian	84/85	25		8	P
	85/86	33		12	P
	86/87	41		8	P
	87/88	11	24	6	P
	88/89	1	1	1	P
Partick T	89/90	1		2	D1
Dunfermline A	89/90	3		1	P

CLARK David

Club	Season	Apps	Sub	Goals	Div
Dundee U	46/47	21			D2
East Fife	47/48				D2
	48/49	6			D1

CLARK Henry
Heart of Midlothian

Club	Season	Apps	Sub	Goals	Div
Dunfermline A	60/61	5			D1
Berwick R	61/62	3			D2

CLARK J

Club	Season	Apps	Sub	Goals	Div
Falkirk	52/53	1			D1

CLARK James
Largs Thistle

Club	Season	Apps	Sub	Goals	Div
Hamilton A	T 48/49	2			D2
Morton	48/49	11			D1
	49/50				D1
Raith R	50/51	2			D1
Glentoran	51/52				
	52/53				

CLARK John
b. Larkhall 13.3.1941 Caps: S - 4
Larkhall Thistle
Birmingham C
Larkhall Thistle

Club	Season				Div
Celtic	59/60	2			D1
	60/61	10			D1
	61/62	12			D1
	62/63	2			D1
	63/64	26			D1
	64/65	27			D1
	65/66	34			D1
	66/67	34			D1
	67/68	18			D1
	68/69	10	1		D1
	69/70	9			D1
	70/71	1			D1
Morton	71/72	24			D1
	72/73	30			D1

CLARK John
Nairn Co

Club	Season				Div
Dundee U	63/64	2			D1
	64/65				D1
Ross Co	65/66				
Nairn Co	66/67				

CLARK Robert
b. Glasgow 12.4.1952
Sighthill Amateurs

Club	Season				Div
Partick T	69/70	17			D1
	70/71	10			D2
	71/72	10			D1
	72/73	22			D1
	73/74	25	2	1	D1
	74/75	11			D1
Queen of the South	75/76	19	1	1	D1
	76/77	38			D1
	77/78	39		1	D1
	78/79	39		1	D1
	79/80	37			D2
	80/81	39			D2
	81/82	38		2	D1
	82/83	18	1	1	D2
	83/84	8	1		D2

CLARK Robert
Alloa A

Club	Season			Div
Stirling A	48/49			D2
	49/50	7		D1

CLARK Robert Brown
b. Glasgow 26.9.1945 Caps: S - 17
Glasgow YMCA

Club	Season			Div
Queen's Park	62/63	18		D2
	63/64	30		D2
	64/65	35		D2
Aberdeen	65/66	33		D1
	66/67	34		D1
	67/68	33		D1
	68/69	14		D1
	69/70	13	1	D1
	70/71	34		D1
	71/72	22		D1
	72/73	33		D1
	73/74	34		D1
	74/75	33		D1
	75/76	20		P
San Antonio Thunder	76	19		NA
Aberdeen	76/77	27		P
	77/78	36		P
	78/79	23		P
	79/80	35		P
	80/81			P
	81/82			P
Clyde	82/83	4		D1

CLARK Ronald
b. Clarkston 21.5.1932
Forth W
Petershill

Club	Season			Div
Kilmarnock	51/52	7	2	D2
	52/53			D2
	53/54			D2
	54/55	5	1	D1
	55/56	4		D1
Gillingham	56/57	20	5	FL
	57/58	13	1	FL
Oldham A	58/59	4		FL
Bedford T				

CLARK William

Club	Season				Div
Hibernian	46/47	1			D1
	47/48				D1
	48/49	1			D1
	49/50	1			D1
	50/51				D1
	51/52				D1
	52/53	14		1	D1
St Johnstone	53/54	12			D2
	54/55	20			D2

CLARK William
Kilsyth R

Club	Season				Div
St Johnstone	65/66	10		1	D1
	66/67	7	1	1	D1

CLARKE Andrew
Shettleston

Club	Season			Div
Partick T	66/67	2		D1
	67/68			D1
Ayr U	68/69			D2

CLARKE David
b. Edinburgh 26.6.1950
Tynecastle BC

Club	Season				Div
East Fife	68/69	33			D2
	69/70	26	1	2	D2
	70/71	32		1	D2
	71/72	32			D1
	72/73	33			D1
	73/74	28			D1
	74/75	23	2	1	D2
	75/76	25			D1
	76/77	35		1	D1
	77/78	33			D1
	78/79	38	1	2	D2
	79/80	37		1	D2
	80/81	37		1	D2
	81/82	22			D2
	82/83	31			D2
	83/84	30	3		D2
	84/85	12			D2
	85/86	1			D1

CLARKE James

Club	Season				Div
Morton	70/71	5	1	1	D1

CLARKE Thomas
b. Ardrossan 12.4.1946
Beith

Club	Season			Div
Airdrieonians	67/68	1		D1
	68/69	2		D1
	69/70	3		D1
Carlisle U	70/71			FL
	71/72	7		FL
	72/73	6		FL
	73/74	1		FL
	74/75	9		FL
Preston NE	75/76	3		FL

CLARKE Walter

Club	Season			Div
Airdrieonians	71/72	23		D1
	72/73	15	1	D1
	73/74	5		D2

CLARKSON William

Club	Season		Div
Third Lanark	61/62	1	D1

CLELAND Peter
Newarthill Hearts

Club	Season			Div
Motherwell	50/51	1		D1
	51/52			D1
	52/53			D1

CLELLAND James

Club	Season		Div
Airdrieonians	64/65	2	D1

CLEMENTS James

Club	Season			Div
Third Lanark	51/52	3		D1
	53/54	2		D2
Dundee U	T 58/59			D2

CLIFFORD John

Club	Season			Div
Clyde	50/51	5	2	D1
	51/52			D2
	52/53	2		D1
Stirling A	53/54			D1

CLINTON Michael
Kilsyth R

Club	Season			Div
Clyde	55/56	5		D1
	56/57			D2
	57/58	31		D1
	58/59	21		D1
	59/60	22	2	D1
	60/61	29	2	D1
Raith R	61/62	24	3	D1
	62/63	8	1	D1
Cowdenbeath	64/65	28		D2
	65/66	31	4	D2
	66/67	32		D2
	67/68	12	2	D2

CLOSS David
Troon Jnrs

Club	Season			Div
Partick T	60/61	13	3	D1
	61/62	7		D1
	62/63	5		D1
	63/64	25		D1
	64/65			D1
	65/66	3		D1

CLUNIE David
b. Edinburgh 16.3.1948
Salvesen BC

Club	Season			Div
Heart of Midlothian	66/67	3		D1
	67/68			D1
	68/69	15		D1
	69/70	34	3	D1
	70/71	29	1	D1
	71/72	5		D1
	72/73	25	1	D1
	73/74	31		D1
	74/75	27		D1
	75/76	26		P
	76/77	29	1	P
Berwick R	77/78	1		D2
St Johnstone	77/78	34		D1

CLUNIE James Robertson
b. Kirkcaldy 4.9.1933 d. 12.5.2003

Club	Season			Div
Raith R	51/52	2		D1
	52/53	3		D1
	53/54	4		D1
Aberdeen	53/54	1		D1
	54/55			D1
	55/56	14	1	D1
	56/57	10		D1
	57/58	25		D1
	58/59	28	1	D1
	59/60	26	7	D1
St Mirren	60/61	34	7	D1
	61/62	33	1	D1
	62/63	33	1	D1
	63/64	31	1	D1
	64/65	34	2	D1
Bury	65/66	10		FL
St Mirren	65/66	8	1	D1
	66/67	6		D1

CLYDESDALE William
b. Fallin 14.9.1935
Petershill

Club	Season	App	Sub	Gls	Div
Aberdeen	57/58	2			D1
	58/59	24		1	D1
	59/60	1			D1
Hartlepools U	60/61	14			FL

COAKLEY Thomas
b. Bellshill 21.5.1947
Glencairn Juveniles
Bellshill Academy

Club	Season	App	Sub	Gls	Div
Motherwell	63/64	3			D1
	64/65	15			D1
	65/66	5		1	D1
Arsenal	66/67	9		1	FL
	67/68				FL
Detroit Cougars	68	20			NA
Morton	68/69	22	1	2	D1
	69/70	19	2	7	D1
Detroit Cougars					
Chelmsford C					

COATES Arnold
Crook T

Club	Season	App	Sub	Gls	Div
Queen of the South	63/64	28		12	D1
	64/65	20		13	D2

COATES James

Club	Season	App	Sub	Gls	Div
Queen's Park	57/58	13		4	D1

COATS James

Club	Season	App	Sub	Gls	Div
Airdrieonians	62/63	14		2	D1
	63/64	4			D1

COATS T

Club	Season	App	Sub	Gls	Div
Albion R	48/49	5			D1
	49/50	5			D2

COBURN John
b. Perth

Club	Season	App	Sub	Gls	Div
Forfar A	61/62	34		17	D2
	62/63				D2
East Stirlingshire	63/64	24		11	D1
ES Clydebank	64/65	12		7	D2
Forfar A	64/65	2			D2
St Johnstone	64/65	9		3	D1
Montrose	65/66	1		2	D2
Ayr U	65/66	12		8	D2

COBURN William S
Crieff Earngrove

Club	Season	App	Sub	Gls	Div
St Johnstone	62/63	3			D2
	63/64	1			D1
	64/65	32			D1
	65/66	29		4	D1
	66/67	32		5	D1
	67/68	33	1		D1
	68/69	30		1	D1
	69/70	32		2	D1
	70/71	16	1		D1
	71/72	28			D1
Forfar A	72/73	32		1	D2
Cowdenbeath	73/74	10	1		D2
	74/75				D2

COCHRANE

Club	Season	App	Sub	Gls	Div
Queen of the South	57/58	1			D1

COCHRANE David
Perth Celtic

Club	Season	App	Sub	Gls	Div
St Johnstone	71/72	4			D1
	72/73				D1
	73/74	2			D1
Nairn Co					

COCHRANE John
b. Glasgow
Renfrew Waverley
Ardrossan Winton R

Club	Season	App	Sub	Gls	Div
Heart of Midlothian	53/54	2	1		D1

COCKBURN James

Club	Season	App	Sub	Gls	Div
Clyde	49/50	2			D1
Raith R	50/51	1			D1
	51/52	3		1	D1
	52/53	3			D1

COGILL Thomas
Fauldhouse U

Club	Season	App	Sub	Gls	Div
Kilmarnock	67/68	4			D1
Queen of the South	68/69			1	D2
Stranraer	68/69			1	D2
	69/70	16	1	1	D2
Hamilton A	70/71	21		4	D2
Shotts Bon Accord					
Blantyre Victoria					

COLEMAN Peter

Club	Season	App	Sub	Gls	Div
ES Clydebank *	64/65	2			D2
E Stirlingshire *	65/66				D2
Alloa A *	66/67	1			D2
Cambuslang R					
Albion R	67/68	14		4	D2
	68/69			8	D2
	69/70	34		14	D2
	70/71			10	D2
Dumbarton	71/72	33	1	4	D2
	72/73	21	4		D1
	73/74	23	2	2	D1
	74/75	19	8		D1
	75/76	5			D1

COLLIER Austin
b. Dewsbury 24.7.1914 d. ?.?.1991
Upton Colliery
Frickley Colliery

Club	Season	App	Sub	Gls	Div
Mansfield T	38/39	21			FL
York C	46/47	10			FL
Queen of the South	46/47	17			D1
Rochdale	46/47	3			FL
	47/48	3			FL
Halifax T	47/48	1			FL
Goole T					
Scarborough					

COLLINS Alan
b. Kilmarnock 24.1.1918
d. Kilmarnock 10.4.2002
Kilmarnock Academicals
Cumnock Jnrs

Club	Season	App	Sub	Gls	Div
Kilmarnock	36/37	11		3	D1
	37/38	34		14	D1
	38/39	16		6	D1
	46/47	19		9	D1
	47/48	30		24	D2
Raith R	48/49				D2
	49/50	25		9	D1
	50/51	5		1	D1
Stenhousemuir	51/52				D2
	52/53	12		6	D2

COLLINS Angus

Club	Season	App	Sub	Gls	Div
Stirling A	55/56	1			D1

COLLINS Peter
St Mungos Academy
Arsenal

Club	Season	App	Sub	Gls	Div
Partick T	49/50				D1
	50/51				D1
	51/52	7			D1
	52/53	7			D1
	53/54				D1
	54/55	5			D1
	55/56				D1
	56/57	11			D1
	57/58	12			D1
	58/59				D1
	59/60	1			D2
Dundee U	59/60	1			D2

COLLINS Ralph Clark
b. Airdrie 16.4.1924
Shettleston
Airdrieonians

Club	Season	App	Sub	Gls	Div
East Stirlingshire	46/47				D3
	47/48				D3
	48/49				D2
	49/50				D2
Kilmarnock	49/50	23			D2
	50/51	28			D2
	51/52	28			D2
	52/53	28			D2
	53/54	28			D2
	54/55	22			D1
	55/56	23			D1
	56/57	28		1	D1
	57/58	24			D1
	58/59	14			D1

COLLINS Robert Young
b. Govanhill 16.2.1931 Caps: S - 31
Polmadie Hawthorn Juveniles
Pollok

Club	Season	App	Sub	Gls	Div
Celtic	49/50	26		7	D1
	50/51	27		15	D1
	51/52	30		12	D1
	52/53	14		3	D1
	53/54	25		10	D1
	54/55	20		5	D1
	55/56	26		4	D1
	56/57	20		5	D1
	57/58	30		19	D1
	58/59	2		1	D1
Everton	58/59	32		7	FL
	59/60	42		14	FL
	60/61	40		16	FL
	61/62	19		5	FL
Leeds U	61/62	11		1	FL
	62/63	41		8	FL
	63/64	41		6	FL
	64/65	39		9	FL
	65/66	10			FL
	66/67	7			FL
Bury	66/67	10			FL
	67/68	43		4	FL
	68/69	21	1	2	FL
Morton	69/70	27		2	D1
	70/71	27		1	D1
Ringwood C					
Hakoah (Aus)					
Wilhelmina					
Oldham A	72/73	6		1	FL
Shamrock R	73/74				

COLLUMBINE Ernest

Club	Season	App	Sub	Gls	Div
Stenhousemuir	61/62	13		1	D2
	62/63				D2
East Stirlingshire	63/64	34			D1
ES Clydebank	64/65	35		2	D2
St Johnstone	65/66	5			D1
Clydebank	66/67	35			D2
	67/68	29	1		D2

COLMAN Michael

Club	Season	App	Sub	Gls	Div
Aberdeen	46/47	1			D1

COLQUHOUN John
b. Stirling 3.6.1940
Maryhill Harp

Club	Season				
Stirling A	59/60	28		14	D1
	60/61				D2
	61/62	1			D1
Oldham A	61/62	41		6	FL
	62/63	46		14	FL
	63/64	35		7	FL
	64/65	41		6	FL
Scunthorpe U	65/66	44		5	FL
	66/67	45		7	FL
	67/68	45		8	FL
	68/69	15		3	FL
Oldham A	68/69	29		3	FL
	69/70	39	2	3	FL
Ashton U					

COLRAIN John James
b. Glasgow 4.2.1937 d. 14.7.1984
St Mungos Academy
Ashfield
Celtic
St Anthonys   L
Duntochter Hibs   L

Club	Season				
Celtic	57/58	4		1	D1
	58/59	25		13	D1
	59/60	17		5	D1
Clyde	60/61	22		7	D1
	61/62				D2
	62/63	22		7	D1
Ipswich T	63/64	15		3	FL
	64/65	23		10	FL
	65/66	17	1	4	FL
Glentoran	66/67				
	67/68				

COLVILLE Henry
b. Kirkcaldy 12.2.1924 d. Glenrothes 16.3.1999
Bayview Boys
Falkirk

Club	Season				
Raith R	46/47				D2
Chester	47/48	4		1	FL
	48/49				FL
Raith R	49/50	30		1	D1
	50/51	30		3	D1
	51/52	30		2	D1
	52/53	28			D1
	53/54	30			D1
	54/55	23			D1
Falkirk	55/56	21			D1
Dunfermline A	55/56	12			D1
	56/57	34			D1
	57/58				D2
	58/59	34			D1
	59/60	17			D1

COMBE James Robert
b. Leith 29.1.1924 d. Cyprus 19.11.1991
Caps: S - 3
Inveresk A

Club	Season				
Hibernian	46/47	2		2	D1
	47/48	29		7	D1
	48/49	21		3	D1
	49/50	30		5	D1
	50/51	27		3	D1
	51/52	28		12	D1
	52/53	30		6	D1
	53/54	29		2	D1
	54/55	28		3	D1
	55/56	30		10	D1
	56/57	9			D1

CONDIE D

Club	Season			
Raith R	50/51	2		D1
	51/52	1		D1
	52/53	5		D1

CONN Alfred
b. Prestonpans 2.10.1926 Caps: S - 1
Bathgate Academy
Prestonpans YMCA
Inveresk A

Club	Season			
Heart of Midlothian	46/47	12	3	D1
	47/48			D1
	48/49	22	13	D1
	49/50	22	13	D1
	50/51	28	19	D1
	51/52	25	12	D1
	52/53	25	11	D1
	53/54	26	11	D1
	54/55	22	10	D1
	55/56	25	17	D1
	56/57	10	2	D1
	57/58	5	4	D1
Raith R	58/59	13	6	D1
	59/60	21	8	D1
Johannesburg Ramblers				

CONN Alfred James
b. Kirkcaldy 5.4.1952 Caps: S - 2
Tynecastle A
Leeds U

Club	Season				
Rangers	67/68				D1
Musselburgh Wind L					
Rangers	68/69	1	1		D1
	69/70	8	4		D1
	70/71	23	2	4	D1
	71/72	21	2	3	D1
	72/73	18	2	12	D1
	73/74	7	4	4	D1
Tottenham H	74/75	16	1	6	FL
	75/76	7	1		FL
	76/77	12	1		FL
Celtic	76/77	13	1	2	P
	77/78	9	1		P
	78/79	12	1	6	P
Derby Co	78/79				FL
Hercules Alicante T	79/80				
Pittsburgh Spirit					
San Jose Earthquake	80	2			NA
Hartford Hellions					
Heart of Midlothian	80/81	13	4	3	P
Blackpool	80/81	3			FL
Motherwell	81/82	17	5	2	D1
	82/83	4	1	1	P
	83/84				P

CONNACHAN Edward Devlin
b. Prestonpans 27.8.1935 Caps: S - 2
Dalkeith Thistle

Club	Season			
Dunfermline A	57/58			D2
	58/59	24		D1
	59/60	31		D1
	60/61	22		D1
	61/62	33		D1
	62/63	16		D1
Middlesbrough	63/64	41		FL
	64/65	38		FL
	65/66	16		FL
Falkirk	66/67	20		D1
	67/68	6		D1
East London				

CONNAGHAN Denis
b. Glasgow 9.1.1945
Celtic
Yoker A
Queen of the Soutl T
Renfrew Jnrs

Club	Season			
St Mirren	66/67	23		D1
Baltimore Bays	67	7		NP
St Mirren	67/68			D2
	68/69	21		D1
	69/70	15		D1
	70/71	33		D1
Celtic	71/72	14		D1
	72/73	4		D1
	73/74	8		D1
	74/75	6		D1
	75/76			P
	76/77			P
Clydebank	76/77			D1
Ayr U	77/78			P
Morton	77/78	25		D1
	78/79	16		P
Clyde	79/80	17		D1
Arthurlie				

CONNELL Anthony

Club	Season				
Third Lanark	63/64	2			D1
	64/65	26		1	D1
	65/66	30		1	D2
	66/67	33			D2
St Mirren	67/68	35			D2
	68/69	30			D1
	69/70	33		1	D1
	70/71	16			D1
Queen of the South	71/72	35		1	D2
	72/73	23	1		D2

CONNELL Peter McArthur
b. East Kilbride 26.11.1927 d. ?.?.1995

Club	Season			
Morton	50/51	3		D1
Northampton T	51/52	13		FL
	52/53			FL

CONNELLY George
b. Fife 1.3.1949 Caps: S - 2
Tulliallan Thistle

Club	Season				
Celtic	64/65				D1
	65/66				D1
	66/67				D1
	67/68				D1
	68/69	6	1	1	D1
	69/70	7			D1
	70/71	22	2	3	D1
	71/72	32			D1
	72/73	32			D1
	73/74	14		1	D1
	74/75	15			D1
	75/76	1	2		P
Falkirk	L 76/77	8		2	D1
Tulliallan Thistle					
Sauchie					

CONNELLY W

Club	Season			
Falkirk	49/50	1		D1
	50/51	1		D1

CONNOLLY John
b. Barrhead 13.6.1950 Caps: S - 1
Glasgow U

Club	Season	Apps	Sub	Goals	Div
St Johnstone	67/68	1		1	D1
	68/69	13		6	D1
	69/70	21		6	D1
	70/71	34		17	D1
	71/72	27		11	D1
Everton	71/72	2			FL
	72/73	41		7	FL
	73/74	26		5	FL
	74/75	22	2	3	FL
	75/76	14	1	1	FL
Birmingham C	76/77	37		5	FL
	77/78	12	8	4	FL
Newcastle U	78/79	34		8	FL
	79/80	8	7	2	FL
Hibernian	80/81	29	3	8	D1
	81/82	1	1		P
Gateshead	81/82				
	82/83				
Blyth Spartans	82/83				
Gateshead	83/84				

CONNOR Francis
b. Blantyre 13.2.1936
Polkemmet Jnrs
Kilmarnock T
Armadale Thistle
Blantyre Celtic

Club	Season	Apps	Sub	Goals	Div
Third Lanark	L 57/58				D1
Dundee U	T 59/60				D2
Celtic	59/60				D1
	60/61				D1
	61/62	2			D1
Portadown	62/63				
	63/64				
St Mirren	63/64	6			D1
Third Lanark	T				
Derry C					
Portadown					
Albion R	68/69				D2

CONNOR John

Club	Season	Apps	Sub	Goals	Div
St Mirren	55/56	2			D1
	56/57				D1
	57/58				D1
	58/59				D1
	59/60	1			D1

CONROY Michael
b. Port Glasgow 5.8.1932
St Columbas Juveniles
St Anthonys

Club	Season	Apps	Sub	Goals	Div
Celtic	52/53	1			D1
	53/54				D1
	54/55	2			D1
	55/56	1			D1
	56/57				D1
	57/58	3			D1
	58/59				D1
	59/60				D1

CONWAY D

Club	Season	Apps	Sub	Goals	Div
Airdrieonians	61/62	5			D1

CONWAY James
b. Motherwell 27.8.1940
Coltness U

Club	Season	Apps	Sub	Goals	Div
Celtic	57/58	3		1	D1
	58/59	9		1	D1
Rangers	L 58/59				
Celtic	59/60	12		6	D1
	60/61	7		1	D1
Norwich C	61/62	30		8	FL
	62/63	4		2	FL
	63/64	8		3	FL
Southend U	63/64	24		8	FL
	64/65	7		1	FL
Partick T	65/66	2		2	D1
Portadown					

COOK I

Club	Season	Apps	Sub	Goals	Div
Morton	47/48	2			D1

COOK James
b. ?.?.1946
Shotts Bon Accord

Club	Season	Apps	Sub	Goals	Div
Heart of Midlothian	65/66				D1
	66/67				D1
Kilmarnock	67/68				D1
	68/69	7		1	D1
	69/70	33	1	5	D1
	70/71	32		6	D1
	71/72	34		10	D1
	72/73	30		4	D1
	73/74	31	1	4	D2
	74/75	1			D1
Dumbarton	74/75	24	5	3	D1
	75/76	25	1	5	D1
	76/77	7	1		D1
Falkirk	76/77	17		1	D1
	77/78	6			D2
Shotts Bon Accord					

COOK William James McLaughlan
b. Galston 26.6.1940 Caps: Aus - 7
Galston Amateurs
Ardrossan Winton R

Club	Season	Apps	Sub	Goals	Div
Kilmarnock	58/59				D1
	59/60	8			D1
	60/61	2			D1
	61/62				D1
	62/63				D1
Port Melbourne					
Slavia					

COOKE Charles
b. St Monance 14.10.1942 Caps: S - 16
Port Glasgow
Renfrew Jnrs

Club	Season	Apps	Sub	Goals	Div
Aberdeen	59/60				D1
	60/61	32		10	D1
	61/62	29		5	D1
	62/63	27		8	D1
	63/64	22		3	D1
	64/65	15		1	D1
Dundee	64/65	18		7	D1
	65/66	29		4	D1
Chelsea	66/67	33		3	FL
	67/68	41		3	FL
	68/69	25	1		FL
	69/70	35		4	FL
	70/71	28	3	1	FL
	71/72	35	3	2	FL
	72/73	7	1	2	FL
Crystal Palace	72/73	29			FL
	73/74	13	2		FL
Chelsea	73/74	17		1	FL
	74/75	38	1	5	FL
	75/76	16	1	1	FL
	76/77	8			FL
Los Angeles Aztecs	77	20		2	NA
Chelsea	77/78	6			FL
Los Angeles Aztecs	78	16		2	NA
Memphis Rogues	78	7			NA
	79	22		2	NA
	80	25		1	NA
California Surf	81	29		3	NA

COOKE Robert

Club	Season	Apps	Sub	Goals	Div
Airdrieonians	47/48	9		2	D1

COOPER Brian
b. 30.11.1950
Aberdeen

Club	Season	Apps	Sub	Goals	Div
Raith R	69/70	24		3	D1
	70/71				D2
	71/72	34		3	D2
	72/73	36			D2
	73/74	34	1		D2
	74/75	30			D2
	75/76	26		1	D2
	76/77	37		3	D2
East Fife	77/78	14			D1
	78/79	15			D2

COOPER Brian G
Arbroath V

Club	Season	Apps	Sub	Goals	Div
Brechin C	70/71			5	D2
	71/72	33		9	D2
	72/73	17		4	D2
Dundee U	72/73	1		2	D1
Forfar A	73/74	22		5	D2
	74/75	33	3	2	D2
Keith					
Montrose	82/83	21	1		D2

COOPER James

Club	Season	Apps	Sub	Goals	Div
Aberdeen	58/59	1			D1

COOPER James Thomson
b. Glasgow 28.12.1939

Club	Season	Apps	Sub	Goals	Div
Raith R	60/61	8			D1
Airdrieonians	61/62	9		2	D1
Brighton & HA	62/63	20		2	FL
	63/64	21		4	FL
	64/65				FL
Hartlepools U	65/66	19		1	FL
Addington					
Cape Town C					

COOPER Neil
b. Aberdeen 12.8.1959

Club	Season	Apps	Sub	Goals	Div
Aberdeen	74/75		1		D1
	75/76	1	1		P
	76/77				P
	77/78	1			P
	78/79	3	4	1	P
	79/80	1			P
Barnsley	79/80	20		3	FL
	80/81	27	3	2	FL
	81/82	10		1	FL
Grimsby T	81/82	16		1	FL
	82/83	24		1	FL
	83/84	7			FL
St Mirren	83/84	23	2		P
	84/85	10			P
	85/86	28	2		P
	86/87	38		1	P
	87/88	27		1	P
	88/89	30			P
Hibernian	89/90	27			P
	90/91	11			P

COOPER William
b. Aberdeen c1910 d. ?.5.1994
St Machar Juveniles
Mugiemoss

Club	Season	Apps	Sub	Goals	Div
Aberdeen	27/28	2			D1
	28/29	3			D1
	29/30	14			D1
	30/31	20			D1
	31/32	37			D1
	32/33	34			D1
	33/34	38		2	D1
	34/35	38			D1
	35/36	38			D1
	36/37	37			D1
	37/38	32			D1
	38/39	14			D1
	46/47	13			D1
	47/48	7			D1
Huntly					

COPELAND James
b. Dumfries 23.8.1941
Kilmarnock Amateurs
Nithsdale W

Club	Season	Apps	Sub	Goals	Div
Kilmarnock	59/60	6			D1
	60/61				D1
	61/62				D1
Dumbarton	62/63				D2
Montrose	62/63				D2
Clyde	63/64				D2
Bermuda					

COPLAND Ernest
b. Montrose

Club	Season	Apps	Subs	Goals	Div
Arbroath	49/50	12		3	D2
Dundee	50/51	5		1	D1
	51/52	1		2	D1
Raith R	51/52	18		8	D1
	52/53	23		17	D1
	53/54	30		24	D1
	54/55	26		11	D1
	55/56	29		17	D1
	56/57	34		24	D1
	57/58	18		4	D1

COPLAND John C
b. Paisley 2.3.1947
Beith

Club	Season	Apps	Subs	Goals	Div
St Mirren	67/68	2			D2
Beith					
Stranraer	69/70	17		10	D2
	70/71			9	D2
Dundee U	70/71	10	2	2	D1
	71/72	24	2	9	D1
	72/73	33		1	D1
	73/74	27		1	D1
	74/75	33		3	D1
	75/76	13		2	P
St Mirren	76/77	12		1	D1
	77/78	31		1	P
	78/79	36		1	P
	79/80	35			P
	80/81	33		2	P
	81/82	36			P
	82/83	18			P

F CORBETT William
b. Falkirk 31.8.1922
Dunipace Thistle
Maryhill Jnrs

Club	Season	Apps	Subs	Goals	Div
Celtic	46/47	19			D1
	47/48	29		3	D1
Preston NE	48/49	19			FL
Leicester C	49/50	16			FL
Yeovil T	50/51				
	51/52				
Dunfermline A	51/52				D2
	52/53	4			D2
Morton	52/53	11			D2

CORMACK Peter Barr
b. Edinburgh 17.7.1946 Caps: S - 9
Tynecastle BC
Heart of Midlothian

Club	Season	Apps	Subs	Goals	Div
Hibernian	62/63	1		1	D1
	63/64	6		1	D1
	64/65	32		9	D1
	65/66	32		15	D1
	66/67	30		13	D1
	67/68	29	1	11	D1
	68/69	29		15	D1
	69/70	23		11	D1
Nottingham F	69/70	1			FL
	70/71	41		9	FL
	71/72	32		7	FL
Liverpool	72/73	30		8	FL
	73/74	40	2	9	FL
	74/75	33	3	3	FL
	75/76	16	1	1	FL
	76/77				FL
Bristol C	76/77	20	1	6	FL
	77/78	25	1	6	FL
	78/79	14	3	3	FL
	79/80	1	3		FL
Hibernian	79/80	10	4		P
	80/81	3	3	1	D1
	81/82				P
	82/83				P
Partick T	83/84			1	D1

CORRIGAN John
b. Loganlea 8.1.1947
Bathgate Thistle

Club	Season	Apps	Subs	Goals	Div
Stirling A	67/68	24	1		D1
Crystal Palace	68/69				FL
Stirling A	69/70	36		2	D2
	70/71			1	D2
Albion R	70/71			2	D2

COSGROVE Charles
Lothian U

Club	Season	Apps	Subs	Goals	Div
Falkirk	63/64	3			D1
	64/65	3			D1

COSH William

Club	Season	Apps	Subs	Goals	Div
Airdrieonians	50/51	14			D1
	51/52	4			D1

COSKER Owen

Club	Season	Apps	Subs	Goals	Div
Falkirk	54/55	2			D1
	55/56	4			D1
	56/57	7			D1
Third Lanark	57/58	13			D1
	58/59	4			D1
	59/60	4			D1

COULSTON Frank
Queen's Park

Club	Season	Apps	Subs	Goals	Div
Stranraer	64/65	9		2	D2
	65/66				
	66/67	14		3	D2
Jordanhill College					
Partick T	67/68	32		10	D1
	68/69	17	4	4	D1
	69/70	4	3	1	D1
	70/71	36		20	D2
	71/72	33		10	D1
	72/73	22	1	4	D1
	73/74	11	5	4	D1
	74/75	9	6	4	D1
Stranraer	75/76	18	2	3	D2
Stenhousemuir	76/77	32	3	7	D2

COURT Harold John
b. Rhymney 13.6.1919 d. ?.?.1975
Llanbradach

Club	Season	Apps	Subs	Goals	Div
Cardiff C	38/39	1			FL
	46/47				FL
	47/48				FL
Dundee U	48/49	6		1	D2
Dundee	48/49	2			D1
	49/50				D1
Swindon T	50/51	16		2	FL

COUSIN Alan
Alloa YM

Club	Season	Apps	Subs	Goals	Div
Dundee	55/56	6		1	D1
	56/57	23		8	D1
	57/58	31		15	D1
	58/59	32		17	D1
	59/60	34		13	D1
	60/61	29		12	D1
	61/62	34		15	D1
	62/63	30		6	D1
	63/64	32		8	D1
	64/65	34		8	D1
	65/66	3			D1
Hibernian	65/66	20		2	D1
	66/67	34			D1
	67/68	11	3		D1
	68/69	19	2		D1

COUSINS Ross
b. Edinburgh
Broxburn A

Club	Season	Apps	Subs	Goals	Div
East Fife	54/55	7			D1
	55/56	2			D1
	56/57				D1
	57/58				D1

COUTTS Douglas
Banks o'Dee

Club	Season	Apps	Subs	Goals	Div
Aberdeen	59/60	5			D1
	60/61	17		1	D1
	61/62	7			D1
	62/63	31		1	D1
	63/64	28			D1
	64/65	11		1	D1
Berwick R	65/66	31			D2
	66/67	32	1		D2
	67/68	35			D2
	68/69			3	D2

COUTTS John

Club	Season	Apps	Subs	Goals	Div
Albion R	48/49	1			D1

F COWAN Ian
b. Falkirk 27.11.1944
Rutherglen Glencairn

Club	Season	Apps	Subs	Goals	Div
Partick T	62/63	24		6	D1
	63/64	20		6	D1
	64/65	15		1	D1
	65/66	5			D1
St Johnstone	65/66	20		2	D1
Falkirk	66/67	25		3	D1
	67/68	5			D1
Dunfermline A	68/69	1	1		D1
	69/70		3	1	D1
Southend U	70/71	3			FL
Australia					
Albion R *	72/73	8		1	D2

COWAN James Clews
b. Paisley 16.6.1926 d. 20.6.1968 Caps: S - 25
Mossvale Jnrs
St Mirren

Club	Season	Apps	Subs	Goals	Div
Morton	46/47	1			D1
	47/48	18			D1
	48/49	17			D1
	49/50	25			D1
	50/51	26			D1
	51/52	29			D1
	52/53	25			D2
Sunderland	53/54	28			FL
	54/55				FL
	55/56				FL
Third Lanark	55/56				D2

COWAN John
b. Canada c1927 d. Canada ?.12.2000
Caps: Canada
Vancouver University

Club	Season	Apps	Subs	Goals	Div
Dundee	49/50	21			D1
	50/51	25			D1
	51/52	23		1	D1
	52/53	26			D1
	53/54	20			D1
Vancouver Halecos					

COWAN Mark G
West Bromwich A

Club	Season	Apps	Subs	Goals	Div
Airdrieonians	69/70	19		7	D1
	70/71	27	2		D1
	71/72	25	3	2	D1
	72/73	30	2	1	D1
	73/74	36		1	D2
	74/75	27			D1
	75/76	18	1	1	D1
	76/77	16	1	1	D1
	77/78	24	2		D1
	78/79	18	2		D1
Clyde	79/80	14	1		D1

COWAN Samuel

Club	Season	Apps	Subs	Goals	Div
Queen's Park	47/48	16		1	D1
	48/49	1			D2
Newton Stewart	49/50				
Kilmarnock	49/50	13		5	D2
	50/51	7			D2
	51/52	9		4	D2

COWIE

Club	Season	Apps	Subs	Goals	Div
St Mirren	56/57	1		1	D1

COWIE Andrew David
b. Motherwell 11.3.1913 d. ?.?.1972

Club	Season	App	Gls	Div
Dundee	35/36	1		D1
	36/37	6		D1
	37/38	36	2	D1
	38/39	17	1	D2
Aberdeen	38/39	16		D1
	46/47	18		D1
	47/48	27		D1
Swindon T	48/49	35	2	FL
	49/50	35	2	FL
	50/51	19		FL

COWIE Douglas
b. Aberdeen 1.5.1926 Caps: S - 20
Caledonian Juveniles
Aberdeen St Clements

Club	Season	App	Gls	Div
Dundee	47/48	15		D1
	48/49	23		D1
	49/50	22	1	D1
	50/51	25		D1
	51/52	23		D1
	52/53	29	1	D1
	53/54	27	4	D1
	54/55	26	2	D1
	55/56	27		D1
	56/57	17	1	D1
	57/58	31	2	D1
	58/59	27		D1
	59/60	29	4	D1
	60/61	17	2	D1
Morton	61/62			D2
	62/63			D2

COWIE William
Kilsyth R

Club	Season	App	Gls	Div
Motherwell	56/57	5		D1
	57/58	2		D1
	58/59	3		D1
Queen of the South	59/60			D2

COX Charles John
b. Glasgow 19.2.1926 Caps: S - 1
Dumbarton Academy
Yoker A

Club	Season	App	Gls	Div
Heart of Midlothian	46/47	21	1	D1
	47/48	10		D1
	48/49	17	1	D1
	49/50	25		D1
	50/51	22	1	D1
	51/52	2		D1
Motherwell	51/52	13		D1
	52/53	28		D1
	53/54	27	2	D2
	54/55	20	1	D1
	55/56	1	1	D1

COX John
b. Darvel 23.11.1922
RAF

Club	Season	App	Gls	Div
Kilmarnock	46/47	1		D1
	47/48	1		D2
Stranraer	48/49			
Tarff Rovers				
Canada				
Hamilton A	T 55/56	1	1	D2

COX Robert
Dundee Osborne

Club	Season	App	Gls	Div
Dundee	56/57	28		D1
	57/58	34		D1
	58/59	34		D1
	59/60	34		D1
	60/61	30	1	D1
	61/62	31		D1
	62/63	27		D1
	63/64	32	1	D1
	64/65	15		D1
	65/66	27		D1
	66/67	29		D1
	67/68	6	1	D1

COX Samuel Richmond
b. Darvel 13.4.1924 Caps: S - 24
Queen's Park
Third Lanark
Dundee

Club	Season	App	Gls	Div
Rangers	46/47	13	2	D1
	47/48	30	1	D1
	48/49	29	2	D1
	49/50	30	4	D1
	50/51	19	1	D1
	51/52	23	4	D1
	52/53	23		D1
	53/54	28		D1
	54/55	12		D1
	55/56			D1
East Fife	56/57	30		D1
	57/58	30	1	D1

COYLE John C
b. Dundee ?.?.1933
St Josephs

Club	Season	App	Gls	Div
Dundee U	50/51			D2
	51/52	3	1	D2
	52/53	2		D2
Brechin C	52/53			D3
Dundee U	53/54	2	1	D2
	54/55	1		D2
	55/56	36	41	D2
	56/57	35	22	D1
	57/58	17	14	D2
Clyde	57/58	21	20	D1
	58/59	30	19	D1
	59/60	13	6	D1

CRABTREE Leonard

Club	Season	App	Gls	Div
St Mirren	51/52	7		D1
	52/53			D1
	53/54	5		D1
	54/55	1		D1

CRAIG James Philip
b. Glasgow 30.4.1943 Caps: S - 1
Glasgow University

Club	Season	App	Gls	Div
Celtic	65/66	15		D1
	66/67	17	1	D1
	67/68	22		D1
	68/69	32	1	D1
	69/70	20	4	D1
	70/71	22		D1
	71/72	16		D1
Hellenic	72			
Sheffield W	72/73	2		FL
	73/74	3	1	FL

CRAIG John
Bridgeton Waverley

Club	Season	App	Gls	Div
Albion R	47/48			D2
	48/49	21	3	D1
	49/50	29	2	D2
	50/51			D2
	51/52			D2
	52/53			D2
Alloa A	52/53	2		D2

CRAIG John V
b. Glasgow 10.4.1953
Chelsea

Club	Season	App	Gls	Div
Aberdeen	73/74	4	4	D1
	74/75	8		D1
Partick T	74/75	4	2	D1
	75/76	26	3	D1
	76/77	31		P
	77/78	30	2	P
	78/79	1		P
Heart of Midlothian	78/79	14	4	P
Morton	79/80	6		P
	80/81	1		P
Keith				
Montrose *	82/83	9	3	D2

CRAIG Joseph
b. Bridge of Allan 14.5.1954 Caps: S - 1
Sauchie Jnrs

Club	Season	App	Sub	Gls	Div
Partick T	72/73	18	4	8	D1
	73/74	32	1	7	D1
	74/75	31		15	D1
	75/76	22	2	14	D1
	76/77	2			P
Celtic	76/77	34		16	P
	77/78	19	1	8	P
	78/79	1			P
Blackburn R	78/79	28	2	5	FL
	79/80	16	1	3	FL
	80/81	1			FL
Hamilton A	80/81	7		3	D1
	81/82	32	1	9	D1
	82/83	11	3	2	D1

CRAIG Robert McAllister
b. Airdrie 8.4.1935
Blantyre Celtic

Club	Season	App	Gls	Div
Third Lanark	57/58	33	14	D1
	58/59	31	10	D1
	59/60	10	7	D1
Sheffield W	59/60	24	9	FL
	60/61	37	12	FL
	61/62	23	4	FL
Blackburn R	61/62	2		FL
Celtic	62/63	17	13	D1
St Johnstone	63/64	11	2	D1
Oldham A	63/64	10	3	FL
	64/65	8	1	FL
Toronto C				
Johannesburg W				
Third Lanark	66/67	9	1	D2

CRAIG Thomas
Kirkintilloch Rob Roy

Club	Season	App	Gls	Div
Dumbarton	55/56			D2
	56/57			D2
	57/58			D2
	58/59			D2
	59/60			D2
East Stirlingshire	60/61			D2
	61/62			D2
	62/63			D2
	63/64	31		D1
ES Clydebank	64/65	36		D2
East Stirlingshire	65/66	36		D2
	66/67	38		D2
	67/68	29	2	D2

CRAIG Thomas Brooks
b. Glasgow 21.11.1950 Caps: S - 1
Avon Villa Juveniles
Drumchapel Amateurs

Club	Season	App	Sub	Gls	Div
Aberdeen	67/68	13	1	1	D1
	68/69	30	1	7	D1
Sheffield W	68/69	1			FL
	69/70	40		5	FL
	70/71	35	4	5	FL
	71/72	36		10	FL
	72/73	39		10	FL
	73/74	37		4	FL
	74/75	22		4	FL
Newcastle U	74/75	19	1	2	FL
	75/76	39	1	9	FL
	76/77	40		8	FL
	77/78	24		3	FL
Aston Villa	77/78	4			FL
	78/79	23		2	FL
Swansea C	79/80	26			FL
	80/81	14	5	3	FL
	81/82				FL
Carlisle U	81/82	18		3	FL
	82/83	30	6	3	FL
	83/84	35		2	FL
	84/85	10		1	FL
Hibernian	84/85	10	1		P

CRAIG William
b. c1936
Dumfries St Josephs
St Anthonys

Celtic	53/54			D1
	54/55			D1
	55/56	6		D1
	56/57	2		D1
Third Lanark	57/58	18	4	D1
	58/59	9	2	D1
Stirling A	T			
Morton	59/60			D2
	60/61			D2

CRAIG William James
b. Aberdeen 11.9.1929

Dundee	50/51	4		D1
	51/52			D1
	52/53			D1
	53/54	1		D1
	54/55	8		D1
	55/56	7		D1
Millwall	56/57	9		FL
	57/58	10	1	FL
	58/59	2		FL

CRAINIE Christopher

Blantyre Victoria

Hamilton A	46/47	4		D1

St Rochs
Vale of Leven
St Anthonys
Bedlay Jnrs

CRAMOND Gordon Alexander
b. Aberdeen 19.3.1949 d. Ayr 11.1.1989
Banks o'Dee

Dundee	67/68				D1
	68/69				D1
Montrose	69/70				D2
	70/71				D2
	71/72	33		3	D2
	72/73	34	1	13	D2
	73/74	8		2	D2
St Johnstone	73/74	27		3	D1
	74/75	33		2	D1
	75/76	25		2	P
Ayr U	75/76	9			P
	76/77	23	4	5	P
	77/78	33	1	4	P
	78/79	39		4	D1
	79/80	18	2	1	D1
Kilmarnock	79/80	15		1	P
	80/81	16	2	2	P
	81/82				D1
Brechin C	82/83	1			D2

CRAMPSEY Francis C
b. Glasgow
Arthurlie

Queen's Park	54/55	24		D2
	55/56	36		D2
	56/57	32		D1
	57/58	18		D1

CRAWFORD Andrew

Dunfermline A	55/56	1		D1

CRAWFORD Andrew

Arsenal

Dumbarton	63/64	8		D2
	64/65	35		D2
	65/66	22		D2
	66/67	33		D2
	67/68	1		D2
Morton	67/68	10		D1
	68/69	10		D1

CRAWFORD James

Arbroath	59/60	15		D1

CRAWFORD John
b. Edinburgh 14.7.1934
Hibernian

Hamilton A	L 53/54	18	3	D1
Heart of Midlothian	54/55	3	1	D1
	55/56	12	5	D1
	56/57	30	11	D1
	57/58	25	10	D1
	58/59	19	8	D1
	59/60	18	12	D1
	60/61	20	11	D1
West Ham U	61/62	19	5	FL
	62/63	5		FL
Scunthorpe U	62/63	15	1	FL
	63/64	20	1	FL
Peterborough U	64/65	34	5	FL
	65/66	46	1	FL
	66/67	46		FL
	67/68	9		FL
	68/69	37		FL

CRAWFORD John Campbell
b. Falkirk 27.6.1922
East Stirlingshire

Morton	47/48	4	1	D1
	48/49	1	1	D1
Raith R	49/50	1		D1
Ayr U	50/51			D2
	51/52			D2
Oldham A	52/53	14	7	FL
	53/54	10	1	FL
Halifax T	54/55	11	2	FL
Macclesfield T	55/56			
Montrose				

CRAWFORD W M

Third Lanark	49/50	7		D1

CRAWFORD William

Govan High School

Partick T	49/50	1		D1
	50/51	10	5	D1
	51/52	17		D1
	52/53	14	1	D1
	53/54	22	6	D1
	54/55	5	1	D1
	55/56	10	3	D1
	56/57			D1
	57/58	8	1	D1
	58/59	2		D1
Queen of the South	59/60			D2

CRERAND Patrick Timothy
b. Glasgow 19.2.1939 Caps: S - 16
Duntochter Hibs

Celtic	58/59	4		D1
	59/60	8	1	D1
	60/61	31	2	D1
	61/62	31	2	D1
	62/63	17		D1
Manchester U	62/63	19		FL
	63/64	41	1	FL
	64/65	39	3	FL
	65/66	41		FL
	66/67	39	3	FL
	67/68	41	1	FL
	68/69	35	1	FL
	69/70	25	1	FL
	70/71	24		FL

CRICHTON J

Morton	47/48	5		D1

CRICHTON J

Airdrieonians	50/51	1		D1

CRICHTON Ronald

Arbroath YM

Dundee	60/61	11	1	D1

Heart of Midlothian

CROMAR Robert L
b. Glasgow

Queen's Park	49/50	4	1	D2
	50/51	19	9	D2
	51/52	2		D2
	52/53	21	2	D2
	53/54	29	1	D2
	54/55	28	3	D2
	55/56	36	3	D2
	56/57	34	4	D1
	57/58	32	4	D1
	58/59	35	3	D2
	59/60	30	5	D2
	60/61	34	3	D2
	61/62	32	3	D2
	62/63	20		D2
	63/64	1	1	D2

CROPLEY Alexander James
b. Aldershot 16.1.1951 Caps: S - 2
Edina Hearts

Hibernian	68/69	2	1	1	D1
	69/70	7	1	2	D1
	70/71	17	1	3	D1
	71/72	20	1	1	D1
	72/73	33		6	D1
	73/74	31		11	D1
	74/75	14		5	D1
Arsenal	74/75	7		1	FL
	75/76	20		4	FL
	76/77	2	1		FL
Aston Villa	76/77	32		3	FL
	77/78	17		2	FL
	78/79	15	2	2	FL
	79/80	1			FL
Newcastle U	79/80	3			FL
	80/81				FL
Toronto Blizzard	81	15		2	NA
Portsmouth	81/82	7	2	2	FL

CROSBIE Robert Crichton
b. Glasgow 2.9.1925 d. ?.2.1994

Bury	47/48	2	2	FL
	48/49	7	3	FL
Bradford PA	49/50	24	6	FL
	50/51	38	27	FL
	51/52	31	14	FL
	52/53	33	16	FL
	53/54	13	9	FL
Hull C	53/54	28	11	FL
	54/55	33	11	FL
Grimsby T	55/56	42	35	FL
	56/57	23	10	FL
Queen of the South	57/58	21	11	D1

CROSS Alexander
b. Rutherglen c1920 d. Kinnesswood 1998
Rutherglen Academy

Queen's Park	38/39	20	2	D1
	46/47	1		D1

CROSS David

Airdrieonians	52/53	21		D1
	53/54	22		D1

CROSS William

St Mirren	52/53	1		D1
	53/54	3		D1

CROSSAN Frank

Dundee	58/59	2	2	D1

CROWE Alexander Allan
b. Motherwell 24.11.1924 d. ?.?.1997

Club	Season	Apps	Sub	Gls	Div
St Mirren	46/47	24		6	D1
	47/48	11		4	D1
	48/49	3			D1
	49/50	10		8	D1
	50/51	5			D1
	51/52	18		2	D1
	52/53				D2
Cowdenbeath	53/54				D2
Ipswich T	53/54	32		6	FL
	54/55	18		3	FL

CROWE Matthew Jackson
b. Bathgate 4.7.1932
Bathgate Thistle

Club	Season	Apps	Sub	Gls	Div
Bradford PA	49/50				FL
	50/51				FL
	51/52				FL
	52/53	1			FL
	53/54				FL
Partick T	54/55	10		5	D1
	55/56	12		3	D1
	56/57	4		2	D1
Norwich C	57/58	33		4	FL
	58/59	45		1	FL
	59/60	45		4	FL
	60/61	42		5	FL
	61/62	21			FL
Brentford	62/63	39			FL
	63/64	34			FL
Port Elizabeth C					

CRUIKSHANK George Philip
b. Malaya 22.7.1931

Club	Season	Apps	Sub	Gls	Div
Queen of the South	50/51				D2
	51/52				D1
	52/53	5			D1
	53/54	1			D1
	54/55	1			D1
	55/56	5			D1
	56/57	3			D1
Carlisle U	57/58	14			FL

CRUIKSHANK James Fergus
b. Glasgow 13.4.1941 Caps: S - 6
Drumchapel Amateurs

Club	Season	Apps	Sub	Gls	Div
Queen's Park	59/60	30			D2
Heart of Midlothian	60/61	4			D1
	61/62	5			D1
	62/63	6			D1
	63/64	34			D1
	64/65	34			D1
	65/66	34			D1
	66/67	34			D1
	67/68	20			D1
	68/69	31			D1
	69/70	29			D1
	70/71	32			D1
	71/72	20			D1
	72/73	11			D1
	73/74	11			D1
	74/75	27			D1
	75/76	35			P
	76/77	27			P
Dumbarton	77/78	3			D1

CULLEN Charles

Club	Season	Apps	Sub	Gls	Div
Third Lanark	64/65	7		5	D1

CUMMING George
Motherwell Bridge Works

Club	Season	Apps	Sub	Gls	Div
Partick T	65/66	1			D1
	66/67	15			D1
	67/68		1		D1
	68/69	14		1	D1
St Mirren	69/70	22		2	D1
Hamilton A	70/71	35		3	D2
Carluke R					

CUMMING Ian
b. Aberdeen
Banks o'Dee

Club	Season	Apps	Sub	Gls	Div
Aberdeen	67/68	5		1	D1
	68/69		1		D1
Inverness Thistle					

CUMMING James

Club	Season	Apps	Sub	Gls	Div
Queen of the South	46/47	4			D1

CUMMING John
b. Carluke 17.3.1930 Caps: S - 9
Castlehill Colliery
Carluke R

Club	Season	Apps	Sub	Gls	Div
Heart of Midlothian	50/51	14		4	D1
	51/52	12		1	D1
	52/53	7		2	D1
	53/54	29			D1
	54/55	29		1	D1
	55/56	34		1	D1
	56/57	25		4	D1
	57/58	20		5	D1
	58/59	33		2	D1
	59/60	32		5	D1
	60/61	32		3	D1
	61/62	33		3	D1
	62/63	20		1	D1
	63/64	20			D1
	64/65				D1
	65/66	16		1	D1
	66/67	2			D1

CUMMING John
Loanhead Mayflower

Club	Season	Apps	Sub	Gls	Div
Stirling A	61/62	3			D1
	62/63				D2
	63/64	18			D2
Morton	63/64	2			D2

CUMMING Richard
Killermont Amateurs

Club	Season	Apps	Sub	Gls	Div
Motherwell	50/51	2			D1
	51/52				D1
Dumbarton	52/53				D2
	53/54	3			D2
Albion R	53/54				D2

CUMMINGS John
b. Greenock 5.5.1944

Club	Season	Apps	Sub	Gls	Div
Aberdeen	64/65	1			D1
Port Vale	65/66	2		1	FL
Ayr U	T 65/66	4		2	D2
Clydebank *	66/67	9	1	2	D2

CUMMINGS Robert Douglas
b. Ashington 17.11.1935
New Hartley Jnrs

Club	Season	Apps	Sub	Gls	Div
Newcastle U	54/55				FL
	55/56				FL
	56/57				FL
Ashington	56/57				
	57/58				
	58/59				
Aberdeen	59/60	6		2	D1
	60/61	6		6	D1
	61/62	15		6	D1
	62/63	30		18	D1
	63/64	5		1	D1
Newcastle U	63/64	16		5	FL
	64/65	24		8	FL
	65/66	3	1	1	FL
Darlington	65/66	37		23	FL
	66/67	15		8	FL
	67/68	21	1	12	FL
Hartlepools U	67/68	18		9	FL
	68/69	30	4	3	FL
Port Elizabeth					

CUNNING Robert Robertson
b. Dunfermline 12.2.1930
Port Glasgow A

Club	Season	Apps	Sub	Gls	Div
Sunderland	50/51				FL
Hamilton A	51/52	9		5	D2
	52/53	30		16	D2
	53/54	19		2	D1
Rangers	54/55	3			D1

CUNNINGHAM David

Club	Season	Apps	Sub	Gls	Div
St Mirren	46/47	20			D1
	47/48	1			D1
	48/49	1			D1
	49/50	1			D1

CUNNINGHAM David

Club	Season	Apps	Sub	Gls	Div
Airdrieonians	63/64	3		1	D1

CUNNINGHAM Dennis
Heart of Midlothian

Club	Season	Apps	Sub	Gls	Div
Motherwell	61/62	1			D1
Berwick R					

CUNNINGHAM George

Club	Season	Apps	Sub	Gls	Div
Airdrieonians	50/51	1			D1

CUNNINGHAM Graham McC

Club	Season	Apps	Sub	Gls	Div
Queen's Park	47/48	18		8	D1
	48/49	30		12	D2
	49/50	25		4	D2
	50/51	10		2	D2

CUNNINGHAM J

Club	Season	Apps	Sub	Gls	Div
Queen of the South	55/56	1			D1

CUNNINGHAM Stewart

Club	Season	Apps	Sub	Gls	Div
Dunfermline A	55/56	2		1	D1

CUNNINGHAM Thomas

Club	Season	Apps	Sub	Gls	Div
Partick T	50/51	3			D1
Albion R	51/52				D2

CUNNINGHAM William
Baillieston Jnrs

Club	Season	Apps	Sub	Gls	Div
Partick T	60/61	10		1	D1
	61/62	33		1	D1
	62/63	32		2	D1
	63/64	30		4	D1
	64/65	27		5	D1
	65/66	26		2	D1
	66/67	27	1	6	D1
	67/68	5	7	1	D1
	68/69	5	1		D1

CUNNINGHAM William

Club	Season	Apps	Sub	Gls	Div
Raith R	61/62	11			D1

CUNNINGHAM William
Lochore Welfare

Club	Season	Apps	Sub	Gls	Div
Raith R	67/68	10		5	D1
	68/69	7			D1
Glenrothes					

CUNNINGHAM William Carruthers
b. Cowdenbeath 22.2.1925
d. Preston 27.11.2000 Caps: S - 8
Crossgates Primrose
Dunfermline A

Airdrieonians	46/47			D2
	47/48	26		D1
	48/49			D1
Preston NE	49/50	30	1	FL
	50/51	31		FL
	51/52	42		FL
	52/53	41		FL
	53/54	30		FL
	54/55	24		FL
	55/56	24		FL
	56/57	41		FL
	57/58	42		FL
	58/59	42	1	FL
	59/60	24	1	FL
	60/61	31		FL
	61/62	29		FL
	62/63	9		FL
	63/64			FL
Southport	64/65	12		FL

CUNNINGHAM William Edward
b. Mallusk 20.2.1930 Caps: NI - 30
Tranent Jnrs
Ardrossan Winton R

St Mirren	50/51	14		D1
	51/52	23	1	D1
	52/53	7		D1
	53/54	9		D1
	54/55	8		D1
Leicester C	54/55	16		FL
	55/56	34		FL
	56/57	1		FL
	57/58	28	3	FL
	58/59	28		FL
	59/60	20	1	FL
Dunfermline A	60/61	19		D1
	61/62	34	1	D1
	62/63	17	3	D1

CUNNINGHAM William Livingstone
b. Paisley 11.7.1938

St Mirren	56/57	1		D1
Third Lanark	57/58	2		D1
	58/59	6		D1
	59/60	32		D1
	60/61	33	1	D1
	61/62	31		D1
	62/63	28	7	D1
	63/64	11		D1
Barnsley	64/65	24		FL
Stirling A	65/66	5		D1
	66/67	18		D1
	67/68	22		D1

CUPPLES David

Partick T

Morton	46/47	13	2	D1
	47/48	18	5	D1
	48/49			D1
Hamilton A	L 48/49	15	8	D2
Morton	49/50			D2
	50/51	12	2	D1
	51/52	13	3	D1

CURLETT David White
b. Stevenston 4.10.1932
Dalry Rosevale
Ardeer Recreation
Dary Thistle

Kilmarnock	49/50			D1
	50/51			D2
	51/52			D2
	52/53	1		D2
	53/54	29	13	D2
	54/55	26	3	D1
	55/56	32	12	D1
	56/57	10	7	D1
	57/58	16	5	D1
Dundee	57/58	8	4	D1
	58/59	21	7	D1
	59/60	18	5	D1
	60/61	2		D1
Ayr U	60/61	17	1	D1
	61/62			D2
	62/63			D2
Portadown				

CURLEY Thomas
b. Glasgow 11.6.1945
Portsmouth

Celtic	61/62			D1
	62/63			D1
	63/64			D1
	64/65	1		D1
Brentford	65/66	14	2	FL
	66/67	26	4	FL
Crewe Alex.	67/68	17	1	FL
	68/69	31	3 7	FL
Hamilton A	69/70	3		D2

CURRAN Hugh Patrick
b. Glasgow 25.9.1943 Caps: S - 5
Home Farm
Manchester U
Shamrock R

Third Lanark	62/63	9	4	D1
Millwall	T			
Morton	T			
Corby T	63/64			
Millwall	63/64	2		FL
	64/65	39	18	FL
	65/66	16	8	FL
Norwich C	65/66	14	6	FL
	66/67	29	7	FL
	67/68	42	16	FL
	68/69	27	17	FL
Wolverhampton W	68/69	10	4	FL
	69/70	38	20	FL
	70/71	27 3	16	FL
	71/72	2 2		FL
Oxford U	72/73	31	15	FL
	73/74	36	12	FL
	74/75	2 1	1	FL
Bolton W	74/75	32 3	11	FL
	75/76	8 1	2	FL
	76/77	3		FL
Oxford U	77/78	29 4	11	FL
	78/79	1 1		FL

CURRAN John
b. Glasgow 22.6.1924 d. Milltimber 24.3.1985

Queen's Park	46/47			D1
	47/48	8		D1
Aberdeen	48/49	14		D1
	49/50	10		D1
	50/51	3		D1
East Fife	50/51	12		D1
	51/52	30		D1
	52/53	27		D1
	53/54	30		D1
	54/55	28		D1
	55/56	29		D1
Shrewsbury T	56/57	24		FL
Watford	57/58	30		FL
Keith				

CURRAN John
b. 21.5.1940
St Mungos Academy
Drumchapel Amateurs
Ruchazie Hearts
Duntochter Hibs

Celtic	58/59			D1
	59/60	3		D1
	60/61	1		D1
	61/62			D1
Derry C				
Maryhill Harp				

CURRAN Peter
b. Saltcoats

Partick T	37/38	21		D1
	38/39	27		D1
	46/47	30		D1
	47/48	18		D1
	48/49	8		D1
Ayr U	49/50	7		D2

CURRAN Peter

Partick T	59/60	5		D1

CURRIE Daniel
b. c1936 d. Brantford, Ontario 28.7.1992

Clyde	54/55	1		D1
	55/56	10	2	D1
	56/57			D2
	57/58	31	12	D1
	58/59	26	5	D1
	59/60	12	4	D1
	60/61	7	1	D1
	61/62			D2
	62/63	28	2	D1
Queen of the South	63/64	31	9	D1
	64/65	27	6	D2
	65/66	3		D2
Brantford Ex-Imperials				

CURRIE David

Duntocher Hibernian
Birmingham C

Hamilton A	58/59	15	4	D2
	59/60	34	14	D2
	60/61	35	14	D2
	61/62	35	17	D2
	62/63	30	6	D2
	63/64	34	14	D2
	64/65	31	6	D2
	65/66	17	1	D1

CURRIE James Adam Campbell
b. Glasgow 25.4.1932

Falkirk	55/56	3		D1
Exeter C	56/57	45	17	FL
	57/58	9	2	FL
Workington	57/58	19	6	FL
	58/59	1	1	FL
	59/60	3	1	FL

CURRIE John

Petershill

Rangers	57/58			D1
	58/59			D1
	59/60			D1
	60/61			D1
Stirling A	61/62	3		D1

CURRIE Kenneth

Bayview YC

Heart of Midlothian	46/47	8		D1
	47/48	16	3	D1
	48/49	6	1	D1
	49/50	4		D1
	50/51			D1
Third Lanark	51/52	1		D1

CURRIE William

Clyde	55/56	2		D1

CUSHLEY John
b. Blantyre 21.1.1943
Blantyre Celtic

Club	Season				Div
Celtic	62/63	2			D1
	63/64	5			D1
	64/65	10			D1
	65/66	12			D1
	66/67	1			D1
West Ham U	67/68	27			FL
	68/69	9			FL
	69/70	2			FL
Dunfermline A	70/71	28			D1
	71/72	21			D1
Dumbarton	72/73	28			D1
	73/74	29		1	D1
	74/75	24		1	D1
	75/76	2			D1

CUTHBERT Ian
Edina Hibs

Club	Season		Div
Hibernian	61/62	1	D1

CUTHBERT Richard
Pollok

Club	Season		Div
Falkirk	68/69	5	D1
Dumbarton			

CUTHBERTSON John G
b. Edinburgh

Club	Season			Div
Hibernian	46/47	9	5	D1
	47/48	9	10	D1
	48/49	15	14	D1
Third Lanark	49/50	26	15	D1
	50/51	21	8	D1
	51/52	16	6	D1
	52/53	19	10	D1
Stenhousemuir				

DAILEY Douglas
b. Isle of Man 6.3.1953
Woodside Jnrs

Club	Season				Div
East Fife	70/71			1	D2
	71/72	9	7	6	D1
	72/73	18	4	6	D1
	73/74	3	2	1	D1
Berwick R	74/75	5	5	1	D2
Raith R	74/75	1	2	1	D2
Forfar A	75/76	4			D2

DALGLEISH W

Club	Season		Div
Airdrieonians	47/48	4	D1

DALGLISH Kenneth Mathieson
b. Dalmarnock 4.3.1951 Caps: S - 102
Glasgow U
Possilpark YMCA
Drumchapel Amateurs
Celtic
Cumbernauld U L

Club	Season				Div
Celtic	69/70	2			D1
	70/71	1		2	D1
	71/72	31		17	D1
	72/73	32		22	D1
	73/74	31	2	18	D1
	74/75	33		16	D1
	75/76	35		24	P
	76/77	35		14	P
Liverpool	77/78	42		20	FL
	78/79	42		21	FL
	79/80	42		16	FL
	80/81	34		8	FL
	81/82	42		13	FL
	82/83	42		18	FL
	83/84	33		7	FL
	84/85	36		6	FL
	85/86	17	4	3	FL
	86/87	12	6	6	FL
	87/88		2		FL
	88/89				FL
	89/90			1	FL

DALLAS William Robert Dempster
b. Glasgow 6.3.1931

Club	Season			Div
Luton T	52/53			FL
	53/54			FL
	54/55			FL
	55/56			FL
St Mirren	56/57	20	2	D1
Wrexham	57/58	8		FL
Nuneaton B				

DALY Patrick
Maryhill Harp

Club	Season			Div
Hamilton A	46/47	26	1	D1
Morton	47/48	5		D1
Clyde	47/48	1		D1
	48/49	4		D1
Workington	49/50			
Ayr U	49/50	4	1	D2

DALZIEL Robert
b. Glasgow
Ardrossan Winton R
Craigmark Bruntonians

Club	Season			Div
Kilmarnock T	48/49	1		D2
Third Lanark	49/50	4	1	D1
Queen's Park	50/51	18	7	D2
	51/52	9		D2
	52/53	29	7	D2
	53/54	27	8	D2
	54/55	28	8	D2
	55/56	7		D2
	56/57	1		D1

D'ARCY Thomas McDonald
b. Edinburgh 22.6.1932 d. ?.?.1985

Club	Season		Div
Hibernian	53/54	3	D1
Bournemouth	54/55		FL
Hibernian	55/56		D1
Southend U	56/57	2	FL
	57/58	2	FL
Queen of the South	58/59	2	D1

DARLING Thomas
b. Clackmannan 14.7.1929
Dalkeith Thistle

Club	Season		Div
Heart of Midlothian	48/49	2	D1
	49/50		D1
	50/51		D1
	51/52		D1
Cowdenbeath	52/53	30	D2
	53/54	7	D2

DARROCH Malcolm

Club	Season			Div
Queen's Park	56/57	4		D1
	57/58	4		D1
	58/59	21	8	D2

DARWOOD Hugh

Club	Season		Div
Clyde	48/49	2	D1

DAVIDSON

Club	Season		Div
Arbroath	59/60	5	D1

DAVIDSON Douglas Bell
b. Dundee 2.12.1918
d. Portsmouth (?) ?.7.1968
Dundee Violet

Club	Season			Div
East Fife	46/47			D2
	47/48			D2
	48/49	3	1	D1
Blackpool	48/49	11		FL
	49/50	5		FL
Reading	49/50	1		FL
	50/51	10	1	FL

DAVIDSON Duncan
b. Elgin 5.7.1954
Lewis U

Club	Season				Div
Aberdeen	73/74		5		D1
	74/75	2	14	2	D1
	75/76				P
	76/77	8	5	5	P
	77/78	17	7	8	P
	78/79	7	2	2	P
	79/80	2	5	2	P
	80/81		4		P
Tulsa Roughnecks	81	9		2	NA
Toronto Blizzard	81	12		2	NA
See Bee	81/82				
Toronto Blizzard	82	9		2	NA
See Bee	82/83				
Manchester C	83/84	2	4	1	FL
Cove R					

DAVIDSON Gordon
Lochgelly Albert

Club	Season			Div
Stirling A	55/56	8	2	D1
	56/57			D2

DAVIDSON Ian
b. Pencaitland 8.9.1937
Ormiston Primrose

Club	Season			Div
Kilmarnock	56/57			D1
	57/58			D1
	58/59			D1
	59/60			D1
	60/61	17	4	D1
	61/62	28	1	D1
	62/63	1		D1
Preston NE	62/63	16		FL
	63/64	37	1	FL
	64/65	14		FL
Middlesbrough	64/65	11		FL
	65/66	27		FL
	66/67	8		FL
Darlington	67/68	27		FL
South Africa				

DAVIDSON James
b. Aberdeen
Aberdeen Cattofield
Clyde

Club	Season			Div
Falkirk	54/55	28	12	D1
	55/56	6	3	D1
	56/57	1		D1

DAVIDSON James

Club	Season		Div
Airdrieonians	55/56	5	D1
	56/57	1	D1

DAVIDSON James Anderson
b. Douglas Water 8.11.1925 d. Ayr 24.1.1996
Caps: S - 8
Muirkirk

Club	Season			Div
Partick T	46/47	1		D1
	47/48	6		D1
	48/49	15	2	D1
	49/50	21	3	D1
	50/51	26		D1
	51/52	26	3	D1
	52/53	27	3	D1
	53/54	23	2	D1
	54/55	24	5	D1
	55/56	29	4	D1
	56/57	27	4	D1
	57/58	26	2	D1
	58/59	21	1	D1
	59/60	9		D1
Inverness Caley	60/61			
	61/62			
	62/63			
	63/64			

DAVIDSON John Arnott
b. Leslie 30.12.1925
Dundee Violet

Club	Season				
Dundee U	46/47	10		2	D2
	47/48				D2
East Fife	47/48	26		5	D2
	48/49	18		6	D1
	49/50	4			D1
Kilmarnock	49/50	4		1	D2
	50/51	2			D2
	51/52				D2
Rhyl A	51/52				
	52/53				
Alloa A	53/54	22		6	D2
	54/55				D2

DAVIDSON Kenneth J
b. Newtongrange 14.2.1952
Loanhead Mayflower

Club	Season				
Hibernian	70/71	11	3	4	D1
	71/72	4	1		D1
	72/73				D1
	73/74				D1
Dunfermline A	74/75	9	8	2	D1
Meadowbank T	75/76	26		7	D2
	76/77	30	4	8	D2
	77/78	35	4	6	D2
	78/79	27	6	6	D2
	79/80	26	6	3	D2
	80/81	21	5	1	D2

DAVIDSON Norman
b. Kintore 25.10.1934
Chelsea
Fraserburgh
Inverurie Loco

Club	Season			
Aberdeen	55/56	9	5	D1
	56/57	17	10	D1
	57/58	28	17	D1
	58/59	19	5	D1
	59/60	23	11	D1
	60/61	14	7	D1
Heart of Midlothian	60/61	6	2	D1
	61/62	8	3	D1
	62/63	13	10	D1
	63/64	9	4	D1
Dundee U	63/64	8	3	D1
Partick T	63/64	7	2	D1
	64/65	1		D1
St Mirren	64/65	1		D1
Boksburg				

DAVIDSON Steven

Club	Season			
East Stirlingshire	63/64	7	1	D1
ES Clydebank	64/65	1		D2

DAVIDSON Thomas
b. Edinburgh
Edinburgh A

Club	Season			
Falkirk	62/63	13	3	D1
	63/64	6		D1
	64/65	2		D1
Bonnyrigg Rose				
Heart of Midlothian	66/67	2	1	D1
Raith R				

DAVIDSON Thomas
Arniston R

Club	Season				
Raith R	67/68	14			D1
	68/69	1			D1
	69/70	3			D1
Berwick R	70/71			1	D2
	71/72	21		2	D2
	72/73	28			D2
	73/74	33	1	2	D2
	74/75	28	1		D2
	75/76	13		1	D2

DAVIDSON Victor Salvatore Ferla
b. Glasgow 8.11.1950
Glasgow U

Club	Season				
Celtic	67/68				D1
Giffnock North	L				
Ashfield	L				
Celtic	68/69				D1
	69/70	1		1	D1
	70/71	6	1	5	D1
	71/72	5		5	D1
	72/73	1	1		D1
	73/74	3			D1
	74/75				D1
Motherwell	75/76	29	6	5	P
	76/77	30	1	6	P
	77/78	29		8	P
Blackpool	78/79	23	2	3	FL
Celtic	78/79	12		2	P
	79/80	5		2	P
	80/81				P
Phoenix Inferno					

DAVIE Alexander Grimmond
b. Dundee 10.6.1945
Butterburn YC

Club	Season		
Dundee U	61/62	2	D1
	62/63	29	D1
	63/64	29	D1
	64/65	8	D1
	65/66	7	D1
	66/67	28	D1
	67/68	14	D1
Luton T	68/69	27	FL
	69/70	31	FL
Southampton	70/71	1	FL
	71/72		FL
Dundee U	72/73	10	D1
	73/74	15	D1
North Shore U			

DAVIE James Graham
b. Cambuslang 7.9.1922 d. ?.?.1984
Newton V
Bridgeton Waverley

Club	Season			
Kilmarnock	46/47	25		D1
	47/48	24	1	D2
Preston NE	48/49	18		FL
	49/50	10		FL
Northampton T	50/51	39	1	FL
	51/52	25		FL
	52/53	11		FL
Shrewsbury T	53/54			

DAVIE William Clark
b. Paisley 7.1.1925 d. ?.?.1996

Club	Season			
St Mirren	47/48	4		D1
	48/49	18	3	D1
	49/50	22	1	D1
	50/51	6		D1
Luton T	50/51	22	8	FL
	51/52	20	3	FL
Huddersfield T	51/52	20	2	FL
	52/53	31	5	FL
	53/54	30	6	FL
	54/55	6		FL
	55/56	21	2	FL
	56/57	5	1	FL
Walsall	57/58	7		FL

DAVIES Ronald
b. Cape Town 23.8.1924 d. ?.?.1973
Caps: South Africa

Club	Season			
Clyde	47/48	7	4	D1
	48/49	27	8	D1
	49/50	10	4	D1
	50/51	16		D1
Luton T	51/52	25	2	FL
	52/53	29	4	FL
	53/54	31	3	FL
	54/55	33	10	FL
	55/56	16	5	FL
	56/57	16		FL
Bedford T				

DAVIN Joseph James
b. Dumbarton 13.2.1942

Club	Season			
Hibernian	59/60	1		D1
	60/61	4		D1
	61/62	6	1	D1
	62/63	6		D1
Ipswich T	63/64	26		FL
	64/65	26		FL
	65/66	25		FL
Morton	66/67	4	5	D2
Dumbarton	67/68	33	1	D2

DAVIS Harold
b. Cupar

Club	Season			
Newburgh Jnrs	52/53			
	53/54			
	54/55			
East Fife	55/56	2		D1
Rangers	56/57	20	1	D1
	57/58	9	1	D1
	58/59	29	2	D1
	59/60	26		D1
	60/61	31	2	D1
	61/62	33		D1
	62/63	16	2	D1
	63/64	4		D1
Partick T	64/65	22		D1
Queen's Park	65/66			D2

DAVIS Joseph
b. Glasgow 22.5.1941
Shettleston

Club	Season			
Third Lanark	61/62	2		D1
	62/63	12		D1
	63/64	34		D1
	64/65	11		D1
Hibernian	64/65	20		D1
	65/66	33	8	D1
	66/67	34	13	D1
	67/68	34	7	D1
	68/69	34	6	D1
	69/70	1		D1
Carlisle U	69/70	20		FL
	70/71	42		FL
	71/72	13	4	FL

DAWSON George
b. Glasgow 13.9.1930
Rutherglen Glencairn

Club	Season			
Motherwell	52/53	14	2	D1
	53/54	2	1	D2
	54/55			D1
QPR	55/56	1		FL

DAWSON James
b. Falkirk 30.10.1909 d. 19.1.1977 Caps: S - 14
Camelon Juniors

Club	Season		
Rangers	29/30		D1
	30/31	1	D1
	31/32	13	D1
	32/33	20	D1
	33/34	30	D1
	34/35	37	D1
	35/36	38	D1
	36/37	38	D1
	37/38	26	D1
	38/39	33	D1
Falkirk	46/47	30	D1
	47/48	27	D1
	48/49	21	D1

DAWSON Kenneth
Sheffield U

Club	Season			
Falkirk	46/47	11	1	D1
	47/48	16	6	D1
	48/49	22	12	D1
	49/50	21	6	D1
	50/51	2		D1

DAWSON W

Club	Season		
Dunfermline A	55/56	1	D1

DEAKIN John

Glentoran	44/45			
	45/46			
St Mirren	46/47	26	9	D1
	47/48	25	1	D1
	48/49	10	1	D1
	49/50	5		D1
Clyde	49/50	16	8	D1
	50/51	1		D1

DEANS John Kelty
b. Linwood 30.7.1946 Caps: S - 2
Neilston V

Motherwell	65/66	2		D1
	66/67	21	11	D1
	67/68	28	11	D1
	68/69	33	30	D2
	69/70	29	16	D1
	70/71	31	9	D1
	71/72	6	2	D1
Celtic	71/72	21	19	D1
	72/73	30	1	21 D1
	73/74	24	2	24 D1
	74/75	18	1	9 D1
	75/76	29	15	P
Luton T	76/77	13	1	6 FL
Carlisle U	L 76/77	4	2	FL
Partick T	T 76/77	4	2	2 P
Adelaide Juventus				
Shelbourne	77/78			
Adelaide C				
USA				
Partick T	T 80/81			P

DEANS Thomas Sneddon
b. Shieldhill 7.1.1922

Clyde	47/48	29	D1
	48/49	13	D1
	49/50	3	D1
Notts Co	49/50	29	FL
	50/51	37	FL
	51/52	40	FL
	52/53	42	FL
	53/54	40	FL
	54/55	42	FL
	55/56	9	FL
Boston U			

DELANEY James
b. Cleland 3.9.1914
d. Cleland 26.9.1989 Caps: S - 13
Cleland St Marys
Wishaw Jnrs T
Stoneyburn Jnrs

Celtic	33/34			D1
	34/35	30	15	D1
	35/36	30	18	D1
	36/37	32	14	D1
	37/38	26	7	D1
	38/39	25	14	D1
Manchester U	46/47	37	8	FL
	47/48	36	8	FL
	48/49	36	4	FL
	49/50	42	4	FL
	50/51	13	1	FL
Aberdeen	50/51	21	4	D1
	51/52	10	4	D1
Falkirk	51/52	20	13	D2
	52/53	7	3	D1
	53/54			
Derry C	54/55			
Cork A	55/56			
Elgin C				

DELANEY Pat
b. c1940
Douglas Water Thistle

Motherwell	58/59			D1
	59/60	5	1	D1
	60/61	22		D1
	61/62	23	13	D1
	62/63	19	1	D1
	63/64	33	1	D1
	64/65	33		D1
	65/66	29	6	D1
Dunfermline A	66/67	21	2	8 D1
	67/68	7	1	D1
Clyde	67/68	8	2	2 D1
	68/69	1	1	D1
Airdrieonians	69/70	32	1	D1
	70/71	14		D1
	71/72	16		D1
Clydebank	72/73	13	1	D2
Albion R	72/73	13		D2
	73/74	3	1	D2

DEMPSEY John
b. Cumbernauld 22.6.1913

Queen of the South	46/47	23	5	D1
	47/48			D1
Ipswich T	48/49	22	5	FL

DEMPSTER Robert

Airdrieonians	61/62	32	D1
	62/63		D1
St Mirren	63/64	8	D1

DENHOLM L

Third Lanark	60/61	1	D1

DENMARK James
b. Glasgow 13.05.1913
Tollcross Clydesdale
Parkhead

Third Lanark	31/32	1		D1
	32/33	1		D1
	33/34	28	1	D1
	34/35			D2
	35/36	35		D1
	36/37	37		D1
Newcastle U	37/38	17		FL
	38/39	34		FL
Queen of the South	46/47	17		D1
Ashington				

DENNY James
b. Paisley 13.3.1950
Yoker A

Rangers	71/72	7	2	D1
	72/73	6		D1
	73/74		1	D1
	74/75	6	1	D1
	75/76	6	3	P
	76/77	5		P
	77/78			P
	78/79			P
Heart of Midlothian	79/80	34		D1
	80/81	19		P
Stirling A	81/82	20		D2
Irvine V				
Dalry Thistle				
Troon				

DEVANNY Alexander Stark
b. 25.7.1930
Dennistoun Juveniles
Glasgow Perthshire

Celtic	49/50		D1
	50/51		D1
	51/52	1	D1
Berwick R	52/53		D3
	53/54		D3
	54/55		D3
Northampton T	55/56		FL
St Mirren	55/56		D1
	56/57		D1
Alloa A	57/58		D2
	58/59		D2
	59/60		D2
	60/61		D2

DEVINE Daniel

Clyde	53/54	1	1	D1
	54/55			
Stirling A	54/55			

DEVINE J Hunter

Queen's Park	53/54	3		D2
	54/55			D2
	55/56	16	14	D2
	56/57	21	12	D1
	57/58	12	4	D1
	58/59			D2
	59/60	27	13	D2
	60/61	16	5	D2

DEVINE Matthew
b. c1919 d. East Kilbride 5.4.1985
Royal Albert

Hibernian	36/37	1		D1
Ayr U	37/38	18	3	D1
Hamilton A	38/39	7	2	D1
	46/47	18		D1
	47/48	29	1	D2
	48/49	10	1	D2
	49/50	1		D2
Stranraer				

DEVINE William
b. Whitletts 22.8.1933
Whitletts Victoria

St Mirren	55/56	3		D1
	56/57	20	6	D1
	57/58	13	1	D1
Watford	57/58	11	3	FL
	58/59	19	3	FL
Partick T	59/60	14	2	D1
Accrington S	60/61	46	6	FL
	61/62			FL
Cambridge C	62/63			

DEVLIN Alan Thomas
b. Edinburgh 10.10.1953
Tynecastle BC

Dundee U	70/71	3	1	2 D1
	71/72	4	1	D1
	72/73			D1
	73/74			D1
Exeter C	73/74	1		FL

DEVLIN David

League Hearts				
Hamilton A	46/47	14	7	D1
	47/48	13	10	D2
	48/49	7	4	D2
	49/50			D2
	50/51	26		D2
	51/52	30		D2
	52/53	27	1	D2
	53/54	3		D1

DEVLIN Dennis
b. Edinburgh

Club	Season	Apps	Gls	Div
Morton	65/66	3		D1
	66/67	1		D2
Falkirk	66/67	3		D1
	67/68	28		D1
	68/69	9		D1
	69/70	6		D2
	70/71	6		D1
	71/72	3		D1
	72/73	6		D1

DEVLIN John
b. Airdrie 11.12.1917 d. Walsall 26.1.2001
Coatsdyke All Saints
Plains Jnrs
Airdrie Jnrs
Coltness U
Hibernian

Club	Season	Apps	Gls	Div
Kilmarnock	46/47	27	5	D1
	47/48	13	2	D2
Walsall	47/48	22	9	FL
	48/49	34	11	FL
	49/50	37	20	FL
	50/51	41	5	FL
	51/52	25	5	FL

Bloxwich Strollers

DEVLIN Joseph
b. Cleland 12.3.1931
Cleland Jnrs

Club	Season	Apps	Gls	Div
Albion R	47/48			D2
	48/49	6		D1
	49/50	7		D2
Falkirk	50/51	1		D1
	51/52	19	2	D2
	52/53	2		D1
Accrington S	53/54	46	3	FL
	54/55	38	9	FL
	55/56	27	5	FL
	56/57	3	1	FL
Rochdale	56/57	27	6	FL
	57/58	11	1	FL
Bradford PA	57/58	20	2	FL
	58/59	16	1	FL
Carlisle U	59/60	5		FL

Nelson
Northwich V

Club	Season	Apps	Gls	Div
Accrington S	61/62			FL

Northwich V
Netherfield

DEWAR John
b. Crieff 1.11.1929
Bayview YC

Club	Season	Apps	Gls	Div
Heart of Midlothian	46/47	3	3	D1
Dundee U	47/48	4		D2
	48/49	20		D2
	49/50	20	9	D2
	50/51	4		D2

DEWAR W

Club	Season	Apps	Gls	Div
Third Lanark	47/48	1		D1
	48/49	1	1	D1

DICK Francis
Cumnock Jnrs

Club	Season	Apps	Gls	Div
Queen of the South	48/49			D1
	49/50	1		D1

DICK George
Hibernian

Club	Season	Apps	Gls	Div
Stirling A	46/47			D3
	47/48			D2
	48/49			D2
	49/50	20	3	D1
	50/51			D1
	51/52	10	1	D1
	52/53	1		D2

DICK Ian C
b. Glasgow
Ardrossan Winton R

Club	Season	Apps	Gls	Div
Kilmarnock	65/66			D1
	66/67	2		D1
	67/68	3		D1
	68/69			D1
Partick T	69/70	9		D1
	70/71			D1
	71/72			D1

Irvine Meadow

Club	Season	Apps	Gls	Div
Albion R	72/73	1		D2
St Mirren	73/74	6		D2

DICK Kenneth

Club	Season	Apps	Sub	Gls	Div
Forfar A	62/63				D2
	63/64	31		13	D2
	64/65	15		7	D2
Dundee U	64/65	6		4	D1
Queen of the South	65/66	35		22	D2
	66/67	26	2	17	D2
Dundee U	66/67	3			D1
Queen of the South	67/68	35		22	D2
Forfar A	68/69			5	D2
	69/70	24	1	9	D2
Brechin C	70/71				D2

DICK Peter Watt
b. Newmains 20.8.1927

Club	Season	Apps	Gls	Div
Third Lanark	49/50	6	3	D1
	50/51	28	8	D1
	51/52	29	17	D1
	52/53	27	12	D1
	53/54	28	21	D2
	54/55	28	26	D2
Accrington S	55/56	40	18	FL
	56/57	44	13	FL
	57/58	18	4	FL
	58/59	23	2	FL
Bradford PA	58/59	22		FL
	59/60	38		FL
	60/61	44		FL
	61/62	46	2	FL
	62/63	3		FL

DICK Sidney
b. c1945
Arbroath BC

Club	Season	Apps	Gls	Div
Dundee U	61/62			D1
	62/63			D1
	63/64	5		D1
	64/65	1		D1
	65/66			D1
	66/67			D1
Forfar A	67/68	24		D2

Inverness Thistle
Jewish Guild

DICK Thomas Woods
b. Glasgow 19.7.1936

Club	Season	Apps	Gls	Div
Third Lanark	58/59	29	16	D1
	59/60	4		D1
Bradford PA	60/61	4		FL

DICKSON Charles
b. Musselburgh
Penicuik A

Club	Season	Apps	Gls	Div
Dunfermline A	54/55			D2
	55/56	19	9	D1
	56/57	27	12	D1
	57/58			D2
	58/59	27	14	D1
	59/60	33	24	D1
	60/61	32	18	D1
	61/62	26	16	D1
	62/63	22	10	D1
	63/64	25	9	D1
Queen of the South	64/65			D2
	65/66			D2

DICKSON J

Club	Season	Apps	Gls	Div
Dundee U	47/48	15	1	D2
	48/49	22	4	D2
Queen of the South	49/50	2		D1

DICKSON John
b. Kirkcaldy 15.5.1949 d. Kirkcaldy 12.1.1998
Leeds U
Lochore Welfare

Club	Season	Apps	Sub	Gls	Div
Cowdenbeath	68/69				D2
	69/70				D2
	70/71	26	3	8	D1
	71/72	33		12	D2
	72/73	7		5	D2
St Mirren	72/73	29		15	D2
	73/74	29	1	7	D2
Ayr U	74/75	13	4	4	D1
	75/76	8	2		P
	76/77				P
Elgin C	77/78				
East Fife	78/79	35		9	D2
	79/80	4		3	D2

DICKSON Robert James
b. Milton of Campsie 6.3.1942

Club	Season	Apps	Gls	Div
Third Lanark	63/64	17		D1
St Johnstone	64/65	2		D1
Stirling A	65/66	29	1	D1
	66/67	9	1	D1

DICKSON William
Bo'ness Jnrs

Club	Season	Apps	Gls	Div
Albion R	47/48			D2
	48/49	11	1	D1
	49/50	9	4	D2
	50/51			D2
	51/52			D2
	52/53	27	2	D2

DICKSON William
b. Larkhall 8.4.1945 Caps: S - 5
Larkhall Academy
Birkenshaw Amateurs

Club	Season	Apps	Sub	Gls	Div
Kilmarnock	64/65	2			D1
	65/66	10			D1
	66/67	8		3	D1
	67/68	9	1	1	D1
	68/69	33		2	D1
	69/70	33		1	D1
	70/71	34		1	D1
	71/72	21		1	D1
	72/73	27		1	D1
	73/74				D2
Motherwell	74/75	10		2	D1
Ayr U	75/76				P
	76/77				P
Hamilton A	77/78	2		1	D1

DINGWALL George

Club	Season	Apps	Gls	Div
Airdrieonians	49/50	27		D2
	50/51	5		D1
	51/52	4		D1

DIVERS John
b. Clydebank 6.8.1911
d. Western Infirmary 8.6.1984 Caps: S - 1
Clydebank BG
Linwood St Convals
Rothesay Royal Victoria
Renfrew Jnrs

Club	Season	Apps	Gls	Div
Celtic	32/33			D1
	33/34	8	2	D1
	34/35			D1
	35/36	2		D1
	36/37	5	4	D1
	37/38	20	19	D1
	38/39	35	17	D1
Oldham A	T			
Morton	46/47	24	4	D1
Oldham A	47/48	1		FL
Morton	47/48	15	7	D1
	48/49	7	1	D1
	49/50	2	1	D2

Portadown

DIVERS John
b. Clydebank 8.3.1940
Glentyan Thistle
Celtic
Renfrew Jnrs   L

Club	Season	App	Sub	Gls	Div
Celtic	57/58	1		1	D1
	58/59	20		8	D1
	59/60	23		12	D1
	60/61	23		8	D1
	61/62	34		19	D1
	62/63	27		12	D1
	63/64	29		15	D1
	64/65	10		3	D1
	65/66	3		1	D1
Partick T	66/67	14		3	D1
	67/68			1	D1
	68/69	14		2	D1

Strathclyde University

DIVERS John

Club	Season	App	Sub	Gls	Div
Hamilton A	58/59	7		2	D2
	59/50	36		26	D2
	60/61	35		22	D2
	61/62	9		5	D2
Clyde	62/63	1		1	D1
Hamilton A	L 62/63	6		3	D2

DIVERS John Rice
b. Glasgow 24.11.1931
Ashfield

Club	Season	App	Sub	Gls	Div
Clyde	53/54	9			D1
	54/55	8		1	D1
	55/56	14		2	D1
Exeter C	56/57	12		1	FL

East Stirlingshire

DIXON Arthur
b. Middleton 17.11.1921
Baillieston
Queen's Park

Club	Season	App	Sub	Gls	Div
Clyde	46/47	28		12	D1
	47/48	2			
Heart of Midlothian	47/48	24		3	D1
	48/49	9		1	D1
	49/50				D1
Northampton T	49/50	23		9	FL
	50/51	43		12	FL
	51/52	2			FL
Leicester C	51/52	8			FL
	52/53	3			FL

Kettering T

DOBBIE George

Club	Season	App	Sub	Gls	Div
Third Lanark	51/52	1		1	D1
	52/53	26		12	D1
Heart of Midlothian	53/54				D1
	54/55				D1
	55/56				D1
	56/57				D1
	57/58				D1
Raith R	58/59	19		6	D1

DOCHERTY Edward
Blantyre Celtic

Club	Season	App	Sub	Gls	Div
Queen of the South	54/55				D1
	55/56				D1
	56/57				D1
	57/58	4			D1

DOCHERTY James
b. Clydebank 22.4.1926
Coatbridge St Patricks
Renfrew Jnrs

Club	Season	App	Sub	Gls	Div
Celtic	47/48				D1
	48/49				D1
	49/50	1			D1
Northampton T	50/51	1			FL
Stirling A	51/52				D1
Arbroath	51/52				D2
Alloa A	52/53	15		3	D2
Llanelly	53/54				
Distillery	54/55				
Stranraer					

DOCHERTY James

Club	Season	App	Sub	Gls	Div
Airdrieonians	52/53	4			D1
	53/54	6			D1

DOCHERTY James
b. 13.4.1934
Duntocher Hibs

Club	Season	App	Sub	Gls	Div
Celtic	54/55				D1
	55/56	1			D1
Alloa A					

DOCHERTY James
b. Clydebank 22.4.1929

Club	Season	App	Sub	Gls	Div
Airdrieonians	49/50	25		1	D2
	50/51	21		3	D1
Doncaster R	51/52	11		4	FL
Third Lanark	51/52	12		2	D1
	52/53	16		3	D1
	53/54	24		11	D2
Stirling A	54/55	19		2	D1
	55/56	1			D1
Third Lanark	55/56				D2
Limerick	56/57				
Crewe Alex.	56/57	2			FL

DOCHERTY John
b. Glasgow 28.2.1935
Petershill

Club	Season	App	Sub	Gls	Div
Stirling A	56/57				D2
	57/58				D2
	58/59	1			D1
St Johnstone	58/59	34		3	D2
	59/60	35		3	D2
	60/61	25		4	D1
Heart of Midlothian	60/61	8		1	D1
	61/62	1			D1
	62/63	3			D1
Colchester U	63/64	35		1	FL
	64/65	41		1	FL

Chelmsford C

DOCHERTY Thomas Henderson
b. Glasgow 24.4.1928 Caps: S - 25
Shettleston Jnrs

Club	Season	App	Sub	Gls	Div
Celtic	48/49	10		3	D1
	49/50				D1
Preston NE	49/50	15			FL
	50/51	42			FL
	51/52	42			FL
	52/53	41			FL
	53/54	26			FL
	54/55	39		3	FL
	55/56	41		1	FL
Third Lanark	L 55/56				D2
Preston NE	56/57	37			FL
	57/58	40		1	FL
Arsenal	58/59	38		1	FL
	59/60	24			FL
	60/61	21			FL

DOHERTY Hugh
b. Buncrana 5.5.1921
Buncrana Celtic
Derry C
Buncrana Celtic

Club	Season	App	Sub	Gls	Div
Dundalk	45/46				
Celtic	46/47	3			D1
Blackpool	47/48				FL
	48/49				FL
Raith R	L 48/49				D2

DOHERTY James
b. c 1952
Sighthill Amateurs

Club	Season	App	Sub	Gls	Div
Partick T	72/73	1			D1
San Antonio Thunder	75	22		2	NA

DOIG Ernest
b. c1924

Club	Season	App	Sub	Gls	Div
Falkirk	46/47	3			D1
	47/48	4			D1
	48/49	1			D1
Kilmarnock	49/50	28			D2
	50/51	17		2	D2
	51/52	7			D2
Dundee U	53/54	1			D2

DOIG John

Club	Season	App	Sub	Gls	Div
Queen of the South	46/47	3		1	D1

DONALD Ian Richard
b. Aberdeen 28.11.1951
Banks o'Dee

Club	Season	App	Sub	Gls	Div
Manchester U	69/70				FL
	70/71				FL
	71/72				FL
	72/73	4			FL
Partick T	72/73	1			D1
Arbroath	73/74	2		1	D1
	74/75			1	D1

DONALDSON Alistair
b. Edinburgh 27.11.1943
Tynecastle A

Club	Season	App	Sub	Gls	Div
Dundee	63/64				D1
	64/65	30			D1
	65/66	29			D1
	66/67	6			D1
	67/68	24			D1
	68/69	33			D1
	69/70	34			D1
	70/71	29			D1
	71/72	3			D1
Falkirk	71/72	13			D1
	72/73				D1
	73/74	34			D1
	74/75	38			D2
	75/76	20			D1
Dundee	76/77	29			D1
	77/78	22			D1
	78/79	39			D1
	79/80	36			P
	80/81				P
Raith R	81/82	18			D1

DONALDSON George
b. Edinburgh 24.11.1954
Tynecastle BC

Club	Season	App	Sub	Gls	Div
Rangers	72/73	3		2	D1
	73/74				D1
Heart of Midlothian	74/75	10	4	1	D1
	75/76	2			P
Dunfermline A	76/77	13	2	1	D2
	77/78				D2
Meadowbank T	78/79	1			D2

DONALDSON James

Club	Season	App	Sub	Gls	Div
Dunfermline A	59/60	1			D1

DONALDSON James
Jeanfield Swifts

Club	Season	App	Sub	Gls	Div
St Johnstone	65/66	4			D1
	66/67	28			D1
	67/68	20			D1
	68/69	6			D1
	69/70	28			D1
	70/71	34			D1
	71/72	16			D1
	72/73	34			D1
	73/74	18			D1

DONALDSON Lewis

Club	Season	App	Sub	Gls	Div
Clyde	46/47	4		1	D1
	47/48	1			D1

DONALDSON Thomas

Musselburgh Windsor

Club	Season	Apps	Sub	Goals	Div
Aberdeen	63/64	2			D1
	64/65				
Montrose	65/66	4			D2

DONLEVY Frank
b. Edinburgh
Eyemouth U

Club	Season	Apps	Sub	Goals	Div
Partick T	54/55	6			D1
	55/56	5			D1
	56/57	7			D1
	57/58	27		1	D1
	58/59	32		2	D1
	59/60	31		4	D1
	60/61	32		1	D1
	61/62	10			D1
St Johnstone	61/62	17		4	D1
Berwick R					

DONNACHIE Frank

Shotts Bon Accord

Club	Season	Apps	Sub	Goals	Div
Motherwell	64/65	7		1	D1
	65/66	1			D1
	66/67	1	1		D1
Stenhousemuir	67/68	26	1	6	D2

DONNACHIE John

St Rochs

Club	Season	Apps	Sub	Goals	Div
Falkirk	63/64	11			D1

DONNELLY Edward

Renfrew Jnrs

Club	Season	Apps	Sub	Goals	Div
St Johnstone	63/64	5			D1
	64/65	1		1	D1
Dumbarton	65/66	6		1	D2

DONNELLY John
b. Broxburn 17.12.1936
Bathgate St Marys
Broxburn Celtic Juveniles
Armadale Thistle

Club	Season	Apps	Sub	Goals	Div
Celtic	57/58	19			D1
	58/59	4			D1
	59/60	5			D1
	60/61	1			D1
	61/62	3			D1
Preston NE	62/63	29		1	FL
	63/64	9			FL
	64/65	7			FL
	65/66	10	2		FL
	66/67	1			FL

DONNELLY Thomas

Rangers

Club	Season	Apps	Sub	Goals	Div
Motherwell	67/68				D1
	68/69	36		5	D2
	69/70	21	2	3	D1
	70/71	15		1	D1
East Stirlingshire	71/72	28	1	1	D2
	72/73	34		8	D2
	73/74	30	1	6	D2
	74/75	34	1	7	D2
	75/76	24		2	D2
	76/77	23	6		D2
	77/78	27	7	2	D2

DOONAN Joseph

Club	Season	Apps	Sub	Goals	Div
St Mirren	58/59	7			D1
	59/60	9			D1
	60/61	4			D1
	61/62	11			D1

DOONAN Thomas
b. West Calder 5.10.1922
Forth W

Club	Season	Apps	Sub	Goals	Div
Albion R	46/47				D2
	47/48				D2
	48/49	9		1	D1
Bradford C	49/50	13		7	FL
Tranmere R	50/51	4		2	FL
Bangor C					

DORNAN Harry

Ardeer Recreation
Kilmarnock
Dumbarton
Celtic
St Mirren

Club	Season	Apps	Sub	Goals	Div
Kilmarnock	46/47	4			D1
Arbroath	47/48				D2
Queen of the South	48/49				D1

DOSSING Finn
b. Denmark ?.?.1941 Caps: Den
Viborg

Club	Season	Apps	Sub	Goals	Div
Dundee U	64/65	19		21	D1
	65/66	34		25	D1
	66/67	24	5	12	D1
	67/68	6	1	2	D1

DOUGAN Robert
b. Glasgow 3.12.1926 Caps: S - 1
Shawfield Jnrs

Club	Season	Apps	Sub	Goals	Div
Heart of Midlothian	47/48	11			D1
	48/49	26			D1
	49/50	28			D1
	50/51	30			D1
	51/52	3			D1
	52/53	18			D1
	53/54	9			D1
Kilmarnock	54/55	18			D1
	55/56	6			D1
	56/57	6			D1
	57/58				D1
	58/59	27			D1
	59/60	4			D1

DOUGLAS

Club	Season	Apps	Sub	Goals	Div
Clyde	69/70	1	1		D1

DOUGLAS Brian Alexander
b. Berwick 13.5.1947

Club	Season	Apps	Sub	Goals	Div
Morton	64/65	1			D1
	65/66				D1
Stirling A	66/67				D1

DOUGLAS George

Albion R
Berwick R

Club	Season	Apps	Sub	Goals	Div
Morton	68/69	4			D1
	69/70				D1
Airdrieonians	70/71				D1
Hamilton A	71/72	3	1	1	D2

DOUGLAS Thomas

Ashfield

Club	Season	Apps	Sub	Goals	Div
Stirling A	53/54	2		1	D1

DOW D

Club	Season	Apps	Sub	Goals	Div
Queen's Park	47/48	16			D1
	48/49	9			D2

DOWNIE Mitchell
b. Irvine 9.2.1923 d. 12.7.2001
Kilmarnock Amateurs
Hibernian
Troon A

Club	Season	Apps	Sub	Goals	Div
Kilmarnock	46/47	28			D1
Airdrieonians	47/48	21			D1
	48/49				D2
	49/50				D2
Bradford PA	50/51	46			FL
	51/52	30			FL
	52/53	36			FL
	53/54	44			FL
Lincoln C	54/55	42			FL
	55/56	41			FL
	56/57	37			FL
	57/58	9			FL
	58/59	28			FL
Goole T					
Bradford C	59/60	35			FL
	60/61	31			FL
	61/62	35			FL
	62/63	33			FL
Doncaster R	63/64	7			FL
Altrincham					
Stalybridge C					

DOWNS G

Club	Season	Apps	Sub	Goals	Div
Third Lanark	48/49	7		2	D1

DOYLE John
b. Uddingston 11.5.1951
d. Kilmarnock 19.10.1981 Caps: S - 1
Viewpark Boys Guild

Club	Season	Apps	Sub	Goals	Div
Ayr U	70/71	10	2	1	D1
	71/72	34		3	D1
	72/73	34		6	D1
	73/74	23		1	D1
	74/75	28		7	D1
	75/76	23		6	P
Celtic	75/76	5			P
	76/77	33	1	4	P
	77/78	20	5	2	P
	78/79	23	2	2	P
	79/80	22	2	7	P
	80/81	1	4		P
	81/82				

DRAINER I K

Club	Season	Apps	Sub	Goals	Div
Queen's Park	57/58	2			D1
	58/59	13			D2
	59/60	1			D2

DRENNAN Hugh

Club	Season	Apps	Sub	Goals	Div
Dundee	58/59	1			D1

DRINKWATER James Arthur
b. Northwich 10.2.1918 d. ?.?.1996

Club	Season	Apps	Sub	Goals	Div
St Mirren	46/47	26		3	D1
	47/48	14			D1
	48/49	27		1	D1
	49/50	23			D1
	50/51	14		1	D1
	51/52	7			D1
Torquay U	52/53	36		1	FL
	53/54	31			FL

DRUMMOND Charles

Lochore Welfare

Club	Season	Apps	Sub	Goals	Div
Raith R	53/54	16			D1
	54/55	11			D1
	55/56	19			D1
	56/57	19			D1
	57/58	27			D1
	58/59	25			D1
	59/60	19			D1
	60/61	3			D1
Cowdenbeath	61/62	12			D2

DRURY James Welsh
b. Cumnock 29.5.1924
Cumnock Home Guard

Club	Season	Apps	Sub	Goals	Div
Kilmarnock	46/47	9		2	D1
	47/48	27		11	D2
	48/49	8		2	D2
Stirling A	48/49				D2
	49/50				D1
	50/51				D2
Rochdale	51/52	4		1	FL
Carlisle U	52/53	19		3	FL
	53/54	16		2	FL
Southport	54/55	24		2	FL
	55/56				FL
Newton Stewart					

DRYBURGH James

Club	Season	Apps	Sub	Goals	Div
Queen of the South	46/47	23			D1

DUCHART Alexander
b. Falkirk 3.5.1933
Petershill

Club	Season	Apps	Sub	Goals	Div
Hibernian	53/54	3			D1
	54/55				D1
	55/56				D1
Southend U	56/57	8		2	FL
East Fife	57/58	26		9	D1
	58/59				D2
Dumbarton	59/60				D2
Falkirk	60/61	18		6	D2
	61/62	21		10	D1
	62/63	4		2	D1
Inverness Caley					

DUDDY Thomas

Club	Season	Apps	Sub	Goals	Div
Airdrieonians	63/64	5			D1
Cowdenbeath *	64/65	18			D2

DUDMAN Leonard
b. Dundee ?? . 12.2.2004
Coupar Angus

Club	Season	Apps	Sub	Goals	Div
Falkirk	56/57	1			D1
	57/58				D1
Coupar Angus					

DUFF William
b. Winchburgh 6.2.1935
Juniper Green YM
Slateford A
Easthouses Lily

Club	Season	Apps	Sub	Goals	Div
Heart of Midlothian	54/55	26			D1
	55/56	32			D1
	56/57	4			D1
Charlton A	56/57	20			FL
	57/58	41			FL
	58/59	33			FL
	59/60	42			FL
	60/61	39			FL
	61/62	38			FL
	62/63				FL
Peterborough U	63/64	39			FL
	64/65	23			FL
	65/66	43			FL
	66/67	13			FL
Dunfermline A	67/68	3			D1
	68/69	15			D1
	69/70	17			D1
	70/71				D1
Raith R	71/72	1			D2
East Stirlingshire	71/72	15			D2
	72/73				D2
Albion R	73/74	3			D2

DUFFY D

Club	Season	Apps	Sub	Goals	Div
Raith R	59/60	1			D1
	60/61	6			D1

DUFFY John
b. Glasgow 24.4.1922
Rutherglen Glencairn

Club	Season	Apps	Sub	Goals	Div
Clyde	46/47	25			D1
	47/48	3			D1
	48/49				
Norwich C	49/50	17			FL
	50/51	38			FL
	51/52	14			FL
	52/53	6			FL
	53/54	3			FL
Great Yarmouth T					

DUFFY John
b. Dunfermline 6.9.1943
Raith R

Club	Season	Apps	Sub	Goals	Div
Dunfermline A	61/62	2			D1
	62/63	3			D1
Darlington	63/64	10		1	FL

DUFFY John Gerard
b. Dundee 24.8.1929
Dunkeld Amateurs

Club	Season	Apps	Sub	Goals	Div
Celtic	48/49				D1
St Anthonys	L				
Celtic	49/50				D1
	50/51				D1
	51/52				D1
	52/53	2			D1
	53/54				D1
Arbroath	L 53/54	28		5	D2
Southend U	54/55	12			FL
	55/56	2		1	FL
	56/57	14			FL
	57/58	16		1	FL
	58/59	41		1	FL
	59/60	29		1	FL
	60/61				FL

DUFFY Neil
Ashfield

Club	Season	Apps	Sub	Goals	Div
Hamilton A	T 57/58	1			D2
East Stirlingshire	58/59				D2
	59/60				D2
Partick T	60/61	29		11	D1
	61/62	33		13	D1
	62/63	33		16	D1
	63/64	33		12	D1
	64/65	6		1	D1
St Johnstone	64/65	23		9	D1
	65/66	29		11	D1
	66/67	7	1		D1
South Africa					

DUFFY Robert
Vale of Leven

Club	Season	Apps	Sub	Goals	Div
St Mirren	66/67	1			D1
	67/68	21	1	3	D2
	68/69	6	3		D1
Vale of Leven					
Stranraer	69/70	9		1	D2
	70/71			1	D2
	71/72	36		6	D2
	72/73	34	2		D2
	73/74	31		1	D2
	74/75	13	1	1	D2
	75/76	18			D2
Brora R					

DUNBAR John

Club	Season	Apps	Sub	Goals	Div
Aberdeen	52/53	2			D1
	53/54	2			D1

DUNCAN Arthur
b. Falkirk 5.12.1947
Gairdoch U

Club	Season	Apps	Sub	Goals	Div
Partick T	65/66	15		9	D1
	66/67	27		6	D1
	67/68	25		5	D1
	68/69	33		9	D1
	69/70	17		4	D1
Hibernian	69/70	17		3	D1
	70/71	24	1	4	D1
	71/72	27	2	11	D1
	72/73	33		10	D1
	73/74	33		6	D1
	74/75	30	1	12	D1
	75/76	35	1	13	P
	76/77	30		2	P
	77/78	28	3	5	P
	78/79	35		1	P
	79/80	26	2		P
	80/81	39		1	D1
	81/82	32		1	P
	82/83	31	4	2	P
	83/84	25	2	2	P
Meadowbank T	84/85	27	6		D1
	85/86				D2
	86/87	1			D2

DUNCAN Ben
b. N Ireland

Club	Season	Apps	Sub	Goals	Div
Airdrieonians	47/48	22		2	D1
	48/49				D2
	49/50	8			D2
	50/51	1			D1

DUNCAN David Millar
b. Milton of Balgonie 21.11.1921
d. 11.1.1991 Caps: S - 3
Woodside Amateurs
Milton o'Balgownie
Lochgelly Albert
Wolverhampton W T
Raith R
Celtic

Club	Season	Apps	Sub	Goals	Div
East Fife	46/47	18		5	D2
	47/48	30		25	D2
	48/49	29		12	D1
	49/50	24		5	D1
	50/51	30		5	D1
	51/52	28		7	D1
	52/53	21		3	D1
	53/54	1			D1
Raith R	53/54	11		4	D1
	54/55	25		9	D1
Crewe Alex.	55/56	22			FL
Brechin C	55/56				D2
	56/57				D2
	57/58				D2
	58/59				D2

DUNCAN George
b. Glasgow 16.1.1937

Club	Season	Apps	Sub	Goals	Div
Rangers	55/56				D1
	56/57				D1
	57/58	8		3	D1
	58/59	3		2	D1
	59/60	1			D1
Southend U	60/61	6		2	FL
Chesterfield	61/62	23		1	FL
	62/63	44		7	FL
	63/64	36		4	FL
	64/65	37		1	FL
Chelmsford C					
Folkestone T					
Cambridge C	68/69				
Braintree T					

DUNCAN James

Club	Season	Apps	Sub	Goals	Div
Third Lanark	52/53	11		1	D1
	53/54	11			D2
	54/55				D2
Cowdenbeath	55/56				D2
	56/57				D2
	57/58				D2

DUNCAN James B
b. c19332
Mearns Amateurs
Strathclyde
Baillieston Jnrs

Club	Season				Div
Celtic	50/51				D1
	51/52				D1
	52/53	2		1	D1
	53/54	6		1	D1
	54/55				D1
St Mirren	55/56				D1
	56/57	2			D1
Dundee U	57/58	11			D2
Albion R	58/59				D2
Dundee U	59/60				D2
	60/61				D1
Stranraer	60/61				D2

DUNCAN John Pearson
b. Dundee 22.2.1949
Dundee
Broughty Thistle L

Club	Season				Div
Dundee	68/69	11		4	D1
	69/70	2			D1
	70/71	13	2	11	D1
	71/72	32		13	D1
	72/73	30	1	23	D1
	73/74	29		13	D1
	74/75	4			D1
Tottenham H	74/75	28		12	FL
	75/76	35	2	20	FL
	76/77	9		4	FL
	77/78	27		16	FL
	78/79	2		1	FL
Derby Co	78/79	16	1	5	FL
	79/80	16		7	FL
	80/81	3			FL
Scunthorpe U	81/82		3		FL
	82/83	3		3	FL

DUNCAN Robert
b. 27.4.1945
Bonnyrigg Rose

Club	Season			Div
Hibernian	63/64	2		D1
	64/65	1		D1
	65/66	13		D1
	66/67	34		D1
	67/68	16		D1
	68/69	9		D1
	69/70	1		D1
	70/71	6	1	D1
East Fife	71/72	32		D1
	72/73	33		D1
	73/74	20		D1

DUNCAN Thomas Montgomerie
b. Portsoy 15.7.1936
Buckie Thistle

Club	Season			Div
Airdrieonians	53/54	1	1	D1
	54/55			D2
	55/56	6	3	D1
	56/57	19	1	D1
	57/58	5	2	D1
Newport Co	L 57/58	1		FL
Airdrieonians	58/59			D1
	59/60	29	8	D1
	60/61	32	8	D1
	61/62	21	7	D1
	62/63	27	10	D1
	63/64			D1
Falkirk	64/65	8	1	D1
Stirling A	65/66	6		D1

DUNCANSON James
b. Glasgow 13.10.1919
d. Glasgow 1.9.1996 Caps: S - 1
Dunoon Milton R

Club	Season			Div
Rangers	46/47	27	18	D1
	47/48	29	12	D1
	48/49	24	10	D1
	49/50	12	1	D1
	50/51	1		D1
St Mirren	50/51	16	3	D1
	51/52	4	1	D1
	52/53	3		D1
Stranraer	53/54			
	54/55			

DUNLOP Andrew

Club	Season			Div
Ayr U	69/70	2	1	D1
Australia				

DUNLOP Frank
b. Glasgow
Benburb

Club	Season		Div
Aberdeen	36/37	25	D1
	37/38	16	D1
	38/39	30	D1
	46/47	27	D1
	47/48	14	D1

DUNLOP William
b. Glasgow

Club	Season			Div
Falkirk	52/53	14	7	D1
	53/54	10	1	D1
	54/55			D1
Dundee U	54/55	19	8	D2
	55/56	1		D2

DUNLOP William Rex
b. Dumfries 21.9.1927

Club	Season			Div
Rangers	50/51	2		D1
	51/52			D1
	52/53	1		D1
Workington	53/54	24	7	FL
	54/55	46	8	FL
	55/56	39	4	FL

DUNN Charles
b. c1943

Club	Season				Div
Arbroath	59/60	17			D1
	60/61				D2
	61/62				D2
Montrose	61/62	25		4	D2
	62/63				D2
	63/64	7			D2
Brechin C	63/64	9		2	D2
	64/65	31		1	D2
	65/66	35		5	D2
	66/67	36		6	D2
	67/68	32	1	5	D2
	68/69			1	D2
	69/70	32		2	D2
	70/71				D2

DUNN Joseph
b. Glasgow 20.9.1925

Club	Season			Div
Clyde	48/49	17		D1
	49/50	7		D1
	50/51	5		D1
Preston NE	51/52	13		FL
	52/53	25	2	FL
	53/54	21		FL
	54/55	3		FL
	55/56	21		FL
	56/57	38		FL
	57/58	37		FL
	58/59	33		FL
	59/60	29		FL
	60/61	4		FL

DUNN Samuel

Club	Season			Div
Clyde	49/50	12	1	D1
	50/51	1		D1
	51/52			D2
	52/53			D1
Albion R	53/54	22	2	D2
	54/55			D2

DUNNE Thomas

Club	Season				Div
Dumbarton	64/65	3			D2
	65/66				D2
Albion R	66/67				D2
	67/68	32	3	7	D2
Dundee U	67/68	1			D1
	68/69	2			D1
	69/70	7			D1
	70/71	1			D1
East Stirlingshire					

DUNSMORE

Club	Season		Div
Arbroath	59/60	2	D1

DUNSMUIR David
b. Ayr
Ayr Albion

Club	Season			Div
Dundee	54/55	14	4	D1
	55/56			D1

DUNNET J

Club	Season		Div
Queen's Park	57/58	1	D1

DURKIN John
b. Hill of Beath 18.4.1930
Hill of Beath Ramblers

Club	Season			Div
Heart of Midlothian	51/52	4		D1
	52/53	5		D1
Gillingham	53/54	27	4	FL
	54/55	3	1	FL
Ramsgate A				

DUTHIE George
b. Edinburgh
Hibernian

Club	Season			Div
Dunfermline A	53/54	6		D2
	54/55			D2
	55/56	31	1	D1
	56/57	34	3	D1
	57/58			D2
	58/59	20	2	D1

DYER L

Club	Season		Div
Queen's Park	57/58	1	D1

DYSON Jack
b. Oldham 6.7.1934
Nelson

Club	Season			Div
Manchester C	52/53			FL
	53/54			FL
	54/55			FL
	55/56	25	13	FL
	56/57	32	12	FL
	57/58			FL
	58/59			FL
	59/60	6	1	FL
	60/61			FL
Stirling A	60/61			D2
	61/62	9	1	D1
Oldham A	62/63			FL

EADIE Angus
Rutherglen Glencairn

Club	Season			Div
Hamilton A	T 68/69	1		D2
St Mirren	69/70	3	2	D1

EADIE David
Bonkle YC

Club	Season		Div
Falkirk	72/73	2	D1

EASSON David

Club	Season			Div
Dundee	54/55	1		D1
	55/56	1		D1
	56/57	3	3	D1
	57/58	1		D1
	58/59			D1
Arbroath	59/60	34	15	D1
Raith R	60/61	16	8	D1

EASSON Gordon

Club	Season				Div
Bayview YC					
East Fife	49/50	1			D1
	50/51	16			D1
	51/52				D1
	52/53				D1
Worcester C	T 53/54				

EASTON James
b. 3.9.1940
Drumchapel Amateurs

Club	Season				Div
Hibernian	60/61	27			D1
	61/62	27			D1
	62/63	10		1	D1
	63/64	15			D1
Dundee	64/65	26			D1
	65/66	34			D1
	66/67	25			D1
	67/68	23	1		D1
	68/69	21			D1
	69/70	23			D1
	70/71	6		1	D1
Queen of the South	71/72	33	1	1	D2
	72/73	23		1	D2
Miami Toros	73	19			NA

EDDIE Brian

Club	Season				Div
Whitburn Jnrs					
Dundee U	72/73	3			D1
Stevenage B					

EDWARDS Alexander
b. 14.3.1946
Rosyth

Club	Season				Div
Dunfermline A	61/62	2			D1
	62/63	16		3	D1
	63/64	30		3	D1
	64/65	24		4	D1
	65/66	29		7	D1
	66/67	29		8	D1
	67/68	28		5	D1
	68/69	32		7	D1
	69/70	25	1	4	D1
	70/71	21	1	1	D1
	71/72	3	1		D1
Hibernian	71/72	16		3	D1
	72/73	26			D1
	73/74	31			D1
	74/75	12	1	1	D1
	75/76	25		1	P
	76/77	22	3		P
	77/78	5	1		P
Arbroath	78/79	6			D1
	79/80	1	2		D1

ELGIN Robert Brown
b. Edinburgh 23.6.1949
Edinburgh A

Club	Season				Div
Heart of Midlothian	67/68	1			D1
	68/69				D1
Stockport Co	69/70	21	4	2	FL
	70/71	9	1	1	FL

ELLIOT Alan
b Glasgow

Club	Season				Div
Rangers	55/56	2			D1
	56/57				D1
Queen of the South	57/58	25			D1
	58/59	7			D1

ELLIOT William

Club	Season				Div
Airdrieonians	53/54	1			D1
	54/55				
	55/56				
	56/57				
Yeovil T	57/58				
	58/59				
Ayr U	59/60	16		1	D1
	60/61	2			D1

ELLIOTT Alex

Club	Season				Div
Cowdenbeath	46/47				D2
	47/48				D2
	48/49				D2
	49/50				D2
Airdrieonians	50/51	19			D1
	51/52	7			D1

ELLIOTT Campbell

Club	Season				Div
Arthurlie					
Stirling A	61/62	2			D1
	62/63				D2

ELLIOTT Maurice
b. Torthorwald 23.11.1942
Dumfries Academy

Club	Season				Div
Queen of the South	59/60				D2
	60/61				D2
Heart of Midlothian	60/61	3			D1
	61/62	7		2	D1
	62/63				D1
Queen of the South	63/64	5			D1
Forfar A *	64/65	33		20	D2
Montrose *	65/66	17		4	D2
Stenhousemuir *	66/67	37		13	D2
	67/68	18	2	3	D2

ELLIOTT T

Club	Season				Div
Airdrieonians	47/48	2		1	D1

ELLIS James
b. Baldridgeburn ?.?.1924 d. ?.?.1999

Club	Season				Div
Airdrieonians	47/48	1			D1
Raith R	48/49				D2
Cowdenbeath	49/50	10		2	D2
	50/51				D2
	51/52				D2

EMERY Donald Kenneth James
b. Cardiff 11.6.1920 d. Aberdeen ?.11.1993
Ely R
Cardiff C

Club	Season				Div
Swindon T	37/38	1			FL
	38/39	8		1	FL
	46/47	23		2	FL
	47/48	37			FL
Aberdeen	48/49	15		5	D1
	49/50	29		5	D1
	50/51	25		4	D1
	51/52	20		3	D1
East Fife	52/53	30		2	D1
	53/54	28		2	D1
	54/55	30		1	D1
	55/56	4			D1
Fraserburgh					

ENGLISH Samuel
b. c1924 d. 1987

Club	Season				Div
Albion R	48/49	30			D1
	49/50	26			D2
	50/51				D2
	51/52				D2
	52/53	5			D2
Dundee U	52/53	19			D2
	53/54	19			D2
	54/55				D2
Gravesend	55/56				
	56/57				
	57/58				
	58/59				
	59/60				
	60/61				

ERSKINE Robert S
b. Bridge of Allan
Hibernian

Club	Season				Div
Stirling A	54/55	2			D1
	55/56	7			D1

EVANS Allan James
b. Dunfermline 12.10.1956 Caps: S - 4
Dunfermline U

Club	Season				Div
Dunfermline A	73/74	6		3	D1
	74/75	25		1	D1
	75/76	26		1	D1
	76/77	37		13	D2
Aston Villa	77/78	9		1	FL
	78/79	36	1	6	FL
	79/80	35		8	FL
	80/81	39		7	FL
	81/82	38		2	FL
	82/83	39	1	4	FL
	83/84	36		7	FL
	84/85	38		6	FL
	85/86	35		3	FL
	86/87	25	1	6	FL
	87/88	18	2	1	FL
	88/89	26	1		FL
Leicester C	89/90	14			FL
Victoria Vistas					
Brisbane U					
Darlington					
Leicester C					

EVANS George Cameron
b. Stevenston
Ardeer Recreation

Club	Season				Div
Rangers	67/68				D1
	68/69				D1
Sheffield U	68/69				FL
Kilmarnock	68/69	7		3	D1
	69/70				D1
Queen of the South	70/71				D2
	71/72	11	3	2	D2
Stranraer	72/73	6	1	1	D2

EVANS Robert
b. Glasgow 16.7.1927
d. Airdrie 01.09.2001 Caps: S - 48
Thornliebank Methodists
St Anthonys

Club	Season				Div
Celtic	46/47	21		4	D1
	47/48	27		3	D1
	48/49	24			D1
	49/50	27		2	D1
	50/51	28			D1
	51/52	25			D1
	52/53	30			D1
	53/54	29			D1
	54/55	30		1	D1
	55/56	31			D1
	56/57	31			D1
	57/58	33			D1
	58/59	20			D1
	59/60	30			D1
Chelsea	60/61	32			FL
Newport Co	61/62	31			FL
Morton	62/63				D2
	63/64				D2
Third Lanark	64/65	7		1	D1
Raith R	65/66	36			D2
	66/67	38			D2
	67/68	4			D1

EWEN Erniest
b. Kemnay

Club	Season				Div
Dundee	46/47	25		24	D2
	47/48	24		13	D1
	48/49	15		5	D1
	49/50	8		1	D1
	50/51	15		5	D1
	51/52	7		2	D1
Aberdeen	52/53	1			D1
St Johnstone	53/54	29		9	D2
	54/55	29		10	D2
	55/56	37		3	D2
	56/57	36		7	D2
	57/58	35		11	D2
	58/59	17			D2

EWEN Richard

Banks o'Dee

Club	Season				
Aberdeen	57/58	23		7	D1
	58/59	26		8	D1
	59/60	11		1	D1
	60/61	18			D1
	61/62	4		2	D1
	62/63				D1
Forfar A	63/64	22		3	D2
Peterhead					
Keith	67/68				

EWING Thomas
b. Larkhall 2.5.1937 Caps: S - 2

Larkhall Thistle

Club	Season				
Partick T	55/56	27		9	D1
	56/57	31		7	D1
	57/58	26		9	D1
	58/59	6		2	D1
	59/60	4		1	D1
	60/61	23		4	D1
	61/62	16		7	D1
Aston Villa	61/62	12		3	FL
	62/63	13			FL
	63/64	14		1	FL
Partick T	64/65	31		14	D1
	65/66	6		1	D1
Morton	66/67	10		3	D2
Hamilton A	67/68	8		4	D2
	68/69				D2
	69/70	2	1	2	D2
	70/71	2			D2

EWING Thomas McCall Halliday
b. Musselburgh 8.8.1934

Club	Season				
Doncaster R	51/52	3			FL
	52/53	1			FL
	53/54				FL
	54/55				FL
	55/56	2			FL
	56/57	23		3	FL
	57/58	10		3	FL
Queen of the South	57/58	12		5	D1
	58/59	24		7	D1
Cowdenbeath	59/60				D2

FALCONER Duncan

Edinburgh Norton

Club	Season				
Hibernian	59/60	10			D1
	60/61	5			D1
	61/62	18		12	D1
	62/63	8		1	D1
	63/64	7		1	D1
APIA Leichardt					

FALCONER George

Clydesdale Amateurs
Royal Albert

Club	Season				
Hamilton A	53/54	1			D1
?	54/55				D1
	55/56				D2
Albion R	55/56				D2
	56/57				D2
Lesmahagow Jnrs					
Hamilton A T	57/58	1			D2
Queen's Park	58/59	13		4	D2
	59/60	6			D2

FALCONER George
b. Dundee

Lochee Harp

Club	Season				
Montrose	65/66	1			D2
	66/67	38		18	D2
Raith R	67/68	26		3	D1
	68/69	30	1	16	D1
	69/70	11		2	D1
Dundee	70/71	1	2		D1
Elgin C	71/72				
	72/73				
Forfar A	73/74	15	4	1	D2

FALLIS Ian B
d. ?.?.1977

Club	Season				
Queen's Park	72/73	18	5	7	D2
	73/74	35		12	D2
Kilmarnock	74/75	10	6	4	D1
	75/76	26		10	D1
	76/77	32	1	10	P
	77/78	4	2		D1

FALLON Henry
b. Paisley 28.4.1942

Neilston V

Club	Season			
St Johnstone	63/64	21		D1
	64/65	10		D1
	65/66			
York C	65/66	32		FL
	66/67	26		FL
	67/68	9		FL
Corby T				

FALLON John
b. Blantyre 16.8.1940

Club	Season		
Celtic	58/59		
Fauldhouse U	L		
Celtic	59/60	14	D1
	60/61	4	D1
	61/62		D1
	62/63		D1
	63/64	24	D1
	64/65	26	D1
	65/66	4	D1
	66/67	1	D1
	67/68	1	D1
	68/69	22	D1
	69/70	16	D1
	70/71	3	D1
Motherwell	71/72	10	D1
Morton	72/73		D1

FALLON Sean
b. Sligo 31.7.1922 Caps: Ei - 8

Sligo St Marys
Craobh Ruadh GAA
Coolers GAA
Longford T
McArthurs
Sligo Distillery

Club	Season			
Sligo R	48/49			
Glenavon				
Celtic	49/50	1		D1
	50/51	27		D1
	51/52	30		D1
	52/53	20	3	D1
	53/54	12	5	D1
	54/55	20		D1
	55/56	20		D1
	56/57	22		D1
	57/58	26		D1

FALLS Robert

Kilmarnock Amateurs
Kilwinning R

Club	Season		
Kilmarnock	55/56		D1
	56/57	2	D1
	57/58	8	D1
	58/59		D1
San Francisco Scots			

FARM George Neil
b. Slateford 13.7.1924 Caps: S - 10

Armadale

Club	Season			
Hibernian	47/48	7		D1
Blackpool	48/49	34		FL
	49/50	42		FL
	50/51	42		FL
	51/52	42		FL
	52/53	39		FL
	53/54	34		FL
	54/55	39		FL
	55/56	42	1	FL
	56/57	42		FL
	57/58	42		FL
	58/59	42		FL
	59/60	25		FL
Queen of the South	60/61			D2
	61/62			D2
	62/63	30		D1
	63/64	15		D1

FARQUHAR John
b. c1924 d. Glasgow 22.11.2000

Club	Season			
Queen's Park	46/47	12	3	D1
	47/48	25	10	D1
Morton	48/49	23	5	D1
	49/50	26	8	D2
	50/51	1		D1
	51/52			D1
	52/53	5	1	D2
Cowdenbeath	53/54	29	1	D2
Albion R	54/55			D2

FARRELL T

Club	Season		
Falkirk	48/49	1	D1
Raith R	49/50	1	D1

FAULDS William

Club	Season			
St Mirren	65/66	10	3	D1
	66/67	1		D1
	67/68			D2
Queen of the South	68/69		5	D2
	69/70	7	3	D2

FEARN John

Accrington S

Club	Season			
Hamilton A	46/47	3	1	D1
Clydebank Jnrs				
Elgin C				
Huntly				

FERGUSON

Club	Season		
Airdrieonians	60/61	3	D1

FERGUSON Alexander C
b. Govan 31.12.1941

Harmony Row

Club	Season				
Queen's Park	58/59	8			D2
	59/60	23		11	D2
St Johnstone	60/61	3			D1
	61/62	12		5	D1
	62/63	12		8	D2
	63/64	10		6	D1
Dunfermline A	64/65	26		15	D1
	65/66	32		31	D1
	66/67	30		20	D1
Rangers	67/68	29		19	D1
	68/69	7	5	6	D1
Falkirk	69/70	21		14	D2
	70/71	28		14	D1
	71/72	27		9	D1
	72/73	28			D1
Ayr U	73/74	18	6	9	D1

FERGUSON Bert

Club	Season				Div
Maybole Jnrs					
Ayr U	73/74	10	1	2	D1
	74/75	1	1		D1
St Mirren	74/75	20		5	D2
	75/76	13	3	2	D1
Stranraer	76/77	39		12	D2
	77/78	37		8	D2
Whitletts Victoria					
Craigmark Bruntonians					
Auchinleck Talbot					
Glenafton A					

FERGUSON Charles
b. Glasgow 22.4.1930

Club	Season				Div
Tollcross YMCA					
Benburb					
Heart of Midlothian	51/52				D1
	52/53	1			D1
Hamilton A	53/54	10			D1
Accrington S	54/55	1			FL
Rochdale	55/56	33			FL
	56/57	39		1	FL
	57/58	46		1	FL
	58/59	32		1	FL
Oldham A	59/60	45			FL
	60/61	12			FL
Rossendale U					

FERGUSON D

Club	Season				Div
Queen's Park	54/55	5			D2
	55/56				D2
	56/57				D1
	57/58	2			D1

FERGUSON Daniel
b. Prestonpans 5.2.1939
d. Prestonpans ?.?.1977

Club	Season				Div
Ormiston Primrose					
Hamilton A	57/58	1			D2
	58/59	16		1	D2
	59/60				D2
Heart of Midlothian	60/61	9			D1
	61/62	26		3	D1
	62/63	26		3	D1
	63/64	16		2	D1
	64/65	18		3	D1
	65/66	17		1	D1
	66/67	16		1	D1
Durban U	67/68				
Morton	68/69	23	2	2	D1
	69/70	31		1	D1
Cowdenbeath	70/71	14		1	D1

FERGUSON Edward Brodie
b. Whitburn 10.9.1949

Club	Season				Div
Tynecastle A					
Dunfermline A	68/69	2			D1
Dumbarton	69/70	26	1	6	D2
	70/71		1		D2
Rotherham U	70/71	2			FL
	71/72	20			FL
Grimsby T	L 71/72	1		1	FL
Rotherham U	72/73	35		5	FL
	73/74	7			FL

FERGUSON George

Club	Season				Div
St Anthonys					
Celtic	46/47				D1
	47/48	5			D1
Dumbarton	48/49				D2
	49/50	28			D2
	50/51				D2
	51/52				D2
	52/53	27			D2
	53/54	27			D2

FERGUSON Graham

Club	Season				Div
Dunfermline A	58/59	6			D1
	59/60	2			D1
Cowdenbeath	60/61				D2
	61/62	10			D2

FERGUSON J

Club	Season				Div
Queen of the South	47/48	1			D1
	48/49				D1
	49/50	2			D1

FERGUSON J

Club	Season				Div
Queen's Park	56/57	2			D1
	57/58	3			D1

FERGUSON James
b. Renfrew

Club	Season				Div
Clydebank Jnrs					
Stirling A	53/54	25			D1
	54/55	5			D1
Cheltenham T					
Stirling A	55/56	1			D1
	56/57				D2
Dundee	56/57	5			D1

FERGUSON James

Club	Season				Div
Petershill					
St Johnstone	60/61	6			D1
	61/62	28			D1
	62/63	16			D2
Falkirk	63/64	4			D1

FERGUSON James Cameron Mars
b. Glasgow 20.2.1935

Club	Season				Div
Dundee	56/57	2			D1
	57/58	2			D1
Third Lanark	57/58	3			D1
Falkirk	58/59	1			D1
Oldham A	59/60	36			FL
Crewe Alex.	60/61	8			FL
	61/62	18			FL
Darlington	62/63	32			FL
Stenhousemuir	63/64	8			D2

FERGUSON John
b. Maybole 29.8.1939

Club	Season				Div
Morton					
Clyde	62/63	9		4	D1
Airdrieonians	63/64	27		4	D1
	64/65	32		4	D1
	65/66				D2
	66/67	28		5	D1
Southend U	67/68	13	1	2	FL
Ayr U	68/69				D2
	69/70	26	1	3	D1
	70/71	10	1	5	D1

FERGUSON Martin Murphy
b. Glasgow 21.12.1942

Club	Season				Div
Kirkintilloch Rob Roy					
Partick T	62/63	7		2	D1
	63/64	4			D1
	64/65	2			D1
Morton	64/65	3		1	D1
Barnsley	65/66	40		17	FL
Doncaster R	66/67	3			FL

FERGUSON Robert
b. Kilwinning 1.3.1945 Caps: S - 7

Club	Season				Div
Kilmarnock Amateurs					
Kilmarnock	64/65	8			D1
	65/66	34			D1
	66/67	31			D1
West Ham U	67/68	39			FL
	68/69	39			FL
	69/70	30			FL
	70/71	23			FL
	71/72	36			FL
	72/73	31			FL
	73/74	9			FL
Sheffield W	L 73/74	5			FL
Leicester C	L 73/74				FL
West Ham U	74/75				FL
	75/76	1			FL
	76/77				FL
	77/78	19			FL
	78/79	11			FL
	79/80	2			FL
	80/81				FL
Port Elizabeth					

√ FERNIE William
b. Kinglassie 22.11.1928 Caps: S - 12

Club	Season				Div
Leslie Hearts					
Aberdeen	T				
Raith R	T				
Celtic	48/49				D1
Kinglassie Colliery	L				
Celtic	49/50	4		1	D1
	50/51	7			D1
	51/52	6			D1
	52/53	24		7	D1
	53/54	26		10	D1
	54/55	23		12	D1
	55/56	32		6	D1
	56/57	32		6	D1
	57/58	27		2	D1
	58/59	13		4	D1
Middlesbrough	58/59	23		2	FL
	59/60	39		1	FL
	60/61	3			FL
Celtic	60/61	22		6	D1
	61/62	3		1	D1
St Mirren	61/62	20		3	D1
	62/63	2			D1
Alloa A	63/64				D2
Fraserburgh					

FERRIER John
b. Edinburgh 6.10.1927

Club	Season				Div
Brighton & HA	46/47	1		1	FL
Ashfield					
Clyde	53/54	7			D1
	54/55	3			D1
	55/56	2			D1
Exeter C	56/57	31			FL
Yeovil T	57/58				

FERRIS Robert

Club	Season				Div
Rutherglen Glencairn					
Clyde	73/74	14	1	3	D1
	74/75	17	14	5	D1
	75/76	1	9	1	D1
	76/77	34		4	D2
	77/78	7		1	D2
	78/79	7	7	1	D1
	79/80	5		1	D1

FERRY Patrick

Club	Season				Div
Morton	69/70	15		2	D1

FIDDES James
b. Grangemouth
Grangemouth R

Club	Season				Div
Rangers	34/35	3			D1
	35/36	17		6	D1
	36/37	4		1	D1
	37/38	14			D1
	38/39	19		6	D1
Falkirk	46/47	19		3	D1
	47/48	29		4	D1
	48/49	30		3	D1
	49/50	27		4	D1
	50/51	25		2	D1
Ross Co	51/52				
Stenhousemuir	51/52				D2
	52/53	28		3	D2

FILHO Jaoquin
b. Venezuela
Juventus (Brz)

Club	Season				Div
Dunfermline A	65/66	1			D1

FILIPPI Joseph
b. Irvine 3.11.1953
Prestwick Star

Club	Season				Div
Coventry C	69/70				FL
Ayr U	70/71	3			D1
	71/72	33		3	D1
	72/73	27			D1
	73/74	31	1	2	D1
	74/75	29	1	2	D1
	75/76	18	1		P
	76/77	34		3	P
	77/78	6	3		P
Celtic	77/78	11	1		P
	78/79	19	1		P
	79/80				P
Clyde	79/80				D1
	80/81	35	1		D2
Glenafton A					

FINDLAY William
b. Motherwell c1921 d. 6.1.2001
Dalzell Steelworks

Club	Season				Div
Albion R	46/47				D2
Rangers	47/48	7		6	D1
	48/49	12		4	D1
	49/50	20		8	D1
	50/51	16		10	D1
	51/52	14		9	D1
	52/53				D1
	53/54	1			D1
	54/55				D1
Albion R	54/55				D2

FINLAY Allan

Club	Season				Div
Third Lanark	64/65	3			D1

FINLAY Allan Jackson
b. Edinburgh 9.1.1939
Dunbar U

Club	Season				Div
Heart of Midlothian	60/61	9		1	D1
Barry T					
Newport Co	61/62	20		1	FL
Duns					

FINLAY William
b. Auchterderran
Bowhill R

Club	Season				Div
East Fife	46/47	21			D2
	47/48	29			D2
	48/49	30			D1
	49/50	26			D1
	50/51	29			D1
	51/52	27			D1
	52/53	30			D1
	53/54	28			D1
	54/55	30			D1
	55/56	31			D1
Clyde	57/58	32			D1
	58/59	31			D1
	59/60	25			D1
	60/61	33			D1
	61/62				D2
	62/63	9		2	D1
Raith R	63/64	12			D2

FINNIE Alexander
b. Aberdeen
Banks o'Dee

Club	Season				Div
Aberdeen	65/66	3			D1
Arbroath	66/67	30	1	3	D2
	67/68	7	2		D2
	68/69	16	3	1	D1
Inverness Caley					
Huntly					

FINNIGAN John
Clydebank Jnrs

Club	Season				Div
Clyde	62/63	8			D1

FINNIGAN William

Club	Season				Div
Hibernian	46/47	18		1	D1
	47/48	15			D1
	48/49	8			D1
Dunfermline A					

FITZSIMMONS John Thomas
b. Glasgow 3.3.1915
Dumfries St Josephs
St Rochs

Club	Season				Div
Celtic	34/35				
	35/36	2			D1
	36/37	2			D1
	37/38	1			D1
	38/39				D2
Alloa A					
Clyde					
Falkirk	46/47	15		6	D1
Hamilton A	46/47	11		3	D1
Clyde	47/48	21		7	D1
	48/49				D1

FITZSIMMONS Patrick

Club	Season				Div
Queen of the South	46/47	26		1	D1
	47/48	19		1	D1
	48/49	2			D1

FLAHERTY Brian
Glasgow Perthshire

Club	Season				Div
Morton	74/75	2	1		D1
	75/76		1		D1

FLANAGAN John
Glasgow Perthshire

Club	Season				Div
Albion R	61/62	12		4	D2
	62/63				D2
St Johnstone	63/64	23		7	D1
	64/65	16		5	D1
Partick T	65/66	9		3	D1
	66/67	26		10	D1
	67/68	34		4	D1
	68/69	30		7	D1
	69/70	31		10	D1
	70/71	3			D2
Clyde	70/71	20		6	D1
	71/72	24	2	7	D1

FLAVELL Robert
b. Annathill 1.9.1921 Caps: S - 2
Eastwood Heatherbell
Kirkintilloch Rob Roy

Club	Season				Div
Airdrieonians	37/38				D2
	38/39				D2
	46/47	26		37	D2
	47/48	13		7	D1
Heart of Midlothian	47/48	17		6	D1
	48/49	26		8	D1
	49/50	26		11	D1
Millionarios	50/51				
Dundee	51/52	21		14	D1
	52/53	27		14	D1
	53/54	12		2	D1
	54/55	8		2	D1
Kilmarnock	54/55	15		3	D1
	55/56	23		10	D1
St Mirren	56/57	21		5	D1
	57/58	1		1	D1

FLECK Neil

Club	Season				Div
Falkirk	47/48	20		3	D1
	48/49	3			D1
Alloa A	49/50	12		1	D2
Llanelly					
Dundee U	51/52	11		1	D2

FLECK Thomas

Club	Season				Div
Partick T	59/60	3			D1
Dumbarton					
Toronto C	63				
Montreal Cantani	63				
Montreal	64				

FLEMING Charles
b. Blairhall 12.7.1927
d. Edinburgh 14.8.1997 Caps: S - 1
Blairhall Colliery

Club	Season				Div
East Fife	47/48	1		2	D2
	48/49	21		13	D1
	49/50	21		11	D1
	50/51	30		12	D1
	51/52	29		15	D1
	52/53	30		30	D1
	53/54	26		25	D1
	54/55	15		9	D1
Sunderland	54/55	13		6	FL
	55/56	39		28	FL
	56/57	40		25	FL
	57/58	15		3	FL
Bath C	58/59				
	64/65				
Trowbridge T					

FLEMING Ian John Hosea
b. Maybole 15.1.1953
Craigmark Bruntonians

Club	Season				Div
Kilmarnock	70/71	1			D1
	71/72	4	1	1	D1
	72/73	12	1	1	D1
	73/74	32	1	33	D2
	74/75	27	2	11	D1
	75/76	9	4	5	D1
Aberdeen	75/76	11	1	2	P
	76/77	13	4	4	P
	77/78	20	5	5	P
Sheffield W	77/78				FL
	78/79	6		1	FL
	79/80	7			FL
Dundee	79/80	16		3	P
	80/81	7	1	1	D1
	81/82	13	3	1	P
	82/83	8			P
Brechin C	82/83	24		4	D2
	83/84	33	5	10	D1
	84/85	15	4		D1
	85/86	35		1	D1
	86/87	15	1		D1

FLEMING James

Kirkintilloch Rob Roy

Club	Season				Div
Stirling A	63/64				D2
	64/65				D2
	65/66	29		8	D1
	66/67	5			D1
Clydebank	67/68				D2

FLEMING James Freeburn
b. Glasgow 7.1.1929
Tollcross

Club	Season				Div
Stirling A	52/53	15			D2
	53/54	4			D1
Workington	54/55	37		1	FL
	55/56	27			FL
	56/57	23			FL
	57/58	1			FL

FLEMING James Paterson
b. Alloa 7.1.1942
Sauchie

Club	Season				Div
Partick T	58/59	8		2	D1
	59/60	33		11	D1
	60/61	7			D1
Luton T	60/61	18		4	FL
	61/62	33		3	FL
	62/63	15		2	FL
Partick T	62/63	14		3	D1
	63/64	18		3	D1
	64/65	12		3	D1
Dunfermline A	64/65	3		2	D1
	65/66	22		11	D1
	66/67	15	2	4	D1
Heart of Midlothian	66/67	9			D1
	67/68	20	2	5	D1
	68/69	13	1	4	D1
Wigan A	69/70	37	1	7	NL
	70/71	30	1	16	NL
	71/72	36	2	11	NL

FLEMING James Shankland
b. Irvine 8.4.1949
Maybole Jnrs

Club	Season				Div
Kilmarnock	71/72	1			D1

Maybole Jnrs
Girvan Amateurs

FLEMING Richard
b. Paisley 29.12.1946
Rangers
Kilwinning R

Club	Season				Div
Ayr U	68/69				D2
	69/70	34			D1
	70/71	34			D1
	71/72	12			D1
	72/73	33		7	D1
	73/74	34		1	D1
	74/75	34		2	D1
	75/76	31		1	P
	76/77	32			P
	77/78	34	1		P
Hibernian	78/79	11	1		P
Berwick R	79/80	12			D1

FLEMING T George
b. Edinburgh 22.9.1948
Salvesen BC

Club	Season				Div
Heart of Midlothian	66/67	16		1	D1
	67/68	19	9	5	D1
	68/69	30	1	5	D1
	69/70	19	5	3	D1
	70/71	26	4	7	D1
	71/72	2	1		D1
Dundee U	71/72	12		1	D1
	72/73	31		3	D1
	73/74	31	1	4	D1
	74/75	25		5	D1
	75/76	30	2	3	P
	76/77	28	3	1	P
	77/78	36		9	P
	78/79	33		3	P
	79/80	23	2	2	P
St Johnstone	80/81	39		1	D1
	81/82	36	1		D1
	82/83	15	4		D1

FLETCHER Christopher Columba
b. Buncrana 14.6.1933
Southend U

Club	Season				Div
Kilmarnock	55/56	15		2	D1
	56/57	4		1	D1
Cheltenham T	57/58				
Brentford	57/58	3			FL
	58/59				FL
Peterborough U	59/60	4		3	ML
Morton	60/61				D2
East Fife	60/61	1			D2

FLETCHER Gavin
b. Bellshill 30.10.1941
Queen's Park

Club	Season				Div
Partick T	60/61	2			D1
Third Lanark	61/62	18		2	D1
	62/63	4			D1
Bradford C	63/64	8		1	FL

FLETCHER John Ernest
b. Royston 11.4.1953

Club	Season				Div
Arbroath	71/72	19		9	D2
	72/73	3		8	D1
	73/74	32		8	D1
	74/75	32	2	4	D1
	75/76	17	2	4	D1
	76/77	33	1	9	D1
	77/78	36		9	D1
	78/79	30	2	5	D1
Dundee	79/80	12	4	1	P
	80/81	6	1	1	D1
Montrose	81/82	15	3	4	D2
	82/83	22	4	4	D2

FLETCHER Leonard Gerald George
b. Hammersmith 28.4.1929
RAF Didcot

Club	Season				Div
Ipswich T	49/50	5			FL
	50/51				FL
	51/52	3			FL
	52/53				FL
	53/54	7			FL
	54/55	5			FL
Falkirk	55/56	12			D1

FLYNN

Club	Season				Div
St Mirren	58/59	11		1	D1

FLYNN James
Hurlford U

Club	Season				Div
Ayr U	70/71	1	1	1	D1
	71/72	2			D1
	72/73	4			D1
Stranraer	73/74	9	6	5	D2

FOLEY Patrick

Club	Season				Div
Alloa A	61/62	33		10	D2
	62/63				D2
	63/64	17		6	D2
Falkirk	63/64	8		2	D1
Dumbarton	64/65	1			D2

FOLLON Gerald
b. ?.3.1919 d. 9.3.1993
Lochee Harp

Club	Season				Div
Dundee	46/47	23			D2
	47/48	28			D1
	48/49	28		1	D1
	49/50	27			D1
	50/51	27			D1
	51/52	24			D1
	52/53	22			D1
	53/54	10			D1
	54/55	17			D1
St Johnstone	55/56	10			D2
	56/57	7			D2

Forfar A
Keith

FORD Donald
b. Linlithgow 25.10.1944 Caps: S - 3
Vale of Avon
Bo'ness U

Club	Season				Div
Heart of Midlothian	64/65	7		2	D1
	65/66	9			D1
	66/67	5			D1
	67/68	29		11	D1
	68/69	23	4	6	D1
	69/70	24	5	8	D1
	70/71	32		11	D1
	71/72	30		15	D1
	72/73	32		9	D1
	73/74	29		18	D1
	74/75	21	1	13	D1
	75/76	2			P
Falkirk	76/77	19	2	5	D1

FORD John
Loanhead Mayflower

Club	Season				Div
East Fife	56/57				D1
	57/58	9			D1
	58/59				D2

FORD Robert Alan Cameron
b. Edinburgh 14.12.1949
Melbourne Thistle

Club	Season				Div
Falkirk	68/69	2			D1
	69/70	19		1	D2
	70/71	6	5	1	D1
	71/72	3			D1
Dundee	71/72	19	1		D1
	72/73	19	4	2	D1
	73/74	31		1	D1
	74/75	28		1	D1
	75/76	29	1	2	P
	76/77	34	3	3	D1
	77/78	13	5		D1
Montrose	78/79	25		1	D1
Raith R	78/79	12		1	D1
	79/80	37		7	D1
	80/81	36	1	1	D1
	81/82	25	8	3	D1
Dunfermline A	82/83	8	2		D1
Meadowbank T	82/83	10	3		D2

Postal U

FORDYCE J

Club	Season				Div
Queen's Park	57/58	1			D1
	58/59	8			D2

FORREST Angus
b. Whitburn
Broxburn A

Club	Season				Div
Falkirk	54/55	4			D1
	55/56	2			D1
Dunfermline A	55/56	8			D1

FORREST R Gordon
b. Edinburgh 3.9.1952
Livingston U

Club	Season	Apps	Sub	Gls	Div
Dunfermline A	73/74	4	2	1	D1
	74/75	12	2	4	D1
Alloa A	75/76	13	9	1	D2
	76/77	34	5	19	D2
	77/78	15	3	2	D1
Raith R	77/78	6	7	5	D2
	78/79	11	16	6	D1
	79/80	1	8		D1
Cowdenbeath	79/80	10	2	3	D2
	80/81	27	6	10	D2
	81/82	30		16	D2
	82/83	14	3	4	D2
East Fife	83/84	3		2	D2
East Stirlingshire	83/84	1			D2
Stenhousemuir	83/84	25		14	D2
	84/85	7	1	2	D2

FORREST James
b. Bothwell 31.3.1927 Caps: S - 1
Newarthill Hearts

Club	Season	Apps	Gls	Div
Motherwell	49/50	3	2	D1
	50/51	29	14	D1
	51/52	17	1	D1
	52/53	29	6	D1
	53/54	30	24	D2
	54/55	6	1	D1
	55/56	21	2	D1
	56/57	30	1	D1
	57/58	24	3	D1
	58/59	10	2	D1
	59/60	15		D1
Stenhousemuir	60/61			D2
	61/62	16	4	D2

FORREST James
b. Glasgow 22.9.1944 Caps: S - 5
Rangers
Drumchapel Amateurs

Club	Season	Apps	Sub	Gls	Div
Rangers	62/63	4			D1
	63/64	24		21	D1
	64/65	30		30	D1
	65/66	30		24	D1
	66/67	17		8	D1
Preston NE	66/67	8		3	FL
	67/68	16		2	FL
Aberdeen	68/69	31		16	D1
	69/70	31	1	15	D1
	70/71	31	1	8	D1
	71/72	21	1	4	D1
	72/73	11		1	D1
Hong Kong R					
San Antonio Thunder	75	4			NA

FORREST Samuel
Baillieston Jnrs

Club	Season	Apps	Gls	Div
Hamilton A	63/64	23		D2
	64/65	24		D2
	65/66	24		D1
	66/67	33	1	D2
	67/68	22	1	D2

FORSYTH Adam
b. Killearnan
Ross Co

Club	Season	Apps	Div
Partick T	46/47	1	D1
	47/48	24	D1
	48/49	27	D1
	49/50	6	D1
	50/51	21	D1
	51/52	3	D1
Third Lanark	51/52	10	D1
	52/53	22	D1

FORSYTH Alexander
b. Swinton 5.2.1952 Caps: S - 10
Possil YMCA

Club	Season	Apps	Sub	Gls	Div
Partick T	68/69	1			D1
	69/70				D1
	70/71	2		4	D2
	71/72	33		4	D1
	72/73	17		1	D1
Manchester U	72/73	8			FL
	73/74	18	1	1	FL
	74/75	39		1	FL
	75/76	28		2	FL
	76/77	3			FL
	77/78	3			FL
Rangers	78/79	16		4	P
	79/80	8	1		P
	80/81	1			P
	81/82				
Motherwell	82/83	18	1		P
Hamilton A	83/84	34		3	D1
	84/85	28	1	6	D1
Queen of the South	85/86	1	1		D2
Blantyre Victoria					

FORSYTH Allan
b. Glasgow 23.04.1955
Larkhall Thistle

Club	Season	Apps	Sub	Gls	Div
Dundee U	74/75	5	1	2	D1
	75/76	14			P
	76/77	5	1		P
	77/78	1			P
Raith R	78/79	31			D1
	79/80	34		3	D1
	80/81	33		5	D1
	81/82	31			D1
	82/83	17			D1
	83/84	9		1	D1
Dunfermline A	83/84	20		1	D2
	84/85	17	1		D2
Leven Jnrs					

FORSYTH John
Newburgh

Club	Season	Apps	Div
Raith R	61/62	33	D1
	62/63	15	D1

FORSYTH Robert Campbell
b. Plean 5.5.1934 Caps: S - 4
Shettleston

Club	Season	Apps	Div
St Mirren	55/56	9	D1
	56/57	33	D1
	57/58	25	D1
	58/59	21	D1
	59/60	24	D1
	60/61	1	D1
Kilmarnock	61/62	4	D1
	62/63	11	D1
	63/64	34	D1
	64/65	26	D1
Southampton	65/66	22	FL
	66/67	8	FL
	67/68	18	FL

FORSYTH Samuel
b. Denny

Club	Season	Apps	Gls	Div
St Johnstone	46/47	15	1	D2
	47/48	2	1	D2
	48/49	28		D2
	49/50	12		D2
Stirling A	50/51			D2
	51/52	2		D1
	52/53	29		D2
	53/54	6		D1
Dunfermline A	53/54	19		D2

FORSYTH Thomas
b. Glasgow 23.1.1949 Caps: S - 22
Stonehouse Thistle

Club	Season	Apps	Sub	Gls	Div
Motherwell	67/68	12		2	D1
	68/69	33		13	D2
	69/70	34			D1
	70/71	33		3	D1
	71/72	32			D1
	72/73	5		1	D1
Rangers	72/73	21			D1
	73/74	18			D1
	74/75	30		1	D1
	75/76	28		1	P
	76/77	25			P
	77/78	31			P
	78/79	17			P
	79/80	16			P
	80/81	15	7		P
	81/82	12			P

FORSYTH William
Kilbirnie Laneside

Club	Season	Apps	Gls	Div
Hamilton A	T 58/59	1		D2
Saltcoats V				
Hamilton A	61/62	10	2	D2
	62/63	31	21	D2
	63/64	27	14	D2
	64/65	36	33	D2
	65/66	7	3	D1
Berwick R	65/66	17	13	D2
	66/67	7	2	D2

FOWLER James
West Bromwich A

Club	Season	Apps	Sub	Gls	Div
Falkirk	73/74	29	1	6	D1
	74/75	32	2	2	D2
	75/76	13	3		D1

FOWLER Leslie

Club	Season	Apps	Div
Airdrieonians	66/67	1	D1

FOX Desmond

Club	Season	Apps	Gls	Div
Hibernian	55/56	1		D1
	56/57			D1
	57/58			D1
	58/59	24	8	D1
	59/60	5		D1
	60/61			D1
Raith R	60/61	10	5	D1
	61/62	15	6	D1

FOX George
Lochore Welfare

Club	Season	Apps	Div
East Fife	55/56	1	D1
	56/57	11	D1

FRAME Harry
Bayview YC

Club	Season	Apps	Div
East Fife	49/50		D1
	50/51		D1
	51/52	1	D1
	52/53		D1
	53/54		D1
	54/55	1	D1
	55/56		D1
	56/57	1	D1
Brechin C			

FRAME James

Club	Season	Apps	Div
Rangers	48/49	1	D1

FRANCHETTI Ray
b. 11.4.1952
Baillieston
Celtic

Club	Season				Div
Airdrieonians	74/75	10	6	1	D1
Albion R	75/76	15	3		D2
	76/77	29		9	D2
	77/78	28	9	20	D2
	78/79	30	5	4	D2
	79/80	24	8	10	D2
	80/81	13	8	6	D2

FRANCHETTI Virgil

Club	Season			Div
Queen's Park	72/73	19	5	D2
Clyde	73/74	1		D1
	74/75	2	1	D1

FRANKS Albert John
b. Boldon 13.4.1936
Boldon Colliery

Club	Season			Div
Newcastle U	53/54			FL
	54/55			FL
	55/56			FL
	56/57	7		FL
	57/58	33	2	FL
	58/59	29	2	FL
	59/60	3		FL
Rangers	59/60	3		D1
	60/61			D1
	61/62			D1
Morton	L 61/62	13	2	D2
Lincoln C	61/62	24		FL
	62/63	34	5	FL
Queen of the South	63/64	10	2	D1
Scarborough	64/65			
	65/66			

FRASER Andrew McKnight
b. Newtongrange 29.8.1940
Craiglee Thistle
Newtongrange Star

Club	Season			Div
Heart of Midlothian	60/61	1		D1
Toronto C	61			
Hartlepools U	61/62	12		FL
	62/63	26		FL
	63/64	44	2	FL

FRASER Anthony R
b. Aberdeen
Banks o'Dee

Club	Season			Div
Aberdeen	64/65	9	4	D1
	65/66	1		D1
Elgin C				
Inverness Thistle				

FRASER Campbell Grant
b. Dundee 22.7.1957
Invergowrie BC

Club	Season				Div
Heart of Midlothian	74/75	3			D1
	75/76	5	10		P
	76/77	20	2		P
	77/78	39		2	D1
	78/79	36		3	P
	79/80	36		12	D1
	80/81		1	1	P
Dundee	80/81	30		5	D1
	81/82	31		6	P
	82/83	34		5	P
	83/84	29		3	P
Rangers	84/85	27	1	3	P
	85/86	7	1	2	P
	86/87	16		1	P
Raith R	87/88	24		1	D1
	88/89	23		3	D1
	89/90	23		2	D1
	90/91	13			D1
Dundee	90/91	7			D1
	91/92	12			D1
Montrose	91/92	8			D1
	92/93	18		5	D2
Lochore Welfare					

FRASER David McLean
b. Newtongrange 6.6.1937

Club	Season			Div
Hull C	55/56	6	6	FL
	56/57	2		FL
	57/58	3	1	FL
Mansfield T	58/59	6	1	FL
Third Lanark	59/60	7	1	D1
Cowdenbeath	60/61			
	61/62	20	17	D2

FRASER Douglas Michael
b. Busby 8.12.1941 Caps: S - 2
Rolls Royce Works
Eaglesham Amateurs
Blantyre Celtic

Club	Season				Div
Aberdeen	59/60	1			D1
	60/61	24			D1
	61/62	28			D1
	62/63	9			D1
	63/64	3		1	D1
West Bromwich A	63/64	33		1	FL
	64/65	33			FL
	65/66	42		1	FL
	66/67	34	1	4	FL
	67/68	40		1	FL
	68/69	34		1	FL
	69/70	33	1		FL
	70/71	6			FL
Nottingham F	70/71	19			FL
	71/72	36			FL
	72/73	30		3	FL
Walsall	73/74	26	1		FL

FRASER James

Club	Season			Div
Dundee	49/50	21	10	D1
	50/51			D1
	51/52	1		D1
Ayr U	52/53	22	13	D2
	53/54	17	11	D2

FRASER James

Club	Season			Div
Arbroath	59/60	33		D1
	60/61			D2
	61/62	35		D2
Clyde	62/63	8		D1
	63/64			D2
	64/65	32		D1
	65/66	32		D1
	66/67	17		D1
	67/68	32		D1
	68/69	25		D1
Dundee	69/70	2		D1
	70/71	2		D1

͑ FRASER James
b. c1946 d. Kirkcaldy 20.3.2002
St Andrews U

Club	Season			Div
Dunfermline A	63/64	2		D1
	64/65	1		D1
	65/66	1		D1
	66/67	19		D1
	67/68	20	5	D1
	68/69	30	4	D1
	69/70	10		D1
	70/71	33	1	D1
	71/72	32	1	D1
Airdrieonians	72/73	23	1	D1

FRASER John

Edinburgh Thistle

Club	Season			Div
Hibernian	54/55	4	3	D1
	55/56	6	1	D1
	56/57	20	9	D1
	57/58	9		D1
	58/59	5	1	D1
	59/60	7	1	D1
	60/61	33		D1
	61/62	29	6	D1
	62/63	26	4	D1
	63/64	25		D1
	64/65	31		D1
	65/66	2		D1

FRASER John

Largs Thistle

Club	Season		Div
St Johnstone	70/71		D1
	71/72	3	D1

FRASER John Cameron
b. Blackford 24.5.1941
Gairdoch

Club	Season			Div
Dunfermline A	59/60	19		D1
	60/61	22		D1
	61/62	33		D1
	62/63	6		D1
Aston Villa	62/63	22	1	FL
	63/64	11		FL
Birmingham C	64/65	5		FL
	65/66	33	1	FL
Falkirk				

FRASER Robert
b. Glasgow 23.1.1917
Dunoon A
Ashfield

Club	Season		Div
Hibernian	37/38		D1
	38/39	34	D1
	46/47	5	D1
Newcastle U	46/47	3	FL
	47/48	20	FL
	48/49	3	FL

FRASER Robert
b. Dundee 21.12.1925
Dundee Anchorage
Lochee Harp

Club	Season			Div
Celtic	47/48	1		D1
	48/49			D1
Heart of Midlothian	49/50			D1
	50/51			D1
Northwich V	51/52			
	52/53			
St Johnstone	53/54	3	1	D2
Montrose				

FRASER Stewart

Banks o'Dee

Club	Season				Div
Dundee U	57/58	26		2	D2
	58/59	4			D2
	59/60	10			D2
	60/61	30		1	D1
	61/62	33		1	D1
	62/63	32		3	D1
	63/64	30		1	D1
	64/65	15		3	D1
	65/66	8			D1
	66/67	1	4		D1
Brora R					

FRASER William A

Club	Season			Div
Morton	46/47	2		D1
Third Lanark				
Arbroath	49/50	19		D2
Ayr U	50/51			D2
	51/52			D2
	52/53	26	2	D2
	53/54	22		D2

FRASER William Alexander
b. Brighton, Australia 24.2.1929
d. Kirkcaldy 7.3.1996 Caps: S - 2
Cowie
Stirling Jnrs

Club	Season	Apps	Sub	Gls	Div
Third Lanark	46/47	19			D1
	47/48	16			D1
	48/49	23			D1
	49/50	5			D1
Airdrieonians	50/51	28			D1
	51/52	30			D1
	52/53	22			D1
	53/54	23			D1
Sunderland	53/54	7			FL
	54/55	38			FL
	55/56	38			FL
	56/57	3			FL
	57/58	33			FL
	58/59	8			FL
Nottingham F	58/59	2			FL

FRASER William Thomas
b. Edinburgh 12.8.1945
Dunfermline A

Club	Season	Apps	Sub	Gls	Div
Huddersfield T	63/64	4		1	FL
	64/65	4		1	FL
Heart of Midlothian	65/66	1		1	D1
Washington Diplomat	66				
	67				
Boston Beacons	68	32		5	NA
	69				
Washington Darts	70	23		2	NA
	71	23		3	NA
Miami Gatos	72	14		1	NA

FRATE F

Club	Season	Apps	Sub	Gls	Div
Queen's Park	46/47	1			D1

FREEBAIRN John
Glasgow University

Club	Season	Apps	Sub	Gls	Div
Partick T	58/59	21			D1
	59/60	26			D1
	60/61	31			D1
	61/62	3			D1
Albion R	62/63				D2
	63/64				D2
	64/65				D2
	65/66				D2
	66/67				D2
Hamilton A	T 67/68	2			D2

FRENCH John

Club	Season	Apps	Sub	Gls	Div
Raith R	59/60	10		2	D1
	60/61	10		1	D1

FREW Gordon
b. South Africa Caps: SAf - 4

Club	Season	Apps	Sub	Gls	Div
Dundee	50/51	2			D1
	51/52	9			D1
	52/53	10			D1
	53/54	23			D1

FRICKLETON James
Linlithgow Rose

Club	Season	Apps	Sub	Gls	Div
Falkirk	68/69	5			D1

FRICKLETON Joseph

Club	Season	Apps	Sub	Gls	Div
East Stirlingshire	63/64	15			D1

FRIEL John Patrick
b. Glasgow 1.9.1923

Club	Season	Apps	Sub	Gls	Div
Third Lanark	49/50	7		2	D1
New Brighton	50/51	3			FL
Queen of the South	51/52				D1
	52/53				D1
Torquay U	53/54				FL

FRYE John Marr
b. Ardrossan 27.7.1933
Largs R
Ardrossan Winton R

Club	Season	Apps	Sub	Gls	Div
Hibernian	55/56	2		1	D1
	56/57				D1
	57/58	6		1	D1
	58/59	6			D1
	59/60	6			D1
St Mirren	59/60	5		1	D1
	60/61	10		5	D1
Sheffield W	60/61				FL
Tranmere R	61/62	21		6	FL
Queen of the South	62/63	26		4	D1
Hamilton A	63/64	34		3	D2
	64/65	30		4	D2
	65/66	19		1	D1
Stranraer	66/67	17	2	4	D2

FULTON J

Club	Season	Apps	Sub	Gls	Div
Queen of the South	46/47	5			D1
	47/48	5			D1

FULTON W

Club	Season	Apps	Sub	Gls	Div
Hibernian	64/65	1			D1

FULTON William
Ayr Albion
Irvine V

Club	Season	Apps	Sub	Gls	Div
Ayr U	57/58				D2
	58/59				D2
	59/60	27		7	D1
	60/61	31		13	D1
	61/62	31		11	D2
Falkirk	62/63	26		3	D1
	63/64	34		5	D1
	64/65	25		3	D1
	65/66	27		6	D1
	66/67	15	2		D1
St Mirren	67/68	34			D2
	68/69	34			D1
	69/70	18	2		D1
	70/71	32			D1
	71/72	12	1		D2

FURY John
Mount Ellen U

Club	Season	Apps	Sub	Gls	Div
Airdrieonians	71/72	4		2	D1
	72/73	7		2	D1

FYFE Andrew

Club	Season	Apps	Sub	Gls	Div
Morton	46/47	28		3	D1
	47/48	14			D1
	48/49	5			D1

FYFE George
b. Glasgow

Club	Season	Apps	Sub	Gls	Div
Third Lanark	64/65	8		1	D1
	65/66	30		18	D2
	66/67	12		9	D2
Airdrieonians	66/67	16		7	D1
	67/68	16		1	D1
	68/69	24		6	D1

FYFE Graham
b. Motherwell 18.8.1951
Ashfield

Club	Season	Apps	Sub	Gls	Div
Rangers	69/70	4			D1
	70/71	11	3	3	D1
	71/72	9	5	6	D1
	72/73	3	3	2	D1
	73/74	7	6	7	D1
	74/75	6	4	4	D1
	75/76	1	2		P
Hibernian	76/77	9	1	1	P
Dumbarton	77/78	28		4	D1
	78/79	25	6	7	D1
Phoenix Inferno					

FYFE Ian
b. Airdrie 11.7.1945
Kilsyth R

Club	Season	Apps	Sub	Gls	Div
Stirling A	63/64	5			D2
	64/65	10		1	D2
	65/66	8		3	D1
Airdrieonians	66/67	2			D1

GABRIEL James
b. Dundee 16.10.1940 Caps: S - 2
Lawside Academy
Tynecastle BC
Dundee NE

Club	Season	Apps	Sub	Gls	Div
Dundee	58/59	34			D1
	59/60	21			D1
Everton	59/60	8			FL
	60/61	40		1	FL
	61/62	42		6	FL
	62/63	40		5	FL
	63/64	33		5	FL
	64/65	37		4	FL
	65/66	24		6	FL
	66/67	31	1	6	FL
Southampton	67/68	40		4	FL
	68/69	38		4	FL
	69/70	39		5	FL
	70/71	37		7	FL
	71/72	36	1	5	FL
Bournemouth	72/73	42		4	FL
	73/74	11			FL
Swindon T	L 73/74	6			FL
Brentford	73/74	9	1		FL
Seattle Sounders	74	19		4	NA
	75	20		2	NA

GALBRAITH Walter McMurray
b. Glasgow 26.5.1918 d. Glasgow ?.11.1995
Strathclyde
Clyde
Queen's Park

Club	Season	Apps	Sub	Gls	Div
Clyde	46/47	27			D1
	47/48	5			D1
New Brighton	48/49	28			FL
	49/50	41			FL
	50/51	40		1	FL
Grimsby T	51/52	40			FL
	52/53	37			FL
Accrington S	53/54	21			FL

GALLACHER Gerard Majella
b. Glasgow 13.04.1953
Campsie Black Watch

Club	Season	Apps	Sub	Gls	Div
East Fife	71/72	1			D1
East Stirlingshire	72/73	12			D2
Stranraer	73/74	36			D2
	74/75				D2
	75/76	1			D2
	76/77				D2
Albion R	77/78	24			D2

GALLACHER G Thomas
b. Renfrew 13.7.1922 d. Dundee 24.11.2001

Club	Season	Apps	Sub	Gls	Div
Queen's Park	46/47	5			D1
Dundee	47/48	19			D1
	48/49	29			D1
	49/50	16			D1
	50/51	13			D1
	51/52	22			D1
	52/53	24		1	D1
	53/54	22		1	D1
	54/55	27			D1
	55/56	18		3	D1

GALLACHER James
b. Armadale

Club	Season	Apps	Sub	Gls	Div
Falkirk	46/47	7			D1
	47/48	9			D1
	48/49	1			D1
	49/50	20			D1
	50/51	27			D1
	51/52	29			D2
	52/53	27			D1
	53/54	17		1	D1
Clyde	54/55	24			D1
	55/56	27		1	D1

GALLACHER John
b. 7.5.1924
Armadale Thistle

Club	Season				Div
Celtic	46/47				D1
	47/48	3			D1
	48/49	19		13	D1
	49/50	1		1	D1
Dunfermline A	L 49/50	7		3	D2
Falkirk	L 50/51	11		2	D1
Carlisle U	T				
Kettering T					

GALLACHER John

Cowlairs Loco
Lesmahagow Jnrs

Club	Season				Div
Hamilton A	52/53				D2
	53/54	2			D1
Kilsyth R					
Dumbarton					

GALLACHER John
b. Falkirk 12.12.1951

Club	Season				Div
Queen's Park	69/70	7			D2
	70/71				D2
Heart of Midlothian	71/72	3			D1
	72/73	5			D1
	73/74	5			D1
	74/75	4			D1
	75/76	14			P
	76/77	35		4	P
	77/78	7			D1
Dumbarton	78/79	39			D1
	79/80	38			D1
	80/81	23			D1
	81/82	31			D1

GALLACHER Michael
b. Arranmore d. USA 3.1.1984 Caps: Ei - 1
Alloa A

Club	Season				Div
Hibernian	48/49	4			D1
	49/50	1			D1
	50/51	4			D1
	51/52	19			D1
	52/53	9			D1
	53/54	12			D1
Ayr U	54/55				D2
	55/56				D2
	56/57	12			D1
Weymouth					

GALLACHER Stuart

Renfrew Jnrs

Club	Season				Div
Airdrieonians	72/73	3	2		D1
	73/74				D2
	74/75	2			D1
	75/76	2			D1
East Stirlingshire	76/77	13			D2

GALLACHER William

Blantyre Victoria

Club	Season				Div
Motherwell	61/62				D1
	62/63				D1
	63/64	1			D1
	64/65	3		2	D1

GALLAGHER Brian

Drumchapel Amateurs

Club	Season				Div
Partick T	64/65	2		1	D1
	65/66	16		3	D1
	66/67	9	2	3	D1
	67/68	8	1	2	D1
Morton	69/70	12		1	D1
Dumbarton	70/71			6	D2
	71/72	10	1	2	D2

GALLAGHER Charles
b. Gorbals 3.11.1940 Caps: Ei - 2
Kilmarnock Amateurs
Yoker A

Club	Season				Div
Celtic	59/60	4			D1
	60/61	15		3	D1
	61/62	1			D1
	62/63	17		3	D1
	63/64	10		2	D1
	64/65	16		3	D1
	65/66	19		4	D1
	66/67	11		2	D1
	67/68	13			D1
	68/69				D1
	69/70				D1
Dumbarton	70/71			9	D2
	71/72	30	1	19	D2
	72/73	6		1	D1

GALLAGHER Hugh

Dumbarton

Club	Season				Div
Clyde	60/61	5		2	D1
Queen of the South	60/61				D2

GALLAGHER John

Benburb

Club	Season				Div
Ayr U	60/61	18			D1
	61/62	10			D2
	62/63				D2
	63/64	25			D2

GALLAGHER William Patrick
b. Renfrew 29.6.1919 d. 16.10.1982
Renfrew Beechwood
St Anthonys

Club	Season				Div
Celtic	38/39				
	46/47	14			D1
	47/48	11			D1
	48/49	4			D1
Falkirk	49/50	4			D1
Ayr U	50/51				D2
	51/52				D2
St Johnstone	52/53				D2
Inverness Thistle					

GALLETLY Peter

Brandon Swift
Clydebank Jnrs

Club	Season				Div
Clyde	46/47	25		8	D1
	47/48	23		8	D1
	48/49	24		6	D1
	49/50	26		3	D1
	50/51	4			D1
	51/52				D2
	52/53	8		3	D1
	53/54	2			D1
Morton	54/55				D2
	55/56				D2

GALLOWAY Robert

Club	Season				Div
Clyde	50/51	5			D1
Third Lanark	51/52	4			D1

GARDINER C

Club	Season				Div
St Mirren	48/49	3			D1
	49/50	4			D1

GARDINER J

Club	Season				Div
Falkirk	48/49	2			D1

GARDINER James Ian
b. Balbeggie 18.9.1928 Caps: S - 1
Balbeggie Amateurs

Club	Season				Div
East Fife	48/49				D1
	49/50	7		2	D1
	50/51	17		9	D1
	51/52	29		19	D1
	52/53	30		20	D1
	53/54	29		8	D1
	54/55	20		7	D1
	55/56	5		1	D1
Motherwell	55/56	30		9	D1
	56/57	33		18	D1
	57/58	27		19	D1
	58/59	5		2	D1
Raith R	58/59	7			D1
East Fife	59/60	28		1	D2
St Johnstone	59/60	5		1	D2
	60/61	23		7	D1
	61/62	13		3	D1
Montrose	61/62				D2
	62/63				D2

GARDINER T

Club	Season				Div
St Mirren	64/65	2			D1

GARDINER William Silcock
b. Larbert 15.8.1929
Bo'ness U

Club	Season				Div
Rangers	51/52	4			D1
	52/53	2		2	D1
	53/54	8		5	D1
	54/55	11		9	D1
Leicester C	55/56	33		34	FL
	56/57	13		4	FL
	57/58	23		10	FL
Reading	58/59	7		2	FL
	59/60	1			FL
Sudbury T					

GARDNER Patrick
b. Dunfermline ?.?.1943
Belshill

Club	Season				Div
Queen of the South	62/63	1			D1
	63/64	19		2	D1
Raith R	64/65	33		8	D2
	65/66	36		6	D2
	66/67	37		29	D2
Dunfermline A	67/68	32		11	D1
	68/69	30		12	D1
	69/70	29	2	7	D1
	70/71	33		8	D1
	71/72	12	2	3	D1
Dundee U	71/72	11			D1
	72/73	33		13	D1
	73/74	21	3	4	D1
	74/75	7		1	D1
Motherwell	74/75	17	1	1	D1
	75/76	12	4	4	P
Arbroath	76/77	32	5	2	D1

GARDNER Robert
b. East Wemyss 8.2.1945
Blairgowrie Jnrs

Club	Season				Div
Stirling A	63/64	5		1	D2
	64/65	15			D2
	65/66	12		2	D1

GARLAND Kenneth
b. Cupar 19.3.1948
Strathmiglo U
Cupar TM
Newburgh Jnrs

Club	Season				Div
Heart of Midlothian	67/68	14			D1
	68/69	3			D1
	69/70	5			D1
	70/71	2			D1
	71/72	14			D1
	72/73	23			D1
	73/74	20			D1
	74/75	7			D1

GARRETT Archibald Campbell E
b. Lesmahagow 17.6.1919 d. Bristol 10.4.1994
Burnbank A
Lesmahagow Jnrs

Club	Season	Apps	Sub	Goals	Div
Preston NE	37/38	2		2	FL
Heart of Midlothian	38/39	18		17	D1
	46/47	4		3	D1
Northampton T	46/47	35		26	FL
	47/48	16		9	FL
Birmingham C	47/48	8		1	FL
	48/49	10		4	FL
Northampton T	48/49	21		8	FL
	49/50	11		7	FL
	50/51	11		1	FL
Wisbech T					
Holbeach U					

GARRETT James Edward
b. Dumfries 15.3.1939
Glenafton

Club	Season	Apps	Sub	Goals	Div
Queen of the South	58/59	19		5	D1
	59/60				D2
	60/61				D2
	61/62				D2
	62/63	10		1	D1
Carlisle U	63/64	1			FL

GARTH James Russell
b. Glasgow 1.5.1922 d. ?.?.1968

Club	Season	Apps	Sub	Goals	Div
Morton	46/47	7		8	D1
Preston NE	46/47	21		8	FL
	47/48	2			FL
Clyde	47/48	9		2	D1
	48/49	23		5	D1
Raith R	49/50	10		2	D1
Morton	50/51	8			D1
	51/52	17		3	D1
Inverness Caley					

GAUGHAN Robert
Shotts
Scunthorpe U

Club	Season	Apps	Sub	Goals	Div
Hamilton A	65/66	18			D1
	66/67	35			D2
	67/68	33			D2
	68/69	33			D2
	69/70	19	1		D2
Larkhall Thistle					

GAULD James
b. Aberdeen 9.5.1929
Aberdeen
Elgin C
Waterford

Club	Season	Apps	Sub	Goals	Div
Charlton A	55/56	34		17	FL
	56/57	13		4	FL
Everton	56/57	23		7	FL
	57/58				FL
Plymouth A	57/58	19		4	FL
	58/59	45		21	FL
Swindon T	59/60	40		14	FL
St Johnstone	60/61	4			D1
Mansfield T	60/61	4		3	FL

GEBBIE Robert Brown Robertson
b. Cambuslang 18.11.1934
Blantyre Victoria

Club	Season	Apps	Sub	Goals	Div
Queen of the South	58/59	25			D1
	59/60				D2
Bradford PA	60/61	34			FL
	61/62	40			FL
	62/63	28			FL
	63/64	10			FL

GEDDES Andrew
b. Craigmark 6.9.1922 d. 12.2.1958
Connelpark R

Club	Season	Apps	Sub	Goals	Div
Kilmarnock	46/47	3			D1
	47/48				D2
St Cuthberts W	48/49				
Bradford C	49/50	22		2	FL
	50/51	8		2	FL
Mansfield T	51/52	11		2	FL
Halifax T	52/53	26		2	FL
	53/54	16		1	FL
	54/55	8		1	FL

GEDDES James George
b. Burntisland 25.5.1942
Kilwinning R

Club	Season	Apps	Sub	Goals	Div
Third Lanark	63/64	20			D1
	64/65	22			D1
Bradford PA	65/66	1			FL

GEMMELL Thomas
b. Tarbolton 2.7.1930
d. Patna 8.1.2004 Caps: S - 2
Irvine Meadow

Club	Season	Apps	Sub	Goals	Div
St Mirren	51/52	21		5	D1
	52/53	30		11	D1
	53/54	24		7	D1
	54/55	29		9	D1
	55/56	28		8	D1
	56/57	25		4	D1
	57/58	33		9	D1
	58/59	26		7	D1
	59/60	27		9	D1
	60/61	14		2	D1
	61/62	7			D1

GEMMELL Thomas
b. Craigneuk 16.10.1943 Caps: S - 18
Meadow Thistle
Coltness U

Club	Season	Apps	Sub	Goals	Div
Celtic	61/62				D1
	62/63	2			D1
	63/64	31			D1
	64/65	30		3	D1
	65/66	34		4	D1
	66/67	34		9	D1
	67/68	34		4	D1
	68/69	31		8	D1
	69/70	29		9	D1
	70/71	19		1	D1
	71/72	3			D1
Nottingham F	71/72	18		5	FL
	72/73	21		1	FL
Miami Toros	73				
Dundee	73/74	30		1	D1
	74/75	25			D1
	75/76	16	3	3	P
	76/77	20		4	D1

GEMMILL Archibald
b. Paisley 24.3.1947 Caps: S - 43
Drumchapel Amateurs

Club	Season	Apps	Sub	Goals	Div
St Mirren	64/65	19		4	D1
	65/66	17			D1
	66/67	29	2	4	D1
Preston NE	67/68	29	3	4	FL
	68/69	18	4	3	FL
	69/70	39		6	FL
	70/71	7			FL
Derby Co	70/71	31		3	FL
	71/72	40		3	FL
	72/73	34		3	FL
	73/74	38		1	FL
	74/75	41			FL
	75/76	42		5	FL
	76/77	30		1	FL
	77/78	5		1	FL
Nottingham F	77/78	32	2	3	FL
	78/79	24		1	FL
Birmingham C	79/80	37		8	FL
	80/81	41		3	FL
	81/82	19		1	FL
Jacksonville Teamen	82	30		2	NA
Wigan A	82/83	11			FL
Derby Co	82/83	25		6	FL
	83/84	38		2	FL

GEOGHEHAN Andrew
b. Glasgow
Petershill

Club	Season	Apps	Sub	Goals	Div
Aberdeen	71/72	5			D1
	72/73	1			D1
	73/74				D1
	74/75	1			D1
	75/76	16			P
Ayr U	76/77	21			P
	77/78	1			P
St Johnstone	77/78	16			D1
	78/79	20			D1
	79/80	2			D1

GEORGE James
Kilbowie Amateurs

Club	Season	Apps	Sub	Goals	Div
St Johnstone	72/73	10			D1
	73/74	2	1		D1
East Fife	74/75	2			D2
	75/76	18		1	D1
	76/77	30	2	3	D1
	77/78	28		1	D1
	78/79	18		1	D2
Queen of the South	79/80	3	1	1	D2
Yoker A					
Dumbarton					

GEORGESON Roderick Bruce
b. Shubra, Egypt 31.7.1948
Bo'ness U

Club	Season	Apps	Sub	Goals	Div
Port Vale	65/66	5		1	FL
	66/67	21	1	5	FL
Dundee	67/68	3	4	1	D1
	68/69	4		1	D1
	69/70	2		1	D1
Hibernian	70/71				D1
Raith R	70/71			10	D2
	71/72	28	2	1	D2
	72/73	25	3	11	D2
Berwick R	73/74	34		9	D2
	74/75	37		18	D2
	75/76	19		9	D2
Dunfermline A	75/76	4		1	D1
	76/77	31	2	11	D2
	77/78	27	6	7	D2
	78/79	2			D2
Montrose	78/79	18		5	D1
Meadowbank T					
Arniston R					
Penicuik A					
Haddington					

GERHARD, Peter
(see Morawiec, Gerhard)

GERRIE Sydney
b. Aberdeen 14.6.1927
Inverurie Loco

Club	Season	Apps	Sub	Goals	Div
Dundee	48/49	11		5	D1
	49/50	25		13	D1
	50/51	5		2	D1
Hull C	50/51	23		11	FL
	51/52	38		24	FL
	52/53	35		13	FL
	53/54	23		6	FL
	54/55	11		3	FL
	55/56	7		1	FL
	56/57	9		1	FL

GIBB Robert
Bo'ness U

Club	Season	Apps	Sub	Goals	Div
Partick T	48/49	10			D1
	49/50	24			D1
	50/51	29			D1
	51/52	18			D1
	52/53	21			D1
	53/54	16			D1
	54/55	12			D1
	55/56	32			D1
	56/57	10			D1

GIBB Thomas
b. Bathgate 13.12.1944
Wallhouse Rose
Armadale Thistle

Club	Season	Apps	Sub	Gls	Div
Partick T	63/64	1			D1
	64/65	11		2	D1
	65/66	32		3	D1
	66/67	33		4	D1
	67/68	34		4	D1
Newcastle U	68/69	41		4	FL
	69/70	42		1	FL
	70/71	42		2	FL
	71/72	26	3	1	FL
	72/73	13	1	1	FL
	73/74	15	4	3	FL
	74/75	11	2		FL
Sunderland	75/76	5	3	1	FL
	76/77	2	2		FL
Hartlepool U	77/78	40		4	FL
	78/79				FL

GIBSON Alexander

Club	Season	Apps	Sub	Gls	Div
Motherwell	46/47	8		2	D1
Morton	46/47	3			D1
Ayr U	L 46/47				D2
Queen of the South	47/48	3		1	D1

GIBSON Alexander Rose
b. Glasgow 25.1.1925
Arthurlie

Club	Season	Apps	Sub	Gls	Div
Clyde	46/47	8			D1
	47/48	24			D1
	48/49	27			D1
	49/50	20			D1
Hull C	49/50	9			FL
	50/51	12			FL
Stirling A	51/52	14			D1
	52/53	29			D2
	53/54	7			D1
	54/55	16			D1
	55/56	33			D1
	56/57				D2
	57/58				D2
	58/59	19			D1

GIBSON Alistair
b. Glasgow
Pollok Jnrs

Club	Season	Apps	Sub	Gls	Div
Queen of the South	54/55	7			D1
	55/56	21		1	D1
	56/57	4			D1
Dundee U	57/58	33			D2
	58/59	21			D2

GIBSON Bert

Club	Season	Apps	Sub	Gls	Div
Aberdeen	58/59	4			D1

GIBSON David Wedderburn
b. Winchburgh 23.9.1938 Caps: S - 7
Livingston U

Club	Season	Apps	Sub	Gls	Div
Hibernian	56/57	1			D1
	57/58	1			D1
	58/59	20		5	D1
	59/60	5			D1
	60/61	3			D1
	61/62	11		3	D1
Leicester C	61/62	5		1	FL
	62/63	36		9	FL
	63/64	37		9	FL
	64/65	35		6	FL
	65/66	42		5	FL
	66/67	40		6	FL
	67/68	41		4	FL
	68/69	29	3	1	FL
	69/70	9	3		FL
Aston Villa	70/71	13	3	1	FL
	71/72	3			FL
Exeter C	71/72	23		1	FL
	72/73	30	1	2	FL

GIBSON George
b. c1946
West Calder

Club	Season	Apps	Sub	Gls	Div
Falkirk	66/67	4			D1
	67/68	34		2	D1
	68/69	34		3	D1
	69/70	36		1	D2
	70/71	33			D1
	71/72	26			D1
	72/73	33		1	D1
	73/74	30			D1
	74/75	35		1	D2
	75/76	26			D1
	76/77	28		1	D1
Sydney Olympic					

GIBSON John
b. Hull 23.12.1950
Clydebank Strollers

Club	Season	Apps	Sub	Gls	Div
Partick T	67/68				D1
	68/69	3		1	D1
	69/70		1		D1
	70/71	9	8		D2
	71/72	13	7	5	D1
	72/73	18	2	3	D1
	73/74	20	6	3	D1
	74/75	3	3	1	D1
Ayr U	74/75	2	3		D1
	75/76				P
St Mirren	76/77		1		D1
Celtic	76/77	1	2		P
	77/78				P
East Fife	78/79	15	9	2	D2
	79/80				D2
	80/81				D2
Forfar A	80/81	4	4		D2
Stirling A	81/82	2	2		D2
Sauchie Jnrs					

GIBSON Robert

Club	Season	Apps	Sub	Gls	Div
Morton	51/52	5			D1
	52/53	27		17	D2
	53/54	19		12	D2
Dumbarton					
Berwick R					
Hamilton A	59/60	4		3	D2

GIBSON Robert Henry
b. Ashington 5.8.1927 d. ?.3.1989
Ashington

Club	Season	Apps	Sub	Gls	Div
Aberdeen	48/49	1			D1
Hull C	49/50	12		5	FL
Ashington	50/51				
Lincoln C	51/52	17		8	FL
	52/53	4		2	FL
	53/54	4		1	FL
	54/55	18		9	FL
Peterborough U	55/56	30		31	ML
	56/57	25		20	ML
Gateshead	56/57	10		8	FL
	57/58	32		14	FL
	58/59	8		4	FL

GIBSON Thomas
Ardeer Rec

Club	Season	Apps	Sub	Gls	Div
Ayr U	59/60	2			D1
	60/61	2			D1
	61/62	9		4	D2
Hamilton A	62/63	4		1	D2
Ardeer Rec					

GIBSON W

Club	Season	Apps	Sub	Gls	Div
Third Lanark	51/52	1			D1

GIBSON William

Club	Season	Apps	Sub	Gls	Div
Morton	47/48	3			D1
	48/49	15			D1
Queen of the South	49/50	4			D1

GIBSON William
b. St Andrews 3.4.1953
Methil Star
Lochore Welfare

Club	Season	Apps	Sub	Gls	Div
Heart of Midlothian	73/74	10	2	6	D1
	74/75	27	3	9	D1
	75/76	24	4	8	P
	76/77	31		15	P
	77/78	36	3	20	D1
	78/79	33	1	6	P
	79/80	39		17	D1
	80/81	30	2	4	P
Partick T	81/82	2		1	P
Raith R	81/82	24	3	9	D1
	82/83	4	2		D1
Cowdenbeath	82/83	22		13	D2

GILCHRIST J

Club	Season	Apps	Sub	Gls	Div
Airdrieonians	47/48	2			D1

GILCHRIST John Skidmore
b. Wishaw 5.9.1939 d. ?.?.1991

Club	Season	Apps	Sub	Gls	Div
Airdrieonians	57/58				D1
	58/59				D1
	59/60	3			D1
	60/61				D1
Millwall	60/61	1			FL
	61/62	31			FL
	62/63	22		2	FL
	63/64	45		1	FL
	64/65	29		1	FL
	65/66	46		1	FL
	66/67	41		1	FL
	67/68	38		2	FL
	68/69	26		2	FL
Fulham	69/70	20	3	1	FL
Colchester U	70/71	28		1	FL
	71/72	13			FL
Tonbridge					

GILCHRIST Robert Cook
b. Bellshill 17.8.1932
Dunfermline A

Club	Season	Apps	Sub	Gls	Div
Aldershot	52/53	2			FL
	53/54				FL
	54/55	1			FL
	55/56	22			FL
	56/57	22			FL
Motherwell	56/57	4			D1
	57/58	6			D1

GILCHRIST Thomas

Club	Season	Apps	Sub	Gls	Div
Stirling A	59/60	2		1	D1
	60/61				D2
St Johnstone					

GILFILLAN Robert Inglis
b. Cowdenbeath 29.6.1938
Dundonald

Club	Season	Apps	Sub	Gls	Div
Cowdenbeath	56/57				D2
	57/58				D2
	58/59				D2
	59/60				D2
Newcastle U	59/60	5			FL
	60/61	2		2	FL
St Johnstone	60/61	9		5	D1
	61/62	5		1	D1
Raith R	61/62	7		2	D1
	62/63	15		1	D1
Southend U	63/64	18		9	FL
	64/65	39		22	FL
	65/66	8	1	2	FL
Doncaster R	65/66	29		6	FL
	66/67	38		8	FL
	67/68	37	3	7	FL
	68/69	31	3	7	FL
	69/70	21	1	1	FL
	70/71	22		5	FL
Northwich V					

GILLAN George
b. 21.6.
Saltcoats V
Arthurlie
Alloa A
Motherwell
Ayr U

Hamilton A	46/47	14	1	D1
	47/48	17		D2
	48/49	29	1	D2
	49/50	29	1	D2
	50/51	5		D2

Berwick R

GILLESPIE Dennis
b. Duntocher 7.1.1936 d. Dundee 4.6.2001
Duntocher Hibs

Alloa A	56/57			D2
	57/58			D2
	58/59			D2
Dundee U	59/60	34	18	D2
	60/61	31	14	D1
	61/62	32	12	D1
	62/63	32	14	D1
	63/64	33	10	D1
	64/65	31	7	D1
	65/66	27	6	D1
	66/67	29	6	D1
	67/68	30	3	D1
	68/69	28		D1
	69/70	34	2	D1
	70/71	3	2 1	D1
	71/72			D1
Brechin C	72/73	29		D2
	73/74	23	2	D2
	74/75	28	1	D2
	75/76	4	1	D2

GILLESPIE Eric J

Carmunnock Downcraig
Cambuslang R

Burnley	69/70			FL
Kilmarnock	70/71	2		D1
Motherwell	71/72	11		D1
Hamilton A	72/73	34	6	D2
	73/74	20	1 3	D2
Albion R	74/75	24	4 2	D2

Cumnock Jnrs

GILLESPIE James

East Stirlingshire	67/68	17	1 5	D2
Raith R	67/68	14	3	D1
	68/69	16	1 1	D1
	69/70	2		D1
Dunfermline A	69/70	14	1 4	D1
	70/71	1		D1
	71/72	21	6 2	D1
	72/73	15	6 1	D2
	73/74	9	4	D1
Alloa A	74/75	10	9 2	D2

GILLESPIE Michael

Irvine Meadow

Clyde	73/74	7	9 3	D1

GILLESPIE Norman
b. Edinburgh 20.4.1940

Arbroath	61/62	16	8	D2
	62/63			D2
Falkirk	63/64	7	1	D1
Wrexham	63/64	3		FL
Berwick R	64/65			D2

GILLICK Torrance
b. Airdrie 19.5.1915 d. 16.12.1971 Caps: S - 5
Petershill

Rangers	33/34	2		D1
	34/35	27	17	D1
Everton	35/36	23	9	FL
	36/37	42	14	FL
	37/38	16	3	FL
	38/39	40	14	FL
Rangers	46/47	27	12	D1
	47/48	21	9	D1
	48/49	8	4	D1
	49/50	2		D1
	505/1			D1
Partick T	51/52	7	1	D1

GILLIES Donald George
b. Glencoe 20.6.1951
Inverness Clachnacuddin

Morton	71/72	22	1 9	D1
	72/73	23	1 14	D1
Bristol C	72/73	11	2	FL
	73/74	28	8 6	FL
	74/75	28	1 9	FL
	75/76	22	3 1	FL
	76/77	37	1 3	FL
	77/78	24	3 4	FL
	78/79	27	1	FL
	79/80	7	1	FL
Bristol R	80/81	30	1	FL
	81/82	26	1	FL

Paulton R
Trowbridge T
Anorthosis
Trowbridge T

Yeovil T	86/87			

Clutton
Bristol Manor Farm

GILLIES John
b. Glasgow 22.10.1918
St Mirren

Brentford	46/47	5		FL
Morton	46/47	2	2	D1
	47/48	2		D1

GILLIES William T
b. 19.1.1951
Leven Jnrs

East Fife	72/73			D1
	73/74	14	1	D1
	74/75	38	1	D1
	75/76	12	1 2	D1
	76/77	33	1 7	D1
	77/78	25	4 3	D1
	78/79	35	2	D2
	79/80	2		D2
Forfar A	80/81	24	2 2	D2

GILLON Robert

Luthrie Amateurs

East Fife	50/51			D1
	51/52			D1
	52/53			D1
	53/54			D1
	54/55			D1
	55/56			D1
	56/57	7	1	D1
	57/58	8	1	D1

Cowdenbeath Royals

Cowdenbeath	58/59			D2

GILMARTIN Hugh

Market Star
Celtic

Hamilton A	46/47	2	1	D1

GILMOUR G

Queen of the South	46/47	9		D1

GILMOUR James

Kyle U

Ayr U	68/69			D2
Troon Jnrs	L 68/69			
Ayr U	69/70			D1
	70/71	3		D1
St Mirren	71/72	10		D2

GILMOUR John M
b. Hamilton 7.1.1944 d. Hamilton 23.9.1980
Motherwell Bridge Works
Wishaw Jnrs

Hamilton A	63/64	9	5	D2
	64/65	36	20	D2
	65/66	27	4	D1
	66/67	36	12	D2
Kilmarnock	67/68	15	1 2	D1
	68/69	32	1	D1
	69/70	29	2 3	D1
	70/71	32	4	D1
	71/72	33	3	D1
	72/73	11		D1
	73/74	3	2 1	D2
Clydebank	73/74	14		D2
	74/75	10		D2
Stirling A	74/75	9	2	D2

Cambuslang R

GILMOUR Robert

Benburb

Queen of the South	52/53	1		D1

GILMOUR Robert

Stoneyburn Jnrs

Partick T	56/57	6	3	D1
	57/58	6	5	D1
Stirling A	58/59	32	22	D1
	59/60	25	12	D1
	60/61			D2
	61/62	15	4	D1
	62/63			D2
	63/64	1	1	D2

Bedford T

GILROY Joseph
b. Glasgow 19.10.1941
Montrose

Queen's Park	59/60	2		D2
Clyde	60/61			D1
	61/62			D2
	62/63			D1
Montrose	63/64	31	6	D2
Clyde	64/65	34	14	D1
	65/66	30	14	D1
	66/67	32	13	D1
	67/68	7	3	D1
Fulham	67/68	18	7	FL
	68/69	5	1 1	FL
Dundee	68/69	24	6	D1
	69/70	14	4	D1
	70/71	14	3	D1

Highlands Park

GILSHAN Hugh

Greenock Jnrs

Celtic	T			
Ayr U	64/65			D2
	65/66			D2
	66/67			D1
	67/68			D2

Johnstone Burgh

St Mirren	68/69	29	6	D1
	69/70	29	5	D1
	70/71	14	2 2	D1

GILZEAN Alan John
b. Coupar Angus 22.10.1938 Caps: S - 22
Coupar Angus Juveniles
Dundee Violet
Dundee
Aldershot   L

Dundee	59/60	8		8	D1
	60/61	33		19	D1
	61/62	29		24	D1
	62/63	27		24	D1
	63/64	30		33	D1
	64/65	7		5	D1
Tottenham H	64/65	20		11	FL
	65/66	40		12	FL
	66/67	40		17	FL
	67/68	32	2	8	FL
	68/69	37		7	FL
	69/70	34	2	10	FL
	70/71	38		9	FL
	71/72	38		11	FL
	72/73	35		5	FL
	73/74	21	4	3	FL

Highlands Park

GLANCEY Patrick
Blackburn R

Albion R	55/56			D2
	56/57			D2
	57/58			D2
	58/59			D2
	59/60			D2
Stirling A	59/60	15	3	D1
	60/61			D2

GLASGOW Henry
Falkirk

Clyde	62/63	2			D1
	63/64				D2
	64/65	30			D1
	65/66	34			D1
	66/67	30		2	D1
	67/68	32		1	D1
	68/69	31		2	D1
	69/70	20		4	D1
	70/71	13	1		D1
	71/72	17	3		D1
Stenhousemuir	72/73	24		2	D2
	73/74	30	2		D2

GLAVIN Ronald Michael
b. Glasgow 27.3.1951 Caps: S - 1
Lochend R

Partick T	68/69			1	D1
	69/70	5	3	2	D1
	70/71	16	6	10	D2
	71/72	29		2	D1
	72/73	33		9	D1
	73/74	31		9	D1
	74/75	11		3	D1
Celtic	74/75	19	1	5	D1
	75/76	10			P
	76/77	34		19	P
	77/78	28		9	P
	78/79	9	1	3	P
Barnsley	79/80	42		20	FL
	80/81	36	1	18	FL
	81/82	26	1	7	FL
	82/83	33	2	17	FL
	83/84	34	1	11	FL
Belenenses	84/85				
Barnsley	85/86	5	1		FL
Stockport Co	86/87	5	5	1	FL
Cowdenbeath	86/87	2			D2

St Louis Steamers
Farsley Celtic

GLEESON Arthur
Bellshill Academy

Stirling A	49/50	1		D1

Ashfield

GLEN Alexander

Queen's Park	55/56	14	3	D2
	56/57	34	1	D1
Dundee	57/58	1		D1
Ayr U	58/59			D2
	59/60	2		D1
	60/61	11	1	D1
	61/62	12		D2

GLEN Archibald
b. Coalburn 16.4.1929
d. Aberdeen 30.8.1998 Caps: S - 2
Cumnock Academy
Ballochmyle Thistle
Annbank U

Aberdeen	48/49	4	1	D1
	49/50	1		D1
	50/51	7		D1
	51/52			D1
	52/53	5		D1
	53/54	27		D1
	54/55	30	4	D1
	55/56	27	4	D1
	56/57	29	4	D1
	57/58	26	2	D1
	58/59	33	7	D1
	59/60	14	2	D1

GLEN James

Morton	65/66	3		D1

GLIDDEN Freddie
b. Newmains 9.7.1928
West Calder Juveniles
Whitburn Jnrs
Heart of Midlothian
Newtongrange Sta L

Heart of Midlothian	51/52	21		D1
	52/53	16	2	D1
	53/54	21		D1
	54/55	30		D1
	55/56	32		D1
	56/57	19		D1
	57/58	13		D1
	58/59	13		D1
Dumbarton	58/59			D2
	59/60			D2
	60/61			D2
	61/62	33		D2

GLOVER Alexander
b. Glasgow 28.2.1922

Partick T	46/47	26	4	D1
	47/48	10	2	D1
Bradford PA	47/48	11		FL
	48/49	31	4	FL
	49/50	6	1	FL
Luton T	49/50	32	2	FL
	50/51	24	4	FL
Blackburn R	51/52	29	2	FL
	52/53	17	1	FL
	53/54	18	1	FL
Barrow	54/55	28	3	FL
	55/56	28	2	FL
	56/57	22	1	FL
	57/58	7	1	FL

GODDARD Raymond
b. Fulham 13.2.1949
Fulham

Leyton Orient	66/67	1		FL
	67/68	41		FL
	68/69	44		FL
	69/70	44		FL
	70/71	42		FL
	71/72	39		FL
	72/73	42		FL
	73/74	25		FL
Morton	74/75	1		D1
Millwall	74/75			FL
	75/76	46		FL
	76/77	26		FL
	77/78	8		FL
Wimbledon	77/78	18		FL
	78/79	45		FL
	79/80	44		FL
	80/81	12	1	FL

Wealdstone

GOLDIE David
Kilsyth Jnrs

Motherwell	61/62	1		D1
	62/63	6	1	D1
Stranraer	63/64	13	5	D2

GOLDIE Hugh

Raith R	49/50	8	2	D1
Ayr U	49/50			D2
	50/51			D2
	51/52			D2

GOLDIE Hugh

Partick T	58/59	3		D1
	59/60	2		D1
Albion R *	60/61			D2
	61/62	2		D2

GOLDIE James

Falkirk	58/59	4		D1

GOLDIE Peter
b. Dumbarton 7.6.1934
Vale Emmet
Duntocher Hibs

Celtic	53/54			D1
	54/55			D1
	55/56	10		D1
	56/57	1		D1
	57/58	2		D1
Aldershot	58/59	5		FL

GOLDIE William
b. Newmains 16.3.1937
Ardeer Thistle
Motherwell   T
Rutherglen Glencairn
Clyde   T

Airdrieonians	55/56	7		D1
	56/57	8		D1
	57/58	13		D1
Army				
Celtic	60/61	1		D1
Albion R	60/61			D2

GOLDTHORP John

Lesmahagow Jnrs

Club	Season				Div
Motherwell	67/68	11		3	D1
	68/69	11	1	9	D2
	69/70	18		4	D1
	70/71	18	1	2	D1
	71/72	22	4	6	D1
	72/73	15	6	3	D1
	73/74	24	2	10	D1
	74/75	23	4	6	D1
	75/76		3		P
Morton	75/76	8		5	D1
	76/77	20	6	11	D1
	77/78	34		20	D1
Airdrieonians	78/79	31		16	D1
St Johnstone	79/80	22	6	7	D1

GOLDTHORPE James

Club	Season				Div
St Mirren	51/52	6		2	D1

GOODALL David

Arniston R

Club	Season				Div
Dunfermline A	60/61	1			D1

GOODALL Ian

Kilsyth R

Club	Season				Div
Motherwell	48/49	16		2	D1
	49/50				D1
Third Lanark	50/51	8		3	D1
	51/52	10		4	D1

GOODFELLOW James Boyd
b. Edinburgh 30.7.1938

Tranent Jnrs

Club	Season				Div
Third Lanark	58/59	11		4	D1
	59/60	18		6	D1
	60/61	31		12	D1
	61/62	32		3	D1
	62/63	24		4	D1
Leicester C	63/64	5		1	FL
	64/65	29		11	FL
	65/66	30	1	9	FL
	66/67	29		5	FL
	67/68	3	1		FL
Mansfield T	67/68	12			FL
	68/69	39		6	FL
	69/70	30		6	FL
	70/71	15	4	2	FL

Weymouth
Durban C
Nuneaton B
AP Leamington

GOODWIN John

Carluke R

Club	Season				Div
Motherwell	62/63	6		1	D1
	63/64	1			D1

GOODWIN Samuel Gourlay
b. Tarbolton 14.3.1943

Craigmark Burntonians

Club	Season				Div
Airdrieonians	64/65	1			D1
	65/66	30		1	D2
	66/67	32			D1
	67/68	32		6	D1
	68/69	32		4	D1
	69/70	34		4	D1
	70/71	29	2	1	D1
	71/72	4			D1
Crystal Palace	71/72	18	7		FL
Motherwell	72/73	27			D1
	73/74	14	1	1	D1
	74/75	20	2	1	D1

Clydebank

GORAM Lewis Albert
b. Edinburgh 2.7.1926 d. ?.?.1989

Club	Season				Div
Third Lanark	49/50	9			D1
Bury	50/51	40			FL
	51/52	24			FL
	52/53	1			FL
	53/54	21			FL
	54/55	9			FL
	55/56	11			FL
	56/57	8			FL
Buxton					

GORDON Alan
b. Edinburgh 14.5.1944

Edina Hearts
Edinburgh A

Club	Season				Div
Heart of Midlothian	61/62	22		5	D1
	62/63	16		12	D1
	63/64	10		1	D1
	64/65	29		19	D1
	65/66	15		6	D1
	66/67	19	1	6	D1
Durban U					
Heart of Midlothian	68/69	15		6	D1
Dundee U	68/69	4			D1
	69/70	25	3	11	D1
	70/71	31		16	D1
	71/72	14	1	7	D1
Hibernian	71/72	13		4	D1
	72/73	33		27	D1
	73/74	27	1	16	D1
	74/75	10		4	D1
Dundee	74/75	13	3	5	D1
	75/76	17	3	3	P

GORDON Henry Alexander
b. Livingston 25.7.1940 d. ?.2.1996

Armadale Thistle

Club	Season				Div
Dundee U	60/61	6			D1
	61/62	27		1	D1
	62/63	19			D1
	63/64	15			D1
	64/65	12			D1
Bradford PA	65/66	27			FL
	66/67	34		2	FL
St Johnstone	67/68	22		2	D1
	68/69	33		1	D1
	69/70	34			D1
	70/71	29			D1
	71/72	30			D1

GORDON Ian
b. Glasgow 13.5.1929

Rob Roy Juveniles
Parkhead Juveniles
Kilsyth R

Club	Season				Div
Heart of Midlothian	51/52	3			D1
	52/53				D1
Airdrieonians	53/54	6			D1

GORDON J

Club	Season				Div
St Mirren	60/61	4			D1

GORDON Stuart

Kilsyth R

Club	Season				Div
Dunfermline A	67/68	2			D1

GORDON T

Club	Season				Div
Queen of the South	47/48	1			D1

GORE Reginald
b. Hepthorne Lane 1.8.1913 d. ?.?.1997

Hepthorne Lane Primitives

Club	Season				Div
Chesterfield	32/33				FL
Birmingham	33/34				FL
Southport	34/35	16		2	FL
South Liverpool					
Rhyl					
Frickley Colliery					
West Ham U	38/39	5		1	FL
St Mirren	46/47	2		1	D1
Cowdenbeath	47/48				D2

GORMAN David
b. Lumphinnans 18.4.1947

Cowdenbeath Royals

Club	Season				Div
Cowdenbeath	64/65				D2
	65/66				D2
Alloa A	66/67	1			D2
St Andrews U					
East Fife	67/68	10			D2
	68/69	26			D2
	69/70	28			D2
	70/71	33			D2
	71/72	33			D1
	72/73	17			D1
	73/74	8			D1
Montrose	74/75	38			D2
	75/76	26			D1
	76/77	39			D1
	77/78	14			D1
	78/79	23			D1
East Fife	79/80	38			D2
	80/81	38			D2
	81/82	30			D2
	82/83	29			D2
	81/82	7			D2

GORMLEY Philip
b. Greenock 13.10.1924

Klondyke A
Kirkintilloch Rob Roy

Club	Season				Div
Celtic	47/48	1			D1
	48/49				D1
	49/50				D1
Aldershot	50/51	15		6	FL
	51/52	32		1	FL
	52/53	18		2	FL
Dundee U					

GOURLAY Archibald

Club	Season				Div
Partick T	46/47	3		2	D1
Clyde	46/47	14		5	D1
	47/48	4		1	D1

GOURLAY Bert

Club	Season				Div
Morton	50/51	4			D1
	51/52	4			D1

GOURLAY Thomas
b. Glasgow

Ashfield

Club	Season				Div
Airdrieonians	70/71	12			D1
	71/72	2			D1
Partick T	72/73				D1
	73/74				D1
East Stirlingshire	74/75	38			D2
	75/76	23			D2

GOURLAY William

Maryhill

Club	Season				Div
Partick T	61/62	1			D1
	62/63	8		4	D1
	63/64	1		1	D1
Falkirk	63/64	20		2	D1
	64/65	17		2	D1
	65/66	2			D1
Stranraer					

GOVAN Thomas John
b. Larkhall 16.1.1923
d. Edinburgh 19.2.1999 Caps: S - 6

Larkhall Thistle

Club	Season				Div
Hibernian	46/47	10			D1
	47/48	29			D1
	48/49	28			D1
	49/50	17			D1
	50/51	23			D1
	51/52	30			D1
	52/53	20			D1
	53/54	6			D1
Ayr U	54/55				D2

GRAHAM Arthur
b. Castlemilk 26.10.1952 Caps: S - 10
Cambuslang R

Club	Season				Div
Aberdeen	69/70	4	1	2	D1
	70/71	31		5	D1
	71/72	27	2	4	D1
	72/73	19	4		D1
	73/74	31	1	3	D1
	74/75	34		11	D1
	75/76	31		4	P
	76/77	35		5	P
Leeds U	77/78	40		9	FL
	78/79	39		8	FL
	79/80	26	1	3	FL
	80/81	40		3	FL
	81/82	38		9	FL
	82/83	39		5	FL
Manchester U	83/84	33	4	5	FL
	84/85				FL
Bradford C	85/86	23	2	2	FL
	86/87	5	1		FL

GRAHAM David
b. Edinburgh c1952
Carrickvale Thistle

Club	Season			Div
Heart of Midlothian	73/74	4		D1
	74/75			D1
	75/76	1		P
Meadowbank T	76/77	4		D2
Berwick R	76/77	3		D2

GRAHAM Gerald
Elgin C

Club	Season			Div
Arbroath	68/69	1	1	D1

GRAHAM James P
Glasgow University
Queen's Park

Club	Season			Div
Kilmarnock	70/71	2	1	D1

GRAHAM John
Arthurlie

Club	Season				Div
Dumbarton	67/68	10		2	D2
	68/69			3	D2
	69/70	36		5	D2
	70/71			2	D2
	71/72	34	1	4	D2
	72/73	33		1	D1
	73/74	15	4		D1
	74/75	28		1	D1
	75/76	22	3	1	D1
	76/77	28	1	1	D1

GRAHAM John Joseph
b. Glasgow 16.7.1946

Club	Season				Div
Morton	65/66	6		1	D1
Dundee U	66/67	13	2	9	D1
	67/68	8	4	1	D1
Guildford C	68/69				
	69/70				
Brentford	70/71	42		6	FL
	71/72	45		7	FL
	72/73	30	1	6	FL
	73/74	31		2	FL
	74/75	43		4	FL
	75/76	38		5	FL
	76/77	42		4	FL
	77/78	35	1	2	FL
	78/79	35		1	FL
	79/80	30	1	1	FL
Addlestone & Weybridge					

GRAHAM John R
b. Glasgow 8.1.1946
Strathclyde

Club	Season				Div
Third Lanark	63/64	31		7	D1
Dundee U	64/65	16		1	D1
Falkirk	64/65	14		4	D1
	65/66	34		17	D1
	66/67	30	1	12	D1
	67/68	29		13	D1
	68/69	23	3	7	D1
Hibernian	69/70	22		10	D1
	70/71	20	2	4	D1
Ayr U	71/72	34		14	D1
	72/73	28		7	D1
	73/74	31		10	D1
	74/75	29	3	12	D1
	75/76	34	1	16	P
	76/77	5	3	3	P
Falkirk	76/77	17	7		D1
	77/78	11	3		D2

GRAHAM Robert
Gateshead

Club	Season			Div
Aberdeen	63/64	14	6	D1
Queen of the South	64/65	12	7	D2

GRAHAM Robert
b. Motherwell 22.11.1944

Club	Season				Div
Liverpool	64/65	14			FL
	65/66	1			FL
	66/67	3		1	FL
	67/68	2	2	1	FL
	68/69	11	1	5	FL
	69/70	42		13	FL
	70/71	13	1	5	FL
	71/72	10	1	2	FL
Coventry C	71/72	13		2	FL
	72/73	6		1	FL
Tranmere R	L 72/73	10		3	FL
Motherwell	73/74	33		13	D1
	74/75	31	1	11	D1
	75/76	34		5	P
	76/77	28	5	8	P
Hamilton A	77/78	38		10	D1
	78/79	38		18	D1
	79/80	30		11	D1
	80/81	9	3	3	D1
Queen of the South					

GRAHAM Thomas R
Shotts Bon Accord

Club	Season		Div
Dundee U	59/60	34	D2
	60/61	12	D1
	61/62	5	D1
Poole T	62/63		
	63/64		
Bath C	64/65		

GRAHAM W
Club	Season		Div
St Mirren	49/50	1	D1
	50/51	3	D1

GRANT Archibald S
b. ?.?.1937
St Anthonys

Club	Season		Div
Kilmarnock	58/59	5	D1
Portadown	59/60		
Beith Jnrs			
Toronto C			

GRANT Bernard
b. Airdrie 23.5.1920 d. ?.?.1984

Club	Season		Div
Third Lanark	46/47	2	D1
Exeter C	47/48		FL
	48/49	2	FL

GRANT Colin
Linlithgow Rose

Club	Season				Div
Hibernian	65/66	5		2	D1
	66/67	1			D1
	67/68		2	1	D1
	68/69	4	2		D1
	69/70	2	4		D1
Chelmsford C					
Peterhead					

GRANT David Bell
b. Edinburgh 31.7.1943

Club	Season				Div
Third Lanark	62/63	21		9	D1
Reading	63/64	8		2	FL
	64/65	9		1	FL
Barnsley	64/65				FL
Stirling A	65/66	11		1	D1
	66/67	27		7	D1
	67/68	19		1	D1
	68/69				D2
	69/70				D2
	70/71				D2
East Stirlingshire	71/72	16	1	2	D2
	72/73	25	1		D2
	73/74	10			D2

GRANT George D
b. Newmains
New Stevenston U
Arbroath

Club	Season			Div
Dundee U	46/47	13	6	D2
	47/48	25	4	D2
	48/49	19	1	D2
	49/50	29	8	D2
	50/51	28	8	D2
	51/52	26	7	D2
	52/53	24	1	D2
	53/54	20	6	D2
	54/55	4	1	D2
Falkirk	54/55	14		D1
	55/56	2		D1
Dundee U	55/56	7		D2
Hamilton A	56/57	6		D2
Fauldhouse U				

GRANT J
Club	Season		Div
Clyde	47/48	2	D1
	48/49	1	D1

GRANT John
b. Edinburgh c1931 Caps: S - 2
Colinton Mains U
Merchiston Thistle

Club	Season			Div
Hibernian	54/55	14		D1
	55/56	19		D1
	56/57	21		D1
	57/58	24	1	D1
	58/59	32		D1
	59/60	22		D1
	60/61	17		D1
	61/62	28		D1
	62/63	25		D1
	63/64	22	1	D1
Raith R	64/65			D2

GRANT John
Merchiston Thistle

Club	Season			Div
Hibernian	63/64	13	1	D1
Raith R	64/65			D2
Ayr U	65/66	31	3	D2
	66/67	19	1	D1
Durban U				

GRANT P
Club	Season			Div
Queen of the South	47/48	4	1	D1

GRANT Richard
Club	Season			Div
Clyde	62/63	9	2	D1
Ayr U	63/64			D2

GRANT Robert
b. Edinburgh 25.9.1940

Club	Season				Div
Rangers	59/60	1			D1
Leyton Orient					
Chelmsford C					
Gloucester C					
Stirling A					
St Johnstone	61/62	3			D1
Carlisle U	62/63	2		1	FL
Queen of the South					

GRANT William

Club	Season				Div
Heart of Midlothian	54/55	1			D1
Stirling A	55/56	3			D1
	56/57				D2
	57/58				D2
	58/59				D1
	59/60	6		1	D1

GRANVILLE Anthony Ralph
b. Glasgow 23.4.1931

Club	Season				Div
Clyde	54/55	9			D1
	55/56	5			D1
	56/57				D2
Gateshead	57/58	1			FL

GRAY Alan

Club	Season				Div
Clyde	62/63	18			D1
	63/64				D2
	64/65	4			D1

GRAY Alexander

Club	Season				Div
Raith R	67/68	34		1	D1
	68/69	29			D1
	69/70	16			D1

GRAY Andrew Mullen
b. Glasgow 30.11.1955 Caps: S - 20
Clydebank Strollers

Club	Season				Div
Dundee U	73/74	25	1	16	D1
	74/75	33		20	D1
	75/76	3			P
Aston Villa	75/76	30		10	FL
	76/77	36		25	FL
	77/78	31	1	13	FL
	78/79	15		6	FL
Wolverhampton W	79/80	35		12	FL
	80/81	25	2	9	FL
	81/82	28	1	5	FL
	82/83	33		10	FL
	83/84	9		2	FL
Everton	83/84	23		5	FL
	84/85	21	5	9	FL
Aston Villa	85/86	35		5	FL
	86/87	18	1		FL
	87/88				FL
Notts Co	L 87/88	3	1		FL
West Bromwich A	87/88	30	2	10	FL
	88/89	2	1		FL
Rangers	88/89	3	10	5	P

GRAY David
b. Coupar Angus 8.2.1922

Club	Season				Div
Rangers	46/47	9			D1
Preston NE	47/48	36			FL
Blackburn R	48/49	38		5	FL
	49/50	38			FL
	50/51	12			FL
	51/52	14			FL
	52/53	5			FL
	53/54				FL
Dundee	54/55	12			D1
	55/56	8			D1
Dundee U	56/57	18			D2
	57/58	18			D2

GRAY Denis
Annbank U

Club	Season				Div
Ayr U	70/71				D1
	71/72				D1
	72/73	1		1	D1
Stranraer	73/74	7	2		D2

GRAY Edward

Club	Season				Div
Hibernian	56/57	1			D1

GRAY George

Club	Season				Div
Raith R	51/52	3			D1

GRAY James
Arthurlie

Club	Season				Div
Partick T	60/61	3			D1
	61/62	22			D1
	62/63				D1
	63/64				D1
	64/65	15			D1
	65/66	14			D1
Raith R	67/68	3			D1

GRAY James

Club	Season				Div
Motherwell	67/68			1	D1

GRAY John
b. Hamilton ?.?.1953
Blantyre Celtic

Club	Season				Div
Dundee	70/71				D1
	71/72				D1
	72/73	3	2	1	D1
	73/74		3		D1
Partick T	74/75	2	5		D1
Australia					
Hamilton A	76/77	2	1		D1
East Fife	76/77	13	2	1	D1

GRAY John
Eastercraig YC
Cumbernauld U

Club	Season				Div
Motherwell	72/73	13	1	1	D1
	73/74	9	2	1	D1
	74/75				D1
	75/76				P
Ayr U	76/77		2		P

GRAY Matthew
b. Renfrew 11.7.1936

Club	Season				Div
Third Lanark	57/58	21		8	D1
	58/59	27		19	D1
	59/60	33		22	D1
	60/61	34		19	D1
	61/62	34		16	D1
	62/63	17		10	D1
Manchester C	62/63	18		6	FL
	63/64	37		8	FL
	64/65	27		5	FL
	65/66	3	3	1	FL
	66/67	2	1	1	FL
Port Elizabeth					

GRAY Robert

Club	Season				Div
St Johnstone	61/62	2			D1

GRAY Robert

Club	Season				Div
Partick T	68/69	28			D1
	69/70	26	1		D1
	70/71	9			D2

GRAY Robert
Bo'ness U

Club	Season				Div
Partick T	70/71	9			D2
	71/72	5	1		D1
	72/73	12			D1

GRAY Thomas Davidson
b. c1913 d. 24.12.1992
Morton

Club	Season				Div
Dundee	46/47	24			D2
	47/48	11			D1
	48/49	11			D1
Arbroath	49/50	17			D2
	50/51				D2
	51/52				D2
	52/53	30		7	D2
	53/54	28			D2

GRAY William

Club	Season				Div
St Mirren	62/63	7			D1
	63/64	8			D1
	64/65	22			D1
Morton	65/66	15		1	D1
	66/67				D2
	67/68	26	1	1	D1
	68/69	32			D1
	69/70	34		1	D1
	70/71	26		1	D1
Dundee U	71/72	26		1	D1
	72/73	3			D1

GREEN J

Club	Season				Div
Queen of the South	49/50	2			D1

GREEN James

Club	Season				Div
Airdrieonians	67/68	1	1		D1

GREEN Michael
b. 1.10.1949
Benburb

Club	Season				Div
Albion R	67/68				D2
	68/69				D2
	69/70				D2
	70/71				D2
Blackpool	71/72				FL
East Fife	72/73	4		1	D1

GREENOCK James
Wishaw Jnrs

Club	Season				Div
Queen of the South	51/52	26			D1
	52/53	29		5	D1
	53/54	30		3	D1
	54/55	22		2	D1
	55/56				D1
	56/57	25		1	D1
	57/58	32		1	D1
	58/59	24		1	D1

GREGAL Anthony

Club	Season				Div
St Mirren	57/58	3			D1
	58/59	17			D1
	59/60	25			D1
	60/61	1			D1
Montrose					

GREIG John
b. Edinburgh 11.9.1942 Caps: S - 44
Edina Hearts
Whitburn

Club	Season				Div
Rangers	61/62	11		7	D1
	62/63	27		5	D1
	63/64	34		4	D1
	64/65	34		4	D1
	65/66	32		7	D1
	66/67	32		2	D1
	67/68	32		11	D1
	68/69	33		6	D1
	69/70	30		7	D1
	70/71	26		8	D1
	71/72	28		8	D1
	72/73	30		7	D1
	73/74	30	2	6	D1
	74/75	21	1	1	D1
	75/76	36		2	P
	76/77	30			P
	77/78	28	1	2	P

GRIERSON Derek D

Club	Season			Div
Queen's Park	48/49	1		D2
	49/50	24	16	D2
	50/51	29	20	D2
	51/52	29	15	D2
Rangers	52/53	30	23	D1
	53/54	21	8	D1
	54/55	18	11	D1
	55/56			D1
	56/57	3		D1
Falkirk	56/57	13	4	D1
	57/58	29	9	D1
	58/59	29	8	D1
Arbroath	59/60	27	8	D1
Stirling A	60/61			D2
Forfar A	60/61			D2
Cowdenbeath	61/62	4		D2

GROZIER James

Glenafton

Club	Season			Div
Motherwell	50/51			D1
	51/52	3	1	D1
	52/53			D1

GRUBB Alan Johnstone

b. Leven 5.2.1928
Largo Villa

Club	Season			Div
East Fife	48/49			D1
	49/50			D1
	50/51	1		D1
Gloucester C	51/52			
Tottenham H	52/53	2		FL
Walsall	53/54	15		FL
Worcester C				

GULLAN Stanley Knox

b. Edinburgh 26.1.1926 d. Aberdeen 29.6.1999
Dumbarton

Club	Season			Div
Clyde	47/48	17		D1
	48/49	29		D1
QPR	49/50			FL
	50/51	22		FL
	51/52	4		FL
	52/53	3		FL
	53/54	13		FL
	54/55	6		FL

Tunbridge Wells
Berwick R
Third Lanark
Montrose
Stenhousemuir

GUNN Alistair Robert

b. Broughty Ferry 2.11.1924
Elmwood

Club	Season			Div
Dundee	46/47	19	6	D2
	47/48	16	2	D1
	48/49	28	10	D1
	49/50	27	5	D1
	50/51	13	3	D1
Huddersfield T	50/51	3		FL
	51/52	24	4	FL
	52/53	33	7	FL
	53/54	23		FL
Bournemouth	54/55	27	2	FL

GUNN Robert H

Club	Season			Div
Queen's Park	47/48	25	4	D1
	48/49	27	21	D2

GUNNING James Michael

b. Helensburgh 25.6.1929 d. ?.?.1993

Club	Season			Div
Hibernian	50/51	1		D1
Manchester C	50/51	4		FL
	51/52	3		FL
	52/53	6		FL
Weymouth	53/54			
Barrow	54/55	10	1	FL
Stockport Co	55/56			FL

GUTHRIE John

Cumnock Jnrs

Club	Season			Div
St Mirren	47/48	1		D1
	48/49	4	3	D1
	49/50	1	1	D1
Ayr U	49/50	10	3	D2
	50/51			D2
Queen of the South				

GUY James

Third Lanark

Club	Season			Div
Stirling A	48/49			D2
	49/50	14	2	D2
	50/51			D2
	51/52			D1
Falkirk				
Dundee U	52/53	2		D2

HADDEN Thomas

Club	Season			Div
Airdrieonians	47/48	6		D1
	48/49			D2
	49/50	1		D2
Stirling A	50/51			D2
	51/52	27		D1

HADDOCK Andrew Edwin Robinson

b. Edinburgh 5.5.1946

Club	Season			Div
Chester	63/64	12		FL
Crewe Alex.	64/65	4		FL
Falkirk	65/66	9		D1
Rotherham U	66/67	4		FL
Chelmsford C	67/68			
Bradford PA	67/68	5		FL
Chester	67/68	10	1	FL
Fleetwood T				

HADDOCK Harry

b. Glasgow 26.7.1925
d. Rutherglen 18.12.1998 Caps: S - 6
Renfrew Jnrs

Club	Season			Div
Clyde	49/50	16		D1
	50/51	8		D1
	51/52			D2
	52/53	30		D1
	53/54	23		D1
	54/55	27		D1
	55/56	33	2	D1
	56/57			D2
	57/58	33	1	D1
	58/59	34		D1
	59/60	34	2	D1
	60/61	30	4	D1
	61/62			D2
	62/63	7		D1

HADDOW John

Club	Season			Div
Partick T	48/49	3		D1
	49/50	1		D1

HAFFEY Francis

b. Glasgow 28.11.1938 Caps: S - 2
Campsie Black Watch
Celtic
Maryhill Harp   L

Club	Season			Div
Celtic	57/58	1		D1
	58/59	14		D1
	59/60	20		D1
	60/61	29		D1
	61/62	32		D1
	62/63	33		D1
	63/64	10		D1
Swindon T	64/65	4		FL
St Georges Budapest				
Hakoah (Aus)				
Sutherland				

HAIG Gordon

Club	Season			Div
Raith R	62/63	19		D1
	63/64	16		D2
	64/65	2		D2
Berwick R	64/65	23		D2
	65/66	31		D2
	66/67	29		D2
	67/68	35		D2
	68/69			D2
	69/70	33		D2
	70/71			D2
	71/72	29	1 1	D2
	72/73	25		D2
	73/74	4	1	D2

HAILSTONES John

Dalkeith Thistle

Club	Season			Div
Stirling A	58/59	14		D1
	59/60	1		D1
	60/61			D2

HAINEY William

Johnstone Burgh

Club	Season			Div
Partick T	61/62	12	2	D1
	62/63	22	4	D1
	63/64	31	11	D1
	64/65	29	10	D1
	65/66	18	2	D1
Dundee U	65/66	9	2	D1
	66/67	23	3 4	D1
	67/68	8	3 2	D1
St Mirren	68/69	13	9 2	D1
Portadown				

HAIR Iain

b. Glasgow 8.8.1954
East Kilbride Burgh

Club	Season			Div
Aberdeen	73/74	18	1	D1
	74/75	26	1 4	D1
	75/76	24	5	P
	76/77	1		P
Montrose	76/77	26	1	D1
	77/78	34		D1
	78/79	30	1 3	D1
	79/80	13		D2
	80/81	19	2	D2

HALL Alexander

Club	Season			Div
Hibernian	46/47	1		D1

HALL Henry Begg

b. Falkirk 22.4.1945
Kirkintilloch Rob Roy

Club	Season			Div
Dundee	64/65			
Stirling A	65/66	29	14	D1
	66/67	22	1 2	D1
	67/68	29	1 3	D1
St Johnstone	68/69	21	19	D1
	69/70	28	1 15	D1
	70/71	31	18	D1
	71/72	26	9	D1
	72/73	34	16	D1
	73/74	28	7	D1
	74/75	17	1 1	D1
Dundee U	75/76	25	1 8	P
	76/77	1	7	P
Forfar A	77/78	37	1	D2
	78/79	25	4 2	D2

HALL James

Club	Season			Div
Queen of the South	51/52	4		D1
	52/53	7		D1
	53/54	2		D1

HALL T

Club	Season			Div
Falkirk	49/50	1		D1

HALLIDAY Chic

Club	Season			Div
Morton	65/66	3		D1

HALLIDAY James

Club	Season	Apps	Sub	Gls	Div
Falkirk	64/65	4		1	D1
	65/66	3			D1
Brechin C	66/67	13	1	1	D2

HALPIN Thomas

Club	Season	Apps	Sub	Gls	Div
Hamilton A	65/66	10			D1
	66/67	28			D2
	67/68	35			D2
	68/69	30		1	D2
	69/70	26	1		D2
	70/71	15		1	D2
Albion R	71/72	13	3		D2
Blantyre Victoria					

HAMILL Arthur
b. 5.4.1939

Club	Season	Apps	Sub	Gls	Div
Brechin C	61/62	3			D2
East Stirlingshire	62/63				D2
	63/64	28		8	D1
ES Clydebank	64/65				D2
East Stirlingshire	65/66	29		7	D2
	66/67	37		1	D2
	67/68	35		1	D2
	68/69			3	D2
	69/70	16	4	2	D2
	70/71			3	D2

HAMILL Charles

Club	Season	Apps	Sub	Gls	Div
Parkhead Jnrs					
Queen of the South	57/58	1			D1

HAMILTON Alexander William
b. Bo'ness 31.1.1939 d. ?.7.1993 Caps: S - 24
Westrigg Bluebell

Club	Season	Apps	Sub	Gls	Div
Dundee	57/58	18			D1
	58/59	15			D1
	59/60	34			D1
	60/61	28			D1
	61/62	34			D1
	62/63	30			D1
	63/64	32		1	D1
	64/65	29			D1
	65/66	22			D1
	66/67	19			D1
Durban U					
East London U					
Addington					

HAMILTON Donald

Club	Season	Apps	Sub	Gls	Div
Hibernian	53/54	17			D1
	54/55	5			D1
Falkirk	55/56	10			D1

HAMILTON George
b. Irvine 7.12.1917 d. Aberdeen 23.5.2001
Caps: S - 5
Irvine Meadow

Club	Season	Apps	Sub	Gls	Div
Queen of the South	37/38	31		9	D1
Aberdeen	38/39	37		17	D1
	46/47	26		17	D1
	47/48	8		2	D1
Heart of Midlothian	47/48	13		6	D1
Aberdeen	48/49	20		10	D1
	49/50	26		9	D1
	50/51	28		17	D1
	51/52	19		13	D1
	52/53	18		15	D1
	53/54	15			D1
	54/55	4		2	D1
Hamilton A	55/56	11		2	D2

HAMILTON Gordon D

Club	Season	Apps	Sub	Gls	Div
Queen's Park	38/39	3			D1
	46/47	11			D1
	47/48				D2
	48/49				D2
	49/50				D2
Morton	50/51	3			D1
	51/52	1			D1

HAMILTON Hugh Hare
b. Newton Mearns 16.6.1942

Club	Season	Apps	Sub	Gls	Div
Falkirk	62/63	2		1	D1
Hartlepools U	63/64	17		4	FL
	64/65	18		3	FL
	65/66	3	1		FL
Scarborough					

HAMILTON Ian

Club	Season	Apps	Sub	Gls	Div
Kirkintilloch Rob Roy					
Ayr U	58/59				D2
	59/60	34			D1
	60/61	16			D1
Queen of the South	61/62				D2
	62/63	3			D1
Falkirk	63/64				D1
East Fife	64/65				D2
	65/66				D2

HAMILTON James
b. Bannockburn 3.2.1951
Dunipace

Club	Season	Apps	Sub	Gls	Div
Aberdeen	68/69	6	1		D1
	69/70	19	3	3	D1
	70/71	5	1	2	D1
East Fife	71/72	30		1	D1
	72/73	33		1	D1
	73/74	17	2	2	D1
	74/75	5	2	1	D1
Dunfermline A					
Peterhead					
Elgin C					

HAMILTON John
b. Larkhall 22.1.1935
Lesmahagow Jnrs

Club	Season	Apps	Sub	Gls	Div
Heart of Midlothian	55/56	22		1	D1
	56/57	26		4	D1
	57/58	4		4	D1
	58/59	27		6	D1
	59/60	27		7	D1
	60/61	20		4	D1
	61/62	27		7	D1
	62/63	33		10	D1
	63/64	34		13	D1
	64/65	32		16	D1
	65/66	26		4	D1
	66/67	15			D1
Watford	67/68	7	1	2	FL

HAMILTON John Turner
b. Glasgow 10.7.1949
Cumbernauld U

Club	Season	Apps	Sub	Gls	Div
Hibernian	69/70	20	2	4	D1
	70/71	8	1	1	D1
	71/72	21	1	6	D1
	72/73	4	4	1	D1
	73/74	4	3	1	D1
Rangers	74/75	2	1		D1
	75/76	22		1	P
	76/77	22	1	3	P
	77/78	3	1		P
Millwall	78/79	1	1		FL
St Johnstone	78/79	18	1	2	D1
	79/80	20	1	3	D1

HAMILTON Richard

Club	Season	Apps	Sub	Gls	Div
Wishaw Jnrs					
Motherwell	47/48				D1
	48/49				D1
	49/50	28			D1
	50/51	7			D1
	51/52	1			D1
	52/53	1			D1
St Mirren	53/54	1			D1

HAMILTON Robert

Club	Season	Apps	Sub	Gls	Div
Baillieston					
Motherwell	74/75	6	1		D1

HAMILTON Robin

Club	Season	Apps	Sub	Gls	Div
St Mirren	54/55	1			D1

HAMILTON Ronald Douglas
b. Kilmarnock 24.4.1945
Saxone Amateurs
Troon Jnrs

Club	Season	Apps	Sub	Gls	Div
Kilmarnock	61/62	4		3	D1
	62/63	11		6	D1
	63/64	4		5	D1
	64/65	28		15	D1
	65/66	13		9	D1
St Mirren	65/66	12		2	D1
	66/67	23		2	D1
	67/68				D2
	68/69				D1
	69/70	10		3	D1
	70/71	26	2	4	D1
Queen of the South	71/72	23		6	D2
	72/73	27	4	9	D2
	73/74	28	6	16	D2
	74/75	1		4	D2

HAMILTON S

Club	Season	Apps	Sub	Gls	Div
Queen's Park	55/56				D2
	56/57	1			D1

HAMILTON William
b. Hamilton 1.9.1918
Blantyre Celtic

Club	Season	Apps	Sub	Gls	Div
Preston NE	37/38				FL
	38/39				FL
	46/47	37			FL
Queen of the South	47/48	8		1	D1
	48/49	27			D1
	49/50	23			D1
	50/51				D2
Hamilton A	50/51	1			D2
Morton	51/52	2			D1

HAMILTON William

Club	Season	Apps	Sub	Gls	Div
Alva BC					
Motherwell	66/67				D1
	67/68	1			D1
	68/69				D2
	69/70		1		D1
	70/71		1		D1
Hakoah (Aus)					

HAMILTON William Murdoch
b. Airdrie 16.2.1938 d. Canada ?.10.1976
Caps: S - 1
Drumpellier Amateurs

Club	Season	Apps	Sub	Gls	Div
Sheffield U	56/57	1			FL
	57/58	8		1	FL
	58/59	19		10	FL
	59/60	37		9	FL
	60/61	14		1	FL
Middlesbrough	60/61	8		1	FL
	61/62	2			FL
Heart of Midlothian	62/63	27		10	D1
	63/64	3		2	D1
Hibernian	63/64	30		10	D1
	64/65	20		5	D1
Aston Villa	65/66	37		9	FL
	66/67	12			FL
Heart of Midlothian	67/68	3	1		D1
	68/69	14	4	7	D1
South Africa					
Ross Co					
Hamilton A	71/72	11		2	D2
Ferranti Thistle					

HANNAH James

Bo'ness U

Stirling A	58/59			D1
	59/60	2		D1
Rothes	60/61			
Airdrieonians	61/62	20		D1
	62/63	25		D1
	63/64	33	2	D1
	64/65	32		D1
	65/66	21	1	D2
St Mirren	66/67	7		D1
	67/68	1		D2
Stranraer	67/68	18	1	D2
	68/69		1	D2
	69/70	32		D2

HANNAH John

Shotts Bon Accord

Queen of the South	52/53			D1
	53/54	1		D1

HANNIGAN Ernest

b. Glasgow 23.1.1943
St Rochs

Queen of the South	61/62				D2
	62/63	33		1	D1
	63/64	31		2	D1
Preston NE	64/65	11			FL
	65/66	29		11	FL
	66/67	42		12	FL
	67/68	15		5	FL
Coventry C	67/68	23		5	FL
	68/69	13	3	1	FL
	69/70	7	1		FL
Torquay U	L 69/70	2			FL
Morton	70/71	29	3	6	D1
New York Cosmos	71	1			NA
Queen of the South	71/72	11			D2
	72/73	2			D2
Raith R	72/73	5		2	D2

HANSEN Allan David

b. Sauchie 13.6.1955 Caps: S - 26
Sauchie Jnrs

Partick T	73/74		1		D1
	74/75	26	3		D1
	75/76	21		2	D1
	76/77	35		4	P
Liverpool	77/78	18	2		FL
	78/79	34		1	FL
	79/80	38		4	FL
	80/81	36			FL
	81/82	35			FL
	82/83	34			FL
	83/84	42		1	FL
	84/85	41			FL
	85/86	41			FL
	86/87	39			FL
	87/88	39		1	FL
	88/89	6			FL
	89/90	31			FL

HANSEN John Angus McDonald

b. Sauchie 3.2.1950 Caps: S - 2
Sauchie BC

Partick T	67/68	2			D1
	68/69	18			D1
	69/70	26	5		D1
	70/71	9	4	1	D2
	71/72	23			D1
	72/73	10	1		D1
	73/74	15	2		D1
	74/75	33		2	D1
	75/76	26		1	D1
	76/77	33	1	2	P
	77/78	3			P

HARDIE James S

b. Glasgow
Ayr Newton R

Queen's Park	46/47	6			D1
	47/48	14		2	D1
	48/49	1			D2
Kilmarnock	49/50	10		2	D2
Third Lanark	50/51				D1
Hamilton A	51/52	2		1	D2

HARKER Christopher Joseph

b. Shiremoor 29.6.1937
Backworth Welfare
West Allotment Celtic

Newcastle U	57/58	1		FL
	58/59			FL
Consett	L 58/59			
Aberdeen	59/60	12		D1
	60/61	8		D1
	61/62	3		D1
Bury	61/62	17		FL
	62/63	42		FL
	63/64	42		FL
	64/65	41		FL
	65/66	23		FL
	66/67	13		FL
Grimsby T	67/68	10		FL
Rochdale	68/69	46		FL
	69/70	46		FL
Stockton				

HARKNESS Samuel

b. Dumfries 23.4.1921
Kello R

Kilmarnock	46/47	2	D1
Airdrieonians	47/48		D1
	48/49		D2
Nithsdale W			
Whitburn Jnrs			

HARLEY Alexander

b. Glasgow 20.4.1936 d. ?.?.1969

Third Lanark	58/59	3		D1
	59/60	16	12	D1
	60/61	33	35	D1
	61/62	33	22	D1
Manchester C	62/63	40	23	FL
Birmingham C	63/64	23	7	FL
	64/65	5	2	FL
Dundee	64/65	10	4	D1
Portadown				

HARLEY Ian

b. Bellshill 3.9.1953
Shotts Bon Accord

Falkirk	71/72	9		3	D1
	72/73				D1
	73/74	18	3	4	D1
Morton	74/75	11	2		D1
	75/76	20	5	5	D1
Cowdenbeath	76/77	33	4	8	D2
	77/78	35	1	15	D2
	78/79	26	6	8	D2
	79/80	11	4	5	D2
Arbroath	79/80	13		5	D1
	80/81	31	1	15	D2
	81/82	20	12	2	D2
	82/83	16	8	6	D2
	83/84	36		18	D2
	84/85	12	8	3	D2
East Stirlingshire	85/86	3	3		D2
Montrose	85/86		3		D1

HARNETT Ian Gerald

b. Broughty Ferry c1927 d. 23.6.2001
Lochee Harp

Queen's Park	46/47	29	1	D1
	47/48	8		D1
	48/49			D2
	49/50			D2
	50/51	1		D2
	51/52	28	1	D2
	52/53	22		D2
	53/54	18		D2
	54/55	29		D2
	55/56	33		D2
	56/57	34		D1
	57/58	32		D1
	58/59	32		D2
	59/60	29		D2
	60/61	8		D2

HARPER Frank

Salts A
Thornliewood U
Fauldhouse U

East Stirlingshire	67/68	8		3	D2
	68/69			8	D2
	69/70	29	1	4	D2
	70/71				D2
Cowdenbeath	70/71	6		2	D1
	71/72				D2
Hamilton A	71/72	19		7	D2

HARPER Ian

Partick T	48/49	4		D1
	49/50			D1
Ayr U	50/51			D2
	51/52			D2
Stirling A	52/53			D2

HARPER Joseph Montgomery

b. Greenock 11.1.1948 Caps: S - 3
Larkfield BC

Morton	64/65	3		1	D1
	65/66	12		6	D1
	66/67	30		29	D2
Huddersfield T	66/67	5		1	FL
	67/68	21	2	3	FL
Morton	68/69	34		25	D1
	69/70	6		4	D1
Aberdeen	69/70	24		6	D1
	70/71	30	1	19	D1
	71/72	34		33	D1
	72/73	13		11	D1
Everton	72/73	20		7	FL
	73/74	20	3	5	FL
Hibernian	73/74	13		9	D1
	74/75	34		12	D1
	75/76	22		5	P
Aberdeen	76/77	34		18	P
	77/78	31		17	P
	78/79	28	3	18	P
	79/80	11	3	3	P
	80/81	1			P
Peterhead					
Keith					

HARRA Hugh

Falkirk	57/58	4		D1
	58/59	2		D1
	59/60			D2
	60/61	1		D2
	61/62	4		D1
Dumbarton	63/64	31	6	D2
	64/65	12		D2
	65/66	27	3	D2
	66/67	28		D2

HARRIS John Robert
b. Glasgow c1923 d. Glasgow 25.8.2000
Queen's Park

Club	Season	Apps	Goals	Div
Aberdeen	46/47	28	10	D1
	47/48	28	4	D1
	48/49	25	1	D1
	49/50	29	1	D1
	50/51	23		D1
	51/52	26	2	D1
	52/53	24		D1
	53/54	5		D1
Airdrieonians				

HARRIS William

Club	Season	Apps	Goals	Div
St Mirren	66/67	11	1	D1

HARROWER James
b. Alva 18.8.1935
Sauchie Jnrs
Kilsyth R
Sauchie Jnrs
Bo'ness U

Club	Season	Apps	Goals	Div
Hibernian	55/56	6		D1
	56/57	12	6	D1
	57/58	18	5	D1
Liverpool	57/58	12	2	FL
	58/59	37	6	FL
	59/60	26	5	FL
	60/61	21	8	FL
Newcastle U	60/61	3		FL
	61/62	2		FL
Falkirk	61/62	12	1	D1
	62/63	9	2	D1
St Johnstone	63/64	24	4	D1
	64/65	18	4	D1
Albion R	65/66	22		D2

HARROWER James Swanson
b. Crossgates 19.6.1924 d. ?.?.1992

Club	Season	Apps	Goals	Div
Dunfermline A	46/47			D2
Third Lanark	47/48	4		D1
	48/49	27	1	D1
	49/50	30		D1
	50/51	29		D1
	51/52	29	1	D1
	52/53	14		D1
	53/54	26		D2
	54/55			D2
Accrington S	54/55	25		FL
	55/56	46		FL
	56/57	32		FL
	57/58	46	1	FL
	58/59	31		FL
	59/60	37	1	FL
	60/61	29		FL

HARVEY Anthony
b. Dundee
Stirling California

Club	Season	Apps	Goals	Div
Dundee	64/65			D1
	65/66	5	1	D1
	66/67			D1
Addington (SAf)				

HARVEY John
Baillieston Jnrs

Club	Season	Apps	Goals	Div
Partick T	51/52	7	1	D1
	52/53	7	1	D1
	53/54	15	3	D1
	54/55	15		D1
	55/56	24	1	D1
	56/57	25	2	D1
	57/58	16	1	D1
	58/59	15	1	D1
	59/60	31		D1
	60/61	28		D1
	61/62	16	1	D1
	62/63	27	1	D1
	63/64	31	2	D1
	64/65	28	1	D1
	65/66	7		D1

HARVEY Robert
Holy Cross BG

Club	Season	Apps	Subs	Goals	Div
Clyde	72/73	2		1	D2
	73/74	2	6		D1
	74/75	16	4	8	D1
	75/76	11	6	3	D1
	76/77	11	5	1	D2
	77/78	2	7		D2

HARVEY William James
b. Clydebank 23.11.1929
Bridgeton Waverley

Club	Season	Apps	Goals	Div
Kilmarnock	54/55	18	3	D1
	55/56	20	2	D1
	56/57	31	5	D1
	57/58	7	1	D1
Dunfermline A	58/59	3		D1
Bradford PA	58/59	18	1	FL
	59/60	8		FL
Arbroath	60/61			D2
Bangor C	61/62			
Inverness Caley	61/62			
	62/63			
Prague				

HASTIE William McKenzie
d. Glasgow 14.11.1995
Gala Fairydean

Club	Season	Apps	Goals	Div
Queen's Park	47/48	5		D1
	48/49	18		D2
	49/50	28	8	D2
	50/51	29	3	D2
	51/52	25		D2
	52/53	25		D2
	53/54	28		D2
	54/55	27		D2
	55/56	35		D2
	56/57	33		D1
	57/58	22		D1
	58/59	7	3	D2

HASTINGS Alex

Club	Season	Apps	Goals	Div
Partick T	59/60	6	2	D1
	60/61	2		D1
Ardeer Thistle				
Airdrieonians	63/64	19	6	D1
	64/65	4		D1
Stranraer *	64/65	11	8	D2

HASTINGS Sam
Nithsdale W

Club	Season	Apps	Subs	Goals	Div
Hamilton A	T 56/57	3		2	D2
	57/58	36		13	D2
	58/59	29		13	D2
	59/60	25		10	D2
	60/61	12		3	D2
	61/62	27		14	D2
	62/63	33		10	D2
	63/64	20		8	D1
Clyde	64/65	33		11	D1
	65/66	29		9	D1
	66/67	29		5	D1
	67/68	33		6	D1
	68/69	31	1	5	D1
	69/70	28	1	4	D1
	70/71	24		1	D1
	71/72	10	3	1	D1
Alloa A	72/73	1			D2
Queen of the South	72/73	6			D2

HATHER John
b. England c1926 d. Co Durham 1.1.1996
Annfield Plain

Club	Season	Apps	Goals	Div
Aberdeen	48/49	14	4	D1
	49/50	17	6	D1
	50/51	10	3	D1
	51/52	10		D1
	52/53	28	14	D1
	53/54	25	7	D1
	54/55	30	9	D1
	55/56	24	10	D1
	56/57	32	7	D1
	57/58	30	9	D1
	58/59	29	7	D1
	59/60	15	2	D1
Horden Colliery				

HAUGH Adam
b. Wishaw
Muirkirk Jnrs

Club	Season	Apps	Goals	Div
Ayr U	55/56			D2
	56/57	25	1	D1
	57/58			D2

HAUGHEY William
b. Glasgow 20.12.1932
Larkhall Thistle

Club	Season	Apps	Goals	Div
Everton	56/57	3	1	FL
	57/58	1		FL
Falkirk	58/59	5	3	D1

HAUGHNEY Michael
b. Paisley 10.12.1926 d. Peoria 22.2.2002
Caps: S - 1
Dalkeith St Davids
Newtongrange Star

Club	Season	Apps	Goals	Div
Celtic	49/50	23	12	D1
	50/51	6	1	D1
Ayr U	L 50/51			D2
Celtic	51/52	1		D1
	52/53	13		D1
	53/54	28	4	D1
	54/55	30	7	D1
	55/56	24	2	D1
	56/57	34	8	D1

HAVERTY Joseph
b. Dublin 17.2.1936 Caps: Ei - 32
Home Farm

Club	Season	Apps	Goals	Div
St Patricks A	53/54			
Drumcondra				
Arsenal	54/55	6		FL
	55/56	8	2	FL
	56/57	28	8	FL
	57/58	15		FL
	58/59	10	3	FL
	59/60	35	8	FL
	60/61	12	4	FL
Blackburn R	61/62	23	1	FL
	62/63	4		FL
Millwall	62/63	35	4	FL
	63/64	33	4	FL
Celtic	T 64/65	1		D1
Bristol R	64/65	13	1	FL
Shelbourne	65/66			
	66/67			
Chicago Spurs	67	16		NA
Kansas City Spurs	68	22	1	NA

HAWKSHAW Ian
Saltcoats V

Club	Season	Apps	Goals	Div
St Johnstone	63/64	11	1	D1
	64/65	8	4	D1
Ayr U	65/66	33	14	D2
	66/67	26	4	D1
	67/68	32	22	D2
Clydebank	68/69		11	D2
East Stirlingshire	69/70	6	1	D2
Montrose	69/70	6	2	D2

HAXTON W

Club	Season	Apps	Goals	Div
Queen of the South	46/47	3		D1

HAY David
b. Paisley 29.1.1948 Caps: S - 27
St Mirins Boys Guild

Club	Season				Div
Celtic	67/68			1	D1
	68/69				D1
	69/70	25			D1
	70/71	27	1	1	D1
	71/72	28			D1
	72/73	21		3	D1
	73/74	25		2	D1
Chelsea	74/75	34			FL
	75/76	27	1	1	FL
	76/77	31		1	FL
	77/78	7			FL
	78/79	8			FL

HAY Hugh

Banks o'Dee

Club	Season				Div
Aberdeen	51/52	2			D1
	52/53	17		8	D1
	53/54	11		6	D1
	54/55				D1
	55/56	6			D1
	56/57	5		5	D1
	57/58	6		4	D1
Dundee U	58/59	14		3	D2
Arbroath	59/60	6		1	D1

HAY Hugh
b. Irvine 6.4.1949

Club	Season				Div
Airdrieonians	70/71	2		1	D1
Stranraer	71/72	29	2	6	D2
	72/73	19	7	4	D2
	73/74	35	1	3	D2
	74/75	36		5	D2
	75/76	23	1	6	D2
	76/77	38		1	D2
	77/78	39			D2
	78/79	38		3	D2
	79/80	30	2	3	D2
	80/81	37		7	D2
	81/82	30	3		D2
	82/83	30		6	D2

HAY Millar A

Club	Season				Div
Queen's Park	64/65	28			D2
	65/66	28		5	D2
	66/67	33		10	D2
	67/68	34		14	D2
	68/69	31		2	D2
Clyde	69/70	11		3	D1
	70/71	18	9	4	D1
	71/72	11	9	1	D1
Hamilton A	72/73	22			D2

HAYES Archibald David Mackie
b. Glasgow 10.6.1953

Club	Season				Div
Morton	69/70	3	1		D1
	70/71	9			D1
	71/72	27			D1
	72/73	30		1	D1
	73/74	34			D1
	74/75	31			D1
	75/76	25			D1
	76/77	37			D1
	77/78	30		2	D1
	78/79	28			P
	79/80	21			P
	80/81	31			P
	81/82	35			P
	82/83	9	1		P
	83/84	4	1		D1
Queen of the South	84/85	6			D2
Partick T	84/85	6			D1
Blantyre Victoria					

HAZEL John
b. Denny
Dunipace Jnrs

Club	Season				Div
Hibernian	70/71	10	1	1	D1
	71/72	19	4	2	D1
	72/73	3	3		D1
	73/74	3	2		D1
Morton	73/74	3			D1
	74/75	17		6	D1
East Stirlingshire	77/78	1			D2
	78/79				D2
Alloa A	79/80	3	2		D2

HAZLETT George
b. Glasgow 10.3.1923
St Marys BG
Blantyre Celtic
Glasgow Perthshire

Club	Season				Div
Celtic	46/47	18		3	D1
	47/48	3			D1
Belfast Celtic	48/49				
Bury	49/50	39		4	FL
	50/51	39		4	FL
	51/52	22		2	FL
Rochdale	52/53				FL
Accrington S	53/54				FL
Guildford C					
Bexleyheath & Welling					

HEAP John

Club	Season				Div
St Mirren	66/67	8			D1
Stranraer	67/68	18			D2
	68/69			1	D2
	69/70	30			D2
	70/71	36			D2
	71/72	35			D2
	72/73	36		2	D2
	73/74	30	3	2	D2
	74/75	25	1		D2
	75/76	7	10		D2
	76/77	4	4		D2

HEDINSSON Atli Thor
b. Iceland
KR Reykjavik

Club	Season				Div
Morton	74/75	1	1		D1

HEGARTY Kevin Michael
b. Edinburgh 30.7.1950
Salvesen BC

Club	Season				Div
Falkirk	67/68				D1
Haddington A					
Heart of Midlothian	69/70				D1
	70/71	13	3	4	D1
Carlisle U	71/72	1	6		FL
East Fife	72/73	34	4	9	D1
	73/74	21	4	4	D1
Morton	73/74	12		1	D1
	74/75	1	10		D1
East Fife	74/75	8	3	2	D2
	75/76	24		8	D1
	76/77	37	1	7	D1
	77/78	34	2	6	D1
	78/79	2	1		D1
Dunfermline A	78/79	22	6	7	D2
	79/80	28	2	2	D1
	80/81	28	1	1	D1
	81/82	29	3	3	D1
	82/83	8		1	D1
Brechin C	L 82/83	3	1		D2
Berwick R	83/84	4	6		D2

HEGARTY Paul Anthony
b. Edinburgh 25.7.1954 Caps: S - 8
Tynecastle BC

Club	Season				Div
Hamilton A	71/72	2			D2
	72/73	36		7	D2
	73/74	31		10	D2
	74/75	12		5	D2
Dundee U	74/75	10	7	4	D1
	75/76	31	2	8	P
	76/77	36		6	P
	77/78	36		4	P
	78/79	36		5	P
	79/80	27			P
	80/81	33		3	P
	81/82	36		3	P
	82/83	36		3	P
	83/84	36		4	P
	84/85	33		2	P
	85/86	36		5	P
	86/87	21	2	4	P
	87/88	40	1	1	P
	88/89	27	2	1	P
	89/90	5			P
St Johnstone	89/90	14		1	D1
Forfar A	90/91	32			D1
	91/92	8		1	D1

HEMPLE Samuel
b. 3.5.1929
Parkhead White Rose
Auchinleck Talbot
Parkhead Jnrs
Rutherglen Glencairn

Club	Season				Div
Celtic	52/53				D1
	53/54	4		2	D1
Albion R	54/55				D2

HENAUGHAN Thomas
b. New Jersey
St Mungos Academy

Club	Season				Div
Queen's Park	49/50				D2
	50/51	9		2	D2
Kilmarnock	51/52	16		3	D2
	52/53	27		6	D2
	53/54	30		13	D2
	54/55	23		5	D1
	55/56	3			D1
Brentford	L 56/57				FL
Kilmarnock	57/58	19		1	D1
	58/59	11		3	D1
	59/60	5			D1
Stirling A	60/61				D2
Morton	60/61				D2

HENDERSON Albert
b. c1930
Aberdeen Lads Club

Club	Season				Div
Dundee	51/52	11		8	D1
	52/53	22		6	D1
	53/54	21		9	D1
	54/55	29		9	D1
	55/56	21		3	D1
	56/57	28			D1
	57/58	26		3	D1
	58/59	30		2	D1
	59/60	18		5	D1
	60/61	11		2	D1
St Mirren	60/61	7		1	D1
	61/62	12		1	D1

HENDERSON Charles

Blairgowrie

Club	Season				Div
Motherwell	46/47	1			D1

HENDERSON George

Wishaw Jnrs
Third Lanark

Club	Season	Apps	Gls	Div
Stirling A	47/48			D2
Dundee U	L 47/48			D2
Stirling A	48/49			D2
Dunfermline A	48/49			D2
St Mirren	49/50	10	5	D1
Stirling A	49/50	6	2	D1
	50/51			D2
	51/52	24	8	D1
	52/53	25	20	D2
Dunfermline A	53/54	20	16	D2
Albion R	53/54	4	1	D2
Alloa A	54/55			D2
Coltness U				
Stirling A	55/56	4		D1

HENDERSON J

Club	Season	Apps	Gls	Div
Airdrieonians	68/69	1		D1

HENDERSON James

Club	Season	Apps	Gls	Div
Falkirk	46/47	21	7	D1
	47/48	27	5	D1
	48/49	4	3	D1

HENDERSON James

Linfield

Club	Season	Apps	Gls	Div
Heart of Midlothian	48/49	2		D1
	49/50	4		D1
	50/51			D1
Stirling A	51/52	19		D1

HENDERSON James
b. c1936
L Pieters

Club	Season	Apps	Gls	Div
Partick T	52/53	2		D1
	53/54	2		D1
	54/55	3		D1
	55/56			D1
	56/57			D1
	57/58	2		D1
	58/59	1		D1
Queen of the South	58/59	6		D1
Worcester C	59/60			
	60/61			
	61/62			
	62/63			
Kidderminster H				

HENDERSON John

Club	Season	Apps	Gls	Div
Clyde	52/53	4		D1
Airdrieonians	53/54	3		D1

HENDERSON John Swinton Pryde
b. Glasgow 13.10.1923

Club	Season	Apps	Gls	Div
Third Lanark	46/47	8	5	D1
	47/48	1		D1
	48/49	16	4	D1
	49/50	30	5	D1
	50/51	17	2	D1
	51/52	30	12	D1
	52/53	19	10	D1
Rotherham U	53/54	22	2	FL
	54/55	25	5	FL
Leeds U	54/55	9	3	FL
	55/56	6	1	FL

HENDERSON Joseph
b. Cleland 21.12.1924
Hibernian

Club	Season	Apps	Gls	Div
Albion R	46/47			D2
	47/48			D2
	48/49	18		D1
Northampton T	49/50			FK
Stenhousemuir	50/51			D2
	51/52			D2
	52/53	30		D2
Accrington S	53/54	14		FL
Alloa A	54/55			D2
Canterbury C				

HENDERSON Joseph

Arthurlie Jnrs

Club	Season	Apps	Gls	Div
St Johnstone	60/61	1		D1
	61/62	13	1	D1
	62/63			D2
Forfar A				

HENDERSON N

Club	Season	Apps	Gls	Div
St Mirren	46/47	4		D1

HENDERSON R

Club	Season	Apps	Gls	Div
Raith R	49/50	2		D1

HENDERSON Robert

Club	Season	Apps	Gls	Div
Falkirk	46/47	22		D1
	47/48	14		D1
	48/49	29		D1
	49/50	26		D1
	50/51	16		D1
Dundee	51/52			D1
	52/53	3		D1

HENDERSON Robert
b. Maryhill
Glasgow Perthshire

Club	Season	Apps	Gls	Div
Partick T	37/38	2		D1
	38/39	7		D1
	46/47			
	47/48	25		D1
	48/49	20		D1
	49/50	14		D1
Dundee	51/52	14		D1
	52/53	22		D1
	53/54	10		D1
	54/55	2		D1
	55/56	4		D1
Dundee U	56/57	1		D2

HENDERSON Ross

Club	Season	Apps	Gls	Div
Morton	46/47	17	10	D1
	47/48	14	2	D1
	48/49	6		D1
Ayr U	49/50	25	4	D2

HENDERSON Roy
b. Wishaw ?.?.1923 d. Dumfries 11.1.1997
Carluke Amateurs
Lanark U
Third Lanark

Club	Season	Apps	Gls	Div
Queen of the South	46/47	14		D1
	47/48	19		D1
	48/49	30		D1
	49/50	29		D1
	50/51			D2
	51/52	29		D1
	52/53	30		D1
	53/54	30		D1
	54/55	30		D1
	55/56	34		D1
	56/57	4		D1
	57/58	12		D1

HENDERSON Samuel
b. Garngad 25.11.1944
St Mungos Academy
Ashfield

Club	Season	Apps	Gls	Div
Celtic	61/62			D1
	62/63			D1
	63/64	2		D1
Morton	L 63/64			D2
Celtic	64/65			D1
	65/66			D1
	66/67			D1
	67/68			D1
Stirling A	67/68	15	1	D1
	68/69		1	D2
	69/70	30	2	D2
	70/71		3	D2
	71/72	22	1	D2
	72/73	23	3	D2
Clydebank	73/74	34	2	D2
	74/75	18	2 1	D2
	75/76	19		D2

HENDERSON Thomas

Club	Season	Apps	Gls	Div
Falkirk	62/63	17	3	D1
	63/64	5	1	D1

HENDERSON Thomas Wedlock
b. Larkhall 25.7.1943
Celtic

Club	Season	Apps	Gls	Div
Heart of Midlothian	60/61	7	1	D1
	61/62			D1
St Mirren	61/62	16	2	D1
	62/63	4	1	D1
Leeds U	62/63	20	1	FL
	63/64	2	1	FL
	64/65	2		FL
Bury	65/66	7	1	FL
Swindon T	65/66	11	3	FL
Stockport Co	66/67	17	2 4	FL

HENDERSON William
b. Baillieston 24.1.1944 Caps: S - 29
Edinburgh A

Club	Season	Apps	Gls	Div
Rangers	60/61	3		D1
	61/62	15	1	D1
	62/63	27	5	D1
	63/64	30	3	D1
	64/65	18	1	D1
	65/66	28	3	D1
	66/67	32	8	D1
	67/68	20	2	D1
	68/69	32	5	D1
	69/70	27	4	D1
	70/71	29	3	D1
	71/72	13	2 1	D1
Sheffield W	72/73	27	2 4	FL
Miami Toros	73	7		NA
Sheffield W	73/74	15	4 1	FL
Hong Kong Rangers				

HENDERSON William

Motherwell

Club	Season	Apps	Gls	Div
St Mirren	70/71	1		D1
Stenhousemuir	71/72	17	1	D2
	72/73	29		D2
	73/74	5	4	D2

HENRY Gordon
b. Troon 9.10.1930

Club	Season	Apps	Gls	Div
St Mirren	53/54	5		D1
	54/55	1		D1
	55/56	13	4	D1
Aldershot	56/57	11	1	FL
	57/58	37	6	FL
	58/59	30	2	FL
	59/60	17		FL
	60/61	12	3	FL
	61/62	7		FL
	62/63	37	3	FL
	63/64	24		FL
Salisbury C				

HENRY Hamilton Stillic
b. Troon 7.7.1916 d. ?.?.1957
Troon A
Glenafton A

Club	Season	Apps	Sub	Gls	Div
Kilmarnock	36/37	3		2	D1
	37/38	4		2	D1
	38/39	5		3	D1
	46/47	8		4	D1
Arbroath	47/48				D2

HENRY James
b. Dundee 24.2.1949
Carnoustie Jnrs

Club	Season	Apps	Sub	Gls	Div
Dundee U	67/68				D1
	68/69				D1
	69/70	24		2	D1
	70/71	29	2	1	D1
	71/72	19		1	D1
	72/73	12		3	D1
	73/74	8			D1
Aberdeen	73/74	6			D1
	74/75	11			D1
	75/76	1			P
San Antonio Thunder	76	18			NA
Forfar A	76/77	4			D2
Team Hawaii	77	24		5	NA
Forfar A	77/78	13		1	D2
	78/79	29	1	2	D2
	79/80	1		1	D2

HEPBURN Anthony
b. 22.5.1932
Clydebank Jnrs

Club	Season	Apps	Sub	Gls	Div
Celtic	52/53	6			D1
	53/54				D1
Dumbarton	L 53/54	15		6	D2
Ayr U	54/55				D2
Distillery	55/56				
	56/57				
Morton	57/58				D2
Boston U					

HEPBURN J

Club	Season	Apps	Sub	Gls	Div
Queen of the South	46/47	2			D1

HEPBURN John
b. Paisley 10.3.1921

Club	Season	Apps	Sub	Gls	Div
Clyde	46/47	18		3	D1
	47/48	9			D1
Morton	47/48	13			D1
	48/49	5			D1
	49/50	4			D2
	50/51				D1
Workington	51/52	1			FL

HEPBURN Michael

Club	Season	Apps	Sub	Gls	Div
Morton	72/73			1	D1
	73/74	10		1	D1
	74/75	1			D1
	75/76	1			D1

HERD George
b. Gartcosh 6.5.1936 Caps: S - 5
Gartcosh Thistle
Inverness Thistle

Club	Season	Apps	Sub	Gls	Div
Queen's Park	56/57	25		6	D1
Clyde	57/58	30		1	D1
	58/59	30		6	D1
	59/60	32		11	D1
	60/61	19		2	D1
Sunderland	60/61	1			FL
	61/62	32		10	FL
	62/63	40		4	FL
	63/64	39		13	FL
	64/65	39		8	FL
	65/66	37	1	5	FL
	66/67	35	2	3	FL
	67/68	28	8	2	FL
	68/69	24		1	FL
	69/70				FL
Hartlepool U	70/71	10		5	FL

HERMISTON James
b. Edinburgh 30.9.1947
Bonnyrigg Rose

Club	Season	Apps	Sub	Gls	Div
Aberdeen	66/67	4			D1
	67/68	6			D1
	68/69	14			D1
	69/70	26		2	D1
	70/71	31		1	D1
	71/72	33		1	D1
	72/73	33		2	D1
	73/74	33		1	D1
	74/75	13	2	3	D1
Grange Thistle					
Brisbane					

HERNON Gerry
Ashfield

Club	Season	Apps	Sub	Gls	Div
Dundee U	66/67	1		1	D1
	67/68				
Stranraer					

HERON Brian
b. Glasgow 19.6.1948
Baillieston

Club	Season	Apps	Sub	Gls	Div
Rangers	69/70	7			D1
Motherwell	69/70	8		2	D1
	70/71	30		5	D1
	71/72	30		12	D1
	72/73	7		1	D1
Dumbarton	72/73	9	1	2	D1
	73/74	24	2	8	D1
Oxford U	74/75	30	2	7	FL
	75/76	7		1	FL
	76/77	3	1		FL
Scunthorpe U	77/78	20	5	1	FL

HERON Gilbert
b. Kingston, Jamaica 9.4.1922
Detroit Wolverines
Chicago Sting
Detroit Corinthians

Club	Season	Apps	Sub	Gls	Div
Celtic	51/52	1			D1
Third Lanark	52/53				D1
Kidderminster H	53/54				
Detroit Corinthians					

HERON Thomas Russell Ferrie
b. Irvine 31.3.1936

Club	Season	Apps	Sub	Gls	Div
Queen's Park	56/57	5		1	D1
Kilmarnock					
Portadown					
Manchester U	57/58	1			FL
	58/59				FL
	59/60	1			FL
	60/61				FL
York C	61/62	44			FL
	62/63	39		3	FL
	63/64	46		3	FL
	64/65	46			FL
	65/66	17			FL
Altrincham					
Droylsden					

HERRIOT James
b. Airdrie 20.12.1939 Caps: S - 8
Douglasdale

Club	Season	Apps	Sub	Gls	Div
Dunfermline A	58/59				D1
	59/60				D1
	60/61	12			D1
	61/62	1			D1
	62/63	18			D1
	63/64	30			D1
	64/65	33			D1
Birmingham C	65/66	35			FL
	66/67	42			FL
	67/68	40			FL
	68/69	38			FL
	69/70	26			FL
Mansfield T	L 70/71	5			FL
Hibernian	71/72	34			D1
	72/73	23			D1
St Mirren	73/74	25			D2
	74/75	6			D2
Partick T	74/75				D1
	75/76				D1
Morton	L 75/76	1			D1
Dunfermline A	76/77				D2
Morton	76/77	3			D1

HERRON Desmond
Duntocher Hibs

Club	Season	Apps	Sub	Gls	Div
Aberdeen	60/61	1			D1
	61/62	2		1	D1
Ayr U	62/63				D2
	63/64	6			D2
Hillingdon B					
Arbroath	T 65/66				D2
Montrose	65/66	22		5	D2
Dumbarton	66/67	8	1		D2
East Stirlingshire	67/68	2		1	D2

HEWITT Michael A
b. Glasgow 14.7.1944

Club	Season	Apps	Sub	Gls	Div
Queen's Park	67/68	14			D2
	68/69	9			D2
	69/70	30			D2
Dundee	70/71	5			D1
	71/72	31			D1
	72/73	5			D1
	73/74	1			D1
Tampa Bay Rowdies	75	10			NA

HEWITT William
Cadder Juveniles

Club	Season	Apps	Sub	Gls	Div
Partick T	46/47	17			D1
	47/48	14			D1
	48/49	19		1	D1
	49/50	26		1	D1
	50/51	11			D1
	51/52	3		1	D1

HEWKINS Kenneth John Robert
b. Pretoria 30.10.1929 Caps: S Afr

Club	Season	Apps	Sub	Gls	Div
Clyde	49/50	15			D1
South Africa	50/51				
	51/52				
	52/53				
	53/54				
Clyde	54/55	15			D1
	55/56	4			D1
Fulham	55/56	6			FL
	56/57	5			FL
	57/58	4			FL
	58/59	5			FL
	59/60	3			FL
	60/61	11			FL
	61/62	4			FL

HEWLETT James

Club	Season	Apps	Sub	Gls	Div
Third Lanark	62/63	1			D1

HIGGINS

Club	Season	Apps	Sub	Gls	Div
Raith R	57/58	2			D1
	58/59	3			D1
	59/60	1			D1

HIGGINS Anthony
b. Glasgow 3.6.1954
Kilsyth St Patricks

Club	Season	Apps	Sub	Goals	Div
Hibernian	72/73	11		3	D1
	73/74	5	3	2	D1
	74/75	5	1	3	D1
	75/76	1	3		P
	76/77	4	1	2	P
	77/78	24		7	P
	78/79	21	2	4	P
	79/80	20	2	2	P
Partick T	79/80	11	1		P
	80/81	21		7	P
	81/82	14	9	2	P
Morton	82/83	3	2		P
	83/84	1	4		D1
Stranraer	84/85	4	6	4	D2
	85/86	15	8	3	D2
	86/87	7	3	2	D2

HIGGINS Charles
b. Bellshill 12.5.1921
Arbroath

Club	Season	Apps	Goals	Div
Chester	46/47	11		FL
Airdrieonians	47/48	8		D1
Motherwell	49/50	18		D1
	50/51	3		D1
	51/52	2		D1
	52/53	4		D1
	53/54	3		D2

HIGGINS Hugh

Club	Season	Apps	Goals	Div
Hibernian	56/57	8		D1
	57/58			D1
Third Lanark	L 57/58	18	3	D1
Hibernian	58/59	2		D1
Dunfermline A	58/59	7	1	D1

HIGGINS John
b. Uddingston 7.1.1933 d. Glasgow 8.6.1994
St Johns Uddingston BG

Club	Season	Apps	Goals	Div
Celtic	49/50			D1
	50/51			D1
	51/52			D1
	52/53			D1
	53/54	14	8	D1
	54/55	14	9	D1
	55/56	7	1	D1
	56/57	19	10	D1
	57/58			D1
	58/59	10	3	D1
Queen of the South	59/60			D2

HIGGINS John Wilson
b. Kilmarnock 27.1.1933

Club	Season	Apps	Goals	Div
Hibernian	54/55	11		D1
	55/56	1		D1
St Mirren	57/58	22		D1
	58/59	1		D1
Swindon T	59/60	27		FL
	60/61	1		FL
Ayr U	T 61/62	1		D2

HIGGINS Laurence

Club	Season	Apps	Goals	Div
Hibernian	50/51	1		D1

HIGGINS William
b. Edinburgh 15.3.1940
Dalkeith Thistle

Club	Season	Apps	Goals	Div
Heart of Midlothian	57/58	1		D1
	58/59	2		D1
	59/60	21	3	D1
	60/61	26		D1
	61/62	28	3	D1
	62/63	31	3	D1
	63/64	26		D1
	64/65	32	1	D1
	65/66	18	1	D1
	66/67	8		D1
Durban C	67/68			
	68/69			
Dundee U	69/70			D1

HILL Alistair Greenwood
b. Glasgow 25.4.1934

Club	Season	Apps	Goals	Div
Clyde	52/53	4		D1
	53/54	20	3	D1
	54/55	26	13	D1
	55/56	18	2	D1
	56/57			D2
	57/58	3	2	D1
Dundee	58/59	16	3	D1
	59/60	7	1	D1
Bristol C	59/60	3		FL
Stirling A	59/60	9	2	D1
Falkirk	60/61	2		D2

HILL George
b. c1921 d. ?.10.2002
Dundee NE

Club	Season	Apps	Goals	Div
Dundee	46/47	18	4	D2
	47/48	24	2	D1
	48/49	18	3	D1
	49/50	17	2	D1
	50/51	15	3	D1
	51/52	12	2	D1
	52/53	10	1	D1
	53/54	15	1	D1
	54/55	10		D1
East Fife	54/55	7		D1

HILL George D
b. Kilmarnock
Dalry Thistle

Club	Season	Apps	Goals	Div
Kilmarnock	54/55			D1
	55/56			D1
	56/57	1		D1
	57/58	1		D1
Ayr U	L 57/58			D2

HILLEY David
b. Glasgow 20.12.1938
Muirend Amateurs
Jordanhill
Pollok Jnrs

Club	Season	Apps	Sub	Goals	Div
Third Lanark	58/59	20		9	D1
	59/60	31		7	D1
	60/61	34		16	D1
	61/62	32		6	D1
Newcastle U	62/63	42		6	FL
	63/64	38		6	FL
	64/65	34		12	FL
	65/66	42		5	FL
	66/67	30		2	FL
	67/68	8	3		FL
Nottingham F	67/68	16	4	3	FL
	68/69	17	9	3	FL
	69/70	37		8	FL
	70/71	2	3		FL
Highlands Park					
Hellenic					
Scarborough	75/76				
South Shields	76/77				
Bedlington Terriers	77/78				

HILLEY Ian

Club	Season	Apps	Goals	Div
Third Lanark	59/60	5	3	D1

HINDMARSH John
Bedlington Mechanics

Club	Season	Apps	Goals	Div
Queen of the South	58/59	3		D1

HINSHELWOOD John

Club	Season	Apps	Goals	Div
Airdrieonians	50/51	1		D1

HINSHELWOOD William
b. Ashgill
Dtonehouse Violet

Club	Season	Apps	Goals	Div
Morton	49/50			D2
	50/51	2		D1
	51/52	1		D1
	52/53	1		D2
	53/54	17	2	D2
	54/55			D2
	55/56			D2
	56/57			D2
	57/58			D2
	58/59			D2
Hamilton A	59/60	13		D2
	60/61	17		D2

HINSHELWOOD William Douglas
b. Chapelhall 11.5.1935
Larkhall Thistle

Club	Season	Apps	Goals	Div
Airdrieonians	61/62	8	1	D1
Tonbridge	62/63			
Hartlepools U	63/64	17	3	FL
Hamilton A	64/65	36	3	D2
	65/66	14		D1

HISLOP Thomas
b. Stirling ?.?.1947
Clackmannan

Club	Season	Apps	Sub	Goals	Div
Raith R	67/68	24			D1
	68/69	17	1		D1
	69/70	16	1		D1
	70/71			1	D2
	71/72	32		3	D2
	72/73	30	1		D2
	73/74	27		2	D2
	74/75	26		1	D2

HODGE Adam

Club	Season	Apps	Goals	Div
Alloa A	63/64	31		D2
	64/65	35		D2
	65/66	35		D2
	66/67	36		D2
	67/68	36		D2
	68/69			D2
Arbroath	68/69	17		D1
	69/70	28		D2

HODGE Lindsay J

Club	Season	Apps	Goals	Div
Queen's Park	46/47	8	1	D1
	47/48			D1
	48/49			D2
Ayr U	49/50	8	2	D2
	50/51			D2
Albion R	51/52			D2
	52/53	22	4	D2
	53/54	20	4	D2
	54/55			D2

HOEY James
Dumbarton

Club	Season	Apps	Goals	Div
Stirling A	47/48			D2
	48/49			D2
	49/50	4		D1

HOGAN Joseph
Newtongrange Star

Club	Season	Apps	Goals	Div
Partick T	55/56	3		D1
	56/57	16	2	D1
	57/58	8		D1
	58/59	30		D1
	59/60	23		D1
	60/61	22	4	D1
	61/62	22		D1
	62/63	21	1	D1
	63/64	18	1	D1
	64/65	27	7	D1
	65/66	9	4	D1
	66/67	1		D1

HOGG David

Tynecastle BC

Club	Season				Div
Hibernian	63/64	2			D1
	64/65	1			D1
	65/66	8		1	D1
	66/67				D1
	67/68				D1
Dundee U	68/69	24	7	6	D1
	69/70	13	1		D1
Berwick R	70/71				D2
Hamilton A	71/72	5	1		D2
Alloa A	72/73	15	1	2	D2

HOGG James

Preston A

Club	Season			Div
Aberdeen	56/57	8		D1
	57/58	27		D1
	58/59	32		D1
	59/60	34		D1
	60/61	14	1	D1
	61/62	18		D1
	62/63	34		D1
	63/64	31		D1
	64/65	15		D1

Inverness Caley

HOGG Robert

Hibernian

Club	Season				Div
Motherwell	67/68	5	2	2	D1

HOGG Robert Brown

b. Larkhall 10.5.1914 d. Paisley 15.4.1975
Caps: S - 1
Larkhall Academy
Royal Albert

Club	Season		Div
Celtic	31/32		D1
	32/33	18	D1
	33/34	38	D1
	34/35	36	D1
	35/36	38	D1
	36/37	35	D1
	37/38	38	D1
	38/39	38	D1
	46/47	26	D1
	47/48	5	D1
Alloa A	48/49		D2

HOGG William

Petershill

Club	Season			Div
Aberdeen	56/57			D1
	57/58	13	4	D1
Rangers	58/59	2	1	D1

HOGGAN Henry Wilson

b. Falkirk 17.7.1948
Linlithgow Rose

Club	Season				Div
Falkirk	68/69	12	4		D1
	69/70	30	1	4	D2
	70/71	28	2	4	D1
	71/72	32		3	D1
	72/73	28	2	3	D1
	73/74	25		3	D1
	74/75	7		3	D2
Dundee	74/75	25		5	D1
	75/76	16	4	5	P
	76/77	23	3	2	D1
	77/78		1		D1
Alloa A	L 77/78	10			D1
Stenhousemuir	77/78	1			D2
Falkirk	78/79	29	4	1	D2
	79/80	17	4		D2
	80/81	34		2	D1
	81/82	39		4	D1
	82/83	28		4	D1

HOLLORAN Thomas

Club	Season		Div
Third Lanark	64/65	7	D1

HOLLYWOOD Ian

Lanark U

Club	Season		Div
Queen of the South	53/54	6	D1
	54/55	1	D1

HOLMES Robert

b. Coatbridge
Campsie Black Watch
Kilsyth R

Club	Season			Div
St Mirren	54/55	26	4	D1
	55/56	27	10	D1
	56/57	29	8	D1
	57/58			D1
	58/59	2		D1

HOLT David Duff

b. Glasgow 3.1.1936
Glentyan Thistle
Newhill Amateurs
Lugar Boswell Thistle

Club	Season			Div
Queen's Park	57/58	18	1	D1
	58/59	15	1	D2
	59/60	28		D2
Heart of Midlothian	60/61	21		D1
	61/62	34		D1
	62/63	32		D1
	63/64	29		D1
	64/65	32		D1
	65/66	21		D1
	66/67	19		D1
	67/68	18	1	D1
	68/69	24		D1
Partick T	69/70	19		D1

HOLT J

Club	Season		Div
Queen of the South	46/47	9	D1

HOLT John W

b. Dundee 21.11.1956
Invergowrie BC

Club	Season				Div
Dundee U	71/72				D1
	72/73				D1
	73/74	2	1		D1
	74/75				D1
	75/76	13	3		P
	76/77	4	4		P
	77/78	13	2	3	P
	78/79	26	1	3	P
	79/80	16	1	4	P
	80/81	22	2		P
	81/82	26	2	1	P
	82/83	18	7	4	P
	83/84	26	6	2	P
	84/85	23	2		P
	85/86	20	7		P
	86/87	15	3		P
	87/88	5	1		P
Dunfermline A	87/88	35		1	P
	88/89	13		1	D1
Dundee	88/89	10	1		P
	89/90	2			P
	90/91	4	4		D1
Forfar A	90/91	14	1		D1
	91/92	36			D1
Deveronvale	92/93				
Montrose	93/94		1		D2

HOLTEN Leif

b. Denmark

Club	Season		Div
Morton	64/65	1	D1

HOLTON Patrick Carr

b. Hamilton 23.12.1935
Cadzow BG
Burnbank A
Douglas Water Thistle

Club	Season			Div
Hamilton A	54/55	5		D2
	55/56	15		D2
Motherwell	56/57	33		D1
	57/58	23		D1
	58/59	13		D1
Chelsea	58/59	1		FL
	59/60			FL
Southend U	60/61	11		FL
St Johnstone	61/62	2		D1
Hamilton A	62/63	27		D2
	63/64	14	1	D2
	64/65	36		D2
	65/66	31		D1
	66/67	9		D2
	67/68	8	2	D2

HONEYMAN Graham

b. Methil 30.5.1953
Ladybank V
Frances Colliery

Club	Season				Div
East Fife	69/70	1		1	D2
	70/71			10	D2
	71/72	27	4	3	D1
	72/73	15	6	5	D1
	73/74	6	3		D1
	74/75	12	15	2	D2
	75/76	9	4	2	D1
West Adelaide Hellas	76/77				
	77/78				
Dundee U	78/79	2	1		P
West Adelaide Hellas					

HOOD Henry Anthony

b. Glasgow 3.10.1944
Campsie Black Watch
St Rochs

Club	Season				Div
Queen's Park	61/62				D2
Brunswick BC					
Clyde	62/63	15		5	D1
	63/64	36		32	D2
	64/65	11		4	D1
Sunderland	64/65	24		8	FL
	65/66				FL
	66/67	7		1	FL
Clyde	66/67	27		10	D1
	67/68	34		13	D1
	68/69	26		7	D1
Celtic	68/69	7		5	D1
	69/70	25	3	8	D1
	70/71	27	3	22	D1
	71/72	24		11	D1
	72/73	22	7	12	D1
	73/74	28	3	7	D1
	74/75	21	6	8	D1
	75/76	7	7	1	P
San Antonio Thunder	76	20		10	NA
Motherwell	76/77	6	9		P
Queen of the South	77/78	31	1	4	D1

HOOD James

b. Kilwinning
Claremont Amateurs
Irvine Meadow

Club	Season			Div
Kilmarnock	46/47	21		D1
	47/48	29		D2
	48/49	28		D2
	49/50	19		D2
	50/51	13	5	D2
	51/52	29	1	D2
	52/53	22		D2
	53/54	20	1	D2
	54/55	9	2	D1

HOOD Neil
b. 30.6.1950
Annbank U

Club	Season				Div
Ayr U	69/70	13	7	7	D1
	70/71		1		D1
Queen of the South	71/72	25		13	D2
Hamilton A	72/73	28	5	20	D2
	73/74	19	14	13	D2
	74/75	20	15	11	D2
Clyde	75/76	20		14	D1
	76/77	33		16	D2
	77/78	38	1	21	D2
	78/79	30	4	7	D1
	79/80	15	8	11	D1
Stranraer	79/80	11		6	D2
	80/81	13	5	4	D2
Clyde	81/82	3	12	2	D2

HOPE J

Club	Season				Div
Queen of the South	46/47	2			D1
	47/48	2			D1

HOPPER Niall

Club	Season				Div
Queen's Park	55/56	19		6	D2
	56/57	5			D1
	57/58	2			D1
	58/59	1			D2
	59/60	29		7	D2
	60/61	29		10	D2
	61/62	31		6	D2
	62/63	14		1	D2
	63/64	22		3	D2
	64/65	32		8	D2
	65/66	23		3	D2
	66/67	32		13	D2
	67/68	26		2	D2
	68/69	17		1	D2
	69/70	4			D2

HORN Ian
Arthurlie

Club	Season				Div
Hamilton A	65/66	16		3	D1
	66/67	23	1	5	D2
	67/68	24	3	5	D2

Renfrew Jnrs

HORN William
b. Glasgow 13.5.1938
Kilmarnock Amateurs
Shettleston
Kirkintilloch Rob Roy

Club	Season				Div
Kilmarnock	56/57				D1
	57/58				D1
	58/59				D1
Brentford	L 58/59	1			FL
Kilmarnock	59/60	6			D1
Third Lanark	60/61				D1
Coleraine	61/62				
	62/63				
	63/64				
Third Lanark	64/65	3			D1
Dumbarton	64/65	4			D2
	65/66				D2
Clydebank	66/67	3			D2
Raith R	66/67	6			D2

HORSBURGH John James
b. Edinburgh 17.11.1936
Penicuik Jnrs

Club	Season				Div
Dundee	59/60	1			D1
	60/61	4			D1
Oldham A	61/62	1			FL

HOSIE James England
b. Aberdeen 3.4.1940

Club	Season				Div
Aberdeen	59/60	2			D1
	60/61	4			D1
	61/62	4			D1
Barnsley	62/63	37			FL

Ross Co

HOSIE Matthew

Club	Season				Div
Airdrieonians	61/62	9		1	D1
	62/63	7			D1

HOTSON John
Gairdoch U

Club	Season				Div
St Johnstone	72/73	14		1	D1
	73/74	17	5	1	D1
	74/75	5	2		D1
	75/76	13	4	1	P
Morton	76/77	10	9	1	D1

HOULISTON William
b. Dumfries 4.4.1921 d. 10.2.1999 Caps: S - 3
Crichton Institute

Club	Season				Div
Queen of the South	46/47	18		9	D1
	47/48	28		17	D1
	48/49	25		18	D1
	49/50	18		7	D1
	50/51				D2
	51/52	8		2	D1
Berwick R	52/53				D3
Third Lanark	53/54	1			D2

HOUSTON Douglas A
b. Glasgow 13.4.1943
Giffnock North

Club	Season				Div
Queen's Park	60/61	29		8	D2
	61/62	27		7	D2
Dundee	62/63	17		4	D1
	63/64	8			D1
	64/65	5			D1
	65/66	15		3	D1
	66/67	11		1	D1
	67/68	25		1	D1
	68/69	32			D1
	69/70	30		2	D1
	70/71	32	1		D1
	71/72	28			D1
	72/73	33		5	D1
Rangers	73/74	9	1		D1
Dundee U	73/74	6			D1
	74/75	25	1	3	D1
	75/76	33		2	P
	76/77	20	1		P
St Johnstone	77/78	39			D1
	78/79	7	1		D1

HOUSTON Hugh
St Rochs

Club	Season				Div
Falkirk	64/65	15		2	D1

HOUSTON Joseph
b. Wishaw 27.2.1926
Newarthill Hearts

Club	Season				Div
Dunfermline A	49/50	24			D2
	50/51				D2
Aldershot	51/52	22			FL
	52/53	25			FL
Hamilton A	53/54	19			D1
	54/55	29			D2
	55/56	3			D2
Stirling A	55/56	8			D1
Morton					

HOUSTON Liam
Vale of Leven

Club	Season				Div
Clyde	71/72	4	1		D1
	72/73	33		5	D2
	73/74	3	2		D1
Clydebank	74/75	4	6		D2

HOUSTON Robert Joseph
b. Glasgow 23.1.1952
Rutherglen Glencairn

Club	Season				Div
Partick T	72/73	9			D1
	73/74	31	2	2	D1
	74/75	33		2	D1
	75/76	22		2	D1
	76/77	18	2	1	P
	77/78	28	4	7	P
	78/79	31	2	4	P
	79/80	3	1		P
Kilmarnock	79/80	24	1	6	P
	80/81	14	1		P
Morton	80/81	3	5		P
	81/82	19	6	4	P
	82/83	35	1	1	P
	83/84	37		3	D1

HOWIE Hugh
b. Glasgow 14.2.1924 d. 14.1.1958 Caps: S - 1
Hallside Juveniles
Newton Jnrs

Club	Season				Div
Hibernian	46/47	29			D1
	47/48	17			D1
	48/49	7			D1
	49/50	6			D1
	50/51	14			D1
	51/52	30			D1
	52/53	27			D1
	53/54	9			D1

HOWIESON Robert
Leeds U

Club	Season				Div
Dundee U	60/61	13			D1
	61/62	8		2	D1
	62/63	15		1	D1
	63/64	24		2	D1
	64/65	7		1	D1
Motherwell	65/66	3			D1

HOWITT Robert Gibb
b. Glasgow 15.7.1929
Vale of Clyde

Club	Season				Div
Partick T	48/49	3			D1
	49/50	25		4	D1
	50/51	7		1	D1
	51/52				D1
	52/53	24		14	D1
	53/54	25		9	D1
	54/55	26		7	D1
Sheffield U	55/56	40		14	FL
	56/57	27		13	FL
	57/58	22		4	FL
Stoke C	58/59	27		10	FL
	59/60	21		4	FL
	60/61	35			FL
	61/62	40			FL
	62/63	10			FL

HOWLEY Frank
Brae Thistle *
Thorniewood U *

Club	Season				Div
Hamilton A *	T 59/60	1			D1
Albion R	59/60	8			D1

Third Lanark

HUBBARD John Gaulton
b. S Africa 16.12.1930 Caps: S Afr

Club	Season				Div
Rangers	49/50	2			D1
	50/51	8		2	D1
	51/52	1			D1
	52/53	24			D1
	53/54	15		1	D1
	54/55	23		14	D1
	55/56	34		17	D1
	56/57	33		15	D1
	57/58	24		18	D1
	58/59	8		10	D1
Bury	59/60	43		9	FL
	60/61	44		17	FL
	61/62	22		3	FL
Ayr U	62/63				D2
	63/64	25		2	D2

HUDSON Ernest

Derby Co

Club	Season	App	Sub	Gls	Div
East Fife	48/49	3			D1
	49/50	2			D1
	50/51				D1
	51/52	1			D1

HUDSON Raymond Wilfred
b. Gateshead 24.3.1955

Club	Season	App	Sub	Gls	Div
Newcastle U	72/73				FL
	73/74	1			FL
	74/75	1			FL
Morton	L 74/75	4			D1
Newcastle U	75/76	7		2	FL
	76/77	4		1	FL
	77/78	4		1	FL
Fort Lauderdale Strike	78	29		7	NA
	79	23		6	NA
	80	31		11	NA
	81	16		3	NA
	82	22		6	NA
	83	30		5	NA
Brighton & HA	83/84				FL
Solingen					
Minnesota Strikers	84	21		2	NA
Edmonton					

HUGHES James

Club	Season	App	Sub	Gls	Div
Queen's Park	57/58	1			D1

HUGHES John
b. Coatbridge 3.4.1943 Caps: S - 8
Kirkshaw Amateurs
Shotts Bon Accord

Club	Season	App	Sub	Gls	Div
Celtic	60/61	19		4	D1
	61/62	31		18	D1
	62/63	16		11	D1
	63/64	22		10	D1
	64/65	29		22	D1
	65/66	23		13	D1
	66/67	19		6	D1
	67/68	31	1	7	D1
	68/69	27		10	D1
	69/70	20	1	10	D1
	70/71	14		5	D1
	71/72		1		D1
Crystal Palace	71/72	10		3	FL
	72/73	10		1	FL
Sunderland	72/73	1			FL

HUGHES Joseph
b. Glasgow 8.12.1942

Club	Season	App	Sub	Gls	Div
Third Lanark	64/65	1			D1
Arthurlie					
Stirling A	67/68	16		7	D1
	68/69			20	D2
	69/70	35		24	D2
	70/71			9	D2
East Fife	70/71			10	D2
	71/72	29	3	8	D1
Dunfermline A	72/73	25	3	12	D2
Montrose	73/74	17	1	11	D2
Clydebank	73/74	13		8	D2
	74/75			5	D2
Cowdenbeath	74/75			6	D2
Stirling A	74/75	4	7	1	D2

HUGHES Patrick

Whitburn

Club	Season	App	Sub	Gls	Div
Hibernian	56/57	12			D1
	57/58	10			D1
	58/59	2			D1
	59/60	15			D1
	60/61	6			D1
	61/62	10			D1
	62/63	12			D1
	63/64	1			D1
Forfar A	64/65	25			D2

HUGHES Patrick Joseph
b. Coatbridge 28.2.1945
Baillieston

Club	Season	App	Sub	Gls	Div
St Mirren	63/64	1			D1
	64/65	5			D1
Barnsley	65/66				FL
Darlington	65/66	3			FL
Hamilton A	T 66/67	1			D2

HUGHES Thomas

Bellshill Academy

Club	Season	App	Sub	Gls	Div
Arbroath	61/62	7			D2
	62/63				D2
	63/64	34			D2
	64/65	34			D2
	65/66	29			D2
	66/67	35		1	D2
	67/68	36			D2
	68/69	28		1	D1
	69/70	28	4		D2
	70/71	32	2	6	D2

HULSTON William Duncan
b. Stirling 18.12.1946
Woodburn A

Club	Season	App	Sub	Gls	Div
Stirling A	63/64	2			D2
Stenhousemuir	64/65	1			D2
Brechin C	64/65	1			D2
	65/66				D2
East Stirlingshire	66/67	36		2	D2
	67/68	35		9	D2
	68/69			19	D2
Clyde	68/69	6		1	D1
	69/70	30	1	9	D1
	70/71	22	1	10	D1
	71/72	21		6	D1
Airdrieonians	72/73	12		4	D1
	73/74	14	7	7	D2
East Stirlingshire	74/75	19	6	1	D2
Stirling A	75/76	12			D2

HUME Ian
b. Glasgow 9.10.1948

Club	Season	App	Sub	Gls	Div
Queen's Park	67/68	3			D2
	68/69	4		1	D2
	69/70	24		2	D2
Airdrieonians	70/71	4		1	D1
Ayr U	71/72				D1
Stirling A	72/73	1			D2
Stenhousemuir	72/73	4			D2
	73/74	6	1	1	D2

HUME Robert
b. Kirkintilloch 18.3.1941 d. Johannesburg 1997
Kirkintilloch Rob Roy

Club	Season	App	Sub	Gls	Div
Rangers	59/60	12		3	D1
	60/61	2			D1
	61/62	3			D1
Middlesbrough	62/63	19		5	FL
Aberdeen	63/64	23		4	D1
	64/65	10			D1
Highlands Park					

HUME Ronald

Club	Season	App	Sub	Gls	Div
Airdrieonians	60/61	1			D1
	61/62	11			D1
	62/63	4		1	D1
Partick T	63/64	2			D1
Motherwell	64/65	5			D1
Highlands Park					

HUME William

Club	Season	App	Sub	Gls	Div
Aberdeen	38/39	3			D1
	46/47	4		1	D1
	47/48	2			D1

HUME William Sanderson
b. Armadale 18.12.1935

Club	Season	App	Sub	Gls	Div
Dunfermline A	56/57	4		1	D1
	57/58				D2
Birmingham C	58/59	2			FL
	59/60	8		2	FL
St Mirren	60/61	8		3	D1

HUMPHRIES Wilson
b. Motherwell 1.7.1928
d. Carluke 22.10.1992 Caps: S - 1

Club	Season	App	Sub	Gls	Div
Motherwell	46/47	26		5	D1
	47/48	30		19	D1
	48/49	13			D1
	49/50	8		4	D1
	50/51	7		4	D1
	51/52	25		4	D1
	52/53	27		9	D1
	53/54	28		18	D2
	54/55	24		4	D1
	55/56	11		2	D1
St Mirren	56/57	22		8	D1
Dundee U	57/58	30		24	D2
	58/59	24		7	D2
Hamilton A	59/60	19		3	D2
	60/61	10			D2

HUNT J

Club	Season	App	Sub	Gls	Div
Falkirk	47/48	2			D1

HUNTER

Club	Season	App	Sub	Gls	Div
Motherwell	71/72	1			D1

HUNTER Alistair Robert
b. Glasgow 4.10.1945 Caps: S - 4
Drumchapel Amateurs

Club	Season	App	Sub	Gls	Div
Rangers	T				
Leicester C	T				
Johnstone Burgh					
Kilmarnock	70/71	30			D1
	71/72	34			D1
	72/73	12			D1
Celtic	72/73	15			D1
	73/74	26			D1
	74/75	18			D1
	75/76	1			P
Motherwell	76/77	8			P
	77/78				P
St Mirren	77/78	7			P
Clydebank	78/79				D1

HUNTER Andrew

Club	Season	App	Sub	Gls	Div
St Mirren	69/70	6			D1

HUNTER Donald
b. Dumbarton 1.4.1955

Club	Season	App	Sub	Gls	Div
Rangers	73/74	3			D1
	74/75				D1
	75/76				P
	76/77				P
St Mirren	L 76/77	39			D1
	L 77/78	19			P
Dumbarton	78/79	15			D1
	79/80	6			D1
	80/81	6			D1
Alloa A	81/82	39			D2
	82/83	39			D1
	83/84	38			D1
	84/85	7			D2

HUNTER Edward
b. Tillicoultry 7.3.1928
Alva Albion R

Club	Season	App	Sub	Gls	Div
Falkirk	52/53	29			D1
	53/54				D1
Accrington S	54/55	44			FL
	55/56	42		2	FL
	56/57	45		2	FL
	57/58	27			FL
	58/59	11			FL

HUNTER George
b. Ayr

Club	Season	App	Sub	Gls	Div
St Mirren	46/47	3			D1
	47/48	3		1	D1
Kilmarnock	48/49	13		4	D2
Irvine Meadow	49/50				
Blantyre V					

HUNTER George Irvine
b. Troon 29.8.1930 d. Nottingham 10.5.1990
Crosshouses Waverley
Riccarton Glencairn
Neilston Jnrs

Celtic	50/51	11		D1
	51/52			D1
	52/53	17		D1
	53/54	4		D1
Derby Co	54/55	19		FL
Exeter C	55/56	43		FL
	56/57	40		FL
	57/58	28		FL
	58/59	36		FL
	59/60			FL
Yiewsley	60/61			
Darlington	61/62	20		FL
Weymouth	62/63			
Burton A	63/64			
	64/65			
Lincoln C	65/66	1		FL
Matlock T				

HUNTER Harry

Queen of the South	47/48	1	D1

HUNTER Hugh
Plains St Davids
Royal Albert

Hamilton A	53/54	1	D1
	54/55		D1
	55/56	2	D2
	56/57	6	D2
Royal Albert			

HUNTER Ian
Lochore Welfare

Dunfermline A	64/65	2			D1
	65/66	7		3	D1
	66/67	10	2	4	D1
	67/68	6		3	D1
Falkirk	68/69	16	2	3	D1
Cambridge C	69/70				
	70/71				
	71/72				
	72/73				

HUNTER Ian
Bellaire A

Morton	73/74	6	1	1	D1
	74/75	1	1		D1

HUNTER J

Morton	46/47	1	D1

HUNTER James

Albion R	48/49	20	D1
	49/50		D2
Morton	49/50	24	D2
	50/51	7	D1
	51/52	19	D1
Falkirk	53/54	22	D1
	54/55	1	D1

HUNTER John
b. Coatbridge 13.4.1916
Coatbridge St Augustines
Lochryn Amateurs
Shettleston Jnrs
Kilsyth Emmet

Kilmarnock	37/38	15	D1
	38/39	38	D1
	46/47	2	D1
	47/48	24	D2
Stenhousemuir	48/49		D2

HUNTER John
b. Leith
Tranent Jnrs

Motherwell	48/49			D1
	49/50	1		D1
	50/51	4	2	D1
	51/52	5	1	D1
	52/53			D1
	53/54	26	28	D2
	54/55	24	8	D1
	55/56	2		D1
	56/57	26	16	D1
	57/58	18	4	D1
Dundee U	58/59	18	10	D2

HUNTER John
Gairdoch Juveniles

Falkirk	58/59	17		D1
	59/60	8		D2
	60/61	11		D2
	61/62	22		D1
	62/63	29	1	D1
	63/64	15		D1
	64/65	23		D1
	65/66	31	2	D1
	66/67	33	2	D1
	67/68	33	1	D1
	68/69	22		D1
Stenhousemuir				

HUNTER Robert Russell
b. Shotts 12.3.1931 d. Wilmslow 8.7.2002
Shotts YMCA

Hamilton A	50/51	25	15	D2
Motherwell	51/52			D1
	52/53			D1
	53/54			D2
Swindon T	54/55	16	3	FL
Motherwell	55/56	2	1	D1
Hamilton A	L 55/56	17	14	D2

HUNTER Stewart
Hillside BC

Arbroath	74/75		2		D1
Forfar A	75/76	5	4	1	D2

HUNTER William
b. Edinburgh 14.2.1940 Caps: S - 3
Edinburgh Norton

Motherwell	57/58	11		4	D1
	58/59	32		9	D1
	59/60	34		4	D1
	60/61	33		6	D1
	61/62	31		6	D1
	62/63	4			D1
	63/64	7		1	D1
	64/65	24		4	D1
	65/66	24		1	D1
	66/67	29		8	D1
Glentoran	67/68				
Detroit Cougars	68	23		4	NA
Hibernian	68/69	5	1	1	D1
	69/70	4			D1
	70/71	2	1		D1
Cape Town C					

HUNTER William Nibb
b. Cambuslang 7.4.1942
Lanark U

Rangers	62/63	1			D1
	63/64				D1
Bradford PA	64/65	14			FL
Hamilton A	66/67	13		4	D2
	67/68	33	1	7	D2
	68/69	33		2	D2
	69/70	6			D2

HUSBAND I

Airdrieonians	52/53	1	D1

HUSBAND John
b. Dunfermline 28.5.1918
d. 30.4.1992 Caps: S - 1
Yoker A

Partick T	38/39	5	D1
	46/47	28	D1
	47/48	25	D1
	48/49	3	D1
	49/50	11	D1

HUTCHINSON Robert
b. Glasgow 19.6.1953
Aberdeen Lads Club

Montrose	71/72	3			D2
	72/73	8	2	1	D2
	73/74	25	3	7	D2
Dundee	74/75	21	2	7	D1
	75/76	18	3	5	P
	76/77	35		12	D1
	77/78	8	1	1	D1
Hibernian	77/78	20		6	P
	78/79	19	3	4	P
	79/80	18	7	3	P
Wigan A	80/81	34	1	3	FL
Tranmere R	81/82	26	3	4	FL
	82/83	6		2	FL
Mansfield T	82/83	25		3	FL
	83/84	10			FL
Tranmere R	83/84	21		4	FL
Bristol C	84/85	31		4	FL
	85/86	42		4	FL
	86/87	18	1	1	FL
Walsall	86/87	8	6		FL
	87/88	2			FL
Blackpool	L 87/88	3	3		FL
Carlisle U	L 87/88	12	1	2	FL

HUTCHISON David

Raith R	56/57	3	1	D1

HUTCHISON Roderick
b. Lennoxtown 25.3.1955
Clydebank BC

Clyde	74/75	1			D1
Pollok Jnrs	75/76				
Morton	76/77	2	2	1	D1
	77/78	21	5	1	D1
	78/79	16	2	1	P
	79/80	31	4	5	P
	80/81	11	5	3	P
	81/82	35	1	5	P
	82/83	30		4	P
Hamilton A	83/84	18		2	D1
Queen of the South	83/84	2			D2
Partick T	83/84	7	1		D1
	84/85	10		2	D1
East Fife	84/85	3			D1
Petershill					
Kilsyth R					

HUTTON Charles
Valleyfield Colliery

East Fife	52/53	3	D1
	53/54		D1
	54/55		D1
	55/56		D1
	56/57		D1
Dundee U	56/57	3	D2
Brechin C	56/57		D2

HUTTON John
b. Bellshill 23.4.1944
Wishaw Jnrs

Hamilton A	61/62	3		2	D2
	62/63	36		11	D2
Scunthorpe U	63/64	6			FL
	64/65	31		4	FL
	65/66	16	1	3	FL
St Mirren	66/67	20	2	2	D1
N Ireland					

HYND John Roger Shankly
b. Falkirk 2.2.1942

Club	Season	Apps	Sub	Gls	Div
Rangers	63/64	1			D1
	64/65	10			D1
	65/66	4			D1
	66/67	1	1	1	D1
	67/68	3	1	3	D1
	68/69	10			D1
Crystal Palace	69/70	29		1	FL
Birmingham C	70/71	40			FL
	71/72	42		1	FL
	72/73	40		1	FL
	73/74	34	2	2	FL
	74/75	6	6		FL
	75/76		1		FL
Oxford U	L 75/76	5			FL
Walsall	75/76	26		1	FL
	76/77	43			FL
	77/78	20			FL

IMRIE Adam
b. Dumfries 1.10.1933
Kello R

Club	Season	Apps	Sub	Gls	Div
Kilmarnock	51/52				D2
	52/53	1			D2
	53/54				D2
	54/55	2		1	D1
	55/56				D1
	56/57				D1
Carlisle U	57/58	10		5	FL
Stranraer	58/59				D2
	59/60				D2
Hamilton A	59/60	15		9	D2
	60/61	2			D2
Berwick R	60/61				D2
Derry C	61/62				
Stranraer	61/62	11		4	D2

IMRIE R

Club	Season	Apps	Sub	Gls	Div
Albion R	48/49	12		1	D1

INGLIS James McDougal
b. Glasgow 14.2.1924

Club	Season	Apps	Sub	Gls	Div
Falkirk	46/47	10		8	D1
	47/48	20		11	D1
	48/49	24		14	D1
	49/50	16		12	D1
Stirling A	49/50	4		1	D1
Bury	50/51	2			FL
Queen of the South	50/51				D2
	51/52	16		4	D1
Ayr U	51/52				D2
	52/53	2			D2
Worcester C	52/53				
Cowdenbeath	53/54	30		29	D2
	54/55				D2
Albion R	55/56				D2

INGRAM Alexander David
b. Edinburgh 2.1.1945

Club	Season	Apps	Sub	Gls	Div
Queen's Park	63/64	27		7	D2
	64/65	17		5	D2
	65/66	25		12	D2
Ayr U	66/67	23	2	4	D1
	67/68	35		16	D2
	68/69			25	D2
	69/70	16		7	D1
Nottingham F	69/70	16		3	FL
	70/71	12			FL
Ayr U	70/71	16		4	D1
	71/72	23	3	5	D1
	72/73	32		5	D1
	73/74	18	3	3	D1
	74/75	26	3	8	D1
	75/76	31	1	5	P
	76/77	6	6	2	P

INGRAM James
Sunnybank

Club	Season	Apps	Sub	Gls	Div
Aberdeen	55/56	2		1	D1
	56/57				D1
East Fife	57/58	17			D1
Inverness Caley					

INNES Norman

Club	Season	Apps	Sub	Gls	Div
Clyde	55/56	12		1	D1
	56/57				D2
	57/58	1			D1
	58/59	1			D1
Stirling A	59/60	2		1	D1
St Johnstone	59/60	25		5	D2
	60/61	26		4	D1
Falkirk	61/62	12		5	D1
	62/63				D1
Albion R	63/64	15		2	D2

IRVIN Derek Vincent
b. Stockton 23.8.1943

Club	Season	Apps	Sub	Gls	Div
Middlesbrough	61/62				FL
	62/63				FL
Falkirk	63/64	4			D1
St Johnstone	64/65				D1
Brechin C	64/65				D2
	65/66	32		12	D2
	66/67	32	1	12	D2
Watford	67/68		2	1	FL
Corby T					

IRVINE Andrew
b. Dundee ?.?.1921 d. ?.1.1972
Dundee Violet

Club	Season	Apps	Sub	Gls	Div
Dundee	47/48	6			D1
	48/49	19			D1
	49/50	3			D1
	50/51	18		1	D1
	51/52	7		1	D1
	52/53	5			D1
	53/54	8			D1
	54/55	28			D1
	55/56	32			D1
	56/57	3			D1
Falkirk	56/57	11			D1
	57/58	29			D1
	58/59	2			D1
Dundee U	58/59	7			D2

IRVINE Archibald
b. Coatbridge 25.6.1946

Club	Season	Apps	Sub	Gls	Div
Airdrieonians	66/67	11		2	D1
	67/68	8		2	D1
	68/69	3			D1
Sheffield W	68/69	18	4	1	FL
	69/70	7			FL
Doncaster R	69/70	23	1	1	FL
	70/71	34	4	5	FL
	71/72	44		5	FL
	72/73	44		4	FL
	73/74	32	3	1	FL
	74/75	43			FL
Scunthorpe U	75/76	22	1	1	FL

IRVINE J

Club	Season	Apps	Sub	Gls	Div
Queen's Park	46/47	15		5	D1

IRVINE James
b. Whitburn 17.8.1940
Edinburgh A
Whitburn R

Club	Season	Apps	Sub	Gls	Div
Dundee U	59/60	34		23	D2
	60/61	14		4	D1
	61/62	25		14	D1
	62/63	28		11	D1
	63/64	25		11	D1
Middlesbrough	64/65	42		20	FL
	65/66	31		15	FL
	66/67	17	1	2	FL
Heart of Midlothian	67/68	23		7	D1
	68/69	5		3	D1
	69/70	5	1	1	D1
Barrow	70/71	33		11	FL
	71/72	34		6	FL

IRVINE Ross G
Drumchapel Amateurs

Club	Season	Apps	Sub	Gls	Div
Morton	74/75	5		1	D1
	75/76	11	2	1	D1

IRVING James
Petershill

Club	Season	Apps	Sub	Gls	Div
Motherwell	46/47	2			D1
St Johnstone	47/48	25		9	D2
	48/49	26		8	D2
	49/50	21		5	D2
Kilmarnock	50/51	16		1	D2
Dundee U	52/53	7			D2

IRVING Gerry

Club	Season	Apps	Sub	Gls	Div
Queen of the South	59/60				D2
	60/61				D2
	61/62				D2
	62/63	28			D1
	63/64	25		1	D1

IRVING William
Bedlay Jnrs

Club	Season	Apps	Sub	Gls	Div
Hamilton A	46/47	6		1	D1
	47/48				D2

JACK Denis
Cowdenbeath Royals

Club	Season	Apps	Sub	Gls	Div
Cowdenbeath	60/61				D2
	61/62	25			D2
	62/63				D2
	63/64	34		1	D2
	64/65	36		1	D2
	65/66	30		1	D2
	66/67	21	2		D2
	67/68	33			D2
	68/69			1	D2
	69/70	36			D2
	70/71	13			D1
Forfar A	71/72	8			D2

JACK James

Club	Season	Apps	Sub	Gls	Div
Arbroath	65/66	19		13	D2
	66/67	35		22	D2
	67/68	36		30	D2
	68/69	33		14	D1
	69/70	22	3	16	D2
	70/71			28	D2
Falkirk	71/72	16	1	4	D1
	72/73	6		1	D1
Raith R	73/74	7	3	5	D2

JACK John
b. Bellshill 9.3.1932 d. 22.10.1988
Mossend BG
Stonehouse Violet

Club	Season	Apps	Sub	Gls	Div
Celtic	50/51				D1
	51/52	3			D1
	52/53	4			D1
	53/54				D1
	54/55				D1
	55/56	4			D1
	56/57	33			D1
	57/58	2			D1
	58/59	1			D1
Morton					

JACK William
b. Glasgow
Glasgow Perthshire
Shawfield Jnrs

Club	Season	Apps	Sub	Gls	Div
St Mirren	47/48	18		11	D1
	48/49	2			D1
Albion R	49/50				D2
	50/51				D2
	51/52	18		7	D2
Kilmarnock	51/52	9		4	D2
	52/53	25		14	D2
	53/54	25		11	D2
	54/55	12		8	D1
	55/56				D1
Stenhousemuir					

JACKSON Andrew
b. Bothwell
Chelsea

Club	Season	Apps	Sub	Gls	Div
Hamilton A	53/54	3		1	D1

JACKSON Colin MacDonald
b. Falkirk 8.10.1946 Caps: S - 8
Rangers
Sunnybank A

Club	Season	Apps	Sub	Goals	Div
Rangers	63/64				D1
	64/65				D1
	65/66	1			D1
	66/67	4		1	D1
	67/68				D1
	68/69	10			D1
	69/70	3			D1
	70/71	34		2	D1
	71/72	24	1	2	D1
	72/73	7			D1
	73/74	18		4	D1
	74/75	33		3	D1
	75/76	33		2	P
	76/77	30		4	P
	77/78	35		3	P
	78/79	28		1	P
	79/80	29		2	P
	80/81	29			P
	81/82	21			P
Morton	82/83	5		1	P
Partick T	82/83	19			D1
Morton	83/84	2			D1

JACKSON Ian B
b. Edinburgh
Loanhead Mayflower

Club	Season	Apps	Sub	Goals	Div
Stirling A	51/52				D1
	52/53	5			D2
	53/54	8		1	D1
	54/55	2			D1
Stenhousemuir	54/55				D2

JACKSON James Potter
b. Glasgow 4.8.1924

Club	Season	Apps	Sub	Goals	Div
Third Lanark	49/50	4			D1
Bury	50/51	1			FL

JACKSON John
Carnoustie Panmure

Club	Season	Apps	Sub	Goals	Div
Dundee U	59/60				D2
	60/61	1			D1

JACKSON Michael
b. Glasgow 25.8.1939
Benburb

Club	Season	Apps	Sub	Goals	Div
Celtic	57/58	1			D1
	58/59	17		3	D1
	59/60	13		8	D1
	60/61	1			D1
	61/62	24		11	D1
	62/63	2		1	D1
St Johnstone	62/63	12		1	D2
	63/64	12		1	D1
Third Lanark	63/64	10		8	D1
	64/65	33		2	D1
	65/66				D2
Drumcondra					
Athlone T					
Partick T	T 66/67				D1
Clyde	66/67	2	1	2	D1
Morton	66/67				
Queen of the South	67/68	34		11	D2
	68/69			5	D2
	69/70	27		6	D2
Clydebank	70/71				D2
Hamilton A	71/72				D2
Benburb					

JAMES George
b. Annan d. Canada (?) ?.?.1970

Club	Season	Apps	Sub	Goals	Div
Queen of the South	46/47	9			D1
	47/48	29			D1
	48/49	30			D1
	49/50	27			D1

JAMIESON Andrew
Dreghorn Jnrs
Kilmarnock Jnrs
Craigmark Bruntonians
Darvel Jnrs

Club	Season	Apps	Sub	Goals	Div
Kilmarnock	56/57				D1
	57/58	1			D1
	58/59				D1
Stranraer	59/60				D2
Newton Stewart					
Kello R					
Saltcoats V					

JAMIESON John Wallace
b. Dumbarton 14.10.1928

Club	Season	Apps	Sub	Goals	Div
Aberdeen	46/47	1			D1
Oswestry T	47/48				
	48/49				
Coventry C	48/49	9		1	FL
	49/50	9		2	FL
	50/51	2			FL
	51/52	14		2	FL
	52/53	3			FL
	53/54	38		1	FL
	54/55	28			FL
	55/56	17			FL
	56/57	25			FL
	57/58	36			FL
Rugby T					

JAPP William
b. c1929

Club	Season	Apps	Sub	Goals	Div
Falkirk	46/47				D1
	47/48				D1
	48/49	1			D1
East Stirlingshire	49/50				D3
Ayr U	50/51				D2
	51/52				D2
	52/53	26		8	D2
	53/54	27		6	D2
	54/55				D2
	55/56				D2
	56/57	20		3	D1
	57/58				D2
East Stirlingshire	57/58				D2
Berwick R	58/59				D2

JARDINE Frederick
b. Edinburgh 27.9.1941

Club	Season	Apps	Sub	Goals	Div
Dundee	58/59	1			D1
	59/60	2			D1
	60/61	3			D1
Luton T	61/62	3			FL
	62/63	18		3	FL
	63/64	16		2	FL
	64/65	29			FL
	65/66	34		1	FL
	66/67	45		1	FL
	67/68	41			FL
	68/69	23	1	2	FL
	69/70	9	1		FL
Torquay U	70/71	2			FL
	71/72	9			FL
Ampthill T					

JARDINE William Pullar
b. Edinburgh 31.12.1948 Caps: S - 38
United Crossroads
Edinburgh A

Club	Season	Apps	Sub	Goals	Div
Rangers	66/67	14		2	D1
	67/68	6	3		D1
	68/69	15	3	4	D1
	69/70	10	4		D1
	70/71	32		1	D1
	71/72	31		5	D1
	72/73	34		2	D1
	73/74	34		3	D1
	74/75	34		9	D1
	75/76	18	7	2	P
	76/77	36		2	P
	77/78	32		5	P
	78/79	35			P
	79/80	35		3	P
	80/81	29	2	3	P
	81/82	36		1	P
Heart of Midlothian	82/83	39		2	D1
	83/84	33			P
	84/85	34			P
	85/86	35			P
	86/87	34		1	P
	87/88	9			P

JARVIE Andrew
b. Annathill 5.10.1948 Caps: S - 3
Kirkstyle
Kilsyth R

Club	Season	Apps	Sub	Goals	Div
Airdrieonians	67/68	18	1	6	D1
	68/69	27		5	D1
	69/70	34		17	D1
	70/71	34		16	D1
	71/72	28		8	D1
Aberdeen	72/73	33	1	15	D1
	73/74	32		13	D1
	74/75	27	5	9	D1
	75/76	30	2	4	P
	76/77	20	2	9	P
	77/78	35		12	P
	78/79	27	3	4	P
	79/80	30	8	12	P
	80/81	23	7	5	P
	81/82	10	7	2	P
Airdrieonians	82/83	19	2	4	D1
	83/84	6		1	D1
St Mirren	83/84	10	3	2	P
	84/85	1			P
	85/86	2		1	P

JEFFERIES James
b. Musselburgh 22.11.1950
Gorgie Hearts
Heart of Midlothian
Haddington A
Gala Fairydean

Club	Season	Apps	Sub	Goals	Div
Heart of Midlothian	71/72	7			D1
	72/73	8			D1
	73/74	23		1	D1
	74/75	27		1	D1
	75/76	26		3	P
	76/77	18	2	3	P
	77/78	38		1	D1
	78/79	26		2	P
	79/80	32		1	D1
	80/81	12		1	P
Berwick R	81/82	22			D2
	82/83	38			D2
Gala Fairydean					

JEFFREY Ian
Whitburn Jnrs

Club	Season	Apps	Sub	Goals	Div
Hamilton A	51/52	2		1	D2
	52/53	15		1	D2
	53/54	1			D1
	54/55	1			D2
Ayr U	54/55				D2
	55/56				D2
Albion R	L 55/56				D2

JEFFREY Robert
b. Ayr 7.11.1942
Coltness U

Club	Season	Apps	Sub	Gls	Div
Celtic	61/62				D1
	62/63	4			D1
	63/64	1		1	D1
Airdrieonians	63/64	9		1	D1
Rhyl					
Altrincham					
Pwllheli					
Colwyn Bay					
Stranraer	66/67				D2
Cambridge C	T				

JENKINS Brian
b. Stenhousemuir 16.6.1956
Armadale Thistle

Club	Season	Apps	Sub	Gls	Div
Dunfermline A	74/75	2			D1
Whitburn					
Stenhousemuir	77/78	2			D2
	78/79	28	3	6	D2
	79/80	33	1	10	D2
	80/81	32		8	D2
	81/82	31		8	D2
	82/83	14		1	D2
East Fife	83/84	39		2	D2
	84/85	38			D1
	85/86	23		1	D1

JENKINS George E
b. Leeds
Montreal CPR
Montreal Maroons

Club	Season	Apps	Sub	Gls	Div
Indiana Flooring	26/27	9		5	AS
Canada					
Rangers	33/34	7			D1
	34/35	1			D1
	35/36				D1
	36/37				D1
	37/38	12			D1
	38/39	5			D1
Kilmarnock					
Hamilton A	46/47	2			D1

JENKINS Harold
Comrie Colliery

Club	Season	Apps	Sub	Gls	Div
Stirling A	50/51				D2
	51/52	27			D1
	52/53	30			D2
	53/54	25			D1
	54/55	7			D1
Brechin C	55/56				D2
Dunfermline A	55/56	9			D1

JENKINS Kenneth
Johnstone Burgh

Club	Season	Apps	Sub	Gls	Div
Albion R	65/66	8		6	D2
	66/67	30		17	D2
	67/68	34		17	D2
	68/69			17	D2
Dumbarton	69/70	28		10	D2
	70/71			1	D2
	71/72	36		1	D2
	72/73	23		1	D1
	73/74	3	3		D1

JENKINS Ross
b. c1955
Letham U

Club	Season	Apps	Sub	Gls	Div
St Johnstone	72/73	1	1		D1
	73/74	2	2		D1
Forfar A	74/75	5			D2
Brechin C	74/75	2			D2

JENKINS Thomas Frederick
b. Stockton 5.12.1925

Club	Season	Apps	Sub	Gls	Div
Queen of the South	47/48	21		6	D1
	48/49	30		8	D1
Chelsea	49/50	5			FL
Barry T					
Kettering T					
Leicester C	54/55				FL
Queen of the South	55/56	9		4	D1

JENSEN Bjarne
b. Denmark
Chang
Aab Aalborg
AGF Aarhus

Club	Season	Apps	Sub	Gls	Div
Morton	67/68	27		11	D1
	68/69	14	2	2	D1
	69/70	2	4		D1
VAV Groningen					

JENSEN Raold
b. Eidsvagnesit 11.1.1943 d. 6.10.1987 Caps: Nor - 31
SK Brann

Club	Season	Apps	Sub	Gls	Div
Heart of Midlothian	64/65	15		3	D1
	65/66	5			D1
	66/67	7			D1
	67/68	15		5	D1
	68/69	22		7	D1
	69/70	5		3	D1
	70/71	5		1	D1
SK Brann					

JOHANSEN Kai
b. Denmark 23.7.1940 Caps: Den - 20
OB Odense

Club	Season	Apps	Sub	Gls	Div
Morton	63/64	3			D2
	64/65	30			D1
Rangers	65/66	32			D1
	66/67	33		1	D1
	67/68	33		1	D1
	68/69	27		1	D1
	69/70	33		1	D1
Arcadia Shepherds					

JOHNSON Jack
b. Denmark 3.7.1924 Caps: Den - 4

Club	Season	Apps	Sub	Gls	Div
Dundee	47/48	1		1	D1
B1909 Odense	48/49				
	49/50				
	50/51				
	51/52				
Dundee	52/53	1			D1

JOHNSON Joseph Robert
b. Greenock 13.9.1920
Arthurlie

Club	Season	Apps	Sub	Gls	Div
Rangers	47/48	1			D1
	48/49				D1
	49/50	20		5	D1
	50/51	2			D1
Falkirk	L 50/51	20		4	D1
Rangers	51/52	9		2	D1
Lincoln C	52/53	11		2	FL
Workington	53/54	38		5	FL

JOHNSTON Charles
b. Glasgow 26.11.1912
Blantyre Victoria

Club	Season	Apps	Sub	Gls	Div
Motherwell	33/34	4		1	D1
	34/35	2			D1
Doncaster R	35/36	14		3	FL
	36/37	22			FL
Mansfield T	37/38	36		4	FL
Dunfermline A	38/39				D2
Rangers					
Queen of the South	46/47	27		3	D1
	47/48	23		3	D1
	48/49	27		5	D1
	49/50	22		6	D1
	50/51				D2
	51/52	14			D1
	52/53	22		4	D1

JOHNSTON David
b. Nairn 28.11.1942 d. 7.4.2004
Nairn Co

Club	Season	Apps	Sub	Gls	Div
Heart of Midlothian	60/61	5		1	D1
Nairn Co	61/62				
	62/63				
	63/64				
	64/65				
	65/66				
Aberdeen	66/67	20		10	D1
	67/68	28		14	D1
	68/69	25	2	8	D1
Inverness Caley					

JOHNSTON Edwin David
b. Arbroath 29.2.1948
Banks o'Dee

Club	Season	Apps	Sub	Gls	Div
Dundee	68/69	4			D1
	69/70	3		1	D1
	70/71	25	3	1	D1
	71/72	33		4	D1
	72/73	18		1	D1
	73/74	25	2		D1
	74/75	22	3		D1
	75/76	32		2	P
	76/77	21	1		D1
	77/78	22	4		D1
Montrose	78/79	21			D1
	79/80	18		2	D2
	80/81	3			D2

JOHNSTON Joseph
b. Motherwell
Renfrew Jnrs

Club	Season	Apps	Sub	Gls	Div
Motherwell	36/37	6		2	D1
	37/38	9		1	D1
	38/39				D1
	46/47	3		2	D1
	47/48	12		4	D1
	48/49	7		1	D1
	49/50				D1
	50/51	9			D1
	51/52	1			D1
Albion R	52/53	6		1	D2

JOHNSTON Leslie Hamilton
b. Glasgow 16.8.1920
d. Clayton ?.10.2001 Caps: S - 2
Hamilton Memorial Church
Clydebank

Club	Season	Apps	Sub	Gls	Div
Clyde	46/47	24		15	D1
Hibernian	46/47	5		3	D1
	47/48	4		5	D1
Clyde	47/48	23		14	D1
	48/49	7		3	D1
Celtic	48/49	22		7	D1
	49/50	1			D1
Stoke C	49/50	27		5	FL
	50/51	38		13	FL
	51/52	9			FL
	52/53	14		4	FL
Shrewsbury T	53/54	16		5	FL
Hinckley A					

JOHNSTON Walter
b. Glasgow

Club	Season	Apps	Sub	Gls	Div
Queen's Park	68/69	1			D2
	69/70	4			D2
Kilmarnock	70/71	1			D1
Alloa A	71/72	11	3	3	D2

JOHNSTON William
Drumchapel Amateurs

Club	Season	Apps	Sub	Gls	Div
Partick T	71/72	1			D1
St Mirren	72/73	36			D2
	73/74	34			D2
	74/75	26			D2
	75/76	13	1		D1
	76/77	34	1		D1
	77/78	2			P
Falkirk	78/79	37			D2
	79/80	26		1	D2
Renfrew					

JOHNSTON William McClure
b. Glasgow 19.12.1946 Caps: S - 22
Lochore Welfare

Club	Season	Apps	Sub	Goals	Div
Rangers	64/65	17		5	D1
	65/66	31		9	D1
	66/67	21		5	D1
	67/68	30	1	18	D1
	68/69	29		18	D1
	69/70	29		12	D1
	70/71	25		9	D1
	71/72	23	1	11	D1
	72/73	4		2	D1
West Bromwich A	72/73	22			FL
	73/74	35		2	FL
	74/75	38		7	FL
	75/76	39		6	FL
	76/77	34		1	FL
	77/78	32		2	FL
	78/79	3	4		FL
Vancouver Whitecaps	79	27		1	NA
Birmingham C	79/80	15			FL
Vancouver Whitecaps	80	14		2	NA
Rangers	80/81	21	6	2	P
	81/82	6	2		P
Vancouver Whitecaps	82	18			NA
Heart of Midlothian	82/83	24	3	6	D1
	83/84	2	19	2	P
	84/85	4	6	1	P
East Fife	84/85	3			D1

JOHNSTONE Alan

Irvine Meadow

Club	Season	Apps	Sub	Goals	Div
Morton	73/74	6	3	1	D1

JOHNSTONE Andrew

Tynecastle U

Club	Season	Apps	Sub	Goals	Div
St Johnstone	66/67	12	2		D1

JOHNSTONE Cyril
b. Hamilton 21.12.1920
Burnbank A

Club	Season	Apps	Sub	Goals	Div
Hamilton A	46/47	2			D1
Exeter C	47/48	40			FL
	48/49	37			FL
	49/50	41			FL
	50/51	16			FL

JOHNSTONE Derek Joseph
b. Dundee 4.11.1953 Caps: S - 14
St Francis BC
St Columbas

Club	Season	Apps	Sub	Goals	Div
Rangers	70/71	13	4	6	D1
	71/72	16	1	7	D1
	72/73	31		4	D1
	73/74	31		1	D1
	74/75	27		14	D1
	75/76	32	1	15	P
	76/77	27		15	P
	77/78	33		25	P
	78/79	31		9	P
	79/80	31	2	14	P
	80/81	23	3	4	P
	81/82	27	1	9	P
	82/83	18		6	P
Chelsea	83/84		2		FL
Dundee U	L 83/84	2	2		P
Chelsea	84/85	1	1		FL
Rangers	84/85	11		1	P
	85/86	8			P
Partick T	86/87	4			D1

JOHNSTONE George
b. Caldercruix 15.12.1914 d. Kirkcaldy 11.9.1974
Bothwellhaugh A
Benburb

Club	Season	Apps	Sub	Goals	Div
Aberdeen	36/37	10			D1
	37/38	38			D1
	38/39	34			D1
	46/47	26			D1
	47/48	28			D1
	48/49	15			D1
Dunfermline A	49/50	5			D2
Raith R	49/50	11			D1
	50/51	28			D1
	51/52	27			D1
	52/53	21			D1
	53/54	14			D1
Dumbarton	54/55	9			D3
Morton	55/56				D2
	56/57				D2
	57/58				D2
Cowdenbeath	58/59	1			D2

JOHNSTONE James Connolly
b. Uddingston 30.9.1944 Caps: S - 23
St Johns Viewpark
Uddingston St Columbas
Celtic
Blanytre Celtic L

Club	Season	Apps	Sub	Goals	Div
Celtic	62/63	4		1	D1
	63/64	25		6	D1
	64/65	24		1	D1
	65/66	32		9	D1
	66/67	25		13	D1
	67/68	29		5	D1
	68/69	30	1	5	D1
	69/70	27		10	D1
	70/71	30		8	D1
	71/72	23		9	D1
	72/73	21	1	7	D1
	73/74	13	2	3	D1
	74/75	15	6	5	D1
Hamilton A	L 74/75				D2
San Jose Earthquake	75	10			NA
Sheffield U	75/76	6			FL
	76/77	5		1	FL
Dundee	77/78	2	1		D1
Shelbourne	77/78				
Elgin C	78/79				
Blantyre Celtic					

JOHNSTONE Jocky
d. Greenock
Royal Albert

Club	Season	Apps	Sub	Goals	Div
Hamilton A	46/47	23			D1
	47/48	12			D2
	48/49	27			D2
	49/50	30			D2
	50/51	30			D2
	51/52	30			D2
	52/53	30		1	D2
	53/54	19			D1

JOHNSTONE John
b. Bo'ness d. Law 21.1.1989
Winchburgh A
Armadale Thistle

Club	Season	Apps	Sub	Goals	Div
Motherwell	46/47	30			D1
	47/48	30			D1
	48/49	30			D1
	49/50	2			D1
	50/51	23			D1
	51/52	29			D1
	52/53	30			D1
	53/54	30			D2
	54/55	1			D1
Hamilton A	55/56				D2

JOHNSTONE Robert
b. Selkirk 7.9.1929
d. Selkirk 22.8.2001 Caps: S - 17
Newtongrange Bluebell
Newtongrange Star

Club	Season	Apps	Sub	Goals	Div
Hibernian	46/47				D1
	47/48				D1
	48/49	2			D1
	49/50	26		9	D1
	50/51	29		12	D1
	51/52	27		22	D1
	52/53	30		16	D1
	53/54	30		12	D1
	54/55	20		12	D1
Manchester C	54/55	8		2	FL
	55/56	31		12	FL
	56/57	31		16	FL
	57/58	33		6	FL
	58/59	18		4	FL
	59/60	3		1	FL
Hibernian	59/60	30		17	D1
	60/61	1			D1
Oldham A	60/61	30		12	FL
	61/62	40		10	FL
	62/63	28		5	FL
	63/64	34		9	FL
	64/65	11			FL
Witton A					

JOHNSTONE Robert

Muirkirk

Club	Season	Apps	Sub	Goals	Div
Stirling A	59/60	28			D1
	60/61				D2
	61/62	29			D1
	62/63				D2
	63/64				D2
Third Lanark	63/64				D1
Airdrieonians	63/64	4			D1
	64/65	1			D1

JOHNSTONE Ronald

Preston Lodge

Club	Season	Apps	Sub	Goals	Div
Partick T	69/70	15			D1

JOHNSTONE William
b. Glasgow
Strathclyde

Club	Season	Apps	Sub	Goals	Div
St Mirren	48/49	1			D1
	49/50	10			D1
	50/51	29			D1
	51/52	10		1	D1
	52/53	20			D1
	53/54	27			D1
	54/55	22			D1
	55/56	20			D1
	56/57	23		1	D1
	57/58	19			D1
Airdrieonians	58/59	32			D1
	59/60	4			D1
	60/61	29			D1
	61/62	13			D1
Hamilton A	62/63	35		1	D2
	63/64	15			D2

JOHNSTONE William A

Club	Season	Apps	Sub	Goals	Div
Queen's Park	46/47	22			D1
	47/48	4			D1
	48/49	2			D2
	49/50	4			D2

JONES Alexander
b. c1943
Coltness U

Club	Season	Apps	Sub	Goals	Div
Motherwell	61/62	1			D1
	62/63				D1
Ayr U	62/63				D2
	63/64	15		5	D2

JONES B

Club	Season	Apps	Sub	Goals	Div
Morton	73/74	3			D1

JONES John
b. Gourock

Club	Season	Apps	Sub	Gls	Div
Third Lanark	46/47	1			D1
Bradford C T	46/47	2		1	FL
Morton	46/47	3			D1

JONES John

Club	Season	Apps	Sub	Gls	Div
Blantyre Victoria					
Third Lanark					
Hamilton A					
Cowdenbeath	46/47			20	D2
	47/48			25	D2
	48/49				D2
Stirling A	48/49				D2
	49/50	18		8	D1
St Mirren	49/50	5		1	D1
Kilmarnock	50/51	15		10	D2
	51/52				D2

JONES John

Club	Season	Apps	Sub	Gls	Div
Maryhill					
Airdrieonians	74/75	3		3	D1
	75/76	6	1	3	D1
	76/77	13	4	2	D1

JONES Mervyn Thomas David
b. Edinburgh 6.10.1949

Club	Season	Apps	Sub	Gls	Div
Edina Hibs					
Hibernian	66/67				D1
	67/68				D1
	68/69				D1
	69/70	13			D1
	70/71	17			D1
Falkirk	71/72	23			D1
Stirling A	72/73	36			D2
	73/74	31		1	D2
	74/75	26		1	D2
Cowdenbeath	75/76	16		1	D2
	76/77	37		2	D2
Newtongrange Star					

JONQUIN Paul
b. c1944 d. Airdrie 29.8.1995

Club	Season	Apps	Sub	Gls	Div
Edinburgh A					
Airdrieonians	61/62	10			D1
	62/63	22			D1
	63/64	25			D1
	64/65	23			D1
	65/66	29			D2
	66/67	32			D1
	67/68	34		2	D1
	68/69	34		1	D1
	69/70	34			D1
	70/71	34			D1
	71/72	26	3		D1
	72/73	32			D1
	73/74	35		7	D2
	74/75	34		8	D1
	75/76	23		7	D1
	76/77	33		1	D1
	77/78	36		2	D1
	78/79	25		1	D1

JORDAN John
b. Glasgow 25.2.1924

Club	Season	Apps	Sub	Gls	Div
Possil Glenfield					
Falkirk T					
Queen's Park	46/47	2			D1
Celtic	46/47	3		1	D1
Edinburgh C	47/48				
Heart of Midlothian T	47/48				D1
Aberdeen T	47/48				D1
Alloa A	47/48				D2
Reading	48/49	3			FL
	49/50				FL
Brentford	49/50				FL
	50/51				FL
Berwick R					

JORDAN Joseph
b. Carluke 15.12.1951   Caps: S - 52

Club	Season	Apps	Sub	Gls	Div
Blantyre Victoria					
Morton	68/69	1	2		D1
	69/70	5	1		D1
	70/71	1	1		D1
Leeds U	70/71				
	71/72	5	7		FL
	72/73	16	10	9	FL
	73/74	25	8	7	FL
	74/75	26	3	4	FL
	75/76	15	2	2	FL
	76/77	32		10	FL
	77/78	20		3	FL
Manchester U	77/78	14		3	FL
	78/79	30		6	FL
	79/80	32		13	FL
	80/81	33		15	FL
Verona	81/82				
	82/83				
	83/84				
Southampton	84/85	34		12	FL
	85/86	12			FL
	86/87	2			FL
Bristol C	86/87	19		3	FL
	87/88	17	11	4	FL
	88/89	2	7	1	FL
	89/90		1		FL

JOYCE Joseph
b. Kilmarnock

Club	Season	Apps	Sub	Gls	Div
Liverpool					
Motherwell	73/74				D1
	74/75		2		D1
Cumnock					

JOYCE Stephen

Club	Season	Apps	Sub	Gls	Div
Ayr U Boys Club					
Ayr U	73/74				D1
	74/75		2		D1
	75/76				P
	76/77		3		P
Cumnock					
Whitletts Victoria					
Maybole					

JOYNER Francis
b. c1919 d. Paisley ?.4.1997

Club	Season	Apps	Sub	Gls	Div
Raith R	37/38				D2
	38/39				D2
	46/47				D2
	47/48				D2
	48/49				D2
	49/50	3			D1
Hamilton A	49/50	9		1	D2
Kettering T	50/51				
	51/52				
Falkirk	52/53	3			D1
Stirling A	53/54				D1
	54/55	1			D1

JUDGE Michael
b. ?.11.1945

Club	Season	Apps	Sub	Gls	Div
Cowdenbeath Royals					
Lochore Welfare					
Dunfermline A	61/62				D1
	62/63				D1
	63/64				D1
	64/65				D1
	65/66				D1
	66/67				D1
Raith R	67/68	13		4	D1
	68/69	9	6	2	D1
	69/70	16	1	5	D1
East Fife T					
Berwick R	70/71			1	D2
Cowdenbeath	70/71		3		D1
	71/72				D2
Alloa A	72/73	1			D2
Glenrothes					

JULIUSSEN Albert Laurence
b. Blyth 20.2.1920

Club	Season	Apps	Sub	Gls	Div
Dundee NE					
Huddersfield T					
Dundee	46/47	15		30	D2
	47/48	20		17	D1
Portsmouth	47/48	7		4	FL
Everton	48/49	10		1	FL
Consett					
Berwick R					
Dundee U	53/54				D2
Brechin C					

KANE Peter
b. Petershill 4.4.1939

Club	Season	Apps	Sub	Gls	Div
Petershill					
Stirling A T	57/58				D2
Hamilton A T	57/58	2		1	D2
Queen's Park	58/59	11		4	D2
	59/60	6		3	D2
Northampton T	59/60	28		16	FL
Arsenal	60/61	4		1	FL
	61/62				FL
	62/63				FL
Northampton T	63/64	18		8	FL
Crewe Alex.	63/64	10		2	FL
	64/65	27		11	FL
	65/66	30	1	6	FL
	66/67	15		5	FL
St Mirren	66/67	12		3	D1
	67/68	27	1	22	D2
	68/69	34		9	D1
	69/70	11	1	2	D1
Clydebank	70/71			15	D2
	71/72	26	2	13	D2

KAPLER Konrad
b. Tychy 25.2.1925 d. Rochdale 23.10.1991

Club	Season	Apps	Sub	Gls	Div
Forres Mechanics					
Celtic	47/48	7			D1
	48/49				D1
Rochdale	49/50	4			FL
Morecambe					
Altrincham					

KARLSEN Geir
b. Norway   Caps: Nor - 32

Club	Season	Apps	Sub	Gls	Div
Rosenborg Trondheim					
Dunfermline A	73/74	21			D1
	74/75	34			D1
Valerengen Oslo					

KAY Robert
b. Edinburgh 24.10.1949

Club	Season	Apps	Sub	Gls	Div
United Crossroads					
Heart of Midlothian	70/71	13			D1
	71/72	18			D1
	72/73	15			D1
	73/74	14		1	D1
	74/75	28			D1
	75/76	23		1	P
	76/77	29		2	P
Celtic	77/78	5			P
York C	78/79	46			FL
	79/80	41		3	FL
	80/81	36		1	FL
	81/82	37		4	FL
Northallerton					

KEAN Samuel
b. Dumbarton c1918 d. Edinburgh 17.4.2003

Club	Season	Apps	Sub	Gls	Div
Kirkintilloch Rob Roy					
Hibernian	37/38	4			D1
	38/39	31		8	D1
	46/47	24			D1
	47/48	13			D1
	48/49	21			D1

KEARNEY

Club	Season	Apps	Sub	Gls	Div
Airdrieonians	56/57	7			D1

KEDDIE John

Chelsea
Lochore Welfare

Club	Season	Apps		Goals	Div
East Fife	53/54	1		1	D1
	54/55				D1
	55/56	4		2	D1
	56/57	3			D1
St Andrews U					

KEENAN James

Club	Season	Apps		Goals	Div
Partick T	57/58	8		3	D1
	58/59	4		1	D1
	59/60	5			D1

KEENAN John
b. Glasgow
Johnstone Burgh

Club	Season	Apps		Goals	Div
Airdrieonians	60/61	31			D1
	61/62	12			D1
	62/63	32			D1
	63/64	30		1	D1
	64/65	30			D1
	65/66	18		3	D2
	66/67	30		1	D1
	67/68	19			D1
	68/69	18			D1
	69/70	4			D1

KEITH George

Club	Season	Apps		Goals	Div
Third Lanark	64/65	1			D1

KEITH William
b. Stonehaven c1922 d. Coventry ?.1.1996
Brig o'Dee Juveniles
Pollok

Club	Season	Apps		Goals	Div
Clyde	46/47	8		4	D1
Dunfermline A	47/48				D2
	48/49				D2
Stirling A	49/50	22		7	D1
Raith R	50/51	1			D1
Cowdenbeath	50/51	6		2	D2

KELLACHAN Daniel
b. 24.1.1953
Blantyre Celtic

Club	Season	Apps	Sub	Goals	Div
Hamilton A	T 71/72				D2
Partick T	72/73	9			D1
	73/74	32	1		D1
	74/75	26			D1
	75/76	25			D1
	76/77				P
	77/78	2			P
Hamilton A	78/79	31			D1
	79/80	25	1		D1
	80/81	3			D1
Petershill					
Glenafton					
Lesmahagow					

KELLY Archibald
b. Paisley 9.12.1921
Arthurlie

Club	Season	Apps		Goals	Div
Heart of Midlothian	46/47	22		12	D1
	47/48	12		5	D1
Aberdeen	47/48	16		10	D1
	48/49	11		6	D1
	49/50	9		5	D1
Motherwell	49/50	19		14	D1
	50/51	26		12	D1
	51/52	30		20	D1
	52/53	29		19	D1
Stirling A	53/54	23		11	D1
	54/55	10		3	D1
Ayr U	54/55	11		7	D2
Cowdenbeath	55/56				D2

KELLY Bernard
b. New Stevenston 21.10.1932
Law Hearts
Muirkirk Jnrs

Club	Season	Apps		Goals	Div
Raith R	51/52	17		5	D1
	52/53	15		4	D1
	53/54	27		8	D1
	54/55	20		7	D1
	55/56	21		4	D1
	56/57	32		24	D1
	57/58	29		14	D1
Leicester C	58/59	24		13	FL
Nottingham F	58/59	2			FL
Aberdeen	59/60	4		1	D1
Raith R	60/61	15		3	D1
Cowdenbeath	61/62	1			D2

KELLY George Lawson
b. Aberdeen 29.6.1933

Club	Season	Apps		Goals	Div
Aberdeen	53/54	1			D1
	54/55				D1
	55/56	1			D1
Stoke C	55/56	4			FL
	56/57	30		13	FL
	57/58	33		22	FL
Cardiff C	58/59	8		4	FL
Stockport Co	59/60	34		4	FL

KELLY John

Pollok

Club	Season	Apps		Goals	Div
Morton	38/39				D2
Coatbridge St Patricks					
Shettleston					
Third Lanark	46/47	29			D1
	47/48	28		1	D1
	48/49	15			D1
	49/50	2			D1
Airdrieonians	L 49/50				
Kilmarnock	50/51	17			D2
	51/52	1			D2
	52/53	2			D2
East Stirlingshire					

KELLY John Carmichael
b. Paisley 21.2.1921 Caps: S - 2
Mearns Amateurs
Arthurlie

Club	Season	Apps		Goals	Div
Celtic	38/39				D1
Morton					
Barnsley	46/47	37		10	FL
	47/48	40		2	FL
	48/49	40		6	FL
	49/50	37		4	FL
	50/51	23		2	FL
	51/52	4			FL
	52/53	36		1	FL
Falkirk	53/54	22			D1
	54/55	4			D1
Morton	55/56				D2
Halifax T	56/57	26		1	FL
	57/58	12			FL
Portadown					

KELLY John Gerald
b. Glasgow 14.12.1935
Eastfield R
Whifflet St Marys
Shettleston Jnrs
Kilmarnock T

Club	Season	Apps		Goals	Div
Third Lanark	57/58	22			D1
	58/59	29			D1
Crewe Alex.	59/60	20		1	FL
Celtic	60/61	3			D1
	61/62				D1
Morton	L 61/62	18		1	D2
	62/63				D2
Barnsley	63/64				FL
	64/65				FL
	65/66				FL
	66/67				FL
Third Lanark	66/67	4			D2

KELLY Robert

Club	Season	Apps		Goals	Div
Aberdeen	58/59	1			D1

KELLY Walter Muir
b. Cowdenbeath 15.4.1929

Club	Season	Apps		Goals	Div
Raith R	49/50	8		1	D1
	50/51	1			D1
	51/52				D1
Bury	52/53	15		7	FL
	53/54	34		17	FL
	54/55	39		16	FL
	55/56	42		28	FL
	56/57	29		9	FL
Doncaster R	57/58	29		6	FL
Stockport Co	57/58	10		4	FL
	58/59	30		7	FL
	59/60	7		1	FL
Chester	59/60	32		12	FL
	60/61	24		12	FL
Rhyl					

KELLY William Muir
b. Cowdenbeath 14.8.1922

Club	Season	Apps		Goals	Div
Morton	46/47	11			D1
Airdrieonians	47/48	27		4	D1
	48/49				D2
	49/50	25		9	D2
	50/51	30		1	D1
	51/52	1			D1
Blackburn R	51/52	33			FL
	52/53	37			FL
	53/54	42		1	FL
	54/55	38			FL
	55/56	22			FL
	56/57	14			FL
Mossley	57/58				
Accrington S	57/58	24			FL

KEMP James

Club	Season	Apps	Sub	Goals	Div
Montrose	61/62	31		23	D2
East Stirlingshire	62/63				D2
	63/64	28		5	D1
ES Clydebank	64/65				D2
Montrose	64/65	11		8	D2
	65/66	22		10	D2
	66/67	33		14	D2
	67/68	31	1	19	D2
	68/69			15	D2
	69/70	32	1	12	D2
	70/71			5	D2
Brechin C	70/71			7	D2
	71/72	21		6	D2

KEMP John
b. Clydebank 11.4.1934

Club	Season	Apps		Goals	Div
Clyde	55/56	12		3	D1
	56/57				D2
	57/58	1			D1
Leeds U	57/58				FL
	58/59	1			FL
Barrow	58/59	10		2	FL
	59/60	42		9	FL
	60/61	26		5	FL
	61/62	39		15	FL
	62/63	34		10	FL
	63/64	19		4	FL
Crewe Alex.	63/64	21		1	FL
	64/65	19		5	FL
	65/66	7		1	FL

KEMP Robert McAlpine
b. Falkirk 15.8.1941
Camelon

Club	Season	Apps	Sub	Goals	Div
Falkirk	59/60	14			D2
	60/61	4			D2
Carlisle U	60/61	1			FL
Montrose	60/61				D2
	61/62	16		9	D2
St Johnstone	61/62	13		2	D1
	62/63	35		14	D2
	63/64	34		11	D1
	64/65	25		1	D1
	65/66	24		5	D1
	66/67	11		3	D1
Heart of Midlothian	66/67	14		5	D1
	67/68	7	1	4	D1
South Africa					

KEMP Roy

Club	Season	Apps	Sub	Gls	Div
St Mirren	62/63	3		1	D1
	63/64	4			D1

KENNEDY Allan

Arbroath LC

Club	Season	Apps	Sub	Gls	Div
Arbroath	59/60				D1
	60/61				D2
	61/62	34		2	D2
	62/63				D2
	63/64	35		8	D2
	64/65	35		2	D2
	65/66	33		9	D2
	66/67	16			D2
	67/68	34		3	D2
	68/69	20	3	1	D1
	69/70				D2
Cowdenbeath	69/70	24	2	1	D2
	70/71	18	1	2	D1
	71/72	2		2	D2
Forfar A	71/72	21		1	D2
	72/73	3		1	D2

KENNEDY Ian

Eastercraigs

Club	Season	Apps	Sub	Gls	Div
Motherwell	73/74	6		6	D1
	74/75	5			D1
	75/76	1		1	P
	76/77	24	5	2	P
	77/78	4	7		P
	78/79	5			P
Clyde	79/80	11		1	D1

Blantyre Victoria
Kilbirnie Ladeside

KENNEDY James
b. Johnstone 31.1.1934 Caps: S - 6
Duntochter Hibs

Club	Season	Apps	Sub	Gls	Div
Celtic	55/56	1			D1
	56/57	4			D1
	57/58	4			D1
	58/59	1			D1
Rangers	L 58/59				D1
Celtic	59/60	20			D1
	60/61	32			D1
	61/62	32			D1
	62/63	25			D1
	63/64	29			D1
	64/65	22			D1
Morton	65/66	23			D1
	66/67				D2
	67/68	18			D1
	68/69				D1

KENNEDY James

Club	Season	Apps	Sub	Gls	Div
Partick T	58/59	4			D1

KENNEDY John
b. Falkirk 3.3.1953
Gairdoch U

Club	Season	Apps	Sub	Gls	Div
Falkirk	71/72	5			D1
	72/73	14			D1
	73/74				D1
Partick T	74/75	1			D1
Stirling A	75/76	22		1	D2
	76/77	34	2	2	D2
	77/78	2	4	2	D1
	78/79	35	1	2	D1
	79/80	31	1	3	D1
	80/81	37		2	D1
	81/82	12			D2
St Johnstone	82/83	16			D1
	83/84	8		3	P

KENNEDY Robert
b. Kilsyth
Kirkintilloch Rob Roy

Club	Season	Apps	Sub	Gls	Div
Third Lanark	52/53	5			D1
	53/54	11		1	D2

KENNEDY Robert
b. Motherwell 23.6.1937
Coltness U

Club	Season	Apps	Sub	Gls	Div
Kilmarnock	57/58	30			D1
	58/59	4			D1
	59/60	20			D1
	60/61	31		1	D1
Manchester C	61/62	42		6	FL
	62/63	41			FL
	63/64	26			FL
	64/65	38		1	FL
	65/66	35		1	FL
	66/67	20	1	1	FL
	67/68	4	2		FL
	68/69	10			FL
Grimsby T	68/69	9		1	FL
	69/70	42			FL
	70/71	33			FL

KENNEDY Stewart J
b. Stirling 31.8.1949 Caps: S - 5
Airth Castle R
Camelon Juniors

Club	Season	Apps	Sub	Gls	Div
Dunfermline A	67/68				D1
	68/69				D1

Linlithgow Rose

Club	Season	Apps	Sub	Gls	Div
Stenhousemuir	71/72	36			D2
	72/73	28			D2
Rangers	73/74	1			D1
	74/75	34			D1
	75/76	12			P
	76/77	31			P
	77/78	22			P
	78/79				P
	79/80				P
Forfar A	80/81	33			D2
	81/82	17			D2
	82/83	37			D2
	83/84	37			D2
	84/85	23			D1
	85/86	13			D1
	86/87	38			D1
	87/88	44			D1
	88/89	31			D1
	89/90	3			D1
	90/91	5			D1
St Johnstone	91/92	1			P

KENNEDY Stuart Robert
b. Grangemouth 31.5.1953 Caps: S - 8
Bothkennor YM

Club	Season	Apps	Sub	Gls	Div
Falkirk	71/72	1			D1
	72/73	34			D1
	73/74	12		1	D1
	74/75	34	2	1	D2
	75/76	26			D1
Aberdeen	76/77	32		1	P
	77/78	34			P
	78/79	32			P
	79/80	35		1	P
	80/81	31			P
	81/82	34		1	P
	82/83	25			P

KEOGH Basil

Club	Season	Apps	Sub	Gls	Div
Clyde	52/53	18		2	D1
	53/54	8		2	D1
	54/55				D1
	55/56	6			D1
	56/57				D2
	57/58	12		7	D1
	58/59	4			D1

KERR Andrew
b. Lugar 29.6.1931 Caps: S - 2
Lugar Boswell Thistle

Club	Season	Apps	Sub	Gls	Div
Partick T	52/53	16			D1
	53/54	20		2	D1
	54/55	20		4	D1
	55/56	33		3	D1
	56/57	33		1	D1
	57/58	19		5	D1
	58/59	26		15	D1
Manchester C	59/60	10			FL
Kilmarnock	59/60	17		8	D1
	60/61	34		34	D1
	61/62	26		23	D1
	62/63	24		25	D1
Sunderland	62/63	8		2	FL
	63/64	10		3	FL
Aberdeen	63/64	1			D1
	64/65	13		7	D1
Glentoran	T 65/66				
Inverness Caley	65/66				
	66/67				

KERR Archibald
b. Motherwell 30.8.1935
Camelon Juniors

Club	Season	Apps	Sub	Gls	Div
Motherwell	53/54	1			D2
	54/55	4			D1
	55/56	17		4	D1
	56/57				D1
Shrewsbury T	56/57	13			FL
Motherwell	57/58	9		2	D1
	58/59				D1
St Mirren	59/60	1			D1
Albion R	60/61				D2
Cowdenbeath	61/62	12		2	D2

KERR David

Club	Season	Apps	Sub	Gls	Div
Raith R	61/62	9		8	D1
	62/63	8		1	D1
	63/64				D2
	64/65				D2
	65/66				D2
	66/67				D2
St Johnstone	67/68	1			D1

KERR Ian R W

Kilbirnie Ladeside
Irvine V

Club	Season	Apps	Sub	Gls	Div
Kilmarnock	73/74		2		D2
	74/75		2		D1

Kilbirnie Ladeside
Irvine V

KERR J

Club	Season	Apps	Sub	Gls	Div
Airdrieonians	64/65	2			D1

KERR James
b. Ormiston ?.?.1919 d. Edinburgh 27.5.2001
Ormiston Primrose

Club	Season	Apps	Sub	Gls	Div
Hibernian	46/47	29			D1
	47/48	12			D1
	48/49	26			D1
	49/50	1			D1
	50/51				D1
	51/52	4			D1

Queen of the South

KERR James

Kello R

Club	Season	Apps	Sub	Gls	Div
Queen of the South	62/63	29			D1
	63/64	34		1	D1
	64/65	33			D2
	65/66	35			D2
	66/67	28			D2
	67/68	34			D2
	68/69			5	D2
	69/70	7		3	D2
	70/71			6	D2

KERR James
b. c1950
Lochend U

Morton	68/69	3		D1

KERR Jerry
b. ?.?.1912
St Bernards

Motherwell	46/47	2		D1
	47/48	2		D1

KERR John
b. Coatbridge

Queen's Park	57/58	7	1	D1
	58/59	2		D2
Albion R	58/59			D2
	59/60			D2
	60/61			D2

KERR R

Queen's Park	46/47	6	2	D1

KERR Robert

Albion R	48/49	13		D1

KERR Robert
b. Coatbridge 29.11.1929
Sunderland

Third Lanark	53/54	13	10	D2
	54/55			D2
Stirling A	55/56	15		D1
Morton				

KERR Ronald

Third Lanark	63/64	1		D1
	64/65	1		D1

KERRAY James Rillay
b. Stirling 2.12.1935
Denny
Dunipace Jnrs

Raith R	57/58	26		9	D1
	58/59	27		9	D1
	59/60	23		10	D1
Dunfermline A	59/60	11		4	D1
Huddersfield T	60/61	28		4	FL
	61/62	26		8	FL
Newcastle U	61/62	15		2	FL
	62/63	23		8	FL
Dunfermline A	62/63	12		3	D1
	63/64	30		15	D1
St Johnstone	64/65	30		11	D1
	65/66	17		7	D1
Stirling A	65/66	10			D1
	66/67	31		8	D1
	67/68	13	1	1	D1
Falkirk	67/68	9			D1
	68/69	4	2	1	D1
Buxton					

KERRIGAN Donald McDonald
b. West Kilbride 7.5.1941 d. ?.12.1990
Drumchapel Amateurs
Johnstone Burgh

St Mirren	58/59	8		2	D1
	59/60	4		1	D1
	60/61	15		5	D1
	61/62	21		14	D1
	62/63	24		9	D1
	63/64	8		2	D1
Aberdeen	63/64	26		12	D1
	64/65	26		14	D1
Heart of Midlothian	65/66	19		6	D1
	66/67	17		4	D1
Dunfermline A	66/67	9			D1
	67/68	1	2		D1
Fulham	67/68	1			FL
	68/69	3	2	1	FL
Lincoln C	L 68/69	12			FL
Portadown					

KICHENBRAND Donald Basil
b. Germiston, S Africa 13.8.1933 Caps: S Afr
Delfos

Rangers	55/56	25		24	D1
	56/57				D1
	57/58	4		2	D1
Sunderland	57/58	10		6	FL
	58/59	40		21	FL
	59/60	3		1	FL
Johannesburg W					
Forfar A	62/63				D2

KIDD Ronald
Campsie Black Watch

Dumbarton	71/72	3		1	D2
	72/73	3	1	1	D1

KIDDIE Alexander Anderson
b. Dundee 27.4.1927
Ashdale Juveniles
Angus Boys Amateurs
Jeanfield Swifts
Dundee Stobswell
Celtic

Aberdeen	46/47	13		5	D1
	47/48	17		4	D1
	48/49	2		1	D1
	49/50	6		1	D1
	50/51				D1
Falkirk	50/51	3			D1
	51/52				D2
	52/53				D1
Dundee	T 52/53				D1
Arbroath	52/53	2			D2
Brechin C	53/54				D3
	54/55				D2
	55/56				D2
Montrose	56/57				D2

KIERNAN James

Morton	61/62	19			D2
	62/63				D2
	63/64	35			D2
	64/65	24			D1
St Mirren	65/66	32		2	D1
	66/67	29			D1
	67/68	6	2		D2
Dumbarton	67/68	7			D2

KIERNAN Thomas
b. Coatbridge 20.10.1918
d. Coatbridge 26.6.1991
Viewpark Celtic
Clydebank Jnrs

Albion R	37/38				D2
	38/39	29		13	D1
Celtic	46/47	22		11	D1
	47/48	1		1	D1
Stoke C	47/48	24		5	FL
	48/49	4		1	FL
Luton T	48/49	23		5	FL
	49/50	24		4	FL
	50/51	8		1	FL
St Mirren	50/51	8		1	D1
Barry T	51/52				
Albion R	52/53	25		3	D2
	53/54	8			D2
Alloa A	54/55				D2

KILGANNON James
b. Bannockburn c1938
d. Bannockburn 24.7.2000
Cowie Juveniles

Falkirk	54/55				D1
	55/56				D1
	56/57				D1
	57/58				D1
Stirling A	58/59	12		1	D1
Dumbarton	59/60				D2
	60/61				D2
	61/62	25			D2
Montrose	62/63				D2
East Stirlingshire	63/64	22			D1
ES Clydebank	64/65				D2
Berwick R	65/66				D2
	66/67				D2
	67/68				D2
Alloa A	68/69				D2

KILGANNON James
Montrose *
Dumbarton *

Third Lanark	64/65	17		2	D1
	65/66	32		12	D2
	66/67	25	2	11	D2

KILGANNON John
b. Bannockburn 5.12.1931
Alva Albion R

Heart of Midlothian	52/53	1		D1
Northampton T	53/54			FL

KILGANNON John
b. Stenhousemuir 26.6.1936 d. 27.2.1967
Cowie Juveniles
St Johnstone
Stenhousemuir

Luton T	58/59	1			FL
	59/60	12		1	FL
	60/61				FL
Stirling A	60/61				D2
	61/62	28		1	D2
Ayr U	62/63				D2
	63/64				D2
Dunfermline A	64/65	13		3	D1
St Johnstone	65/66	7		3	D1
	66/67	23		7	D1

KILMARNOCK William
b. Irvine
Irvine Meadow
Renfrew Jnrs

Motherwell	46/47	30		3	D1
	47/48	28		3	D1
	48/49	29		1	D1
	49/50	29			D1
	50/51	30			D1
	51/52	30			D1
	52/53	26		2	D1
	53/54	30		1	D2
	54/55	30		2	D1
	55/56	34			D1
Airdrieonians	56/57	23			D1
	57/58	9			D1

KILPATRICK Robin
Queen's Park

Partick T	64/65	7	1	D1
	65/66	3	1	D1

KILPATRICK William

Morton	46/47	2	1	D1

KING Allan
Hamilton Amateurs
Rangers

Hamilton A	65/66	22	D1

KING Andrew
b. Crookedholm
Saxone Amateurs
Dreghorn Jnrs

Club	Season			
Kilmarnock	61/62	4		D1
	62/63	4		D1
	63/64	32	3	D1
	64/65	33	1	D1
	65/66	33	1	D1
	66/67	32		D1
	67/68	14	1	D1
	68/69	33		D1
	69/70	33		D1
	70/71	3		D1
	71/72		2	D1

KING Robert Edward
b. Edinburgh 7.9.1941
Shettleston

Club	Season			
Rangers	61/62	2		D1
	62/63			D1
Southend U	63/64	36		FL
	64/65	20	2	FL
	65/66	21	2	FL
Romford				

KING Wallace
b. Kilmarnock 20.2.1932
Bonnyton YC
Muirkirk

Club	Season			
Heart of Midlothian	53/54			D1
	54/55			D1
Queen of the South	55/56	5		D1
	56/57	4		D1
	57/58	4		D1
	58/59	22	3	D1

KINGSMORE B

Club	Season			
Queen's Park	57/58	4	1	D1

KINLOCH Robert
b. Forres
Forres Mechanics
Inverness Caley

Club	Season			
Hibernian	60/61	11	10	D1
	61/62	6	2	D1
	62/63			D2
Berwick R	63/64	16	1	D2
Morton				
Cowdenbeath	T 67/68			D2
Raith R	67/68	12		D1
Dunfermline A	67/68	3		D1

KINLOCH Thomas Sutherland
b. Glasgow 22.2.1927 d. Milngavie 13.2.1994
Anderston Benburb
Falkirk
Glasgow Secondary Juveniles

Club	Season			
Dundee U	46/47	1		D2
	47/48	1		D2
	48/49	1		D2
Falkirk	48/49			D1
	49/50	4	1	D1
Carlisle U	50/51	11		FL
	51/52	17		FL
	52/53	20	1	FL
	53/54	46	2	FL
	54/55	46	5	FL
	55/56	42	7	FL
Workington	56/57	45	7	FL
	57/58	25	5	FL
Southport	57/58	13		FL
	58/59	40		FL
Wigan A				
Colwyn Bay U				

KINNEAR David
b. Kirkcaldy 22.2.1917 d. Crewe ?.5.2001
Burntisland U

Club	Season			
Raith R	33/34			D2
Rangers	34/35	4		D1
	35/36	12	3	D1
	36/37	37	8	D1
	37/38	26	12	D1
	38/39	26	9	D1
Third Lanark	46/47	4		D1
Dunfermline A	47/48			D2
	48/49			D2
Stirling A	T 49/50	3		D1

KINNEAR Harry
b. Buckhaven 5.3.1949

Club	Season			
Forfar A	69/70	17	4	7 D2
	70/71		2	D2
Heart of Midlothian	71/72	4	2	D1
	72/73	2		D1
	73/74	1		D1
East Fife	73/74	14	4	D1
	74/75	33	1 11	D2
	75/76	9	5	D1
	76/77	22	13 2	D1
	77/78	3	1	D1
Falkirk	77/78	17	6 10	D2
Forfar A	78/79	13	4	D2
Leven Jnrs				
Wemyss Hearts				

KINNELL Andrew
b. Cowdenbeath
Cowdenbeath Royals
Sauchie Jnrs

Club	Season			
Cowdenbeath	65/66	18	1	D2
	66/67	36		D2
	67/68	36	4	D2
	68/69			D2
	69/70	36		D2
	70/71	32	4	D1
	71/72	36		D2
St Johnstone	72/73	20		D1
	73/74	15	4	D1
	74/75	29	1	D1
	75/76	25		P
Forfar A	76/77			D2

KINNELL Bert
d. ?.?.1994
Keltyhill A
Lochgelly Violet

Club	Season			
Dunfermline A	46/47			D2
	47/48			D2
Partick T	47/48	5	2	D1
	48/49	14	5	D1
	49/50	27		D1
	50/51	10	2	D1
	51/52	6		D1
Cowdenbeath	52/53	14		D2
	53/54	18		D2
	54/55			D2

KINNELL George
b. Dunfermline 22.12.1937
Kirkford Juveniles
Crossgates Primrose

Club	Season			
East Fife	T			
Raith R	T			
Aberdeen	59/60	21	1	D1
	60/61	31	3	D1
	61/62	32	3	D1
	62/63	34	10	D1
	63/64	11	3	D1
Stoke C	63/64	24	3	FL
	64/65	40	1	FL
	65/66	25	2 2	FL
Oldham A	66/67	12	8	FL
Sunderland	66/67	29		FL
	67/68	35	3 3	FL
	68/69	3		FL
Middlesbrough	68/69	12	1 1	FL
Sydney Juventus				

KINNINMONTH Alexander
b. Methil 6.9.1941
St Andrews Swifts

Club	Season			
Dundee U	T 60/61			D1
Dundee	60/61			D1
	61/62			D1
	62/63			D1
	63/64			D1
	64/65	2		D1
	65/66	6		D1
	66/67	17	4 5	D1
	67/68	5	3	D1
	68/69	20	2 5	D1
	69/70	26	3 3	D1
	70/71	25	2 3	D1
	71/72	9	5 1	D1
Dunfermline A	72/73	36	7	D2
	73/74	34	3	D1
	74/75	34	5	D1
	75/76	16	1	D1
Forfar A	76/77	6	1	D2
Raith R	76/77			D1

KINSELLA James
Greenock Jnrs

Club	Season			
East Fife	66/67			D2
	67/68			D2
	68/69			D2
	69/70			D2
East Stirlingshire	69/70			D2
Ayr U	70/71		1	D1

KIRK Henry Joseph
b. Saltcoats 25.8.1944
Ardeer Recreation

Club	Season			
Middlesbrough	63/64	1		FL
Third Lanark	64/65	19	1	D1
Falkirk	65/66	5	1	D1
Dumbarton	66/67	32	13	D2
Darlington	67/68	30	1 3	FL
	68/69	24	1 4	FL
	69/70	5		FL
Hartlepool U	69/70	30	1 4	FL
	70/71	12	2 1	FL
Scunthorpe U	70/71	21	4	FL
	71/72	46	4	FL
	72/73	45	8	FL
Stockport Co	73/74	34	4 5	FL
	74/75	26	4 2	FL

KIRK James
b. Tarbolton 12.11.1925

Club	Season			
St Mirren	47/48	13		D1
	48/49	26		D1
	49/50	19		D1
	50/51	28		D1
Bury	51/52	18		FL
	52/53	41		FL
	53/54	21		FL
Colchester U	54/55	32		FL
Torquay U	55/56	39		FL
Aldershot	56/57	5		FL
Tonbridge				

KIRK Robert
b. Arniston 12.8.1927
Newtongrange Hearts
Arniston Thistle
Edinburgh Thistle
Arniston R
Dunfermline A

Club	Season			
Raith R	53/54	15		D1
	54/55	21	2	D1
Heart of Midlothian	55/56	31	2	D1
	56/57	27	2	D1
	57/58	30	2	D1
	58/59	33		D1
	59/60	34		D1
	60/61	30		D1
	61/62	28	2	D1
Gala Fairydean				

KIRKLAND James William
b. Bedford 30.10.1946
Birkenshaw Amateurs

Team	Season				Div
Aberdeen	69/70	13			D1
Grimsby T	70/71	12			FL

KIRKPATRICK Robert
b. Troon
Troon A

Team	Season				Div
Kilmarnock	46/47	12		1	D1
	47/48				D2
	48/49				D2
Stirling A	T 48/49				D2
St Cuthberts W					
Glenluce					
Wigton & Bladnoch					
Tarff Rovers					

KIRKWOOD Ian
b. Edinburgh 29.11.1932
Wokingham T

Team	Season				Div
Reading	52/53	11			FL
	53/54	20			FL
	54/55	4		1	FL
East Fife	55/56	11		4	D1
Arbroath					

KNOX Archibald
b. Dundee 1.5.1947
Errol R

Team	Season				Div
Forfar A	64/65	2			D2
	65/66	32		6	D2
	66/67	34	1	9	D2
	67/68	31		7	D2
	68/69			11	D2
	69/70			9	D2
	70/71			9	D2
St Mirren	70/71	28		7	D1
	71/72	20	1	4	D2
Dundee U	71/72	11		3	D1
	72/73	10		1	D1
	73/74	21	7	8	D1
	74/75	1	4		D1
	75/76	2			P
Montrose	76/77	13		3	D1
Forfar A	76/77	21		3	D2
	77/78	33	1	3	D2
	78/79	27	4	2	D2
	79/80	29	3		D2

KNOX James Hay
b. Brechin 26.11.1935

Team	Season				Div
Raith R	56/57	5			D1
	57/58	8			D1
Coventry C	57/58	2			FL
	58/59				FL
Rugby T					
Lockheed Leamington					
Corby T					

KNOX John
Kelty R

Team	Season				Div
Cowdenbeath	50/51				D2
	51/52				D2
	52/53	16		2	D2
Preston NE	53/54				FL
	54/55				FL
Queen of the South	55/56				D1
	56/57	3			D1
	57/58	3			D1
	58/59	26		3	D1
Cowdenbeath	59/60				D2

KNOX Kenneth
Hibernian
Kirkintilloch Rob Roy

Team	Season				Div
Dumbarton *	63/64	1			D2
Kirkintilloch Rob Roy					
Clyde	64/65	18		7	D1
	65/66	20		7	D1
	66/67	8	1	2	D1
	67/68	11	2	3	D1

KNOX R

Team	Season				Div
Airdrieonians	50/51	1			D1

KNOX Thomas
b. Glasgow 5.9.1939

Team	Season				Div
East Stirlingshire	61/62	21		7	D2
Chelsea	62/63	6			FL
	63/64	1			FL
	64/65	13			FL
Newcastle U	64/65	9		1	FL
	65/66	8			FL
	66/67	7	1		FL
Mansfield T	66/67	13		2	FL
	67/68	21		3	FL
Northampton T	67/68	16			FL
	68/69	12		2	FL
St Mirren	69/70	1			D1
Tonbridge					

KOPEL Frank
b. Falkirk 28.3.1949

Team	Season				Div
Manchester U	67/68	1		1	FL
	68/69	7		1	FL
Blackburn R	68/69	4		2	FL
	69/70	5			FL
	70/71	11			FL
	71/72	3			FL
Dundee U	71/72	8		1	D1
	72/73	32	1	1	D1
	73/74	31	1	1	D1
	74/75	30		1	D1
	75/76	29	1		P
	76/77	30	2		P
	77/78	33			P
	78/79	11	3	2	P
	79/80	31		1	P
	80/81	27	6		P
	81/82	6	1		P
Arbroath	81/82	18			D2
	82/83	35		1	D2
	83/84	9			D2
Dundee U	83/84				P

KURILA John
b. Glasgow 10.4.1941
St Francis BG
Celtic
Blantyre Victoria L

Team	Season				Div
Celtic	58/59	1			D1
	59/60	1			D1
	60/61	3			D1
	61/62				D1
Northampton T	62/63	40		1	FL
Hamilton Steelers	63				
Bristol C	63/64	6			FL
Northampton T	63/64	18		1	FL
	64/65	1			FL
	65/66	20		1	FL
	66/67	37		1	FL
	67/68	29	3		FL
Southend U	68/69	46		1	FL
	69/70	41	1		FL
Colchester U	70/71	44		2	FL
	71/72	9		2	FL
Lincoln C	71/72	23		1	FL
	72/73				FL
Atherstone U					

KYLE John
Heart of Midlothian

Team	Season				Div
Stirling A	53/54	5			D1
Rosyth Rec	54/55				
	55/56				
	56/57				
Cowdenbeath	57/58				D2
Stenhousemuir					

LACHLAN James

Team	Season				Div
Falkirk	54/55	2			D1
	55/56				D1
	56/57				D1
	57/58	11			D1
	58/59	20		1	D1
St Johnstone	59/60	22		1	D2
	60/61	30			D1
	61/62	34			D1
	62/63	33			D2
	63/64	8			D1
Dumbarton	63/64	4			D2
	64/65	2			D2
Stenhousemuir *	65/66	23			D2

LAFFERTY James
Barrhead St Josephs
Arthurlie

Team	Season				Div
Celtic	50/51				D1
	51/52	6		3	D1
	52/53	1		1	D1
Lincoln C	53/54				FL
Larne	53/54				
Worcester C					
Los Angeles Danes					

LAING Alan
Newtongrange Star

Team	Season				Div
Stirling A	66/67	7	1		D1
	67/68	4	1	1	D1

LAING Brian
Liverpool

Team	Season				Div
Heart of Midlothian	70/71	1		1	D1
Queen of the South	71/72	4	1		D2

LAING David
b. Strathmiglo 20.2.1925
Bayview YC

Team	Season				Div
Heart of Midlothian	46/47	9			D1
	47/48	29		2	D1
	48/49	28		3	D1
	49/50	26		1	D1
	50/51	27		3	D1
	51/52	26		1	D1
	52/53	23		1	D1
	53/54	23			D1
Bath C					
Clyde	54/55	27		1	D1
	55/56	16		3	D1
Hibernian	56/57	6			D1
Gillingham	57/58	38		2	FL
	58/59	44		3	FL
Margate					

LAING Derek
b. Dundee
Lochee BC

Team	Season				Div
Dundee	74/75	1			D1
	75/76	18		1	P
	76/77	2	7	1	D1
	77/78		2		D1
Sydney Olympic					

LAING William
Greig Park R
Rangers

Team	Season				Div
Cowdenbeath	70/71	17		1	D1
	71/72	33	1	13	D2
	72/73	34		15	D2
	73/74	30		21	D2
	74/75	26		14	D2
	75/76	5	4	4	D2
Dunfermline A	75/76	3	3		D1
Lossiemouth					
Berwick R	76/77	16	2	8	D2
	77/78	22	10	14	D2
Brechin C	78/79	2	2	1	D2

LAIRD Alexander
b. Newmains 2.6.1926
East Fife
Fauldhouse U

Stirling A	49/50	8	2	D1
	50/51			D2
	51/52	6		D1
Chelsea	52/53			FL
Notts Co	53/54	1		FL
Stirling A	54/55	21	2	D1

LAIRD Alexander Watson
b. Edinburgh 23.10.1928
Hibernian

Dunfermline A	53/54	10	D2
	54/55		D2
	55/56	33	D1
	56/57	18	D1
Barrow	57/58	22	FL
Scunthorpe U	58/59		FL

LAIRD C

Falkirk	49/50	3	1	D1

LAIRD David Sands
b. Rutherglen 11.2.1936

St Mirren	54/55	4	1	D1
	55/56	18	5	D1
	56/57	1		D1
Aldershot	57/58			FL
St Mirren	57/58			D1
	58/59	14	3	D1
	59/60	6	1	D1
Northampton T	60/61	12	1	FL
Folkestone				
Corby T				

LAIRD William
b. Carronshore c1918 d. Falkirk ?.9.1999
Gairdoch Juveniles
East Stirlingshire

East Fife	37/38	18		D2
	38/39	34	1	D2
	46/47	23		D2
	47/48	30		D2
	48/49	25		D1
	49/50	26		D1
	50/51			D1
Dunfermline A	51/52			D2

LAIRD William

East Stirlingshire	61/62	28		D2
	62/63			D2
	63/64	11		D1
ES Clydebank	64/65	5		D2
East Stirlingshire	65/66	34	2	D2
	66/67	7		D2

LAMB Peter
b. New Monkland 6.6.1925
Arthurlie
St Anthonys

Celtic	46/47	1	D1
Alloa A	47/48		D2
	48/49		D2
Wigtown & Bladnoch			

LAMBIE Duncan
b. Whitburn
Armadale Thistle

Dundee	70/71	1			D1
	71/72	20	3	1	D1
	72/73	12	2		D1
	73/74	24	7	6	D1
	74/75	1	1	1	D1
St Johnstone	74/75	27	1	4	D1
	75/76	26		3	P
	76/77	15	1	1	D1
FC Furth	77/78				
Hibernian	78/79	4	2		P
	79/80	9	1		P

LAMBIE John
b. Whitburn 2.3.1941
Whitburn Jnrs

Falkirk	60/61	12		5	D2
	61/62	10			D1
	62/63	19		5	D1
	63/64	14			D1
	64/65	32		1	D1
	65/66	26		3	D1
	66/67	29		1	D1
	67/68	31		1	D1
	68/69	25			D1
St Johnstone	69/70	26		2	D1
	70/71	23	2	1	D1
	71/72	19			D1
	72/73	27		1	D1
	73/74	6			D1

LAMONT William Paul
b. Larkhall 12.5.1936
Bellshill YM
Douglas Water Thistle
Carluke R
Bellshill Academy

Albion R	58/59			D2
	59/60			D2
	60/61			D2
	61/62	33	3	D2
Cheltenham T	62/63			
Hamilton A	63/64	25		D2
	64/65	36		D2
	65/66	28		D1
	66/67	35		D2
	67/68	32		D2
	68/69	32		D2
	69/70	1		D2
Albion R	69/70	15		D2
	70/71			D2
Hamilton A	71/72	6		D2

LANDSBOROUGH Murray
b. Thornhill 30.12.1915 d. ?.?.1987

Queen of the South	38/39		
Kilmarnock	46/47	23	D1
Carlisle U	47/48	1	FL
Nithsdale W	48/49		
	49/50		

LANG R

Third Lanark	46/47	1	D1

LANNON Brian

Wishaw Jnrs

Ayr U	70/71	1		1	D1
	71/72				D1
	72/73	1			D1
	73/74	3			D1
	74/75	8	1		D1
Hamilton A	75/76	12	2		D1
Auchinleck Talbot					

LAPSLEY David
b. Kirkintilloch 7.4.1924 d. Falkirk 15.1.2001
High Bonnybridge Rose
Bathgate Thistle

St Mirren	46/47	2		D1
	47/48	2	1	D1
	48/49	24		D1
	49/50	29	10	D1
	50/51	25	3	D1
	51/52	23	1	D1
	52/53	30	2	D1
	53/54	27	3	D1
	54/55	28	4	D1
	55/56	34	9	D1
	56/57	30	2	D1
	57/58	16	2	D1
	58/59	33	9	D1

LAPSLEY John
b. Edinburgh 24.11.1951
Linlithgow Rose

Airdrieonians	72/73			D2
	73/74			D2
	74/75	25	1	1	D1
	75/76	14	3	1	D1
	76/77	28	2	2	D1
	77/78	32	7		D1
	78/79	38		6	D1
	79/80	30		11	D1
Partick T	79/80	2	1		P
	80/81	14	9		P
	81/82	18	5		P
	82/83		1		P
Ayr U	82/83	4	1		D1
East Stirlingshire	82/83	3			D2
Stenhousemuir	82/83	1			D2
Cowdenbeath	82/83	1			D2
Hamilton A	82/83	2			D1
Falkirk	82/83	2			D1
Dunfermline A	83/84	17		1	D2
Brechin C	84/85	6			D1

LATCHFORD Peter William
b. Kings Heath 27.9.1952
Monyhull Hospital
Redditch U
Sutton Coldfield T
Finn Harps GAA

West Bromwich A	69/70				FL
	70/71				FL
	71/72				FL
	72/73	26			FL
	73/74	42			FL
	74/75	13			FL
Celtic	L 74/75	10			D1
	75/76	35			P
	76/77	31			P
	77/78	36			P
	78/79	27			P
	79/80	36			P
	80/81				P
	81/82				P
	82/83				P
	83/84	3			P
	84/85	2			P
	85/86	6			P
	86/87	1			P
Clyde	87/88	12			D1

LAUGHTON Denis
b. Dingwall 22.1.1948
Ross Co

Morton	67/68	2	1		D1
	68/69	5			D1
	69/70	21	2	1	D1
	70/71	11		1	D1
	71/72	23	1	2	D1
	72/73	9			D1
	73/74	4			D1
Newcastle U	73/74	6			FL
	74/75	1			FL
Whitley Bay					

LAURIE Ian
b. Falkirk 12.10.1946
Falkirk

Stirling A	67/68	5	1		D1
Linlithgow Rose					
Alloa A	70/71				D2
	71/72	11	5	3	D2

LAURIE J S

Queen of the South	47/48	5	D1
	48/49	6	D1

LAURIE Robert

Rangers

Falkirk	72/73	1		D1
	73/74			D1
St Mirren	74/75	15	3	D2

LAVELLE John

St Ninians BC

Club	Season	App	Sub	Gls	Div
Morton	69/70	4		1	D1
	70/71				D1
	71/72	2			D1
	72/73	17	3	1	D1
	73/74	10		2	D1

LAVERY Daniel O'Donnell
b. Sydney 24.8.1925 d. Chorley 19.3.1979
Antrim GAA

Club	Season	App	Sub	Gls	Div
Celtic	47/48	2		1	D1
	48/49	2			D1
Glentoran	L 48/49				
Ballymena U					
Dundalk	49/50				
	50/51				
Leyland Motors					

LAW John

Club	Season	App	Sub	Gls	Div
Airdrieonians	31/32	29		4	D1
	32/33	33		4	D1
	33/34	25			D1
	34/35	27		5	D1
	35/36	38		9	D1
Queen of the South	36/37	34		8	D1
	37/38	37		16	D1
	38/39	29		11	D1
	46/47	19		3	D1
	47/48	17		1	D1
	48/49	1			D1

LAW John

Kello R

Club	Season	App	Sub	Gls	Div
Queen of the South	62/63	9			D1
	63/64	11		1	D1
	64/65	36		10	D2
	65/66	31		10	D2
	66/67	26	1	4	D2
Stranraer	67/68	13	3	2	D2

LAWLOR John Boscoe
b. Bellshill 30.1.1937
Kilmarnock Amateurs
Shettleston

Club	Season	App	Sub	Gls	Div
Kilmarnock	55/56	6		2	D1
	56/57	1			D1
	57/58	2			D1
	58/59				D1
Aldershot	59/60	32		11	FL
	60/61	25		7	FL
Stirling A	61/62	20		8	D1
	62/63				D2
	63/64	7		5	D2
Dumbarton	63/64	25		7	D2
Falkirk	64/65	5		1	D1
ES Clydebank	64/65	5		1	D2
Alloa A	64/65	15		3	D2
	65/66	11		3	D2
East Fife	65/66	17		4	D2
	66/67	33	1	15	D2
	67/68	4		2	D2
Stranraer	67/68	13			D2
Hamilton A	68/69	17	2	2	D2
Hamilton Steelers					

LAWRIE Robert

Irvine Meadow

Club	Season	App	Sub	Gls	Div
Ayr U	T 68/69				D2
Partick T	69/70	20			D1
	70/71	31		9	D2
	71/72	29	3	1	D1
	72/73	20	4	2	D1
	73/74	15	3	1	D1
	74/75	10	5	1	D1
	75/76		1		D1
Stranraer	75/76	14	1	3	D2

LAWSON

Club	Season	App	Sub	Gls	Div
Raith R	59/60	4			D1

LAWSON Allan

Club	Season	App	Sub	Gls	Div
St Mirren	49/50	1			D1

LAWSON Kirkland

Clyde R
Lanark U
Shettleston
Blantyre Victoria

Club	Season	App	Sub	Gls	Div
Motherwell	70/71	16	2	2	D1
	71/72	16	4	7	D1
	72/73	17	1	5	D1
	73/74	2	4	1	D1
Falkirk	73/74	27		7	D1
	74/75	32	1	10	D2
	75/76	23	1	2	D1
Hamilton A	76/77	23	3	6	D1
Shettleston					

LAWSON William
b. Dundee 28.11.1947
Brechin C

Club	Season	App	Sub	Gls	Div
Sheffield W	69/70	8			FL
	70/71	1	1		FL
St Mirren	70/71	5		1	D1
	71/72	3	2	1	D2
	72/73				D2
Arbroath	73/74	3	2		D1

LAYBURN Stuart
b. Kilmarnock
Kilmarnock Amateurs
Troon Jnrs

Club	Season	App	Sub	Gls	Div
Kilmarnock	61/62				D1
	62/63				D1
	63/64	5			D1
	64/65				D1
	65/66	1			D1
	66/67				D1
Airdrieonians	67/68				D1

LECKIE John

Bellfield BC

Club	Season	App	Sub	Gls	Div
Kilmarnock	70/71	1			D1
Darvel Jnrs					

LECKIE Samuel
b. Monkton
Annbank U

Club	Season	App	Sub	Gls	Div
Ayr U	56/57	1			D1

LEDGERWOOD Thomas
b. Coldstream
Coldstream

Club	Season	App	Sub	Gls	Div
Partick T	46/47	2			D1
	47/48	5			D1
	48/49	1			D1
	49/50	16			D1
	50/51	30		1	D1
	51/52	29			D1
	52/53	20			D1
	53/54	23			D1
	54/55	25			D1
	55/56	13			D1
	56/57	15			D1
	57/58	17			D1
	58/59	11			D1

LEE Alan

Renfrew Jnrs

Club	Season	App	Sub	Gls	Div
Kilmarnock	71/72	1			D1
	72/73	12		1	D1

LEGGAT Graham
b. Aberdeen 20.6.1934 Caps: S - 18
Banks o'Dee

Club	Season	App	Sub	Gls	Div
Aberdeen	53/54	26		15	D1
	54/55	26		11	D1
	55/56	18		19	D1
	56/57	24		12	D1
	57/58	15		7	D1
Fulham	58/59	36		21	FL
	59/60	28		18	FL
	60/61	36		23	FL
	61/62	31		13	FL
	62/63	33		10	FL
	63/64	25		15	FL
	64/65	17		4	FL
	65/66	32	1	15	FL
	66/67	13	2	8	FL
Birmingham C	66/67	9		1	FL
	67/68	4	3	3	FL
Rotherham U	68/69	13	2	7	FL
Bromsgrove R					
Toronto Metros	71	11		2	NA

LEIFSSON Gudgeir
b. Iceland Caps: Ice - 39

Club	Season	App	Sub	Gls	Div
Morton	74/75	4			D1

LEIGH Andrew
b. Rothesay c1929 d. Dunfermline 24.5.2003
Dunoon A

Club	Season	App	Sub	Gls	Div
Raith R	48/49	13			D2
	49/50	10			D1
	50/51	28			D1
	51/52	27		1	D1
	52/53	18			D1
	53/54	21			D1
	54/55	27			D1
	55/56	31			D1
	56/57	30			D1
	57/58	34			D1
	58/59	28			D1
	59/60	3			D1
	60/61	28			D1
	61/62	18		1	D1
	62/63	8			D1

LEISHMAN James
b. ?.?.1953
Dunfermline U

Club	Season	App	Sub	Gls	Div
Dunfermline A	71/72	6	1	2	D1
	72/73	29	1	1	D2
	73/74	28	1	1	D1
	74/75				D1
	75/76		1		D1
Cowdenbeath	76/77	11			D2

LEISHMAN Robert
b. Edinburgh
Broxburn A

Club	Season	App	Sub	Gls	Div
East Fife	54/55	18		3	D1
	55/56	17		4	D1
	56/57	33		6	D1
	57/58	20		1	D1
Raith R	59/60	2			D1

LEISHMAN Thomas
b. Stenhousemuir 3.9.1937
Camelon Juniors

Club	Season	App	Sub	Gls	Div
St Mirren	57/58	2			D1
	58/59	11		1	D1
	59/60	2			D1
Liverpool	59/60	15			FL
	60/61	40		4	FL
	61/62	41		1	FL
	62/63	13		1	FL
Hibernian	62/63	13		1	D1
	63/64	14			D1
	64/65	3			D1
Linfield	65/66				
	66/67				
Stranraer	67/68	4			D2
	68/69			2	D2
	69/70	21	2	2	D2

LEISHMAN William
b. Motherwell 17.4.1953 d. Carluke 21.8.2002

Motherwell	73/74	3		D1
	74/75	1		D1
	75/76			P
	76/77			P
Albion R	77/78	31		D2
	78/79	35	5	D2
	79/80	39	8	D2
	80/81			D2
Dunfermline A	80/81	25	2	D1
	81/82	4		D1
Albion R	81/82	13	2	D2
	82/83	25	1	D2

LEITCH William

Wishaw High School

Motherwell	46/47	5	5	D1
	47/48			D1
	48/49			D1

LEMAY Thomas

East Stirlingshire	63/64	2		D1
Cowdenbeath	64/65	1		D2

LENNON James S.R.

Falkirk	50/51	16	1	D1
Linfield	51/52			
Cowdenbeath	52/53			D2

LENNOX Guy
b. Kirkmuirhill

Kirkmuirhill
Wishaw Jnrs

Airdrieonians	51/52	20	18	D1
	52/53	6	5	D1
Morton				

English Non-League
Douglas Water Thistle

Hamilton A	54/55	1		D2
Clyde	55/56	12	7	D1
Ayr U	56/57	3		D1
Hamilton A	57/58	24	18	D2

LENNOX Robert
b. Saltcoats 30.8.1943 Caps S-10

Star of the Sea Amateurs
Ardeer Recreation

Celtic	61/62	1		D1
	62/63	4		D1
	63/64	7	1	D1
	64/65	22	9	D1
	65/66	24	15	D1
	66/67	26	1	13 D1
	67/68	28		32 D1
	68/69	27	1	12 D1
	69/70	19	1	14 D1
	70/71	22	2	10 D1
	71/72	24	2	12 D1
	72/73	15	8	11 D1
	73/74	17	2	12 D1
	74/75	9	5	5 D1
	75/76	25	5	10 P
	76/77	2	3	2 P
	77/78	1	2	P
Houston Hurricanes	78	30		3 NA
Celtic	78/79	6	8	4 P
	79/80	19	10	6 P

LESLIE John

Tranent Jnrs

St Johnstone	70/71	6	1	3 D1
	71/72	1		D1
Berwick R	72/73	3		D2

LESLIE Lawrence Grant
b. Edinburgh 17.3.1935 Caps: S - 5

Newtongrange Star				
Hibernian	56/57	12		D1
	57/58	33		D1
	58/59	31		D1
Airdrieonians	59/60	11		D1
	60/61	31		D1
West Ham U	61/62	37		FL
	62/63	20		FL
Stoke C	63/64	25		FL
	64/65	41		FL
	65/66	12		FL
Millwall	66/67	42		FL
	67/68	25		FL
Southend U	68/69	13		FL

LESLIE Matthew

Arthurlie

Stirling A	54/55	4	2	D1

LESZ Alfons
b. Poland

Forres Mechanics

St Mirren	47/48	27	8	D1
	48/49	24	6	D1
	49/50	18	2	D1
	50/51	17	1	D1
	51/52	14	5	D1
Worcester C	52/53			
Kidderminster H				

LETHAM David

Queen's Park	46/47	25	1	D1
	47/48	30		D1
	48/49			D2
	49/50	10		D2
	50/51	9		D2

LEWIS William

Morton

Third Lanark	56/57			D2
	57/58	32	1	D1
	58/59	19		D1
	59/60	27		D1
	60/61	27	2	D1
	61/62	24		D1
	62/63	9		D1
	63/64	10		D1

LIDDELL

Dundee U	70/71		1	D1

LIDDELL Colin McD
b. Glasgow 10.6.1925 d. Kilmarnock 24.2.1997

Queen's Park	46/47	17	6	D1
Morton	46/47			D1
	47/48	30	7	D1
	48/49	28	7	D1
Heart of Midlothian	49/50	11	1	D1
	50/51	1		D1
	51/52	2		D1
Rangers	51/52	24	6	D1
	52/53	6	2	D1
	53/54	5		D1
Heart of Midlothian	54/55			D1
Stirling A	55/56	13		D1
Morton				

LIDDELL Daniel

Clydebank Juveniles

St Johnstone	58/59	20	1	D2
	59/60	20	7	D2
	60/61	1		D1
Corby T				

LIDDELL George

St Mirren	53/54	4		D1

LIDDELL John

Third Lanark	52/53	8	1	D1

LIDDELL John Cairney
b. Stirling 13.12.1933
d. Grangemouth 16.3.1999

Kilsyth R
Cambuslang R

St Johnstone	58/59	3	4	D2
	59/60	31	27	D2
	60/61	1		D1
Oldham A	60/61	18	9	FL
	61/62	5	1	FL
Worcester C				
Mossley				

LIDDELL Thomas
b. Edinburgh 15.1.1931

Musselburgh A

East Fife	52/53			D1
	53/54	4		D1
	54/55	6		D1
	55/56	2		D1

LINDORES William Robert Hope
b. Newcastleton 3.5.1933

Edinburgh Thistle
Dunbar U

Heart of Midlothian	56/57	2		D1
	57/58	1		D1
	58/59			
Barrow	59/60	4		FL
Gala Fairydean				

LINDSAY David
b. Dumbarton 23.9.1919 d. ?.?.1993

St Mirren	46/47	24		D1
	47/48	20		D1
Luton T	48/49	7		FL
Barnsley	48/49	6		FL
	49/50	35	1	FL
	50/51	19	2	FL
	51/52	18		FL
Wisbech T				

LINDSAY George

Carluke Jnrs

Motherwell	60/61	18	2	D1
	61/62	8	2	D1
	62/63	34	4	D1
	63/64	27	8	D1
	64/65	20	3	D1
	65/66	15	4	D1
	66/67	19	1	6 D1
	67/68	17	2	D1
Queen of the South	68/69			2 D2

LINDSAY James

Heart of Midlothian

Hamilton A	46/47	18		D1
St Johnstone	47/48	26		D2
	48/49	28	2	D2
	49/50	23	2	D2
	50/51	26	1	D2
	51/52	14		D2

LINDSAY John

Clyde	48/49	3		D1
	49/50	9		D1
	50/51	24		D1
	51/52			D2
	52/53	16		D1

LINDSAY John

Lugar Boswell Thistle
Heart of Midlothian

Hamilton A	53/54	5		D1
Ayr U	54/55			D2

LINDSAY John Smith
b. Auchinleck 8.8.1924 d. ?.12.1991

Club	Season				Div
Rangers	46/47	2			D1
	47/48	3			D1
	48/49	4			D1
	49/50	2			D1
	50/51	6			D1
Everton	50/51	4			FL
	51/52	40			FL
	52/53	30			FL
	53/54	31		2	FL
Worcester C	54/55				
	55/56				
Bury	56/57	7			FL
South Liverpool					

LINDSAY Kenneth

Club	Season				Div
Penicuik A					
Raith R	69/70	19	2	1	D1
	70/71			1	D2
	71/72	24		2	D2

LINDSAY W

Club	Season				Div
Queen's Park	57/58	7		1	D1

LINEY Patrick
b. Paisley 14.7.1936
Dalry Thistle

Club	Season				Div
Dundee	57/58	1			D1
	58/59	2			D1
	59/60	33			D1
	60/61	30			D1
	61/62	34			D1
	62/63	2			D1
St Mirren	64/65	32			D1
	65/66	16			D1
Bradford PA	66/67	11			FL
Bradford C	67/68	42			FL
	68/69	21			FL
	69/70	31			FL
	70/71	35			FL
	71/72	18			FL
Bradford PA					

LINWOOD Alexander Bryce
b. Drumsmudden 13.3.1920
d. Renfrew 26.10.2003 Caps: S - 1
Muirkirk A

Club	Season				Div
St Mirren	38/39	4			D1
Middlesbrough	46/47	14		3	FL
Hibernian	47/48	24		15	D1
	48/49	12		8	D1
Clyde	48/49	14		6	D1
	49/50	29		12	D1
	50/51	13		2	D1
Morton	51/52	24		19	D1
	52/53	24		17	D2
	53/54	28		22	D2
	54/55				D2

LISTER Ian T
b. Kirkcaldy
Smeaton BC

Club	Season				Div
Aberdeen	63/64	12		1	D1
	64/65	10		1	D1
Raith R	67/68	10	1	3	D1
Dunfermline A	67/68	8	1	2	D1
	68/69	8	1	3	D1
	69/70		3		D1
St Mirren	69/70	25		5	D1
	70/71	24	1	7	D1
Raith R	71/72	18	7	1	D2
Berwick R	72/73	31	2	6	D2
	73/74	13	3	1	D2

LITTLE Adam
b. Blantyre
Blantyre Victoria
Queen's Park

Club	Season				Div
Rangers	37/38				D1
	38/39	4			D1
	46/47				D1
	47/48	1			D1
	48/49				D1
	49/50				D1
	50/51	1			D1
Morton	51/52	30			D1
	52/53	27			D2
	53/54	28		1	D2

LITTLE Alexander

Club	Season				Div
Holytown U					
Stirling A	49/50	4			D1

LITTLE James

Club	Season				Div
Rutherglen Glencairn					
Stirling A	58/59				D1
	59/60	24			D1
St Johnstone	60/61	32			D1
	61/62	30			D1
	62/63	12			D2
Third Lanark	62/63	8			D1
	63/64	2			D1
	64/65	29			D1

LITTLE R John
b. Calgary 7.7.1930 Caps: S - 1

Club	Season				Div
Queen's Park	48/49	8			D2
	49/50	18			D2
	50/51	29			D2
Rangers	51/52	28			D1
	52/53	30			D1
	53/54	25		1	D1
	54/55	21			D1
	55/56	25			D1
	56/57	5			D1
	57/58	12			D1
	58/59	1			D1
	59/60	31			D1
	60/61				D1
	61/62				D1
Morton					

LITTLE William
b. Dumfries 4.2.1940
Dumfries St Vincent

Club	Season				Div
Aberdeen	57/58	8		4	D1
	58/59	29		13	D1
	59/60	30		9	D1
	60/61	29		12	D1
	61/62	30		17	D1
	62/63	16		6	D1
	63/64	9			D1
	64/65	21		3	D1
	65/66	34		10	D1
	66/67	14		1	D1
	67/68	13	2	3	D1
	68/69	1			D1
Juventus (Aus)					
Inverness Caley					
Falkirk	70/71	4		2	D1
Stirling A	71/72	14	4	3	D2
East Stirlingshire	72/73	13	5	1	D2

LITTLEJOHN Alistair

Club	Season				Div
Blairgowrie					
St Johnstone	65/66	8		3	D1
	66/67	1	1		D1
	67/68				D1
	68/69				D1
Brechin C	69/70	21	3	8	D2
	70/71			1	D2
	71/72	31		2	D2
	72/73	12	1	2	D2
	73/74	5		1	D2

LIVINGSTONE B

Club	Season			Div
Dumbarton	71/72	1		D2
	72/73	1		D1

LLOYD Graham
b. Liverpool 10.1.1951

Club	Season			Div
Liverpool	68/69			FL
	69/70			FL
	70/71			FL
	71/72			FL
	72/73			FL
	73/74			FL
Motherwell	74/75	9		D1
Portsmouth	75/76	33		FL
	76/77	41		FL
	77/78			FL
Runcorn				

LOCHHEAD Ian
b. 26.9.1939
Drumchapel Amateurs
Partick Avondale

Club	Season			Div
Celtic	58/59	7	2	D1
	59/60	1		D1
	60/61			D1
Dumbarton	61/62	4		D2

LOCHRIE Archibald

Club	Season			Div
Cumbernauld U				
Partick T	72/73	1		D1
	73/74			D1
	74/75			D1
Queen of the South	75/76	3		D1
Kirkintilloch Rob Roy				

LOCKERBIE James

Club	Season			Div
Raith R	57/58	9		D1
	58/59	2		D1
	59/60	1		D1

LODGE Thomas Joseph
b. Huddersfield 16.4.1921
d. Huddersfield ?.?.2002

Club	Season			Div
Huddersfield T	46/47	1		FL
	47/48	1		FL
Goole T	48/49			
	49/50			
St Johnstone	50/51	4		D2

LOGAN Alexander
b. 4.11.1928 d. ?.12.2003
Edinburgh Waverley

Club	Season			Div
Falkirk	47/48			D1
	48/49	17	6	D1
	49/50	4		D1
	50/51			D1
	51/52			D2
Hamilton A	52/53	17	8	D2

LOGAN John

Club	Season			Div
Dunfermline A	58/59	1		D1

LOGAN Robert

Club	Season			Div
Tranent Jnrs				
Motherwell	65/66	1		D1
	66/67			D1
Berwick R	67/68	2		D2
	68/69		2	D2

LOGIE William

Club	Season			Div
Rangers	56/57	16		D1
	57/58			D1
Aberdeen	58/59	5		D1
Arbroath	59/60	2		D1

LOGUE Samuel Walker
b. Glasgow 9.4.1934
Renfrew Jnrs

Club	Season			Div
Clyde	59/60	1		D1
Accrington S	60/61	2		FL

LONG Hugh

b. Glasgow 2.1.1923 Caps: S - 1

Club	Season	Apps	Sub	Gls	Div
Mearns Amateurs					
Maryhill Harp					
Celtic					
Clyde	46/47	30		1	D1
	47/48	25		2	D1
	48/49	15			D1
	49/50	18			D1
	50/51	29		1	D1
	51/52				D2
	52/53	26			D1
	53/54	7			D1
Worcester C	54/55				
	55/56				

LONIE James

Club	Season	Apps	Sub	Gls	Div
Grangemouth U					
Motherwell	62/63	1		1	D1
	63/64				D1

LORIMER W

Club	Season	Apps	Sub	Gls	Div
Morton	47/48	1			D1

LORNIE James

b. Aberdeen

Club	Season	Apps	Sub	Gls	Div
Aberdeen St Clements					
St Mirren	52/53	1			D1
	53/54				D1
	54/55	29			D1
	55/56	25			D1
	56/57	1			D1
	57/58	9			D1
Inverness Caley					

LOUGH John

Club	Season	Apps	Sub	Gls	Div
Preston A					
Heart of Midlothian	58/59	11			D1
	59/60				D1
	60/61	3			D1
Arbroath					

LOUGHLAN John

b. Coatbridge 12.6.1943

Club	Season	Apps	Sub	Gls	Div
Leicester C					
Morton	64/65	1			D1
	65/66	22			D1
	66/67				D2
	67/68	30			D1
Crystal Palace	68/69	29			FL
	69/70	26			FL
	70/71	3			FL
	71/72		2		FL
Wrexham	L 71/72	5			FL
Wimbledon					
Kettering T					

LOURIE Ian

Club	Season	Apps	Sub	Gls	Div
Linlithgow Rose					
Raith R	61/62	7		1	D1
	62/63	13		2	D1
	63/64	27		12	D2
	64/65	18		1	D2
ES Clydebank	64/65	7			D2
Falkirk	65/66	3			D1
	66/67				D1
Stranraer *	67/68	2			D2

LOVE John

b. 21.7.1952

Club	Season	Apps	Sub	Gls	Div
Penicuik A					
East Fife	70/71				D2
	71/72	16		3	D1
	72/73	11	1	1	D1
	73/74	30	2	2	D1
	74/75	16	2	4	D2
	75/76	7		4	D1
	76/77	14	10	2	D1

LOVE John Thomson

b. Edinburgh 18.3.1924

Club	Season	Apps	Sub	Gls	Div
Leith A					
Albion R	47/48				D2
	48/49	20		6	D1
Nottingham F	48/49	13		7	FL
	49/50	37		11	FL
	50/51	4		1	FL
	51/52	5		2	FL
Llanelly	52/53				
	53/54				
Walsall	54/55	16		2	FL
	55/56	24		8	FL

LOWRIE Thomas

b. Glasgow 14.1.1928

Club	Season	Apps	Sub	Gls	Div
Troon A					
Manchester U	48/49	8			FL
	49/50	3			FL
Aberdeen	50/51	5			D1
	51/52	24		1	D1
Oldham A	52/53	38			FL
	53/54	29		5	FL
	54/55	12			FL

LOWRIE Walter Scott

b. Edinburgh

Club	Season	Apps	Sub	Gls	Div
Hawick Royal Albert					
Stirling A	67/68	3			D1
Stenhousemuir					

LOWRY Thomas

b. N Ireland

Club	Season	Apps	Sub	Gls	Div
Ballymena U					
Falkirk	59/60	25			D2
	60/61	29			D2
	61/62	7			D1
	62/63	13			D1
	63/64	6			D1

LUCAS Oliver Henry

b. Paisley 14.1.1923

Club	Season	Apps	Sub	Gls	Div
St Mirren	47/48	2			D1
Leyton Orient	48/49	1			FL
	49/50	1			FL

LUKE William

b. Aberdeen 19.4.1932

Club	Season	Apps	Sub	Gls	Div
Hall Russell					
East Fife	52/53				D1
	53/54	3			D1
	54/55	1			D1
Crewe Alex.	55/56	1			FL

LUMSDEN James Murdoch

b. Glasgow 7.11.1947

Club	Season	Apps	Sub	Gls	Div
Leeds U	66/67	1			FL
	67/68	1			FL
	68/69				FL
	69/70	1	1		FL
Southend U	70/71	12	1		FL
Morton	71/72	34		1	D1
	72/73	5	3	2	D1
St Mirren	72/73	13		1	D2
Cork Hibernian	73/74				
Morton	74/75	28		2	D1
Clydebank	75/76	23	1	1	D2
	76/77	27	1	1	D1
	77/78	20	4	1	P

LUNN John

b. c1944 d. ?.12.1973

Club	Season	Apps	Sub	Gls	Div
Blairhall Colliery					
Dunfermline A	61/62				D1
	62/63	12			D1
	63/64	32		1	D1
	64/65	27			D1
	65/66	31		1	D1
	66/67	18			D1
	67/68	34		2	D1
	68/69	29		1	D1
	69/70	32			D1
	70/71	31			D1
	71/72	3			D1

LYNCH Andrew

b. Glasgow 3.3.1951

Club	Season	Apps	Sub	Gls	Div
Glasgow U					
Renfrew Jnrs					
Queen's Park	68/69				D2
Kirkintilloch Rob Roy					
Heart of Midlothian	69/70	13		2	D1
	70/71	20		4	D1
	71/72	16	1	2	D1
	72/73	7	3	3	D1
Celtic	72/73	1			D1
	73/74	1	2		D1
	74/75	5	2	2	D1
	75/76	34		1	P
	76/77	30		2	P
	77/78	26	1	3	P
	78/79	27	1	7	P
	79/80	1			P
Philadelphia Fury	80	23		4	NA
Montreal Manic	81	27		4	NA
	82	1			NA

LYNCH John

b. Uddingston 22.9.1917

Club	Season	Apps	Sub	Gls	Div
Dundee	46/47	8			D2
	47/48	19			D1
	48/49	23			D1
	49/50	20			D1
	50/51	19			D1
St Mirren	51/52	23			D1
Workington	52/53	2			FL

LYNCH Matthew

b. 29.11.1916

Club	Season	Apps	Sub	Gls	Div
Linwood St Convals					
St Anthonys					
Celtic	34/35				D1
	35/36				D1
	36/37				D1
	37/38	14		1	D1
	38/39	16		1	D1
	46/47	14			D1
	47/48				D1
Dumbarton	48/49				D2

LYNCH W

Club	Season	Apps	Sub	Gls	Div
Clyde	55/56	1		1	D1

LYNN Ross

b. Dunblane 30.5.1946

Club	Season	Apps	Sub	Gls	Div
Jeanfield Swifts					
Stirling A	66/67				D1
	67/68	10		3	D1
Jeanfield Swifts					

MACARI Luigi

b. Edinburgh 7.6.1949 Caps: S - 24

Club	Season	Apps	Sub	Gls	Div
Kilmarnock Amateurs					
Kilwinning R					
Celtic	66/67				D1
	67/68				D1
	68/69	1		1	D1
	69/70	12	3	7	D1
	70/71	8	3	5	D1
	71/72	19	1	10	D1
	72/73	10	1	3	D1
Manchester U	72/73	16		5	FL
	73/74	34	1	5	FL
	74/75	36	2	11	FL
	75/76	36		12	FL
	76/77	38		9	FL
	77/78	32		8	FL
	78/79	31	1	6	FL
	79/80	39		9	FL
	80/81	37	1	9	FL
	81/82	10	1	2	FL
	82/83	2	7	2	FL
	83/84		5		FL
Swindon T	84/85				FL
	85/86				FL

MACK John

Club	Season	Apps	Sub	Gls	Div
Falkirk	50/51	3		1	D1

MACKLE Thomas
b. 21.3.1938
Renfrew St James BG
Barrhead St Johns
Johnstone Burgh

Club	Season	Apps	Sub	Gls	Div
Celtic	59/60	3		1	D1
	60/61				D1
Dundee	61/62				D1
	62/63	3			D1
	63/64				D1
Forfar A	64/65	34		10	D2
	65/66	35		15	D2
	66/67	25		4	D2
Raith R	66/67	14		4	D2
	67/68	13		1	D1
Forfar A	67/68	3		1	D2
	68/69			4	D2
	69/70	32	1	7	D2

MADDEN Duncan

Club	Season	Apps	Sub	Gls	Div
Airdrieonians	67/68	10		1	D1
	68/69	3			D1

MADDEN Richard Michael
b. Blantyre 27.7.1944
Blantyre Celtic

Club	Season	Apps	Sub	Gls	Div
Celtic	62/63	1			D1
	63/64				D1
Albion R	64/65				D2
	65/66	36			D2
	66/67	18			D2
Clydebank	67/68	27			D2
	68/69				D2
	69/70	9			D2

MADSEN John
b. Denmark 14.5.1937 Caps: Den - 20
Esbjerg

Club	Season	Apps	Sub	Gls	Div
Morton	65/66	31			D1
	66/67	10		3	D2
Hibernian	66/67	18			D1
	67/68	32			D1
	68/69	21			D1
Esbjerg					

MAGUIRE James Smith
b. Eaglesham 3.2.1932
Ashfield

Club	Season	Apps	Sub	Gls	Div
Queen of the South	55/56	9			D1
	56/57	12		2	D1
	57/58				D1
Rochdale	58/59	15			FL

MAGUIRE V

Club	Season	Apps	Sub	Gls	Div
Raith R	61/62	3			D1
	62/63	5			D1

MAILER Ronald George
b. Auchterarder 18.5.1932

Club	Season	Apps	Sub	Gls	Div
Dunfermline A	50/51				D2
	51/52				D2
	52/53	24		6	D2
	53/54	8			D2
	54/55				D2
Darlington	L 54/55				FL
Dunfermline A	55/56	25		4	D1
	56/57	28		1	D1
	57/58				D2
	58/59	21		2	D1
	59/60	26		3	D1
	60/61	34		4	D1
	61/62	21		1	D1
	62/63	4			D1
	63/64	2			D1

MAIN David
b. Motherwell 17.2.1952

Club	Season	Apps	Sub	Gls	Div
Motherwell	70/71	10	1	2	D1
	71/72	5	1		D1
	72/73				D1
	73/74				D1
Albion R	74/75	21		1	D2
	75/76	19	3	1	D2
	76/77	37			D2
	77/78	18	2		D2
	78/79	38		2	D2
	79/80	32	2		D2
	80/81	29			D2
	81/82	19	1		D2
	82/83	20	2	3	D2

MAIR Hugh
Ardeer Thistle

Club	Season	Apps	Sub	Gls	Div
Airdrieonians	63/64	1			D1
Stranraer	64/65	15			D2
	65/66	19			D2

MALCOLM Walter Grant Lees
b. Musselburgh 25.10.1940
Dalkeith Thistle

Club	Season	Apps	Sub	Gls	Div
Newcastle U	57/58				FL
	58/59				FL
	59/60	1			FL
Raith R	60/61	8		1	D1
	61/62	8		1	D1
Airdrieonians	62/63	1			D1

MALCOLMSON Samuel
Caps: NZ

Club	Season	Apps	Sub	Gls	Div
Airdrieonians	71/72	1			D1
Queen of the South	72/73	8			D2
Albion R	73/74	24	1	1	D2

MALEY Matthew

Club	Season	Apps	Sub	Gls	Div
Morton	46/47	20			D1
	47/48	3			D1

MALLAN John
b. Glasgow 25.1.1927 d. Glasgow 27.5.1969
St Marys BG
Pollok

Club	Season	Apps	Sub	Gls	Div
Celtic	46/47	14			D1
	47/48	24			D1
	48/49	21			D1
	49/50	9			D1
	50/51	19			D1
	51/52	3			D1
	52/53	1			D1
St Mirren	53/54	18			D1
	54/55	15			D1
	55/56	32			D1

MALLOCH James
Wolverhampton W

Club	Season	Apps	Sub	Gls	Div
Dundee	48/49	4		1	D1
St Johnstone	49/50	15		7	D2
	50/51	24		13	D2
	51/52	2			D2
Dumbarton *	52/53	24		17	D2
	53/54	23		13	D2

MALLON James Gillan
b. Glasgow 28.8.1938

Club	Season	Apps	Sub	Gls	Div
Partick T	56/57	1			D1
	57/58	8		7	D1
Oldham A	58/59	12		4	FL
	59/60	19		4	FL
Morton	60/61				D2
	61/62				D2
	62/63	8		2	D2
	63/64	34		2	D2
	64/65	11			D1
Barrow	65/66	36			FL
	66/67	45		2	FL
	67/68	41	1	1	FL
	68/69	27			FL
Altrincham					

MALLON William

Club	Season	Apps	Sub	Gls	Div
Airdrieonians	72/73	5	1		D1

MALLOY Daniel
b. Loanhead 6.11.1930
Camelon

Club	Season	Apps	Sub	Gls	Div
Dundee	53/54	29		1	D1
	54/55	30		3	D1
	55/56	13		3	D1
Cardiff C	55/56	23			FL
	56/57	42		1	FL
	57/58	36			FL
	58/59	42			FL
	59/60	41			FL
	60/61	42			FL
Doncaster R	61/62	42			FL
Clyde	62/63	14			D1

MALLOY John
Provan Star
Larkhall Thistle

Club	Season	Apps	Sub	Gls	Div
Kilmarnock	56/57	2			D1

MALONE Francis C
b. Carfin
Fauldhouse U

Club	Season	Apps	Sub	Gls	Div
Kilmarnock	61/62				D1
	62/63				D1
	63/64				D1
	64/65	2			D1
	65/66				D1
Addington					

MALONE Richard Philip
b. Carfin 22.8.1947
Shotts Bon Accord

Club	Season	Apps	Sub	Gls	Div
Ayr U	64/65	11			D2
	65/66	36			D2
	66/67	26			D1
	67/68	25		6	D2
	68/69				D2
	69/70	33		5	D1
	70/71	6			D1
Sunderland	70/71	21	2	1	FL
	71/72	41			FL
	72/73	41			FL
	73/74	42			FL
	74/75	42		1	FL
	75/76	39			FL
	76/77	9			FL
Hartlepool U	77/78	33		2	FL
	78/79	3			FL
Blackpool	78/79	29	1	1	FL
	79/80	19			FL
North Shields					
Queen of the South	80/81	30			D2
	81/82	12	1		D1

MANDERSON William B

Club	Season	Apps	Sub	Gls	Div
Queen's Park	46/47	1			D1

MANN Andrew

Club	Season	Apps	Sub	Gls	Div
Motherwell	61/62	1			D1
Hamilton A	62/63	22			D2
	63/64	21		1	D2

K

MANN Arthur Fraser
b. Burntisland 23.1.1948
d. Birmingham 3.2.1999
Lochore Welfare

Club	Season				Div
Heart of Midlothian	67/68	21			D1
	68/69	11			D1
Manchester C	68/69	7	1		FL
	69/70	9			FL
	70/71	16	2		FL
Blackpool	71/72	3			FL
Notts Co	72/73	41	1	1	FL
	73/74	39	1	5	FL
	74/75	27	1	1	FL
	75/76	31		3	FL
	76/77	40	1	5	FL
	77/78	29	2	3	FL
	78/79	37	3	3	FL
Shrewsbury T	79/80	8		1	FL
Mansfield T	79/80	35			FL
	80/81	44		2	FL
	81/82	35	2	1	FL
Boston U					
Telford U					
Kettering T					

MANSON J

Club	Season				Div
Falkirk	47/48	1			D1

MARCH James A
b. Glasgow 21.4.1954
St Rochs

Club	Season				Div
Airdrieonians	74/75	2	5	4	D1
	75/76	11	7	1	D1
	76/77	32		2	D1
	77/78	12		2	D1
	78/79	25	2	4	D1
	79/80	17	4		D1
	80/81	22	2	3	P
	81/82	28	2		P
	82/83	21	2	1	D1
	83/84	20	2		D1
Ayr U	84/85	12	1		D1
	85/86	27	2		D1
Pollok					

MARCHBANK J

Club	Season				Div
Queen of the South	63/64	1			D1

MARINELLO Peter
b. Edinburgh 20.2.1950
Salvesen BC

Club	Season				Div
Hibernian	67/68	11			D1
	68/69	17	2	1	D1
	69/70	14		4	D1
Arsenal	69/70	14		1	FL
	70/71	1	2		FL
	71/72	4	4	1	FL
	72/73	13		1	FL
Portsmouth	73/74	39		3	FL
	74/75	38	1	2	FL
	75/76	15	2	2	FL
Motherwell	75/76	16	2	3	P
	76/77	16	6	3	P
	77/78	31	4	5	P
	78/79	14		1	P
Fulham	78/79	8	1		FL
	79/80	17	1	1	FL
Phoenix Inferno	80				
	81				
Heart of Midlothian	81/82	10	8	2	D1
	82/83	2	2		D1
Partick T	83/84	1	5		D1
Whitburn Jnrs					

MARJORIBANKS Brian
Airth Castle R

Club	Season				Div
Hibernian	61/62	4		3	D1
Heart of Midlothian					

MARKEY James P
b. Edinburgh 6.3.1953
Whitehill Welfare

Club	Season				Div
Dunfermline A	74/75	19			D1
	75/76	18	2	1	D1
	76/77	20		2	D2
Cowdenbeath	77/78	32	4	4	D2
	78/79	37		3	D2
	79/80	34		3	D2
	80/81	38		1	D2
	81/82	17	1	1	D2
	82/83		1		D2
Arbroath	82/83	1			D2
East Fife	82/83	1	1		D2

MARKIE John
b. Bo'ness 16.12.1944
Bathgate St Marys

Club	Season				Div
Newcastle U	62/63				FL
	63/64	2			FL
Falkirk	64/65	21			D1
	65/66	24			D1
	66/67	31		1	D1
	67/68	33		3	D1
	68/69	33			D1
	69/70	30		1	D2
	70/71	32		1	D1
	71/72	34		1	D1
	72/73	32		2	D1
	73/74	33			D1
	74/75	36			D2
	75/76	7	1		D1
Clyde	76/77	22			D2
Stenhousemuir	77/78	12		1	D2

MARKLAND Stewart

Club	Season				Div
Berwick R	66/67	8		3	D2
	67/68	23	2	3	D2
Dundee U	68/69	6			D1
	69/70	13	2	1	D1
	70/71	18			D1
	71/72	21	1		D1
	72/73	12	4	1	D1
Montrose	73/74	23	3		D2
	74/75	34	2		D2
	75/76	24		3	D1
	76/77	39		1	D1
	77/78	22	1	2	D1
Sydney Olympic					
Montrose	80/81	10		1	D2

MARR John Gerard
b. Glasgow 3.6.1955
Petershill

Club	Season				Div
Partick T	74/75		1		D1
	75/76	14	5		D1
	76/77	31	1		P
	77/78	33	1		P
	78/79	29			P
	79/80	10			P
	80/81	2	2		P
Morton	80/81	6	1		P
	81/82		1		P

MARSHALL Alexander Stewart
b. Alloa 27.11.1935
Sauchie Jnrs

Club	Season				Div
Stirling A	56/57				D2
	57/58				D2
	58/59	1			D1
	59/60				D1
	60/61				D2
Accrington S	60/61	8		2	FL

MARSHALL David
St Rochs

Club	Season				Div
Rangers	46/47				D1
	47/48	4		3	D1
	48/49	3		1	D1
	49/50	1			D1
	50/51	5		2	D1
	51/52	1		1	D1

MARSHALL David
b. Westrigg
Linlithgow Rose

Club	Season				Div
Airdrieonians	63/64	2			D1
	64/65	27		5	D1
	65/66	27		24	D2
	66/67	32		14	D1
	67/68	24		10	D1
	68/69	29	2	9	D1
	69/70	22		13	D1
Cowdenbeath	70/71	10		1	D1
	71/72	1		1	D2
Forfar A	71/72	7	3	2	D2

MARSHALL Gerard
b. 20.8.1955
Dalry Thistle

Club	Season				Div
Clyde	73/74		2		D1
	74/75	15	7	2	D1
	75/76	4	1		D1
	76/77	19	4	8	D2
	77/78	20	9	6	D2
	78/79	25	6	7	D1
	79/80	1	4		D1
Dumbarton	80/81	1	1		D1

MARSHALL Gordon
b. Farnham 2.7.1939
Balgreen R
Heart of Midlothian
Dalkeith Thistle L

Club	Season				Div
Heart of Midlothian	56/57	11			D1
	57/58	31			D1
	58/59	31			D1
	59/60	33			D1
	60/61	30			D1
	61/62	29			D1
	62/63	28			D1
Newcastle U	63/64	33			FL
	64/65	42			FL
	65/66	33			FL
	66/67	30			FL
	67/68	39			FL
Nottingham F	68/69	7			FL
Hibernian	68/69	3			D1
	69/70	33			D1
	70/71	11			D1
Celtic	71/72				D1
Aberdeen	71/72	7			D1
Arbroath	72/73	34			D1
	73/74	32			D1
	74/75	18			D1
Newtongrange Star					
Arbroath	75/76	16			D1
	76/77	39			D1
	77/78	3			D1
Newtongrange Star					

MARSHALL Michael
b. Methil (or St Andrews) ?.?.1942
Kennoway R

Club	Season				Div
East Fife	59/60				D2
	60/61	1			D2
Jordanhill TC					
Glenrothes					
Alloa A	65/66	30		7	D2
	66/67	36		14	D2
Falkirk	67/68	13	2		D1
	68/69	11	1	1	D1
Alloa A	69/70				D2
	70/71				D2

P

MARSHALL Robert
b. Grangemouth
Hibernian

Club	Season				Div
Stirling A	49/50	7			D1
	50/51				D2
Stenhousemuir	51/52				D2
	52/53	25		1	D2
	53/54	17			D2

MARTIN Alexander

Hull C

Club	Season	Apps	Sub	Gls	Div
Motherwell	70/71	6	6	1	D1
	71/72	11		4	D1
	72/73	13		4	D1
	73/74	27	2	6	D1
	74/75	3		1	D1

MARTIN Bent
b. Denmark
Sonderborg

Club	Season	Apps	Gls	Div
Celtic	65/66			D1

AGF Aarhus

Club	Season	Apps	Gls	Div
Dunfermline A	66/67	18		D1
	67/68	31		D1
	68/69	19		D1
	69/70	6		D1

Rapid Vienna

MARTIN David

Club	Season	Apps	Gls	Div
Albion R	48/49	19		D1

MARTIN Eric
b. Perth 31.3.1946
Blairhall Colliery

Club	Season	Apps	Gls	Div
St Johnstone	T			
Cowdenbeath	T 63/64			D2
Dunfermline A	64/65	1		D1
	65/66	34		D1
	66/67	16		D1
Southampton	66/67	11		FL
	67/68	24		FL
	68/69	8		FL
	69/70	35		FL
	70/71	41		FL
	71/72	42		FL
	72/73	42		FL
	73/74	35		FL
	74/75	10		FL
Washington Diplomat	75	10		NA
	76	24		NA
	77	24		NA

MARTIN Fred
b. Carnoustie 13.5.1929 Caps: S - 6
Carnoustie Panmure

Club	Season	Apps	Gls	Div
Aberdeen	46/47			D1
	47/48			D1
	48/49			D1
	49/50	2		D1
	50/51	24		D1
	51/52	23		D1
	52/53	28		D1
	53/54	25		D1
	54/55	27		D1
	55/56	32		D1
	56/57	26		D1
	57/58	9		D1
	58/59	8		D1
	59/60	2		D1
	60/61			

MARTIN John
b. Carstairs
Lesmahagow Jnrs

Club	Season	Apps	Gls	Div
Hamilton A	47/48	29	20	D2
	48/49	30	5	D2
	49/50	30	12	D2
	50/51	30	2	D2
	51/52	30		D2
	52/53	30		D2
	53/54	20	3	D1
	54/55	29	2	D2
	55/56	4		D2

MARTIN Joseph

Club	Season	Apps	Gls	Div
St Mirren	46/47	3		D1
	47/48	24		D1
	48/49	28		D1
	49/50	29	2	D1
	50/51	6	1	D1
	51/52	10		D1

MARTIN Neil
b. Tranent 20.10.1940 Caps: S - 3
Tranent Jnrs

Club	Season	Apps	Sub	Gls	Div
Alloa A	59/60				D2
	60/61				D2
Queen of the South	61/62				D2
	62/63	25		8	D1
Hibernian	63/64	28		20	D1
	64/65	31		25	D1
	65/66	6		8	D1
Sunderland	65/66	24		8	FL
	66/67	41		20	FL
	67/68	21	1	10	FL
Coventry C	67/68	15		8	FL
	68/69	25		9	FL
	69/70	40		14	FL
	70/71	26		9	FL
Nottingham F	70/71	12			FL
	71/72	23	2	5	FL
	72/73	19		6	FL
	73/74	36		6	FL
	74/75	26	1	10	FL
Brighton & HA	75/76	13	4	8	FL
Crystal Palace	75/76	8	1	1	FL
St Patricks A	76/77				

MARTIN Norman

Dalry Thistle

Club	Season	Apps	Gls	Div
Hamilton A	T 57/58	1		D2

Dalry Thistle

Club	Season	Apps	Gls	Div
Rangers	58/59			D1
	62/63	1		D1
	63/64			D1
	64/65	9		D1
	65/66	1		D1
	66/67	28		D1
	67/68	4		D1
	68/69	31		D1
	69/70	1		D1
East Fife	70/71	2		D2
Queen of the South	70/71			D2
Hamilton A	70/71	3		D2

MARTIN Thomas
b. Glasgow 21.12.1924
Shettleston

Club	Season	Apps	Gls	Div
Heart of Midlothian	46/47	2		D1
	47/48	4	2	D1
	48/49	1		D1
Stirling A	49/50	17	2	D1
Doncaster R	50/51	26	2	FL
	51/52	32	5	FL
	52/53	13	2	FL
Nottingham F	52/53	18	3	FL
	53/54	11	1	FL
	54/55	19		FL
Hull C	55/56	25	2	FL
	56/57	7		FL
Rothes	57/58			
	58/59			
Stirling A	59/60	7	1	D1

MARTIS John
b. Motherwell 30.3.1940 Caps: S - 1
Royal Albert

Club	Season	Apps	Gls	Div
Motherwell	57/58	16		D1
	58/59	30		D1
	59/60	33		D1
	60/61	31		D1
	61/62	27		D1
	62/63	28		D1
	63/64	23	1	D1
	64/65	8		D1
	65/66	32		D1
	66/67	33	1	D1
	67/68	33	1	D1
	68/69	1		D2

Hellenic

Club	Season	Apps	Gls	Div
East Fife	69/70	32		D2
	70/71			D2
	71/72	34		D1
	72/73	34		D1
	73/74	29		D1
	74/75	36		D2

MASON James
b. Glasgow 18.6.1919 d. ?.12.1971 Caps: S - 7
Mossvale YMCA

Club	Season	Apps	Gls	Div
Third Lanark	36/37	18	3	D1
	37/38	19	4	D1
	38/39	32	4	D1
	46/47	17	3	D1
	47/48	28	7	D1
	48/49	26	5	D1
	49/50	25	5	D1
	50/51	27	2	D1
	51/52	12	1	D1
	52/53	3		D1

MASON James
b. Glasgow 17.4.1933
Rutherglen Glencairn

Club	Season	Apps	Gls	Div
Dundee	53/54			D1
	54/55	1		D1
Accrington S	55/56	4		FL
	56/57	10	1	FL
Chester	57/58	29	4	FL
	58/59	35	3	FL
Chelmsford C	59/60			
Crystal Palace	60/61			FL

MASON Joseph Paul Smith
b. Kilmarnock 17.8.1940
Saxone Amateurs
Dreghorn Jnrs
Lugar Boswell

Club	Season	Apps	Sub	Gls	Div
Kilmarnock	60/61				D1
	61/62	13		3	D1
	62/63	17		13	D1
	63/64	4		2	D1
	64/65	4		2	D1
	65/66	9		3	D1
Morton	66/67	36		34	D2
	67/68	31		15	D1
	68/69	28	2	4	D1
	69/70	23	2	9	D1
	70/71	28	1	9	D1
	71/72	34		6	D1
	72/73	6		1	D1
Rangers	72/73	12	4	3	D1

F

MASON William
b. Grangemouth c1931
Linlithgow Rose

Club	Season	Apps	Gls	Div
Motherwell	54/55	20		D1
	55/56	6		D1
Hamilton A	56/57	17		D2

MASSIE Alan
b. Aberdeen

Club	Season	Apps	Sub	Gls	Div
Aberdeen	48/49	8			D1
Dundee	49/50	6			D1
	50/51	2			D1
	51/52				D1
	52/53	1			D1
	53/54				D1
	54/55				D1
Dundee U	54/55	22		1	D2
	55/56	18		2	D2

MATHERS David Cochrane
b. Glasgow 23.10.1931 Caps: S - 1
Govan High School

Club	Season	Apps	Gls	Div
Partick T	48/49			D1
	49/50	2		D1
	50/51	9		D1
	51/52	28		D1
	52/53	16		D1
	53/54	26	1	D1
	54/55	8	2	D1
	55/56	20	2	D1
	56/57	26		D1
	57/58	27	1	D1
	58/59	18	3	D1
Headington U	59/60	34		SL
	60/61	13		SL
Partick T	60/61			D1
East Stirlingshire	61/62	11	1	D2

MATHESON Dougal
b. Glasgow 22.6.1924
Yoker Fernlea
Cunard Thistle
Fauldhouse U

Club	Season	Apps	Sub	Gls	Div
Heart of Midlothian	47/48	24			D1
	48/49	20			D1
	49/50	8			D1
Inverness Thistle					

MATHIE

Club	Season	Apps	Sub	Gls	Div
Motherwell	69/70	1			D1

MATHIE David
b. Motherwell 15.8.1919
d. Law Hospital 3.1.1954
Larkhall Thistle

Club	Season	Apps	Sub	Gls	Div
Motherwell	38/39	30		20	D1
Hibernian					
Dumbarton					
Motherwell					
Clyde	46/47	5		2	D1
Partick T	46/47	17		18	D1
	47/48	21		9	D1
Motherwell	47/48	2		1	D1
	48/49	26		14	D1
	49/50	2			D1
Llanelly	50/51				
Kilmarnock	51/52				D2
	52/53	7		4	D2
	53/54				D2
Workington	53/54	2			FL

MATHIE Ross C

Club	Season	Apps	Sub	Gls	Div
Aberdeen	64/65				
Cambuslang R					
Kilmarnock	69/70	34		21	D1
	70/71	16	4	4	D1
	71/72	26		15	D1
Dumbarton	72/73	10	1	7	D1
	73/74	9	5	6	D1
	74/75	2			D1
	75/76	1			D1
Motherwell	75/76				P
Falkirk	75/76				D1
Berwick R	76/77	28	7	3	D2
	77/78				D2
	78/79				D2
	79/80				D1

MATHIESON Ian
b. c1954
Hibernian

Club	Season	Apps	Sub	Gls	Div
Dundee	L 72/73	1			D1

MATHIESON William
b. Cardenden 20.7.1948
St Andrews U

Club	Season	Apps	Sub	Gls	Div
Rangers	65/66	3			D1
	66/67	1			D1
	67/68	26		1	D1
	68/69	26			D1
	69/70	14			D1
	70/71	14		1	D1
	71/72	30			D1
	72/73	34			D1
	73/74	26			D1
	74/75				D1
Arbroath	75/76	21	4	3	D1
Raith R	76/77	13			D1

MATTHEW Andrew
b. Kirkcaldy ?.?.1932 d. Kinross 4.10.1992
Bayview YC

Club	Season	Apps	Sub	Gls	Div
East Fife	50/51				
	51/52	1		1	D1
	52/53	9		2	D1
	53/54	28		5	D1
	54/55	15		1	D1
	55/56	30		5	D1
	56/57	31		7	D1
	57/58	32		7	D1
Rangers	58/59	18		5	D1
	59/60	10		2	D1
Raith R	60/61	12		3	D1
Dunfermline A	61/62	3			D1
Cowdenbeath	62/63				D2
	63/64	34		12	D2
	64/65	34		4	D2
	65/66	28		2	D2
	66/67	14	2	4	D2

MAULE John
b. 1922 d. Kirkcaldy 22.1.1998

Club	Season	Apps	Sub	Gls	Div
Raith R	46/47				D2
	47/48				D2
	48/49				D2
	49/50	29		6	D1
	50/51	29		2	D1
	51/52	29		3	D1
	52/53	20		1	D1
	53/54	1			D1
Third Lanark	53/54	7		1	D2

MAXWELL C

Club	Season	Apps	Sub	Gls	Div
Morton	46/47	1			D1

MAXWELL Hugh
b. Rigghead 14.5.1938
Shotts Bon Accord

Club	Season	Apps	Sub	Gls	Div
Stirling A	60/61				D2
	61/62	14		1	D1
Bradford PA	61/62	2		1	FL
	62/63	10		4	FL
Falkirk	62/63	20		12	D1
	63/64	33		17	D1
	64/65	10		7	D1
Celtic	64/65	8		2	D1
St Johnstone	65/66	1			D1
Dunfermline A	65/66	6			D1
	66/67	4	2	2	D1
Hellenic (SAf)					

MAXWELL Samuel George
b. Stevenston 9.6.1950
Irvine Royal Academy
Kilmarnock Amateurs
Dreghorn Jnrs

Club	Season	Apps	Sub	Gls	Div
Kilmarnock	68/69				D1
	69/70	1	1		D1
	70/71	17	2	1	D1
	71/72	34		8	D1
	72/73	33		4	D1
	73/74	35		9	D2
	74/75	29	2	6	D1
	75/76	15	3		D1
	76/77	25	5	2	P
	77/78	35		9	D1
	78/79	33	1	11	D1
	79/80	19	3	3	P
	80/81	9	7		P
	81/82				D1
Queen of the South	82/83	7		3	D2
Stranraer	82/83	14		1	D2
Whitletts Victoria					

MAY Donald

Club	Season	Apps	Sub	Gls	Div
Third Lanark	64/65	14			D1
	65/66	13			D2
	66/67	16	2	1	D2
Dumbarton	67/68	20			D2

MAYS Gerard Joseph
b. Craigneuk 18.7.1921
Shieldmuir Celtic

Club	Season	Apps	Sub	Gls	Div
Hibernian	38/39				D1
Hamilton A					
Hibernian	46/47				D1
St Johnstone	47/48				D2
Dunfermline A	48/49				D2
	49/50	27		10	D2
	50/51				D2
	51/52				D2
Kilmarnock	52/53	29		20	D2
	53/54	19		8	D2
	54/55	14		5	D1
	55/56	25		9	D1
	56/57	27		18	D1
	57/58	22		15	D1
	58/59	16		4	D1

MEECHAN Francis
b. Condorrat 27.10.1929 d. Croy 20.8.1976
Holy Cross BG
Glenboig St Josephs
Holy Cross BG
Armadale Thistle

Club	Season	Apps	Sub	Gls	Div
Petershill	T				
Notts Co	T				
Petershill					
Hibernian	51/52				D1
Celtic	52/53	19			D1
	53/54	24			D1
	54/55	18			D1
	55/56	6			D1
	56/57	8			D1
	57/58	9			D1
Stirling A	L 58/59	6			D1

MEEK Ian

Club	Season	Apps	Sub	Gls	Div
Clyde	59/60	12		4	D1

MEHARRY David

Club	Season	Apps	Sub	Gls	Div
Falkirk	64/65	1			D1

MELROSE

Club	Season	Apps	Sub	Gls	Div
Dunfermline A	56/57	10			D1

MELROSE George

Club	Season	Apps	Sub	Gls	Div
St Mirren	55/56	3			D1

MELROSE Harry M
b. Edinburgh ?.?.1935
Dalkeith Thistle
Rangers

Club	Season	Apps	Sub	Gls	Div
Dunfermline A	58/59	32		21	D1
	59/60	31		8	D1
	60/61	27		13	D1
	61/62	34		17	D1
	62/63	26		2	D1
	63/64	10		2	D1
	64/65	18		12	D1
	65/66	1			D1
Aberdeen	65/66	29		6	D1
	66/67	27		5	D1
	67/68	8		2	D1
	68/69				D1
Berwick R	69/70	29		3	D2
	70/71			4	D2
	71/72	25		6	D2
	72/73	6	1	1	D2

MENMUIR William Fraser
b. Glasgow 3.2.1952

Club	Season	Apps	Sub	Gls	Div
Bristol C	69/70	1			FL
	70/71				FL
Heart of Midlothian	71/72				D1
	72/73	13		1	D1
	73/74				D1
Dumbarton	74/75	6	1		D1
Alloa A	75/76		1		D2

MENNIE Francis
b. Coatbridge 30.10.1923
Coatbridge St Patricks

Queen's Park	38/39			D1
Kilmarnock	46/47			D1
	47/48	25	1	D2
	48/49	7		D2
Clyde	48/49	15		D1
	49/50	15		D1
	50/51	24	1	D1
	51/52			D2
	52/53			D1
Portadown	53/54			
Merthyr Tydfil				

MENZIES Alexander
b. Cowdenbeath d. ?.11.1990
Cowdenbeath Welfare BC
Kelty St Josephs
Lochgelly Violet

Dumbarton	47/48			D2
	48/49			D2
Cowdenbeath	48/49			D2
	49/50			D2
	50/51			D2
	51/52			D2
	52/53			D2
	53/54			D2
	54/55			D2
St Johnstone	55/56	37	5	D2
	56/57	12		D2
	57/58			D2
Stirling A	57/58			D2
	58/59	16		D1
Alloa A	59/60			D2
Stirling A	60/61			D2

MENZIES Brian

Raith R	62/63	10	D1

MENZIES Gordon
Kilsyth St Patricks

Dumbarton	72/73	28	1	D1
	73/74	21		D1

MENZIES James

Raith R	59/60	2	D1
	60/61	1	D1
St Johnstone	61/62	4	D1

MENZIES John
Partick T

Airdrieonians	66/67	4		D1
	67/68		1	D1
	68/69	5	4	2 D1
	69/70	18	4	D1
	70/71	34		3 D1
	71/72	34		D1
	72/73	23	2	D1
	73/74	30	2	1 D2
	74/75	22	5	1 D1
	75/76	10		1 D1

MERCER Bonar Brown Lamond
b. 19.1.1953
Dunfermline U

Dunfermline A	70/71			D1
	71/72	32		D1
	72/73	1		D2
Montrose	73/74	19	2	D2
Stirling A	74/75	17	4	1 D2
	75/76			D2
Dunfermline A	76/77			D2
	77/78	29	1	1 D2
	78/79	35	1	1 D2
	79/80	31	3	D1
	80/81	34		D1
	81/82	4		D1

MERCER James
Bothkenner YMCA

St Johnstone	70/71			D1
	71/72	7	3	D1
	72/73	9		D1
Falkirk	73/74	2		D1

MERCHANT George
b. Dundee
Third Lanark
Aberdeen

Dundee	51/52	11		D1
	52/53	3		D1
	53/54	10	6	D1
	54/55	18	11	D1
	55/56	20	12	D1
	56/57	3	2	D1
Falkirk	56/57	14	14	D1
	57/58	8	4	D1
	58/59	1		D1

MICHIE Andrew
Sauchie Jnrs

St Johnstone	65/66	15	D1
	66/67	10	D1
	67/68	1	D1
	68/69		D1
Cowdenbeath	69/70	4	D2

MIDDLEMASS James B
b. Glasgow ?.?.1920
Shawfield Jnrs
Petershill

Kilmarnock	49/50	24	1	D2
	50/51	19		D2
	51/52	25	3	D2
	52/53	21	8	D2
	53/54	20	5	D2
	54/55	8		D1

MIDDLETON James
b. Blackridge 25.4.1922

Third Lanark	46/47	11		D1
	47/48	2		D1
	48/49	2	1	D1
Bradford C	49/50	8		FL

MILLAN Thomas
Renfrew Jnrs

Stirling A	59/60	1	D1
	60/61		D2
	61/62		D1

MILLAR Brian

East Stirlingshire	63/64	5	D1
ES Clydebank	64/65	9	D2
East Stirlingshire	65/66	28	D2
	66/67	34	D2
	67/68	33	D2

MILLAR David A
b. Gourock

Queen's Park	63/64	35		7 D2
	64/65	35		6 D2
Aberdeen	65/66	6		D1
	66/67	9		D1
	67/68	2		D1
Raith R	67/68	11		D1
	68/69	34		4 D1
	69/70	15		D1
	70/71			D2
St Mirren	70/71	18		2 D1
	71/72	32		1 D2
	72/73	21	2	1 D2
	73/74	17	2	1 D2
Stranraer	74/75	17	1	2 D2

MILLAR Hugh G

Queen's Park	46/47	17		6 D1
	47/48	5		D1

MILLAR Ian

Morton	63/64	17	D2
	64/65	3	D1
Ayr U	65/66	22	D2
	66/67	21	D1
Stenhousemuir	67/68		D2

MILLAR J

St Mirren	65/66	4	D1

MILLAR James
b. Edinburgh 20.11.1934 Caps: S - 2
Merchiston Thistle

Dunfermline A	52/53	5	3	D2
	53/54	19		D2
	54/55			D2
Rangers	54/55	2		D1
	55/56	1		D1
	56/57			D1
	57/58	25	5	D1
	58/59	5	2	D1
	59/60	30	21	D1
	60/61	21	9	D1
	61/62	23	15	D1
	62/63	31	27	D1
	63/64	22	6	D1
	64/65	21	4	D1
	65/66	10	1	D1
	66/67	5	1	2 D1
Dundee U	67/68	14	2	3 D1
	68/69	2		D1

MILLAR John Ross
b. Armadale 25.10.1923 d. ?.?.1986

Albion R	48/49	4	D1
Bradford C	49/50	6	FL

MILLAR Peter
b. Motherwell
Forth W

Arbroath	68/69			D1
	69/70	5	3	2 D2
Dunfermline A	69/70			D1
	70/71	5	4	D1
	71/72	15	3	3 D1
Motherwell	72/73	17	1	5 D1
	73/74	30	1	2 D1
	74/75	27	1	4 D1
	75/76	23	5	4 P
	76/77	31	1	P
	77/78	24	5	1 P
	78/79	13		1 P
Dundee	78/79	16		D1
	79/80	26	2	2 P
Phoenix Inferno				
Cleveland Force				

MILLAR Sam
St Lukes BG
Rutherglen Glencairn

Clyde	70/71	7	1	D1
	71/72	10	1	1 D1
	72/73	34		9 D1
	73/74	34		5 D1
	74/75	32		6 D1

MILLAR Thomas Thomson
b. Edinburgh 3.12.1938 d. ?.8.2001
Slateford A
Edina Hearts
Armadale Thistle
Bo'ness U

Club	Season				
Colchester U	59/60	5			FL
	60/61	14			FL
	61/62	29		5	FL
Dundee U	61/62	7			D1
	62/63	32		2	D1
	63/64	34		5	D1
	64/65	34			D1
	65/66	33		1	D1
	66/67	33			D1
	67/68	20	1		D1
	68/69	12	3		D1
Cowdenbeath	69/70	28		1	D2
Berwick R	70/71				D2
	71/72	1	1		D2
Hamilton A	71/72	3	1		D2

MILLAR William
b. Irvine 24.7.1924 d. ?.?.1995
Annbank U
Partick T

Club	Season				
Aberdeen	46/47	5		2	D1
	47/48	15		2	D1
	48/49	4			D1
	49/50	3			D1
Stirling A	49/50	16		4	D1
Swindon T	50/51	30		4	FL
	51/52	25		5	FL
	52/53	20		8	FL
Gillingham	53/54	19		7	FL
	54/55	42		18	FL
	55/56	30		10	FL
Accrington S	56/57	26		11	FL
Kettering T					
Macclesfield T					

MILLER A
Club	Season				
Third Lanark	51/52	5			D1

MILLER Alan
b. 23.7.1946
Camelon

Club	Season				
Raith R	67/68	3			D1
	68/69	4			D1
	69/70	21	1	2	D1
East Stirlingshire	70/71			9	D2
	71/72	26	3	7	D2
	72/73	2	3		D2

MILLER Alexander
Club	Season				
Morton	47/48	22			D1
	48/49	13			D1

MILLER Alexander
b. Glasgow 7.4.1949
Clydebank Strollers

Club	Season				
Rangers	68/69			1	D1
	69/70				D1
	70/71	21		1	D1
	71/72	2			D1
	72/73	2	1	2	D1
	73/74				D1
	74/75	15	3	2	D1
	75/76	25	2	1	P
	76/77	17	7	4	P
	77/78	16	8	2	P
	78/79	10	7		P
	79/80	13	5	3	P
	80/81	24	1	2	P
	81/82	14	2		P
South China	82/83				
Morton	83/84	8		1	D1

MILLER Andrew
Club	Season				
Queen's Park	47/48	13		1	D1
	48/49	2			D2

MILLER Archibald B
b. Larkhall 5.9.1913 Caps: S - 1
Royal Albert

Club	Season				
Heart of Midlothian	31/32	2		1	D1
	32/33	3		2	D1
	33/34	5		2	D1
	34/35	12		1	D1
	35/36	9			D1
	36/37	16		1	D1
	37/38	36		2	D1
	38/39	19		1	D1
Heart of Midlothian	46/47	20		1	D1
Blackburn R	47/48	6			FL
Kilmarnock	48/49	16			D2
	49/50				D2
Carlisle U	50/51	1			FL
Heart of Midlothian	51/52				D1
Workington	51/52				FL

MILLER David
Club	Season				
Partick T	51/52	2		1	D1

MILLER G
Club	Season				
Falkirk	52/53	1			D1

MILLER G A
Club	Season				
Queen's Park	46/47	1			D1
	47/48				D1

MILLER George
b. Larkhall 20.5.1939
Royal Albert

Club	Season				
Dunfermline A	59/60	30			D1
	60/61	30		1	D1
	61/62	33		7	D1
	62/63	33			D1
	63/64	31		4	D1
	64/65	9		3	D1
Wolverhampton W	64/65	28		3	FL
	65/66	9			FL
Heart of Midlothian	65/66	17			D1
	66/67	20		1	D1
	67/68	31		4	D1
	68/69		4		D1
Falkirk	68/69	22		3	D1
	69/70	34		14	D2
	70/71	34		5	D1
	71/72	16		3	D1

MILLER George
Dalry Thistle

Club	Season				
St Johnstone	65/66	1			D1
	66/67	9			D1
	67/68	23			D1
	68/69	31			D1
	69/70	4	1		D1
Brechin C	70/71			1	D2
	71/72	27	3		D2
Jeanfield Swifts					

MILLER James
b. Greenock 4.1.1953
Leicester C

Club	Season				
Aberdeen	73/74	4	1		D1
Queen of the South	74/75	38			D2
	75/76	17	4	1	D1
	76/77	27		1	D1
Motherwell	76/77	14	1		P
	77/78	3	5	1	P
Morton	77/78	14			D1
	78/79	33			P
	79/80	20	1		P
Clyde	80/81	28	2		D2
	81/82	1			D2
Queen of the South	81/82	16	1		D1
	82/83	2			D2
Albion R	83/84	2			D2

MILLER James Alistair Williamson
b. Glasgow 24.1.1936
Third Lanark

Club	Season				
St Mirren	56/57				D1
	57/58	11		1	D1
	58/59	15		2	D1
	59/60	34		11	D1
	60/61	33		5	D1
	61/62	19		2	D1
Brighton & HA	61/62	1			FL
Norwich C	62/63	21		2	FL
	63/64	2			FL
Berwick R	64/65				D2
Dumbarton	65/66	21		5	D2
Hamilton A	66/67	34		3	D2

MILLER John
b. c1938
Cowdenbeath

Club	Season				
Dunfermline A	55/56	20		8	D1
	56/57	9		3	D1

MILLER John
Club	Season				
Airdrieonians	55/56	27			D1
	56/57	10			D1
	57/58	15			D1
	58/59	34			D1
	59/60	24			D1
	60/61	1			D1

MILLER Robert
b. Lochgelly 25.1.1949
Lochore Welfare

Club	Season				
East Fife	66/67	33		7	D2
	67/68	30	2	4	D2
	68/69			8	D2
	69/70	27		10	D2
	70/71	36		18	D2
	71/72	2			D1
Aberdeen	71/72	20	3	3	D1
	72/73	13	4	2	D1
	73/74	5	2	1	D1
East Fife	73/74	14		4	D1
	74/75	35	2	8	D2
	75/76	6		3	D1
Montrose	75/76	20		6	D1
	76/77	36	3	9	D1
	77/78	23	9	3	D1
	78/79	18	11	6	D1
Raith R	79/80	37		6	D1
	80/81	26	4	3	D1
	81/82	4	2		D1
Cowdenbeath	81/82	14	2	1	D2
	82/83	14	5	5	D2
	83/84	13	4	3	D2

MILLER T
Club	Season				
Falkirk	61/62	2			D1

MILLER William
b. Glasgow 20.11.1924 Caps: S - 6
St Rollox U
Maryhill Harp

Club	Season				
Celtic	46/47	29			D1
	47/48	27			D1
	48/49	21			D1
	49/50	17			D1
Clyde	50/51	22			D1
	51/52				D2
Stirling A	L 51/52				D1
Clyde	52/53	1			D1
Hibernian	53/54	2			D1
	54/55	1			D1
	55/56				D1

MILLER William
Club	Season				
St Mirren	48/49	4			D1
	49/50	11			D1
	50/51	2			D1

MILLER William Ferguson
b. Glasgow 2.5.1955 Caps: S - 65
Eastercraig U

Club	Season	Apps	Sub	Gls	Div
Aberdeen	71/72				D1
Peterhead	L 71/72				
Aberdeen	72/73			1	D1
	73/74	31		1	D1
	74/75	34		1	D1
	75/76	36			P
	76/77	36			P
	77/78	36			P
	78/79	34			P
	79/80	31		1	P
	80/81	33		2	P
	81/82	36			P
	82/83	36		2	P
	83/84	34		2	P
	84/85	34		3	P
	85/86	33		1	P
	86/87	36		2	P
	87/88	42		3	P
	88/89	21		1	P
	89/90	15			P

MILLIGAN Robert
b. Troon
Dalry Thistle

Club	Season	Apps	Gls	Div
Clyde	47/48	15		D1
	48/49	1		D1
	49/50	18		D1
	50/51	7		D1
	51/52			D2
Queen of the South	52/53			D1
Stirling A	53/54	30		D1
	54/55	13		D1
	55/56	10		D1
Hamilton A	55/56	7		D2

MILLIGAN Thomas
Lesmahagow

Club	Season	Apps	Div
Motherwell	61/62	1	D1
	62/63		D1

MILLOY Frederick Walker
b. Kilmarnock c1913 d. Kilmarnock c1979
Portland U
Kilmarnock Winton
Parkhead Jnrs

Club	Season	Apps	Gls	Div
Kilmarnock	32/33	37		D1
	33/34	38		D1
	34/35	37		D1
	35/36	32	2	D1
	36/37	23		D1
	37/38	36		D1
	38/39	33	1	D1
	45/46	23		D1
	46/47	3		D1
	47/48			D2

St Cuthberts W

MILLOY William James
b. Kilmarnock ?.?.1933
Bonnyton YC
Largs Thistle

Club	Season	Apps	Div
Kilmarnock	51/52		D2
	52/53	7	D2
	53/54	6	D2
	54/55		D1
	55/56		D1
	56/57	1	D1
	57/58	4	D1

MILLSOPP John
b. 17.7.1930 d. Glasgow 17.9.1952
Eastfield Star
Rutherglen Glencairn
Blantyre Celtic

Club	Season	Apps	Gls	Div
Celtic	47/48			D1
Fraserburgh	L 48/49			
Celtic	48/49			D1
	49/50			D1
	50/51	6		D1
	51/52	12	2	D1
	52/53	1		D1

MILNE Andrew
b. Renfrew 17.7.1948
Arsenal

Club	Season	Apps	Sub	Gls	Div
Heart of Midlothian	66/67				D1
	67/68	1			D1
Cape Town C					
Durban C					
East Fife	76/77	11	4	1	D1
	77/78	6	4		D1

MILNE Arthur
b. Brechin c1915 d. Edinburgh ?.5.1997
Brechin V
Chester T
Brechin C T

Club	Season	Apps	Gls	Div
Dundee U	34/35	18	23	D2
	35/36	27	32	D2
	36/37	28	22	D2
Liverpool	L 36/37			FL
Hibernian	37/38	31	17	D1
	38/39	35	20	D1
	46/47	3	1	D1
St Mirren	46/47	19	6	D1
	47/48	18	6	D1
	48/49	23	10	D1
	49/50	11	2	D1
Coleraine				

MILNE James
b. Arbroath c1930 d. Arbroath 2.3.2004
Brechin V

Club	Season	Apps	Gls	Div
Arbroath	49/50	6		D2
Heart of Midlothian	50/51			D1
	51/52	26		D1
	52/53	14		D1
	53/54			D1
	54/55	1		D1
	55/56	2		D1
	56/57	15		D1
	57/58	21	3	D1
	58/59	20		D1
	59/60	25		D1
	60/61	19		D1
Falkirk	61/62	12		D1

MILNE James
Arbroath LC

Club	Season	Apps	Sub	Gls	Div
Arbroath	69/70	2			D2
	70/71			1	D2
	71/72	34		2	D2
	72/73	31		1	D1
	73/74	28		1	D1
	74/75	25	3	1	D1
	75/76	26			D1
	76/77	20			D1

ƒ
MILNE Robert
b. Camelon 27.4.1921
d. 29.6.1998 Caps: USA - 1
Dunipace Thistle
Polkemmet Jnrs

Club	Season	Apps	Div
Celtic	46/47	29	D1
	47/48	23	D1
	48/49	24	D1
	49/50	15	D1
	50/51	16	D1

New York Americans
Los Angeles Danes

MIRFIN Alex

Club	Season	Apps	Div
Airdrieonians	63/64	1	D1

MITCHELL Barrie
b. Aberdeen 15.3.1947
Arbroath

Club	Season	Apps	Sub	Gls	Div
Dunfermline A	67/68	10	1	2	D1
	68/69	28	1	11	D1
	69/70	32	1	4	D1
	70/71	31		8	D1
	71/72	34		7	D1
Aberdeen	72/73	12		1	D1
	73/74			1	D1
Tranmere R	73/74	16		4	FL
	74/75	19	5	2	FL
Vancouver Whitecaps	75	18		5	NA
Tranmere R	75/76	42	1	4	FL
Vancouver Whitecaps	76				
Preston NE	76/77	7	4	2	FL
York C	T 77/78	1	2		FL

MITCHELL David
b. Paisley 18.5.1948
Stoke C

Club	Season	Apps	Gls	Div
Ayr U	T 64/65	5		D2
St Mirren	64/65	9	1	D1
	65/66	13	1	D1
	66/67			D1
Rochester Lancers	67			
	68			
	69			
	70	24	2	NA
	71	23	1	NA
	72	14	2	NA
	73	18		NA
	74	20		NA
	75	22		NA
New York Cosmos	76	7		NA
Team Hawaii	77	23		NA
Tulsa Roughnecks	78	25		NA
Toronto Blizzard	79	30		NA

MITCHELL Douglas
Ayr Albion
Leeds U
Crosshill Thistle

Club	Season	Apps	Sub	Gls	Div
Ayr U	66/67	25	1	2	D1
	67/68	28	2	5	D2
	68/69				D2
	69/70	34		1	D1
	70/71	27		2	D1
	71/72	12	1	2	D1
	72/73	8		3	D1
	73/74	22	3	2	D1
	74/75	1	3		D1
Partick T	74/75	2	3		D1

MITCHELL George

Club	Season	Apps	Gls	Div
Morton	46/47	2		D1
	47/48			D1
	48/49	3		D1
	49/50	15	1	D2
	50/51	5		D1
Stirling A	51/52	22		D1
Oldham A				

ƒ
MITCHELL Ian
b. Falkirk 9.5.1946 d. Broughty Ferry 2.4.1996
Woodburn A

Club	Season	Apps	Sub	Gls	Div
Dundee U	62/63	26		7	D1
	63/64	25		12	D1
	64/65	14		3	D1
	65/66	19		12	D1
	66/67	28	1	17	D1
	67/68	27		13	D1
	68/69	31		12	D1
	69/70	32	1	18	D1
Newcastle U	70/71	2		1	FL
Dundee U	71/72	14		5	D1
	72/73	17	4	2	D1
	73/74	3		1	D1
Falkirk	74/75	23	2	9	D2
	75/76	13	3	4	D2
	76/77	9	10	2	D2

MITCHELL J

Raith R	50/51	4		D1
	51/52	1		D1

MITCHELL James Ronald
b. Renfrew 27.5.1925
Yoker A
Renfrew Waverley

Celtic	46/47			D1
	47/48	1		D1
	48/49			D1
Exeter C	49/50	2		FL
Third Lanark				

MITCHELL James S
b. Glasgow d. Glasgow 11.3.2004

Queen's Park	46/47	21		D1
Morton	47/48	26		D1
	48/49	26		D1
	49/50	30		D2
	50/51	30		D1
	51/52	30		D1
Aberdeen	52/53	29		D1
	53/54	26		D1
	54/55	29		D1
	55/56	24		D1
	56/57	19		D1
	57/58	2		D1

MITCHELL John
b. Avonbridge
Crieff Earngrove

Stirling A	54/55	11		D1
	55/56	4		D1

MITCHELL John
b. Dundee 26.10.1954
Hillside BC

Arbroath	73/74		1		D1
	74/75	6			D1
	75/76	6	9		D1
	76/77	13	9	1	D1
	77/78	10	7	1	D1
	78/79	4	8	1	D1
Forfar A	79/80	37	1	11	D2
	80/81	13	2	6	D2
	81/82	2			D2

MITCHELL Robert
b. Campbeltown 17.1.1927

Third Lanark	50/51	1		D1
Exeter C	51/52	3		FL
	52/53			FL
	53/54			FL
Bath C	54/55			

MITCHELL Robert
Bellshill Academy

Partick T	66/67	1		D1

MITCHELL Robert Carmichael
b. Glasgow 16.8.1924
d. Tyneside 8.4.1993 Caps: S - 2
Market Star

Third Lanark	46/47	26	22	D1
	47/48	27	12	D1
	48/49	17	8	D1
Newcastle U	48/49	13	3	FL
	49/50	38	8	FL
	50/51	40	7	FL
	51/52	30	9	FL
	52/53	35	10	FL
	53/54	35	14	FL
	54/55	40	19	FL
	55/56	29	5	FL
	56/57	25	2	FL
	57/58	36	12	FL
	58/59	16		FL
	59/60	15		FL
	60/61	15	6	FL
Berwick R	61/62	33	5	D2
Gateshead	62/63			
	63/64			

MITCHELL Stewart Anderson
b. Glasgow 3.3.1933
Benburb

Newcastle U	54/55	4		FL
	55/56			FL
	56/57	7		FL
	57/58	7		FL
	58/59	11		FL
	59/60	9		FL
	60/61	5		FL
	61/62			FL
	62/63	2		FL
Third Lanark	63/64	15		D1
	64/65	8		D1

MITCHELL William
Leven Hibs

Raith R	69/70	5		3	D1
	70/71			9	D2
Celtic	71/72				D1
	72/73				D1
Dunfermline A	73/74		1		D1
Raith R	73/74	8		5	D2
Alloa A	74/75	5	8	1	D2

MOCHAN Dennis
b. Falkirk 12.12.1935
Kilsyth R

East Fife	57/58	23	2	D1
	58/59			D2
Raith R	59/60	31	1	D1
	60/61	20		D1
	61/62	34		D1
Nottingham F	62/63	15	1	FL
	63/64	36		FL
	64/65	38		FL
	65/66	19		FL
Colchester U	66/67	31	3	FL
	67/68	40	2	FL
	68/69	41		FL
	69/70	1		FL

MOCHAN Neil
b. Larbert 6.4.1927
d. Falkirk 28.8.1994 Caps: S - 3
Dunipace Thistle

Morton	48/49	24	13	D1
	49/50	30	24	D2
	50/51	28	20	D1
Middlesbrough	51/52	29	12	FL
	52/53	9	2	FL
Celtic	53/54	22	20	D1
	54/55	17	9	D1
	55/56	31	15	D1
	56/57	31	11	D1
	57/58	26	7	D1
	58/59	33	5	D1
	59/60	29	13	D1
	60/61	2	1	D1
Dundee U	60/61	23	14	D1
	61/62	32	12	D1
	62/63	14	4	D1
Raith R	63/64	18	4	D2

MOFFAT Angus
b. 15.5.1948
Southampton

Motherwell	65/66	10		1	D1
	66/67	27	1	5	D1
	67/68	3			D1
Detroit Cougars	68	10			NA
Falkirk	68/69	1			D1
Dumbarton	69/70				D2
	70/71				D2
	71/72				D2
Toronto Metros	72	14		1	NA

MOLES William

Rangers	57/58	3		D1
	58/59			D1
Third Lanark	59/60	3		D1

MOLLER Rene
b. Randers 15.2.1946 Caps: Den - 5
Randers Freja

Heart of Midlothian	67/68	8	3	D1
	68/69	13	2	D1
	69/70	32	7	D1
Randers Freja				

MOLLISON Harry
St Francis BC

Dundee U	71/72	2		D1
Forfar A				

MONAN Edward
Ardeer Recreation
Irvine Meadow

Ayr U	63/64	2			D2
	64/65	27			D2
	65/66	32		1	D2
	66/67	22	1	2	D1
	67/68	23	1	2	D2
Partick T	68/69				D1
Queen of the South	69/70	5	1		D2

MONTGOMERIE John
Ashfield

Queen of the South	58/59	2		D1

MONTGOMERY James
Maryhill

Airdrieonians	72/73	8		D1
	73/74			D1
Albion R	74/75	24		D2

MOODIE John
b. c1919 d. 1.1.1994
Lochore Welfare

Heart of Midlothian	37/38	3		D1
Raith R				
Dunfermline A				
East Fife				
Cowdenbeath				
Airdrieonians	46/47	24		D2
	47/48	9		D1
Cowdenbeath				

MOONEY Harry

Third Lanark	46/47	26		D1
	47/48	30	1	D1
	48/49	19		D1
	49/50	30		D1
	50/51	11		D1
	51/52	27		D1
	52/53	27		D1
	53/54	5		D2

MOONIE George

Airdrieonians	64/65	21	4	D1

MOORE Edward
Beith Jnrs

Ayr U	63/64	6	4	D2
	64/65	31	23	D2
	65/66	20	13	D2
	66/67	11	2	D1
Clydebank	67/68	31	8	D2

MOORE James

Dundee U	63/64	2		D1
	64/65			D1
	65/66			D1
	66/67	2		D1
	67/68	1		D1
Cowdenbeath	68/69			D2
	69/70	33		D2
	70/71	34		D1
	71/72	34		D2
	72/73	36		D2

MOORE John
b. Harthill 21.12.1943
North Motherwell

Club	Season	Apps	Sub	Goals	Div
Motherwell	63/64	2			D1
	64/65	2			D1
Luton T	65/66	43		5	FL
	66/67	43	1	2	FL
	67/68	45		4	FL
	68/69	29	4	1	FL
	69/70	22	1		FL
	70/71	35		1	FL
	71/72	36	3		FL
	72/73	11	1		FL
Brighton & HA L	72/73	5			FL
Luton T	73/74				FL
Northampton T	74/75	14			FL
Hitchin T					

MOORE Neil
b. Motherwell
Muirkirk

Club	Season	Apps	Goals	Div
St Mirren	52/53	7		D1
	53/54	4		D1
	54/55	9		D1
	55/56	9	2	D1
	56/57	4		D1

MORAN Douglas Walter
b. Musselburgh 29.7.1934
Musselburgh Union

Club	Season	Apps	Sub	Goals	Div
Hibernian	53/54	1		1	D1
	54/55	2			D1
	55/56				D1
Falkirk	56/57	14		2	D1
	57/58	30		12	D1
	58/59	33		16	D1
	59/60	26		15	D2
	60/61	32		30	D2
Ipswich T	61/62	42		14	FL
	62/63	32		9	FL
	63/64	30		8	FL
Dundee U	64/65	3		1	D1
Falkirk	64/65	17		2	D1
	65/66	29		7	D1
	66/67	30	1		D1
	67/68		1		D1
Cowdenbeath					
Gala Fairydean					

MORAN Thomas
b. Edinburgh 5.2.1930

Club	Season	Apps	Goals	Div
Cowdenbeath	52/53	20	8	D2
	53/54	3		D2
Carlisle U	54/55	18	2	FL
	55/56	17	2	FL
Darlington	56/57	43	8	FL
	57/58	27	5	FL
Falkirk	58/59	1		D1

MORAWIEC Gerhard (aka Gerhard, Peter)
b. Poland ?.?.1920 d. Falkirk 23.8.2002

Club	Season	Apps	Div
East Stirlingshire	47/48		D2
	48/49		D2
Stirling A	49/50	21	D1
East Stirlingshire			

MORELAND William

Club	Season	Apps	Div
Falkirk	66/67	1	D1
	67/68	11	D1
	68/69	1	D1

MORGAN Joseph
b. Edinburgh 22.3.1953
Salvesen BC

Club	Season	Apps	Sub	Goals	Div
Heart of Midlothian	70/71		1		D1
	71/72				D1
	72/73				D1
	73/74				D1
Meadowbank T	74/75	4		2	D2

MORRIS Eric
b. Stranraer 30.9.1951
Troon
Muirkirk

Club	Season	Apps	Sub	Goals	Div
Hamilton A T	69/70	1		1	D2
Irvine Meadow					
Rangers	73/74	5	1		D1
	74/75				D1
	75/76				P
	76/77	1			P
	77/78				P
	78/79	1			P
Ayr U	79/80	34		11	D1
	80/81	36		10	D1
	81/82	36	2	8	D1
	82/83	26	1		D1
	83/84	18			D1
	84/85	31	2	1	D1
	85/86	1	1		D1
Cumnock					
Craigmark Burntonians					

MORRIS Henry Miller
b. Dundee 17.12.1919
d. Kirkcaldy 13.3.1993 Caps: S - 1
Lochee Central
Dundee Violet

Club	Season	Apps	Goals	Div
East Fife	46/47	25	20	D2
	47/48	29	41	D2
	48/49	26	15	D1
	49/50	26	18	D1
	50/51	14	5	D1
	51/52	1		D1
	52/53			D1
Dundee U	53/54			D2
Portadown				

MORRISON D

Club	Season	Apps	Div
Third Lanark	46/47	1	D1

MORRISON Derek G
b. Tradeston ?.?.1954
Kilwinning R

Club	Season	Apps	Sub	Goals	Div
Kilmarnock	74/75		1		D1
	75/76		3		D1
Queen of the South					
Largs Thistle					
Svendborg					
Hamilton A	78/79	7	2	3	D1
	79/80		1		D1

MORRISON Edward McCallum
b. Gourock ?.?.1948
Port Glasgow Jnrs

Club	Season	Apps	Sub	Goals	Div
Kilmarnock	66/67	1		1	D1
	67/68	24		14	D1
	68/69	33		13	D1
	69/70	34		19	D1
	70/71	26	4	5	D1
	71/72	28	1	10	D1
	72/73	34		16	D1
	73/74	35		25	D2
	74/75	32	1	11	D1
	75/76	14	1	7	D1
Morton	75/76	4		2	D1
	76/77	36	1	6	D1

MORRISON Reginald
b. Aberdeen
Lewis U

Club	Season	Apps	Div
Aberdeen	52/53	2	D1
	53/54	5	D1
	54/55	3	D1
	55/56	2	D1
	56/57	8	D1
	57/58	25	D1
	58/59	23	D1
Dundee	59/60		D1
Stirling A	59/60	29	D1
	60/61		D2
Deveronvale			

MORRISON Robert Crosson
b. Chapelhall 16.2.1933
Dalry Thistle

Club	Season	Apps	Goals	Div
Falkirk	52/53	6	3	D1
	53/54	18	4	D1
	54/55	29	8	D1
	55/56	13	2	D1
	56/57	13	2	D1
Rangers	56/57	5	6	D1
	57/58			D1
Nottingham F	58/59	1		FL
Workington	59/60	41	17	FL
	60/61	12	3	FL

MORRISON Thomas
b. Kilsyth 6.3.1943
Kilsyth R

Club	Season	Apps	Goals	Div
Aberdeen	63/64	9	2	D1
	64/65	12	5	D1
Port Vale	65/66	5	1	FL
Sligo R	65/66			

MORRISON William

Club	Season	Apps	Goals	Div
Falkirk	50/51	12	3	D1
	51/52	1		D2
	52/53	1		D1

MORRISON William

Craigen Juveniles
Loanhead Mayflower

Club	Season	Apps	Div
Celtic	51/52	1	D1
	52/53		D1
Leith A L	52/53		D3
Loanhead Mayflower			

MORRISON William
b. Kilsyth 10.10.1939
Croy Guilds

Club	Season	Apps	Div
Portsmouth	58/59	3	FL
	59/60		FL
Queen of the South	60/61		D2
	61/62		D2
	62/63	34	D1
	63/64	32	D1
	64/65	3	D2
	65/66	22	D2
	66/67	7	D2

MORROW Richard

Club	Season	Apps	Div
Queen of the South	56/57	4	D1

MORTENSEN Leif
b. Copenhagen
KB Copenhagen
Udinese

Club	Season	Apps	Goals	Div
Aberdeen	64/65	14	1	D1
	65/66	1		D1

MUIR Alec

Burnbank A

Club	Season	Apps	Goals	Div
Albion R	46/47			D2
	47/48			D2
	48/49	15		D1
	49/50	26	3	D2
Stirling A L	49/50	24		D1
Albion R	50/51			D2
	51/52			D2
	52/53	23		D2

MUIR George

Club	Season	Apps	Div
Hibernian	55/56	1	D1
	56/57	24	D1
	57/58	20	D1
	58/59	1	D1
	59/60	3	D1

MUIR George
b. Stirling ?.?.1940 d. Stirling 13.12.1999
Sauchie Jnrs

Club	Season	Apps	Sub	Goals	Div
Partick T	58/59	3			D1
	59/60	0			D1
	60/61	20		1	D1
	61/62	12		1	D1
	62/63	13			D1
	63/64	12			D1
	64/65	19			D1
	65/66	34		1	D1
	66/67	34			D1
	67/68	26			D1
Dumbarton	68/69				D2
	69/70	36		1	D2
	70/71			1	D2
	71/72	9			D2

MUIR Henry
St Andrews U

Club	Season	Apps	Sub	Goals	Div
Dunfermline A	63/64	1			D1

MUIR Ian Baker
b. Motherwell 16.6.1929
Bishop Auckland

Club	Season	Apps	Sub	Goals	Div
Motherwell	50/51	3			D1
	51/52	4			D1
	52/53				D1
Bristol R	53/54	1			FL
	54/55	9			FL
	55/56	14			FL
	56/57	2			FL
Oldham A	57/58	35			FL
Rhyl					

MUIR James
b. c1948
Irvine V

Club	Season	Apps	Sub	Goals	Div
Motherwell	67/68	2			D1
	68/69	15	4	8	D2
	69/70	3		8	D1
	70/71	23	1	6	D1
	71/72	13	1	4	D1
	72/73	13	1	2	D1
	73/74	24		2	D1
Dumbarton	74/75	27	1	3	D1
	75/76	18		4	D1
	76/77	26	1	8	D1
	77/78	29	1	5	D1
	78/79	9	2	2	D1

MUIR John
b. Irvine 21.7.1948
Rotherham U

Club	Season	Apps	Sub	Goals	Div
Motherwell	69/70	1			D1
	70/71				D1
	71/72	21		1	D1
	72/73	8	1		D1
	73/74	13	2	1	D1
	74/75	7	1		D1
Stranraer	75/76	24		4	D2
	76/77	38			D2
	77/78	36			D2
	78/79	34			D2
	79/80	10			D2
Dunfermline A	79/80	23		1	D1
	80/81	3			D1

MUIR John
b. 4.9.1947
Blairhall Colliery

Club	Season	Apps	Sub	Goals	Div
Alloa A	67/68			2	D2
	68/69			16	D2
	69/70	16		9	D2
St Johnstone	69/70	3	3		D1
	70/71	7		1	D1
	71/72	5	2	1	D1
	72/73	19	4	6	D1
	73/74	25	7	12	D1
	74/75	32	1	14	D1
	75/76	24	2	3	P
Alloa A	76/77	32	4	11	D2
	77/78	14	1	4	D1
	78/79	7		2	D2
	79/80	13	3	3	D2

MUIR Joseph
b. Cambuslang
St Rochs

Club	Season	Apps	Sub	Goals	Div
Third Lanark	50/51	5		1	D1
	51/52				D1
	52/53				D1
	53/54	14			D2
	54/55				D2
	55/56				D2
Albion R	55/56				D2

MUIR William McKie
b. Kilwinning ?.?.1934
Irvine Royal Academy
Kilmarnock Amateurs
Neilston Jnrs

Club	Season	Apps	Sub	Goals	Div
Kilmarnock	56/57	29		6	D1
	57/58	18		1	D1
	58/59	20		3	D1
	59/60	24		10	D1
	60/61	28		5	D1
	61/62	18		3	D1
	62/63	1		1	D1
Clyde	62/63	15		4	D1
Queen of the South	63/64	13			D1
Ayr U	64/65	26		2	D2
Dumbarton	65/66	18		2	D2
Irvine Meadow					

MUIR William Nelson
b. Port Glasgow 14.8.1934

Club	Season	Apps	Sub	Goals	Div
St Mirren	55/56	1			D1
Aldershot	56/57	8		4	FL
Nuneaton B					

MUIRHEAD William

Club	Season	Apps	Sub	Goals	Div
Hibernian	59/60	15			D1
	60/61	6			D1
	61/62				D1
Toronto C	62				
Raith R	62/63	3			D1
Toronto C	63				
	64				
	65				

MULHALL George
b. Falkirk 8.5.1936 Caps: S - 3
Denny YMCA
Kilsyth R

Club	Season	Apps	Sub	Goals	Div
Aberdeen	53/54				D1
	54/55				D1
	55/56	7		3	D1
	56/57	2		1	D1
	57/58	4		1	D1
	58/59	4		1	D1
	59/60	27		5	D1
	60/61	32		10	D1
	61/62	32		9	D1
	62/63	2			D1
Sunderland	62/63	35		7	FL
	63/64	42		8	FL
	64/65	41		9	FL
	65/66	35	2	8	FL
	66/67	33		12	FL
	67/68	33	3	4	FL
	68/69	30	1	7	FL
Cape Town C					
Morton	71/72	1			D1

MULHERON Edward

Club	Season	Apps	Sub	Goals	Div
Clyde	63/64	30			D2
	64/65	31			D1
	65/66	23			D1
	66/67	20			D1
	67/68				D1
	68/69	26			D1
	69/70	17	1	1	D1
	70/71	33		1	D1
	71/72	13			D1

MULHOLLAND James
b. Glasgow 10.4.1938

Club	Season	Apps	Sub	Goals	Div
East Stirlingshire	61/62	35		20	D2
Chelsea	62/63	4		1	FL
	63/64	7		1	FL
Morton	64/65	2		1	D1
Barrow	65/66	44	1	15	FL
	66/67	40		18	FL
	67/68	37	1	10	FL
	68/69	11		3	FL
Stockport Co	68/69	18	1	3	FL
	69/70	10	3	2	FL
Crewe Alex.	70/71				

MULKERRIN James
b. Dumbarton 25.12.1931

Club	Season	Apps	Sub	Goals	Div
Hibernian	50/51	2		1	D1
	51/52	1			D1
	52/53	1			D1
	53/54	2		3	D1
Cheltenham T	53/54				
Hibernian	54/55				D1
	55/56	8		5	D1
	56/57	1			D1
Accrington S	56/57	12		8	FL
	57/58	30		19	FL
	58/59	28		9	FL
Tranmere R	59/60	23		7	FL
	60/61	15		1	FL
Northwich V					

MULLEN John

Club	Season	Apps	Sub	Goals	Div
East Stirlingshire	63/64	1			D1

MULLIN James
b. Glasgow
Eastercraigs

Club	Season	Apps	Sub	Goals	Div
Partick T	71/72	3		1	D1
	72/73	3			D1
	73/74	1			D1
East Stirlingshire	74/75	35	1	12	D2
	75/76	20	2	8	D2
	76/77	20		5	D2
Dunfermline A	76/77	13		4	D2
	77/78	21	2	7	D2
	78/79	33	3	12	D2
	79/80	2	3		D1

MULLEN Terry
b. Stirling 26.2.1956

Club	Season				Div
Dumbarton	73/74	8	1		D1
	74/75	16	1		D1
	75/76	10	2		D1
Falkirk	76/77	7	4		D1
Stenhousemuir	77/78	31	1		D2
	78/79	36			D2
	79/80	25			D2
	80/81	29	1		D2
	81/82	28	1		D2
	82/83	13			D2
	83/84	20	3		D2
East Stirlingshire	84/85	3			D2

MULLEN William
Kilsyth R

Club	Season				Div
Cowdenbeath	68/69			3	D2
	69/70	36		18	D2
	70/71	10	2		D1
	71/72	22	4	10	D2
Montrose	72/73	11		2	D2

MUNN William
Camelon

Club	Season				Div
Stenhousemuir	61/62	27		21	D2
Stirling A	61/62	7		1	D1
	62/63				D2
	63/64				D2

MUNRO Alan
Clydebank Strollers

Club	Season				Div
Clydebank	68/69			15	D2
	69/70	34		14	D2
	70/71			12	D2
	71/72	35		16	D2
	72/73	6			D2
Partick T	72/73	1			D1
	73/74				D1
Dundee U	74/75	2		1	D1
St Mirren	74/75	21	2	10	D2
	75/76	6	2		D1
Clydebank	76/77		2		D1
Queen of the South	77/78		4	1	D1

MUNRO Alexander Iain Fordyce
b. Bellshil 24.8.1951 Caps: S - 7
Drumchapel Amateurs

Club	Season				Div
St Mirren	68/69				
	69/70	4	1		D1
	70/71	30	2	3	D1
	71/72	36		6	D2
	72/73	31	1	7	D2
Hibernian	73/74	8	6	2	D1
	74/75	28	2	8	D1
	75/76	17			P
St Mirren	L 75/76	6	2		D1
Rangers	76/77	3	2		P
	77/78				P
St Mirren	77/78	24		3	P
	78/79	33			P
	79/80	32			P
	80/81				P
Stoke C	80/81	32		1	FL
Sunderland	81/82	34			FL
	82/83	37			FL
	83/84	9	3		FL
Dundee U	83/84	9			P
	84/85	5			P
Hibernian	84/85	6			P
	85/86	26			P

MUNRO Bruce
b. Perth 24.6.1946
Perth Celtic

Club	Season				Div
St Johnstone	66/67	2			D1
Stirling A	67/68	6	2	3	D1

MUNRO Francis Michael
b. Broughty Ferry 25.10.1947 Caps: S - 9

Club	Season				Div
Chelsea	62/63				FL
Dundee U	63/64				D1
	64/65	19		1	D1
	65/66	28		13	D1
	66/67	2	1		D1
Aberdeen	66/67	29		6	D1
	67/68	13	1	2	D1
Wolverhampton W	67/68	7		1	FL
	68/69	12	4	2	FL
	69/70	32	1	1	FL
	70/71	36			FL
	71/72	37		3	FL
	72/73	32		2	FL
	73/74	36		2	FL
	74/75	35		3	FL
	75/76	30			FL
	76/77	33		1	FL
Hereford U	L 76/77				FL
Celtic	77/78	14			P

MUNRO J

Club	Season				Div
Hibernian	50/51	1			D1

MUNRO William

Club	Season				Div
East Stirlingshire	61/62	29		14	D2
	62/63				D2
	63/64	2			D1
ES Clydebank	64/65	12		2	D2

MURDOCH Robert White
b. Rutherglen 17.8.1944
d. 14.5.2001 Caps: S - 12
Cambuslang R

Club	Season				Div
Celtic	61/62				D1
	62/63	19		4	D1
	63/64	26		15	D1
	64/65	32		8	D1
	65/66	31		5	D1
	66/67	31		4	D1
	67/68	34		6	D1
	68/69	30		4	D1
	69/70	24	2	5	D1
	70/71	21	2	2	D1
	71/72	15		4	D1
	72/73	24		4	D1
Middlesbrough	73/74	33	1	5	FL
	74/75	39		1	FL
	75/76	21	1		FL

MURDOCH William

Club	Season				Div
Motherwell	63/64	3			D1

MURNEY Bernard

Club	Season				Div
Raith R	55/56	9		4	D1
	56/57				D1
	57/58	1			D1

MURNEY Hugh

Club	Season				Div
Queen of the South	62/63	4		1	D1

MURPHY

Club	Season				Div
Raith R	59/60	4		1	D1

MURPHY Albert
b. Dublin ?.11.1930 Caps: Ei - 1
Transport

Club	Season				Div
Clyde	49/50	6			D1
Shamrock R	50/51				
Clyde	50/51	4			D1
	51/52				D2
	52/53	16			D1
	53/54	29			D1
	54/55	29			D1
	55/56	29			D1
	56/57				D2
	57/58	34			D1
	58/59	30			D1

MURPHY Edward
b. Hamilton 13.5.1924
Hibernian

Club	Season				Div
Morton	47/48	7		3	D1
	48/49	9			D1
Northampton T	49/50	41		13	FL
	50/51	30		2	FL
Barnsley	50/51	10		1	FL
	51/52	8		1	FL
Exeter C	52/53	38		7	FL
	53/54	12		1	FL
	54/55	25		2	FL
	55/56	19		3	FL
Bridgwater T					
Trowbridge T					

MURPHY Edward Cullinane
b. Glasgow 1.6.1934

Club	Season				Div
Clyde	53/54	9			D1
	54/55				D1
	55/56	17			D1
Oldham A	56/57	39			FL
	57/58	13			FL
	58/59	20			FL
Bangor C					

MURPHY James Baird
b. Glasgow 29.11.1942
Larkhall Academy
Larkhall V
Lesmahagow Jnrs
Burnbank A
Stonehouse Violet
Larkhall Thistle
Alloa A

Club	Season				Div
Heart of Midlothian	63/64	6		7	D1
	64/65	1			D1
	65/66	7		2	D1
	66/67	20	1	7	D1
Raith R	67/68	10	1	1	D1
Notts Co	67/68	16		3	FL
	68/69	17		4	FL
Motherwell	68/69	4	6	1	D2
	69/70	16	3	3	D1
Hamilton A	70/71	27		8	D2
East Stirlingshire	71/72	32		6	D2
	72/73	34		2	D2
	73/74	1	1		D2

MURPHY John
b. Halbeath
Crossgates Primrose
Cowdenbeath

Club	Season				Div
Queen of the South	59/60				D2
	60/61				D2
	61/62				D2
	62/63	24		5	D1
	63/64	26		3	D1
	64/65	19		9	D2
	65/66	23		5	D2
	66/67	19		2	D2

MURPHY John
Darvel Jnrs

Club	Season				Div
Ayr U	63/64	33		1	D2
	64/65	35		1	D2
	65/66	27			D2
	66/67	34		1	D1
	67/68	36			D2
	68/69			2	D2
	69/70	32			D1
	70/71	34			D1
	71/72	34			D1
	72/73	34		1	D1
	73/74	27	1	1	D1
	74/75	34			D1
	75/76	35		1	P
	76/77	24	1		P
	77/78	5			P
East Stirlingshire	78/79	1			D2

MURPHY John
b. Edinburgh 26.11.1949

Club	Season				Div
Hibernian	68/69	1			D1
	69/70	5	3	1	D1
	70/71	1			D1
Morton	71/72	32	2	2	D1
	72/73	26	2	1	D1
Stirling A	73/74	23	2	5	D2
	74/75	26	1	5	D2
Cowdenbeath	75/76	24		10	D2

MURPHY P

Club	Season			Div
Airdrieonians	52/53	2		D1

MURRAY Cameron
Drumchapel Amateurs

Club	Season				Div
St Mirren	62/63	34			D1
	63/64	34			D1
	64/65	34			D1
	65/66	30			D1
	66/67	33			D1
	67/68	26		3	D2
	68/69	28			D1
	69/70	34			D1
	70/71	32			D1
	71/72	36			D2
Motherwell	72/73	7	2	1	D1
Arbroath	73/74	34			D1
	74/75	33	1		D1
	75/76	21	4		D1
	76/77	24	7		D1
	77/78	20	3		D1

MURRAY Donald James
b. Elgin 18.1.1946
Burghead Thistle

Club	Season				Div
Cardiff C	62/63	1			FL
	63/64	21			FL
	64/65	31			FL
	65/66	32			FL
	66/67	40			FL
	67/68	40		1	FL
	68/69	42		1	FL
	69/70	42		1	FL
	70/71	42		1	FL
	71/72	36			FL
	72/73	36		1	FL
	73/74	35		1	FL
	74/75	9			FL
Swansea C	L 74/75	5			FL
Heart of Midlothian	74/75	16			D1
	75/76	22			P
	76/77				P
Newport Co	76/77	16	2		FL
Barry T					
Cardiff C					

MURRAY Eric McIntyre
b. Symington ?.?.1941
Saxone Amateurs
Dreghorn Jnrs

Club	Season				Div
Kilmarnock	60/61				D1
	61/62	6			D1
	62/63	9			D1
	63/64	29		14	D1
	64/65	34		4	D1
	65/66	31		4	D1
	66/67	15		2	D1
	67/68	21		2	D1
St Mirren	68/69	24			D1
	69/70	13	3		D1
	70/71		1		D1
Cumnock Jnrs					

MURRAY George
b. Bellshill
Kilmarnock Amateurs

Club	Season				Div
Motherwell	62/63	5		1	D1
	63/64	25		1	D1
	64/65	28		1	D1
	65/66	34		6	D1
	66/67	21	3	5	D1
	67/68	12		1	D1
Aberdeen	67/68	9	1	1	D1
	68/69	9	1		D1
	69/70	34		2	D1
	70/71	4	1		D1
	71/72	23		1	D1
	72/73	7			D1

MURRAY James

Club	Season				Div
Airdrieonians	47/48	8		1	D1
	48/49				D2
	49/50	23		1	D2
	50/51	2			D1
	51/52	5			D1

MURRAY James
b. Edinburgh 4.2.1933 Caps: S - 5
Merchiston Thistle
Newtongrange Star

Club	Season			Div
Heart of Midlothian	50/51			D1
	51/52	1	1	D1
	52/53			D1
Reading	53/54	2	1	FL
	54/55	5	2	FL
Heart of Midlothian	54/55	4		D1
	55/56	4		D1
	56/57	12	7	D1
	57/58	33	27	D1
	58/59	30	12	D1
	59/60	18	11	D1
	60/61	13	5	D1
Falkirk	61/62	14	4	D1
Clyde	62/63	14		D1
	63/64			

MURRAY John

Club	Season			Div
Airdrieonians	51/52	17		D1
	52/53	8		D1

MURRAY John
Dailly Amateurs

Club	Season				Div
Motherwell	67/68	4		1	D1
	68/69	17	3	1	D2
	69/70	2	5	1	D1
	70/71				D1
	71/72				D1
Stranraer	72/73	16	1	3	D2

MURRAY John Anthony
b. Saltcoats 5.2.1949

Club	Season				Div
Morton	65/66	2			D1
	66/67	4	2	1	D2
	67/68	8		1	D1
	68/69				D1
	69/70	14		1	D1
	70/71	17	1		D1
Cambridge U	71/72	3			FL
Queen of the South	72/73	1			D2
	73/74	21	1	1	D2
	74/75	6	2		D2

MURRAY John McCann
b. Glasgow 9.3.1945
Kirkintilloch Rob Roy

Club	Season				Div
Stirling A	64/65	10		1	D2
	65/66	7		1	D1
	66/67				D1
Lincoln C	T 66/67	4			FL

MURRAY Leslie
b. Kinghorn 29.9.1928 d. ?.?.1993

Club	Season			Div
Raith R	49/50	2	1	D1
	50/51	24	6	D1
	51/52	2		D1
Arbroath	51/52			D2
Rochdale	52/53	16	3	FL
Cowdenbeath	53/54	26	12	D2

MURRAY Matthew
b. Paisley 25.12.1929
St Mirren BC
Camelon Juniors
Queen's Park

Club	Season			Div
Kilmarnock	52/53	26	8	D2
	53/54	13	1	D2
	54/55	26	5	D1
	55/56	9	1	D1
Ayr U	56/57	11	1	D1
Raith R				
St Mirren	57/58	3		D1
Barrow	58/59	33	2	FL
Carlisle U	59/60	28	4	FL
Morton				

MURRAY Maxwell
b. Falkirk 7.11.1935
Camelon Juniors

Club	Season			Div
Queen's Park	49/50	2		D2
	50/51	1		D2
	51/52	17	3	D2
	52/53			D2
	53/54	23	14	D2
	54/55	26	10	D2
Rangers	55/56	8	6	D1
	56/57	30	29	D1
	57/58	28	19	D1
	58/59	22	17	D1
	59/60	2	1	D1
	60/61	5	5	D1
	61/62	8	3	D1
West Bromwich A	62/63	3		FL
Third Lanark	63/64	30	13	D1
	64/65	31	4	D1
Clyde	65/66	6	2	D1
Distillery				

MURRAY Neil
b. Fraserburgh 24.10.1950
Lossiemouth
Ross Co

Club	Season				Div
Heart of Midlothian	69/70	8		1	D1
	70/71	2			D1
	71/72	8	2	1	D1
	72/73	3			D1
Morton	72/73	14		3	D1
	73/74	17	4	4	D1
	74/75	3	4	1	D1

MURRAY Robert
Lincoln C

Club	Season			Div
Dunfermline A	64/65	1		D1
Nuneaton B				

MURRAY Robert
b. Winchburgh 5.12.1944
Chelmsford C

Club	Season			Div
Stirling A	67/68	3		D1

MURRAY Ronald

Club	Season			Div
Arbroath	59/60	5		D1
	60/61			D2
	61/62			D2
	62/63			D2
	63/64	33	15	D2
	64/65	11	3	D2

MURRAY Stephen
b. Dumbarton 9.10.1944 Caps: S - 1
Dumbarton St Patricks

Club	Season	Apps		Gls	Div
Dundee	63/64	2			D1
	64/65	23		5	D1
	65/66	33		8	D1
	66/67	32		1	D1
	67/68	33			D1
	68/69	31		1	D1
	69/70	25		3	D1
Aberdeen	69/70	7			D1
	70/71	33		6	D1
	71/72	32		10	D1
	72/73	29		4	D1
Celtic	73/74	32		3	D1
	74/75	28		8	D1
	75/76	2	1		P
	76/77				P
	77/78				P
	78/79				P
Dundee U	79/80	2	1		P
Clydebank	T 79/80				D1

MURRAY Thomas
b. Bellshill 14.1.1933
Dalry Thistle

Club	Season	Apps		Gls	Div
Falkirk	55/56				D1
	56/57	19		4	D1
	57/58	24		4	D1
	58/59	24		5	D1
Queen of the South	59/60				D2
Leeds U	60/61	7		2	FL
Tranmere R	60/61	9		1	FL
	61/62	1			FL
Queen of the South	62/63	12		4	D1

MURRAY Thomas
b. Caldercruix 1.6.1943
Edinburgh A

Club	Season	Apps		Gls	Div
Airdrieonians	60/61	1			D1
	61/62	18		6	D1
	62/63	29		13	D1
	63/64	30		10	D1
	64/65	33		11	D1
	65/66	35		33	D2
	66/67	26		7	D1
Carlisle U	66/67	10		4	FL
	67/68	31	2	15	FL
	68/69	39	2	12	FL
	69/70	30	7	4	FL
	70/71	12		2	FL
Heart of Midlothian	71/72	29		10	D1
	72/73	27	1	5	D1
	73/74	15	7		D1
	74/75	18	5	2	D1
Eastern					
Brisbane C					
Arbroath	77/78	4	3		D1
Raith R	77/78	8	2	3	D2
	78/79	18	4	1	D1

MURRAY William
b. Glasgow 12.10.1942
Kilsyth R

Club	Season	Apps		Gls	Div
Stirling A	65/66	10			D1
	66/67	32			D1
	67/68	31			D1
	68/69				D2

MURRAY William
b. Edinburgh 28.8.1954
Salvesen BC

Club	Season	Apps		Gls	Div
Hibernian	73/74	1		6	D1
	74/75	3		5	D1
	75/76	6	3	1	P
	76/77	11	3	1	P
	77/78	21	1	3	P
	78/79	6	1		P
	79/80	12	1	2	P
	80/81	1	1		D1
Cowdenbeath	80/81	3			D2
Sydney C					

MYLES Alexander

Club	Season	Apps		Gls	Div
St Mirren	60/61	5			D1
Stirling A	61/62	8			D1
Alloa A					

MYLES Neil Thomson
b. Falkirk 17.6.1927 d. ?.?.1993

Club	Season	Apps		Gls	Div
Third Lanark	48/49	1			D1
Ipswich T	49/50	3		2	FL
	50/51	4		2	FL
	51/52	10		3	FL
	52/53	46			FL
	53/54	46		3	FL
	54/55	33		1	FL
	55/56	26		1	FL
	56/57	41		2	FL
	57/58	6			FL
	58/59	4		1	FL
	59/60	4			FL
Clacton T					

MYLES Walter
b. Bridge of Allan 8.10.1947
Bonnybridge

Club	Season	Apps		Gls	Div
Stirling A	67/68	3			D1

McADAM Colin C
b. Glasgow 28.8.1951

Club	Season	Apps		Gls	Div
Dumbarton	71/72	11	1		D2
	72/73	4			D1
	73/74	19	3	5	D1
	74/75	18	1	6	D1
Motherwell	75/76	15		9	P
	76/77	24		4	P
	77/78	9	1	3	P
Partick T	77/78	10	2	3	P
	78/79	22	4	4	P
	79/80	32		17	P
Rangers	80/81	31		12	P
	81/82	15	7	2	P
	82/83	2	2		P
	83/84	8		1	P
Adelaide C	84/85				
Heart of Midlothian	85/86	6			P
Partick T	86/87	16	3	1	D1
	87/88	20	5		D1
Irvine Meadow					
Maryhill					

McADAM John

Club	Season	Apps		Gls	Div
Renfrew					
Falkirk	61/62	2			D1

McADAM Thomas Ian
b. Glasgow 9.4.1954
Clydebank Colts
Weirs Recreation

Club	Season	Apps		Gls	Div
Dumbarton	70/71				D2
	71/72				D2
	72/73	16	2	9	D1
	73/74	16	3	5	D1
	74/75	32	1	11	D1
	75/76	6		4	D1
Dundee U	75/76	26		12	P
	76/77	29	4	9	P
	77/78		2		P
Celtic	77/78	32	1	8	P
	78/79	24	4	7	P
	79/80	34		8	P
	80/81	35		4	P
	81/82	33	1	5	P
	82/83	35		3	P
	83/84	28		1	P
	84/85	25	1		P
	85/86	5			P
Stockport Co	T 86/87	5		1	FL
Hamilton A	T 86/87	3			P
Motherwell	86/87	31		1	P
	87/88	33	1	1	P
	88/89	28		1	P
	89/90	6			P
Airdrieonians	89/90	15		1	D1
	90/91	9			D1

McALEER Francis
b. Glasgow 16.10.1945
Renfrew Jnrs

Club	Season	Apps		Gls	Div
Clydebank	66/67	1			D2
	67/68	17		1	D2
	68/69				D2
Morton	69/70	2			D1
Barrow	70/71	9		1	FL
Ayr U	70/71			1	D1
	71/72	8			D1
Stirling A	72/73	32		1	D2
	73/74	13			D2
	74/75	28		4	D2

McALINDON John
b. Carlisle 25.12.1930 d. 10.2.2002
Carlisle Catholic Youth
Penrith

Club	Season	Apps		Gls	Div
Celtic	48/49				D1
Albion R	L 48/49				D1
Celtic	49/50				D1
	50/51	5		2	D1
	51/52	4		1	D1
	52/53				D1
Worcester C	L 52/53				
Celtic	53/54				D1
	54/55				D1
	55/56	4		2	D1
	56/57	3		2	D1
Shrewsbury T	57/58	12		3	FL

McALLISTER

Club	Season	Apps		Gls	Div
Airdrieonians	60/61	1		1	D1

McALOON Gerald Padua
b. Glasgow 13.9.1916 d. Bridgeton 13.4.1987
St Francis Jnrs

Club	Season	Apps		Gls	Div
Brentford	37/38	7			FL
	38/39	14		3	FL
Wolverhampton W	38/39	2		1	FL
Brentford	46/47	7		4	FL
Celtic	46/47	19		12	D1
	47/48	1			D1
Belfast Celtic					

McALPINE Hamish
b. Kilspindie 21.1.1948
Dundee U

Club	Season	Apps		Gls	Div
Montrose	L 67/68	25			D2
Dundee U	68/69	1			D1
	69/70				D1
	70/71	24			D1
	71/72	29			D1
	72/73	24			D1
	73/74	19			D1
	74/75	34			D1
	75/76	36	1		P
	76/77	36	2		P
	77/78	35			P
	78/79	36			P
	79/80	29			P
	80/81	36			P
	81/82	35			P
	82/83	36			P
	83/84	34			P
	84/85	25			P
	85/86	8			P
Dunfermline A	85/86	1			D2
Raith R	86/87	37			D2
	87/88	35	1		D1
Arbroath	88/89	10			D2

McALPINE William James
b. Edinburgh 14.10.1950
Sighthill Thistle
Gorgie Hearts

Club	Season	Apps		Gls	Div
Heart of Midlothian	68/69	12			D1
	69/70	1			D1
	70/71				D1
	71/72				D1
Arbroath	72/73	18	1		D1
Stirling A	73/74	12	2		D2

McANESPIE Alexander

Craigmark Bruntonians

Club	Season				Div
Ayr U	64/65	24		5	D2
	65/66	29		2	D2
	66/67	18			D1
	67/68	12	2		D2
	68/69		1		D2
	69/70	13	2		D1
	70/71	13	1	1	D1
	71/72	18			D1
	72/73	33		1	D1
	73/74	31			D1
	74/75	24	2		D1
	75/76	23			P
	76/77	19			P
	77/78	20			P

McARA Atholl
b. Glasgow 13.7.1921 d. Glasgow ?.1.1981
Benburb

Club	Season				Div
Heart of Midlothian	46/47	2			D1
Celtic					
Raith R					
Portadown					

McARTHUR J

Club	Season				Div
Airdrieonians	50/51	2			D1

McARTHUR James
b. Dunfermline 27.2.1952
Halbeath BC

Club	Season				Div
Cowdenbeath	67/68	2			D2
	68/69				D2
	69/70	3			D2
	70/71	11			D1
	71/72	35			D2
	72/73	10			D2
Hibernian	72/73	11			D1
	73/74	27			D1
	74/75	30			D1
	75/76	20			P
	76/77				P
	77/78				P
	78/79	18			P
	79/80	29			P
	80/81	37			D1
	81/82	33			P
	82/83	12			P
Meadowbank T	L 82/83	1			D2
Cowdenbeath	83/84	1			D2
Morton	83/84	3			D1
Raith R	83/84	12			D1

McAULEY Alexander J

Club	Season				Div
Queen's Park	46/47	12			D1
	47/48	3		1	D1
	48/49	28		17	D2
	49/50	27		14	D2
Dunfermline A	50/51				D2
	51/52				D2
	52/53	6		2	D2
East Fife	53/54	2			D1

MacAULEY James

Club	Season				Div
Dunfermline A	59/60	2			D1

McAULEY Patrick Comerford
b. Motherwell 31.7.1921 d. Newarthill 16.3.1970
Douglas Hawthorn Juveniles
Benburb T
Celtic
Arthurlie

Club	Season				Div
Celtic	46/47	10			D1
	47/48	27		2	D1
	48/49	24		1	D1
	49/50	17		1	D1
Luton T	50/51	8		1	FL
	51/52				FL
Kettering T	52/53				
	53/54				
Albion R	53/54	3			D2

McAVOY Douglas Haig
b. Kilmarnock 29.11.1918
d. Kilmarnock 15.4.1988
Kilmarnock Academicals
Cumnock Jnrs

Club	Season				Div
Kilmarnock	36/37	1			D1
	37/38	26		5	D1
	38/39	32		7	D1
	46/47	17		5	D1
	47/48	10		3	D2
Liverpool	47/48	1			FL
	48/49	1			FL
Queen of the South	48/49				D1
	49/50	15		2	D1
	50/51				D2

McBAIN Douglas

Club	Season				Div
Queen's Park	47/48	20			D1
Queen of the South	48/49	22			D1
	49/50	28			D1
	50/51				D2
	51/52	22		1	D1
	52/53	16			D1
	53/54	23			D1
	54/55	23		2	D1

McBAIN Gordon Archibald
b. Glasgow 4.12.1934
Shotts Bon Accord

Club	Season				Div
Kilmarnock	56/57	1			D1
	57/58				D1
Rochdale	58/59	10		1	FL
	59/60				FL
Third Lanark	60/61				D1
Cowdenbeath	60/61				D2
	61/62	13		4	D2
Hamilton A	T 61/62	3		2	D2
Brechin C	62/63				D2
Stirling A	63/64	9		7	D2

McBEATH Frank

Club	Season				Div
Partick T	46/47	1			D1

McBETH Andrew Joseph
Pollok Jnrs

Club	Season				Div
Stirling A	63/64	9		10	D2
Morton	64/65	10		2	D1
Dumbarton	65/66	21		8	D2
	66/67	6		1	D2

McBLAIN Gordon
Hibernian

Club	Season				Div
Stirling A	55/56	1			D1

McBRIDE John
b. Kilsyth 31.12.1923
Third Lanark

Club	Season				Div
Reading	47/48	11			FL
	48/49	11			FL
	49/50	19			FL
	50/51	28			FL
	51/52	9			FL
	52/53	22			FL
Shrewsbury T	52/53	3			FL
	53/54	44			FL
	54/55	22			FL
	55/56	9			FL
Kidderminster H	56/57				
	57/58				
	58/59				
Aberdeen	59/60	2			D1

McBRIDE John

Club	Season				Div
Clyde	69/70	4			D1

McBRIDE Joseph
b. Glasgow 10.6.1938 Caps: S - 2
Kilmarnock Amateurs
Kirkintilloch Rob Roy
Shettleston

Club	Season				Div
Kilmarnock	57/58	15		8	D1
	58/59	29		10	D1
	59/60	13		6	D1
Wolverhampton W	59/60				FL
Luton T	59/60	13		6	FL
	60/61	12		3	FL
Partick T	60/61	22		14	D1
	61/62	33		14	D1
	62/63	3		2	D1
Motherwell	62/63	25		16	D1
	63/64	33		18	D1
	64/65	32		21	D1
Celtic	65/66	30		31	D1
	66/67	14		18	D1
	67/68	4	3	4	D1
	68/69	4		1	D1
Hibernian	68/69	23		19	D1
	69/70	33		20	D1
	70/71	11		5	D1
Dunfermline A	70/71	17		8	D1
	71/72		3		D1
Clyde	71/72	12		5	D1

McCABE Bernard J
b. Whitburn
Bathgate Thistle

Club	Season				Div
Aberdeen	66/67	1			D1
	67/68				D1
	68/69				D1
Berwick R	69/70	33			D2
	70/71				D2
	71/72	26	1	2	D2
	72/73	13	1		D2
	73/74	17	2	1	D2
	74/75	35	2	1	D2
	75/76	22	1		D2
Alloa A	76/77	7	4		D2

McCABE James
Bargeddie Amateurs

Club	Season				Div
Motherwell	69/70	2	1		D1
	70/71				D1
	71/72	17	1	7	D1
	72/73	24		4	D1
	73/74	17	1		D1
	74/75	6	2	1	D1
Stranraer	75/76	24	1	11	D2
	76/77	28	1	17	D2
	77/78	9			D2
Albion R	77/78	14	3	3	D2

McCABE Joseph
Kilbirnie Ladeside

Club	Season				Div
Stirling A	50/51				
	51/52	5			D1
	52/53	4			D2
	53/54				D1
	54/55				D1
	55/56				D1
	56/57				D2
Morton	57/58				D2
Hamilton A	58/59	6			D2

McCABE Joseph
Airdrie BC

Club	Season				Div
Airdrieonians	72/73	1			D1

McCABE Thomas
b. Douglas Water
Douglas Water Thistle

Club	Season	Apps	Sub	Goals	Div
Hibernian	46/47	13			D1
	47/48				D1
	48/49				D1
Hamilton A	L 48/49	22			D2
Falkirk	49/50	15			D1
	50/51	5			D1
	51/52	15		4	D2
	52/53	9		1	D1
Stirling A	52/53				D2

McCALL Alexander

Club	Season	Apps	Sub	Goals	Div
Arsenal					
Motherwell	66/67	2		1	D1
	67/68	19	1	2	D1
Kansas City Spurs	68	8		1	NA
Partick T	68/69	1			D1
Ayr U	69/70	2		1	D1

McCALL C Walker
b. Irvine 29.3.1954
Hurlford U

Club	Season	Apps	Sub	Goals	Div
Aberdeen	73/74	4	3	2	D1
	74/75	10	4	6	D1
	75/76	1	1		P
Ayr U	76/77	32	1	16	P
	77/78	34	1	12	P
San Diego Sockers	78	19		11	NA
St Johnstone	78/79	5			D1
San Diego Sockers	79	17		6	NA
	80	11		1	NA
Atlanta Chiefs	80	14		2	NA
Aberdeen	80/81	15	4	10	P
	81/82	6	2	4	P
	82/83		2		P
South China					
Dundee	83/84	30	1	13	P
	84/85	14	10	1	P
	85/86		2		P

McCALL John
b. Dalmellington
Ayr Albion
Dalry T

Club	Season	Apps	Sub	Goals	Div
Aberdeen	59/60	1			D1
Ayr U	60/61				D1

McCALL Ronald

Irvine V

Club	Season	Apps	Sub	Goals	Div
Ayr U	68/69				D2
	69/70	5	1	2	D1
Stranraer	70/71	36		3	D2
	71/72	36		5	D2
	72/73	35		4	D2
	73/74	32	1	5	D2
	74/75	26	7	2	D2
	75/76	12	4		D2
	76/77	14	3	5	D2
	77/78	2	10		D2
Irvine Meadow					

McCALL William
b. Glasgow 14.11.1920

Club	Season	Apps	Sub	Goals	Div
Aberdeen	46/47	29		5	D1
	47/48	13		3	D1
Newcastle U	47/48	15		4	FL
	48/49	1			FL
Motherwell	48/49	14		4	D1
	49/50	14		4	D1
Third Lanark	50/51	15		5	D1
	51/52	6			D1

McCALLION Daniel

Kilsyth R

Club	Season	Apps	Sub	Goals	Div
Morton	73/74	17	4	2	D1

McCALLUM Angus

Bellahouston Academy

Club	Season	Apps	Sub	Goals	Div
Rangers	70/71	1			D1
Irvine V					

McCALLUM Archibald

Yoker A

Club	Season	Apps	Sub	Goals	Div
Partick T	47/48	10		3	D1
	48/49	9		1	D1
	49/50	14		3	D1
	50/51	10		6	D1
	51/52				D1
	52/53	1			D1

McCALLUM David

Westrigg Bluebell

Club	Season	Apps	Sub	Goals	Div
Stirling A	59/60	3			D1

McCALLUM George

Club	Season	Apps	Sub	Goals	Div
Third Lanark	58/59	8			D1
	59/60	9			D1
	60/61	5			D1
	61/62	9			D1

McCALLUM Robert
d. Poole 14.8.1999
Bellshill Academy

Club	Season	Apps	Sub	Goals	Div
Motherwell	58/59	3			D1
	59/60	4		1	D1
	60/61				D1
	61/62	6			D1
	62/63	28		2	D1
	63/64	25			D1
	64/65	33			D1
	65/66	34		6	D1
	66/67	28		2	D1
	67/68	1			D1

McCALLUM W

Club	Season	Apps	Sub	Goals	Div
St Mirren	65/66	2			D1

McCALLUM William
b. c1942 d. 13.3.2003
Douglas Water Thistle

Club	Season	Apps	Sub	Goals	Div
Motherwell	60/61	3			D1
	61/62	6			D1
	62/63	7			D1
	63/64	1			D1
	64/65	17			D1
	65/66	14			D1
	66/67	34		1	D1
	67/68	31	1		D1
	68/69	35			D2
	69/70	32			D1
	70/71	32			D1
	71/72	26			D1
	72/73	33			D1
St Mirren	73/74	7			D2
Dunfermline A	73/74	15		1	D1
	74/75	7			D1
Raith R	74/75	18		1	D2

McCALMAN J

Club	Season	Apps	Sub	Goals	Div
Morton	50/51	1			D1

McCANN Kevin
b. Coatbridge 10.6.1953
Carluke R

Club	Season	Apps	Sub	Goals	Div
Airdrieonians	72/73	11	1	1	D1
	73/74	27		3	D2
	74/75	26	1	1	D1
	75/76	10	3		D1
	76/77	16	5	5	D1
	77/78	27	2	2	D1
	78/79	14	1	2	D1
Queen of the South	78/79	9		1	D1
	79/80	29		4	D2
	80/81	31	2	2	D2
	81/82	25	2	4	D1
	82/83	9	9	1	D2
Stenhousemuir	83/84	6		5	D2
Workington					

McCANN Robert Johnston
b. Dundee 15.10.1932 Caps: S - 5
Dundee Violet
Dundee NE

Club	Season	Apps	Sub	Goals	Div
Dundee U	53/54	27		4	D2
Queen's Park	54/55	25		15	D2
	55/56	26		7	D2
Motherwell	56/57	29		7	D1
	57/58	23		1	D1
	58/59	33			D1
	59/60	30		1	D1
	60/61	32		3	D1
	61/62	17			D1
	62/63	28		4	D1
	63/64	31		5	D1
	64/65	24		1	D1
Hamilton A	65/66	26		2	D1

McCARDLE James

Queen's Park

Club	Season	Apps	Sub	Goals	Div
Queen of the South	48/49				D1
	49/50	12			D1

McCARRON Francis Paul
b. Kinning Park 1.10.1943
Lourdes School Cardonald

Club	Season	Apps	Sub	Goals	Div
Celtic	62/63	1			D1
Parkhead Jnrs	L				
Celtic	63/64				D1
	64/65				D1
	65/66				D1
	66/67				D1
Carlisle U	67/68	7	2	1	FL
	68/69				FL

McCARRY William
b. Tillicoultry 4.12.1938

Club	Season	Apps	Sub	Goals	Div
Falkirk	57/58	3			D1
	58/59	1			D1
	59/60	14			D2
	60/61	26			D2
	61/62	2			D1
	62/63	15			D1
St Johnstone	63/64	31		5	D1
	64/65	31		2	D1
	65/66	29		2	D1
	66/67	31	1	1	D1
	67/68	33		5	D1
	68/69	25	1	3	D1
	69/70	26		4	D1
	70/71	13	3	1	D1
Stirling A	71/72	32		1	D2
	72/73	34			D2

McCARTHY Edward

Club	Season	Apps	Sub	Goals	Div
Raith R	69/70	3		1	D1
	70/71				D2

McCHESNEY Ian
b. 29.7.1944
Kello R

Queen of the South	61/62			D2
	62/63			D1
	63/64	14		D1
	64/65	17	4	D2
	65/66	7		D2
	66/67	34	8	D2
	67/68	32	4	D2
	68/69		11	D2
	69/70	34	7	D2
	70/71		10	D2
	71/72	31	10	D2
	72/73	16	3	3 D2
	73/74	29	2	2 D2
	74/75	30		1 D2
	75/76	19	3	D1
	76/77	30	1	D1
	77/78	29	3	3 D1
	78/79	32		3 D1
	79/80	21		1 D2
	80/81	23	1	D2
	81/82		1	D1
	82/83			D2

McCLARE Peter

Motherwell Bridge Works
Motherwell
Larkhall Thistle

Hamilton A	64/65	16	2	D2
	65/66	23	4	D1
	66/67	25	5	D2
	67/68	9	2	D2

Lanark U

McCLELLAND Joseph
b. Edinburgh 12.10.1935 d. Edinburgh ?.4.1999
Edinburgh Thistle
Armadale Jnrs
Newtongrange Star

Hibernian	54/55	1		D1
	55/56	2		D1
	56/57	1		D1
	57/58	9		D1
	58/59	30		D1
	59/60	33	1	D1
	60/61	31	1	D1
	61/62	30		D1
	62/63	32		D1
	63/64	13		D1
Wrexham	64/65	32		FL
Rhyl				
Barmouth & Dyffryn				

McCLOY Peter
b. Girvan 16.11.1946 Caps: S - 4
Crosshill Thistle

Motherwell	63/64		D1
	64/65	5	D1
	65/66	32	D1
	66/67	32	D1
	67/68	34	D1
	68/69	19	D2
	69/70	15	D1
Rangers	69/70.	7	D1
	70/71	31	D1
	71/72	34	D1
	72/73	33	D1
	73/74	30	D1
	74/75		D1
	75/76	24	P
	76/77	5	P
	77/78	14	P
	78/79	36	P
	79/80	34	P
	80/81	26	P
	81/82	10	P
	82/83	17	P
	83/84	26	P
	84/85	21	P
	85/86	2	P

McCLURE Duncan
b. Troon 10.6.1913 d. Grangemouth ?.5.1991
Parkhead Jnrs

Heart of Midlothian	33/34	26		D1
	34/35	29		D1
	35/36	14		D1
	36/37	29		D1
	37/38	27	1	D1
	38/39	37		D1
	46/47	16		D1
	47/48	1		D1
	48/49			D1
	49/50			D1
	50/51			D1

McCLURE James
b. Glasgow
Parkhead Jnrs

Kilmarnock	35/36	11		D1
	36/37	25		D1
	37/38	25		D1
Albion R	L 38/39	22		D1
Kilmarnock	46/47	5		D1
Albion R	46/47			D2
	47/48			D2

McCLURE James

St Mirren	49/50	1		D1

McCLURE John

Airdrieonians	53/54	2		D1

McCLUSKEY J

Morton	50/51	1		D1

McCLUSKEY Patrick
b. Kilsyth 13.4.1952

Millwall	T				
Berwick R	T				
Albion R	T				
Chelsea	T				
Glasgow U		67/68			
Maryhill Jnrs		68/69			
Celtic		69/70			D1
Maryhill Jnrs	L	69/70			
Sligo R	L	69/70			
Celtic		70/71			D1
		71/72	2	2	D1
		72/73	14	1	3 D1
		73/74	23	2	1 D1
		74/75	28	1	3 D1
		75/76	34		3 P
		76/77	4	4	P
Dumbarton		77/78	38		1 D1
		78/79	38		3 D1
		79/80	36		8 D1
Darmstadt	T				
Airdrieonians		80/81	27		P
		81/82	19		P
Pittsburgh Spirit		82/83			
Queen of the South		83/84	34		1 D2
		84/85	17		D2

McCLUSKEY Ronald
b. Johnstone 3.11.1936
Rosyth Rec

East Fife	55/56			D1
	56/57	24		D1
	57/58	24		D1
	58/59			D2
	59/60			D2
Accrington S	60/61	4		FL
Gravesend U	61/62			
Gloucester C				
Cinderford T				
Biggleswade				
Potton A				
Kempston R				

McCLYMONT W

Morton	50/51	4		D1
	51/52	1		D1

McCLYMONT William

Cumbernauld U

Motherwell	71/72	2	2	1	D1
	72/73	11	2	6	D1
	73/74	25	1	1	D1
	74/75		5		D1
Stranraer	75/76	24		6	D2
	76/77	23	2	2	D2

McCOLE John
b. Glasgow 18.9.1936

Falkirk	56/57	12	4	D1
	57/58	18	15	D1
	58/59	1	1	D1
Bradford C	58/59	34	28	FL
	59/60	8	4	FL
Leeds U	59/60	33	22	FL
	60/61	35	20	FL
	61/62	10	3	FL
Bradford C	61/62	26	10	FL
	62/63	20	5	FL
Rotherham U	62/63	14	5	FL
Shelbourne	63/64			
Newport Co	64/65	6	2	FL
Cork Hibernian	64/65			
	65/66			

McCOLL Duncan John
b. Glasgow 28.12.1945

Partick T	63/64	3		D1
	64/65			D1
	65/66			D1
Barnsley	65/66	5		FL
Ballymena U				

McCOLL James

Queen's Park	46/47	16		D1
	47/48	13		D1
Queen of the South	48/49	22		D1
	49/50	4		D1
Falkirk	50/51	5		D1
Cowdenbeath	51/52			D2
Berwick R	52/53			D3

McCOLL John

Airdrieonians	62/63	19	3	D1
	63/64	9		D1
	64/65	11	2	D1
Dumbarton	65/66	21	2	D2

McCOLL John Miller
b. Alexandria 7.6.1927 Caps: S - 14
Vale of Leven Jnrs
Queen's Park

Rangers	46/47	19	1	D1
	47/48	29	1	D1
	48/49	30		D1
	49/50	30		D1
	50/51	25	1	D1
	51/52	29	1	D1
	52/53	29	3	D1
	53/54	27	2	D1
	54/55	26		D1
	55/56	34	1	D1
	56/57	34		D1
	57/58	32	1	D1
	58/59	11		D1
	59/60	5		D1

McCOLLIGAN John

Clyde	70/71	14	3	2	D1
	71/72	5	1		D1

McCONNACHIE John

Aberdeen	59/60	2		D1

McCOOL Robert

Third Lanark	60/61	3		D1
	61/62			D1
Hamilton Steelers	62			

McCORMACK Francis Adamson
b. Glasgow 25.9.1924

Club	Season	Apps	Sub	Goals	Div
Clyde	46/47	29			D1
	47/48	28		1	D1
	48/49	25			D1
Oldham A	49/50	14			FL
Morton					

McCORMACK John

Club	Season	Apps	Sub	Goals	Div
Falkirk	55/56	7		1	D1
	56/57	7		1	D1
	57/58	2			D1
	58/59	15			D1

McCORMACK Roy
b. Glasgow 12.2.1949
Glasgow U
Yoker A

Club	Season	Apps	Sub	Goals	Div
Dumbarton	66/67	14		5	D2
	67/68	33		21	D2
	68/69			26	D2
	69/70	34		13	D2
	70/71			22	D2
	71/72	36		19	D2
	72/73	32		11	D1
	73/74	23		4	D1
	74/75	4	2		D1
Apia					
Dundee	77/78		2		D1
Airdrieonians	L 78/79	3		1	D1
East Stirlingshire	78/79	21	1	7	D2
	79/80	12	6	1	D2

McCORMICK John
b. Glasgow 18.7.1936
St Rochs

Club	Season	Apps	Sub	Goals	Div
Third Lanark	59/60	1			D1
	60/61	19			D1
	61/62	33			D1
	62/63	21			D1
	63/64	31			D1
	64/65	7			D1
Aberdeen	64/65	23			D1
	65/66	5			D1
Crystal Palace	66/67	2			FL
	67/68	27		1	FL
	68/69	42		3	FL
	69/70	41		1	FL
	70/71	32			FL
	71/72	35		1	FL
	72/73	15			FL
Wealdstone					

McCRAE Alexander
b. Whitburn 2.1.1920
Haddington Jnrs

Club	Season	Apps	Sub	Goals	Div
Heart of Midlothian	46/47	24		9	D1
Charlton A	47/48	39		8	FL
	48/49	4			FL
Middlesbrough	48/49	20		2	FL
	49/50	36		14	FL
	50/51	32		21	FL
	51/52	24		6	FL
	52/53	10		4	FL
Falkirk	52/53	5		1	D1
	53/54	23		10	D1
	54/55	24		9	D1
	55/56	34		11	D1
	56/57	7		1	D1
Ballymena U					

McCREADIE Bernard Thomas
b. Dumbarton 23.4.1937
Dumbarton St Patricks
Renfrew Jnrs

Club	Season	Apps	Sub	Goals	Div
St Mirren	T 54/55				D1
Hibernian	T 54/55				D1
Celtic	55/56				D1
	56/57	1			D1
Rochdale	57/58	12			FL
	58/59	17			FL
Oldham A	58/59	7			FL
Clyde	T 59/60				D1

McCREADIE William Harvey
b. Glenluce 1.10.1942
Girvan Amateurs
Stranraer

Club	Season	Apps	Sub	Goals	Div
Accrington S	58/59	1			FL
	59/60	27		10	FL
Luton T	59/60	1			FL
Wrexham	60/61	10		2	FL
Northwich V	61/62				
Mossley	61/62				
Hibernian	62/63	9		3	D1
Altrincham					

McCREARY J

Club	Season	Apps	Sub	Goals	Div
Falkirk	46/47	5			D1

McCREDIE Norman James
b. Glasgow 17.5.1928
Yoker A

Club	Season	Apps	Sub	Goals	Div
Partick T	48/49	2		1	D1
	49/50	7		1	D1
	50/51	11		2	D1
	51/52	9		2	D1
	52/53	5		2	D1
	53/54	2			D1
	54/55	1			D1
Third Lanark	L 54/55				D2
Accrington S	55/56	42		3	FL
	56/57	9			FL
Southport	57/58	33		2	FL
Barrow	58/59	23			FL
Bacup Borough					

McCUBBIN Robert
b. Ayr

Club	Season	Apps	Sub	Goals	Div
Airdrieonians	61/62	4			D1
Ayr U	62/63				D2

McCUE Alexander Bain
b. Greenock 25.11.1927 d. ?.?.1989

Club	Season	Apps	Sub	Goals	Div
Falkirk	49/50	11		1	D1
	50/51	1			D1
Carlisle U	50/51	28		11	FL
Grimsby T	51/52	12		2	FL
	52/53	25		13	FL
Shrewsbury T	53/54	34		15	FL
	54/55	35		9	FL
	55/56	22		4	FL

McCULLIE Colin
Gairdoch U

Club	Season	Apps	Sub	Goals	Div
Cowdenbeath	70/71	17	1		D1
	71/72	1			D2
Stenhousemuir	72/73	16	3	1	D2
	73/74	34		1	D2
	74/75	20	9	4	D2
	75/76	18	5	3	D2
Raith R	76/77	5			D1

McCULLOCH

Club	Season	Apps	Sub	Goals	Div
Falkirk	70/71	1			D1

McCULLOCH Adam Andrew Ball Ross
b. Crossford 4.6.1920

Club	Season	Apps	Sub	Goals	Div
Third Lanark	46/47	24		13	D1
	47/48	16		5	D1
	48/49	13		6	D1
Northampton T	49/50	34		15	FL
	50/51	41		13	FL
	51/52	14		8	FL
Shrewsbury T	51/52	18		8	FL
	52/53	28		10	FL
Aldershot	52/53	12		4	FL
	53/54	44		19	FL
	54/55	23		9	FL
Ramsgate					

McCULLOCH Alan William
b. Barrhead 19.8.1953
Kilbirnie Ladeside

Club	Season	Apps	Sub	Goals	Div
Kilmarnock	72/73				D1
	73/74	1			D2
	74/75	16			D1
	75/76				D1
	76/77	1			P
	77/78				D1
St Mirren	L 77/78	10			P
Kilmarnock	78/79	39			D1
	79/80	36			P
	80/81	19			P
	81/82	39			D1
	82/83	35			P
	83/84	39			D1
	84/85	38			D1
	85/86	38			D1
	86/87	40			D1
	87/88	36			D1
	88/89	39			D1
	89/90	24			D2

McCULLOCH David
b. Glasgow 28.6.1949
Kilsyth R

Club	Season	Apps	Sub	Goals	Div
Ayr U	67/68	2			D2
	68/69			7	D2
	69/70	33		2	D1
	70/71	9	3	1	D1
	71/72	8			D1
	72/73	30	2	4	D1
	73/74	31	1	2	D1
	74/75	29	2	5	D1
	75/76	25	4	4	P
	76/77	29	3	2	P
	77/78	17	4	2	P
Clydebank	78/79	3	4		D1
Hamilton A	78/79	14		2	D1
	79/80	20	3	1	D1

McCULLOCH Iain John Balfour
b. Kilmarnock 28.12.1954
Hurlford U

Club	Season	Apps	Sub	Goals	Div
Kilmarnock	73/74	4	5	2	D2
	74/75	26	2		D1
	75/76	26			D1
	76/77	27		3	P
	77/78	28		8	D1
Notts Co	77/78				FL
	78/79	42		8	FL
	79/80	38		6	FL
	80/81	39		11	FL
	81/82	39	1	16	FL
	82/83	34		10	FL
	83/84	20	2		FL
	84/85				FL
	85/86				FL

McCULLOCH J

Club	Season	Apps	Sub	Goals	Div
Queen's Park	46/47				D1
	47/48	6			D1
	48/49	9			D2
	49/50	9			D2
	50/51	8			D2
	51/52	11			D2
	52/53				D2
	53/54				D2
	54/55	1			D2

McCULLOCH James
Meadow Thistle
Lanark U

Club	Season	Apps	Sub	Goals	Div
Hamilton A	68/69	1		1	D2
Kilmarnock	69/70				D1
	70/71	12	2	6	D1
	71/72	8	1		D1
	72/73		2	1	D1
	73/74				D2

McCULLOCH John

Club	Season	Apps	Sub	Gls	Div
Wishaw Jnrs					
Airdrieonians	58/59	4			D1
	59/60	4			D1
	60/61	9			D1

McCULLOCH Thomas
b. Glasgow 25.12.1921

Club	Season	Apps	Sub	Gls	Div
Airdrieonians	47/48	17		2	D1
Queen of the South	48/49	25		4	D1
Northampton T	49/50	34		15	FL
Bradford C	50/51	19		3	FL
	51/52	29		2	FL
	52/53	23		2	FL
	53/54	38		2	FL
Crewe Alex.	54/55	28		5	FL

McCULLOCH Thomas
Bridgeton Waverley

Club	Season	Apps	Sub	Gls	Div
Clyde	57/58	28			D1
	58/59	32			D1
	59/60	22			D1
	60/61	28			D1
	61/62				D2
	62/63	34			D1
	63/64				D2
	64/65	34			D1
	65/66	16			D1
	66/67	23			D1
	67/68	8			D1
	68/69	14			D1
	69/70	23			D1
	70/71	26			D1
	71/72	18			D1
Hamilton A	72/73	12			D2

McCULLOCH William
b. Glasgow

Club	Season	Apps	Sub	Gls	Div
Rangers	49/50	10		1	D1
	50/51				D1
	51/52	6		1	D1
	52/53	12		3	D1
	53/54	9		2	D1
	54/55	12		2	D1
Falkirk	58/59	11		2	D1

McCULLOCH William

Club	Season	Apps	Sub	Gls	Div
Clyde	60/61	14		2	D1

McCULLOCH William
b. Bannockburn 7.1.1948
Camelon

Club	Season	Apps	Sub	Gls	Div
Alloa A	68/69			1	D2
	69/70	33		2	D2
	70/71	36		5	D2
	71/72	33		2	D2
	72/73	25	1	10	D2
	73/74	10		4	D2
Airdrieonians	73/74	25		5	D2
	74/75	28	2	7	D1
	75/76	16	3	2	D1
	76/77	35		7	D1
	77/78	10			D1
	78/79	7	1	1	D1
	79/80	17	5	5	D1
	80/81	11	5	3	P
Berwick R	81/82	27	6	6	D2
Cowdenbeath	82/83				D2

McCULLOCH William B
b. Ayr
Annbank U
Muirkirk Jnrs

Club	Season	Apps	Sub	Gls	Div
Kilmarnock	46/47	1			D1
	47/48				D2
	48/49	8		3	D2
	49/50				D2
Cumnock Jnrs	50/51				
Airdrieonians	50/51	15		7	D1
	51/52	28		8	D1
Ayr U	L 51/52				D2
Airdrieonians	52/53	29		7	D1
	53/54	25		3	D1
	54/55				D2
	55/56	32		11	D1
	56/57	18		7	D1
St Mirren	56/57	9		1	D1
	57/58	22		4	D1
	58/59	4			D1
Morton	58/59				D2
	59/60				D2
Newton Stewart					

McCULLY Charles
b. Motherwell 30.4.1947
Cambuslang R

Club	Season	Apps	Sub	Gls	Div
Stirling A	65/66	1			D1
	66/67				D1
	67/68				D1
Boston Beacons	68	6			NA
	69				
	70				
	71				
New York Cosmos	72	7			NA

McDAID James
b. New Stevenston
Shotts Bon Accord

Club	Season	Apps	Sub	Gls	Div
Motherwell	66/67	2			D1

McDERMENT William Stirling
b. Paisley 5.1.1943
Johnstone Burgh

Club	Season	Apps	Sub	Gls	Div
Leicester C	61/62				FL
	62/63	2			FL
	63/64	3			FL
	64/65	12		1	FL
	65/66	2	2		FL
	66/67	1	1		FL
Luton T	67/68	13	6		FL
	68/69	15	6	1	FL
Notts Co	69/70	2	1		FL
Morton	69/70	13		1	D1
	70/71	20	3		D1
	71/72	4			D1
St Mirren	71/72	7	1		D2

McDICKEN Derrick Schendal
b. Auchinleck 4.4.1955
Ayr Boswell
Bellfield BC
Troon Jnrs
Darvel Jnrs

Club	Season	Apps	Sub	Gls	Div
Kilmarnock	72/73				D1
	73/74	5	5	1	D2
	74/75	33		4	D1
	75/76	16	1	1	D1
	76/77	29	1	4	P
	77/78	36			P
	78/79	36		2	D1
	79/80	34		1	P
	80/81	33		1	P
	81/82	20	7	8	D1
	82/83	27	4	1	P
	83/84	30	4	7	D1
	84/85	22	2		D1
Clyde	85/86	7	4		D1
Auchinleck Talbot					

MacDONALD Alan
b. Glasgow
Drumchapel Amateurs
Arniston R

Club	Season	Apps	Sub	Gls	Div
Heart of Midlothian	66/67	15			D1
	67/68	7			D1
	68/69	20	1	2	D1
	69/70	16	2	2	D1
Kilmarnock	69/70	11		1	D1
	70/71	27			D1
	71/72	2			D1

MacDONALD Alexander
b. Glasgow 17.3.1948 Caps: S - 1
Luncarty Jnrs
Glasgow U

Club	Season	Apps	Sub	Gls	Div
St Johnstone	65/66	8		3	D1
	66/67	16		3	D1
	67/68	29	1	9	D1
	68/69	11		2	D1
Rangers	68/69	8	1	1	D1
	69/70	15		2	D1
	70/71	27	6	6	D1
	71/72	31	1	11	D1
	72/73	27	2	4	D1
	73/74	29	1	3	D1
	74/75	29	1	2	D1
	75/76	34	1	4	P
	76/77	29	1	9	P
	77/78	34		3	P
	78/79	33		5	P
	79/80	23	3	1	P
	80/81	28		3	P
Heart of Midlothian	80/81	28		3	P
	81/82	15	1	1	D1
	82/83	29	2	5	D1
	83/84	19	5	1	P
	84/85	14	8	2	P
	85/86			1	P

McDONALD Andrew

Club	Season	Apps	Sub	Gls	Div
Raith R	52/53	2			D1
	53/54	1			D1

McDONALD Daniel
b. Hamilton 11.1.1954
Muirkirk Jnrs

Club	Season	Apps	Sub	Gls	Div
Ayr U	73/74	2		1	D1
	74/75	9		1	D1
	75/76	20	2	1	P
	76/77	14	6	1	P
	77/78	4		1	P
Stranraer	78/79	37		6	D2
	79/80	35		2	D2
	80/81	36			D2
	81/82	38		2	D2
	82/83	36		3	D2
	83/84	37		8	D2
	84/85	25	2	1	D2
	85/86	10			D2

McDONALD Donald

Club	Season	Apps	Sub	Gls	Div
Rangers	47/48				D1
Stirling A	L 47/48				D2
Rangers	48/49				D1
	49/50				D1
	50/51				D1
Stirling A	51/52	1			D1

McDONALD Donald

Club	Season	Apps	Sub	Gls	Div
Clyde	62/63	6			D1

McDONALD Frank

Club	Season	Apps	Sub	Gls	Div
Aberdeen	46/47	1			D1

McDONALD Iain
b. Edinburgh 26.8.1952
Carrickvale Thistle

Club	Season				Div
Rangers	69/70	1		1	D1
	70/71	3			D1
	71/72	7		1	D1
	72/73				D1
	73/74				D1
Dundee U	74/75	25	2	6	D1
	75/76	1	2		P

MacDONALD Ian Campbell Aitken
b. Rintein 30.8.1953
Elgin C

Club	Season				Div
St Johnstone	72/73	14		1	D1
	73/74	30		1	D1
	74/75	33		1	D1
	75/76	30			P
Carlisle U	76/77	42		2	FL
	77/78	34		2	FL
	78/79	41		1	FL
	79/80	40		1	FL
	80/81	27	5	1	FL
Dundee	81/82	17		2	P
	82/83	34			P
	83/84	18	3	1	P
Arbroath	84/85	20		1	D2
	85/86	6			D2

McDONALD James

Club	Season				Div
St Mirren	61/62	8		3	D1

MacDONALD John

Club	Season				Div
Third Lanark	64/65	2			D1

MacDONALD John

Club	Season				Div
Clyde	71/72	1		1	D1

McDONALD Joseph
b. Blantyre 10.2.1929
d. Australia 7.9.2003 Caps: S - 2
Bellshill Academy

Club	Season			Div
Falkirk	51/52	29		D2
	52/53	27		D1
	53/54	23		D1
Sunderland	53/54	3		FL
	54/55	41		FL
	55/56	39		FL
	56/57	35	1	FL
	57/58	19		FL
Nottingham F	58/59	35		FL
	59/60	36		FL
	60/61	38		FL
Wisbech T				
Ramsgate				

McDONALD Kenneth
Kansas City Spurs

Club	Season		Div
Raith R	68/69	17	D1
	69/70	8	D1

MacDONALD Malcolm
b. Glasgow 26.10.1913 d. 26.9.1999
Linwood St Convals
St Anthonys

Club	Season			Div
Celtic	31/32	1	2	D1
	32/33	7		D1
	33/34	15	1	D1
	34/35	30	1	D1
	35/36	10		D1
	36/37	12	1	D1
	37/38	27	12	D1
	38/39	30	14	D1
Kilmarnock	46/47	8		D1
Brentford	46/47	16	1	FL
	47/48	41		FL
	48/49	30		FL

McDONALD P

Club	Season		Div
St Mirren	51/52	1	D1

McDONALD Patrick
b. Cambuslang 19.4.1922
St Brides BG
Shawfield Jnrs
Airdrieonians

Club	Season		Div
Celtic	46/47	9	D1
Raith R	L 46/47		D2
Celtic	47/48		D1
Dunfermline A	47/48		D2
	48/49		D2
	49/50		D2

McDONALD Robert

Club	Season			Div
Raith R	59/60	2	1	D1
	60/61	10		D1
	61/62	9		D1

McDONALD Robert

Club	Season		Div
Falkirk	64/65	2	D1
	65/66	4	D1
	66/67	4	D1

MacDONALD Roderick D W
b. Alness 30.8.1954
Invergordon Academy
Easter Ross
Brora R

Club	Season				Div
Celtic	72/73				D1
	73/74	2			D1
	74/75	12	3		D1
	75/76	27		3	P
	76/77	24		2	P
	77/78	36		7	P
	78/79	18		2	P
	79/80	27	2	6	P
	80/81	14		1	P
Heart of Midlothian	81/82	35		6	D1
	82/83	39		3	D1
	83/84	34		2	P
	84/85	28		1	P
	85/86	10	1	2	P
	86/87	27		5	P
Morton	87/88	31			P
	88/89	26		2	D1
Partick T	89/90	17			D1
Queen of the South	T 90/91	8		2	D2
Irvine Meadow					

McDONALD Roger Brown
b. Glasgow 2.2.1933 d. ?.?.1996

Club	Season			Div
St Mirren	53/54	9	1	D1
	54/55	3	1	D1
Mansfield T	54/55	6		FL
	55/56	7		FL
Cheltenham T	56/57			
	57/58			
Crystal Palace	57/58			FL

McDONALD Thomas
Cleland St Marys
St Rochs

Club	Season			Div
Third Lanark	46/47	4	1	D1
	47/48			D1
Celtic	47/48	13	7	D1
Alloa A	48/49			D2
Arbroath	T 49/50			D2
Crusaders	T			

McDONALD Thomas
b. Cowdenbeath 24.5.1930
Hill of Beath

Club	Season			Div
Hibernian	49/50	1		D1
	50/51			D1
	51/52			D1
	52/53	1		D1
	53/54	14	6	D1
Wolverhampton W	54/55	1		FL
	55/56	4	1	FL
Leicester C	56/57	31	7	FL
	57/58	22	5	FL
	58/59	29	4	FL
	59/60	31	11	FL
Dunfermline A	60/61	27	6	D1
	61/62	24	6	D1
	62/63	5		D1
Raith R	62/63	14	1	D1
Queen of the South	63/64	2		D1
Stirling A	63/64	7	1	D2
Cowdenbeath	63/64	3		D2

McDONALD William
St Josephs

Club	Season			Div
Dundee U	56/57	9	3	D2
	57/58	25	10	D2
	58/59	26	11	D2
	59/60	11	1	D2
	60/61	2		D1
	61/62	2		D1
Stirling A	61/62	6	2	D1
Montrose				

McDONALD William
Blairhall Colliery

Club	Season		Div
St Johnstone	64/65	3	D1

McDOUGALL Ian
b. New Stevenston 14.8.1954

Club	Season				Div
Rangers	73/74	8		1	D1
	74/75	11	3	2	D1
	75/76	3	1	1	P
	76/77	1	3		P
Dundee	77/78	36	1	1	D1
	78/79	8	8	1	D1
	79/80				
Berwick R	80/81	2			D1
Albion R	80/81	1	3		D2

McDOWALL Daniel
b. Kirkintilloch 22.5.1929
Kirkintilloch Rob Roy

Club	Season			Div
Middlesbrough	47/48			FL
	48/49			FL
	49/50			FL
Kilmarnock	49/50	6	1	D2
Celtic	50/51	1		D1
Workington	51/52	44	14	FL
	52/53	38	9	FL
Lincoln C	53/54	17	4	FL
Millwall	54/55	5		FL
	55/56	5	1	FL

McDOWELL Donald
b. Glasgow 11.9.1952
Sighthill YC

Club	Season				Div
Partick T	71/72				D1
	72/73				D1
	73/74	5	3	1	D1
	74/75				D1
St Mirren	74/75	22			D2
	75/76	24		12	D1
	76/77	27	6	12	D1
	77/78	1			P
Kilmarnock	77/78	36		13	D1
	78/79	5	3	2	D1
Falkirk	78/79	11	1	3	D2
	79/80	12	7	6	D2
	80/81		1		D1
Arbroath	80/81	6	2	1	D2

McEWAN Andrew P
b. Bridge of Allan 10.3.1933

Club	Season	Apps	Sub	Gls	Div
Queen's Park	54/55	3			D2
	55/56	7			D2
	56/57	30		12	D1
	57/58	29		9	D1
Rangers	58/59	1			D1
Queen of the South	59/60				D2
Stirling A	60/61				D2
	61/62				D1

McEWAN J

Club	Season	Apps	Sub	Gls	Div
St Mirren	51/52	3			D1

MacEWAN James
b. Dundee 22.3.1929

Club	Season	Apps	Sub	Gls	Div
Arbroath	49/50	9		1	D2
	50/51				D2
Raith R	51/52	26		5	D1
	52/53	16		2	D1
	53/54	25		4	D1
	54/55	14		2	D1
	55/56	31		9	D1
	56/57	32		8	D1
	57/58	32		8	D1
	58/59	33		16	D1
Aston Villa	59/60	28		5	FL
	60/61	11			FL
	61/62	24		5	FL
	62/63	19		6	FL
	63/64	27		2	FL
	64/65	4		1	FL
	65/66	4	1	1	FL
Walsall	66/67	10		1	FL

McEWAN William Johnston McGowan
b. Cleland 20.6.1951
Pumpherston Jnrs

Club	Season	Apps	Sub	Gls	Div
Hibernian	69/70	19			D1
	70/71	19			D1
	71/72	15	1	2	D1
	72/73	6	1		D1
Blackpool	73/74	4			FL
Brighton & HA	73/74	15		3	FL
	74/75	12			FL
Chesterfield	74/75	22		1	FL
	75/76	5	1	2	FL
	76/77	22		4	FL
Mansfield T	76/77	23		3	FL
	77/78	9			FL
Peterborough U	77/78	29		1	FL
	78/79	33	1	2	FL
Rotherham U	79/80	30	2	7	FL
	80/81				FL
	81/82	21		3	FL
	82/83	18	5		FL
	83/84	17	1		FL

McFADDEN Andrew
Port Glasgow R

Club	Season	Apps	Sub	Gls	Div
St Mirren	66/67	1			D1
	67/68	28			D2
	68/69	27			D1
	69/70	27			D1
	70/71	19		2	D1
	71/72	6			D2

McFADYEN Charles
Rutherglen Glencairn

Club	Season	Apps	Sub	Gls	Div
St Johnstone	55/56	11			D2
	56/57				D2
	57/58	25			D2
	58/59	22			D2
	59/60	29		1	D2
	60/61	34			D1
	61/62	32		1	D1
	62/63	35		1	D2
	63/64	31			D1
	64/65	34			D1
	65/66	9			D1

McFADYEN Ian

Club	Season	Apps	Sub	Gls	Div
Dundee U	50/51				
Motherwell	54/55	1			D1
	55/56	21			D1
	56/57	4			D1
	57/58	13			D1
Dundee U	58/59				D2
	59/60	13			D2

McFADZEAN James
b. Kilmarnock 20.8.1938
Kilmarnock YMCA
Troon Jnrs

Club	Season	Apps	Sub	Gls	Div
Heart of Midlothian	56/57	4		1	D1
	57/58				D1
	58/59	3		2	D1
	59/60	5		1	D1
	60/61	13		1	D1
St Mirren	60/61	5		1	D1
	61/62	2			D1
Raith R	61/62	9		1	D1
	62/63	17		3	D1
Kilmarnock	63/64	14			D1
	64/65	26		3	D1
	65/66	19		4	D1
	66/67	29	2	1	D1
	67/68	30		3	D1
	68/69	6	2	1	D1
Ayr U	69/70	2	3		D1
	70/71	22			D1
	71/72	18			D1
	72/73	4			D1

McFARLANE Fraser

Club	Season	Apps	Sub	Gls	Div
Airdrieonians	68/69	1	1		D1

McFARLANE Graham
Strathclyde

Club	Season	Apps	Sub	Gls	Div
Clyde	60/61				D1
	61/62				D2
	62/63	10		5	D1
	63/64	28		11	D2
	64/65	3		2	D1
	65/66	17		7	D1
	66/67	32		8	D1
	67/68	29		3	D1
	68/69	28		1	D1
	69/70	20	2		D1
	70/71	7		1	D1
Clydebank	71/72	12			D2

McFARLANE Ian
b. Lanark 26.1.1933

Club	Season	Apps	Sub	Gls	Div
Aberdeen	55/56	16			D1
Chelsea	56/57	30			FL
	57/58	10			FL
Leicester C	58/59	1			FL
Bath C	59/60				
	66/67				

McFARLANE John
Wishaw Jnrs

Club	Season	Apps	Sub	Gls	Div
Hamilton A	46/47	12		2	D1
Wishaw Jnrs					

McFARLANE W

Club	Season	Apps	Sub	Gls	Div
Third Lanark	50/51	1			D1

McFARLANE William
b. Fallin 1.10.1923 d. Ayr 13.10.1998 Caps: S - 1
Bathgate Thistle

Club	Season	Apps	Sub	Gls	Div
Heart of Midlothian	46/47	14		2	D1
	47/48	17		2	D1
	48/49	7		1	D1
	49/50				D1
	50/51				D1
Stirling A	51/52	13			D1
	52/53	26		5	D2
	53/54	3			D1
Kilmarnock	T 53/54	1			D2
Inverness Caleys					

McFARLANE William

Club	Season	Apps	Sub	Gls	Div
Hibernian	53/54	19			D1
	54/55	14			D1
	55/56	32			D1
	56/57	7		2	D1
	57/58	6			D1
Raith R	58/59	27		1	D1
	59/60	8		2	D1
	60/61	1			D1

McFEAT Archibald
b. Kincardine 23.1.1924
d. Grangemouth 1.4.1996
Polkemmet Jnrs

Club	Season	Apps	Sub	Gls	Div
Morton	46/47	29			D1
	47/48	6			D1
Torquay U	48/49	9			FL
	49/50				FL
Albion R	50/51				D2
	51/52				D2
	52/53	11			D2
Falkirk	52/53	19			D1
	53/54	27			D1
Stenhousemuir					

McFEDRIES John
Hurlford U

Club	Season	Apps	Sub	Gls	Div
Partick T	66/67	2			D1
Hurlford U					

McGANN William
Lochee Harp

Club	Season	Apps	Sub	Gls	Div
Forfar A	63/64	1			D2
Dundee Downfield	64/65				
East Fife	65/66	15			D2
	66/67	29			D2
	67/68	24			D2
	68/69				D2
	69/70				D2
St Mirren	69/70	8			D1
	70/71	1			D1
Cowdenbeath	70/71	4			D1
	71/72	1			D2
Hamilton A	72/73	3			D2
Forfar A	72/73	4			D2

McGARR Ernest
b. Glasgow 9.3.1944 Caps: S - 2
Kilbirnie Ladeside

Club	Season	Apps	Sub	Gls	Div
Aberdeen	65/66				D1
	66/67				D1
	67/68	1			D1
	68/69	20			D1
	69/70	22			D1
	70/71				D1
Dunfermline A	70/71	14			D1
	71/72	11			D1
	72/73				D2
East Fife	72/73	17			D1
	73/74	26			D1
	74/75	31			D2
	75/76	26			D1
	76/77	18			D1
Cowdenbeath	77/78	39			D2
	78/79	5			D1
Airdrieonians	78/79	33			D1
	79/80	39			D1
	80/81	3			P
Berwick R	80/81	6			D1

McGARRITY John
Blairhall Colliery

Club	Season	Apps	Sub	Gls	Div
East Fife	48/49	1			D1
	49/50	7			D1
	50/51				D1
	51/52				D1
Cowdenbeath	52/53	18			D2
	53/54	4			D2

McGARRITY Thomas Welsh
b. Glasgow 24.11.1922 d. Oxford 17.3.1999
Arthurlie

Club	Season				
Morton	46/47	16		4	D1
	47/48	10		1	D1
	48/49	19		3	D1
	49/50	27		9	D2
	50/51	29		5	D1
	51/52	27		12	D1
Southampton	52/53	5		1	FL
Headington U	53/54	11		3	SL
Banbury Spencer					

McGARRY Daniel

Morton	46/47	7			D1
Stirling A	47/48				D2

McGARTY John
Burnley

Hibernian					D1
Dunfermline A	66/67				D1
	67/68	3			D1
	68/69	3	1		D1
	69/70	17			D1
	70/71	2			D1
Hamilton A	T 71/72	1			D2

McGARVEY Francis Peter
b. Glasgow 17.3.1956
Colston Amateurs
Kilsyth R

St Mirren	74/75		1		D2
	75/76	16	9		D1
	76/77	37	1	17	D1
	77/78	35		17	P
	78/79	33		13	P
Liverpool	79/80				FL
Celtic	79/80	11	1	2	P
	80/81	34		23	P
	81/82	25	1	10	P
	82/83	32	2	17	P
	83/84	28	2	10	P
	84/85	30	3	15	P
St Mirren	85/86	35		6	P
	86/87	38	2	10	P
	87/88	18	7	2	P
	88/89	18	13	2	P
	89/90	2	1		P
Queen of the South	90/91	12	7	6	D2
Clyde	91/92	12		6	D2
	92/93	33	1	16	D2

F

McGEACHIE George
b. Falkirk 9.9.1939
Falkirk High

Dundee	56/57	4			D1
	57/58	5			D1
	58/59	23		3	D1
	59/60	31		5	D1
	60/61	10			D1
	61/62	3			D1
	62/63	1			D1
Darlington	63/64	15		3	FL
	64/65	43		4	FL
	65/66	46		2	FL
	66/67	15			FL

McGEACHY Joseph
b. Glasgow 21.4.1920 d. ?.?.1985

Third Lanark	47/48	7		1	D1
Leyton Orient	48/49	38		2	FL
	49/50	20		1	FL
	50/51	16		1	FL
Hereford U	51/52				
Workington	52/53	2		1	FL

McGEOGH Thomas
Linlithgow Rose

Falkirk	65/66				D1
	66/67				D1
St Johnstone	67/68	2	2		D1

McGHEE Alexander J
Edinburgh Thistle

Hibernian	71/72	1			D1
	72/73				D1
Morton	73/74	12		2	D1
	74/75	27		3	D1
Hibernian	75/76	5	1	3	P
	76/77	7	2		P
	77/78	9	1	3	P
Dundee	78/79	20		2	D1
	79/80		1		P
Cowdenbeath	80/81	3	1		D2

McGHEE James William
b. Motherwell 21.8.1930
Forth W

Kilmarnock	49/50	3		2	D2
	50/51	3		2	D2
	51/52				D2
Darlington	52/53	15		4	FL
Barry T	53/54				
Newport Co	54/55	10		1	FL
Morton	55/56				D2
Ballymena U	56/57				
Ardrossan Winton R	57/58				
Ayr U	58/59				D2
	59/60	34		15	D1
	60/61	22		2	D1
	61/62	27		5	D2
Queen of the South	62/63	2			D1
St Mirren	62/63	2			D1

McGIFFEN Ian
b. Ayr 26.10.1956
Ayr U Boys Club
Troon Jnrs

Ayr U	74/75	13			D1
	75/76				P
	76/77				P
	77/78	4			P
Largs Thistle					
Ardrossan Winton R					

McGILL Andrew
b. Glasgow 11.7.1924 d. ?.?.1988
Florida Amateurs
Third Lanark
Queen's Park

Clyde	46/47	3			D1
	47/48	1			D1
Bradford C	47/48	26		5	FL
	48/49	36		5	FL
	49/50	38		11	FL
	50/51	42		1	FL
	51/52	22		2	FL
Scunthorpe U	52/53	46		2	FL
	53/54	28		2	FL
	54/55	43		5	FL
	55/56	31		3	FL
	56/57	35		3	FL

McGILL Austin Michael
b. Dumfries 29.1.1935
Nithsdale W

Queen of the South	58/59	7		3	D1
Carlisle U	59/60	29		12	FL

McGILL Duncan
b. Bellshill
Duntocher Hibs

St Mirren	51/52	3		1	D1
	52/53	26		6	D1
	53/54	12		3	D1
Stirling A	54/55	25		7	D1
	55/56	4			D1
St Mirren	55/56	17		1	D1
	56/57	21		9	D1
	57/58	19		7	D1
Stirling A	58/59	2			D1
Albion R	59/60				D2
	60/61				D2
	61/62	16		7	D2
Stranraer	62/63				D2
	63/64	6		1	D2
Albion R	63/64	5			D2

McGILL James
b. Kilsyth 10.3.1926
Kilsyth R
Maryhill Harp
Kilsyth R

Bury	46/47	1			FL
Derby Co	46/47	4			FL
	47/48	4			FL
	48/49				FL
	49/50				FL
Kilmarnock	49/50	11		2	D2
	50/51	5			D2
Berwick R	50/51				D3
	51/52				D3
	52/53				D3
Queen of the South	53/54	30		6	D1
	54/55	22		4	D1
Berwick R	L 54/55				D3
Heart of Midlothian	L 54/55				D1
Queen of the South	55/56	29		6	D1
	56/57	31		8	D1
	57/58	10			D1
	58/59				D1
Cowdenbeath	59/60				D2

McGILL John
b. Irvine 2.11.1935
Larkhall Thistle

Hamilton A	T 56/57	1			D2
Airdrieonians	57/58	15		9	D1
	58/59	27		12	D1
	59/60	24		11	D1
	60/61	4			D1
East Stirlingshire	61/62	21		6	D2
Hamilton A	62/63	10		1	D2
Stranraer	63/64				D2
Stirling A	64/65	10		4	D2

McGILLIVRAY Findlay
b. Newtongrange 19.3.1940
Newtongrange Star

Third Lanark	59/60	1			D1
	60/61	31		2	D1
	61/62	25			D1
	62/63	34			D1
	63/64	26			D1
	64/65	4			D1
Rangers	65/66				D1
Bradford PA	66/67	38	1	1	FL
St Johnstone	67/68	31			D1
	68/69	10			D1
	69/70	3			D1

McGLYNN Anthony
Edinburgh Thistle

Hibernian	61/62	1		1	D1
	62/63				D1
	63/64	2		1	D1
Airdrieonians					

McGOLDRICK Joseph
St Mirrins BG

Clyde	69/70	6	1		D1
	70/71	28			D1
	71/72	13	1		D1
	72/73	16	2		D2
	73/74	1	2		D1

McGOVERN Philip
b. Glasgow
St Anthonys

Albion R	67/68	2	1		D2
	68/69			14	D2
	69/70	20	1	9	D2
Newcastle U	69/70				FL
Ayr U	70/71	20		4	D1
	71/72	7	5	1	D1
	72/73	5	5		D1
Kilmarnock	72/73	12			D1
	73/74	1	2		D2
Clydebank	73/74	15		5	D2
	74/75	12	2	6	D2
	75/76				D2
Albion R	76/77		1		D2

McGOWAN James
b. Whiterigg

Club	Season				Div
Partick T	46/47	29			D1
	47/48	30			D1
	48/49	27			D1
	49/50	22			D1
	50/51	27			D1
	51/52	28		1	D1
	52/53	23			D1
	53/54	25			D1
	54/55	22			D1
	55/56	10			D1

McGOWAN P

Club	Season				Div
Clyde	53/54	1			D1

McGOWAN Samuel

Morton

Club	Season				Div
Motherwell	46/47	1			D1
Morton	46/47	4			D1
St Johnstone	47/48	13		1	D2

McGRAIN Danny

Blantyre Victoria

Club	Season				Div
Clyde	70/71		1		D1
	71/72	29	1	2	D1
	72/73	36		2	D2
	73/74	21		2	D1
	74/75				D1

McGRAIN Daniel Fergus
b. Glasgow 1.5.1950 Caps: S - 62
Celtic
Maryhill Jnrs L

Club	Season				Div
Celtic	70/71	7			D1
	71/72	2	1		D1
	72/73	30			D1
	73/74	29	1	1	D1
	74/75	30			D1
	75/76	35			P
	76/77	36			P
	77/78	7			P
	78/79	18		2	P
	79/80	34			P
	80/81	33			P
	81/82	27			P
	82/83	34		1	P
Blackpool	L 82/83				FL
Celtic	83/84	33			P
	84/85	30			P
	85/86	27	1		P
	86/87	21	5		P
Rochdale Rovers	87				
Hamilton A	87/88	20	1		D1

McGRATH K

Club	Season				Div
Airdrieonians	47/48	4			D1

McGRAW Allan

Renfrew Jnrs
Army

Club	Season				Div
Morton	61/62				D2
	62/63	15		15	D2
	63/64	35		51	D2
	64/65	23		12	D1
	65/66	28		9	D1
Hibernian	66/67	20	1	13	D1
	67/68	34		5	D1
	68/69	6	2	1	D1
Linfield					

McGREGOR Alexander

Club	Season				Div
Albion R	48/49	11			D1
Raith R	49/50	17			D1

McGREGOR Alexander George Penman
b. Glasgow 12.11.1950
Troon

Club	Season				Div
Ayr U	69/70	1	1		D1
	70/71	1	2		D1
	71/72	19	1	1	D1
	72/73	3	1		D1
Hibernian	73/74				D1
Shrewsbury T	74/75	18		4	FL
	75/76	28	3	3	FL
West Ham U	T 76/77				FL
Aldershot	76/77	34		5	FL
	77/78	38	1	3	FL
	78/79	41		2	FL
	79/80	30	2	5	FL
	80/81	18	6	2	FL
	81/82	7			FL
Farnborough T					

McGREGOR Frank

Club	Season				Div
Clyde	59/60	2			D1

McGREGOR Ian

Club	Season				Div
Raith R	57/58	2			D1
	58/59	3			D1
	59/60	7			D1
	60/61	2			D1

McGREGOR Ian

Club	Season				Div
Dumbarton	74/75	18			D1
	75/76				D1
	76/77	1			D1
Stenhousemuir	77/78	1			D2

McGREGOR James

Grangemouth U

Club	Season				Div
Stirling A	60/61				D2
	61/62	12			D1
	62/63				D2
	63/64	30		2	D2
Dumbarton	64/65	16		1	D2
East Stirlingshire	65/66	29		6	D2
Stenhousemuir	66/67	32		12	D2

McGREGOR James
b. 4.8.1949 d. 7.11.1979
Partick T

Club	Season				Div
Clyde	67/68	3			D1
	68/69	12			D1
	69/70	3			D1
East Stirlingshire	70/71				D2
	71/72	30			D2
	72/73	12			D2
	73/74	35		1	D2
	74/75	27	2		D2
	75/76	26			D2
	76/77	25		1	D2
Falkirk	76/77	10			D1
	77/78	7			D2
Albion R	78/79	37			D2
	79/80	16			D2

McGREGOR James Gordon
b. Glasgow 15.11.1956

Club	Season				Div
St Johnstone	73/74		2		D1
	74/75		2		D1
	75/76	15	9	2	P
	76/77	11	6	2	D1
St George (Aus)	77/78				
Partick T	78/79		1		P
	79/80	3	1		P
Stirling A	80/81	6	1		D1
Clyde	80/81		1		D2

McGROGAN Felix

Pollok Jnrs

Club	Season				Div
Hamilton A	T 61/62	1			D2
Raith R	62/63	9		2	D1
	63/64	33		14	D2
	64/65	9		2	D2
St Johnstone	64/65	16		3	D1
	65/66	9		1	D1
Addington (SAf)					

McGRORY Frank

East Craigie Jnrs

Club	Season				Div
Arbroath	55/56				D2
	56/57				D2
	57/58				D2
Dundee	57/58	5		1	D1
Forfar A	58/59				D2
Dundee U	59/60	1			D2

McGRORY John
b. Linwood 31.8.1928 d. Linwood 12.11.1991
Maryhill Harp

Club	Season				Div
Celtic	49/50	25			D1
	50/51	3			D1
	51/52				D1
	52/53	10		3	D1
Albion R	L 53/54	27		16	D2
St Mirren	54/55	17		9	D1
	55/56				D1
Albion R	T 56/57				D2

McGRORY John
b. Glasgow 15.11.1941 Caps: S - 3
Kilmarnock Amateurs
Dreghorn Jnrs

Club	Season				Div
Kilmarnock	60/61	2			D1
	61/62	6			D1
	62/63	34			D1
	63/64	34			D1
	64/65	32			D1
	65/66	30			D1
	66/67	34			D1
	67/68	34			D1
	68/69	34			D1
	69/70	29			D1
	70/71	33			D1
	71/72	33			D1
	72/73	1			D1

McGUGAN John Hannah
b. Airdrie 12.6.1939
Pollok Jnrs

Club	Season				Div
St Mirren	56/57				D1
	57/58				D1
	58/59	34			D1
	59/60	29		3	D1
Leeds U	60/61	1			FL
Tranmere R	60/61	14			FL
	61/62	21			FL
Cambridge C	61/62				
Ayr U	61/62	10			D2
	62/63				D2
	63/64	10			D2

McGUIGAN James
b. Addiewell 1.3.1924
d. Chesterfield 30.3.1988
Bonnyrigg Rose

Club	Season				Div
Hamilton A	46/47	11		2	D1
Sunderland	47/48	1			FL
	48/49	2		1	FL
Stockport Co	49/50	39		8	FL
	50/51	4		1	FL
Crewe Alex.	50/51	36		4	FL
	51/52	40		13	FL
	52/53	38		10	FL
	53/54	30		4	FL
	54/55	25			FL
	55/56	38		1	FL
Rochdale	56/57	26		1	FL
	57/58	34		1	FL
	58/59	10			FL

McGUIGAN John Joseph
b. Motherwell 29.10.1932
Muirkirk Jnrs
Bo'ness Jnrs

Team	Season	Apps	Sub	Goals	Div
St Mirren	53/54	14		3	D1
	54/55	7		1	D1
Southend U	55/56	46		13	FL
	56/57	41		10	FL
	57/58	38		11	FL
Newcastle U	58/59	21		5	FL
	59/60	1			FL
	60/61	17		5	FL
	61/62	11		5	FL
Scunthorpe U	61/62	17		10	FL
	62/63	40		7	FL
Southampton	63/64	21		8	FL
	64/65	12			FL
Swansea T	64/65	10		1	FL
	65/66	18		3	FL

McGUINNESS David
Johnstone Burgh

Team	Season	Apps	Sub	Goals	Div
Ayr U	59/60	5		2	D1
	60/61	6		2	D1

McGUINNESS John
b. Coatbridge 21.6.1937
Hozier Thistle

Team	Season	Apps	Sub	Goals	Div
Albion R	55/56				D2
	56/57				D2
	57/58				D2
	58/59				D2
	59/60				D2
	60/61				D2
Stirling A	60/61				D2
	61/62	34			D1
	62/63				D2
	63/64	29			D2
	64/65	36			D2
	65/66	28			D1
	66/67	27	1	2	D1
	67/68	9			D1
East Stirlingshire	68/69				D2
	69/70	17			D2

McGUINNESS Robert Francis
b. Motherwell 29.1.1954
Lesmahagow Jnrs

Team	Season	Apps	Sub	Goals	Div
Motherwell	73/74	1		3	D1
	74/75	2		1	D1
Portsmouth	75/76	26	2	3	FL
	76/77	1		2	FL

McGUIRE Benny

Team	Season	Apps	Sub	Goals	Div
East Stirlingshire	68/69			17	D2
Raith R	69/70	23	1	2	D1
	70/71			10	D2
	71/72	33	1	6	D2
Clydebank	72/73	13			D2

McGUIRE J

Team	Season	Apps	Sub	Goals	Div
Airdrieonians	52/53	4			D1
	53/54	5			D1

McGUIRE James C
b. Plains ?.?.1927
St Margarets BG
Wolverhampton W
Hibernian

Team	Season	Apps	Sub	Goals	Div
Alloa A	L 46/47				D2
Hibernian	46/47				D1
Aberdeen	47/48				D1
Celtic	48/49	10			D1
	49/50	4			D1
Shamrock R	50/51				
Waterford	51/52				
Kidderminster H	52/53				
	53/54				
	54/55				
Berwick R	55/56				D2
Stranraer	56/57				D2
	57/58				D2

McGUIRE John
Celtic

Team	Season	Apps	Sub	Goals	Div
Third Lanark	64/65	6			D1
	65/66				D2
	66/67				D2
Hamilton A	T 67/68	1			D2

McGURK D

Team	Season	Apps	Sub	Goals	Div
Hibernian	49/50	1			D1

McGURK James
d. ?.7.1999
Stonehouse Violet

Team	Season	Apps	Sub	Goals	Div
Hamilton A	37/38	13			D1
	38/39	11			D1
	46/47	27			D1
	47/48	28			D2
	48/49	21			D2
	49/50	14			D2
	50/51	1			D2

McGURN William
b. c1925 d. Dunfermline 22.1.2001
Thornton Hibernian

Team	Season	Apps	Sub	Goals	Div
Cowdenbeath	48/49	25		10	D2
	49/50	19		5	D2
Airdrieonians	50/51	18		7	D1
	51/52	15		5	D1
	52/53	9		3	D1
Brechin C	53/54				D3

McHARD Archibald
b. Dumbarton 10.6.1934

Team	Season	Apps	Sub	Goals	Div
Clyde	55/56	10		1	D1
	56/57				D2
	57/58	4		1	D1
	58/59	3		1	D1
Bradford PA	59/60	25		2	FL
	60/61	2			FL

McHUGH John
b. Glasgow
Dennistoun Waverley

Team	Season	Apps	Sub	Goals	Div
Clyde	62/63	20		1	D1
	63/64				D2
	64/65	33			D1
	65/66	34		2	D1
	66/67	33			D1
	67/68	30		1	D1
	68/69	34		1	D1
	69/70	30		1	D1
	70/71	33		1	D1
	71/72	29	1	1	D1
	72/73	7	2		D2
	73/74	31	1		D1
	74/75		2		D1
Forfar A	75/76	26			D2
	76/77	36	2	1	D2

McILHATTON John
b. Ardrossan 3.1.1921 d. ?.?.1954
Albion R

Team	Season	Apps	Sub	Goals	Div
Everton	46/47	37		1	FL
	47/48	13			FL
	48/49	5			FL
Dundee	49/50	5			D1
	50/51				D1
Raith R	50/51	9			D1

McILMOYLE Hugh
b. Port Glasgow 29.1.1940
Port Glasgow A

Team	Season	Apps	Sub	Goals	Div
Leicester C	60/61	7		4	FL
	61/62	13		1	FL
Rotherham U	62/63	12		4	FL
Carlisle U	62/63	17		7	FL
	63/64	45		39	FL
	64/65	15		1	FL
Wolverhampton W	64/65	25		7	FL
	65/66	41		15	FL
	66/67	24		13	FL
Bristol C	66/67	12		2	FL
	67/68	8		2	FL
Carlisle U	67/68	27		11	FL
	68/69	42		17	FL
	69/70	10		3	FL
Middlesbrough	69/70	29		6	FL
	70/71	40	1	13	FL
Preston NE	71/72	35		10	FL
	72/73	24	1		FL
Morton	73/74	27	1	8	D1
Carlisle U	74/75	15	3	2	FL

McILRAVEY James
Hillside BC

Team	Season	Apps	Sub	Goals	Div
Arbroath	74/75	3		3	D1
	75/76	7		2	D1
East Fife	76/77	6			D1
	77/78	2		1	D1

McILROY James
b. Glasgow 19.7.1930
Partick U
Duntochter Hibs

Team	Season	Apps	Sub	Goals	Div
Celtic	50/51				D1
	51/52				D1
	52/53	8		3	D1
	53/54	3			D1
	54/55				D1
	55/56				D1
Third Lanark	55/56				D2
Barrow	56/57				FL

McILROY James Brian
Wallace Castle
Kirkintilloch Rob Roy

Team	Season	Apps	Sub	Goals	Div
Rangers	57/58				D1
	58/59				D1
	59/60				D1
Kilmarnock	60/61	14		3	D1
	61/62	19		9	D1
	62/63	20		6	D1
	63/64	34		24	D1
	64/65	29		9	D1
	65/66	32		20	D1
	66/67	23		16	D1
	67/68	17	2	5	D1
	68/69	28		13	D1
Aberdeen	69/70	6	1	1	D1
	70/71				D1
Hamilton A	71/72				D2

McILWRAITH James
b. Glasgow 17.4.1954
Troon Jnrs
Kilwinning R

Team	Season	Apps	Sub	Goals	Div
Motherwell	73/74				D1
	74/75	18	5	5	D1
	75/76	3	2	1	P
Bury	75/76	19	4	3	FL
	76/77	29	2	11	FL
	77/78	32	3	7	FL
Portsmouth	78/79	16	3		FL
Ayr U	L 78/79	2			D1
Bury	79/80	28	1	3	FL
Halifax T	80/81	29		5	FL
	81/82	4	3	1	FL

McINALLY James

Team	Season	Apps	Sub	Goals	Div
Third Lanark	62/63	4			D1
Stirling A	63/64				D2
	64/65				D2

McINALLY John Whitfield Milligan
b. Ayr ?.?.1936
Kello R
Minishant Amateurs
Scots Greys
Crosshill Thistle

Club	Season	App	Sub	Gls	Div
Kilmarnock	59/60	29		16	D1
	60/61	28		14	D1
	61/62	21		8	D1
	62/63	5		1	D1
	63/64	27		16	D1
	64/65	32		11	D1
	65/66	31		10	D1
	66/67	32		8	D1
	67/68	6	1	2	D1
Motherwell	67/68	18		6	D1
	68/69	26		13	D2
	69/70	33		8	D1
	70/71	17	1	7	D1
	71/72	22	1	4	D1
	72/73	15	2		D1
Hamilton A	73/74	27	4	12	D2
	74/75	30	5	9	D2

McINNES Graham James
b. Aberdeen 7.4.1938

Club	Season	App	Gls	Div
Aberdeen	58/59	1		D1
Bury	59/60			FL
	60/61	1		FL
Toronto Italia	61			
Morton	61/62	7	3	D2
Inverness Caley				

McINNES John
b. Ayr 29.3.1923

Club	Season	App	Gls	Div
Partick T	46/47	5	2	D1
	47/48	3		D1
	48/49			D1
Bradford C	49/50	18	5	FL
	50/51	3	1	FL

McINNES John Smith
b. Glasgow 11.8.1927 d. ?.10.1973

Club	Season	App	Gls	Div
Morton	46/47	21	5	D1
Chelsea	46/47	3	1	FL
	47/48	15		FL
	48/49	18	6	FL
	49/50	1		FL
Bedford T				

McINNES Joseph Clarke
b. Glasgow 9.12.1932
Larkhall Thistle

Club	Season	App	Gls	Div
Hamilton A	T 50/51	1		D2
Larkhall Thistle				
Partick T	52/53	7	2	D1
	53/54	19	5	D1
	54/55	1		D1
	55/56	7	1	D1
Accrington S	55/56	14	2	FL
Third Lanark	56/57			D2
	57/58	28	2	D1
	58/59	26	8	D1
	59/60	30	6	D1
	60/61	34	8	D1
	61/62	16	2	D1
	62/63	15	4	D1
Stirling A	63/64	20	1	D2

McINNES William
b. Douglas 20.5.1931
Kirkmuirhill
Stonehouse Violet

Club	Season	App	Gls	Div
Falkirk	52/53	3		D1
	53/54	1		D1
Alloa A	L 54/55			D2
Lesmahagow				
Accrington S	55/56	11		FL
	56/57	11		FL
	57/58	43		FL
	58/59	35		FL
	59/60	17		FL
	60/61	36		FL
Southport	61/62	16		FL
	62/63	10		FL

McINTOSH James
b. c1937
Forres Mechanics

Club	Season	App	Gls	Div
Falkirk	55/56	24	1	D1
	56/57	21	1	D1
	57/58	20		D1
	58/59	5		D1
	59/60	25		D2
	60/61	19		D2
	61/62	32		D1
	62/63	11	1	D1

MacINTOSH John
b. Uddingston 17.7.1935
Larkhall Thistle

Club	Season	App	Gls	Div
Heart of Midlothian	58/59	1		D1

McINTOSH John McGregor
b. Glasgow 14.9.1933
Petershill

Club	Season	App	Gls	Div
Partick T	53/54	1	1	D1
	54/55			D1
	55/56			D1
	56/57	24	11	D1
	57/58	3		D1
Bury	57/58	12	10	FL
	58/59	17	4	FL
Weymouth				

McINTOSH William
b. 30.7.1939
Heart of Midlothian

Club	Season	App	Gls	Div
Cowdenbeath	60/61			D2
	61/62	36	7	D2
East Stirlingshire	62/63			D2
	63/64	33	6	D1
Aberdeen	64/65	7	1	D1
Highlands Park				
Atlanta Chiefs *	68	31	4	NA

McINTYRE Alistair
b. c1938
Irvine Meadow

Club	Season	App	Gls	Div
Ayr U	56/57	6		D1
	57/58			D2
	58/59			D2
	59/60	10	1	D1
	60/61	32	9	D1
	61/62	16	4	D2
St Johnstone	61/62	8	2	D1
	62/63	35	16	D2
	63/64	34	10	D1
St Mirren	64/65	11		D1
Morton	65/66	11		D1
Stranraer	66/67	33	7	D2

McINTYRE George
Kirkintilloch Rob Roy

Club	Season	App	Gls	Div
Ayr U	58/59			D2
	59/60	5		D1
	60/61	11		D1
	61/62	9	2	D2

McINTYRE Ian

Club	Season	App	Gls	Div
Rangers	49/50	2		D1
Airdrieonians				

McINTYRE James
b. c1924 d. Aberdeen ?.6.1993
Kilbirnie Ladeside

Club	Season	App	Gls	Div
Aberdeen	49/50	2		D1
Deveronvale				
Arbroath				
Buckie Thistle				

McINTYRE James
b. Motherwell 22.3.1933
Forth W

Club	Season	App	Gls	Div
Motherwell	53/54			D1
	54/55	17		D1
	55/56			D1
	56/57			D1
Accrington S	56/57	4		FL

McINTYRE James

Club	Season	App	Div
Dumbarton	73/74	1	D1

McINTYRE John

Club	Season	App	Gls	Div
Raith R	51/52	16	4	D1
	52/53	16	4	D1
	53/54	6		D1
	54/55	1		D1

McINTYRE William
Port Glasgow Jnrs

Club	Season	App	Gls	Div
Ayr U	57/58			D2
	58/59			D2
	59/60	30	8	D1
	60/61	26	5	D1
	61/62	34	5	D2

McIVOR Arthur
Bonnybridge

Club	Season	App	Gls	Div
Dundee	55/56	3		D1
	56/57			D1
	57/58	3		D1
Stirling A	T 57/58			D2
East Fife	58/59	22	4	D2

MacIVOR Ronald William
b. Edinburgh 23.3.1951
Bonnyrigg Rose

Club	Season	App	Sub	Gls	Div
East Fife	72/73	5		1	D1
	73/74	19	6	2	D1
	74/75	29	4	1	D2
	75/76	25			D1
	76/77	24	2		D1
	77/78	26	3	1	D1
	78/79	34	1	4	D2
	79/80				D2
Wigan A	79/80	3		1	FL

McKAY Alan

Club	Season	App	Sub	Gls	Div
Third Lanark	63/64	1			D1
	64/65	2			D1
	65/66	31		1	D2
	66/67	31	1	1	D2
Motherwell	67/68	31		1	D1
	68/69	7		2	D2
Dumbarton	69/70	33			D2
	70/71				
	71/72	22			D2
	72/73	11			D1
	73/74	14		2	D1

MACKAY Alistair
b. Glasgow
Imrie Memorial Juveniles
Vale of Clyde

Club	Season	App	Gls	Div
Kilmarnock	48/49			D1
	49/50			D2
	50/51			D2
	51/52			D2
	52/53	1		D2
	53/54			D2
	54/55	16	2	D1
	55/56	25	1	D1
	56/57	30	1	D1
	57/58	12		D1
	58/59	22		D1
	59/60	10		D1
Falkirk	59/60	10		D2
	60/61	5		D2
Cowdenbeath	61/62	19		D2

MACKAY David Craig
b. Edinburgh 14.11.1934 Caps: S - 22
Slateford A
Newtongrange Star

Club	Season				Div
Heart of Midlothian	53/54	4			D1
	54/55	25		2	D1
	55/56	28		4	D1
	56/57	31		5	D1
	57/58	28		12	D1
	58/59	19		4	D1
Tottenham H	58/59	4			FL
	59/60	38		11	FL
	60/61	37		4	FL
	61/62	26		8	FL
	62/63	37		6	FL
	63/64	17		3	FL
	64/65				FL
	65/66	41		6	FL
	66/67	39		3	FL
	67/68	29		1	FL
Derby Co	68/69	41		1	FL
	69/70	39		2	FL
	70/71	42		2	FL
Swindon T	71/72	25	1	1	FL

McKAY Derek
b. Banff 13.12.1949
Deveronvale

Club	Season				Div
Dundee	66/67	7	2	1	D1
	67/68	3			D1
	68/69	1			D1
Aberdeen	69/70	10	3		D1
	70/71	2			D1
Barrow	71/72	18			FL

McKAY Desmond

Drumchapel Amateurs

Club	Season				Div
Airdrieonians	70/71	21	1	1	D1
	71/72	13	2		D1

MACKAY Donald Scrimgeour
b. Glasgow 19.3.1940
Jeanfield Swifts

Club	Season			Div
Forfar A	58/59			D2
	59/60			D2
	60/61			D2
	61/62	27		D2
Dundee U	62/63	5		D1
	63/64	5		D1
	64/65	26		D1
	65/66	27		D1
	66/67	6		D1
	67/68	20		D1
	68/69	33		D1
	69/70	34		D1
	70/71	10		D1
	71/72	5		D1
Southend U	72/73	8		FL
	73/74	6		FL

McKAY Duncan
b. Springburn 14.7.1937 Caps: S - 14
St Marys BG
Maryhill Harp

Club	Season			Div
Celtic	55/56			D1
	56/57			D1
	57/58			D1
	58/59	30		D1
	59/60	29		D1
	60/61	32		D1
	61/62	32		D1
	62/63	29	4	D1
	63/64	9	1	D1
	64/65	1		D1
Third Lanark	64/65	20		D1
Croatia Melbourne				
St Anthonys				

MACKAY George

Dundee Elmwood
Dundee U

Club	Season			Div
Dundee	47/48	6	2	D1
	48/49	3	1	D1
East Fife	49/50	5		D1
Morton				

McKAY George

Petershill

Club	Season		Div
Arbroath	69/70		D2
	70/71		D2
	71/72	28	D2
	72/73	5	D1

McKAY James
Caps: Aus - 31
Bonnyrigg Rose

Club	Season			Div
Airdrieonians	64/65	5	1	D1
Melbourne Croatia				
Sydney Hakoah				
South Melbourne Hellas				

McKAY Peter Walker
b. Newburgh 23.2.1925 d. Corby 23.11.2000
Newburgh WE

Club	Season			Div
Dundee U	47/48	19	14	D2
	48/49	27	25	D2
	49/50	27	21	D2
	50/51	30	32	D2
	51/52	29	28	D2
	52/53	23	15	D2
	53/54	30	23	D2
Burnley	54/55	4		FL
	55/56	34	25	FL
	56/57	22	11	FL
St Mirren	56/57	12	4	D1
	57/58	22	15	D1
Corby T				

McKEAN Robert Munro
b. East Kilbride 8.12.1952
d. 15.3.1978 Caps: S - 1
Blantyre Victoria

Club	Season				Div
St Mirren	69/70				
	70/71	20	3	2	D1
	71/72	28		8	D2
	72/73	33	2	6	D2
	73/74	34		19	D2
Rangers	74/75	25	1	5	D1
	75/76	32	1	5	P
	76/77	14	8	2	P
	77/78	6	4		P

McKECHIE John
b. Glasgow
Benburb

Club	Season		Div
Stirling A	53/54	4	D1
	54/55	14	D1
	55/56	3	D1
	56/57		D2
	57/58		D2
	58/59	29	D1
	59/60	32	D1
Dunfermline A			

McKELLAR David

Club	Season		Div
Third Lanark	49/50	8	D1

McKELLAR Hugh

Bellfield BC
Ardeer Recreation

Club	Season				Div
Celtic	67/68				D1
	68/69				D1
Kilmarnock	68/69	1	1	1	D1

McKENNA John

Petershill

Club		Season		Div
Stirling A	T	52/53	1	D2
Clyde		53/54	1	D1
		54/55	3	D1
Stirling A		54/55		D1
Worcester C		55/56		
Albion R				

McKENNA Patrick
b. Glasgow 26.4.1920 d. Aberdeen 16.11.1995
Blantyre Celtic

Club	Season		Div
Aberdeen	46/47	25	D1
	47/48	30	D1
	48/49	26	D1
	49/50	28	D1
	50/51	13	D1
	51/52	12	D1
Plymouth A	52/53	1	FL
Arbroath	52/53	1	D2
Derry C			
Fraserburgh			

McKENNAN Peter Stewart
b. Airdrie 16.7.1918 d. Dundonald 28.9.1991
Whitburn Jnrs

Club	Season			Div
Partick T	35/36	19	6	D1
	36/37	33	20	D1
	37/38	35	20	D1
	38/39	34	24	D1
	46/47	4	1	D1
	47/48	6	5	D1
West Bromwich A	47/48	11	4	FL
Leicester C	47/48	11	4	FL
	48/49	7	3	FL
Brentford	48/49	24	6	FL
Middlesbrough	49/50	33	15	FL
	50/51	7	3	FL
Oldham A	51/52	38	16	FL
	52/53	32	10	FL
	53/54	8	2	FL
Coleraine				

McKENZIE Alan W
b. Dundee 3.6.1953
Downfield

Club	Season				Div
Arbroath	72/73	1			D1
	73/74		1		D1
	74/75	3	4		D1
	75/76	9	5	3	D1
	76/77	10	4		D1
	77/78	25	4	1	D1
	78/79	39		1	D1
	79/80	32	2		D1
	80/81	20	1	2	D2
	81/82	12	1		D2
	82/83	39		3	D2
	83/84	20	1		D2
	84/85	19		1	D2
Brechin C	85/86	32	1	1	D1

McKENZIE Donald C

Club	Season			Div
Arbroath	52/53	6	6	D2
	53/54	30	13	D2
	54/55			D2
Stirling A	55/56	7	2	D1

McKENZIE G

Club	Season		Div
Queen's Park	57/58	2	D1

McKENZIE George

Club	Season		Div
Rangers	54/55	1	D1

McKENZIE Gilbert					
Rangers					
Queen of the Soutl	L 36/37	20		2	D1
	37/38	15			D1
Hamilton A	38/39	26			D1
Dundee	46/47	24		2	D2
	47/48	1			D1
Airdrieonians	47/48	9			D1
Dundee U	47/48	10			D2
	48/49	3			D2
Kilmarnock	49/50	2			D2
Berwick R					
Bangor C					
Linfield					
Portadown					

McKENZIE Gordon					
b. c1930					
Rangers					
Worcester C	L 50/51				
Rangers	51/52				D1
	52/53				D1
	53/54				D1
	54/55	9			D1

McKENZIE Ian					
Arbroath	59/60	2			D1

McKENZIE J Roderick					
b. Kilkeen Caps: NI - 1					
Drumchapel Amateurs					
Airdrieonians	63/64	6			D1
	64/65	2			D1
	65/66	36			D2
	66/67	34			D1
	67/68	33			D1
	68/69	32			D1
	69/70	31			D1
	70/71	22			D1
	71/72	32			D1
	72/73	28			D1
Hibernian	73/74	7			D1
	74/75				D1
Clydebank	75/76	26			D2
	76/77	3			D1

MacKENZIE John Archibald						
b. Glasgow 4.9.1925 Caps: S - 9						
Petershill						
Partick T	46/47					
Bournemouth	L 47/48	38			9	FL
Partick T	48/49	25			1	D1
	49/50	9			1	D1
	50/51	26			5	D1
	51/52	18			5	D1
	52/53	21			2	D1
	53/54	28			4	D1
	54/55	27			2	D1
	55/56	29			8	D1
	56/57	28			3	D1
	57/58	8			2	D1
Fulham	57/58					FL
Partick T	58/59	23			1	D1
	59/60	16				D1
Dumbarton	60/61					D2
	61/62	16			4	D2
Derry C						

McKENZIE Ralph					
b. Old Kilpatrick					
Aberdeen	46/47	2			D1
	47/48				D1
Dundee U	L 47/48	5			D2
Aberdeen	48/49				D1
	49/50	10			D1
Falkirk	50/51	11			D1
	51/52	18			D2
	52/53	30			D1
	53/54	21			D1
	54/55	24			D1
	55/56	7			D1
Dundee	56/57	30			D1
	57/58	31			D1
Inverness Caley					

McKENZIE Thomas					
b. Edinburgh d. Peterborough ?.11.1967					
Pentland R					
Haddington A					
Heart of Midlothian	46/47	21		1	D1
	47/48	25			D1
	48/49	28			D1
	49/50	26			D1
	50/51	27			D1
	51/52	23			D1
	52/53	24			D1
	53/54	7			D1
	54/55	22		1	D1
	55/56	22			D1
	56/57	21		1	D1
	57/58	8			D1
Wisbech T					
March T					

MacKENZIE William					
Banks o'Dee					
Aberdeen	59/60	2			D1

McKEOWN Anthony					
Limerick					
Aberdeen	49/50	2			D1

McKEOWN Joseph Francis					
b. Bannockburn 9.4.1924					
Rutherglen Glencairn					
Stirling A	45/46				
	46/47				D3
	47/48				D2
	48/49				D2
	49/50	25			
Hartlepools U	50/51	46		7	FL
Ayr U	51/52				D2
	52/53	9		1	D2
Stirling A	53/54	1			D1

McKEOWN Thomas					
b. Cleland 2.10.1930					
Cumnock Jnrs					
Queen of the South	50/51				D2
	51/52	6		2	D1
	52/53				D1
	53/54				D1
Accrington S	54/55	12		2	FL
Netherfield					
Nelson					
Berwick R	57/58				D2

McKERNAN John					
Sighthill Amateurs					
Blantyre Victoria					
Morton	72/73	1	2		D1
Hamilton A	72/73	1			D2
	73/74	25			D2
San Antonio Thunder	75	20			NA

MACKIE Kenneth					
b. Kirkcaldy 29.3.1955					
Dunfermline U					
Dunfermline A	71/72	9		4	D1
	72/73	35		21	D2
	73/74	34		8	D1
	74/75	16	3	3	D1
	75/76	18	4	10	D1
Falkirk	76/77	33	2	3	D1
	77/78	2			D2
East Fife	77/78	33		11	D1
	78/79	34	2	17	D2
	79/80	27	1	7	D2
	80/81	8		1	D2

MACKIE Sinclair D				
b. Edinburgh d. 30.5.1997				
Hibernian	48/49			D1
	49/50			D1
	50/51			D1
	51/52			D1
	52/53			D1
Dunfermline A	53/54	26		D2
	54/55			D2
	55/56	12		D1
	56/57			D1
Stirling A	57/58			D2

McKILLOP Alistair					
Morton	46/47	17		6	D1
	47/48	6		1	D1
Albion R	47/48				D2
Morton	48/49	2			D1

McKIMMIE George					
Lochee BC					
Dundee Violet					
Dunfermline A	68/69	3			D1
	69/70	9	1		D1
	70/71	4	2		D1
Highland Park (SAf)					

MACKIN Joseph				
b. Forth				
Luton T				
Corby T				
Dunfermline A	53/54	10		D2
	54/55			D2
	55/56	25		D1
	56/57	34		D1
Ayr U	57/58			D2
	58/59			D2
Motherwell	59/60	19		D1

McKINLAY Colin					
b. Edinburgh c1927					
Morton					
Tranent Jnrs					
St Johnstone	49/50	7		3	D2
	50/51	26		12	D2
	51/52				D2
	52/53	19		1	D2
Dunfermline A	53/54	13		3	D2
	54/55				D2
	55/56	9		1	D1
	56/57	11		1	D1
St Johnstone	58/59	4			D2

McKINLAY Columb					
Vale of Leven					
Airdrieonians	70/71	13	2	2	D1
	71/72	18			D1
	72/73	12	1	2	D1
	73/74	1	3		D2
	74/75	13	1		D1
Dumbarton	75/76	19	1		D1
	76/77	28	1		D1
	77/78	12	1		D1

McKINLAY Hector					
Falkirk					
Armadale					
Dundee U	62/63	1		1	D1
	63/64	1			D1
Dumbarton					

McKINLAY Ian				
Third Lanark	61/62	5		D1
	62/63	9		D1

McKINNEY Victor J
b. N Ireland d. S Africa ?.?.1989 Caps: NI - 1
Glenavon

Club	Season				Div
Falkirk	64/65	11		2	D1
	65/66	26		2	D1
	66/67	24	1	4	D1
Addington (SAf)					

McKINNON Daniel
b. Glasgow 26.1.1943

Club	Season				Div
Morton	63/64	1			D2
Stirling A	64/65	36		21	D2
	65/66	21		2	D1
	66/67	18			D1
	67/68	16	1	1	D1
	68/69				D2

McKINNON Donald
Rutherglen Glencairn

Club	Season			Div
Partick T	60/61	9		D1
	61/62	33		D1
	62/63	8		D1
	63/64	3		D1
	64/65	5		D1
	65/66	28		D1
	66/67	30		D1
	67/68	32		D1
	68/69	26	1	D1
	69/70	17		D1
	70/71	28		D2
	71/72	1		D1
	72/73	6		D1

McKINNON Neil
Rangers

Club	Season			Div
Dundee U	46/47	7	1	D2
Albion R	46/47			D2
	47/48			D2
	48/49	19	2	D1
Queen of the South	49/50	6	1	D1
Ayr U	T 50/51			D2

McKINNON Ronald
b. Glasgow 20.8.1940 Caps: S - 28
Benburb
Dunipace Jnrs

Club	Season			Div
Rangers	59/60			D1
	60/61	2		D1
	61/62	6		D1
	62/63	32		D1
	63/64	32		D1
	64/65	34		D1
	65/66	33		D1
	66/67	31	1	D1
	67/68	34	1	D1
	68/69	28		D1
	69/70	30		D1
	70/71	32		D1
	71/72	7		D1
	72/73			
Durban C				
Australia				

McKINVEN John James
b. Campbeltown 1.5.1941

Club	Season				Div
Raith R	59/60	6		2	D1
Southend U	60/61	22		4	FL
	61/62	36		3	FL
	62/63	37		12	FL
	63/64	42		6	FL
	64/65	38		11	FL
	65/66	29		5	FL
	66/67	24		3	FL
	67/68	44		16	FL
	68/69	10	2	2	FL
	69/70	2			FL
Cambridge U	70/71	18		2	FL

McKINVEN Ronald

Club	Season			Div
Queen's Park	53/54	8	3	D2
	54/55	1	1	D2
Stirling A	55/56	4		D1
Queen's Park	56/57	1		D1
	57/58	25		D1
St Johnstone	59/60	32		D2
	60/61	16	1	D1
	61/62	25	1	D1
	62/63	34	7	D1
	63/64	35	1	D1
	64/65	32		D1
	65/66	32	1	D1

McKIRDY Robert
Neilston Jnrs

Club	Season			Div
Queen's Park	48/49	1		D2
	49/50	4	1	D2
	50/51	3		D2
	51/52	10	1	D2
Hamilton A	52/53	3		D2
Albion R	52/53			D2
Hamilton A	53/54	2		D1

McKNIGHT James
Lugar Boswell

Club	Season		Div
Queen of the South	47/48		D1
	48/49		D1
	49/50	1	D1
	50/51		D2
	51/52	4	D1

McLAFFERTY Maurice
b. Baillieston 7.8.1922

Club	Season		Div
St Mirren	50/51	1	D1
Sheffield U	51/52	18	FL
Brighton & HA	52/53	21	FL
Dartford			
Hastings U			
Newhaven			

McLARDIE James

Club	Season				Div
St Mirren	65/66	10			D1
	66/67	4	1		D1
Stranraer	67/68	31		1	D2
	68/69			1	D2
	69/70	31	1	1	D2

McLAREN David
b. Auchterarder 12.6.1934
Comrie A
St Johnstone Jnrs

Club	Season		Div
Dundee	56/57	1	D1
Leicester C	56/57	14	FL
	57/58	24	FL
	58/59	37	FL
	59/60	10	FL
Plymouth A	60/61	11	FL
	61/62	40	FL
	62/63	28	FL
	63/64	29	FL
	64/65	23	FL
Wolverhampton W	64/65	9	FL
	65/66	34	FL
	66/67	1	FL
Southampton	66/67	22	FL
Worcester C			

McLAREN Malcolm
b. Bridgeton c 1918
Strathclyde
Blackpool
Kilmarnock

Club	Season			Div
St Mirren	46/47	13	3	
AS Cannes	47/48			
AS Roma	48/49			
Forfar A	49/50	19	5	D2

McLAREN Stewart
b. Larkhall 6.4.1953
West Bromwich A

Club	Season				Div
Motherwell	74/75	22			D1
	75/76	29	2	2	P
	76/77	25	2		P
	77/78	29	2	2	P
	78/79	12		1	P
Dundee	78/79	21		4	D1
	79/80	28		3	P
	80/81	31			D1
Heart of Midlothian	81/82	34			D1
	82/83	8	6		D1
	83/84	18	1		P
	84/85	1			P

McLAREN William R
b. Glasgow 7.6.1948
Kirkintilloch Rob Roy

Club	Season				Div
Dunfermline A	69/70	15	1	1	D1
	70/71	12	1	1	D1
East Fife	71/72	14		1	D1
Raith R	72/73	18	5	4	D2
Queen of the South	73/74	35		3	D2
	74/75	35	1		D2
	75/76	25		2	D1
	76/77	35		3	D1
	77/78	35		5	D1
	78/79	2	1		D1
Morton	78/79	18	1		P
	79/80	25	4	1	P
	80/81	7	1		P
Hibernian	80/81	18			D1
	81/82	18	2		P
Clyde	82/83	14	2	1	D1
Queen of the South	82/83	5			D2
	83/84	24	1		D2
Partick T	84/85	5			D1

McLAUGHLAN Alexander Donaldson
b. Kilwinning 17.7.1936
Ardeer Recreation

Club	Season		Div
Kilmarnock	60/61	24	D1
	61/62	30	D1
	62/63	23	D1
	63/64		
Sunderland	64/65	30	FL
	65/66	13	FL
Kilmarnock	66/67		
	67/68	31	D1
	68/69	34	D1
	69/70	34	D1
	70/71	4	D1
Troon Jnrs			

McLAUGHLAN J

Club	Season		Div
St Mirren	53/54	1	D1

McLAUGHLAN William
b. c1951 d. East Wemyss ?.5.1972
Greig Park R

Club	Season			Div
Cowdenbeath	68/69		1	D2
Jubilee A	L 68/69			
Cowdenbeath	69/70	33		D2
	70/71	33		D1
	71/72	36		D2

McLAUGHLIN Alexander

Club	Season			Div
St Mirren	65/66	4	1	D1
	66/67	12	1	D1

McLAUGHLIN Brian
b. Falkirk 7.10.1954
Celtic
Linlithgow Rose   L

Club	Season				Div
Celtic	71/72				D1
	72/73		2		D1
	73/74	2	1	1	D1
	74/75		1		D1
	75/76				P
Finn Harps L	75/76				
Celtic	76/77				P
	77/78	1			P
Ayr U	77/78	22	2	5	P
	78/79	38	1	19	D1
	79/80	5		1	D1
Motherwell	79/80	34		11	D1
	80/81	32	4	6	D1
	81/82	36	1	19	D1
	82/83	6	3	1	P
Hamilton A	82/83	15		8	D1
	83/84				D1
Falkirk	83/84	5	6		D1
	84/85		1		D1
West Adelaide					
Ayr U	86/87	15	3	1	D2

McLAUGHLIN Hugh
b. Glasgow 2.9.1943
St Rochs

Club	Season				Div
Brentford	63/64	2			FL
	64/65	2			FL
	65/66	1			FL
	66/67				FL
St Mirren	67/68	11	1	3	D2
	68/69	11	4	6	D1
	69/70	19	2	1	D1
	70/71	21	2	1	D1
	71/72	27			D2
Queen of the South	72/73	21	2	1	D2

McLAUGHLIN James
b. Paisley 11.2.1926

Club	Season				Div
Celtic	47/48	2		1	D1
Walsall	48/49	5			FL
	49/50	9			FL

McLAUGHLIN James

Club	Season				Div
Falkirk	48/49	9		1	D1
	49/50	1			D1
	50/51	2			D1
	51/52				D2
Stirling A	51/52				D1

McLAUGHLIN John
b. Lennoxtown 13.11.1936

Club	Season				Div
Clyde	59/60	9		13	D1
	60/61	23		7	D1
	61/62				D2
	62/63	4		1	D1
Millwall	63/64	21		5	FL
Dunfermline A	64/65	24		11	D1
Motherwell	65/66	18		4	D1

McLAUGHLIN John Ian
b. Stirling 3.1.1948
Gowanhill U

Club	Season				Div
Falkirk	64/65				D1
	65/66				D1
	66/67				D1
	67/68	31		4	D1
	68/69	26	2	4	D1
	69/70	13	2	2	D2
	70/71	30	1		D1
	71/72	4			D1
Everton	71/72	27			FL
	72/73	7			FL
	73.74	21		1	FL
	74/75	2	1		FL
	75/76	2	1		FL
Falkirk	75/76	2	2		D1
	76/77	30		2	D1

McLAUGHLIN Joseph
b. c1920
Douglas Water Thistle
Bo'ness Cadora
Blairhall Colliery
Celtic
St Anthonys   L

Club	Season				Div
Hamilton A	46/47	10			D1
Aberdeen	46/47	19			D1
	47/48	9			D1
	48/49	19			D1
Raith R	49/50	15		4	D1
	50/51	29		5	D1
	51/52	7		1	D1
	52/53				D1
Albion R	53/54				D2
Sligo R	54/55				

McLAY James
Gairdoch U

Club	Season				Div
Falkirk	68/69	1			D1

McLEAN

Club	Season				Div
Arbroath	59/60	5			D1

McLEAN Adam
b. Langloan
Baillieston Jnrs

Club	Season				Div
Albion R	46/47				D2
	47/48				D2
Leith A L	47/48				D2
Albion R	48/49	4		1	D1

McLEAN Alistair
Ardrossan Winton R

Club	Season				Div
Ayr U	70/71				D1
	71/72	12			D1
	72/73	4			D1
	73/74	29			D1
	74/75	10			D1
	75/76				P
Aberdeen	76/77	9			P
Ayr U	77/78	3			P
St Mirren	78/79	2			P
Partick T	78/79	1			P
Aberdeen	79/80				P
Motherwell	80/81	1			D1

McLEAN Angus

Club	Season				Div
Clyde	69/70	13			D1

McLEAN Desmond

Club	Season				Div
Airdrieonians	52/53	2			D1

McLEAN Donald H

Club	Season				Div
Queen's Park	55/56	7		3	D2
	56/57	10		2	D1
	57/58	5			D1
	58/59	23		2	D2
	59/60	3			D2

McLEAN George Roy
b. Paisley 16.9.1937
Cambuslang R

Club	Season				Div
Rangers	59/60	2			D1
	60/61	6		3	D1
	61/62				D1
Norwich C	61/62				FL
Grimsby T	62/63	31		15	FL
	63/64	27		7	FL
	64/65	33		19	FL
Exeter C	65/66	34		11	FL
	66/67	13		1	FL
Workington	66/67	15		4	FL
	67/68	38		11	FL
Barrow	68/69	26	1	9	FL
Boston U					

McLEAN George Tomlinson
b. Paisley 26.5.1943 Caps: S - 1
Drumchapel Amateurs

Club	Season				Div
St Mirren	59/60				D1
	60/61	3		2	D1
	61/62	22		7	D1
	62/63	21		2	D1
Rangers	62/63	9		2	D1
	63/64	19		10	D1
	64/65	8		4	D1
	65/66	24		25	D1
	66/67	9		8	D1
Dundee	67/68	32		23	D1
	68/69	20	2	2	D1
Dunfermline A	68/69	6	1	3	D1
	69/70	28	1	15	D1
	70/71	7		4	D1
Ayr U	70/71	9	2	1	D1
	71/72	11	6	5	D1
	72/73	24		16	D1
	73/74	25	5	6	D1
Vancouver Whitecaps	74	19		5	NA
Ayr U	74/75	10	1	4	D1
Hamilton A T	75/76	1			D1

McLEAN J

Club	Season				Div
St Mirren	47/48	3			D1
	48/49	1			D1

McLEAN James
Baillieston Jnrs

Club	Season				Div
Ayr U	57/58				D2
	58/59				D2
	59/60	23			D1
	60/61	26			D1
	61/62	25			D2
Dunfermline A	61/62	4			D1
	62/63	28			D1
	63/64	29			D1
	64/65	33			D1
	65/66	32			D1
	66/67	12			D1

McLEAN James Yuille
b. Ashgill ?.?.1937
Larkhall Thistle

Club	Season				Div
Hamilton A	55/56	1			D2
	56/57	20		5	D2
	57/58	25		8	D2
	58/59	32		21	D2
	59/60	26		11	D2
	60/61	24		12	D2
Clyde	60/61	8		3	D1
	61/62				D2
	62/63	26		4	D1
	63/64	29		8	D2
	64/65	30		16	D1
	65/66	1			D1
Dundee	65/66	27		6	D1
	66/67	29		13	D1
	67/68	34		9	D1
Kilmarnock	68/69	31		6	D1
	69/70	24	1	1	D1

McLEAN Stewart Donald
b. Glasgow 13.12.1955
Kilmarnock Star
Darvel Jnrs

Club	Season	App	Sub	Gls	Div
Kilmarnock	73/74				D2
	74/75	19	1		D1
	75/76	20	2	2	D1
	76/77	15		6	P
	77/78	30	1		D1
	78/79	38			D1
	79/80	34			P
	80/81	32	2	1	P
	81/82	28	4	1	D1
	82/83	19	2	2	P
	83/84	19	3		D1
	84/85	33	3	2	D1
	85/86	31	1	3	D1
	86/87	34	4	2	D1
	87/88	44			D1
	88/89	29	3		D1
	89/90	19	2		D2

McLEAN Thomas
b. Ashgill 2.6.1947 Caps: S - 6
Birkenshaw Amateurs

Club	Season	App	Sub	Gls	Div
Kilmarnock	62/63				D1
	63/64				D1
	64/65	19		3	D1
	65/66	33		9	D1
	66/67	31		8	D1
	67/68	34		4	D1
	68/69	33		5	D1
	69/70	33		9	D1
	70/71	33		10	D1
Rangers	71/72	21	1	1	D1
	72/73	22	2	5	D1
	73/74	21	3	4	D1
	74/75	32	1	14	D1
	75/76	34	1	4	P
	76/77	36		1	P
	77/78	29	2	1	P
	78/79	34	1	1	P
	79/80	22	6	2	P
	80/81	23	5		P
	81/82	2	1	1	P

McLEAN William
Larkhall Thistle
Stonehouse Violet

Club	Season	App	Sub	Gls	Div
Hamilton A	T 55/56	1			D2
Alloa A	55/56				D2
Airdrieonians	56/57	11		2	D1
	57/58	9			D1
Sheffield W					
Alloa A					
Queen of the South	61/62				D2
	62/63	15		5	D1
	63/64				D1
Alloa A	64/65	6		1	D2
Raith R	64/65	21		1	D2
	65/66				D2
	66/67				D2
	67/68			1	D1

McLEISH John
b. Gorbals ?.?.1921
Dennistoun Waverley

Club	Season	App	Sub	Gls	Div
Kilmarnock	46/47	12		3	D1
	47/48	15			D2
	48/49	6		1	D2

McLELLAN William

Club	Season	App	Sub	Gls	Div
Airdrieonians	66/67	5	1	3	D1
	67/68	6	1		D1

McLELLAND

Club	Season	App	Sub	Gls	Div
St Mirren	57/58	1			D1

McLELLAND Charles
b. Glasgow 24.3.1953
Eastercraigs

Club	Season	App	Sub	Gls	Div
Aberdeen	73/74	15		1	D1
	74/75	33		1	D1
	75/76	29	1		P
	76/77	25		1	P
	77/78	25			P
	78/79	25	1		P
Motherwell	79/80	34		1	D1
	80/81	15	2		D1
Dundee	81/82	15			P
	82/83			1	P
Motherwell	82/83	14	1	1	P
Montrose	83/84	29			D2
	84/85	36	1		D2
	85/86	28			D1
	86/87	33	1		D1
	87/88	27			D2
	88/89	16			D2
	89/90	3	2		D2

McLENNAN Daniel
b. Stirling
Rangers

Club	Season	App	Sub	Gls	Div
Stirling A	45/46				
Falkirk	46/47	6			D1
East Fife	46/47				D2
	47/48				D2
	48/49				D2
	49/50	2			D1
	50/51	22			D1
	51/52	29		2	D1
	52/53	11			D1
	53/54	25			D1
	54/55	18		1	D1
	55/56	31			D1
	56/57	25		3	D1
Dundee	57/58				D1
Berwick R	58/59				D2
	59/60				D2

McLEOD Alexander

Club	Season	App	Sub	Gls	Div
Third Lanark	47/48	3			D1
Albion R	48/49	14			D1

MacLEOD Alexander Hector McMillan
b. Glasgow 1.1.1951
Renfrew Jnrs

Club	Season	App	Sub	Gls	Div
St Mirren	69/70				D1
	70/71	9	1	3	D1
	71/72	36		27	D2
	72/73	34		23	D2
Southampton	73/74	2		1	FL
	74/75				FL
Huddersfield T	L 74/75	3	1	1	FL
Hibernian	74/75	9	1	3	D1
	75/76	16	1	7	P
	76/77	19		7	P
	77/78	35	1	16	P
	78/79	36		8	P
	79/80	25	1	8	P
	80/81	27	3	15	D1
	81/82	33	1	7	P
	82/83				P
Dundee U	T 82/83				P
Hamilton A	82/83	1		2	D1

MacLEOD Alistair Reid
b. Glasgow 26.2.1931 d. Ayr 1.2.2004

Club	Season	App	Sub	Gls	Div
Third Lanark	49/50	11		2	D1
	50/51				D1
	51/52	22		1	D1
	52/53	21		1	D1
St Mirren	55/56	22		3	D1
Blackburn R	56/57	41		7	FL
	57/58	38		17	FL
	58/59	40		4	FL
	59/60	39		8	FL
	60/61	35		11	FL
Hibernian	61/62	34		5	D1
	62/63	18		1	D1
Third Lanark	63/64	24		1	D1
Ayr U	64/65				D2
	65/66				D2

McLEOD Donald A
b. Edinburgh 1.11.1917 d. Penicuik 20.6.1999
Arniston Star
Whitburn Jnrs

Club	Season	App	Sub	Gls	Div
Motherwell	38/39	2			D1
	46/47	30			D1
	47/48	29			D1
	48/49	17			D1
	49/50	21		1	D1
	50/51	29			D1
	51/52	17		1	D1

McLEOD Duncan
b. Tobermory 23.5.1949
Southampton

Club	Season	App	Sub	Gls	Div
Dundee	72/73				D1
Dundee U	73/74	12	1	3	D1
	74/75	7		5	D1
St Johnstone	75/76	1		1	P
Brechin C	76/77	33	1	2	D2
	77/78	33			D2
	78/79	18			D2
	79/80	20		1	D2
	80/81	18		1	D2

McLEOD Iain Alasdair
b. Edinburgh 11.5.1952
Bonnyrigg Rose

Club	Season	App	Sub	Gls	Div
Dunfermline A	74/75	1			D1
Bonnyrigg Rose					
Berwick R	76/77	33	2	4	D2
	77/78	27	6	2	D2
	78/79	37		5	D2
	79/80	36	1	5	D1
	80/81	21	8	2	D1
Stirling A	81/82	14		2	D2
Meadowbank T	81/82		1		D2
Linlithgow Rose					
Bonnyrigg Rose					

McLEOD James

Club	Season	App	Sub	Gls	Div
Airdrieonians	63/64	1			D1

MacLEOD John Murdoch
b. Edinburgh 23.11.1938 Caps: S - 4
Edinburgh Thistle
Armadale

Club	Season	App	Sub	Gls	Div
Hibernian	57/58	8		4	D1
	58/59	10		2	D1
	59/60	33		13	D1
	60/61	34		8	D1
Arsenal	61/62	37		6	FL
	62/63	33		9	FL
	63/64	30		7	FL
	64/65	1		1	FL
Aston Villa	64/65	33		2	FL
	65/66	36		4	FL
	66/67	34	1	8	FL
	67/68	20	1	2	FL
Mechelen	68/69				
	69/70				
	70/71				
Raith R	71/72	14	1	5	D2
Newtongrange Star					

McLEOD Thomas
Ardeer Thistle

Club	Season	App	Sub	Gls	Div
Dundee U	60/61	7		2	D1
Toronto White Eagles	61				
Morton	61/62	1			D2
Inverness Caley					

McLEOD Thomas
b. Edinburgh 12.11.1951
Musselburgh A

Club	Season	Apps	Sub	Gls	Div
Falkirk	70/71	1			D1
	71/72	5	3		D1
	72/73	1			D1
	73/74	11	3	1	D1
	74/75	21	2	1	D2
	75/76	6			D1
Dunfermline A	76/77	15	2	1	D2
Brisbane C					
Stirling A	78/79	1			D1
Tranent Jnrs					
Ormiston Primrose					

McLEVY Tom
Blairgowrie

Club	Season	Apps	Div
Arbroath	59/60	34	D1
	60/61		D2
Brechin C	61/62	36	D2
	62/63		D2
	63/64	35	D2
	64/65	36	D2
	65/66	26	D2
	66/67	21	D2

McLINDON Daniel
Bellshill Academy

Club	Season	Apps	Sub	Gls	Div
Dunfermline A	60/61	13		2	D1
	61/62	4			D1
	62/63	6			D1
	63/64	6			D1
St Johnstone	64/65	7		3	D1
Partick T	64/65	17		3	D1
	65/66	24		5	D1
	66/67	25		3	D1
	67/68	9	2	1	D1
	68/69	34		1	D1
	69/70	11		1	D1
Stranraer	70/71			2	D2
East Stirlingshire	71/72	24	3	4	D2

McLURE Malcolm
b. Glasgow
Heart of Midlothian

Club	Season	Apps	Div
Raith R	49/50	13	D1
	50/51	26	D1
	51/52	17	D1
	52/53	25	D1
	53/54	15	D1
	54/55	26	D1
	55/56	20	D1
	56/57	4	D1

McMAHON Eamon
b. Lurgan 16.1.1933
Lurgan GAA

Club	Season	Apps	Div
Celtic	53/54		D1
	54/55	1	D1
Glentoran	55/56		
	56/57		
	57/58		
	58/59		

McMAHON Patrick
b. Kilsyth 19.9.1945
Ashfield
Yoker A
Kilsyth R

Club	Season	Apps	Sub	Gls	Div
Celtic	67/68	2		1	D1
	68/69		1	1	D1
Aston Villa	69/70	20	4	4	FL
	70/71	36	1	8	FL
	71/72	15	3	5	FL
	72/73	28	1	3	FL
	73/74	20		5	FL
	74/75	2			FL
	75/76				FL
Portland Timbers	76	19		1	NA
	77	23		1	NA
Colorado Caribous	78	25			NA
Atlanta Chiefs	79	22			NA

McMANUS J

Club	Season	Apps	Div
Airdrieonians	55/56	1	D1
	56/57	2	D1

McMANUS James
Edinburgh Norton

Club	Season	Apps	Gls	Div
Dundee U	62/63			D1
	63/64	8	2	D1
	64/65	3		D1
Falkirk	65/66	23	2	D1
	66/67	12	1	D1
	67/68	22	2	D1
	68/69	3		D1
Raith R	69/70		1	D1

McMANUS Stanley
b. Carlisle 31.10.1932
Carlisle Catholic Youth

Club	Season	Apps	Div
Carlisle U	48/49		FL
	49/50		FL
Penrith	50/51		
	51/52		
	52/53		
Canterbury C	53/54		
	54/55		
Bury	55/56		FL
	56/57		FL
Southport	57/58	5	FL
Queen of the South	57/58	2	D1
Netherfield			
West End Celtic			

McMANUS William
Letham Juveniles

Club	Season	Apps	Sub	Gls	Div
St Johnstone	70/71	4			D1
	71/72	6			D1
	72/73	9	2		D1
	73/74	3			D1
Forfar A	74/75	16	1	1	D2

McMASTER John
b. Greenock 23.2.1955
Port Glasgow Jnrs

Club	Season	Apps	Sub	Gls	Div
Aberdeen	72/73				D1
	73/74				D1
	74/75	1	1		D1
	75/76	18	3	3	P
	76/77	2	1		P
	77/78	32	2	4	P
	78/79	27	3	3	P
	79/80	34	2	4	P
	80/81	10		2	P
	81/82	31	10	1	P
	82/83	25	6	2	P
	83/84	12	1		P
	84/85	1	1		P
	85/86	7	2		P
	86/87		2		P
Morton	86/87	5	4		D1
	87/88	19	1	2	P

McMASTER William

Club	Season	Apps	Gls	Div
St Mirren	53/54	12	1	D1
	54/55	21	8	D1

McMICHAEL James
Bathgate Thistle

Club	Season	Apps	Gls	Div
Dundee U	60/61	7	1	D1
	61/62	1		D1

McMILLAN A

Club	Season	Apps	Div
Third Lanark	47/48	8	D1

McMILLAN Duncan
b. Glasgow 18.1.1922 d. Grimsby 20.5.1992
Maryhill Harp

Club	Season	Apps	Gls	Div
Celtic	46/47	12		D1
	47/48	5		D1
	48/49	2		D1
Grimsby T	48/49	8		FL
	49/50	40		FL
	50/51	26	1	FL
	51/52	43		FL
	52/53	45	1	FL
	53/54	22		FL
	54/55	4		FL
Dundee	T 54/55			D1

McMILLAN George Sneddon
b. Motherwell 15.3.1930
Bolton W

Club	Season	Apps	Div
Aberdeen	50/51	1	D1
	51/52		D1
Wrexham	52/53	1	FL
Brechin C	53/54		D3
	54/55		D2
	55/56		D2
Newport Co	56/57		FL

McMILLAN Hamish
b. Airdrie

Club	Season	Apps	Gls	Div
Raith R	55/56	23	7	D1
	56/57	3		D1
	57/58	3	1	D1
	58/59	4	2	D1

McMILLAN John Livingstone
b. Airdrie 18.3.1931 Caps: S - 6
Airdrie Academy

Club	Season	Apps	Gls	Div
Airdrieonians	48/49			D2
	49/50	9	5	D2
	50/51	15	9	D1
	51/52	28	8	D1
	52/53	30	11	D1
	53/54	26	5	D1
	54/55			D2
	55/56	31	23	D1
	56/57	28	13	D1
	57/58	27	8	D1
Rangers	58/59	26	8	D1
	59/60	27	14	D1
	60/61	28	8	D1
	61/62	24	4	D1
	62/63	12	1	D1
	63/64	10	1	D1
Airdrieonians	64/65	20	4	D1
	65/66	33		D2
	66/67			D1

McMILLAN P Hunter
b Glasgow

Club	Season	Apps	Gls	Div
Rangers	53/54	1		D1
	54/55	4	1	D1
	55/56			D1
Queen of the South	56/57	24	5	D1
Falkirk	57/58	23	2	D1
	58/59	8		D1

McMILLAN Samuel
b. c1937
Ballochmyle Thistle

Club	Season	Apps	Gls	Div
Ayr U	T 52/53	1		D2
Irvine Meadow	53/54			
	54/55			
Ayr U	55/56			D2
	56/57	30	4	D1
	57/58			D2
	58/59			D2
	59/60	33	10	D1
	60/61	29	6	D1
	61/62	34	14	D2
	62/63			D2
	63/64	32	10	D2
	64/65	31	1	D2
	65/66	35	15	D2
	66/67	27		D1
	67/68	16	2	D2
Corby T				

McMILLAN Thomas
b. Glasgow 12.2.1931
Garrowhill Amateurs
Baillieston Jnrs

Club	Season				Div
Celtic	52/53				D1
	53/54	2			D1
Norwich C	54/55	19		2	FL
Albion R	T 55/56				D2
Workington	55/56	1			FL
Albion R	T 56/57				D2
Cowdenbeath	56/57	1			D2

McMILLAN Thomas
b. Paisley
Neilston Jnrs

Club	Season				Div
Aberdeen	65/66	32			D1
	66/67	32			D1
	67/68	33			D1
	68/69	16			D1
	69/70	24			D1
	70/71	27		1	D1
	71/72	8			D1
Falkirk	72/73	32			D1
Inverness Thistle					

McMILLAN William
Dalry Thistle

Club	Season				Div
Dundee	59/60	6			D1

McMORRAN James Wilson
b. Muirkirk 29.10.1942

Club	Season				Div
Aston Villa	60/61	5			FL
	61/62	9		1	FL
Third Lanark	62/63	15			D1
	63/64	26		9	D1
	64/65	3			D1
Walsall	64/65	26		1	FL
	65/66	25		3	FL
	66/67	20	1	1	FL
	67/68	22		4	FL
Swansea T	68/69	14		1	FL
Walsall	68/69	9	1	1	FL
Notts Co	69/70	6			FL
Halifax T	70/71				
Worcester C					
Redditch U					

McNAB Neil
b. Greenock 4.6.1957

Club	Season				Div
Morton	72/73	3			D1
	73/74	8	3		D1
Tottenham H	73/74		1		FL
	74/75	2			FL
	75/76	11	4		FL
	76/77	6	4		FL
	77/78	42		3	FL
	78/79	2			FL
Bolton W	78/79	22	1	3	FL
	79/80	11	1	1	FL
Brighton & HA	79/80	15	1		FL
	80/81	33		1	FL
	81/82	38	2	3	FL
	82/83	14			FL
Leeds U	L 82/83	5			FL
Manchester C	83/84	33		1	FL
	84/85	15	3		FL
	85/86	37		4	FL
	86/87	42		4	FL
	87/88	36	1	2	FL
	88/89	42		5	FL
	89/90	11	1		FL
Tranmere R	89/90	22		1	FL
	90/91	39	1	3	FL
	91/92	3	9		FL
Huddersfield T	L 91/92				FL
Tranmere R	92/93	30	1	2	FL
Ayr U	92/93				D1
Darlington	93/94	4			FL
Derry C					

McNAB Thomas Copeland
b. Glasgow 15.7.1933
Baillieston Jnrs

Club	Season				Div
Partick T	51/52	4			D1
	52/53	13			D1
	53/54	1			D1
Nottingham F	53/54				FL
Partick T	54/55	1			D1
	55/56	5			D1
	56/57	6			D1
Wrexham	56/57	11			FL
	57/58	27		5	FL
	58/59	5			FL
Barrow	58/59	8			FL
	59/60	25		3	FL
	60/61	10		1	FL
East Stirlingshire	61/62	35			D2
	62/63				D2
	63/64	17		1	D1
Eastern Suburbs (NZ)					

McNAMARA John
b. Glasgow 19.9.1952
Eastercraigs Amateurs
Cumbernauld U

Club	Season				Div
Celtic	70/71				D1
	71/72				D1
	72/73				D1
	73/74	1	1		D1
	74/75	1			D1
	75/76	16	2	2	P
Hibernian	76/77	10	1		P
	77/78	33	1		P
	78/79	35			P
	79/80	30			P
	80/81	36		1	D1
	81/82	27	2		P
	82/83	27	1	1	P
	83/84	10			P
	84/85	23			P
Morton	85/86	23			D1
	86/87	26	1	2	D1
	87/88	7			P

McNAMEE John
b. Coatbridge 11.6.1941
Bellshill Academy

Club	Season				Div
Celtic	60/61	1			D1
	61/62	5			D1
	62/63	19		2	D1
	63/64	2			D1
Hibernian	63/64	2		1	D1
	64/65	32			D1
	65/66	31		2	D1
	66/67	12		1	D1
Newcastle U	66/67	19		1	FL
	67/68	31		2	FL
	68/69	23	1	3	FL
	69/70	13	1	1	FL
	70/71	27		1	FL
	71/72	2			FL
Morton	72/73				D1
	73/74				D1
Hartlepool U	73/74	2			FL
Lancaster C	74/75				
Workington	75/76	2			FL

McNAMEE John James
b. Watford 31.7.1942

Club	Season				Div
Raith R	61/62	4			D1
	62/63	11		3	D1
Montrose	62/63				D2
	63/64				D2
	63/64	24		11	D2
Reading	64/65				FL
	65/66				FL
	66/67				FL
Tranmere R	67/68	14	2	3	FL
	68/69	35		6	FL
	69/70	18	3	3	FL

McNAUGHT John

Club	Season				Div
Queen of the South	63/64	4			D1
Stranraer	64/65	28		1	D2
	65/66	30			D2

McNAUGHT William
b. Dumfries 7.5.1922 Caps: S - 5
Dumfries Park Rovers

Club	Season				Div
Raith R	46/47				D2
	47/48				D2
	48/49				D2
	49/50	25			D1
	50/51	28			D1
	51/52	28			D1
	52/53	29			D1
	53/54	29			D1
	54/55	21			D1
	55/56	31			D1
	56/57	34			D1
	57/58	31			D1
	58/59	33			D1
	59/60	24			D1
	60/61	26			D1
	61/62	1			D1
Brechin C	62/63				D2

McNAUGHTON John
Auchinleck Talbot

Club	Season				Div
Stirling A	59/60	2			D1

McNEE Christopher

Club	Season				Div
Rangers	46/47	10		3	D1

McNEIL John
Blantyre Victoria
Hibernian

Club	Season				Div
Motherwell	54/55	5			D1
Airdrieonians	55/56	26			D1
	56/57	16		3	D1
	57/58				D1
	58/59				D1
	59/60	6			D1
	60/61	34		2	D1
	61/62	23		4	D1
	62/63	4		1	D1

McNEIL Matthew Alexander
b. Glasgow 28.7.1927 d. Glasgow 22.4.1977

Club	Season				Div
Hibernian	47/48				D1
	48/49				D1
	49/50	1			D1
Newcastle U	49/50				FL
	50/51	9			FL
Barnsley	51/52	38		1	FL
	52/53	30			FL
Brighton & HA	53/54	10			FL
	54/55	29			FL
	55/56	14			FL
Norwich C	55/56	12			FL
	56/57	32		2	FL
Cambridge U					

McNEIL Ronald

Club	Season				Div
Raith R	53/54	12		1	D1

McNEILL George Forsyth
b. Tranent 19.2.1947
Tranent Jnrs

Club	Season					Div
Hibernian	65/66	1				D1
	66/67					D1
	67/68					D1
Morton	68/69	4	1		1	D1
Stirling A	68/69				4	D2
	69/70					D2
	70/71					D2

McNEILL John McKeand
b. Glasgow 24.2.1932
Bridgeton Waverley

Club	Season	Apps	Sub	Gls	Div
Aberdeen	50/51	2		1	D1
	51/52				D1
	52/53	3			D1
	53/54				D1
	54/55				D1
	55/56	2			D1
Leicester C	55/56	5		1	FL
	56/57	38		18	FL
	57/58	17		6	FL
	58/59	12		1	FL
Brighton & HA	58/59	7		2	FL
	59/60	35		5	FL
	60/61	38		4	FL
	61/62	36		1	FL
Southend U	62/63	36		3	FL
	63/64	5			FL
Ross Co					
Dover A					

McNEILL Tom
b. Paisley 2.8.1955
Johnstone Burgh

Club	Season	Apps	Sub	Gls	Div
Morton	74/75	11	1		D1
	75/76	24	1	2	D1
	76/77	22	5	2	D1
	77/78	12	9	1	D1
St Johnstone	78/79	36	1	3	D1
	79/80	31	1	3	D1
	80/81	19	2	2	D1
	81/82	29	1	3	D1
	82/83	17		1	D1

McNEILL William
b. Bellshill 2.3.1940 Caps: S - 29
Blantyre Victoria

Club	Season	Apps	Sub	Gls	Div
Celtic	57/58				D1
	58/59	17			D1
	59/60	19			D1
	60/61	31		1	D1
	61/62	29		1	D1
	62/63	28		1	D1
	63/64	28			D1
	64/65	22			D1
	65/66	25			D1
	66/67	33			D1
	67/68	34		6	D1
	68/69	34		3	D1
	69/70	31		5	D1
	70/71	31		1	D1
	71/72	34		3	D1
	72/73	30			D1
	73/74	30			D1
	74/75	30		1	D1

McNICHOL David
b. Dundee 23.9.1951
Butterburn YC

Club	Season	Apps	Sub	Gls	Div
Dunfermline A	69/70	20			D1
	70/71	24	1	2	D1
	71/72	34		1	D1
	72/73	36		2	D2
	73/74	8			D1
	74/75	9		1	D1
Montrose	75/76	26		3	D1
	76/77	31		3	D1
	77/78	12			D1
Heart of Midlothian	77/78	27		1	D1
	78/79	16		1	P
St Johnstone	79/80	16	1	1	D1
Inverness Clachnacuddin					

McNICHOL Robert Hugh
b. Dumbarton 13.2.1933 d. Tenerife 25.4.1980
Vale of Leven

Club	Season	Apps	Sub	Gls	Div
Stirling A	53/54	3			D1
	54/55	21			D1
	55/56	32		1	D1
Accrington S	56/57	46		1	FL
	57/58	46		1	FL
	58/59	42		3	FL
Brighton & HA	59/60				FL
	60/61				FL
	61/62				FL
Gravesend U	62/63				
Carlisle U	63/64	1			FL
Stalybridge C					
Great Harwood					

McPARLAND David
b. Tullibody
Larkhall Thistle

Club	Season	Apps	Sub	Gls	Div
Partick T	53/54	1		1	D1
	54/55	30		3	D1
	55/56	8		2	D1
	56/57	8			D1
	57/58	34		13	D1
	58/59	32		4	D1
	59/60	33		8	D1
	60/61	33		13	D1
	61/62	33		8	D1
	62/63	34		1	D1
	63/64	34		5	D1
	64/65	34		5	D1
	65/66	31		3	D1
	66/67	24		1	D1
	67/68	18	1	2	D1
	68/69	26		3	D1

McPHAIL George

Club	Season	Apps	Sub	Gls	Div
Clyde	58/59	1			D1
	59/60	10			D1
	60/61	3			D1

McPHAIL John
b. Lambhill 27.5.1923
d. Glasgow 8.11.2000 Caps: S - 5
St Mungos Academy
Strathclyde

Club	Season	Apps	Sub	Gls	Div
Celtic	46/47	3			D1
Ballymoney U	L 46/47				
Celtic	47/48	24		4	D1
	48/49	18		4	D1
	49/50	22		11	D1
	50/51	17		13	D1
	51/52	21		11	D1
	52/53	15		5	D1
	53/54	15		4	D1
	54/55	4		2	D1
	55/56	2		1	D1

McPHAIL John
b. Glasgow
Ashfield

Club	Season	Apps	Sub	Gls	Div
Albion R	53/54	29			D2
	54/55				D2
	55/56				D2
	56/57				D2
	57/58				D2
Airdrieonians	57/58	12			D1
Albion R	58/59				D2

McPHAIL William S
b. Glasgow 2.2.1928 d. Glasgow 4.4.2003

Club	Season	Apps	Sub	Gls	Div
Queen's Park	46/47	12		2	D1
Clyde	47/48	21		7	D1
	48/49				D1
	49/50	10		3	D1
	50/51	16		5	D1
	51/52	25		34	D2
	52/53	26		19	D1
	53/54	15		10	D1
	54/55	11		5	D1
	55/56	13		5	D1
Celtic	55/56				
	56/57	13		5	D1
	57/58	20		9	D1

McPHEAT William
b. Caldercruix 4.9.1942
Calder Youth

Club	Season	Apps	Sub	Gls	Div
Sunderland	60/61	26		11	FL
	61/62	29		7	FL
	62/63	3		1	FL
	63/64				FL
	64/65				FL
	65/66				FL
Hartlepools U	65/66	13	2	2	FL
Airdrieonians	66/67	14		5	D1
	67/68	17	3	7	D1
	68/69	23		8	D1
	69/70	22	5	4	D1
	70/71	11		1	D1

McPHEE Ian
b. c1943
Duntocher Hibs

Club	Season	Apps	Sub	Gls	Div
East Stirlingshire	63/64	13			D1
ES Clydebank	64/65	34		3	D2
St Johnstone	65/66	6			D1
	66/67	32		3	D1
	67/68	27	3	6	D1
	68/69	25	3	2	D1
	69/70	33		2	D1
	70/71	29	1	2	D1
	71/72	12	2	3	D1
	72/73	3		1	D1
Toronto Metros	73	19			NA
Arbroath	72/73	4			D1
Raith R	72/73	4		1	D2
Toronto Metros	75	11			NA

McPHEE John
b. Motherwell 21.11.1937
Douglas Water Thistle
North Mothewell

Club	Season	Apps	Sub	Gls	Div
Motherwell	55/56				D1
	56/57	1			D1
	57/58	9		3	D1
	58/59	1			D1
	59/60	9		6	D1
	60/61	23		1	D1
	61/62	32		6	D1
Blackpool	62/63	37		6	FL
	63/64	30		5	FL
	64/65	26		1	FL
	65/66	26		4	FL
	66/67	25		1	FL
	67/68	42		1	FL
	68/69	38	1	1	FL
	69/70	25	4	1	FL
Barnsley	70/71	26		3	FL
Southport	71/72	44			FL
	72/73	41		1	FL

McPHEE Matthew
b. Edinburgh 16.10.1949
Musselburgh A

Club	Season	Apps	Sub	Gls	Div
Stirling A	66/67				D1
	67/68	17	1	1	D1
	68/69	8			D2
	69/70	34	1	15	D2
	70/71	35		9	D2
	71/72	33	3	8	D2
	72/73	30	3	7	D2
	73/74	26	5	4	D2
	74/75	27	8	4	D2
	75/76	18	6	1	D2
	76/77	39		9	D2
	77/78	37	2	11	D1
	78/79	33	4	4	D1
	79/80	39		3	D1
	80/81	24	12	3	D1
Meadowbank T	81/82	8	16	2	D2

McPHEE Robert
Newburgh

Club	Season	Apps	Sub	Gls	Div
Stirling A	57/58				D2
	58/59	20		6	D1
	59/60	21		5	D1
East Fife	59/60				D2
	60/61				D2

McPHEE William
b. Methil 12.6.1949
Bowhill YC

Club	Season	Apps		Gls	Div
Rangers	69/70	1			D1
East Fife	70/71	36		22	D2
	71/72	26	2	9	D1
	72/73	34		16	D1
	73/74	25	4	2	D1
	74/75	15		4	D2
	75/76	17	1	2	D1
	76/77	7	4		D1
Berwick R	77/78	21	4	7	D2

McPHERSON John

Club	Season	Apps	Gls	Div
Rangers	47/48	1	1	D1
	48/49			D1
Ayr U	49/50	7	2	D2

McPHIE James
b. Bonnybridge 25.8.1920 d. Falkirk 24.2.2002

Club	Season	Apps		Gls	Div
Falkirk	37/38	1			D1
	38/39	9	2		D1
	46/47	24			D1
	47/48	28			D1
	48/49	30			D1
	49/50	21			D1
	50/51	19		1	D1
	51/52	28			D2
	52/53	6			D1

McPIKE William
Kilmarnock Amateurs
Mauchline Colliery
Irvine Meadow

Club	Season	Apps	Gls	Div
Kilmarnock	56/57			D1
	57/58			D1
	58/59	2	2	D1
	59/60	1		D1
Hamilton A	59/60	8	6	D2
	60/61	10	2	D2

Cumnock Jnrs
Irvine Meadow

McQUADE Denis
b. Glasgow 6.1.1951
St Rochs

Club	Season	Apps		Gls	Div
Partick T	69/70			1	D1
	70/71	28	4	12	D2
	71/72	26	6	12	D1
	72/73	23	7	5	D1
	73/74	3	6		D1
	74/75	33		7	D1
	75/76	16	6	7	D1
	76/77	16	4	4	P
	77/78	10	4	1	P
	78/79	13	9	4	P
Heart of Midlothian	78/79	13	9	4	P
Hamilton A	79/80	7	6	2	D1

McQUADE John
Kilsyth St Patricks

Club	Season	Apps		Gls	Div
St Johnstone	73/74	9	3	1	D1
	74/75				D1
Hamilton A	75/76	2	3		D1

McQUADE Peter M
b. High Valleyfield 4.11.1948
Valleyfield Colliery

Club	Season	Apps		Gls	Div
East Fife	67/68	1			D2
	68/69			1	D2
	69/70	23	3		D2
	70/71			3	D2
	71/72	30	1		D1
	72/73	10		1	D1
Dumbarton	73/74	4			D1
Berwick R	73/74	11			D2
	74/75	36		3	D2
	75/76	14	1	2	D2

McQUEEN Gordon
b. Kilwinning 26.6.1952 Caps: S - 30
Largs Thistle

Club	Season	Apps	Gls	Div
Rangers	T			
Liverpool	T			
St Mirren	70/71	18		D1
	71/72	34	5	D2
	72/73	6		D2
Leeds U	72/73	6		FL
	73/74	36		FL
	74/75	33	2	FL
	75/76	10	1	FL
	76/77	34	7	FL
	77/78	21	5	FL
Manchester U	77/78	14	1	FL
	78/79	36	6	FL
	79/80	33	9	FL
	80/81	11	2	FL
	81/82	21		FL
	82/83	37		FL
	83/84	20	1	FL
	84/85	12	1	FL
Seiko Hong Kong				

McQUEEN John
Troon Jnrs

Club	Season	Apps	Gls	Div
Stirling A	54/55	2		D1

McQUEEN John
Vale of Leven

Club	Season	Apps		Gls	Div
Hamilton A	60/61	18		2	D2
	61/62	33			D2
	62/63	10			D2
East Stirlingshire	62/63				D2
	63/64	32		1	D1
ES Clydebank	64/65	34			D2
East Stirlingshire	65/66	22			D2
Stranraer	66/67	33	1	2	D2
	67/68	21		1	D2
Blantyre Victoria					

McQUEEN Thomas
b. West Calder 21.2.1929
Kilbirnie Ladeside

Club	Season	Apps	Gls	Div
Hibernian	52/53	3		D1
Queen of the South	53/54			D1
Accrington S	54/55	14		FL
	55/56	35		FL
	56/57	31		FL
East Fife	56/57	6		D1
	57/58			D1
Berwick R	57/58			D2

MacRAE Keith Alexander
b. Glasgow 5.2.1951
Lanark GS

Club	Season	Apps		Gls	Div
Motherwell	67/68	1			D1
	68/69	19		1	D2
	69/70	20	2		D1
	70/71	33			D1
	71/72	14			D1
	72/73	30			D1
	73/74	7			D1
Manchester C	73/74	25			FL
	74/75	27			FL
	75/76	1			FL
	76/77				FL
	77/78				FL
	78/79				FL
	79/80				FL
	80/81	3			FL
Portland Timbers	81				
Leeds U	81/82				FL

McROBERTS Alistair Dove
b. Newmains 17.9.1954
Bonkle YC

Club	Season	Apps		Gls	Div
Airdrieonians	72/73	12	2	1	D1
	73/74	36		23	D2
	74/75	6	6	1	D1
	75/76	19	4	5	D1
	76/77	8		1	D1
Falkirk	77/78	35	1	13	D2
	78/79	32	4	11	D2
	79/80	29	2	8	D1
	80/81	19		1	D1
	81/82	3	4	1	D1
Dumbarton	81/82	4	4		D1
Stirling A	82/83	18	3	1	D2
Stenhousemuir L	82/83	7		1	D2
Darvel					

McROBERTS William

Club	Season	Apps	Gls	Div
Motherwell	46/47	3	2	D1
	47/48	2		D1
St Johnstone	48/49	23	10	D2
	49/50	16	5	D2

McRORIE Alexander

Club	Season	Apps	Div
St Johnstone	63/64	2	D1
Alloa A	64/65	2	D2

McSEVENEY William
b. Shotts
Wishaw Jnrs

Club	Season	Apps	Gls	Div
Dunfermline A	52/53	29	1	D2
	53/54	20	10	D2
Motherwell	53/54	4	5	D2
	54/55	12	4	D1
	55/56	21	4	D1
	56/57	30		D1
	57/58	29	3	D1
	58/59	34		D1
	59/60	23		D1
	60/61	17	4	D1
	61/62	24		D1
	62/63	2		D1

McSHERRY James
b. Larkhall 12.2.1952
Fairholm Amateurs
Lesmahagow

Club	Season	Apps		Gls	Div
Kilmarnock	70/71	7	2		D1
	71/72	33		1	D1
	72/73	27		4	D1
	73/74	32	1	3	D2
	74/75	12	1		D1
Ayr U	75/76	28	5		P
	76/77	29	3	2	P
	77/78	21	5		P
	78/79	27	5	5	D1
	79/80	31	4	3	D1
	80/81	9	7		D1
	81/82	12	4		D1
Berwick R	82/83	24		1	D2
Stirling A	82/83	7			D2
Pezoporikos	83/84				
Stirling A	84/85	7	4		D2

McSORLEY Daniel
b. Cambuslang
Shettleston

Club	Season	Apps	Gls	Div
Clyde	54/55	3	1	D1

McSPADYEN Alexander
b. Carfin 19.12.1914 d. ?.10.1978
Holytown Thistle

Club	Season	Apps	Gls	Div
Partick T	34/35	6		D1
	35/36	16		D1
	36/37	32	6	D1
	37/38	31	1	D1
	38/39	38	5	D1
	46/47			D1
	47/48	1		D1
Portadown				

McSPADYEN Thomas
b. Cleland 21.1.1920
Newarthill Hearts
Rutherglen Glencairn

Club	Season				Div
Heart of Midlothian	46/47	20			D1
	47/48	10			D1
	48/49				D1
Raith R	49/50	17			D1
Heart of Midlothian	50/51	3			D1
	51/52	4			D1

McTAVISH John Robert
b. Glasgow 2.2.21932
Dalry Thistle

Club	Season				Div
Manchester C	52/53				FL
	53/54	20			FL
	54/55	3			FL
	55/56	5			FL
	56/57	8			FL
	57/58	6			FL
	58/59	16			FL
	59/60	35			FL
St Mirren	60/61	14		2	D1
	61/62	32			D1
	62/63	28			D1
	63/64	17			D1

McTURK John
b. Cumnock 11.7.1936
Lugar
Auchinleck Thistle
Auchinleck Talbot

Club	Season				Div
St Mirren	54/55	3			D1
	55/56	2			D1
	56/57	14			D1
	57/58	10			D1
Wrexham	57/58	2			FL
St Mirren	58/59	10			D1
	59/60	9		3	D1
	60/61	1			D1
Queen of the South	61/62				D2
	62/63	11			D1
Ayr U	T 62/63				D2
Morton	63/64	4		1	D2
Stirling A	64/65	17		5	D2
Albion R	65/66	22		3	D2
Lugar					
Cumnock					

McVAKE Alexander
Rangers

Club	Season				Div
Ayr U	74/75	3		1	D1

McVEAN Hugh

Club	Season				Div
Aberdeen	47/48	4			D1
	48/49	5			D1

McVIE William
b. Glasgow 7.8.1948
Lesmahagow Jnrs

Club	Season				Div
Clyde	68/69	4			D1
	69/70	7	1		D1
	70/71	5	1		D1
	71/72	16	1	2	D1
	72/73	12	3	5	D2
	73/74	24	2	2	D1
	74/75	34		1	D1
Motherwell	75/76	32		1	P
	76/77	12	1	1	P
	77/78	25	1		P
	78/79	16			P
Toronto Blizzard	79	25			NA
	80	3			NA
Heart of Midlothian	80/81	12			P
Blantyre Victoria					

McVINISH Thomas
b. Inverness 1.1.1921
Inverness Caleys

Club	Season				Div
Hamilton A	46/47	11		2	D1
	47/48	27		9	D2
Preston NE	48/49				FL
	49/50				FL
Darlington	50/51	1			FL
Morton	50/51	23		3	D1
	51/52	17			D1
St Johnstone	52/53	7			D2

McVITTIE Matthew
b. Calderbank 30.9.1937
Calderbank BG
Wishaw Jnrs
Celtic

Club	Season				Div
Albion R	L 53/54				D2
Celtic	54/55				D1
	55/56	4		2	D1
	56/57				D1
	57/58	11		4	D1
	58/59	17		5	D1
	59/60	1			D1
St Johnstone	59/60	13		1	D2
	60/61	27		8	D1
	61/62	25		2	D1
Cambridge T					

McVITTIE Michael
b. Kirriemuir
Brechin Matrix

Club	Season				Div
Brechin C	63/64	35			D2
	64/65	12			D2
St Johnstone	64/65	24			D1
	65/66	30			D1
	66/67	5			D1

McWILLIAM Gerald
Airdrieonians

Club	Season				Div
Dunfermline A	56/57	13		7	D1
	57/58				D2
	58/59	10		3	D1
	59/60	1			D1
Stirling A	59/60	2			D1
Cowdenbeath	60/61				D2

McWILLIAMS David
b. 29.4.1952
Johnstone Burgh

Club	Season				Div
Alloa A	71/72	31			D2
	72/73	34			D2
Airdrieonians	73/74	35			D2
	74/75	34			D1
	75/76	25			D1
	76/77	3			D1
	77/78	9			D1
Hamilton A	L 77/78	3			D1
Forfar A	78/79	38			D2
	79/80	10			D2
Clyde	79/80	19			D1
	80/81	17			D2

McWILLIAMS Walter
b. Pumpherston c1935
Livingston U
Ards
Distillery

Club	Season				Div
Hibernian	56/57	2		1	D1
Cowdenbeath	57/58				D2
	58/59				D2
Peebles R					
Pumpherston Welfare					
Mid Calder Welfare					

NAPIER Alexander Stevenson
b. Kirkcaldy 8.8.1935

Club	Season				Div
Raith R	53/54	1			D1
	54/55				D1
Darlington	55/56	1			FL

NAPIER Charles
Bonnybridge

Club	Season				Div
Dunfermline A	58/59	10		3	D1
Stirling A	59/60	3			D1

NAREY David
b. Dundee 12.6.1956 Caps: S - 35
St Columba BC
Dundee
Chelsea

Club	Season				Div
Dundee U	73/74	10	2		D1
	74/75	31		6	D1
	75/76	33			P
	76/77	32		2	P
	77/78	35			P
	78/79	36		5	P
	79/80	35		1	P
	80/81	32			P
	81/82	34		1	P
	82/83	36		5	P
	83/84	34		1	P
	84/85	29		1	P
	85/86	35			P
	86/87	33			P
	87/88	39			P
	88/89	33			P
	89/90	31			P
	90/91	4			P
	91/92	24			P
	92/93	27	1		P
	93/94	6			P
Raith R	94/95	21		1	D1

NEE R

Club	Season				Div
Raith R	51/52	1			D1

NEEF Gerhard
b. Hausham ?.?.1946
Dusseldorf

Club	Season				Div
Aberdeen	T				
Rangers	68/69	3			D1
	69/70	26			D1
	70/71	3			D1
	71/72				D1
	72/73	1			D1
1FC Nuremburg					

NEIL David Knox
b. Stewarton 7.10.1929
Stewarton U

Club	Season				Div
Kilmarnock	50/51	1			D2
	51/52				D2
Kilmarnock Jnrs	52/53				
	53/54				
	54/55				
Girvan Amateurs	55/56				
Kilmarnock	56/57	1			D1
	57/58				D1
Rangers	58/59				D1
Stirling A	58/59				D1
Hamilton A	59/60				D2

NEIL Hugh Moorhead
b. Cumnock 2.01.1936
Rangers

Club	Season				Div
Falkirk	56/57	7			D1
	57/58				D1
	58/59				D1
	59/60				D2
St Johnstone	60/61	5			D1
Carlisle U	61/62	46			FL
	62/63	34			FL
	63/64	45			FL
	64/65	44		1	FL
	65/66	17			FL
	66/67	28	1	1	FL
	67/68	32			FL
	68/69	4		1	FL

NEIL William

Club	Season	Apps	Gls	Div
Airdrieonians	56/57	3		D1
	57/58	5		D1
	58/59	28		D1
	59/60	8		D1
	60/61	5		D1

NEIL William

Club	Season	Apps	Gls	Div
Kilmarnock	56/57	1		D1
	57/58			D1
Stirling A	58/59	1		D1

NEIL William Marshbanks
b. Lanark 20.4.1924

Club	Season	Apps	Gls	Div
Morton	46/47	11	9	D1
Stirling A	T 47/48			D2
Bradford PA	47/48	3		FL

NEILLANDS John
b. Edinburgh.

Club	Season	Apps	Gls	Div
Rangers	51/52	3		D1
	52/53			D1
	53/54	2		D1
	54/55	1		D1
	55/56			D1
Queen of the South	56/57	9		D1

NEILSON John
b. Newtongrange
Newtongrange Star

Club	Season	Apps	Gls	Div
St Mirren	49/50	10	1	D1
	50/51	23		D1
	51/52	25		D1
	52/53	26		D1
	53/54	26	1	D1
	54/55	29		D1
	55/56	27		D1
	56/57	5		D1
	57/58	34		D1
	58/59	23		D1
	59/60	13		D1

NEILSON John Crane
b. Hamilton 2.8.1921 d. ?.?.1988

Club	Season	Apps	Gls	Div
Clyde	47/48	1		D1
Bradford C	47/48	24	10	FL
	48/49	5	1	FL
Wrexham	48/49			FL
Queen of the South	49/50	9		D1
	50/51			D2
	51/52	20	4	D1
	52/53	11	2	D1
Airdrieonians				

NEILSON Thomas
b. Armadale 28.7.1922
Armadale Thistle

Club	Season	Apps	Gls	Div
Heart of Midlothian	46/47	6		D1
	47/48			D1
Ipswich T	48/49	1		FL

NEILSON Thomas
Arniston R

Club	Season	Apps	Gls	Div
Heart of Midlothian	53/54			D1
	54/55			D1
	55/56			D1
	56/57			D1
East Fife	57/58	28	4	D1
	58/59			D2
Dundee U	59/60	23	2	D2
	60/61	34	2	D1
	61/62	32	1	D1
	62/63	25	2	D1
	63/64	28	1	D1
	64/65	21		D1
	65/66	33	1	D1
	66/67	32		D1
	67/68	9	2	D1

NEILSON W

Club	Season	Apps	Gls	Div
St Mirren	53/54	4		D1

NELSON Andrew
b. c1943
Newport Co

Club	Season	Apps	Gls	Div
St Mirren	60/61	1		D1
	61/62	6	1	D1
Worcester C	62/63			
Weymouth	63/64			
Ayr U	64/65	7		D2
Dumbarton	64/65	25	18	D2
	65/66	35	8	D2
	66/67	30	8	D2
East Fife	66/67			D2
	67/68	35	8	D2
	68/69		2	D2

NELSON Dennis
b. Edinburgh 25.2.1950
Broxburn A

Club	Season	Apps		Gls	Div
Hibernian	71/72	1			D1
Dunfermline A	72/73	27	2	13	D2
	73/74	11	8	4	D1
Crewe Alex.	74/75	36	2	6	FL
	75/76	29	4	12	FL
Reading	75/76	10		3	FL
	76/77	9	5	1	FL
	77/78	34	1	2	FL
Crewe Alex.	78/79	31	4	5	FL
	79/80	42	1	8	FL
	80/81	24	5	2	FL

NELSON James

Club	Season	Apps	Gls	Div
Third Lanark	46/47	11	6	D1
Airdrieonians	47/48	7	3	D1

NELSON John

Club	Season	Apps		Gls	Div
Morton	71/72	2	1		D1
	72/73	4	1		D1
	73/74	29		2	D1
	74/75	6		1	D1
	75/76	1	1		D1
Hamilton A	76/77	5	2		D1
	77/78		1		D1

NELSON Maxwell
Muirkirk Amateurs

Club	Season	Apps	Gls	Div
Motherwell	55/56	1		D1
	56/57			D1

NELSON T

Club	Season	Apps	Gls	Div
Airdrieonians	53/54	4	1	D1

NEVILLE David

Club	Season	Apps	Gls	Div
Airdrieonians	55/56	4		D1
Ayr U				
Inverness Caley				

NEWBIGGIN Thomas
b. Larkhall
Larkhall U
Forth W
Larkhall U

Club	Season	Apps	Gls	Div
Kilmarnock	54/55	3		D1
	55/56			D1
Morton	T 56/57			D2

NEWLANDS Douglas Haigh
b. Edinburgh 29.10.1931

Club	Season	Apps	Gls	Div
Aberdeen	51/52	3		D1
	52/53			D1
St Johnstone	L 53/54	27	8	D2
Burnley	54/55	1		FL
	55/56	10	2	FL
	56/57	36	6	FL
	57/58	41	11	FL
	58/59	10	2	FL
Stoke C	59/60	32	8	FL
St Johnstone	60/61	25	5	D1
Airdrieonians	61/62	25	6	D1
	62/63	17	3	D1
	63/64	19	3	D1
	64/65	15	6	D1

NEWLANDS Malcolm
b. Wishaw 28.3.1925 d. ?.?.1996
Carluke R

Club	Season	Apps	Div
St Mirren	46/47	26	D1
	47/48	5	D1
Preston NE	48/49	26	FL
	49/50	19	FL
	50/51	15	FL
	51/52	8	FL
	52/53	12	FL
Workington	52/53	25	FL
	53/54	41	FL
	54/55	27	FL
	55/56	24	FL
	56/57	40	FL
	57/58	30	FL
	58/59	27	FL
	59/60	36	FL

NICOL David

Club	Season	Apps	Div
Falkirk	57/58	3	D1

NICOL George
b. Bannockburn 20.7.1923

Club	Season	Apps	Div
Falkirk	48/49	5	D1
	49/50	23	D1
	50/51	10	D1
Aldershot	51/52	19	FL
Alloa A	52/53	30	D2
	53/54	21	D2
Stenhousemuir	53/54		D2
Stirling A	54/55	12	D1
Brechin C			

NICOL Robert Benjamin Mathieson
b. Edinburgh 11.5.1936

Club	Season	Apps	Gls	Div
Hibernian	55/56	1		D1
	56/57	20	1	D1
	57/58	3		D1
	58/59	11		D1
	59/60	1	1	D1
	60/61			D1
	61/62	1		D1
Barnsley	62/63	29		FL
	63/64	8	1	FL
Berwick R	63/64	15		D2
Toronto C	64			
	65			

NICOLL David

Club	Season	Apps	Div
Brechin C	72/73	1	D2
Montrose	73/74	2	D2
Dundee Osborne			
St Johnstone	74/75	2	D1
	75/76	4	P
	76/77	6	D1
Forfar A	77/78	32	D2

NIELSEN Flemming
b. Denmark 24.2.1934 Caps: Den - 26
B93 Copenhagen
AB Copenhagen
Atalanta

Club	Season	Apps	Gls	Div
Morton	64/65	9		D1
	65/66	20	2	D1

NIELSEN Leif
b. Denmark 28.5.1942 Caps: Den - 28
Frem Copenhagen
Houston Stars

Club	Season	Apps	Div
Morton	68/69	14	D1
	69/70	33	D1
	70/71	7	D1

NIMMO Archibald

Club	Season	Apps	Gls	Div
Partick T	59/60	5	3	D1

NIMMO William

Club	Season	Apps	Div
Partick T	46/47	10	D1

NIVEN George
b. Blairhall
Coupar Angus

Club	Season	Apps	Gls	Div
Rangers	51/52	1		D1
	52/53	30		D1
	53/54	9		D1
	54/55	22		D1
	55/56	31		D1
	56/57	34		D1
	57/58	5		D1
	58/59	34		D1
	59/60	33		D1
	60/61	22		D1
Partick T	61/62	9		D1
	62/63	34		D1
	63/64	34		D1
	64/65	17		D1
	65/66	20		D1
	66/67	31		D1
	67/68	34		D1

NIVEN John Gordon
b. Coatbridge 15.5.1921
Renfrew Jnrs
Dundee

Club	Season	Apps	Gls	Div
East Fife	46/47	24		D2
	47/48	30		D2
	48/49	23		D1
	49/50	22		D1
	50/51	2		D1
Kilmarnock	51/52	30		D2
	52/53	30		D2

NOBLE Andrew
Polbeth A

Club	Season	Apps	Gls	Div
East Fife	71/72			
	72/73	3	4	D1
	73/74	1		D1

NORMAN Eric
Sauchie

Club	Season	Apps	Gls	Div
Partick T	63/64	3		D1
	64/65			
	65/66	2		D1
Adelaide C				

NORRIS Robert
b. c1938 d. ?.3.2003
Rutherglen Glencairn

Club	Season	Apps	Gls	Div
Dundee U	58/59	2		D2
	59/60	24	5	D2
	60/61	1		D1
South Shields				

NUORANEN Semi
b. Finland Caps: FIN - 33

Club	Season	Apps	Gls	Div
Partick T	65/66	1		D1

NUTLEY Robert
b. Paisley 10.9.1916

Club	Season	Apps	Gls	Div
Hibernian	46/47	1		D1
Portsmouth	46/47	9	1	FL
Queen of the South	47/48	15	3	D1

OAKES John
b. Hamilton 6.12.1919
Queen of the South
Huddersfield T

Club	Season	Apps	Gls	Div
Queen of the South	46/47	22	7	D1
Blackburn R	46/47	16	2	FL
	47/48	19	7	FL
Manchester C	48/49	34	5	FL
	49/50	22	1	FL
	50/51	21	3	FL
Queen of the South	51/52	26	5	D1
	52/53	28	5	D1
	53/54	28	2	D1
	54/55	26	3	D1
	55/56	17	3	D1
	56/57	30	6	D1
	57/58	25	4	D1
	58/59	26	3	D1

O'BRIEN Andrew

Club	Season	Apps	Gls	Div
Falkirk	63/64	1		D1

O'BRIEN George
b. Dunfermline 22.11.1935
Blairhall Colliery

Club	Season	Apps	Gls	Div
Dunfermline A	55/56	24	4	D1
	56/57	14	5	D1
Leeds U	56/57	8		FL
	57/58	18	3	FL
	58/59	17	3	FL
Southampton	59/60	42	23	FL
	60/61	41	22	FL
	61/62	38	28	FL
	62/63	42	22	FL
	63/64	24	16	FL
	64/65	41	32	FL
	65/66	16	11	FL
Leyton Orient	65/66	7		FL
	66/67	10	3	FL
Aldershot	66/67	20	4	FL
	67/68	18	3	4 FL

O'CONNOR Derek A
b. Edinburgh 8.1.1955
Edinburgh A

Club	Season	Apps	Sub	Gls	Div
East Fife	73/74	9	4	2	D1
	74/75	18	1	7	D2
	75/76	17	1	4	D1
	76/77	14	1	4	D1
St Johnstone	76/77	12	1	3	D1
	77/78	37	1	19	D1
	78/79	11		1	D1
Heart of Midlothian	78/79	18		8	P
	79/80	25	2	12	D1
	80/81	13	3	4	P
	81/82	12	2	4	D1
Berwick R	L 81/82	10		6	D2
Heart of Midlothian	82/83	37	1	17	D1
	83/84	5	6	1	P
	84/85		3	1	P
Meadowbank T	L 84/85	6		1	D1
Dunfermline A	84/85	9		1	D2
Brechin C	84/85	5	2	1	D1
Berwick R	85/86	12	2	6	D2
	86/87	24	7	6	D2
Broxburn A					
Penicuik A					

O'CONNOR Patrick
Kilmarnock Amateurs
Clydebank Jnrs

Club	Season	Apps	Gls	Div
Kilmarnock	57/58			D1
	58/59	3		D1
	59/60	14	1	D1
	60/61	1		D1
	61/62	3		D1
	62/63	25	5	D1
	63/64	23	1	D1
	64/65	1	1	D1
	65/66	7		D1
	66/67	29	1	D1
Chicago Spurs	67	4	1	NA
Kansas City Spurs				

O'DONNELL Edward
b. Falkirk 4.3.1947

Club	Season	Apps	Gls	Div
Falkirk	63/64	16	1	D1
	64/65	3		D1
Heart of Midlothian	65/66	3		D1
St Johnstone	66/67	8	2	2 D1
Brechin C	67/68	24	4	D2
	68/69		2	D2
Gala Fairydean				

O'DONNELL James
Weirs Recreation

Club	Season	Apps	Gls	Div
Morton	73/74	1		D1

O'DONNELL William
b. Clydebank 9.8.1924
Yoker A

Club	Season	Apps	Gls	Div
Partick T	46/47	28	15	D1
	47/48	11	5	D1
	48/49	23	7	D1
	49/50			D1
	50/51	12	9	D1
Northampton T	51/52	22	10	FL
	52/53	46	27	FL
	53/54	37	7	FL
Shrewsbury T	54/55	42	13	FL
	55/56	41	19	FL
	56/57	34	12	FL
	57/58	13	1	FL

OGILVIE Duncan Henderson
b. Glasgow 8.10.1911 d. c1970 Caps: S - 1
Alva Albion R

Club	Season	Apps	Gls	Div
Motherwell	32/33	19	8	D1
	33/34			D1
	34/35			D1
Huddersfield T	35/36	10		FL
	36/37	18	4	FL
Motherwell	37/38	36	18	D1
	38/39	36	9	D1
Falkirk	46/47	4		D1
Hamilton A	46/47	12	4	D1
	47/48	3		D2
Dundee U	48/49	19		D2

OGILVIE John Forrest
b. Motherwell 28.10.1928
Thornliewood U

Club	Season	Apps	Gls	Div
Hibernian	48/49	6		D1
	49/50	5		D1
	50/51	23		D1
	51/52			D1
	52/53			D1
	53/54	1		D1
	54/55			D1
Sheffield U	T 55/56			FL
Leicester C	55/56	24		FL
	56/57	38		FL
	57/58	15		FL
	58/59	5	2	FL
Mansfield T	59/60	17		FL
	60/61	7	1	FL

OGSTON John Kessack
b. Aberdeen 15.1.1939
Banks o'Dee

Club	Season	Apps	Gls	Div
Aberdeen	58/59	3		D1
	59/60	16		D1
	60/61	26		D1
	61/62	31		D1
	62/63	34		D1
	63/64	34		D1
	64/65	34		D1
	65/66	1		D1
Liverpool	65/66			FL
	66/67	1		FL
	67/68			FL
Doncaster R	68/69	31		FL
	69/70	38		FL
	70/71	1		FL
Buckie Thistle				
Huntly				

O'HARA Albert Edward
b. Glasgow 28.10.1935
Shettleston Jnrs

Club	Season	Apps	Gls	Div
Falkirk	55/56	32	6	D1
	56/57	31	4	D1
	57/58	32	8	D1
Everton	58/59	21	2	FL
	59/60	8		FL
Rotherham U	59/60	11	2	FL
	60/61	9	1	FL
Morton	61/62	29	5	D2
Barnsley	62/63	45	16	FL
	63/64	41	10	FL
	64/65	41	10	FL
Bloemfontein				

O'HARA Alexander C
b. Glasgow 21.10.1956

Club	Season				Div
Rangers	73/74	18	1	4	D1
	74/75	2	2	1	D1
	75/76	1		3	P
	76/77	5		2	P
Partick T	77/78	25	3	10	P
	78/79	26	8	8	P
	79/80	33	1	5	P
	80/81	32		7	P
	81/82	17	6	3	P
	82/83	32		3	D1
	83/84	21	3	8	D1
Morton	84/85	24	3	1	P
	85/86	32	1	4	D1
	86/87	40		2	D1
	87/88	35	5	1	P
	88/89	21	2		D1
	89/90	19	10	3	D1
Hamilton A	90/91	19	5	1	D1
Glenafton A					

O'HARA Daniel
b. Airdrie 28.8.1937
Fauldhouse U

Club	Season				Div
Celtic	59/60	6		1	D1
	60/61				D1
Cork Hibernian	L 60/61				
Celtic	61/62				D1
Mansfield T	L 61/62	3		1	FL
Albion R	62/63				D2
Coltness U	T				
Armadale Thistle					

O'HARA George
Shettleston

Club	Season				Div
Dundee	55/56	12		5	D1
	56/57	28		9	D1
	57/58	15		5	D1
Southend U	58/59				FL
Queen of the South	58/59	10			D1

O'HARA Ray

Club	Season				Div
Arbroath	73/74		3		D1
	74/75	1	2		D1
Peterhead					
Keith					

OLIPHANT Charles
Petershill
Kilsyth R
Johnstone Burgh

Club	Season				Div
Ayr U	64/65	13		3	D2
	65/66	32			D2
	66/67	16	2	1	D1
Albion R	67/68	34	1	1	D2
	68/69				D2
	69/70	15	2		D2

f **OLIVER James Robert**
b. Maddiston 3.12.1941
Woodburn A
Linlithgow Rose

Club	Season				Div
Falkirk	58/59	5		1	D1
	59/60	27		3	D2
	60/61	13		1	D2
	61/62	32		7	D1
Norwich C	62/63	27		7	FL
	63/64	9		4	FL
	64/65	4		3	FL
Brighton & HA	64/65	5			FL
	65/66	23	6	3	FL
	66/67	6		2	FL
	67/68	3		1	FL
Colchester U	67/68	14	1		FL
	68/69	34	7	9	FL
	69/70	17	2	1	FL
Kings Lynn					
Lowestoft T					
Gorleston T					

OLIVER Peter Francis Raeside
b. Dunfermline 14.8.1948
Lochore Welfare

Club	Season				Div
Heart of Midlothian	65/66				D1
	66/67				D1
	67/68				D1
	68/69				D1
	69/70	33			D1
	70/71	20			D1
	71/72	7	1		D1
	72/73	15	2		D1
	73/74	1			D1
York C	74/75	34			FL
	75/76	7			FL
Huddersfield T	76/77	41		1	FL

OMAND William
b. Glasgow
Giffnock Park

Club	Season				Div
Queen's Park	51/52	20		3	D2
	52/53	29		8	D2
	53/54	29		13	D2
	54/55	19		5	D2
	55/56	26		11	D2
	56/57	21		6	D1
	57/58	17		3	D1
	58/59	23		5	D2
	59/60	31		4	D2
	60/61	27		4	D2
	61/62	16		1	D2
	62/63	1			D2

O'NEIL Joseph
b. Glasgow 15.8.1931
Bridgeton Waverley

Club	Season				Div
Aberdeen	50/51	1			D1
	51/52				D1
	52/53				D1
Southend U	L 52/53	16		7	FL
	53/54	8		4	FL
Aberdeen	53/54	10		5	D1
	54/55	12		4	D1
	55/56				D1
Leicester C	55/56				FL
	56/57				FL
	57/58	5		2	FL
Northampton T	57/58	6		3	FL
	58/59	22		1	FL
Bath C	59/60				
	60/61				

O'NEILL George
Dunoon

Club	Season				Div
Partick T	66/67	5		2	D1
	67/68	31	1	4	D1
	68/69	29		1	D1
	69/70	4			D1
Morton	69/70	19	1	2	D1
	70/71	15		2	D1
Dunfermline A	70/71	7		1	D1
	71/72	18		2	D1
St Mirren	72/73	2			D2

O'NEILL William
b. Glasgow 30.12.1940
St Anthonys

Club	Season				Div
Celtic	60/61	2			D1
	61/62	2			D1
	62/63	13			D1
	63/64	5			D1
	64/65	4			D1
	65/66				D1
	66/67	18			D1
	67/68	6	1		D1
	68/69	4			D1
Carlisle U	69/70	15			FL

ORMOND Gilbert

Club	Season				Div
Airdrieonians	57/58	23		10	D1
	58/59	34		10	D1
	59/60	8		1	D1
Albion R	59/60				D2
Dundee U	60/61	8		3	D1
	60/61	30		3	D1
	61/62	6		1	D1
	62/63				D1
Cowdenbeath	63/64	6		1	D2
Alloa A	63/64	17		9	D2
	64/65	12		4	D2

ORMOND Hugh

Club	Season				Div
St Mirren	48/49	2			D1
	49/50	1			D1
Dundee U	50/51	1			D2
	51/52	6			D2

f **ORMOND Robert**
b. Falkirk
Grange R

Club	Season				Div
Falkirk	54/55	23		9	D1
	55/56	21		10	D1
	56/57	8		3	D1
	57/58				D1
Airdrieonians	58/59	6		4	D1
	59/60	4			D1

f **ORMOND William Esplin**
b. Falkirk 23.2.1927 d. 4.5.1984 Caps: S - 6
Gairdoch Juveniles
Stenhousemuir

Club	Season				Div
Hibernian	46/47	15		4	D1
	47/48	23		12	D1
	48/49	12		2	D1
	49/50	30		11	D1
	50/51	23		7	D1
	51/52	19		13	D1
	52/53	26		9	D1
	53/54	26		12	D1
	54/55	30		12	D1
	55/56	29		18	D1
	56/57	25		8	D1
	57/58	25		8	D1
	58/59	26		5	D1
	59/60	26		8	D1
	60/61	15		3	D1
Falkirk	61/62	23		4	D1
	62/63	3			D1

O'ROURKE James
b. Edinburgh
Holycross Academy

Club	Season				Div
Hibernian	62/63	17		2	D1
	63/64	10		3	D1
	64/65	1			D1
	65/66	21		10	D1
	66/67	23		6	D1
	67/68	13	5	4	D1
	68/69	27	2	6	D1
	69/70	8	3	1	D1
	70/71	18		6	D1
	71/72	25	2	11	D1
	72/73	25	3	17	D1
	73/74	16	3	14	D1
St Johnstone	74/75	34		15	D1
	75/76	34		8	P
Motherwell	76/77	19	4	9	P
	77/78	15	8	5	P

ORR Anderson
b. Glasgow 19.12.1923

Club	Season				Div
Third Lanark	47/48	10		3	D1
	48/49	27		1	D1
	49/50	28		3	D1
	50/51	20		2	D1
Nottingham F	51/52	24			FL
	52/53	3			FL
	53/54	15			FL
	54/55	4			FL

ORR James

Club	Season				Div
Airdrieonians	47/48	3		1	D1
	48/49				D2
	49/50	18			D2
	50/51	10		4	D1
Albion R	50/51				D2
	51/52				D2
	52/53	11		4	D2

ORR John
b. Lennoxtown 2.3.1947
Rutherglen Glencairn

Club	Season				Div
Stirling A	66/67	4			D1
	67/68	8	1		D1
	68/69				D2
Stranraer	68/69			5	D2
	69/70	29	2	6	D2
	70/71			1	D2

ORR Robert

Club	Season			Div
Rangers	58/59	1		D1

ORR Thomas Bingham
b. Greenock 21.4.1924 d. ?.?.1972 Caps: S - 2
Morton Jnrs

Club	Season			Div
Morton	46/47	2	1	D1
	47/48	26	14	D1
	48/49	21	5	D1
	49/50	26	8	D2
	50/51	20	11	D1
	51/52	22	8	D1
	52/53	13	4	D2
	53/54	23	3	D2
	54/55			D2
	55/56			D2
	56/57			D2
	57/58			D2

OSBORNE Brian
Glasgow U

Club	Season				Div
St Mirren	70/71		2		D1
	71/72	9			D2
	72/73	5	1	1	D2

OSBORNE William
Dunoon A

Club	Season				Div
Morton	69/70	17	1	11	D1
	70/71	20	1	8	D1
	71/72	21	1	8	D1
	72/73	20	4	8	D1
	73/74	11	6	5	D1
	74/75	15	8	5	D1
Stranraer	75/76	10	3		D2

O'SULLIVAN Patrick
Saltcoats V
St Anthonys
Airdrieonians

Club	Season		Div
Celtic	46/47	4	D1
Alloa A	47/48		D2
Stirling A	48/49		D2

Newton Stewart
Coleraine
Wigtown & Bladnoch

OWENS James

Club	Season		Div
Aberdeen	47/48	1	D1

OWER John Campion Taylor
b. Glasgow 2.1.1939
Kirkintilloch Rob Roy

Club	Season		Div
St Johnstone	60/61	5	D1
	61/62	1	D1
	62/63	11	D2
Workington	62/63	22	FL
	63/64	46	FL
	64/65	37	FL
	65/66	45	FL
	66/67	24	FL
	67/68	25	FL

PALMER Alexander

Club	Season		Div
Third Lanark	46/47	21	D1
	47/48	12	D1
Dundee U	48/49		D2
Clyde	49/50		D1
	50/51		D1
Airdrieonians	50/51		D1

PALMER Charles Gardner
b. Paisley 21.5.1947
Johnstone Burgh

Club	Season			Div
St Mirren	69/70	3	1	D1
	70/71	3		D1
Stirling A	71/72	20		D2
Washington Diplomats				
Vancouver Whitecaps	74	15	1	NA
	75	6	1	NA
Morton	75/76		1	D1

PARK Donald J
b. Inverness 19.7.1953
Inverness Caley

Club	Season				Div
Heart of Midlothian	72/73	16	2	6	D1
	73/74	13	2	4	D1
	74/75	7	4	1	D1
	75/76	18	8	3	P
	76/77	26	7	3	P
	77/78	32	1	6	D1
	78/79	2	1	1	P
Partick T	78/79	30	1	2	P
	79/80	29	2	3	P
	80/81	31	2	3	P
	81/82	34	2	5	P
	82/83	33		12	D1
Heart of Midlothian	83/84	26	4	4	P
	84/85	16	6	3	P
Brechin C	85/86	21	12	1	D1
	86/87	4	1		D1
Meadowbank T	86/87	12	2	2	D2
	87/88	27	4	3	D1
	88/89	5	12	2	D1
	89/90	9	11	4	D1
	90/91	2			D1

PARK John
Shotts Bon Accord

Club	Season			Div
Stirling A	60/61			D2
	61/62	11	7	D1
	62/63			D2
	63/64	10		D1
Raith R	63/64	12	8	D2
	64/65	15	12	D2
Forfar A *	65/66	18	11	D2
	66/67	2		D2
Montrose *	67/68	4	2	D2

PARK Robert

Club	Season		Div
Queen of the South	51/52	1	D1
St Mirren	52/53	28	D1
	53/54	23	D1

PARKE John
b. Bangor 6.8.1937 Caps: NI - 14
Cliftonville
Linfield

Club	Season			Div
Hibernian	63/64	10		D1
	64/65	11		D1
Sunderland	64/65	24		FL
	65/66	31	2	FL
	66/67	7	5	FL
	67/68	21		FL
Mechelen				

PARKER Alexander Hershaw
b. Irvine 2.8.1935 Caps: S - 15
Kello R

Club	Season			Div
Falkirk	52/53	3		D1
	53/54	3	2	D1
	54/55	24		D1
	55/56	32		D1
	56/57	30		D1
	57/58	28		D1
Everton	58/59	26	1	FL
	59/60	38	2	FL
	60/61	41		FL
	61/62	31		FL
	62/63	33	2	FL
	63/64	17		FL
	64/65	12		FL
Southport	65/66	38		FL
	66/67	32		FL
	67/68	6		FL
Ballymena U				

PARKER Robert
b. Newbridge c1924 d. Edinburgh ?.3.1997
Edinburgh Waverley
Bathgate Thistle

Club	Season			Div
Partick T	46/47	11		D1
Heart of Midlothian	47/48	25	1	D1
	48/49	15		D1
	49/50	28	2	D1
	50/51	27	1	D1
	51/52	29	6	D1
	52/53	27	2	D1
	53/54	26	2	D1
	54/55	30	4	D1
	55/56	14		D1
	56/57	22	1	D1
	57/58	4		D1

PARLANE Derek James
b. Helensburgh 5.5.1953 Caps: S - 12
Queen's Park

Club	Season				Div
Rangers	70/71	2	2		D1
	71/72	2			D1
	72/73	29	1	19	D1
	73/74	28	1	14	D1
	74/75	30	1	17	D1
	75/76	17	7	5	P
	76/77	31	2	16	P
	77/78	6	16	5	P
	78/79	21	3	4	P
	79/80	2	1		P
Leeds U	79/80	11		3	FL
	80/81	22	4	5	FL
	81/82	12		2	FL
	82/83		1		FL
Hong Kong	L 82/83				
Manchester C	83/84	40	1	16	FL
	84/85	7		4	FL
Swansea C	84/85	21		3	FL
Racing Jet	85/86				
Rochdale	86/87	23		7	FL
	87/88	19		3	FL
Airdrieonians	87/88	9		4	D1

PARLANE James

Club	Season			Div
Rangers	46/47	4	2	D1
	47/48	1	1	D1
Airdrieonians	47/48	10	7	D1
	48/49			D2
	49/50	4	1	D2

PATERSON Alec

Club	Season	Apps	Goals	Div
St Mirren	54/55	1		D1
Albion R	55/56			D2

PATERSON Alexander
b. Bridge of Allan
Kilsyth R

Club	Season	Apps	Goals	Div
Stirling A	54/55	9	1	D1
	55/56	3		D1

PATERSON Alexander C

Club	Season	Apps	Goals	Div
Stenhousemuir	52/53	3		D2
	53/54	30		D2
	54/55			D2
	55/56			D2
Ayr U	56/57	18		D1

PATERSON Arthur
b. Glasgow
Inverurie Loco

Club	Season	Apps	Goals	Div
Aberdeen	58/59	2		D1

Irvine Meadow

Club	Season	Apps	Goals	Div
Ayr U	64/65	25	5	D2
	65/66	35	15	D2
	66/67	10	3	D1

Clydebank

PATERSON Edward
Larkhall Thistle
Arthurlie
Portsmouth

Club	Season	Apps	Goals	Div
Hamilton A	46/47	2		D1

PATERSON Ian

Club	Season	Apps	Goals	Div
Third Lanark	63/64	4	1	D1

PATERSON James
Dunfermline U

Club	Season	Apps	Goals	Div
Dunfermline A	71/72	23	3	D1

PATERSON John
b. Colchester ?.?.1926 d. Edinburgh 14.1.2000
Penicuik Thistle

Club	Season	Apps	Goals	Div
Hibernian	46/47			D1
	47/48			D1
	48/49	11		D1
	49/50	25		D1
	50/51	30		D1
	51/52	30		D1
	52/53	28		D1
	53/54	29		D1
	54/55	30		D1
	55/56	32		D1
	56/57	28		D1
	57/58	27		D1
	58/59	13		D1
Ayr U	59/60	26		D1
	60/61	7		D1

PATERSON John

Club	Season	Apps	Goals	Div
Albion R	48/49	19	1	D1
	49/50	3		D2

PATERSON John

Club	Season	Apps	Goals	Div
Dumbarton	72/73	3		D1
	73/74	15 2	2	D1

Cambuslang R

PATERSON Robert
b. Glasgow

Club	Season	Apps	Goals	Div
Queen's Park	49/50	1		D2
	50/51	4		D2
	51/52	11		D2
	52/53			D2
Aberdeen	53/54	2		D1
	54/55	1		D1
	55/56	5		D1

PATERSON Robin

Club	Season	Apps	Goals	Div
Motherwell	59/60	1		D1

PATERSON William Alexander Kennedy
b. Kinlochleven 25.2.1930
Inverness Thistle
Ransome & Marles

Club	Season	Apps	Goals	Div
Doncaster R	49/50			FL
	50/51	1		FL
	51/52	24		FL
	52/53	35		FL
	53/54	41		FL
	54/55	12		FL
Newcastle U	54/55	4		FL
	55/56	15	1	FL
	56/57	1		FL
	57/58	2		FL
Rangers	58/59	3		D1
	59/60	23		D1
	60/61	30		D1
	61/62	11		D1
Morton	62/63			D2

Cheltenham T
Inverness Caley
Hamilton Steelers

PATIENCE Alistair
Inverness Clachnacuddin

Club	Season	Apps	Goals	Div
Aberdeen	58/59	2		D1

Inverness Caley

PATON Andrew
b. Dreghorn 2.1.1923 Caps: S - 2
Irvine Meadow
Kello R

Club	Season	Apps	Goals	Div
Motherwell	46/47	27		D1
	47/48	28		D1
	48/49	29		D1
	49/50	29		D1
	50/51	26		D1
	51/52	23		D1
	52/53	28		D1
	53/54	29		D2
	54/55	16		D1
	55/56	33		D1
	56/57	29		D1
	57/58	5		D1
Hamilton A	58/59	32		D2
	59/60	1		D2

PATON David P

Club	Season	Apps	Goals	Div
Stenhousemuir	49/50	21	1	D2
	50/51			D2
Stirling A	51/52	27		D1
	52/53	1		D2
Stenhousemuir	53/54	20		D2

PATON Gordon
Petershill
Glasgow Perthshire

Club	Season	Apps	Goals	Div
Kilmarnock	49/50	19	4	D2
	50/51	6		D2
Morton	51/52	2		D1
Cowdenbeath	52/53	25	1	D2

PATON George

Club	Season	Apps	Goals	Div
Heart of Midlothian	47/48	3		D1

PATON John
Burnbank Swifts
Shettleston

Club	Season	Apps	Goals	Div
Dunfermline A	62/63	1		D1
Yiewsley	63/64			
Hamilton A	64/65	20	1	D2
Montrose	65/66	25		D2
	66/67	6		D2

PATON John Aloysius
b. Glasgow 2.4.1923
St Marys Calton
Dennistoun Waverley
Celtic

Club	Season	Apps	Goals	Div
Chelsea	46/47	18	3	FL
Celtic	47/48	28	6	D1
	48/49	24	6	D1
Brentford	49/50	23	5	FL
	50/51	31	4	FL
	51/52	36	5	FL
Watford	52/53	33	2	FL
	53/54	37	11	FL
	54/55	14	4	FL

PATON Robert
Leeds U

Club	Season	Apps	Goals	Div
Dunfermline A	61/62	8	5	D1
	62/63	11	3	D1
	63/64			D1
	64/65	10	5	D1
	65/66	18	15	D1
	66/67	26	7	D1
	67/68	32	13	D1
	68/69	26	12	D1
	69/70	10	2	D1
	70/71			D1
	71/72	2		D1
Berwick R	72/73	5		D2

PATON Robert Simpson Reid
b. West Calder 27.1.1936
Woodmuir Colliery
Newtongrange Star

Club	Season	Apps	Goals	Div
Heart of Midlothian	57/58	3	1	D1
	58/59	5		D1
	59/60			D1
	60/61			D1
	61/62	17	4	D1
	62/63	19	11	D1
	63/64	6	2	D1
Oxford U	64/65	2	1	FL
Bedford T				
Cambridge C	69/70			
Washington Darts	71	5		NA
Atlanta Chiefs	71	7		NA
	72	13	2	NA
Atlanta Apollo	73	18	2	NA

PATON William

Club	Season	Apps	Goals	Div
Rangers	47/48	4	1	D1
	48/49	19	9	D1
	49/50	7	2	D1
	50/51	19	5	D1
	51/52	15	5	D1
	52/53	6	5	D1
	53/54	19	9	D1
	54/55	19	3	D1
	55/56	1	1	D1
	56/57	1		D1
Ayr U	56/57	30	4	D1
	57/58			D2
	58/59			D2
	59/60	26	3	D1
	60/61	3		D1
	61/62	5		D2

PATON William
Ayr U Boys Club

Club	Season	Apps	Goals	Div
Ayr U	74/75	1		D1
	75/76	11		P
	76/77	2		P

PATON William J
Bo'ness U

Club	Season	Apps	Goals	Div
Motherwell	47/48	5	1	D1
	48/49	1		D1
	49/50	5		D1
	50/51			D1
	51/52			D1

PATTERSON James

Luncarty

Club	Season			Div
Queen of the South	49/50	9	3	D1
	50/51			
	51/52	29	19	D1
	52/53	30	19	D1
	53/54	15	16	D1
	54/55	25	9	D1
	55/56	31	26	D1
	56/57	29	17	D1
	57/58	30	17	D1
	58/59	32	7	D1
	59/60			D2
	60/61			D2
	61/62			D2
	62/63	9		D1

PATTIE George

Blairgowrie Jnrs

Club	Season			Div
Dundee U	61/62	1		D1
	62/63	5	1	D1
	63/64			D1
Brechin C	64/65	15	2	D2
Montrose	64/65	10	3	D2

PATTILLO John
b. c1915 d. Perth ?.8.2002

Mugiemoss
Hall Russells

Club	Season			Div
Aberdeen	38/39	9	11	D1
Dundee	46/47	23	14	D2
	47/48	26	13	D1
	48/49	25	9	D1
	49/50	21		D1
	50/51	13	4	D1
	51/52	15	3	D1
Aberdeen	52/53			
St Johnstone	52/53	8	2	D2

PATTISON Frank McKay
b. Barrhead 23.12.1930

St Rochs
Arthurlie
Hibernian
Alloa A

Club	Season			Div
Barnsley	51/52	16	2	FL
	52/53			FL
	53/54	9	2	FL
	54/55	4	1	FL
Stirling A	55/56	21	1	D1
	56/57			D2
Albion R				
St Johnstone	58/59	3		D2

PAUL William

Bonnyrigg Rose

Club	Season		Div
Third Lanark	63/64	19	D1
East Fife	64/65	17	D2

PAUL William Alexander
b. Glasgow 21.2.1947

Club	Season			Div
Rangers	66/67		1	D1
	67/68			D1
Aberdeen	68/69		1	D1
Stirling A	69/70	8	3	D2

PAYNE Graeme
b. Dundee 13.2.1956

Club	Season				Div
Dundee U	73/74	18	5	1	D1
	74/75	8	3		D1
	75/76	15	4	2	P
	76/77	34	2	1	P
	77/78	31	2	1	P
	78/79	19	7	3	P
	79/80	18	1		P
	80/81	19	3	3	P
	81/82	3	3	1	P
	82/83	2	1		P
Morton L	82/83	16	2	2	P
Dundee U	83/84		1		P
Arbroath	83/84	12		1	D2
	84/85	32		3	D2
Brechin C	84/85	5	2	2	D1
	85/86	23	6	1	D1
	86/87	2	2		D1
St Johnstone	86/87	18	8	5	D2

PAYNE Kenneth M
b. Dundee 14.1.1952

St Columbas BC

Club	Season				Div
Arbroath	70/71			2	D2
	71/72	34	1	12	D2
	72/73	34		8	D1
	73/74	7	8	1	D1
	74/75	3	6	2	D1
Forfar A	75/76	11		1	D2
	76/77	19	3	7	D2
	77/78	17	4	3	D2

PEACOCK Ernest Anderson
b. Renfrew 10.8.1942

Troon

Club	Season		Div
Falkirk	61/62	3	D1
	62/63		D1
	63/64		D1
Workington	63/64	1	FL

PEACOCK Robert
b. Coleraine 29.9.1928 Caps: NI - 31

Coleraine YMCA
Coleraine
Glentoran 48/49

Club	Season			Div
Celtic	49/50	4		D1
	50/51	30	5	D1
	51/52	25	6	D1
	52/53	22	8	D1
	53/54	30	1	D1
	54/55	29		D1
	55/56	33	1	D1
	56/57	31		D1
	57/58	31	2	D1
	58/59	27	3	D1
	59/60	33	2	D1
	60/61	24	4	D1
Coleraine	61/62			
Morton L	61/62			D2
Hamilton Steelers	62			

PEARSON James

Club	Season			Div
East Stirlingshire	61/62	3		D2
Aberdeen	61/62	3	1	D1
Greenock				

PEARSON James Findlay
b. Falkirk 24.3.1953

Gairdoch U

Club	Season				Div
St Johnstone	69/70				D1
	70/71	13	1	7	D1
	71/72	22	7	11	D1
	72/73	32	1	13	D1
	73/74	29		9	D1
Everton	74/75	17	9	3	FL
	75/76	26	3	5	FL
	76/77	12	4	4	FL
	77/78	21	1	3	FL
Newcastle U	78/79	9		3	FL
	79/80	2			FL
Barrow					
Gateshead					
North Shields					
Gateshead					
Workington					

PEARSON Thomas Usher
b. Edinburgh 6.3.1913 d. ?.3.1998 Caps: S - 2

Murrayfield A

Club	Season			Div
Heart of Midlothian T	32/33			D1
Newcastle U	33/34	4	1	FL
	34/35	25	13	FL
	35/36	40	12	FL
	36/37	37	7	FL
	37/38	41	4	FL
	38/39	6	2	FL
	46/47	38	4	FL
Aberdeen	47/48	9	1	D1
	48/49	15	2	D1
	49/50	19	3	D1
	50/51	19	3	D1
	51/52	20	1	D1
	52/53	2		D1

PEAT J

Club	Season		Div
Partick T	49/50	1	D1

PEAT William

Club	Season			Div
Hibernian	46/47	11	3	D1

PEDEN George Wright Watson
b. Rosewell 12.4.1943

Arniston R

Club	Season				Div
Heart of Midlothian	65/66	1			D1
	66/67	12			D1
Lincoln C	66/67	2			FL
	67/68	46		4	FL
	68/69	46		5	FL
	69/70	42		2	FL
	70/71	27		1	FL
	71/72				FL
	72/73	26	1	3	FL
	73/74	10	1		FL
Worksop T					
Lincoln U					
Skegness T					

PEDEN James

Club	Season			Div
Airdrieonians	47/48	4	1	D1
Falkirk	48/49	1		D1

PEEBLES George
B. c1936
Gowanhill U
Dunipace Jnrs

Club	Season	Apps		Gls	Div
Stirling A	T 52/53				D2
Dunfermline A	53/54				D2
	54/55				D1
	55/56	25		2	D1
	56/57	26		5	D1
	57/58				D2
	58/59	32		4	D1
	59/60	33		9	D1
	60/61	34		7	D1
	61/62	34		7	D1
	62/63	30		3	D1
	63/64	32		9	D1
	64/65	13		2	D1
	65/66	9		2	D1
Stirling A	66/67	31		5	D1
	67/68	28	2	5	D1
	68/69			5	D2
	69/70	2			D2
	70/71				D2

PEEBLES James

Club	Season	Apps	Gls	Div
Raith R	60/61	1		D1

PENMAN Andrew
b. Rosyth 20.2.1943 d. Rosyth 20.7.1994
Caps: S - 1
Everton

Club	Season	Apps		Gls	Div
Dundee	58/59	2			D1
	59/60	19		5	D1
	60/61	16		4	D1
	61/62	32		17	D1
	62/63	34		10	D1
	63/64	29		16	D1
	64/65	34		24	D1
	65/66	33		15	D1
	66/67	16		9	D1
Rangers	67/68	24	2	8	D1
	68/69	26		15	D1
	69/70	25	5	10	D1
	70/71	3	5		D1
	71/72	10	1	3	D1
Arbroath	72/73	9			D1
	73/74	32		3	D1
	74/75	24	3	5	D1
	75/76	10	1	2	D1
Inverness Caley	75/76				
	76/77				
	77/78				
	78/79				

PENMAN William

Club	Season	Apps	Gls	Div
Raith R	48/49			D2
	49/50	22	9	D1
	50/51	23	11	D1
	51/52	12	1	D1
	52/53	25	12	D1
	53/54	5	1	D1
Stirling A	53/54			D1
Raith R				
Montrose				
Dundee U	55/56	5		D2

PENMAN William Salmond Thomson
b. Wemyss 7.8.1939
St Andrews U

Club	Season	Apps		Gls	Div
Rangers	60/61	3			D1
	61/62				D1
	62/63				D1
Newcastle U	62/63	6		3	FL
	63/64	23		8	FL
	64/65	22		7	FL
	65/66	11	1		FL
Swindon T	66/67	39	1	10	FL
	67/68	34	4	6	FL
	68/69	13	8	1	FL
	69/70	1			FL
Walsall	70/71	39		1	FL
	71/72	38	2	2	FL
	72/73	41	3	3	FL
Dundalk	73/74				
Seattle Sounders	74	13		1	NA
Redditch U					

PERRIE David

Club	Season	Apps	Gls	Div
Falkirk	48/49	1	1	D1

PERRY Edward

Club	Season	Apps	Gls	Div
Queen's Park	57/58	11	1	D1
Falkirk				
Raith R	58/59	5		D1

PERSSON Orjan
b. Sweden 27.8.1942 Caps: Swe - 47
Orgryte

Club	Season	Apps		Gls	Div
Dundee U	64/65	20		4	D1
	65/66	29		2	D1
	66/67	30		9	D1
Rangers	67/68	32		14	D1
	68/69	28	3	8	D1
	69/70	9			D1
Orgryte					

PETERS John

Club	Season	Apps	Gls	Div
Airdrieonians	47/48	23		D1

PETERSEN Jens
b. Esbjerg 22.12.1941 Caps: Den - 21
Esbjerg

Club	Season	Apps		Gls	Div
Aberdeen	64/65	3			D1
	65/66	23			D1
	66/67	30		1	D1
	67/68	32		3	D1
	68/69	34		1	D1
	69/70	17	3	2	D1
Rapid Vienna					

PETRIE John

Club	Season	Apps	Gls	Div
Third Lanark	46/47	11		D1
	47/48	14		D1
	48/49	7		D1
	49/50	8		D1
	50/51	8		D1
	51/52	10		D1
Ayr U	51/52			D2
St Johnstone	51/52	2		D2
	52/53			D2
	53/54	2		D2

PETTIGREW Thomas

Club	Season	Apps	Gls	Div
Queen's Park	56/57			D1
	57/58			D1
Stirling A	58/59	28		D1
	59/60	34		D1
	60/61			D2
	61/62	17		D1
Chelmsford C				

PETTIGREW William H
b. Motherwell 29.9.1953 Caps: S - 5
Bonkle Amateurs
Hibernian
East Kilbride Thistle

Club	Season	Apps		Gls	Div
Motherwell	73/74	10	1	4	D1
	74/75	21	7	20	D1
	75/76	35		22	P
	76/77	35	1	21	P
	77/78	26		7	P
	78/79	30		6	P
Dundee U	79/80	34	1	14	P
	80/81	14	6	6	P
Heart of Midlothian	81/82	35		16	D1
	82/83	26	7	10	D1
Morton	83/84	17		9	D1
	84/85	10	5	1	P
Hamilton A	84/85	3			D1

PHILLIBEN Thomas
b. Stirling
Gowanhill U

Club	Season	Apps	Gls	Div
Stirling A	54/55			D1
	55/56	8		D1
	56/57			D2

PHILLIP Iain Frederick
b. Broughty Ferry 14.2.1951
Broughty U
Broughty A

Club	Season	Apps		Gls	Div
Dundee	69/70				D1
	70/71	29	1		D1
	71/72	32			D1
	72/73	4			D1
Crystal Palace	72/73	30		1	FL
	73/74	5			FL
Dundee	73/74	26			D1
	74/75	17			D1
	75/76	23	4		P
	76/77	36		1	D1
	77/78	14	1		D1
	78/79	8		1	D1
Dundee U	78/79	9	1		P
	79/80	26		1	P
	80/81	28	2		P
	81/82	14	1		P
	82/83	5			P
Raith R	83/84	3	6		D1
	84/85	39			D2
	85/86	22			D2
Arbroath	86/87	36			D2
	87/88	24	1		D2

PHILLIPS Gerald G
b. Cheltenham 28.4.1956
Cumnock Jnrs

Club	Season	Apps		Gls	Div
Ayr U	74/75	13	2	4	D1
	75/76	12	3	4	P
	76/77	4	8		P
	77/78	7	3	2	P
	78/79	21	6	14	D1
Queen of the South	79/80	21		11	D2
	80/81	17	2	6	D2
	81/82	24	2	12	D1
Cumnock Jnrs					
Hamilton A	82/83	21		4	D1
	83/84	33	3	8	D1
	84/85	27	7	6	D1
	85/86	6	12	1	D1
	86/87	14	6	2	P
Cumnock Jnrs					

PHILLIPS John
b. Glasgow
Everton

Club	Season	Apps		Gls	Div
Dundee	64/65	4			D1
	65/66				D1
Airdrieonians	66/67	15		1	D1
	67/68	29		8	D1
	68/69	4	1	1	D1

PHILLIPS Samuel
b. Cumnock
Annbank U

Club	Season	Apps	Gls	Div
Third Lanark	52/53	10		D1
	53/54	15	3	D2

PHILP James

b. Lumphinnans c1914 d. Kirkcaldy 25.3.1998

Methil Hearts					
Denbeath Star					
Crossgates Primrose					
St Bernards	36/37				D2
	37/38				D2
	38/39				D2
East Fife	46/47				D2
	47/48				D2
	48/49	30			D1
	49/50	27			D1
	50/51	23			D1
	51/52	1			D1
Brechin C	52/53				D3
	53/54				D3
	54/55				D2

PICKEN Sammy

Airdrieonians	47/48	18		2	D1
	48/49				D2
	49/50	14		3	D2
	50/51	11		3	D1

PIERSON James

b. Glasgow

Corkerhill U					
Stirling A	55/56	11		1	D1
	56/57				D2
	57/58				D2
	58/59	30			D1
	59/60	27			D1
Falkirk	60/61	17			D2
	61/62	31		1	D1
	62/63	32			D1
	63/64	34			D1
	64/65	11			D1
Arbroath	65/66	29			D2
	66/67	33	1		D2
	67/68	28			D2
	68/69	8	5		D1

PINKERTON Robert

Craigmark Burntonians					
St Mirren	65/66	20		3	D1
	66/67	25	2	3	D1
	67/68	32	1	14	D2
	68/69	30	2	2	D1
	69/70	16	2	3	D1
	70/71	1	1		D1
Stranraer	70/71			3	D2
Maybole					

PINKERTON William J

Queen's Park	51/52	2			D2
	52/53	1			D2
	53/54				D2
	54/55	2			D2
	55/56				D2
	56/57				D1
	57/58	13			D1
	58/59	27			D2
	59/60	3			D2
	60/61	16			D2
	61/62	25			D2

PIRIE William J

b. Aberdeen 2.4.1949

Banks o'Dee					
Arcadia Shepherds					
Huntly					
Arbroath	71/72	10		7	D2
	72/73	34		14	D1
	73/74	24		12	D1
Aberdeen	73/74	9			D1
	74/75	7	4	4	D1
	75/76	8	10	7	P
Dundee	76/77	33		38	D1
	77/78	39		35	D1
	78/79	30	1	16	D1
	79/80	9		4	P

PIRRIE Alex

Partick T	46/47	1			D1
	47/48	1		1	D1
	48/49	13			D1

PITHIE James

b. Edinburgh ?.?.1928

Chesser U					
Hutcheson Vale					
Newtongrange Star					
Heart of Midlothian	46/47	4			D1

PLENDERLEITH John Boyd

b. Bellshill 6.10.1937 Caps: S - 1

Ferndale A					
Armadale Thistle					
Hibernian	54/55	22			D1
	55/56	24			D1
	56/57	24			D1
	57/58	9			D1
	58/59	22			D1
	59/60	22			D1
Manchester C	60/61	34			FL
	61/62	2			FL
	62/63	5			FL
Queen of the South	63/64	5			D1
Cape Town C					
Hellenic					

PLUMB Angus

b. Woolwich

Armadale Thistle					
Hibernian	48/49	7		7	D1
Falkirk	49/50	15		6	D1
	50/51	18		9	D1
	51/52	29		25	D2
	52/53	19		7	D1
	53/54	19		11	D1
	54/55	3			D1
East Fife	54/55	9		11	D1
	55/56	22		10	D1
	56/57	29		12	D1
East Stirlingshire	57/58				D2

POLLAND William

b. Armadale 28.7.1934

Wallhouse Rose					
Linlithgow Rose					
Raith R	55/56	24			D1
	56/57	34			D1
	57/58	34		1	D1
	58/59	32			D1
	59/60	31			D1
	60/61	33			D1
Heart of Midlothian	60/61	2			D1
	61/62	30			D1
	62/63	26			D1
	63/64	26		1	D1
	64/65	31			D1
	65/66	20		1	D1
	66/67	11	1		D1
Raith R	67/68	11			D1
	68/69	32			D1
	69/70	24	1	1	D1

POLLOCK Alan

Airdrie BC					
Airdrieonians	72/73	2			D1

POLLOCK Stewart

b. Bellshill 25.9.1933

Glenafton					
Partick T	53/54				D1
	54/55				D1
	55/56				D1
Motherwell	55/56	2			D1
Gillingham	56/57	10			FL
Ramsgate A					
Hamilton A	60/61	4			D2

PORTERFIELD John

b. Dunfermline 11.2.1946

Lochgelly Albert					
Lochore Welfare					
Leeds U					
Heart of Midlothian T					
Rangers T					
Cowdenbeath T	63/64	1			D2
Raith R	64/65	28			D2
	65/66				D2
	66/67				D2
	67/68	16		1	D1
Sunderland	67/68	8			FL
	68/69	22	9	1	FL
	69/70				FL
	70/71	37	3	2	FL
	71/72	36	1	5	FL
	72/73	41		5	FL
	73/74	40		2	FL
	74/75	14		1	FL
	75/76	20	2	1	FL
Reading L	76/77	5			FL
Sheffield W	77/78	38			FL
	78/79	45	1	2	FL
	79/80	20	2	1	FL
Rotherham U	79/80				FL

POULTON William Marshall

b. Coatbridge 23.12.1954

Airdrie BC					
Airdrieonians	72/73	6			D1
	73/74	1			D2
	74/75				D1
	75/76	1			D1
	76/77	32			D1
	77/78	28			D1
	78/79	6			D1
Queen of the South	78/79	10			D1
Stirling A	79/80				
Lesmahagow					

PRENTICE

Hibernian	59/60	1			D1

PRENTICE David

Queen's Park					
St Mirren	70/71	2	1		D1

PRENTICE John

b. Shotts

Carluke R					
Heart of Midlothian	49/50	2			D1
	50/51	4			D1
Rangers	50/51	1			D1
	51/52	19		2	D1
	52/53	30		8	D1
	53/54	18		5	D1
	54/55	18		2	D1
	55/56	10		1	D1
Falkirk	56/57	31		2	D1
	57/58	22		1	D1
	58/59	29		2	D1
Dumbarton					

PRENTICE Robert

b. Douglas Water 27.9.1953

Edina Hibs					
Dundee	71/72				D1
Newtongrange Star					
Celtic	72/73				D1
Heart of Midlothian	73/74	26	2	3	D1
	74/75	5	9	2	D1
	75/76	30	3	4	P
	76/77	25	8	2	P
	77/78	17	7	2	D1
	78/79	6	6		P
Toronto Blizzard	79	5			NA
	80	24			NA

PRESSLIE Allan Smith

b. 21.11.1940

Arbroath	59/60	4			D1
Inverness Caley					

PRESTON James
b. South Africa 1.5.1919

Club	Season				Div
Aberdeen	46/47	2			D1
	47/48				D1
	48/49	1			D1

PRESTON Thomas

Newtongrange Thistle

Club	Season				Div
Hibernian	53/54	3			D1
	54/55	23		3	D1
	55/56	19			D1
	56/57	17		2	D1
	57/58	28		7	D1
	58/59	29		3	D1
	59/60	17		12	D1
	60/61	27		5	D1
	61/62	29		1	D1
	62/63	21		1	D1
	63/64	15			D1
St Mirren	64/65	1			D1

PRICE Peter

Craigmark Bruntonians
Celtic   T

Club	Season				Div
St Mirren	51/52	2			D1
Gloucester C					
Darlington	L				
Ayr U	55/56			40	D2
	56/57	32		20	D1
	57/58			46	D2
	58/59			37	D2
	59/60	32		17	D1
	60/61	19		5	D1
	61/62	12		6	D2
Raith R	61/62	10		1	D1
Albion R	62/63				
Gladesville (Aus)					

PRICE William
b. Tarbolton 5.10.1934

Annbank U

Club	Season				Div
Airdrieonians	52/53				D1
	53/54				D1
	54/55				D2
	55/56	33		3	D1
	56/57	33		7	D1
	57/58	28		6	D1
Falkirk	58/59	10			D1
Celtic	61/62	23			D1
	62/63	27		3	D1
	63/64	1			D1
Berwick R	64/65				D2

PRINGLE Alexander
b. Edinburgh 8.11.1948

Club	Season				Div
Hibernian	68/69	1			D1
	69/70				D1
	70/71	5	3		D1
	71/72	1	1		D1
Dundee	72/73	9	1		D1
	73/74	5	5	1	D1
Clyde	74/75	6	1		D1
Tampa Bay Rowdies	75	14		1	NA
	76	22			NA
	77	1			NA
Washington Diplomat	77	17			NA
	78	11			NA

PRINTY Ian J D
b. 28.2.1950

Newtongrange Star

Club	Season				Div
East Fife	72/73	22			D1
	73/74	28			D1
	74/75	22	1		D2
Meadowbank T	75/76	18	2		D2
	76/77	37			D2
	77/78	30	1		D2

PRIOR Peter

Fauldhouse U

Club	Season				Div
Raith R	58/59	4		1	D1
Dundee U	59/60	5		2	D2
Hamilton A	60/61				D2
Fauldhouse U					

PROUDFOOT Archibald

Club	Season			Div
Edinburgh C				
East Fife	48/49	4		D1
	49/50	2		D1
	50/51	17		D1
Linfield				
Gloucester C				

PROUDFOOT J

Club	Season			Div
Third Lanark	47/48	1		D1

PROVAN Andrew McKelvie Hughes
b. Greenock 1.1.1944

Port Glasgow R

Club	Season				Div
St Mirren	61/62	3		1	D1
	62/63	5			D1
Barnsley	63/64	3			FL
York C	64/65	46		18	FL
	65/66	26		2	FL
	66/67	40	1	15	FL
	67/68	44		13	FL
	68/69	3		1	FL
Chester	68/69	33	4	12	FL
	69/70	45		6	FL
Wrexham	70/71	30	2	7	FL
	71/72	19		3	FL
Southport	72/73	43		21	FL
Philadelphia Atoms	73	19		11	NA
Southport	73/74	39	1	7	FL
Philadelphia Atoms	74	20		9	NA
Torquay U	74/75	35	3	6	FL
	75/76	29	4	5	FL
	76/77	19	1	3	FL
Bath C	77/78				
	78/79				
Totnes Birdwatchers					
Windsor U					

PROVAN David
b. Falkirk 11.3.1941 Caps: S - 5

Bonnyvale Star

Club	Season				Div
Rangers	58/59	1			D1
	59/60				D1
	60/61	2			D1
	61/62	3			D1
	62/63	12			D1
	63/64	33		3	D1
	64/65	34			D1
	65/66	33			D1
	66/67	33		4	D1
	67/68	2			D1
	68/69	8			D1
	69/70	9		2	D1
Crystal Palace	70/71	1			FL
Plymouth A	70/71	14			FL
	71/72	43		4	FL
	72/73	44		4	FL
	73/74	20	1	2	FL
	74/75	7			FL
St Mirren	74/75	22			D2

PROVAN David Alexander
b. Gourock 8.5.1956 Caps: S - 10

Port Glasgow A

Club	Season				Div
Kilmarnock	74/75	20	2	1	D1
	75/76	23	1	3	D1
	76/77	34		1	P
	77/78	36		3	D1
	78/79	4		1	D1
Celtic	78/79	30		4	P
	79/80	35		1	P
	80/81	31	2	7	P
	81/82	19	1	4	P
	82/83	33		5	P
	83/84	14	4	2	P
	84/85	19	6	2	P
Sydney Olympic	L 85				
Celtic	85/86	11	1	2	P

PRUDHAM Charles Edward
b. Felling 12.4.1952

Club	Season				Div
Sheffield W	70/71	1			FL
	71/72	1			FL
	72/73	2		1	FL
	73/74	6	4	1	FL
	74/75	4		1	FL
Partick T	74/75	3	1	3	D1
Carlisle U	74/75	5	1	1	FL
	75/76	9	1	1	FL
	76/77	1			FL
Hartlepool U	76/77	3			FL
Workington	76/77	15		6	FL
Stockport Co	77/78	37		12	FL
	78/79	19	5	1	FL
	79/80	24	2	9	FL
Bournemouth	80/81	2	2		FL

PRYDE

Club	Season			Div
Airdrieonians	68/69	2		D1

PRYDE James
b Leuchars.

Club	Season			Div
Rangers	51/52	3		D1
	52/53	3		D1
	53/54			D1
	54/55	5		D1

PRYDE William

Club	Season			Div
Airdrieonians	51/52	11		D1
	52/53	27	1	D1
	53/54	13		D1

PURCELL Patrick

Club	Season			Div
Dundee U	67/68	1		D1
Raith R	68/69	1		D1

PURDIE Ian
b. Bellshill 7.3.1953

Larkhall Thistle

Club	Season				Div
Aberdeen	71/72		1		D1
	72/73	3		2	D1
	73/74	6	2	1	D1
	74/75	27		7	D1
Dundee	75/76	22	3		P
	76/77	33	1	7	D1
Motherwell	77/78	11	5	3	P
Wigan A	78/79	46		11	FL
	79/80	8	1	1	FL
Portsmouth	79/80	4	1	1	FL
Canberra C					

QUA

Club	Season			Div
Falkirk	58/59	1		D1

QUEEN Gerald
b. Glasgow 15.1.1945

Johnstone Burgh

Club	Season				Div
St Mirren	62/63	8		1	D1
	63/64	7		3	D1
	64/65	28		6	D1
	65/66	20		1	D1
Kilmarnock	65/66	14		6	D1
	66/67	22		3	D1
	67/68	30	1	14	D1
	68/69	28		6	D1
Crystal Palace	69/70	31	2	2	FL
	70/71	29	2	9	FL
	71/72	31	2	5	FL
	72/73	4	2	1	FL
Leyton Orient	72/73	11			FL
	73/74	34	2	12	FL
	74/75	32	2	4	FL
	75/76	32		6	FL
	76/77	18	3	2	FL
Arcadia Shepherds					

QUEEN John

Petershill

Club	Season	App	Gls	Div
Rangers	55/56	1		D1
	56/57			D1
	57/58	1		D1

QUIGLEY Michael

Club	Season	App	Gls	Div
Airdrieonians	55/56	34		D1
	56/57	26	1	D1
	57/58	24		D1
	58/59	9		D1
	59/60	17	2	D1

QUIGLEY Thomas Cook
b. East Calder 26.3.1932

Barry T

Club	Season	App	Gls	Div
Airdrieonians	53/54	13	3	D1
Albion R	54/55			D2
Portsmouth	55/56			FL
QPR	56/57	16	7	FL

Worcester C

QUINN Francis
b. Saltcoats 12.9.1926

Saltcoats V

Club	Season	App	Gls	Div
Celtic	46/47	5	1	D1
	47/48			
Dundee U	48/49	22	9	D2
	49/50	28	15	D2
	50/51	29	21	D2
	51/52	29	18	D2
	52/53	29	19	D2
	53/54	20	8	D2
Hamilton A	54/55	25	15	D2
Cowdenbeath	55/56			D2
	56/57			D2

Stranraer

QUINN Henry

Burnley

Club	M	Season	App	Sub	Gls	Div
St Mirren		62/63	5		1	D1
		63/64	1			D1
		64/65	15		3	D1
Celtic		65/66				
Clyde		66/67	2	2		D1
Dundee U	T	67/68				D1

QUINN James
b. Croy 23.11.1947 d. 24.4.2002

Kirkintilloch St Ninians
Croy Amateurs
Holy Cross Croy BG

Club	M	Season	App	Sub	Gls	Div
Celtic		63/64				D1
Maryhill Harp	L	64/65				
Celtic		65/66				D1
		66/67				D1
		67/68	2		1	D1
		68/69				D1
Clyde	L	68/69	9	1	2	D1
Celtic		69/70	1			D1
		70/71		2		D1
		71/72	9			D1
		72/73	9	1		D1
		73/74	3			D1
Sheffield W		74/75	10			FL
		75/76	36		1	FL
Australia						
Hamilton A		76/77				D1

QUINN John

Club	Season	App	Gls	Div
Airdrieonians	50/51	3		D1
	51/52	18	3	D1
	52/53	21	5	D1
	53/54	20	6	D1
	54/55			D2
	55/56	21	2	D1
	56/57	18	1	D1
	57/58	27		D1
	58/59	32		D1
	59/60	28		D1
	60/61	3		D1

QUINN Patrick
b. Glasgow 26.4.1936 Caps: S - 4

Bridgeton Waverley

Club	M	Season	App	Sub	Gls	Div
Albion R	T	55/56				D2
Motherwell		55/56	12		4	D1
		56/57	29		13	D1
		57/58	14		3	D1
		58/59	31		13	D1
		59/60	34		17	D1
		60/61	33		17	D1
		61/62	34		16	D1
		62/63	9		3	D1
Blackpool		62/63	25		8	FL
		63/64	9		1	FL
Hibernian		63/64	19		2	D1
		64/65	25		8	D1
		65/66	16		2	D1
		66/67	21	1		D1
		67/68	31		5	D1
		68/69	16		2	D1
East Fife		69/70	29	2	2	D2
		70/71			4	D2

QUINN Robert
b. Earnock 16.1.1923

Burnbank A
Blantyre Victoria
Blantyre Celtic

Club	Season	App	Gls	Div
Celtic	46/47	2		D1
	47/48	4		D1
Arbroath	47/48			D2
	48/49			D2
	49/50	24	5	D2
Cowdenbeath	50/51			D2
	51/52			D2
Morton	52/53	30	7	D2
	53/54	20	1	D2
Hamilton A	54/55	30	1	D2
	55/56	33	6	D2
	56/57	34	1	D2
	57/58	16	1	D2
Stenhousemuir	58/59			D2
	59/60			D2
	60/61			D2

QUINN Stanley

Shettleston

Club	Season	App	Div
Ayr U	66/67	23	D1
	67/68		D2
	68/69		D2
	69/70	24	D1
	70/71	24	D1
	71/72	22	D1
	72/73	3	D1
St Mirren	73/74	8	D2

QUINN Thomas

Club	Season	App	Gls	Div
Arbroath	59/60	26	3	D1

RAE Alexander McFarlane
b. Glasgow 23.8.1946

Renfrew Jnrs

Club	Season	App	Sub	Gls	Div
East Fife	64/65	3			D2
	65/66	20		4	D2
	66/67	22	1	2	D2
	67/68	22		8	D2
	68/69			2	D2
Bury	69/70	10		1	FL
Partick T	70/71	28	3		D2
	71/72	34		3	D1
	72/73	25			D1
	73/74	1			D1
East Fife	73/74	13	5		D1
	74/75	11		3	D2
Cowdenbeath	75/76	18		3	D2
	76/77	20	6		D2
Forfar A	77/78	37		11	D2
	78/79	33	1	11	D2
	79/80	22	5	5	D2
	80/81	3		1	D2

RAE Ian
b. Cambusnethan

Larkhall Thistle
Larkhall Albert

Club	Season	App	Gls	Div
Hamilton A	51/52	25	11	D2
	52/53	30	20	D2
	53/54	10		D1

Elgin C
Lossiemouth

F RAE Ian Johnstone
b. Grangemouth 19.1.1933

Dunipace Jnrs

Club	Season	App	Gls	Div
Falkirk	50/51			D1
	51/52	3		D2
	52/53	24		D1
	53/54	18		D1
	54/55	25		D1
	55/56	30	1	D1
	56/57	32		D1
	57/58	3		D1
Bristol C	57/58	12		FL
Falkirk	58/59	7		D1
	59/60	36	1	D2
	60/61	7	2	D2
	61/62	26		D1
	62/63	32		D1
	63/64	32		D1
	64/65	14		D1
	65/66	3		D1
Stenhousemuir	66/67	37		D2
	67/68	16		D2

RAE James

Gorgie Hearts

Club	Season	App	Div
Falkirk	66/67	2	D1

RAE Joseph
b. Partick 6.3.1925 d. 1.5.1987

Arthurlie

Club	M	Season	App	Gls	Div
Celtic		46/47	15	10	D1
		47/48	4	1	D1
Raith R	L	47/48			D2
Rosario Central					
Torquay U		48/49	20	4	FL
Raith R		48/49			D2
		49/50	2		D1
Kilmarnock	T	49/50	2		D2
Yeovil T		49/50			
		50/51			

RAE Thomas M
b. Allanton 17.2.1946

Club	Season	App	Sub	Gls	Div
Partick T	63/64	2			D1
	64/65	1		1	D1
	65/66	7			D1
	66/67	25	1	9	D1
	67/68	33		15	D1
Aberdeen	68/69	8		1	D1
	69/70	2	2	1	D1
Partick T	69/70	21	1	8	D1
	70/71	5	1		D2
	71/72	3	10	3	D1
	72/73	8	1	2	D1
	73/74	26	3	2	D1
	74/75	1	1		D1
Cowdenbeath	75/76	7		1	D2
Morton	75/76	8	2	1	D2
East Stirlingshire	75/76	2	1		D2
	76/77	20	6	2	D2

RAE William
b. Glasgow
Petershill

Club	Season	Apps	Gls	Div
Rangers	46/47	19		D1
	47/48	19		D1
	48/49	1		D1
	49/50	7	1	D1
	50/51	25	2	D1
	51/52	2	1	D1
	52/53	3		D1
	53/54	8		D1
	54/55	19	1	D1
	55/56	27	1	D1
Queen of the South	56/57	6		D1
	57/58	8		D1

RAINEY Graham
Kilsyth R

Club	Season	Apps	Div
Partick T	64/65	1	D1
East Fife	65/66	4	D2

RALSTON Brian
Leicester C

Club	Season	Apps	Gls	Div
Partick T	70/71	14		D2
	71/72	3		D1
	72/73	11		D1
	73/74	2	1	D1
Stranraer	73/74	9	1	D2
	74/75	19		D2

RALSTON Peter
b. Fauldhouse 31.1.1929
Fauldhouse U

Club	Season	Apps	Gls	Div
Falkirk	50/51	6	1	D1
	51/52			D2
	52/53			D1
	53/54	11		D1
	54/55	13		D1
	55/56	2		D1
	56/57	12		D1
Accrington S	57/58	2		FL
	58/59	4		FL
Bangor C				

RAMAGE George McIntosh
b. Newtongrange 29.1.1937

Club	Season	Apps	Div
Third Lanark	57/58	5	D1
	58/59	32	D1
	59/60	1	D1
	60/61		D1
	61/62		D1
Colchester U	62/63	12	FL
	63/64	26	FL
Leyton Orient	64/65	4	FL
Luton T	65/66	7	FL

RAMSEY Robert
b. Motherwell
North Motherwell A

Club	Season	Apps	Gls	Div
Motherwell	62/63	3		D1
	63/64			D1
	64/65	1		D1
Airdrieonians	66/67	32	2	D1
	67/68	27	2	D1
	68/69	1		D1

RANKIN Brian C
b. 27.3.1953
Vale of Clyde

Club	Season	Apps	Subs	Gls	Div
Dundee U	71/72				D1
	72/73				D1
	73/74	2			D1
	74/75				D1
Hamilton A	74/75	15	5	7	D2
East Fife	75/76	14	3	3	D1
Alloa A	76/77	6	2	1	D2
Forfar A	76/77	14		2	D2
	77/78	32		5	D2
	78/79				D2
	79/80				D2
	80/81	6			D2
	81/82	5		1	D2

RANKIN George
Kilsyth R

Club	Season	Apps	Gls	Div
Airdrieonians	55/56	27	7	D1
	56/57	18	5	D1
	57/58	29	11	D1
	58/59	25	11	D1
	59/60	27	9	D1
	60/61	33	2	D1
	61/62	6		D1
St Johnstone	61/62	18	4	D1
	62/63	1		D2
Stenhousemuir	63/64	20	5	D2
	64/65	28	3	D2
	65/66	5		D2

RANKIN John
b. Glasgow
Rutherglen Glencairn

Club	Season	Apps	Div
Stirling A	54/55	4	D1
	55/56	22	D1
	56/57		D2
	57/58		D2
	58/59	2	D1
Berwick R			

RANKIN Robert
Wishaw

Club	Season	Apps	Gls	Div
Queen of the South	55/56	4		D1
	56/57	1		D1
	57/58	3	3	D1
	58/59	8		D1
Heart of Midlothian	58/59	5	9	D1
Third Lanark	59/60	9	3	D1
Queen of the South				
Stenhousemuir				

RANKIN Stanley Matthews
Glasgow U

Club	Season	Apps	Subs	Gls	Div
Morton	66/67	1			D2
	67/68	17	2		D1
	68/69	19	2		D1
	69/70	28		1	D1
	70/71	31			D1
	71/72	9			D1
	72/73	13		2	D1
	73/74	18	1	1	D1
	74/75	26			D1
	75/76				D1
St Johnstone	76/77	14			D1
Clyde	77/78	27		1	D2

RATTRAY Norman
b. Kelty c1939 d. Barbados ?.9.1999
Crossgates Primrose

Club	Season	Apps	Gls	Div
Dunfermline A	56/57			D1
	57/58			D2
	58/59	19	1	D1
	59/60	11	1	D1
	60/61	1		D1
St Johnstone	60/61	14		D1
	61/62	5		D1
	62/63			D1
Alloa A	63/64	3		D2

RATTRAY Peter Kerr
b. Bannockburn 7.11.1925
Rutherglen Glencairn

Club	Season	Apps	Gls	Div
Dundee	46/47	5	7	D2
	47/48	7	3	D1
	48/49	3		D1
	49/50	15	5	D1
	50/51			D1
Plymouth A	50/51	13	3	FL
	51/52	41	19	FL
Norwich C	52/53	23	5	FL
	53/54	1		FL
Stirling A	53/54	11	2	D1
	54/55	9	1	D1
St Johnstone	55/56	3		D2
	56/57	6	4	D2

RAVN Jorgen
b. Copenhagen
KB Copenhagen

Club	Season	Apps	Gls	Div
Aberdeen	64/65	12	6	D1
	65/66	13	3	D1

RAY

Club	Season	Apps	Div
Morton	70/71	1	D1

REA Wallace
b. Uddingston 21.8.1935
Larkhall Royal Albert

Club	Season	Apps	Gls	Div
Third Lanark	54/55			D2
Motherwell	55/56	9	1	D1
	56/57	2	1	D1
	57/58	3	2	D1
	58/59			D1
Bradford C	59/60	11	2	FL

REDPATH Alan
b. Edinburgh
Edinburgh A

Club	Season	Apps	Gls	Div
Falkirk	62/63	19	5	D1
	63/64	32	6	D1
	64/65	2		D1
St Mirren	64/65	13	2	D1
	65/66	13	4	D1

REDPATH William Yates
b. Stoneyburn 8.8.1922
d. 20.1.1989 Caps: S - 9
Polkemmet Jnrs

Club	Season	Apps	Gls	Div
Motherwell	46/47	22	2	D1
	47/48	28	1	D1
	48/49	21	1	D1
	49/50	27	1	D1
	50/51	28	2	D1
	51/52	29		D1
	52/53	17	1	D1
	53/54	30	10	D2
	54/55	23	1	D1
	55/56	2		D1
Third Lanark	56/57			D2

REED Ernest

Club	Season	Apps	Gls	Div
Arbroath	69/70			D2
St Mirren	70/71	3	1	D1

REID Alan
United Crossroads

Club	Season	Apps	Subs	Gls	Div
Dunfermline A	74/75	15		2	D1
	75/76	3	6	1	D1
Newtongrange Star					

REID Brian
b. Arbroath 5.5.1954
Brechin V

Club	Season	Apps	Subs	Gls	Div
Arbroath	73/74	1		1	D1
	74/75	8	10	3	D1
Brechin C	75/76	14	1	1	D2
	76/77	25	4	1	D2
	77/78	35	2	1	D2
	78/79	28	4	1	D2
	79/80	35		2	D2
	80/81	12		3	D2
	81/82	38	1	1	D2
	82/83	37			D2
	83/84	21		5	D1
	84/85	24	1	1	D1
	85/86			1	D1

REID David

Club	Season	Apps	Div
Dunfermline A	59/60	1	D1

REID David

Club	Season	Apps	Gls	Div
Dundee U	60/61	2	1	D1
Hakoah (Aus)				

REID Dennis Alexander
b. Glasgow 2.3.1947
Glasgow Perthshire

Rangers	64/65				D1
	65/66				D1
	66/67	2		2	D1
Dundee U	68/69	31	3	3	D1
	69/70	20		1	D1
	70/71	29	1	6	D1
	71/72	6	1	1	D1
Newcastle U	71/72	12	6		FL
	72/73	3	2		FL
Morton	L 72/73	7		1	D1
Morton	73/74	25	1	5	D1
	74/75	22		4	D1
	75/76	17		1	D1
Dundee U	75/76	8	2	3	P
	76/77		1		P
Ayr U	76/77	2			P

REID George McC
b. Aberfoyle
Tranent Jnrs

Celtic	35/36				D1
Dunfermline A	L 36/37	24		7	D1
Kilmarnock	37/38	14		3	D1
	38/39	38		17	D1
	46/47	17		1	D1

REID Hugh
b. Dundee
Carnoustie Panmure

Dundee	54/55	1		D1
	55/56	27		D1
	56/57	32	1	D1
	57/58	16		D1
	58/59	19		D1
	59/60			D1
	60/61	10		D1
	61/62			D1
	62/63	4		D1
	63/64	3		D1
	64/65	7		D1

REID Ian
b. Caldercrux

Motherwell	52/53	4		D1
Cowdenbeath				

REID Ian

Arbroath	68/69	26	2	D1

REID Ian
Bonkle YC

Partick T	69/70	28		D1
	70/71	32		D2
	71/72	5		D1
	72/73	5		D1
	73/74			D1
St Mirren	74/75	24	1	D2
	75/76	8		D1

REID Ian
Drumchapel Amateurs
Queen of the South
Nottingham F

Dundee U	70/71	3			D1
	71/72	4	2	1	D1
	72/73	4	1	2	D1
Queen of the South	73/74	33		22	D2
	74/75	38		27	D2
	75/76	24	1	11	D1
	76/77	37	1	13	D1
	77/78	18	2	6	D1
Airdrieonians	77/78	7		2	D1
Forfar A	78/79	25	1	7	D2
	79/80	2	1		D2

REID John
b. Edinburgh 23.7.1935
Tranent Jnrs

Airdrieonians	55/56	11			D1
Watford	L 56/57	1		1	FL
Airdrieonians	57/58	7			D1
Norwich C	58/59				FL
Barrow	59/60	20		4	FL

REID John Holt
b. Edinburgh 22.5.1934
Armadale Thistle

Celtic	52/53				D1
	53/54				D1
	54/55	3		1	D1
	55/56	1			D1
Alloa A	L 55/56				D2
Celtic	56/57				D1
Airdrieonians	57/58	3			D1
Alloa A					

REID Joseph
Polkemmet Jnrs

Motherwell	46/47	1			D1
	47/48	3			D1
	48/49				D1
Falkirk	49/50	7		3	D1

REID Robert Bell Alexander
b. Dundee 18.11.1936 d. Kirkcaldy 29.7.2000
Lochee Harp
Downfield Jnrs

Swansea T	57/58	13		FL
	58/59	1		FL
	59/60	3		FL
Raith R	60/61			D1
	61/62			D1
	62/63			D1
	63/64	36		D2
	64/65	33		D2
	65/66	18		D2
	66/67	38		D2
	67/68	29		D1
	68/69	31		D1
	69/70	29		D1
	70/71		1	D2
	71/72	13		D2
	72/73	4		D2

REID Samuel
b. Craigneuk

Motherwell	56/57	12		2	D1
	57/58	2			D1
	58/59	27		11	D1
	59/60	19		6	D1
Liverpool	59/60				FL
Falkirk	60/61	33		20	D2
	61/62	28		4	D1
	62/63	9		1	D1
Clyde	62/63	16		3	D1
	63/64	28		7	D2
	64/65	4			D1
	65/66	9			D1
Berwick R	66/67	18	3	7	D2
Dumbarton	67/68	12	2	2	D2

REID Walter

St Mirren	47/48	22		4	D1
	48/49	13		2	D1
Stirling A	49/50	5			D1
Stranraer	50/51				D3
Dundee U	51/52				D2

REID William

Third Lanark	47/48	4		2	D1
	48/49	3			D1

REID William

St Mirren	47/48	9		2	D1
	48/49	19		4	D1
	49/50	25		1	D1
	50/51	21		3	D1
	51/52	14			D1
	52/53	21			D1
	53/54	7			D1

REID William
b. Craigneuk

Motherwell	54/55	1			D1
	55/56	13		5	D1
	56/57	9		3	D1
	57/58				D1
	58/59	2		2	D1
	59/60	23			D1
	60/61	8			D1
Airdrieonians	61/62	22		1	D1
	62/63	25			D1
	63/64	28		1	D1
	64/65	32		3	D1

REID William
b. Baillieston 6.1.1939
Kirkintilloch Rob Roy

Stirling A	63/64				D2
	64/65				D2
	65/66	29		1	D1
	66/67	27	1	1	D1
	67/68	17	1		D1

REID William

Airdrieonians	65/66	12		D2
	66/67	2		D1
	67/68	1		D1

REILLY Felix McCairney
b. Musselburgh 12.9.1933
Shotts Bon Accord

Dunfermline A	53/54	7			D2
	54/55				D2
	55/56	28		6	D1
	56/57	29		9	D1
Dundee	56/57	1			D1
	57/58	4			D1
East Fife	57/58	9		2	D1
	58/59				D2
	59/60				D2
Portsmouth	59/60				FL
Bradford PA	59/60	12		4	FL
	60/61	18		8	FL
	61/62	1			FL
Crewe Alex.	61/62	6			FL

REILLY James

Clyde	58/59	6			D1
Third Lanark	59/60	34		3	D1
	60/61	34		5	D1
	61/62	27		1	D1
	62/63	27		2	D1
Morton	63/64	28		3	D2
	64/65	11			D1

REILLY John
Caps: Aus - 15
Inverurie Loco

Hibernian	65/66	1		D1
	66/67	1		D1
Washington Whips	68	17		NA
Melbourne Juventus				
Fitzroy				
South Melbourne Hellas				

REILLY Lawrence
b. Edinburgh 28.10.1928 Caps: S - 38
Edinburgh Thistle

Club	Season				Div
Hibernian	46/47	5		2	D1
	47/48	6		4	D1
	48/49	20		14	D1
	49/50	29		16	D1
	50/51	29		22	D1
	51/52	29		27	D1
	52/53	28		30	D1
	53/54	18		14	D1
	54/55	20		15	D1
	55/56	29		23	D1
	56/57	26		16	D1
	57/58	14		2	D1

RENNET William James
b. Perth 25.10.1924
Perth Celtic
Beechwood Jnrs
Lochee Harp

Club	Season				Div
Stirling A	T 45/46				
Perth Celtic					
Stenhousemuir	T 47/48				D2
Aberdeen	T 48/49				D1
Celtic	49/50	14		4	D1
	50/51				D1
Blackburn R	T 50/51				FL
Arbroath	51/52				D2
	52/53	24		9	D2
	53/54	25		3	D2
	54/55				D2
	55/56				D2
	56/57				D2

RENNIE Alexander
b. Westquarter 27.9.1948
United Crossroads

Club	Season					Div
Rangers	64/65					D1
	65/66					D1
	66/67					D1
Stirling A	67/68	3				D1
St Johnstone	67/68	5				D1
	68/69	16	8		3	D1
	69/70	9	4		1	D1
	70/71	32			1	D1
	71/72	33			2	D1
	72/73	32				D1
	73/74	30				D1
	74/75	28				D1
Dundee U	75/76	25	2			P
	76/77	18				P
	77/78	17	1			P
	78/79					P

RENNIE Gilbert
b. Aberdeen

Club	Season				Div
St Mirren	49/50	1			D1
	50/51	15		5	D1
	51/52	2		3	D1
Brechin C					

RENNIE Gordon

Club	Season				Div
St Mirren	46/47	4			D1
	47/48	12			D1
St Johnstone	48/49	30			D2
	49/50	11			D2

RENNIE Stuart
b. Edinburgh 24.4.1947
Royston BC

Club	Season				Div
Falkirk	67/68				D1
	68/69	25			D1
	69/70	31			D2
	70/71	29			D1
	71/72	18			D1
	72/73	29			D1
	73/74				D1
Motherwell	73/74	27			D1
	74/75	25			D1
	75/76	36			P
	76/77	26			P
	77/78	32			P
	78/79	28			P
Ayr U	79/80	39			D1
	80/81	39			D1
	81/82	29			D1
	82/83	18			D1
Postal U					

RENTON Derek
b. Duns 7.1.1952
Duns
Arniston R
Rangers

Club	Season					Div
Heart of Midlothian	71/72	17			5	D1
	72/73	9	1		2	D1
Germiston Callies	73					
Queen of the South	73/74	28			7	D2
	74/75	11	5			D2
	75/76	4	3			D2
Stenhousemuir	76/77	32	3		3	D2
	77/78	7	4			D2

RENTON William
b. Cardenden 4.2.1942
Lochore Welfare

Club	Season					Div
St Johnstone	62/63	2				D2
	63/64	9				D1
	64/65	33				D1
	65/66	32			3	D1
	66/67	4		1		D1
St Mirren	66/67	15				D1
	67/68	31	1		3	D2
Dunfermline A	68/69	29	1		2	D1
	69/70	24	1		4	D1
	70/71	2				D1
Barrow	70/71	11			1	FL
	71/72	12	1		1	FL
Cowdenbeath	71/72	1		1		D2

RENUCCI Alfredo
b. Glasgow d. ?.?.1985

Club	Season				Div
Partick T	57/58	6			D1
	58/59	2			D1
Falkirk	58/59				D1
East Fife	58/59	1			D2
Hamilton A	58/59				D2
	59/60	3			D2

REYNOLDS Hugh
b. Wishaw 19.9.1926

Club	Season				Div
Morton	46/47	4			D1
	47/48				D1
Torquay U	48/49	3			FL

REYNOLDS Thomas
Ayr Albion

Club	Season				Div
Ayr U	69/70	13		2	D1
	70/71	25	1	1	D1
	71/72	5	1		D1
	72/73				D1
Airdrieonians	73/74	9	13	1	D2
	74/75	27	1	1	D1
	75/76	12	6	1	D1

RICE H

Club	Season			Div
Falkirk	46/47	19		D1

RICE Peter
Hibernian

Club	Season				Div
Aberdeen	48/49	16		2	D1
	49/50	7		1	D1
St Mirren	50/51	7		2	D1
	51/52	15		5	D1
	52/53	21		5	D1
	53/54	3			D1
Raith R	53/54	5		1	D1
	54/55	5		1	D1
Albion R	55/56				D2

RICHARDSON Ian
Lochore Welfare

Club	Season			Div
Raith R	67/68	2		D1
	68/69	2		D1

RICHMOND James C
b. Blantyre
Beith Jnrs

Club	Season				Div
Hamilton A	55/56	33		1	D2
	56/57	36			D2
	57/58	35		1	D2
Falkirk	58/59	33			D1
Kilmarnock	59/60	17			D1
	60/61	34		1	D1
	61/62	34		2	D1
	62/63	30		1	D1
	63/64	1			D1
St Johnstone	63/64	24		2	D1
	64/65	11		1	D1
	65/66	16		1	D1
Lossiemouth					
Rothes					

RICHMOND T

Club	Season			Div
Queen of the South	46/47	1		D1

RIDDELL Ian
Jordanhill College

Club	Season				Div
St Mirren	58/59	9			D1
	59/60	25		6	D1
	60/61	22			D1
	61/62	2			D1
	62/63	16			D1
	63/64	17			D1
	64/65	17			D1
	65/66	18			D1
	66/67				D1
	67/68				D2
Arbroath	68/69	8			D1

RIDDLE Alistair

Club	Season				Div
Montrose	61/62	32		2	D2
Dundee U	62/63	4			D1
Montrose	63/64				D2
	64/65				D2
	65/66	36		6	D2
	66/67	14	1	1	D2

RILEY John

Club	Season			Div
Clyde	46/47	5		D1
	47/48	11	3	D1
	48/49	3		D1

RING Thomas
b. Glasgow 8.8.1930 d. ?.10.1997 Caps: S - 12
Springburn U
Ashfield

Clyde	50/51	21		8	D1
	51/52				D2
	52/53	28		16	D1
	53/54	30		17	D1
	54/55	27		10	D1
	55/56	34		10	D1
	56/57				D2
	57/58	32		12	D1
	58/59	32		5	D1
	59/60	12		1	D1
Everton	59/60	16		2	FL
	60/61	11		4	FL
Barnsley	61/62	20		1	FL
	62/63	1			FL
Aberdeen	62/63	2			D1
Fraserburgh					
Stevenage T					

RITCHIE Andrew
b. Bellshill 23.2.1956
Bellshill Academy
Bellshill YMCA

Celtic	71/72					D1
Kirkintilloch Rob R	L 71/72					
	72/73					
Celtic	73/74			1		D1
	74/75					D1
	75/76	5	3		1	P
	76/77					P
Morton	76/77	26		1	22	D1
	77/78	37			20	D1
	78/79	35			22	P
	79/80	34			19	P
	80/81	29	3		8	P
	81/82	23	2		6	P
	82/83	16	7		3	P
Motherwell	83/84	6	2		1	P
Clydebank	T 83/84	1				D1
East Stirlingshire	T 83/84	1				D2
Hannover 96	T 83/84					
Albion R	83/84	2	1		1	D2
	84/85	2	1		1	D2

RITCHIE D

Airdrieonians	50/51	1		D1

RITCHIE Grahame
b. 3.7.1954
Arniston R

East Fife	73/74	12	3	1	D1
	74/75	1			D2
Meadowbank T	74/75	7		1	D2

RITCHIE James

St Mirren	50/51	13	2	D1

RITCHIE James

Giffnock North
Alloa A

Hamilton A	52/53	27		D2
	53/54	5		D1

Third Lanark

RITCHIE Stephen Kilcar
b. Edinburgh 17.2.1954

Bristol C	71/72				FL
	72/73	1			FL
Morton	72/73	11		1	D1
	73/74	26		1	D1
	74/75	28		1	D1
Hereford U	75/76	46		1	FL
	76/77	32		1	FL
	77/78	24		1	FL
Aberdeen	77/78	9			P
	78/79	1			P
Torquay U	78/79	17			FL
	79/80	41		2	FL
Yeovil T	80/81				
	81/82				
	82/83				
Trowbridge T					

RITCHIE William
b. Newtongrange 11.9.1936 Caps: S - 1
Bathgate Thistle

Rangers	57/58	29		D1
	58/59			D1
	59/60	1		D1
	60/61	12		D1
	61/62	34		D1
	62/63	33		D1
	63/64	34		D1
	64/65	25		D1
	65/66	33		D1
	66/67	6		D1
Partick T	68/69	34		D1
	69/70	23		D1
Motherwell	70/71	1		D1
	71/72	8		D1
	72/73	4		D1
	73/74			D1
	74/75			D1
Stranraer	75/76	23		D2

RITCHIE William

Largs Thistle

St Johnstone	72/73	2		D1
	73/74	28	2	D1
	74/75	12	1	D1
	75/76	21	1	P
Clyde	76/77	6	2	D2

RITCHIE William Saunders
b. Dundee 13.11.1932
Dundee Osborne

Dundee U	T 54/55	1			D2
Dundee	55/56	12		6	D1
Stirling A	56/57				D2
Bury	57/58	13		7	FL
Stockport Co	58/59	12		4	FL
	59/60	40		8	FL

ROBB Angus

Newburgh Jnrs

East Fife	54/55			D1
	55/56			D1
	56/57			D1
	57/58	2		D1
	58/59			D2
	59/60			D2
	60/61			D2
Brechin C	61/62	14	2	D2

ROBB David Thomson
b. Broughty Ferry 15.12.1947 Caps: S - 5
Chelsea
Newburgh Jnrs

Aberdeen	65/66				D1
	66/67	2	1	1	D1
	67/68	16	2	4	D1
	68/69	24	2	9	D1
	69/70	34		16	D1
	70/71	32		9	D1
	71/72	34		10	D1
	72/73	19		4	D1
	73/74	21		11	D1
	74/75	6		4	D1
	75/76	30	2	4	P
	76/77	13	7	1	P
Tampa Bay Rowdies	77	15		8	NA
Aberdeen	77/78	13		5	P
Tampa Bay Rowdies	78	27		13	NA
Norwich C	78/79	4	1	1	FL
Philadelphia Fury	79	30		16	NA
Vancouver Whitecaps	80	15			NA
Tulsa Roughnecks	80	12		4	NA
Dunfermline A	80/81	3			D1

ROBB James Fraser
b. Glasgow 30.3.1935
Strathclyde

Queen's Park	53/54	3			D2
	54/55	27		4	D2
	55/56	22		2	D2
	56/57	21		5	D1
	57/58	24		2	D1
Third Lanark	58/59	27			D1
	59/60	15		1	D1
	60/61	2			D1
	61/62	13			D1
	62/63	10			D1
	63/64	2			D1
Charlton A	63/64				FL
Stirling A	64/65	34		3	D2
	65/66	11			D1
Stenhousemuir	66/67	12	1	1	D2

ROBB William Lawson
b. Rutherglen 23.12.1927

Aberdeen	49/50	4			D1
Leyton Orient	50/51	5			FL
Albion R	51/52				D2
	52/53	27		5	D2
	53/54	22			D2
Bradford C	54/55	25		2	FL
	55/56	39		1	FL
	56/57	46		1	FL
	57/58	17			FL

ROBERTS Philip

Arsenal
Grimsby T

St Johnstone	74/75	2			D1
	75/76	20	1		P
	76/77	32	1	1	D1
Crieff					

ROBERTS Robert
b. Edinburgh 2.9.1940
Edinburgh Norton

Motherwell	58/59	1			D1
	59/60	5		2	D1
	60/61	19		6	D1
	61/62	32		8	D1
	62/63	31		9	D1
	63/64	3		2	D1
Leicester C	63/64	17		2	FL
	64/65	27		8	FL
	65/66	41		2	FL
	66/67	42		7	FL
	67/68	41		6	FL
	68/69	25	3		FL
	69/70	31	2	1	FL
Mansfield T	70/71	39		2	FL
	71/72	37	4	2	FL
Coventry C	72/73				FL
Colchester U	73/74				FL

ROBERTSON

Club	Season	Apps	Sub	Goals	Div
Queen of the South	58/59	5			D1

ROBERTSON Allan David
b. Irvine 22.9.1952
Eastercraigs BC
Troon Jnrs

Club	Season	Apps	Sub	Goals	Div
Kilmarnock	72/73	27			D1
	73/74	34		1	D2
	74/75	33			D1
	75/76	26			D1
	76/77	36		2	P
	77/78	28		1	D1
	78/79	37			D1
	79/80	24			P
	80/81	18	1		P
	81/82	37	2	2	D1
	82/83	13			P
	83/84	38			D1
	84/85	30		1	D1
	85/86	32			D1
	86/87	26			D1
	87/88	27			D1
	88/89	12			D1

ROBERTSON Archibald Clark
b. Busby 15.9.1929 d. 28.1.1978 Caps: S - 5
Rutherglen Glencairn

Club	Season	Apps	Sub	Goals	Div
Clyde	47/48				D1
	48/49				D1
	49/50	1			D1
	50/51	11		2	D1
	51/52				D2
	52/53	28		13	D1
	53/54	30		3	D1
	54/55	29		10	D1
	55/56	26		8	D1
	56/57				D2
	57/58	34		25	D1
	58/59	33		20	D1
	59/60	20		9	D1
	60/61	22		7	D1
Morton	61/62	31		15	D2
	62/63				D2
	63/64				D2
Cowdenbeath	64/65	5		3	D2

ROBERTSON Charles
Armadale

Club	Season	Apps	Sub	Goals	Div
Motherwell	46/47	5		3	D1
	47/48	1			D1
	48/49	3		1	D1
	49/50	8		2	D1

ROBERTSON David
Saltcoats V

Club	Season	Apps	Sub	Goals	Div
Ayr U	71/72	3		1	D1
	72/73		1		D1

ROBERTSON Derek
Petershill

Club	Season	Apps	Sub	Goals	Div
St Johnstone	66/67	1			D1
	67/68	14			D1
	68/69	28			D1
	69/70	6			D1
	70/71				D1
	71/72	18			D1
	72/73				D1
	73/74	16			D1
	74/75	32			D1
	75/76	32			P
	76/77	33			D1
	77/78	23			D1
	78/79	20			D1
Hibernian	79/80				P

ROBERTSON George
Tranent Jnrs

Club	Season	Apps	Sub	Goals	Div
Heart of Midlothian	58/59	1			D1
Morton					

ROBERTSON Hugh
b. Auchinleck 29.11.1939 Caps: S - 1
Auchinleck Talbot

Club	Season	Apps	Sub	Goals	Div
Dundee	57/58	23		3	D1
	58/59	32		9	D1
	59/60	32		13	D1
	60/61	34		9	D1
	61/62	33		6	D1
	62/63	16		1	D1
	63/64	21		2	D1
	64/65	32		5	D1
Dunfermline A	65/66	28		10	D1
	66/67	33		10	D1
	67/68	31	1	14	D1
	68/69	32	1	4	D1
	69/70	13	2	2	D1
	70/71	28	3	8	D1
Arbroath	71/72	34	1	5	D2
	72/73	1		4	D1

ROBERTSON James
b. Leith 7.7.1940
Edinburgh Thistle

Club	Season	Apps	Sub	Goals	Div
Aberdeen	60/61	2			D1
Newport Co	61/62	29		5	FL
Bath C	62/63				
Motherwell	63/64	21		2	D1
	64/65	3			D1
Durban C					

ROBERTSON James
Tulliallan Jnrs

Club	Season	Apps	Sub	Goals	Div
Stirling A	61/62	2		1	D1
	62/63				D2

ROBERTSON James Gillen
b. Glasgow 17.12.1944 Caps: S - 1
Middlesbrough

Club	Season	Apps	Sub	Goals	Div
Cowdenbeath	60/61				D2
	61/62	25		7	D2
St Mirren	62/63	23		4	D1
	63/64	29		9	D1
Tottenham H	63/64	3		1	FL
	64/65	36		7	FL
	65/66	33		6	FL
	66/67	40		5	FL
	67/68	33	1	5	FL
	68/69	8	3	1	FL
Arsenal	68/69	18	1	3	FL
	69/70	27		4	FL
Ipswich T	69/70	7		3	FL
	70/71	40		5	FL
	71/72	40		2	FL
Stoke C	72/73	27	4	5	FL
	73/74	37		3	FL
	74/75	9	5	3	FL
	75/76	12	6	1	FL
	76/77	14			FL
Walsall	77/78	16			FL
Crewe Alex.	78/79				

ROBERTSON John B
b. Edinburgh 21.5.1926 d. Edinburgh 31.3.2004
Armadale Thistle

Club	Season	Apps	Sub	Goals	Div
Third Lanark	51/52	15			D1
	52/53	30			D1
	53/54	30			D2
	54/55				D2
	55/56				D2
	56/57				D2
	57/58	26			D1
	58/59	2			D1
	59/60	33			D1
	60/61	34			D1
	61/62	29			D1
	62/63	25			D1
Berwick R	63/64	9			D2

ROBERTSON Thomas
b. Kincardine ?.?.1935 d. Melbourne 4.9.2001
Rangers

Club	Season	Apps	Sub	Goals	Div
Dundee	58/59	4		1	D1
	59/60	1			D1
Queen of the South	60/61				D2
Cowdenbeath	61/62	1			D2

ROBERTSON Thomas Smith
b. Coventry 28.9.1944
Petershill

Club	Season	Apps	Sub	Goals	Div
St Mirren	63/64	18		3	D1
	64/65	30		3	D1
	65/66	31		11	D1
Crystal Palace	66/67	5			FL

ROBERTSON Walter
Bayview YC

Club	Season	Apps	Sub	Goals	Div
East Fife	49/50	1			D1
	50/51				D1
	51/52				D1
Forfar A	52/53				D2

ROBERTSON William
Nairn Co

Club	Season	Apps	Sub	Goals	Div
Stirling A	55/56	21			D1
	56/57				D2
Brechin C	57/58				D2
Dunfermline A	58/59	4			D1

ROBINSON Gordon
b. Chesterfield
Sheffield U

Club	Season	Apps	Sub	Goals	Div
Motherwell	51/52	1			D1
	52/53	6		3	D1

ROBINSON Robert Sharp
b. Edinburgh 10.11.1950
d. Forfar 24.12.1996 Caps: S - 4
Newtongrange

Club	Season	Apps	Sub	Goals	Div
Falkirk	71/72	2			D1
Dundee	72/73	31		2	D1
	73/74	30	2	4	D1
	74/75	33		6	D1
	75/76	17	3	2	P
	76/77	20	14	2	P
Dundee U	77/78	14	5		P
	78/79	8	3		P
Heart of Midlothian	79/80	31	4	1	D1
	80/81	13	6		P
Raith R	81/82	25	3	2	D1
	82/83	21		1	D1
Forfar Albion					
Coupar Angus					

ROBSON Benjamin Thomas
b. Gateshead 31.1.1922
Carr Hill Jnrs
St Marys BC
Felling Red Star

Club	Season	Apps	Sub	Goals	Div
Aberdeen	46/47	1			D1
	47/48				D1
	48/49				D1
Southport	49/50	2			FL
Annfield Plain					
Stockton					
New Gateshead U					

RODGER Allan
Kello R

Club	Season	Apps	Sub	Goals	Div
Aberdeen	51/52	2			D1
Ayr U	52/53	15			D2
	53/54	19			D2
	54/55				D2
	55/56				D2
	56/57	1			D1

RODGER Ian
b. Newburgh

Club	Season	Apps	Sub	Goals	Div
Aberdeen	49/50	2			D1
	50/51	1			D1
	51/52	11		8	D1
	52/53	17		5	D1
St Johnstone	53/54	28		30	D2
	54/55	29		21	D2
	55/56	27		20	D2
	56/57	31		16	D2
	57/58	20		6	D2
Forfar A					

RODGER James

Larkhall Thistle
Whitburn

Club	Season				Div
Heart of Midlothian	47/48	15			D1
	48/49	3			D1
Stirling A	L 49/50	6			D1
Third Lanark	50/51	1			D1
Airdrieonians	51/52	21			D1
	52/53	25			D1
	53/54	19			D1
Morton					

RODGER James McPhail
b. Cleland 15.9.1933
Cumnock Jnrs
Douglas Water Thistle

Club	Season				Div
Rangers	53/54	1			D1
	54/55	2			D1
St Mirren	55/56	16		3	D1
	56/57	4		1	D1
Newport Co	L 56/57	1			FL
	57/58	4		1	FL
St Mirren	57/58	2			D1
	58/59	10		5	D1
	59/60	30		5	D1
	60/61	29		8	D1
	61/62	16		2	D1
Heart of Midlothian	61/62	7		1	D1
	62/63	13		6	D1
Queen of the South	63/64	5		1	D1
East Fife	64/65	19		7	D2

RODGERS W

Club	Season				Div
Falkirk	49/50	2			D1

RODMAN Brian William
b. Kilmarnock 3.5.1949
Bellfield BC
Dreghorn Jnrs

Club	Season				Div
Kilmarnock	66/67	1			D1
	67/68	8	1		D1
	68/69		1		D1
	69/70	8			D1
	70/71	11	1		D1
	71/72	33			D1
	72/73	29		1	D1
	73/74	36			D2
	74/75	34			D1
	75/76	20	2	2	D1
Ayr U	76/77	8			P
	77/78	18			P
Partick T	78/79		1		P

ROE John
b. Broxburn 7.1.1938 d. ?.?.1996
West Calder

Club	Season				Div
Colchester U	58/59				FL
	59/60	2			FL
Dundee U	60/61	2			D1
	61/62	2			D1
	62/63	5			D1
St Johnstone	63/64	11			D1

ROGERSON Andrew
b. Whins of Milton 7.2.1941

Club	Season				Div
Alloa A	63/64	36		3	D2
	64/65	36		2	D2
	65/66	2			D2
Stirling A	65/66	25			D1
	66/67	27		2	D1
	67/68	27			D1
Albion R	68/69			5	D2
	69/70	31			D2
Stenhousemuir	70/71			3	D2
	71/72	31	1		D2
Ayr U	72/73	1			D1
St Mirren	72/73	18			D2
Raith R	72/73	2			D2
	73/74	23	3		D2
	74/75	7			D2

ROLLAND Andrew
b. Cardenden 12.11.1942

Club	Season				Div
Cowdenbeath	61/62	7		3	D2
	62/63				D2
	63/64				D2
	64/65	27		4	D2
	65/66	23		3	D2
	66/67	37		7	D2
	67/68	6		1	D2
Dundee U	67/68	29		3	D1
	68/69	34		4	D1
	69/70	32		2	D1
	70/71	33		1	D1
	71/72	30		5	D1
	72/73	24	1	3	D1
	73/74	24	2	4	D1
	74/75	30	2	3	D1
	75/76	32	1	1	P
	76/77	29		2	P
	77/78	22	1	1	P
Fort Lauderdale Strike	78	15		1	NA
Los Angeles Aztecs	78	12			NA
Dunfermline A	78/79	31		1	D2
	79/80	11			D2
Cowdenbeath	79/80	24		3	D2
	80/81	33			D2
	81/82	19	2		D2

ROLLO Alexander
b. Dumbarton 18.9.1926
Springburn U
Ashfield

Club	Season				Div
Celtic	50/51	14			D1
	51/52	17			D1
	52/53	5		1	D1
	53/54	1			D1
Kilmarnock	54/55	25			D1
	55/56	25			D1
Dumbarton	56/57				D2
Workington	57/58	44			FL
	58/59	38		1	FL
	59/60	43		2	FL
Sligo R					

ROLLO James Shepherd
b. Helmsdale 16.11.1937
Blairgowrie Jnrs
Jeanfield Swifts

Club	Season				Div
Hibernian	55/56	1			D1
	56/57	1			D1
Poole T	57/58				
	58/59				
	59/60				
Oldham A	60/61	29			FL
	61/62	20			FL
	62/63	10			FL
Southport	63/64	38			FL
Bradford C	64/65	32			FL
	65/66	5			FL
Scarborough					

RONALDSON Kenneth
b. Leith 27.9.1945
Tynecastle Jnrs

Club	Season				Div
Aberdeen	64/65	1			D1
Bristol R	65/66	9	2	2	FL
	66/67	23		3	FL
	67/68	23		7	FL
	68/69	17	2	3	FL
Gillingham	69/70	5			FL
	70/71	1			FL

ROONEY Benjamin

Petershill

Club	Season				Div
Celtic	60/61				D1
	61/62				D1
	62/63				D1
Dundee U	63/64	8		2	D1
	64/65	4			D1
	65/66	10		3	D1
St Johnstone	65/66	7		2	D1
	66/67	22			D1
	67/68	31	1		D1
	68/69	32		1	D1
	69/70	34		1	D1
	70/71	30		2	D1
	71/72	26	2	2	D1
	72/73	34		4	D1
	73/74	2	1		D1
Partick T	73/74	22			D1
	74/75	20		1	D1
	75/76	20		2	D1

ROONEY R

Club	Season				Div
Clyde	47/48	2			D1

ROSS Charles

Club	Season				Div
Stenhousemuir	61/62	33			D2
	62/63				D2
Falkirk	63/64	1			D1

ROSS David
b. Methilhill 2.5.1951
Kennoway U

Club	Season				Div
Cowdenbeath	69/70	34		10	D2
	70/71	30		4	D1
	71/72	30	3	7	D2
	72/73	35		5	D2
	73/74	33	1	7	D2
	74/75	30	1	2	D2
	75/76				D1
St Johnstone	76/77	20	1		D1
	77/78	23	7	1	D1
	78/79	5	1		D1
Forfar A	78/79	8		1	D2
	79/80	6	7		D2

ROSS Ian John

Kilwinning R

Club	Season				Div
Kilmarnock	57/58	3			D1
	58/59	1			D1
	59/60				D1
	60/61				D1
Raith R	61/62				D1

ROSS John

Kilsyth R

Club	Season				Div
Partick T	68/69	3	1		D1

ROSS Louis Alexander
b. Dublin 19.9.1920 d. ?.?.1990

Club	Season				Div
Hibernian	46/47	1			D1
Queen of the South	47/48	10			D1
Walsall	48/49	8			FL

ROSS Robert Cochrane
b. Edinburgh 9.9.1941
Arniston R

Club	Season				Div
East Fife	59/60				D2
	60/61				D2
	61/62	28		4	D2
	62/63				D2
St Mirren	62/63	6			D1
	63/64	26		3	D1
	64/65	23		2	D1
Grimsby T	65/66	27		4	FL
	66/67	37	1	2	FL
	67/68	44		3	FL
	68/69	30		4	FL
	69/70	43		1	FL
	70/71	27	3	4	FL
Gainsborough T					

ROSS Robert Herdman

b. Edinburgh 18.5.1942					
Tynecastle A					
Musselburgh A					
Heart of Midlothian	60/61	3			D1
	61/62	13		2	D1
	62/63	8		1	D1
Shrewsbury T	63/64	39		5	FL
	64/65	44		16	FL
	65/66	16		5	FL
Brentford	65/66	17			FL
	66/67	46		9	FL
	67/68	41		2	FL
	68/69	44		6	FL
	69/70	46		13	FL
	70/71	46		15	FL
	71/72	45		13	FL
	72/73	7			FL
Cambridge U	72/73	32		9	FL
	73/74	25	8	5	FL
Hayes					

ROSS Samuel

Airdrieonians	59/60	3			D1
	60/61	3			D1
	61/62	5			D1
Brechin C					
Inverness Caley					

ROSS W Lindsay

b. Hamilton					
Glasgow University					
Queen's Park	47/48	7			D1
	48/49	26			D2
	49/50	17		2	D2
	50/51	4			D2
	51/52	4			D2
	52/53	14			D2
	53/54	4			D2
	54/55	5			D2
	55/56	3			D2

ROTHERA Walter

b. c1921 d. 1.4.1990					
Shawfield Jnrs					
Hamilton A	46/47	17			D1
	47/48	30		3	D2
	48/49	30		4	D2
	49/50	30			D2
	50/51	30		4	D2
Queen of the South	51/52	26		7	D1
	52/53	11		1	D1
	53/54	26		18	D1
	54/55	16		3	D1
	55/56	24		11	D1
	56/57	3			D1

ROUGH Alan Roderick

b. Gorbals 25.11.1951 Caps: S - 53					
Lincoln Amateurs					
Partick T					
Sighthill Amateurs	L				
Partick T	69/70	2			D1
	70/71	36			D2
	71/72	34			D1
	72/73	34			D1
	73/74	34			D1
	74/75	19			D1
	75/76	26			D1
	76/77	36			P
	77/78	36			P
	78/79	35			P
	79/80	34			P
	80/81	33			P
	81/82	36			P
	82/83	15			D1
Hibernian	82/83	24			P
	83/84	27			P
	84/85	35			P
	85/86	36			P
	86/87	42			P
	87/88	11			P
Orlando Lions	88				
Celtic	88/89	5			P
Hamilton A	88/89	5			P
Ayr U	89/90	1			D1
Glenafton A					

ROUGH Robert Hendry

Dundee					
Ayr U	68/69				D2
	69/70	20		3	D1
	70/71	9	2	1	D1
	71/72	8	1		D1
	72/73				D1
Stirling A	73/74	4			D2

ROUND Frederick Leonard

b. Kingswinford 21.5.1928					
Ayr U	46/47				D2
	47/48				D2
	48/49				D2
	49/50	11			D2
	50/51				D2
	51/52				D2
	52/53	28			D2
	53/54	29			D2
	54/55				D2
	55/56				D2
	56/57	19			D1
Hull C	57/58	17			FL
Sittingbourne					

ROWAN Brian

b. Glasgow 28.6.1948					
Baillieston R					
Aston Villa	69/70	1			FL
	70/71				FL
Toronto Metros	71	23			NA
Watford	71/72	8	4		FL
Toronto Metros	72	9			NA
Morton	72/73	2			D1
Toronto Metros	73	17			NA
	74	19		1	NA
Toronto Metros-Croat	75	13			NA
New York Cosmos	75	3			NA

ROWAN James

b. Glasgow 29.6.1934					
Shettleston					
Celtic	54/55	1		1	D1
	55/56	1			D1
Stirling A	L 55/56	18		2	D1
Clyde	56/57				D2
	57/58	1			D1
	58/59	3			D1
Dunfermline A	59/60	8		4	D1
Stirling A	59/60	10		2	D1
	60/61				D2
	61/62	24			D1
Airdrieonians	62/63	32		9	D1
	63/64	31		12	D1
	64/65	24		6	D1
Falkirk	65/66	32		1	D1
	66/67	12		2	D1
	67/68				D1
	68/69	1			D1
Partick T	69/70	9			D1

ROXBURGH Andrew

Queen's Park	61/62	9		2	D2
	62/63	10		8	D2
East Stirlingshire	63/64	2			D1
ES Clydebank	64/65				D2
Partick T	65/66	31		16	D1
	66/67	8	1	3	D1
	67/68	6		1	D1
	68/69	2			D1
Falkirk	69/70	23		17	D2
	70/71	24		6	D1
	71/72	7	1	2	D1
Clydebank	72/73	13	1	5	D2
	73/74	25		5	D2
	74/75	3	2	2	D2

ROY Joseph

b. Bo'ness					
Falkirk					
Clydebank					
Dundee	54/55	15		1	D1
	55/56	4			D1
Third Lanark	56/57				
Dundee U	57/58	14		1	D2

ROY William

St Mirren	46/47	11			D1
Aberdeen	47/48	8			D1
	48/49	13			D1
	49/50	4			D1
Dundee	50/51	2			D1
Elgin C					

RUDDY Dennis

Glasgow U					
Clydebank	67/68	4			D2
	68/69				D2
	69/70	36			D2
	70/71			1	D2
	71/72	20	2		D2
Dumbarton	72/73		1		D1
	73/74	28	1		D1
	74/75	28	2	1	D1
	75/76	2	1		D1
Stenhousemuir	75/76	15	2	2	D2

RUGG John

Queen of the South	62/63	30			D1
	63/64	25			D1

RUSSELL F

Raith R	61/62	1			D1
	62/63	1			D1

RUSSELL John
b. Glasgow
Pollok Jnrs

Motherwell	46/47	11		D1
	47/48	3		D1
	48/49	21	1	D1
	49/50	3		D1
Kilmarnock	50/51	25		D2
	51/52	25	1	D2
	52/53	29	1	D2
	53/54	30	1	D2
	54/55	11		D1
	55/56	2		D1

RUSSELL Robert
Darvel Jnrs

Motherwell	62/63	16	9	D1
	63/64	2		D1
Arbroath				

RUSSELL Robert

Aberdeen	59/60	1	D1
	60/61		D1
	61/62		D1
	62/63		D1
Stenhousemuir	63/64	24	D2
	64/65	17	D2
Third Lanark	65/66	12	D2
	66/67	24	D2
Morton	67/68	21	D1
	68/69	13	D1

RUTHERFORD Andrew
b. Edinburgh 4.10.1953
Salvesen BC

East Fife	70/71				D2
	71/72				D1
	72/73				D1
	73/74	13	4		D1
	74/75	23	4	4	D2
	75/76	19	2	8	D1
	76/77	18	3	3	D1
St Johnstone	76/77	14			D1
	77/78	39			D1
	78/79	39		7	D1
	79/80	38		3	D1
	80/81	35			D1
	81/82	37		6	D1
	82/83	39		2	D1
	83/84	34			P
	84/85	21	2		D1
Cowdenbeath	85/86	30	2		D2
	86/87		2		D2

RUTHERFORD Derek
b. Keith 23.10.1946
Keith
Leicester C

Heart of Midlothian	66/67	2	D1
East London U			

RUTHERFORD Edward
b. Glasgow 8.2.1921 Caps: S - 1
Mossvale Amateurs

Rangers	46/47	5	1	D1
	47/48	20	5	D1
	48/49	27	2	D1
	49/50	22	7	D1
	50/51	17	3	D1
	51/52	4	1	D1
Heart of Midlothian	51/52	20	8	D1
	52/53	4	1	D1
	53/54	14	2	D1
Raith R	54/55	4		D1
Hamilton A	55/56	21	6	D2

RUTHERFORD Harry

Alloa A	64/65	34		22	D2
	65/66	31		13	D2
	66/67	14		7	D2
Ayr U	66/67	11	1	1	D1
Clydebank					
Alloa A	67/68	7		1	D2

RUTHERFORD William John
b. Bellshill 23.1.1930 d. Southport 29.4.1980
Bellshill

Ayr U	49/50	4		D2
	50/51			D2
Stirling A	51/52	8		D1
Darlington	52/53	45		FL
	53/54	41	1	FL
	54/55	40	1	FL
	55/56	43	1	FL
	56/57	30		FL
	57/58	44		FL
	58/59	8		FL
Southport	59/60	40	2	FL
	60/61	45	3	FL
	61/62	42		FL
	62/63	38	1	FL
	63/64	11	1	FL
Kirkby T				

RYAN Vincent
b. Irish Rep c1936
Home Farm

Celtic	53/54	1		D1
	54/55			D1
	55/56			D1
	56/57	15	3	D1
	57/58	6		D1
St Mirren	57/58	12	4	D1
	58/59	12	1	D1
Drumcondra	59/60			

RYCE James
Dalkeith Thistle

Stirling A	57/58			D2
	58/59	20	3	D1
	59/60	3		D1

RYDEN George Joseph
b. Alexandria 14.07.1940
Duntocher Hibs

Dundee	58/59			D1
	59/60			D1
	60/61			D1
	61/62			D1
	62/63	9	2	D1
	63/64	31		D1
	64/65	8		D1
	65/66	4		D1
St Johnstone	66/67	12		D1
	67/68	8		D1
	68/69	5		D1
Stirling A	69/70			D2

RYLANCE Derek
b. Perth 6.4.1952
Kinnoull

Arbroath	72/73	34		D1
	73/74	34	1	D1
	74/75	32	2	D1
	75/76	26		D1
	76/77	38	3	D1
	77/78	33		D1
	78/79	39		D1
	79/80	15		D1
	80/81	17	5	D2

SAMSON James
b. c1935
Darvel Jnrs

Hamilton A	55/56	25	D2
	56/57	35	D2
	57/58	33	D2
	58/59	36	D2
	59/60	33	D2
	60/61	28	D2
	61/62	31	D2
Airdrieonians	62/63	34	D1
	63/64	28	D1
	64/65	32	D1
Arbroath *	65/66	28	D2
Stenhousemuir	66/67	25	D2
	67/68	11	D2
Darvel Jnrs			

SAMUEL George
b. Broxburn c1929

Aberdeen	51/52	4	1	D1
	52/53			D1
Dunfermline A	53/54	11		D2
	54/55			D2
	55/56	31		D1
	56/57	22		D1

SAMUEL John

Morton	46/47	3		D1
	47/48	1		D1
Meadowbank				
Third Lanark	50/51	30		D1
	51/52	16		D1
	52/53	11		D1
Dundee U	53/54	4	1	D2

SANDEMAN Frank
b. Dundee 28.8.1936

Montrose	55/56				D2
	56/57				D2
	57/58				D2
	58/59				D2
	59/60				D2
	60/61				D2
	61/62	30		2	D2
	62/63				D2
East Stirlingshire	63/64	28		2	D1
Heart of Midlothian	63/64	5			D1
	64/65				D1
Arbroath	65/66	18		4	D2
	66/67				D2
Brechin C	67/68	29	5	4	D2
	68/69			5	D2
	69/70	23	4	1	D2
	70/71				D2

SANG George
b. c1940 d. Aberdeen 8.12.2003
Rosemount Juniors

Aberdeen	59/60	3	D1
Arbroath	60/61		D2
Peterhead			
Buckie Thistle			
Fraserburgh			
Ross County			

SANSOM J

Queen of the South	62/63	3	D1

SAVAGE

Third Lanark	57/58	2	D1

SAVAGE William
d. c1961
Motherwell Jnrs

Club	Season	App	Sub	Goals	Div
Queen of the South	32/33				
	33/34	36			D1
	34/35	36			D1
	35/36	32			D1
	36/37	36			D1
	37/38	36		3	D1
	38/39	35		1	D1
	46/47	28			D1
	47/48	8			D1

SCALLY D

Club	Season	App	Sub	Goals	Div
St Mirren	46/47	1			D1

SCHAEDLER Erich Peter
b. Biggar 6.8.1949 d. 24.12.1985
Whitehill Welfare
Peebles R
Melbourne Thistle

Club	Season	App	Sub	Goals	Div
Stirling A	68/69	3			D2
	69/70	15		1	D2
Hibernian	69/70	5			D1
	70/71	15			D1
	71/72	29			D1
	72/73	32		1	D1
	73/74	31			D1
	74/75	30	1		D1
	75/76	32	1	1	P
	76/77	24			P
	77/78	10			P
Dundee	77/78	15			D1
	78/79	27	1	1	D1
	79/80	27			P
	80/81	31	1		D1
	81/82	1			P
Hibernian	81/82	23	5		P
	82/83	6	1		P
	83/84	29			P
	84/85	23			P
Dumbarton	85/86	14			D1

SCOBIE Wallace

Club	Season	App	Sub	Goals	Div
Queen's Park	56/57	5			D1
	57/58	14		1	D1

SCOTT Alexander Silcock
b. Falkirk 22.11.1936 d. ?.9.2001 Caps: S - 16
Camelon Thistle
Bo'ness U

Club	Season	App	Sub	Goals	Div
Rangers	54/55	7		3	D1
	55/56	34		9	D1
	56/57	29		12	D1
	57/58	23		4	D1
	58/59	34		7	D1
	59/60	29		12	D1
	60/61	33		12	D1
	61/62	23		7	D1
	62/63	4		1	D1
Everton	62/63	17		4	FL
	63/64	40		7	FL
	64/65	36		6	FL
	65/66	35		5	FL
	66/67	21		1	FL
Hibernian	67/68	22			D1
	68/69	16	2	2	D1
Falkirk	69/70	12	1	1	D2
	70/71	9	1		D1
	71/72	1			D1

SCOTT Alistair B
b. Glasgow 26.8.1950

Club	Season	App	Sub	Goals	Div
Queen's Park	72/73	33		11	D2
Rangers	73/74	21	3	8	D1
	74/75	7	2	1	D1
	75/76	1		1	P
Hibernian	76/77	23	8	3	P
	77/78	5	2	1	P
Morton	78/79	24	6	3	P
	79/80	13	13	3	P
	80/81	1	1		P
Partick T	80/81		2		P
Queen of the South	80/81	6		1	D2
East Stirlingshire	81/82	3			D1

SCOTT Charles

Club	Season	App	Sub	Goals	Div
Aberdeen	47/48	1			D1

SCOTT Edward
Sunnybank

Club	Season	App	Sub	Goals	Div
Aberdeen	55/56	1			D1

SCOTT George
Hibernian

Club	Season	App	Sub	Goals	Div
Hamilton A	53/54	29			D1
	54/55				D2
	55/56	8			D2
	56/57	6			D2
	57/58				D2
Blackpool	58/59				FL
Bath C	59/60				
	60/61				

SCOTT George William
b. Aberdeen 25.10.1944

Club	Season	App	Sub	Goals	Div
Liverpool	61/62				FL
	62/63				FL
	63/64				FL
	64/65				FL
Aberdeen	65/66	2			D1
Port Elizabeth					
Tranmere R	68/69	18			FL
	69/70	17		1	FL

SCOTT Ian
b. Montrose
Montrose

Club	Season	App	Sub	Goals	Div
Raith R	52/53	8			D1
	53/54	16		3	D1
	54/55	9			D1
	55/56	17			D1

SCOTT Ian
b. Musselburgh ?.?.1946
Musselburgh A

Club	Season	App	Sub	Goals	Div
Dundee U	66/67	1			D1
	67/68	19	1	7	D1
	68/69	8	9	2	D1
	69/70	20	9	5	D1
	70/71	2	3		D1
Dundee	71/72	14	2	6	D1
	72/73	25	1	3	D1
	73/74	9	6		D1
	74/75	7	5	3	D1

SCOTT James
b. Falkirk 21.8.1940 Caps: S - 1
Denny R
Falkirk
Bo'ness U

Club	Season	App	Sub	Goals	Div
Hibernian	58/59	3			D1
	59/60	7			D1
	60/61	18		6	D1
	61/62	10		1	D1
	62/63	24		4	D1
	63/64	25		6	D1
	64/65	22		15	D1
	65/66	31		8	D1
	66/67	31	1	8	D1
Newcastle U	67/68	35	1	3	FL
	68/69	23	2	2	FL
	69/70	12	1	1	FL
Crystal Palace	69/70	11			FL
	70/71	21	5	4	FL
	71/72	4	2	1	FL
Falkirk	71/72	2			D1
	72/73	9	1	7	D1
Hamilton A	73/74	22		2	D2
	74/75				

SCOTT James
b. 19.11.1953
Leven Royal Colts

Club	Season	App	Sub	Goals	Div
Dunfermline A	70/71	1	1		D1
	71/72	26	1	1	D1
	72/73	31		6	D2
	73/74	27	5	1	D1
	74/75	31		1	D1
	75/76	26		1	D1
	76/77	33	2	4	D2
	77/78	30	2	1	D2
	78/79	7	8		D2
	79/80	5	1		D1
East Fife	80/81	26	1	1	D2

SCOTT John

Club	Season	App	Sub	Goals	Div
Third Lanark	47/48	6			D1
	48/49	15		8	D1
	49/50	5			D1
Cowdenbeath	50/51				D2
Dundee U	51/52				D2
Haddington U	52/53				
Hamilton A	53/54	23		5	D1
Eyemouth U					

SCOTT John
b. Aberdeen 14.1.1948 Caps: S - 2
Chelsea

Club	Season	App	Sub	Goals	Div
Dundee	64/65	6		6	D1
	65/66	7			D1
	66/67	20		12	D1
	67/68	19	3	6	D1
	68/69	32	1	10	D1
	69/70	32		9	D1
	70/71	33		16	D1
	71/72	34		12	D1
	72/73	31	1	12	D1
	73/74	30		22	D1
	74/75	32		8	D1
	75/76				P
Aberdeen	75/76	28	4	14	P
	76/77	13	6	3	P
Seattle Sounders	77	17		6	NA
Aberdeen	77/78	1			P
Dundee	77/78	19	1	4	D1
Seattle Sounders	78	22		3	NA
Dundee	78/79	1	4		D1
	79/80				P
	80/81	2			D1

SCOTT Kenneth
Musselburgh A

Club	Season	App	Sub	Goals	Div
Falkirk	64/65	28		3	D1
	65/66	11		2	D1
	66/67	3			D1
	67/68	13	1		D1

SCOTT Robert

Club	Season				Div
St Mirren	46/47	17		1	D1
Queen of the South	47/48	19			D1
St Johnstone	T 48/49	1			D2

SCOTT Walter
b. Douglas 23.6.1932
Douglasdale Jnrs

Club	Season				Div
Falkirk	50/51	14			D1
	51/52	27			D2
	52/53	8			D1
Hamilton A	53/54	2			D1
Dumbarton	53/54	13			D2
Halifax T	54/55	13			FL

SEAWRIGHT David

Club	Season				Div
Airdrieonians	49/50	27	13		D2
	50/51	9		2	D1
	51/52	6			D1
	52/53	17		5	D1
	53/54	4			D1

SEEMANN Finn
Caps: Nor - 15
Lyn Oslo

Club	Season				Div
Dundee U	65/66	14		3	D1
	66/67	15	3	5	D1
	67/68	22		4	D1

DWS Amsterdam

SEITH James
Hill of Beath

Club	Season				Div
Motherwell	62/63	1			D1

SEITH Robert
b. Coatbridge 9.3.1932

Club	Season				Div
Burnley	49/50				FL
	50/51				FL
	51/52				FL
	52/53				FL
	53/54	23			FL
	54/55	13			FL
	55/56	33			FL
	56/57	41		1	FL
	57/58	32		2	FL
	58/59	42		3	FL
	59/60	27			FL
Dundee	60/61	33		2	D1
	61/62	34		2	D1
	62/63	28			D1
	63/64	32		1	D1
	64/65	7			D1

SELFRIDGE Henry
Methil Star

Club	Season				Div
Raith R	64/65	12			D2
	65/66	21			D2
	66/67	6			D2
	67/68	3			D1

SELKIRK Alexander
Stonehouse Violet

Club	Season				Div
Queen of the South	56/57	26			D1

SELLARS Eric
Carnoustie Panmure

Club	Season				Div
Arbroath	66/67	30		9	D2
	67/68	14	1	1	D2
	68/69	27	3	8	D1
	69/70	28	2	8	D2
	70/71			7	D2
	71/72	26	1	6	D2
	72/73	34		8	D1
	73/74	34		21	D1
	74/75	27	4	3	D1
	75/76	14	7	4	D1
St Johnstone	76/77	11	3	1	D1
Brechin C	76/77	10	1	2	D2
	77/78	16	4	1	D2

SELWAY Ronald
b. Dundee
Preston N E

Club	Season				Div
Dundee	66/67	9			D1
	67/68	2			D1
	68/69	4	1		D1
	69/70	29			D1
	70/71	15	1		D1
	71/72	3	1		D1
Raith R	72/73	31			D2
	73/74	17			D2

SEMPLE William
b. Bellshill
Edinburgh A

Club	Season				Div
Rangers	67/68	2			D1
	68/69				D1
	69/70	4		2	D1
	70/71	2			D1
Durban U					
Dundee	72/73	2	3		D1
	73/74	1	5		D1
	74/75				D1
	75/76				P
Albion R	76/77	26	2	13	D2

SETTERINGTON Denis Grant
b. Edinburgh 17.11.1945

Club	Season				Div
Rangers	61/62				D1
	62/63				D1
	63/64				D1
	64/65				D1
	65/66	1			D1
	66/67	6		3	D1
	67/68				D1
	68/69				D1
	69/70	4	2	1	D1
Falkirk	70/71	25	4	4	D1
	71/72	17	4	6	D1
	72/73	25	4		D1
	73/74				D1
Stirling A	74/75	12	4	2	D2
	75/76	3	2		D2

SHANKLAND David
Cowdenbeath

Club	Season				Div
Airdrieonians	49/50	8		1	D2
	50/51	24			D1
	51/52	25		2	D1
	52/53	15			D1
	53/54	15			D1

SHANKS James

Club	Season				Div
Airdrieonians	52/53	1			D1
	53/54	7			D1
	54/55				D2
	55/56	9			D1
	56/57	27			D1
	57/58	32			D1
	58/59	3			D1
	59/60	27			D1
	60/61	31			D1
	61/62	32			D1
	62/63	16			D1
Stranraer *	63/64	20			D2
	64/65	15		1	D2
	65/66	34		3	D2
	66/67	33			D2

SHARKEY James
b. 12.2.1934
Haverill R
Celtic
Rutherglen Glenca L

Club	Season				Div
Celtic	54/55				D1
	55/56	19		7	D1
	56/57	3		1	D1
	57/58	1			D1
Airdrieonians	57/58	12		4	D1
	58/59	33		12	D1
	59/60	28		7	D1
	60/61	24		7	D1
Raith R	61/62				D1
Portadown	T 61/62				
Cambridge T					
Wisbech T					
Corby T					
Bury T					
Newmarket T					
Girton U					

SHARP Frank
b. Edinburgh 28.5.1947
Tynecastle A

Club	Season				Div
Heart of Midlothian	65/66	6		1	D1
Carlisle U	66/67	1			FL
	67/68	27		1	FL
	68/69	4		1	FL
Southport	T 68/69				FL
Cardiff C	68/69	6			FL
	69/70	7			FL
Barnsley	70/71	43		3	FL
	71/72	42			FL
	72/73	40		4	FL
Grimsby T	73/74	26	3	2	FL
Port Vale	74/75	17	7	2	FL
Northwich V					

SHARP Ronald
b.30.1.1948 d. Mexico 15.4.2002
Glenrothes Jnrs

Club	Season				Div
Cowdenbeath	68/69			4	D2
	69/70	15		3	D2
	70/71	1	1		D1
	71/72	15	1	3	D2
	72/73	4		2	D2
Miami Toros	74	20		2	NA
	75	21		1	NA
	76	21		1	NA
Fort Lauderdale Strike	77	1			NA

SHARP William
Shettleston

Club	Season				Div
Partick T	46/47	28		13	D1
	47/48	26		6	D1
	48/49	27		11	D1
	49/50	18		4	D1
	50/51	29		8	D1
	51/52	30		4	D1
	52/53	26		1	D1
	53/54	28		22	D1
	54/55	13		6	D1
	55/56	22		13	D1
	56/57	7		2	D1

SHARPE Douglas
b. Dumfries c1926 d. ?.?.1974
Greystone R

Club	Season	Apps	Sub	Gls	Div
Queen of the South	46/47				
	47/48	18		1	D1
	48/49	13			D1
	49/50	17			D1
	50/51				D2
	51/52	23			D1
	52/53	29			D1
	53/54	29			D1
	54/55	28			D1
	55/56	32			D1
	56/57	33			D1
	57/58	20			D1
	58/59	33			D1
	59/60				D2
	60/61				D2
	61/62				D2
	62/63				D1
	63/64				D1
	64/65				D2
	65/66				D2

K

SHARPE Robert
b. Kirkcaldy 20.12.1925

Club	Season	Apps	Sub	Gls	Div
Raith R	51/52	1			D1
Darlington	52/53	14			FL

SHAW Archibald Hamilton Rammage
b. Craigneuk d. 11.2.1985
Wishaw Jnrs

Club	Season	Apps	Sub	Gls	Div
Motherwell	46/47	30			D1
	47/48	25			D1
	48/49	28			D1
	49/50	12			D1
	50/51	25			D1
	51/52	28			D1
	52/53	26			D1
	53/54	25			D2
	54/55	29			D1
	55/56	19			D1
	56/57				D1
	57/58	9			D1

SHAW D

Club	Season	Apps	Sub	Gls	Div
Airdrieonians	55/56	2			D1

SHAW David
b. Annathill 5.5.1917 d. ?.?.1977 Caps: S - 8
Banknock Juveniles
Grange R

Club	Season	Apps	Sub	Gls	Div
Hibernian	38/39	1			D1
	46/47	28			D1
	47/48	28			D1
	48/49	14			D1
	49/50	15			D1
Aberdeen	50/51	23			D1
	51/52	14		1	D1
	52/53	13			D1

SHAW Graham
b. Edinburgh 8.10.1951
Edina Hibs
Albion BC
Musselburgh

Club	Season	Apps	Sub	Gls	Div
Dunfermline A	71/72	1			D1
	72/73	36		26	D2
	73/74	28	1	8	D1
	74/75	33		12	D1
	75/76	18		6	D1
Heart of Midlothian	75/76	13		2	P
	76/77	30	5	7	P
	77/78	23	3	3	D1
	78/79	8		1	P
	79/80	15	5	2	D1
Arbroath	80/81	31	2	3	D2
	81/82	25	5	6	D2
	82/83	37	1	12	D2
	83/84	8		4	D2
	84/85	15	1	1	D2

SHAW John
b. Annathill 29.11.1912
d. Glasgow 13.6.2000 Caps: S - 4
Benburb

Club	Season	Apps	Sub	Gls	Div
Airdrieonians	33/34	37			D1
	34/35	37			D1
	35/36	35		1	D1
	36/37	31		2	D2
	37/38	34		2	D2
Rangers	38/39	36			D1
	46/47	28			D1
	47/48	28		1	D1
	48/49	27			D1
	49/50	29			D1
	50/51	18			D1
	51/52	2			D1
	52/53	1			D1

SHEARER John
Hamilton Cross
Ardeer Rec

Club	Season	Apps	Sub	Gls	Div
Hamilton A	T 56/57	1			D2

Burnbank A

Club	Season	Apps	Sub	Gls	Div
Hamilton A	T 58/59	1			D2
Clyde	59/60	8		4	D1
	60/61				D1
	61/62				D2
Albion R	62/63				D2

East Kilbride Thistle
Baillieston Jnrs
Royal Albert

SHEARER Robert
b. Hamilton 29.12.1931 Caps: S - 4
Burnbank A

Club	Season	Apps	Sub	Gls	Div
Hamilton A	50/51				D2
	51/52	5			D2
	52/53				D2
	53/54	22		5	D1
	54/55	30		3	D2
	55/56	17		6	D2
Rangers	55/56	16			D1
	56/57	34			D1
	57/58	28		2	D1
	58/59	34			D1
	59/60	21			D1
	60/61	33			D1
	61/62	34			D1
	62/63	34			D1
	63/64	31			D1
	64/65	3			D1
Queen of the South	65/66	30			D2

SHEED Ronald McLean
b. Provan 8.5.1947
East Kilbride Thistle

Club	Season	Apps	Sub	Gls	Div
Kilmarnock	69/70	1			D1
	70/71	1			D1
	71/72	1			D1
	72/73	4	5	1	D1
	73/74	36		3	D2
	74/75	32		9	D1
	75/76	16	1	1	D1
	76/77	18	3	1	P
Partick T	77/78	1			P
	78/79	1	1	1	P
	79/80		1		P

Duncanrigg Amateurs

SHEEHY Sean
Preston N E

Club	Season	Apps	Sub	Gls	Div
Dundee U	73/74	2	1		D1

SHEPHERD G

Club	Season	Apps	Sub	Gls	Div
Clyde	49/50	2			D1

SHERRINGTON Edward R
Dunblane R
Edinburgh C
Queen's Park

Club	Season	Apps	Sub	Gls	Div
Stirling A	47/48				D2
	48/49				D2
	49/50	1			D1

SHERRY A

Club	Season	Apps	Sub	Gls	Div
Airdrieonians	55/56	1			D1

SHEVLANE Anthony Christopher
b. Edinburgh 6.5.1942
Edina Hearts
Heart of Midlothian
Loanhead Mayflow L

Club	Season	Apps	Sub	Gls	Div
Heart of Midlothian	60/61				D1
	61/62				D1
	62/63	10			D1
	63/64	31			D1
	64/65	25			D1
	65/66	23			D1
	66/67	15		1	D1
Celtic	67/68	2			D1
Hibernian	68/69	25		1	D1
	69/70	32		1	D1
	70/71	8	1		D1
Morton	71/72	17			D1
	72/73	18			D1
	73/74	2	1		D1

SHEWAN Alistair J
b. Turriff
Formartine

Club	Season	Apps	Sub	Gls	Div
Aberdeen	60/61				D1
	61/62	7			D1
	62/63	12			D1
	63/64	32			D1
	64/65	34			D1
	65/66	34		2	D1
	66/67	34		1	D1
	67/68	34		3	D1
	68/69	34		2	D1

St Georges Budapest
Elgin C

SHIELDS James
St Mungos Academy

Club	Season	Apps	Sub	Gls	Div
Celtic	46/47	3			D1
Raith R	T 46/47				D2
Dumbarton	47/48				D2

SHIELDS W

Club	Season	Apps	Sub	Gls	Div
Queen of the South	62/63	2			D1

F

SHIRRA James W
b. Falkirk 10.6.1950
Gairdoch Juveniles

Club	Season	Apps	Sub	Gls	Div
Falkirk	67/68				D1
	68/69		1		D1
	69/70	8	1		D2
	70/71	32		2	D1
	71/72	31		3	D1
	72/73	32			D1
	73/74	30	3	1	D1
	74/75	23	4	14	D2
	75/76	25	3	5	D1
	76/77	11		2	D1
Aberdeen	76/77	20		6	P
	77/78	8			P
Dundee	77/78	22	1	2	D1
	78/79	30	2	5	D1
	79/80	27	4	3	P
	80/81	15	5	4	D1
South Melbourne Hell	81/82				
	82/83				
Stirling A	83/84	27	2		D2

SHIRREFFS Gilbert

Club	Season	Apps	Sub	Gls	Div
Arbroath	59/60	34		6	D1

SIEVWRIGHT George Edgar Smollett
b. Broughty Ferry 10.9.1937
Broughty A

Club	Season	Apps	Sub	Gls	Div
Dundee U	61/62	7			D1
	62/63	1			D1
Oldham A	63/64	37		4	FL
Tranmere R	64/65				FL
Rochdale	65/66	31	1	1	FL
Macclesfield T					

SIEVWRIGHT Gordon

Falkirk	53/54	15		D1
	54/55	4		D1

SILCOCK James
b. Falkirk
Camelon

Falkirk	48/49	3		D1
	49/50	6	1	D1
Stirling A	49/50	1	1	D1
	50/51			D2
	51/52	16	3	D1
Stenhousemuir	52/53	25	14	D2
	53/54	25	11	D2

SIM Gordon

Aberdeen	59/60	7		D1
	60/61	14		D1
Highlands Park				

SIM Ian

Clyde	57/58	2		D1
	58/59	3		D1
	59/60	10		D1
	60/61	15		D1

SIMPSON Archibald
b. Dundee 8.6.1933

Dundee	53/54	1		D1
	54/55			D1
Newcastle U	55/56			FL
Barrow	56/57	38	1	FL
	57/58	27		FL
	58/59	11		FL

SIMPSON David

Third Lanark	52/53	1		D1
	53/54	2		D2
Coventry C				

SIMPSON Robert

Rangers	50/51	2	2	D1

SIMPSON Robert

Ayr U	56/57	1		D1
	57/58			D2
Stranraer	L 57/58			D2

SIMPSON Ronald
Greengairs U
Armadale

Dundee U	62/63			D1
	63/64	3		D1
Stranraer				

SIMPSON Ronald Campbell
b. Glasgow 11.10.1930 d. 4.2004 Caps: S - 5

Queen's Park	46/47	19		D1
	47/48	22		D1
	48/49	17		D2
	49/50	20		D2
Third Lanark	50/51	21		D1
Newcastle U	51/52	39		FL
	52/53	37		FL
	53/54	42		FL
	54/55	35		FL
	55/56	37		FL
	56/57	35		FL
	57/58	34		FL
	58/59			FL
	59/60	3		FL
Hibernian	60/61	28		D1
	61/62	34		D1
	62/63	30		D1
	63/64	31		D1
Celtic	64/65	8		D1
	65/66	30		D1
	66/67	33		D1
	67/68	33		D1
	68/69	12		D1
	69/70	2		D1

SIMPSON Thomas
b. Airdrie 31.7.1931
Burnbank A

Hamilton A	53/54	3		D1
Dundee U	54/55	5	1	D2
	55/56			D2
Darlington	56/57	3		FL
	57/58	1		FL
Weymouth				

SIMPSON William
Edina Hibs

Hibernian	63/64	4			D1
	64/65	5			D1
	65/66	20			D1
	66/67		1		D1
	67/68	15			D1
	68/69				D1
	69/70				D1
Falkirk	70/71	2			D1
Albion R	71/72	17	2	1	D2
Alloa A	72/73	26	1	5	D2
	73/74	21	2	3	D2
	74/75	12			D2
Cowdenbeath	75/76	19	1		D2
	76/77	27	3	1	D2

SIMPSON William J
b. Belfast Caps: NI - 12
Linfield

Rangers	50/51	19	13	D1
	51/52	3	1	D1
	52/53	21	21	D1
	53/54	18	11	D1
	54/55	25	18	D1
	55/56	32	10	D1
	56/57	32	21	D1
	57/58	16	11	D1
	58/59	6	7	D1
Stirling A	58/59	7	1	D1
	59/60	1		D1
Partick T	59/60	6		D1

SINCLAIR

Arbroath	59/60	5		D1

SINCLAIR Allan A
b. Canada
Loudoun Star

Kilmarnock	46/47	2		D1
	47/48			D2
	48/49	7	3	D2
Annbank U				
Craigmark Bruntonians				
Inverness Clachnacuddin				

SINCLAIR Andrew
Armadale Thistle

Motherwell	46/47			
	47/48	7		D1
	48/49	4		D1
	49/50			D1

SINCLAIR Colin MacLean
b. Edinburgh 1.12.1947
Whitston Star
Linlithgow Rose

Raith R	69/70	21		4	D1
	70/71			4	D2
Darlington	71/72	24	1	8	FL
	72/73	46		9	FL
	73/74	38		9	FL
	74/75	43		10	FL
	75/76	43	1	21	FL
	76/77	7		2	FL
Hereford U	76/77	7			FL
	77/78	13		2	FL
Newport Co	77/78	15		1	FL
	78/79	14	1	4	FL
Linlithgow Rose					
IFK Vasteras					

SINCLAIR Duncan Eric
b. Haggs 13.1.1954
Kilsyth R

Dundee	74/75	1			D1
	75/76	9	3	2	P
	76/77	30	2	11	D1
	77/78	27	6	13	D1
	78/79	27	4	10	D1
	79/80	35		8	P
	80/81	36		19	D1
	81/82	24	1	7	P
	82/83	25	6	6	P
	83/84	1			P
St Mirren	83/84	2	1		P
Airdrieonians	83/84	14	2	1	D1

SINCLAIR John Evens Wright
b. Culross 21.7.1943 Caps: S - 1
Blairhall Colliery

Dunfermline A	60/61	1			D1
	61/62	5		4	D1
	62/63	16		5	D1
	63/64	14		8	D1
	64/65	25		16	D1
Leicester C	65/66	42		22	FL
	66/67	41		21	FL
	67/68	20		7	FL
Newcastle U	67/68	16		3	FL
	68/69	20	1	3	FL
	69/70	6			FL
Sheffield W	69/70	19		3	FL
	70/71	38		7	FL
	71/72	37	3	4	FL
	72/73	3	1		FL
Chesterfield	L 72/73	10		3	FL
Dunfermline A	73/74	24		4	D1
	74/75	23	5	5	D1
Stenhousemuir	75/76	17	1	1	D2

SINCLAIR John R
Dalkeith Thistle

Stirling A	58/59	18	1	D1
	59/60	13		D1
	60/61			D2
	61/62	5		D1
Cowdenbeath	62/63			D2
	63/64	32		D2

SINCLAIR Malcolm JM

Third Lanark	38/39	3		
	46/47	2		
Falkirk	46/47	10	1	
Dundee U	47/48	16	2	D2

SINCLAIR William Inglis
b. Glasgow 21.3.1947

Club	Season				Div
Morton	63/64				D2
Chelsea	64/65	1			FL
	65/66				FL
Glentoran	65/66				
	66/67				
Kilmarnock	67/68	7			D1
	68/69	1	2		D1
Glentoran					
Linfield					

SINCLAIR William Mearns
b. Blairhall 14.10.1934
Aberdeen

Club	Season				Div
Falkirk	53/54	29		9	D1
	54/55	8			D1
	55/56	30		8	D1
	56/57	11		3	D1
	57/58	8			D1
	58/59	3			D1
Huddersfield T	58/59	8		2	FL
	59/60	7		3	FL
Tranmere R	60/61	4			FL
Halifax T	60/61				FL
Stirling A	61/62	18		3	D1

SIRREL James
b. Glasgow 2.2.1922
Bridgeton Waverley
Renfrew Jnrs

Club	Season				Div
Celtic	46/47	6		1	D1
	47/48	4		1	D1
	48/49	3			D1
Bradford PA	49/50	5		1	FL
	50/51	7		1	FL
Brighton & HA	51/52	27		7	FL
	52/53	9		1	FL
	53/54	19		8	FL
Aldershot	54/55	30		3	FL
	55/56				
	56/57	1			FL

SKINNER Edwin
Arbroath

Club	Season				Div
Dundee	56/57	1			D1
East Fife	56/57	6			D1

SKOVDAM Kenny
b. Denmark

Club	Season				Div
Morton	74/75	25	3	3	D1

SLATER Malcolm
b. Buckie 22.10.1939
Buckie Thistle

Club	Season				Div
Celtic	58/59	4		1	D1
	59/60	1			D1
Buckie Thistle	59/60				
	60/61				
Inverness Caley	61/62				
	62/63				
Montrose	62/63				D2
	63/64				D2
Southend U	63/64	10			FL
	64/65	31		2	FL
	65/66	35		4	FL
	66/67	6			FL
Leyton Orient	66/67	22		1	FL
	67/68	35		2	FL
	68/69	45		1	FL
	69/70	9			FL
Colchester U L	69/70	4			FL

SLATER Robert
b. Musselburgh 5.5.1936
Airth Castle R
Tranent Jnrs
Broughton Star

Club	Season				Div
Falkirk	53/54	2			D1
	54/55	30			D1
	55/56	24			D1
	56/57	17			D1
	57/58	28			D1
	58/59	33			D1
Liverpool	59/60	28			FL
	60/61	42			FL
	61/62	29			FL
Dundee	62/63	32			D1
	63/64	34			D1
	64/65	4			D1
Watford	65/66	46			FL
	66/67	38			FL
	67/68	46			FL
	68/69	4			FL

SLAVEN

Club	Season				Div
Hibernian	57/58	2			D1

SLINGSBY Geoff

Club	Season				Div
Airdrieonians	53/54	5			D1
	54/55				D2
	55/56	7			D1
	56/57	11			D1
Third Lanark	57/58	28		1	D1
	58/59	4			D1

SLOAN Thomas
b. Barrhead 13.10.1925
Arthurlie

Club	Season				Div
Heart of Midlothian	46/47	18		5	D1
	47/48	10		3	D1
	48/49	23		4	D1
	49/50	28		5	D1
	50/51	29		7	D1
	51/52	2			D1
Motherwell	51/52	16		7	D1
	52/53	29		5	D1
	53/54	28		10	D2
	54/55	12		2	D1
	55/56	15		6	D1
	56/57	12		5	D1
Gloucester C					

SMALL James
Yoker A

Club	Season				Div
Hamilton A	63/64	16			D2
	64/65	36			D2
	65/66	27			D1
	66/67	37			D2
	67/68	27			D2
	68/69	24			D2
	69/70	20			D2

SMELLIE James

Club	Season				Div
Third Lanark	51/52	10		1	D1
	52/53	1			D1

SMITH Alexander
b. Ayr
Muirkirk

Club	Season				Div
Queen of the South	51/52	1			D1
	52/53	30			D1
	53/54	25			D1
	54/55	30			D1
	55/56	32		1	D1
	56/57	30		1	D1
	57/58	25			D1
	58/59	30			D1

SMITH Alexander
b. c1940
Dunbar U

Club	Season				Div
Dunfermline A	57/58				D2
	58/59	24		7	D1
	59/60	29		10	D1
	60/61	24		7	D1
	61/62	25		13	D1
	62/63	28		15	D1
	63/64	22		5	D1
	64/65	24		6	D1
	65/66	34		5	D1
Rangers	66/67	33		19	D1
	67/68	6	2	1	D1
	68/69				D1
Aberdeen	69/70		1		D1

SMITH Alexander
Luncarty Jnrs

Club	Season				Div
St Johnstone	74/75	11			D1
	75/76	23	1		P
	76/77	27			D1
Wigan A					

SMITH Archibald
b. Larkhall 23.10.1924 d. ?.?.1995
Larkhall Rangers
Royal Albert

Club	Season				Div
Hamilton A	46/47	13		4	D1
	47/48	12		5	D2
Exeter C	48/49	20		7	FL
	49/50	31		9	FL
	50/51	41		21	FL
	51/52	23		6	FL
Carlisle U	52/53	21		7	FL
	53/54	10		1	FL

SMITH Archibald
Bayview YC

Club	Season				Div
East Fife	50/51				D1
	51/52	2			D1
	52/53				D1
Dundee U	53/54				D2

SMITH Brian Watson
b. Glasgow 27.7.1946
Renfrew Jnrs

Club	Season				Div
Stirling A	66/67	9			D1
	67/68	11			D1
Charlton A	68/69				FL
Stirling A	68/69				D2

SMITH Charles
Gairdoch U

Club	Season				Div
Falkirk	65/66	5			D1
	66/67	21			D1
	67/68	11	1	2	D1
	68/69	34		3	D1
Partick T	69/70	33		2	D1
	70/71	33		6	D2
	71/72	11	1		D1
	72/73	3			D1
Marist Bros					
Falkirk	73/74	8	1		D1
	74/75	23	4	6	D2
St Johnstone	75/76	8	1	3	P

SMITH Colin
Glasgow College of Building

Club	Season				Div
Queen's Park	71/72	16		5	D2
Partick T	72/73	2	3		D1
	73/74	1			D1
Stranraer	74/75	10	3	3	D2

SMITH Daniel
Grangemouth U

Club	Season				Div
Dunfermline A	61/62	1			D1
Alloa A					

SMITH David

Carrickvale Thistle

Club	Season	Apps	Sub	Gls	Div
Dunfermline A	74/75	1		3	D1
	75/76*	2		1	D1
	76/77	2	6	3	D2

Vale of Leithen
Gala Fairydean
Whitehill Welfare

SMITH David Bruce
b. Aberdeen 14.11.1943 Caps: S - 2
Aberdeen Lads Club

Club	Season	Apps	Sub	Gls	Div
Aberdeen	61/62	2			D1
	62/63	31		3	D1
	63/64	33		2	D1
	64/65	33			D1
	65/66	34		3	D1
Rangers	66/67	34		2	D1
	67/68	34		2	D1
	68/69	22	1	2	D1
	69/70	22	3		D1
	70/71	9	2		D1
	71/72	30		1	D1
	72/73	29			D1
	73/74	7	2	1	D1
Los Angeles Aztecs	74				
Arbroath	74/75	20			D1
	75/76				D1
Berwick R	75/76				D2
	76/77	27			D2
	77/78	39		1	D2
	78/79	39		3	D2
	79/80	39		5	D1
	80/81	16		1	D1
Meadowbank T	80/81	11			D2
Hamilton A	80/81	6			D1
Peterhead					

SMITH Douglas B
b. Aberdeen ?.?.1937
Aberdeen Lads Club

Club	Season	Apps	Sub	Gls	Div
Dundee U	59/60	1			D2
	60/61	6			D1
	61/62	33			D1
	62/63	34		1	D1
	63/64	33			D1
	64/65	34			D1
	65/66	34			D1
	66/67	34			D1
	67/68	34			D1
	68/69	34			D1
	69/70	34		1	D1
	70/71	34		5	D1
	71/72	25		2	D1
	72/73	31		5	D1
	73/74	26		3	D1
	74/75	20	2	1	D1
	75/76	7			P

SMITH Edward

Club	Season	Apps	Sub	Gls	Div
St Johnstone	68/69			1	D1

SMITH Eric

Club	Season	Apps	Sub	Gls	Div
Queen's Park	57/58	1			D1

SMITH Frederick Adamson
b. Aberdeen 14.2.1926
Hall Russells

Club	Season	Apps	Sub	Gls	Div
Aberdeen	48/49	1			D1
	49/50	1			D1
Hull C	49/50	9		1	FL
	50/51	8			FL
Sheffield U	50/51	1			FL
	51/52	36		11	FL
	52/53	3			FL
Millwall	52/53	15		4	FL
	53/54	31		6	FL
	54/55	28		8	FL
	55/56	18		2	FL
Chesterfield	56/57	7		1	FL
Montrose					

SMITH George
b. Bathgate
Wallhouse Rose
Torpichen Juveniles

Club	Season	Apps	Sub	Gls	Div
Partick T	53/54	2			D1
	54/55	25		12	D1
	55/56	14		2	D1
	56/57	26		8	D1
	57/58	23		8	D1
	58/59	27		12	D1
	59/60	32		17	D1
	60/61	20		3	D1
	61/62	28		9	D1
	62/63	26		6	D1
	63/64	5			D1
Dundee U	63/64	5		1	D1
	64/65				D1
Ballymena U					

SMITH Gordon
b. Edinburgh 25.5.1924 Caps: S - 18
Kirriemuir Juveniles
Roselea
Dundee NE

Club	Season	Apps	Sub	Gls	Div
Hibernian	46/47	23		7	D1
	47/48	29		19	D1
	48/49	29		15	D1
	49/50	29		25	D1
	50/51	25		10	D1
	51/52	29		8	D1
	52/53	28		13	D1
	53/54	12		5	D1
	54/55	28		9	D1
	55/56	30		7	D1
	56/57	17		3	D1
	57/58	16		3	D1
	58/59	15		1	D1
Heart of Midlothian	59/60	29		11	D1
	60/61	13		2	D1
Dundee	61/62	32		7	D1
	62/63	29		3	D1
	63/64	9			D1
Drumcondra					

SMITH Gordon Duffield
b. Kilwinning 29.12.1954
Kilmarnock Star

Club	Season	Apps	Sub	Gls	Div
Kilmarnock	71/72				D1
	72/73	34		4	D1
	73/74	34		11	D2
	74/75	31	2	5	D1
	75/76	25		9	D1
	76/77	32	2	7	P
Rangers	77/78				P
	78/79				P
	79/80				P
Brighton & HA	80/81	36	2	10	FL
	81/82	24	3	2	FL
	82/83	26	3	6	FL
Rangers	L 82/83				P
Brighton & HA	83/84	11	4	4	FL
Manchester C	83/84	9		1	FL
	84/85	31	1	12	FL
	85/86	1			FL
Oldham A	85/86	14	1		FL
Admira Wacker	86/87				
FC Basel	87/88				
Stirling A	88/89	3			D2
Oldham A					

SMITH Gordon Melville
b. Glasgow 3.7.1954
Rangers BC

Club	Season	Apps	Sub	Gls	Div
St Johnstone	72/73	12	1		D1
	73/74	33	1	5	D1
	74/75	32	1	1	D1
	75/76	32		2	P
Aston Villa	76/77	32	2		FL
	77/78	38			FL
	78/79	6	1		FL
Tottenham H	78/79	1	1		FL
	79/80	14			FL
	80/81	18	2	1	FL
	81/82	1	1		FL
Wolverhampton W	82/83	24	3	2	FL
	83/84	11		1	FL
S Africa					
Pittsburgh Spirit					

SMITH Hugh

Club	Season	Apps	Sub	Gls	Div
Third Lanark	60/61	1			D1

SMITH Ian R
b. Ormiston 25.12.1952
Haddington A

Club	Season	Apps	Sub	Gls	Div
Dundee	72/73	1	1		D1
	73/74				D1
Berwick R	74/75	36		8	D2
	75/76	24		10	D2
	76/77	32	3	4	D2
	77/78	32	4	7	D2
	78/79	13	7	1	D2
	79/80	5	5		D1
Alloa A	79/80	17	1		D2
	80/81	14	1	1	D2
	81/82	34		2	D2
	82/83	22	2	1	D1
	83/84	22	2	3	D2
Berwick R	84/85	20	5		D2
	85/86	4	1		D2
Meadowbank T	85/86	11			D2
	86/87	4	1		D2

SMITH Ivor

Club	Season	Apps	Sub	Gls	Div
Aberdeen	53/54	1			D1
	54/55				D1
Dundee	55/56	15		9	D1
	56/57	3			D1

SMITH James

Bo'ness U

Club	Season	Apps	Sub	Gls	Div
Raith R	62/63	7			D1

SMITH James

Club	Season	Apps	Sub	Gls	Div
Partick T	46/47	4		1	D1
	47/48	2	.		D1
Albion R	48/49	17		1	D1

SMITH James

Club	Season	Apps	Sub	Gls	Div
Queen's Park	55/56				D2
	56/57				D1
	57/58	6		3	D1
	58/59	2			D2

SMITH James
b. Glasgow 20.1.1947 Caps: S - 4
Benburb

Club	Season	Apps	Sub	Gls	Div
Aberdeen	65/66	7		1	D1
	66/67	30		10	D1
	67/68	33		9	D1
	68/69	33		1	D1
Newcastle U	69/70	21	1	3	FL
	70/71	24		3	FL
	71/72	1	2	1	FL
	72/73	32		5	FL
	73/74	27		1	FL
	74/75	19	2		FL
	75/76				FL
Celtic	L 75/76				P
Whitley Bay					

SMITH James Christopher Reginald (born Schmidt)

b. Battersea 20.1.1912
d. Letchworth 6.1.2004
Hitchin T
Crystal Palace   T
Tottenham H
St Albans C

Club	Season	Apps	Sub	Gls	Div
Millwall	35/36	30		7	FL
	36/37	19		4	FL
	37/38	31		7	FL
	38/39	37		3	FL
Dundee	46/47	26		4	D2
	47/48	19		2	D1
Corby T					
Dundee	48/49	8			D1

SMITH James T

Inverness Caley

Club	Season	Apps	Sub	Gls	Div
Stirling A	55/56	1			D1
	56/57				D2
	57/58				D2
	58/59	17			D1
	59/60	9			D1

SMITH John

b. Greenock
Ardeer Recreation

Club	Season	Apps	Sub	Gls	Div
Stirling A	50/51				D2
	51/52	21		3	D1
	52/53	30		6	D2
	53/54	20			D1
	54/55	25		5	D1
	55/56	31		1	D1
	56/57				D2
Dumbarton					

SMITH John Eric

b. Glasgow 29.7.1934 d. Dubai 12.6.1991
Caps: S - 2
St Andrews Juveniles
Pollok
Benburb

Club	Season	Apps	Sub	Gls	Div
Celtic	54/55	3		1	D1
	55/56	13		1	D1
	56/57	10		1	D1
	57/58	23		4	D1
	58/59	27		5	D1
	59/60	21			D1
Leeds U	60/61	18		2	FL
	61/62	41		1	FL
	62/63	6			FL
Morton	64/65	18			D1
	65/66	16		3	D1
	66/67	1			D2

SMITH Joseph F

b. Glasgow 11.11.1953
St Gregorys BC
Aberdeen
Banks o'Dee   L

Club	Season	Apps	Sub	Gls	Div
Aberdeen	72/73	13		1	D1
	73/74	23	2	1	D1
	74/75	23	3	1	D1
	75/76	33	2		P
	76/77	35	3		P
	77/78	7			P
	78/79		2		P
Arbroath L	78/79	4			D1
Motherwell	78/79	14			P
	79/80	22	2		D1
	80/81	19			D1
	81/82				D1
	82/83				P
Peterhead					
Dunfermline A	83/84	1			D2

SMITH P

Club	Season	Apps	Sub	Gls	Div
Albion R	48/49	12		3	D1

SMITH Paul

Club	Season	Apps	Sub	Gls	Div
Morton	71/72	4	1	2	D1

SMITH Robert

Club	Season	Apps	Sub	Gls	Div
Raith R	49/50	15		3	D1

SMITH Robert

Burnley

Club	Season	Apps	Sub	Gls	Div
Dundee U	61/62				D1
	62/63				D1
	63/64	6		1	D1
	64/65				D1
	65/66	1			D1
St Johnstone	66/67	11			D1
	67/68				D1
Montrose	67/68	11			D2
	68/69				D2
	69/70	16		1	D2
	70/71				D2
	71/72	23			D2

SMITH Robert Nisbet

b. Dalkeith 21.12.1953
Musselburgh Windsor

Club	Season	Apps	Sub	Gls	Div
Hibernian	72/73	5	4		D1
	73/74	5	6	2	D1
	74/75	16	5	3	D1
	75/76	20	3	6	P
	76/77	36		8	P
	77/78	32	3		P
	78/79	17			P
Leicester C	78/79	17		6	FL
	79/80	35		12	FL
	80/81	17	2	1	FL
	81/82	2	2		FL
Peterborough U L	81/82	5			FL
Leicester C	82/83	26		1	FL
Hibernian L	82/83	4	1		P
Leicester C	83/84	35	1		FL
	84/85	30			FL
	85/86	13	1	1	FL
Hibernian	86/87	9	1		P
Dunfermline A	87/88	33	2		P
	88/89	32	1	1	D1
Partick T	89/90	29	1	1	D1
Berwick R	90/91	24	2		D2

SMITH Samuel

Club	Season	Apps	Sub	Gls	Div
St Mirren	46/47	16			D1
	47/48	28		1	D1
	48/49	8			D1

SMITH Stirton

b. Gorebridge 28.10.1926
Edinburgh Thistle

Club	Season	Apps	Sub	Gls	Div
Heart of Midlothian	46/47	1			D1
	47/48				D1
Third Lanark	48/49	1			D1
Dunfermline A	49/50	12			D2
Arniston R					
Newtongrange Star					
NCB Amateurs					

SMITH Walter

b. Lanark 24.2.1948
Ashfield

Club	Season	Apps	Sub	Gls	Div
Dundee U	66/67	1			D1
	67/68	2			D1
	68/69				D1
	69/70	4		1	D1
	70/71	17			D1
	71/72	14		4	D1
	72/73	14		1	D1
	73/74	30	2	1	D1
	74/75	16	2		D1
	75/76	2			P
Dumbarton	75/76	21			D1
	76/77	23			D1
Dundee U	76/77	17	1		P
	77/78		1		P
	78/79	5			P
	79/80	1			P
	80/81	1			P

SMITH William

b. Aberdeen
Sunnybank

Club	Season	Apps	Sub	Gls	Div
Aberdeen	51/52	4			D1
	52/53	25			D1
	53/54	9			D1
	54/55	25			D1
	55/56				D1
	56/57	8			D1
Third Lanark	57/58	31		3	D1
	58/59	9			D1
	59/60	4			D1

SMITH William

b. Armadale
Linlithgow Rose

Club	Season	Apps	Sub	Gls	Div
Partick T	53/54	6			D1
	54/55	2			D1
	55/56	21			D1
	56/57	19			D1
Queen of the South	57/58	22			D1
	58/59	9			D1

SMITH William

Club	Season	Apps	Sub	Gls	Div
Rangers	57/58	2			D1
	58/59				
Dundee	59/60	26			D1
	60/61	6			D1
Forfar A					

SMITH William

b. Aberdeen 23.12.1938

Club	Season	Apps	Sub	Gls	Div
Raith R	62/63	9		2	D1
Darlington	63/64	26		7	FL
Inverness Caley					
Nairn Co					

SNEDDON David

b. Kilwinning 24.4.1936
Kilwinning R

Club	Season	Apps	Sub	Gls	Div
Dundee	54/55	1			D1
	55/56	1			D1
	56/57	3		1	D1
	57/58	23		6	D1
	58/59	32		6	D1
Preston NE	58/59	1			FL
	59/60	40		11	FL
	60/61	37		5	FL
	61/62	13		1	FL
Kilmarnock	61/62	19		2	D1
	62/63	20		5	D1
	63/64	31		4	D1
	64/65	28		5	D1
	65/66	9			D1
	66/67	5	1		D1
Raith R	67/68	23	5	5	D1
	68/69	29	1	3	D1
	69/70	17	4	1	D1
	70/71				D2

SNEDDON Ian

b. Duntocher 30.11.1946
Drumchapel Amateurs

Club	Season	Apps	Sub	Gls	Div
Heart of Midlothian	67/68	31			D1
	68/69	9			D1
	69/70	4	1		D1
	70/71	7			D1
	71/72	31			D1
	72/73	22		1	D1
	73/74	18			D1
	74/75	6			D1
Denver Dynamos	75	21			NA
Morton	75/76	20			D1
	76/77	2	1		D1
Ontario					

SNEDDON William

Hurlford U

Club	Season	Apps	Sub	Gls	Div
Motherwell	50/51	1		1	D1
	51/52				D1

SOMERVILLE Robert

Club	Season			Div
Clyde	50/51	22		D1
	51/52			D2
	52/53			D1
Albion R	53/54	1		D2

SOMERVILLE Thomas

Coltness U

Club	Season			Div
Falkirk	50/51	6		D1

SOMNER Douglas
b. Edinburgh 4.7.1951
East Kilbride R
East Kilbride Thistle

Club	Season				Div
Falkirk	71/72	23	2	6	D1
	72/73	10	2	6	D1
	73/74	6	2	1	D1
Ayr U	74/75	3	2	1	D1
Partick T	74/75	21		8	D1
	75/76	26		16	D1
	76/77	33		11	P
	77/78	31		15	P
	78/79	31	2	11	P
St Mirren	79/60	32		25	P
	80/81	29		13	P
	81/82	14	2	2	P
	82/83	15	7	5	P
Hamilton A	83/84	33	3	9	D1
Montrose	84/85	31	3	12	D2
	85/86	30	2	3	D1

SORENSEN Erik Lykke
b. Denmark 22.1.1940 Caps: Den - 15
B1913 Odense

Club	Season			Div
Morton	63/64	5		D2
	64/65	31		D1
	65/66	31		D1
	66/67	35		D2
Rangers	67/68	30		D1
Morton	70/71	27		D1
	71/72	34		D1
	72/73	10		D1

SORENSEN Jorn
b. Denmark 17.10.1936 Caps: Den - 31
Nibe
KB Copenhagen
Metz

Club	Season			Div
Morton	64/65	22	9	D1
Rangers	65/66	12	3	D1
Bellinzona				

SOUNESS James McGill
b. Leith 9.11.1928 d. Switzerland 2.9.1990
Murrayfield A
Edinburgh Thistle
Hibernian

Club	Season			Div
Falkirk	L 49/50	9	1	D1
Hibernian	50/51	2	2	D1
	51/52	1		D1
	52/53	1	1	D1
Heart of Midlothian	52/53	5		D1
	53/54	14	6	D1
	54/55	28	8	D1
	55/56	1		D1

SOUTAR David
b. Dundee
Carnoustie Panmure

Club	Season				Div
Dundee U	T 58/59	1			D2
Arbroath	59/60	2			D1
	60/61				D2
	61/62				D2
	62/63				D2
	63/64	30		3	D2
	6465	8		1	D2
Clyde	64/65	13		3	D1
	65/66	15			D1
	66/67	18	1	1	D1
	67/68	28		1	D1
	68/69	11	3	2	D1
	69/70	13	1		D1
Dundee	70/71	9	1		D1

SOUTAR Douglas
Butterburn YC

Club	Season			Div
Dundee U	62/63	2		D1
	63/64			D1
	64/65	3	1	D1
Forfar A	L 64/65			D2
Dundee U	65/66			D1
East Fife	66/67			D2
	67/68			D2
	68/69			D2
	69/70			D2
	70/71			D2
Elgin C				

SPALDING Derek
b. Dundee 20.12.1954

Club	Season				Div
Hibernian	72/73	2			D1
	73/74	13			D1
	74/75	21	1	1	D1
	75/76	16	1		P
	76/77	18	2		P
	77/78				P
Chicago Sting	78	29		2	NA
	79	23		7	NA
	80	30		4	NA
	81	28		2	NA
	82	9			NA
Toronto Blizzard	83	24			NA
	84	10			NA

SPENCE Ian
Armadale Thistle

Club	Season			Div
Stirling A	58/59	31	11	D1
	59/60	6	2	D1
Raith R	59/60	26	8	D1
	60/61	11	2	D1
Stirling A	61/62	26	3	D1
Stenhousemuir	62/63			D2
Third Lanark	62/63	17	4	D1
Berwick R	63/64	17	1	D2

SPROAT Hugh
b. Ayr 16.11.1952
Auchinleck Talbot

Club	Season			Div
Ayr U	74/75	11		D1
	75/76	36		P
	76/77	15		P
	77/78	28		P
	78/79	38		D1
Motherwell	79/80	39		D1
	80/81	34		D1
	81/82	35		D1
	82/83	21		P
	83/84	17		P
Ayr U	84/85	37		D1
	85/86	24		D1
Clyde	86/87			

ST JOHN Ian
b. Motherwell 7.6.1938 Caps: S - 21
Motherwell Bridge Works
Douglas Water Thistle

Club	Season			Div
Motherwell	57/58	22	17	D1
	58/59	30	24	D1
	59/60	32	20	D1
	60/61	29	18	D1
Liverpool	61/62	40	18	FL
	62/63	40	19	FL
	63/64	40	21	FL
	64/65	27	4	FL
	65/66	41	10	FL
	66/67	39	9	FL
	67/68	41	5	FL
	68/69	41	4	FL
	69/70	25	1 5	FL
	70/71		1	FL
Hellenic	71			
Coventry C	71/72	18	3	FL
Tranmere R	72/73	9	1	FL

STABLES Ian

Club	Season			Div
Dundee	52/53	6	1	D1
	53/54			D1
	54/55			D1
	55/56	20	5	D1

STAITE Richard
Broxburn Strollers

Club	Season				Div
Partick T	62/63	3			D1
	63/64	5		2	D1
	64/65	11			D1
Clyde	65/66	8		1	D1
	66/67	24	2	2	D1
	67/68	31		8	D1
	68/69	20	4	2	D1
	69/70	22	3	6	D1
	70/71	1	1		D1
Raith R	71/72	22	1	2	D2
	72/73	12			D2

STANNERS Duncan
b Denny.
Dunipace Jnrs

Club	Season			Div
Rangers	51/52	1		D1
	52/53	3		D1
	53/54	8		D1
	54/55	7		D1
	55/56	1		D1
Stirling A	55/56	16		D1
	56/57			D2

STANTON Dennis
Musselburgh A

Club	Season				Div
Arbroath	69/70	1			D2
	70/71			2	D2
	71/72	24	2	2	D2
	72/73	5		2	D1
Forfar A	73/74	15	3	2	D2
Alloa A	73/74	6	1		D2

STANTON Patrick Gordon
b. Edinburgh 13.9.1944 Caps: S - 16
United Crossroads
Salvesen BC
Dunfermline A   T
Edina Hearts
Bonnyrigg Rose

Club	Season			Div
Hibernian	63/64	15	1	D1
	64/65	33		D1
	65/66	34	2	D1
	66/67	33	1	D1
	67/68	26		D1
	68/69	33	1	D1
	69/70	31	6	D1
	70/71	30	3	D1
	71/72	32	9	D1
	72/73	33	8	D1
	73/74	32	9	D1
	74/75	34	6	D1
	75/76	31	2 5	P
Celtic	76/77	36		P
	77/78	1		P

STAROSCIK Felix
b. Silesia 20.5.1920
Wolverhampton W

Club	Season			Div
Third Lanark	47/48	23	12	D1
	48/49	20	9	D1
	49/50	18	7	D1
	50/51	20	5	D1
Northampton T	51/52	24	6	FL
	52/53	1	1	FL
	53/54	2	1	FL
	54/55	22	11	FL
Bedford T				

STEAD Angus
d. Glasgow ?.?.1999
St Mirren
Dumbarton

Club	Season			Div
Rangers	46/47	3		D1
Morton	47/48	4		D1

STEADWARD James J

Queen's Park

Club	Season	Apps	Gls	Div
Partick T	46/47	18		D1
Dundee	47/48	1		D1
	48/49			D1
Hamilton A	L 48/49	18		D2
Dundee	49/50			D1
Stirling A	50/51			D2
	51/52	3		D1
East Fife	51/52			D1

STEEDMAN William

Dalkeith Thistle

Club	Season	Apps	Gls	Div
East Fife	55/56	5		D1
	56/57	3		D1

STEEL John
b. Holytown
Carnoustie Panmure

Club	Season	Apps	Gls	Div
Hamilton A	46/47	7		D1
Brechin C				

STEEL Robert
b. Larkhall
Royal Albert

Club	Season	Apps	Gls	Div
Clyde	59/60	1		D1
	60/61	22	10	D1
	61/62			D2
	62/63	12	3	D1
Queen of the South	62/63			D1
Hamilton A	63/64	14	2	D2

STEEL W

Club	Season	Apps	Gls	Div
Clyde	60/61	1		D1

STEEL William
b. Denny 1.5.1923 d. Los Angeles 13.5.1982
Caps: S - 30
Dunipace Thistle
Bo'ness Cadora
Leicester C
St Mirren

Club	Season	Apps	Gls	Div
Morton	46/47	9	1	D1
Derby Co	47/48	37	8	FL
	48/49	38	14	FL
	49/50	34	5	FL
Dundee	50/51	26	7	D1
	51/52	21	6	D1
	52/53	22	8	D1
	53/54	25	6	D1
Los Angeles Danes				
Hollywood				

STEEL William

Wallhouse Rose

Club	Season	Apps	Gls	Div
Partick T	54/55	1		D1
	55/56			D1
	56/57	1		D1

STEELE James
b. Edinburgh 11.3.1950

Club	Season	Apps	Sub	Gls	Div
Dundee	67/68	1			D1
	68/69	3	1	1	D1
	69/70	23		2	D1
	70/71	28		1	D1
	71/72	19		1	D1
Southampton	71/72	16			FL
	72/73	38		1	FL
	73/74	34	1		FL
	74/75	27			FL
	75/76	32		1	FL
	76/77	13			FL
Rangers	L 76/77	5			P
Washington Diplomat	77	15			NA
	78	22			NA
	79	17		1	NA
Memphis Rogues	80	7			NA
Chicago Sting					
Pittsburgh					

STEELE Russell

Larkhall Thistle
Rangers

Club	Season	Apps	Gls	Div
Clyde	67/68	2		D1
	68/69			D1
	69/70			D1
	70/71			D1
Hamilton A	71/72	2		D2
Carluke R				

STEEN John M
b. Dundee 20.12.1954
Blackpool

Club	Season	Apps	Sub	Gls	Div
Dundee U	72/73	1			D1
	73/74	2			D1
	74/75				D1
Forfar A	75/76	24		1	D2
Stranraer	76/77	31	1	2	D2
	77/78	36	2	2	D2
	78/79	26	2	2	D2
Raith R	79/80	11		3	D1
	80/81	33	2	2	D1
	81/82	14	1		D1
	82/83	8	2		D1
East Stirlingshire	82/83	12	2	1	D2
	83/84	28			D2
	84/85	21			D2

STEIN Colin Anderson
b. Philipstoun 10.5.1947 Caps: S - 21
Broxburn Strollers
Armadale Thistle

Club	Season	Apps	Sub	Gls	Div
Hibernian	65/66	13		8	D1
	66/67	18		9	D1
	67/68	32		21	D1
	68/69	7		3	D1
Rangers	68/69	18		13	D1
	69/70	33		24	D1
	70/71	30		12	D1
	71/72	28		11	D1
	72/73	2	1		D1
Coventry C	72/73	31		10	FL
	73/74	28		5	FL
	74/75	24		6	FL
Rangers	74/75	8		3	D1
	75/76	3	3	1	P
	76/77	1	1		P
	77/78				P
Kilmarnock	L 77/78	23	1	8	D1

STEIN John
b. Earnock 6.10.1922 d. Cardiff 10.9.1985
Blantyre Victoria

Club	Season	Apps	Gls	Div
Albion R	46/47			D2
	47/48			D2
	48/49	15	2	D1
	49/50	7		D2
Llanelly	50/51			
	51/52			
Celtic	51/52	17		D1
	52/53	28		D1
	53/54	27	1	D1
	54/55	28	1	D1
	55/56	6		D1
	56/57			D1

STEIN Robert
b. Philipstoun 19.9.1939
Broxburn A

Club	Season	Apps	Sub	Gls	Div
Raith R	60/61	20			D1
	61/62	27		1	D1
	62/63	26			D1
	63/64	26			D2
	64/65	31			D2
	65/66	34		5	D2
	66/67	37		5	D2
	67/68	32		1	D1
	68/69	4	4	1	D1
Montrose	69/70	34		6	D2
East Stirlingshire	70/71			1	D2
	71/72	33		3	D2
	72/73	23	1	2	D2
	73/74	29	1	2	D2
	74/75	35	2	2	D2
	75/76	17	2	2	D2
	76/77	26	3	2	D2

STENHOUSE Alan

Edina Hearts

Club	Season	Apps	Gls	Div
Motherwell	57/58	3	1	D1
	58/59	1		D1
	59/60	1		D1
	60/61			D1
	61/62			D1

STENHOUSE James
b. Lochgelly
Lochgelly Violet

Club	Season	Apps	Gls	Div
St Mirren	46/47	16	1	D1
	47/48	9	1	D1
Aberdeen	47/48	3		D1
	48/49	17		D1
	49/50	9	1	D1
	50/51	2		D1

STENHOUSE Robin
b. Gilmerton 29.3.1942
Edina Hibs
Loanhead Mayflower

Club	Season	Apps	Gls	Div
Heart of Midlothian	61/62	3	3	D1
Hamilton Steelers	62			
Third Lanark	62/63	9	8	D1
Penicuik A				

STEPHEN A

Club	Season	Apps	Gls	Div
Queen of the South	47/48	7	1	D1

STEPHENS

Club	Season	Apps	Gls	Div
Arbroath	59/60	2		D1

STEVEN Thomas
b. Edinburgh 5.9.1954
Dunbar U

Club	Season	Apps	Sub	Gls	Div
Hibernian	71/72				D1
	72/73	1			D1
	73/74				D1
Hamilton A	74/75	6		1	D2
Berwick R	74/75	27		6	D2
	75/76	10			D2
East Fife	75/76	9		2	D1
	76/77	2			D1
Forfar A	76/77	26	1	2	D2

STEVENS A

Club	Season	Apps	Gls	Div
Hibernian	72/73	1		D1

STEVENS Gregor MacKenzie
b. Glasgow 13.1.1955
Baillieston

Club	Season				Div
Motherwell	74/75	4		1	D1
	75/76	30	3	4	P
	76/77	36		2	P
	77/78	35		6	P
	78/79	31		6	P
Leicester C	79/80	4			FL
Rangers	79/80	31		1	P
	80/81	7	2		P
	81/82	13			P
	82/83	10			P
	83/84	1			P
Heart of Midlothian L	83/84	3			P
Motherwell	84/85	8			D1
Partick T	84/85	1			D1
	85/86	2			D1
Brechin C	86/87	32			D1
	87/88	35			D2
	88/89	21			D2
	89/90	7			D2
Dumbarton	89/90	8			D2

STEVENSON David

Club	Season	Apps	Div
Morton	47/48	6	D1
	48/49	2	D1

STEVENSON Eric
Edina Hearts
Heart of Midlothian

Club	Season			Div
Hibernian	60/61	8	1	D1
	61/62	32	9	D1
	62/63	20	2	D1
	63/64	24	8	D1
	64/65	16	1	D1
	65/66	27	10	D1
	66/67	31	8	D1
	67/68	30	10	D1
	68/69	30	2	D1
	69/70	27	1	D1
	70/71	11	1	D1
	71/72	1	1	D1
Ayr U	71/72	16 1	3	D1
	72/73	11		D1

STEVENSON Hugh

Club	Season	Apps		Div
Queen's Park	57/58	3	2	D1

STEVENSON James

Club	Season	Apps	Div
Airdrieonians	47/48	22	D1

STEVENSON James

Club	Season	Apps	Div
Dundee	55/56	10	D1
	56/57		D1
	57/58		D1
	58/59		D1
Dunfermline A	59/60	14	D1
	60/61	14	D1
	61/62	2	D1

STEVENSON James

Club	Season	Apps		Div
St Mirren	56/57	1		D1
	57/58			D1
	58/59			D1
Raith R	59/60	10		D1
	60/61	7		D1
	61/62	11		D1
	62/63	24	1	D1

STEVENSON James
b. Bellshill 4.8.1946

Club	Season	Apps		Div
Hibernian	64/65	5		D1
	65/66	6	1	D1
	66/67			D1
Southend U	67/68	33	1	FL
Brentwood T				

STEVENSON James Rae
b. Galston 30.9.1923
Loudoun Star
Glenafton A
Kilmarnock Jnrs

Club	Season	Apps		Div
Kilmarnock	46/47	15	3	D1
	47/48	6	2	D2
Morton	48/49	3		D1
Stranraer	49/50			D3
	50/51			D3
	51/52			D3

STEVENSON John
b. Uddingston 17.6.1953

Club	Season				Div
Coventry C	71/72				FL
Heart of Midlothian	72/73	5			D1
	73/74	30		4	D1
	74/75	10	6	1	D1
St Johnstone	75/76	1	2		P

STEVENSON Morris John
b. Tranent 16.4.1943
Cockenzie Star

Club	Season			Div
Motherwell	60/61	2		D1
	61/62	10	3	D1
Hibernian	62/63	20	4	D1
Morton	63/64	33	8	D2
	64/65	32	6	D1
	65/66	26	4	D1
	66/67	36	4	D2
	67/68	27	4	D1
	68/69	6		D1
Luton T	68/69	1		FL
Dundee U	69/70	7	1	D1
	70/71	20	2	D1
	71/72	5		D1
Berwick R	72/73	5		D2

STEVENSON Robert
Auchinleck Talbot

Club	Season	Apps		Div
Ayr U	55/56			D2
	56/57	4	2	D1
	57/58			D2
	58/59			D2
	59/60	1		D1
Kilwinning R				

STEVENSON Robert
b. Irvine 1.2.1953
Irvine Meadow

Club	Season				Div
Kilmarnock	70/71				D1
	71/72				D1
	72/73	3			D1
	73/74	4	2	2	D2
Irvine Meadow					
Cumnock Jnrs					
Largs Thistle					

STEVENSON William
b. Leith 26.10.1939
Edina Hearts
Dalkeith Thistle

Club	Season			Div
Rangers	58/59	26		D1
	59/60	34	1	D1
	60/61	8		D1
	61/62	5		D1
Liverpool	62/63	28	2	FL
	63/64	38	1	FL
	64/65	39	3	FL
	65/66	41	5	FL
	66/67	41	3	FL
	67/68	1	1	FL
Stoke C	67/68	18		FL
	68/69	30 2	3	FL
	69/70	18 2	2	FL
	70/71	3 2		FL
	71/72	12 5		FL
	72/73	1 1		FL
Tranmere R	73/74	20		FL
Vancouver Whitecaps	74	19		NA

STEWART

Club	Season	Apps	Div
Motherwell	58/59	1	D1

STEWART Alexander

Club	Season			Div
Airdrieonians	59/60	16	2	D1
	60/61	1		D1
Dundee U	60/61			D1
Albion R	61/62	20	3	D2
	62/63			D2
	63/64			D2
	64/65			D2
Brechin C	65/66	25	1	D2
	66/67	12	1	D2

STEWART David
Larkhall Thistle

Club	Season	Apps	Div
Hamilton A	46/47	16	D1
	47/48	5	D2
Queen's Park	48/49	4	D2
	49/50		D2
	50/51		D2
	51/52	2	D2

Larkhall Thistle
Eaglesham Amateurs

STEWART David Steel
b. Glasgow 11.3.1947 Caps: S - 1
Kilsyth R

Club	Season	Apps	Div
Ayr U	67/68	36	D2
	68/69		D2
	69/70	34	D1
	70/71	31	D1
	71/72	22	D1
	72/73	30	D1
	73/74	5	D1
Leeds U	73/74	3	FL
	74/75	14	FL
	75/76	2	FL
	76/77	16	FL
	77/78	17	FL
	78/79	3	FL
West Bromwich A	78/79		FL
	79/80		FL
Swansea C	79/80	15	FL
	80/81	42	FL
Ryoden			

STEWART George
b. Edinburgh 29.8.1947
Tynecastle BC

Club	Season			Div
Dundee	66/67	9		D1
	67/68	23		D1
	68/69	24	1	D1
	69/70	21 1		D1
	70/71	9		D1
	71/72	16	1	D1
	72/73	33	2	D1
	73/74	11		D1
	74/75	28	2	D1
	75/76	25		P
Hibernian	76/77	29		P
	77/78	36	1	P
	78/79	27 2	1	P
	79/80	13		P
	80/81	2		D1
Cowdenbeath	80/81	13	1	D2
	81/82			D2
	82/83			D2
	83/84	1		D2

STEWART George Scott
b. Larkhall 16.11.1932
Petershill

Club	Season	Apps	Div
Raith R	51/52		D1
	52/53	9	D1
	53/54		D1
	54/55	10	D1
	55/56	15	D1
	56/57	15	D1
	57/58	1	D1
Stirling A	58/59	16	D1
Bradford C	59/60	7	FL
	60/61	15	FL

STEWART George Thompson Scott
b. Buckie 17.2.1927
Buckie Thistle

Club	Season	Apps	Sub	Gls	Div
Dundee	46/47				D2
	47/48	5			D1
	48/49	2		2	D1
	49/50	4		2	D1
	50/51				D1
St Mirren	50/51	15		7	D1
	51/52	16		6	D1
	52/53	26		13	D1
	53/54	18		12	D1
Worcester C	54/55				
Accrington S	54/55	33		28	FL
	55/56	46		35	FL
	56/57	40		33	FL
	57/58	44		27	FL
	58/59	19		13	FL
Coventry C	58/59	25		15	FL
	59/60	15		8	FL
Carlisle U	60/61	7		2	FL

STEWART Hugh
b. Glasgow
St Rochs

Club	Season	Apps	Sub	Gls	Div
Aberdeen	63/64	1			D1
	64/65	8			D1
	65/66	1			D1
Third Lanark	66/67	32	1	11	D2

STEWART Ian

Perth Celtic

Club	Season	Apps	Sub	Gls	Div
Arbroath	64/65	4		1	D2
	65/66	5		2	D2
Dundee U	65/66	1		1	D1
Morton					
Arbroath					
Forfar A	67/68	35		8	D2
	68/69			4	D2
	69/70	20	1	5	D2
	70/71	35		13	D2
	71/72	29		7	D2
	72/73	17	1		D2
	73/74	12			D2
Montrose	73/74	16	3	5	D2
	74/75	18	10	6	D2
	75/76	14	6	2	D1
	76/77	29	3	5	D1
	77/78	9	1	2	D1
Brechin C	77/78	12	1	1	D2
	78/79	2			D2
	79/80	2			D2
Montrose	84/85	1			D2
	85/86				D1
	86/87	1			D1

STEWART Ian
b. Aberdeen c1940 d. Aberdeen 18.5.1998
Banks o'Dee

Club	Season	Apps	Sub	Gls	Div
East Fife	59/60				D2
	60/61				D2
	61/62	34		20	D2
	62/63				D2
	63/64	35		20	D2
	64/65	34		7	D2
Clyde	65/66	25		10	D1
	66/67	32		18	D1
	67/68	27	1	8	D1
	68/69	12	5		D1
	69/70	9	3		D1
Arbroath	70/71	22	9	7	D2
	71/72	10	1	3	D2

STEWART J

Club	Season	Apps	Sub	Gls	Div
Third Lanark	62/63	3			D1

STEWART James

Club	Season	Apps	Sub	Gls	Div
Falkirk	46/47	9		1	D1

STEWART James
b. Glasgow d. 3.11.1989
Irvine Meadow

Club	Season	Apps	Sub	Gls	Div
Kilmarnock	55/56				D1
	56/57	17			D1
	57/58	25			D1
	58/59	2			D1
	59/60				D1
Dunfermline A	60/61	2			D1
Hamilton A	60/61	11			D2

STEWART James Garven
b. Kilwinning 9.3.1954 Caps: S - 2
Troon Jnrs

Club	Season	Apps	Sub	Gls	Div
Kilmarnock	70/71				D1
	71/72				D1
Rangers	L 71/72				D1
Kilmarnock	72/73	22			D1
	73/74	35			D2
	74/75	18			D1
	75/76	26			D1
	76/77	35			P
	77/78	39			D1
Middlesbrough	78/79	27			FL
	79/80	5			FL
	80/81	2			FL
Rangers	80/81	10			P
	81/82	26			P
	82/83	18			P
	83/84	2			P
Dumbarton	L 83/84	2			D1
St Mirren	84/85	6			P
	85/86	3			P
Partick T	86/87	8			D1

STEWART John
b. Armadale 23.1.1929 d. Edinburgh 10.1.2004
Royal Albert

Club	Season	Apps	Sub	Gls	Div
Dunfermline A	50/51				D2
East Fife	50/51	10		1	D1
	51/52	30		9	D1
	52/53	30		4	D1
	53/54	30		5	D1
	54/55	28		7	D1
	55/56	25		3	D1
	56/57	28		4	D1
Walsall	57/58	28		4	FL

STEWART John

Club	Season	Apps	Sub	Gls	Div
Dundee	53/54	7			D1
	54/55				D1
	55/56				D1
	56/57	1			D1
Airdrieonians	58/59	3			D1
	59/60	25			D1
	60/61	31		1	D1
	61/62	16			D1
	62/63	14			D1
	63/64	14			D1
	64/65	5			D1

STEWART John

Shotts Bon Accord

Club	Season	Apps	Sub	Gls	Div
Falkirk	62/63	5		1	D1
	63/64	19			D1
	64/65	14			D1

STEWART John

Club	Season	Apps	Sub	Gls	Div
Motherwell	62/63	2			D1

STEWART John

Cadzow St Anne's
Blantyre V

Club	Season	Apps	Sub	Gls	Div
Hamilton A	T 67/68	1			D2
Blantyre V					
Airdrieonians	69/70	18	4	3	D1
Shotts Bon Accord					

STEWART John Gebbie
b. Lochgelly 04.09.1921 d. ?.?.1990
Lochgelly Welfare
Donibristle YC
Raith R

Club	Season	Apps	Sub	Gls	Div
Birmingham C	47/48	17		7	FL
	48/49	37		11	FL
	49/50	31		4	FL
	50/51	25		9	FL
	51/52	37		9	FL
	52/53	33		5	FL
	53/54	22		9	FL
	54/55	1			FL
Raith R	54/55	6			D1

STEWART Patrick

Sighthill YC

Club	Season	Apps	Sub	Gls	Div
Partick T	68/69	2		1	D1
	69/70	1			D1
	70/71	1			D2
Alloa A	71/72	24	4	1	D2
Hamilton A	72/73	8		3	D2

STEWART Robert

Club	Season	Apps	Sub	Gls	Div
Morton	72/73	1			D1

STEWART Robert Edward Thorburn
b. Kilmarnock 7.10.1932
Bonnyton Thistle YC
Dreghorn Jnrs

Club	Season	Apps	Sub	Gls	Div
Kilmarnock	51/52	2			D2
	52/53	9		1	D2
	53/54				D2
	54/55				D1
	55/56	15			D1
	56/57	24			D1
	57/58	21		1	D1
	58/59	26		5	D1
	59/60	13		1	D1
	60/61	3			D1
St Mirren	60/61	16			D1
	61/62	19			D1
Ayr U	62/63				

STEWART Ronald

Club	Season	Apps	Sub	Gls	Div
Airdrieonians	62/63	1			D1

STEWART Samuel
b. Musselburgh ?.5.1920 d. 27.6.1995
Tranent Jnrs

Club	Season	Apps	Sub	Gls	Div
East Fife	38/39	3		1	D2
	46/47	23			D2
	47/48	29			D2
	48/49	30		1	D1
	49/50	28		1	D1
	50/51	26			D1
	51/52	30			D1
	52/53	29			D1
	53/54	30			D1
	54/55	29			D1
	55/56	34			D1
	56/57	33			D1
	57/58	13			D1
	58/59	30			D2
	59/60	23		1	D2
	60/61	2			D2

STEWART Thomas H

Woodburn A

Club	Season	Apps	Sub	Gls	Div
Stirling A	60/61				D2
	61/62	1			D1

STEWART William
b. Clydebank 10.3.1922 d. ?.6.1987

Club	Season	Apps	Sub	Gls	Div
St Mirren	48/49	23		7	D1
	49/50	11		1	D1
	50/51	8		1	D1
Stirling A	L 50/51				D2
Aldershot	51/52	8		2	FL
	52/53	18		2	FL
	53/54	1			FL
Yeovil T	54/55				

STILLIE Daniel
b. c1927 d. 7.6.1999
Newarthill Hearts
Royal Albert
Auchinleck Talbot
Lesmahagow Jnrs
Bellshill Academy

Club	Season				Div
Hamilton A	51/52	1			D2
	52/53	20		4	D2
	53/54	4			D1
Albion R					

STIRLING Alexander
Reading

Club	Season				Div
Stirling A	48/49				D2
	49/50	1		1	D1
East Stirlingshire	49/50				D2
Dumbarton	49/50	11		4	D2
Bo'ness U					

STIRLING Ian

Club	Season				Div
Arbroath	63/64	36			D2
	64/65	32			D2
	65/66	36			D2
	66/67	38		3	D2
	67/68	36		4	D2
	68/69	34			D1
	69/70	36		9	D2
	70/71				D2

STIRLING John

Club	Season				Div
Raith R	49/50	6			D1

STIRLING Robert

Club	Season				Div
Queen's Park	46/47	1			D1
Hibernian	46/47	2		2	D1
Third Lanark	47/48	6		1	D1
	48/49	6		5	D1

STIRRAT N

Club	Season				Div
Airdrieonians	51/52	4			D1

STIRRAT Robert
Whitburn Jnrs

Club	Season				Div
East Fife	55/56				D1
	56/57				D1
	57/58	8			D1
	58/59				D2
	59/60				D2
	60/61				D2
	61/62	36			D2
	62/63				D2
	63/64				D2
	64/65				D2
	65/66				D2

STOBO William

Club	Season				Div
East Stirlingshire	63/64	5			D1
ES Clydebank	64/65	32			D2
Berwick R	65/66	34			D2
	66/67	8			D2

STOCKDALE Douglas

Club	Season				Div
Raith R	50/51	4		2	D1
Ayr U	50/51				D2
	51/52				D2
	52/53				D2
Forfar A	52/53	22		5	D2

STORRIE James
b. Kirkintilloch 31.3.1940
Kilsyth R

Club	Season				Div
Airdrieonians	57/58	4		2	D1
	58/59	14		2	D1
	59/60	13		4	D1
	60/61	30		21	D1
	61/62	28		19	D1
Leeds U	62/63	38		25	FL
	63/64	15		3	FL
	64/65	37		16	FL
	65/66	30		13	FL
	66/67	3	3	1	FL
Aberdeen	66/67	6		1	D1
	67/68	6		2	D1
Rotherham U	67/68	19		3	FL
	68/69	42	1	14	FL
	69/70	9		2	FL
Portsmouth	69/70				FL
	70/71				FL
	71/72	4			FL
Aldershot L	71/72	5		1	FL
St Mirren	72/73	7	2	3	D2
Waterlooville					

STORRIER R

Club	Season				Div
Airdrieonians	52/53	2			D1

STOTT Alexander
b. Newbigging d. 19.12.1998
Portsmouth

Club	Season				Div
Dundee	47/48				D1
	48/49	23		30	D1
	49/50				D1
Partick T	49/50	23		16	D1
	50/51	13		11	D1
	51/52	25		16	D1
	52/53	23		16	D1
Hamilton A	53/54	2		1	D1

STRACHAN Gordon David
b. Edinburgh 9.2.1957
Edinburgh Thistle

Club	Season				Div
Dundee	71/72				D1
	72/73				D1
	73/74				D1
	74/75	1			D1
	75/76	17	6	6	P
	76/77	33	3	7	D1
	77/78	5		4	D1
Aberdeen	77/78	10	2	2	P
	78/79	26	5	5	P
	79/80	33		10	P
	80/81	20		6	P
	81/82	30		7	P
	82/83	32		12	P
	83/84	24	1	13	P
Manchester U	84/85	41		15	FL
	85/86	27	1	5	FL
	86/87	33	1	4	FL
	87/88	33	3	8	FL
	88/89	21		1	FL
Leeds U	88/89	11		3	FL
	89/90	46		16	FL
	90/91	34		7	FL
	91/92	35	1	4	FL
	92/93	25	6	4	FL
	93/94	32	1	3	FL
	94/95	5	1		FL
Coventry C	94/95	5			FL
	95/96	5	7		FL
	96/97	3	6		FL

STRACHAN Hugh Mair
b. Crookedholm ?.?.1939
Saxone Amateurs
Troon Jnrs
Cumnock Jnrs

Club	Season				Div
Motherwell	58/59	3		3	D1
	59/60	10		1	D1
	60/61	10			D1
	61/62	3			D1
	62/63	1			D1
Morton	63/64	36		1	D2
	64/65	34		2	D1
	65/66	31		1	D1
	66/67	37			D2
	67/68	33			D1
	68/69	21	2		D1
Kilmarnock	69/70	18	1	1	D1
Partick T	70/71	32			D2
	71/72	34			D1
	72/73	32			D1
	73/74	2			D1

STRAITON Archibald

Club	Season				Div
St Mirren	55/56	7		2	D1

STREET Robert John Wainwright
b. Gourock 29.10.1953
Port Glasgow Jnrs

Club	Season				Div
Aberdeen	72/73	1	1		D1
	73/74	1	1		D1
	74/75	3			D1
	75/76		1		P
Montrose	76/77	26	4	12	D1
	77/78	9	8	3	D1
Kilmarnock	78/79	12	6	5	D1
	79/80	26	5	9	P
	80/81	13		2	P
Keith	81/82				
Peterhead	81/82				
	82/83				
Montrose	83/84	23	11	2	D2
	84/85		2		D2
Brechin C	84/85	4	6		D1
Huntly					

STRICKLAND John
Strathclyde

Club	Season				Div
Ayr U	52/53				D2
	53/54				D2
	54/55				D2
	55/56				D2
	56/57	1			D1
Hamilton A	57/58	33			D2
	58/59	34		1	D2
	59/60	36			D2
	60/61	24		1	D2
	61/62	13			D2
	62/63	32		1	D2
	63/64	27			D2

STROUD Arthur

Club	Season				Div
Arbroath	59/60	1			D1

STUART Alexander
b. c1940
Aberdeen EE

Club	Season				Div
Dundee	58/59				D1
	59/60				D1
	60/61	3			D1
	61/62	2			D1
	62/63	8			D1
	63/64	32		5	D1
	64/65	34		4	D1
	65/66	32		3	D1
	66/67	30		5	D1
	67/68	20		4	D1
	68/69	5			D1
Dundee U	69/70		1		D1
Montrose	69/70	16		2	D2
	70/71			2	D2
	71/72	28	1	3	D2
	72/73		1		D2

STURROCK Paul Whitehead
b. Ellon 10.10.1956
Grandtully Vale
Vale of Atholl
Bankfoot Jnrs

Club	Season	Apps	Sub	Gls	Div
Dundee U	74/75	9	3	6	D1
	75/76	10	7	3	P
	76/77	36		15	P
	77/78	32	1	3	P
	78/79	31	2	6	P
	79/80	31	2	4	P
	80/81	35		13	P
	81/82	31		15	P
	82/83	28		8	P
	83/84	15	2	4	P
	84/85	28	2	14	P
	85/86	31	1	8	P
	86/87	30		6	P
	87/88	8	1	3	P
	88/89	5	5	1	P

SULLIVAN Dominick
b. Glasgow 1.4.1951
Provanmill Gasworks
St Rochs

Club	Season	Apps	Sub	Gls	Div
Clyde	69/70				D1
	70/71	28			D1
	71/72	27	2	3	D1
	72/73	30	3	7	D2
	73/74	33	1	1	D1
	74/75	34		4	D1
	75/76	12	4	1	D1
Aberdeen	76/77	28	4	3	P
	77/78	25	4	3	P
	78/79	32		5	P
	79/80	2	3		P
Celtic	79/80	15		3	P
	80/81	30		3	P
	81/82	31		3	P
	82/83	7	1	1	P
Dundee U	T 83/84				P
Manchester C	T 83/84				FL
Morton	83/84	24	1	3	D1
	84/85	23	4	3	P
Alloa A	85/86	20	2	1	D1
	86/87	21	2	3	D2
	87/88	14			D2

SUTHERLAND James
b. Falkirk
Camelon

Club	Season	Apps	Sub	Gls	Div
Airdrieonians	55/56	1			D1

SUTHERLAND Robert F G
b. Broxburn 21.5.1942
Rangers

Club	Season	Apps	Sub	Gls	Div
Stirling A	64/65				D2
	65/66	8		1	D1

SUTHERLAND Thomas
Shotts Bon Accord

Club	Season	Apps	Sub	Gls	Div
Aberdeen	69/70	5			D1
Hamilton A	70/71	4			D2

SWAN Alan
Shettleston

Club	Season	Apps	Sub	Gls	Div
Clyde	69/70	3			D1
	70/71	2			D1
	71/72	10			D1
	72/73	30	1	2	D2
	73/74	34		1	D1
	74/75	30	1	1	D1
	75/76	16		2	D1

SWAN David
b. Edinburgh ?.?.1948
Cowdenbeath
Edina Hearts

Club	Season	Apps	Sub	Gls	Div
Dundee	65/66	3			D1
	66/67				D1
	67/68	9			D1
	68/69	18			D1
	69/70	11			D1
Kilmarnock	70/71	2			D1

Highlands Park

SWAN Ronald McDonald
b. Plean 8.1.1941
Camelon Juniors

Club	Season	Apps	Sub	Gls	Div
East Stirlingshire	60/61				D2
	61/62	2			D2
	62/63				D2
	63/64	16			D1
Oldham A	64/65	27			FL
	65/66	33			FL
	66/67	4			FL
Luton T	66/67	14			FL

Buxton

SWANSON John
b. Greenock
Kilbirnie Ladeside

Club	Season	Apps	Sub	Gls	Div
Stirling A	53/54	22		3	D1
	54/55	9			D1
	55/56	24		3	D1
	56/57				
	57/58				

Morton

SWEENEY Gerald
b. Renfrew 10.7.1945
Renfrew Jnrs

Club	Season	Apps	Sub	Gls	Div
Morton	66/67	12		3	D2
	67/68	31	2	2	D1
	68/69	33		1	D1
	69/70	27		4	D1
	70/71	34		6	D1
Bristol C	71/72	33	4	3	FL
	72/73	40	1	2	FL
	73/74	42		3	FL
	74/75	42		6	FL
	75/76	32	2	5	FL
	76/77	43		2	FL
	77/78	38		1	FL
	78/79	42			FL
	79/80	40	1		FL
	80/81	38			FL
	81/82	8	2		FL
York C	81/82	12			FL

SWEENEY John
b. c1935
Edina Hearts

Club	Season	Apps	Sub	Gls	Div
Dunfermline A	54/55				D2
	55/56				D1
	56/57				D1
	57/58				D2
	58/59	33			D1
	59/60	27		1	D1
	60/61	16			D1

SWEENEY Walter
b. Glasgow
Leeds U

Club	Season	Apps	Sub	Gls	Div
Morton	68/69	3			D1

SWEENEY William
b. Port Glasgow
Irvine Meadow

Club	Season	Apps	Sub	Gls	Div
Queen of the South	52/53	9			D1
	53/54	3			D1
	54/55	1			D1
	55/56	19			D1

SWEENEY William Clerihew
b. St Andrews 23.10.1918

Club	Season	Apps	Sub	Gls	Div
Clyde	46/47	30			D1
	47/48	11			D1
Carlisle U	47/48	15			FL
	48/49	22			FL

SYMINGTON James
Pumpherston

Club	Season	Apps	Sub	Gls	Div
Stirling A	65/66	4			D1
	66/67	17	2	2	D1
	67/68	9			D1
Stranraer	68/69			10	D2
	69/70	30		6	D2
	70/71			5	D2
	71/72				D2
	72/73				D2
	73/74				D2
	74/75	11		4	D2

SYMON James Scotland
b. Errol 9.5.1911 d. Glasgow 30.4.1985
Errol Amateurs
Perth NE
Dundee Violet

Club	Season	Apps	Sub	Gls	Div
Dundee	30/31	21			D1
	31/32	32		2	D1
	32/33	26			D1
	33/34	35			D1
	34/35	36			D1
Portsmouth	35/36	34		3	FL
	36/37	23		2	FL
	37/38	9		1	FL
Rangers	38/39	22		3	D1
	46/47	10			D1

SZPULA Jan
b. Poland
Alloa A

Club	Season	Apps	Sub	Gls	Div
Stirling A	48/49				D2
	49/50	9			D1

TAGGART George McGrory
b. Glasgow ?.?.1937
Kilmarnock Amateurs
Kilwinning R

Club	Season	Apps	Sub	Gls	Div
Kilmarnock	55/56	17			D1
	56/57	3			D1
	57/58				D1
St Johnstone	T 58/59	1			D2
Rutherglen Glencairn	59/60				
	60/61				
Clydebank Jnrs	61/62				
Berwick R	61/62	3			D2
	62/63				D2
	63/64				D2
Dumbarton	63/64	27		2	D2

Ballymena U

TAINSH

Club	Season	Apps	Sub	Gls	Div
Raith R	57/58	3		2	D1

TAIT Robert
b. Kilmarnock 23.7.1954
Crosshouse Waverley
Hibernian
Crosshouse Waverley

Club	Season	Apps	Sub	Gls	Div
Ayr U	72/73			1	D1
	73/74	7	2	1	D1
	74/75	3		1	D1
	75/76	7			P
	76/77	6		1	P
	77/78	6			P
Stranraer	78/79	28	1	2	D2
	79/80	24		2	D2

Cumnock
Annbank U

TAIT Robert James
b. Edinburgh 4.10.1938
Loanhead Mayflower

Club	Season	Apps	Sub	Gls	Div
Aberdeen	60/61	2			D1
	61/62				D1
Notts Co	62/63	34		6	FL
	63/64	26		5	FL
Barrow	64/65	45		14	FL
	65/66	33	1	15	FL
Chesterfield	66/67	27	1	2	FL

Arnold
Long Eaton U

TASKER Robert

Stenhousemuir

Club	Season	App	Sub	Gls	Div
Queen of the South	57/58	23		5	D1
	58/59	1			D1
Falkirk	58/59	2			D1

TAYLOR Anthony
b. Glasgow 6.9.1946
Barrhead Thistle

Club	Season	App	Sub	Gls	Div
Kilmarnock	62/63				D1
	63/64				D1
Celtic	64/65				D1
	65/66				D1
	66/67				D1
Morton	67/68	14	3	6	D1
	68/69	6		2	D1
Crystal Palace	68/69	25		2	FL
	69/70	30	2	1	FL
	70/71	36	1	2	FL
	71/72	41		2	FL
	72/73	40		1	FL
	73/74	20			FL
Southend U	74/75	40		1	FL
	75/76	16			FL
Hamilton A	L 75/76	8		2	D1
Swindon T	76/77	20	6		FL
Athlone T					
Bristol R	77/78	12			FL
Portsmouth	77/78	17			FL
	78/79				FL
Kilmarnock	T 78/79	2			D1
Albion R	78/79	3			D2
Northampton T	79/80	4			FL
Toronto Blizzard					

TAYLOR Duncan

Club	Season	App	Sub	Gls	Div
St Mirren	66/67	5	1		D1
Stranraer	67/68	21		5	D2

TAYLOR George Alexander
b. Aberdeen 9.6.1915 d. ?.?.1982
Hall Russells

Club	Season	App	Sub	Gls	Div
Aberdeen	37/38	1			D1
	38/39	5			D1
	46/47	28		3	D1
	47/48	29		3	D1
Plymouth A	48/49	26		1	FL
	49/50	22		1	FL

TAYLOR Ian W
b. Aberdeen
Banks o'Dee

Club	Season	App	Sub	Gls	Div
Aberdeen	66/67	12	1	3	D1
	67/68	14	1	5	D1
	68/69	13	1	1	D1
	69/70	1			D1
	70/71	14	2	4	D1
	71/72	10	5	2	D1
	72/73	18		4	D1
	73/74	14	3	3	D1
Motherwell	73/74	2			D1
	74/75	20	3	1	D1
	75/76	17	7	4	P
St Johnstone	76/77	23	1	2	D1
	77/78	12	2	1	D1
Fraserburgh					
Elgin C					
Peterhead					

TAYLOR James
Luncarty
St Johnstone

Club	Season	App	Sub	Gls	Div
Cowdenbeath	66/67	35		1	D2
	67/68	31		6	D2
	68/69				
	69/70	2	8	1	D2
	70/71	30		1	D1
	71/72	33	1	2	D2
	72/73	31		5	D2
St Mirren	73/74	13	2	2	D2
Forfar A	74/75	10			D2
Raith R	74/75	29		2	D2
	75/76	24			D2
	76/77	31	1	1	D1
	77/78	38		2	D2
	78/79	15	1	1	D1

TAYLOR John A.C.
b. Ayr 22.6.1949
Ayr Albion

Club	Season	App	Sub	Gls	Div
Queen's Park	66/67	26			D2
	67/68	15			D2
	68/69	15			D2
	69/70				D2
	70/71	9			D2
	71/72	17			D2
	72/73	24			D2
Dumbarton	73/74	9			D1
Stranraer	74/75	37			D2
	75/76	1			D2
	76/77	39			D2
	77/78	30			D2
	78/79	35			D2
	79/80	34			D2
	80/81	11			D2
	81/82	1			D2

TAYLOR John
b. Ayr
Leeds U

Club	Season	App	Sub	Gls	Div
Ayr U	73/74	2	3		D1
	74/75	7			D1
Clyde	75/76	16		1	D1

TAYLOR Raymond

Club	Season	App	Sub	Gls	Div
Morton	74/75	12		4	D1
	75/76	6		2	D1

TAYLOR Samuel McGregor
b. Glasgow 23.9.1933

Club	Season	App	Sub	Gls	Div
Falkirk	54/55	24		3	D1
Preston NE	55/56	15		2	FL
	56/57	37		12	FL
	57/58	36		14	FL
	58/59	17		3	FL
	59/60	34		10	FL
	60/61	10			FL
Carlisle U	61/62	29		6	FL
	62/63	30		3	FL
	63/64	36		2	FL
Southport	64/65	36		3	FL

TAYLOR W

Club	Season	App	Sub	Gls	Div
Raith R	52/53	3			D1

TAYLOR William
Glencairn Juveniles

Club	Season	App	Sub	Gls	Div
Celtic	47/48				D1
	48/49				D1
	49/50	14		4	D1
	50/51				D1
Carlisle U	T 50/51				FL
Alloa A	51/52				D2
	52/53	4			D2
Ayr U	52/53				D2

TAYLOR William Donnachie
b. Kirkconnel 3.6.1938
Cumnock

Club	Season	App	Sub	Gls	Div
St Johnstone	57/58	10			D2
	58/59	36			D2
	59/60	31			D2
	60/61	29			D1
	61/62	33			D1
	62/63	25			D2
	63/64	14			D1
Stirling A	64/65	36			D2
	65/66	24			D1
	66/67	2			D1
Partick T	66/67	1			D1
Luton T	67/68	3			FL
	68/69	3			FL
Epping T					

TEES Matthew
b. Johnstone 13.10.1939
Penaleen A
Cambuslang R

Club	Season	App	Sub	Gls	Div
Airdrieonians	61/62	14		2	D1
	62/63	29		10	D1
Grimsby T	63/64	21		5	FL
	64/65	26		9	FL
	65/66	43		28	FL
	66/67	23		9	FL
Charlton A	66/67	9		4	FL
	67/68	38		13	FL
	68/69	35	1	15	FL
	69/70	6			FL
Luton T	69/70	3	2	11	FL
	70/71	3		2	FL
Grimsby T	70/71	23		10	FL
	71/72	43		27	FL
	72/73	17		5	FL
Boston U					

TELFER John
Douglas Water Thistle

Club	Season	App	Sub	Gls	Div
Ayr U	56/57	5			D1
	57/58				D2
	58/59				D2
	59/60	18		1	D1
	60/61	1			D1

TELFER William

Club	Season	App	Sub	Gls	Div
Falkirk	46/47	12		3	D1
	47/48	4			D1
	48/49	16			D1

TELFER William Douglas
b. Larkhall 26.10.1925 Caps: S - 1
Larkhall Rangers
Burnbank A

Club	Season	App	Sub	Gls	Div
St Mirren	46/47	26			D1
	47/48	27		2	D1
	48/49	27			D1
	49/50	28			D1
	50/51	30		3	D1
	51/52	30		1	D1
	52/53	27		3	D1
	53/54	27		6	D1
	54/55	29		6	D1
	55/56	33		5	D1
	56/57	28		1	D1
	57/58	10		1	D1
Rangers	57/58	28			D1
	58/59	31			D1
	59/60	11			D1
Queen of the South	60/61				D2
Hamilton A	61/62	28		1	D2

TELFORD William

Club	Season	App	Sub	Gls	Div
St Mirren	46/47	23		5	D1
	47/48	8			D1
	48/49	8		1	D1
Third Lanark	48/49	8			D1
Motherwell	49/50	7			D1
Ayr U					
Cheltenham T					

TENNANT D

Club	Season				Div
Morton	50/51	3			D1

THOM Gordon

Club	Season				Div
Third Lanark	48/49	1			D1
Morton	50/51	19			D1
	51/52	21			D1

THOM Lewis McDonald
b. Stornaway 10.4.1944
Banks o'Dee

Club	Season				Div
Aberdeen	61/62	2			D1
	62/63	23		4	D1
	63/64	10		1	D1
Dundee U	64/65	11		2	D1
Shrewsbury T	65/66	35	1	4	FL
	66/67	13	2	1	FL
Lincoln C	66/67	1		1	FL
	67/68	38	1	3	FL
	68/69	6	1		FL
Bradford PA	69/70	31		1	FL
Altrincham					
Elgin C					
Inverness Clachnacuddin					
Huntly					

THOMAS Graham
b. Eastbourne
Crystal Palace

Club	Season				Div
Morton	73/74	11	3	2	D1
Bath C	74/75				

THOMAS William
b. Larkhall
Bonkle Amateurs
Bellshill Academy
West Bromwich A

Club	Season				Div
Falkirk	73/74	11	11	2	D1
	74/75	8	12	3	D2
Hamilton A	75/76	13	9	14	D1
	76/77	12	5	3	D1
Morton	77/78	7	9	2	D1
St Johnstone	78/79	9	14	1	D1
	79/80	6	2		D1
Shettleston					
Larkhall Thistle					

THOMS John H
Stobswell
Brechin C

Club	Season				Div
Stirling A	60/61				D2
	61/62				D1
Bath C	61/62				
	62/63				
Raith R	63/64	5		1	D2
Brechin C	63/64	23		21	D2
	64/65	11		4	D2
Stirling A	64/65	21		10	D2
	65/66	5		2	D1
East Fife	65/66	16		7	D2
	66/67	3		1	D2

THOMSON Adam

Club	Season				Div
Airdrieonians	61/62	4			D1
	62/63	22			D1
	63/64	6			D1
Ayr U	64/65				D2
	65/66	19			D2
	66/67	23			D1
	67/68				D2

THOMSON Alexander

Club	Season				Div
Rangers	55/56	1			D1
	56/57				D1
East Stirlingshire	57/58				D2

THOMSON Andrew
Airdrie BC

Club	Season				Div
Airdrieonians	72/73	11	3		D1

THOMSON Arthur Campbell
b. Edinburgh 2.9.1948 d. Edinburgh 7.3.2002

Club	Season				Div
Chelsea	63/64				FL
Heart of Midlothian	64/65				D1
	65/66				D1
	66/67	14			D1
	67/68	30			D1
	68/69	14			D1
	69/70				D1
Oldham A	69/70	18	1		FL
	70/71	9			FL
Raith R	70/71	11			D2
	71/72	15	1	1	D2
Dalkeith Thistle					

THOMSON Charles Richard
b. Perth 2.3.1930

Club	Season			Div
Clyde	49/50	15		D1
	50/51	1		D1
	51/52			D2
	52/53	1		D1
Chelsea	52/53	15		FL
	53/54	7		FL
	54/55	16		FL
	55/56	8		FL
	56/57			FL
Nottingham F	57/58	39		FL
	58/59	35		FL
	59/60	31		FL
	60/61	16		FL
Rugby T				

THOMSON Colin
Kirkintilloch Rob Roy

Club	Season				Div
Clyde	70/71	5		1	D1
	71/72	7	1	1	D1
	72/73				D2
Stenhousemuir	73/74	20	6	6	D2

THOMSON David

Club	Season			Div
Partick T	57/58	11		D1
Clyde	58/59	2		D1
	59/60	12		D1
	60/61	6		D1

THOMSON David

Club	Season			Div
Clyde	59/60	4		D1
	60/61	13	2	D1
	61/62			D2
	62/63	6	1	D1

THOMSON David Laing
b. Bothkennar 2.2.1938
Bo'ness U

Club	Season			Div
Dunfermline A	59/60	2		D1
	60/61	6	5	D1
Leicester C	61/62	1	1	FL
	62/63			FL
Queen of the South	63/64	10	3	D1

THOMSON Edward
b. Rosewell 25.2.1947 d. Sydney 20.2.2003
Whitehill Welfare
Penicuik A
Whitehill Welfare
Penicuik A

Club	Season				Div
Heart of Midlothian	66/67	9			D1
	67/68	9		1	D1
	68/69	34			D1
	69/70	23			D1
	70/71	34			D1
	71/72	29		2	D1
	72/73	23	1	1	D1
Aberdeen	72/73	7			D1
	73/74	31	1	1	D1
	74/75	16	1		D1
	75/76	26	2		P
San Antonio Thunder	76	19		3	NA
Aberdeen	76/77	3	4		P
Hakoah Eastern Suburbs					

THOMSON George
Blantyre Celtic

Club	Season			Div
Dunfermline A	73/74	1		D1
	74/75			D1
Morton	75/76			D1
Albion R	76/77	22		D2
	77/78	13		D2

THOMSON George Matthewson
b. Edinburgh 19.10.1936
Edinburgh C

Club	Season				Div
Heart of Midlothian	56/57	7			D1
	57/58	30			D1
	58/59	34		10	D1
	59/60	34		4	D1
	60/61	12			D1
Everton	60/61	22			FL
	61/62	32		1	FL
	62/63	19			FL
Brentford	63/64	23		1	FL
	64/65	41			FL
	65/66	44		2	FL
	66/67	25			FL
	67/68	29	1	2	FL

THOMSON Ian
Musselburgh Windsor

Club	Season				Div
Motherwell	62/63	7			D1
	63/64	7			D1
	64/65	2			D1
	65/66	28		10	D1
	66/67	8		1	D1
	67/68	2			D1
	68/69				D2
	69/70				D1
Morton	70/71	15	1	2	D1
East Fife	71/72	6			D1

THOMSON Ian
Port Glasgow A

Club	Season			Div
Rangers	71/72			D1
	72/73			D1
	73/74			D1
Morton	74/75	10	4	D1

THOMSON James

Club	Season			Div
Hibernian	53/54	3	1	D1
	54/55	7		D1
	55/56	25	2	D1
	56/57	12	4	D1
	57/58	5	1	D1
	58/59			D1
Ayr U	59/60	2		D1

THOMSON James

Club	Season			Div
St Mirren	56/57	2		D1
	57/58	2		D1
	58/59	11		D1
	59/60	15		D1
	60/61	12		D1
Dunfermline A	61/62	17		D1
	62/63	34		D1
	63/64	22	1	D1
	64/65	24		D1
	65/66	30	2	D1
	66/67	26	1	D1
	67/68	26	1	D1
	68/69	8	1	D1
	69/70	4	1	D1
	70/71	22	3	D1

THOMSON James Donaldson
b. Glasgow 17.3.1931

Club	Season			Div
Raith R	53/54	1		D1
	54/55	4		D1
	55/56	19	7	D1
Southend U	56/57	30	7	FL
	57/58			FL
	58/59	10	3	FL
Headington U	59/60	35	9	SL

THOMSON John Ballantyne
b. Muirhead 22.10.1934
Armadale Thistle

Club	Season				Div
Heart of Midlothian	55/56	1			D1
	56/57				D1
	57/58				D1
Workington	58/59	11		1	FL

THOMSON Kenneth
b. Dunfermline 9.11.1951
Dunfermline U

Club	Season				Div
Dunfermline A	70/71	3			D1
	71/72	13	2		D1
	72/73	35			D2
	73/74	30			D1
	74/75	34			D1
	75/76	26			D1
	76/77	37		1	D2
	77/78	39			D2
	78/79	39			D2
	79/80	39			D1
	80/81	39			D1
	81/82	11		5	D1
	82/83	39			D1
Alloa A	83/84	27		3	D1
	84/85	39			D2
	85/86	36			D1
	86/87	39			D2
	87/88	3			D2
St Johnstone	87/88	36			D2
	88/89	33			D1
	89/90	24			D1
Cowdenbeath	90/91	20			D2

THOMSON Kenneth Gordon
b. Aberdeen 25.2.1930
d. Castle Eden ?.?.1969
Banks o'Dee

Club	Season				Div
Aberdeen	48/49	3			D1
	49/50	2			D1
	50/51	4			D1
	51/52	20			D1
Stoke C	52/53	38		2	FL
	53/54	40		2	FL
	54/55	41			FL
	55/56	37			FL
	56/57	40			FL
	57/58	37			FL
	58/59	38		2	FL
	59/60	7			FL
Middlesbrough	59/60	18			FL
	60/61	38			FL
	61/62	25		1	FL
	62/63	3			FL
Hartlepools U	62/63	28		2	FL

THOMSON Lawrence James
b. Menstrie 26.8.1936
Bo'ness U

Club	Season				Div
Partick T	55/56	1			D1
	56/57				D1
	57/58	1			D1
	58/59	4			D1
	59/60	7		1	D1
Carlisle U	59/60	13		1	FL
St Johnstone	60/61	8		2	D1
	61/62	9		2	D1

THOMSON Leslie Grant
b. Dalrachnock ?.?.1936
Armadale Thistle

Club	Season				Div
Falkirk	55/56	2			D1
	56/57	12		2	D1
	57/58	11			D1
	58/59	8			D1
	59/60	7			D2
	60/61	36		3	D2
	61/62	30		7	D1
	62/63	26		1	D1
	63/64	6			D1
Stirling A	64/65				D2
	65/66				D1
	66/67				D1
	67/68				D1
	68/69				D2
Stenhousemuir	69/70				D2
	70/71				D2
	71/72	18			D2

THOMSON Matthew
Ardeer Thistle

Club	Season				Div
Motherwell	61/62	26			D1
	62/63	24			D1
	63/64	25			D1
	64/65	28			D1
	65/66	28			D1
	66/67	25		2	D1
	67/68	11		1	D1

THOMSON Robert
b. Glasgow
Springburn U

Club	Season				Div
Partick T	48/49	10		1	D1
	49/50	13			D1
	50/51	16			D1
	51/52	16			D1
	52/53	11			D1
	53/54	7			D1
	54/55	12			D1
	55/56	6			D1
	56/57	1			D1
	57/58	2			D1
	58/59	2			D1
	59/60	1			D1

THOMSON Robert
b. Maybole c1928
Craigmark Bruntonians

Club	Season				Div
Ayr U	51/52				D2
	52/53	12			D2
	53/54	1			D2
	54/55				D2
	55/56				D2
	56/57	30		1	D1
	57/58				D2
	58/59				D2
	59/60	16			D1
	60/61	21			D1

THOMSON Robert

Club	Season				Div
Dunfermline A	58/59	4			D1
	59/60	2			D1

THOMSON Robert

Club	Season				Div
Airdrieonians	59/60	7			D1

THOMSON Robert
b. Glasgow 21.3.1955
St Lukes BG
Glasgow U

Club	Season				Div
St Johnstone	73/74	5		1	D1
	74/75	8		6	D1
	75/76	23	3	3	P
	76/77	35	1	7	D1
	77/78	35	1	7	D1
Morton	78/79	30		11	P
	79/80	27		11	P
	80/81	29		2	P
	81/82	4		1	P
Middlesbrough	81/82	18	2	2	FL
Hibernian	82/83	29	1	5	P
	83/84	16		4	P
	84/85	10	6	3	P
Morton	84/85	11		2	P
Blackpool	85/86	14	2	2	FL
	86/87	36		4	FL
Hartlepool U	87/88	3			FL
Hamilton A	87/88	22		4	D1
Queen of the South					

THOMSON Robert Gillies McKenzie
b. Dundee 21.3.1937

Club	Season				Div
Albion R	52/53	8			D2
	53/54				D2
Airdrieonians	53/54	1			D1
Wolverhampton W	54/55				FL
	55/56				FL
	56/57	1		1	FL
	57/58				FL
	58/59				FL
Aston Villa	59/60	34		20	FL
	60/61	1			FL
	61/62	28		12	FL
	62/63	34		12	FL
	63/64	5			FL
Birmingham C	63/64	21		2	FL
	64/65	25		9	FL
	65/66	27	1	6	FL
	66/67	35	1	6	FL
	67/68	1	1		FL
Stockport Co	68/69				FL

THOMSON Robert P
b. Kirkcaldy 30.9.1949
Lochgelly Albert

Club	Season				Div
Cowdenbeath	69/70	3			D2
	70/71	10	3	1	D1
	71/72	9	6	4	D2
	72/73	28	4	5	D2
	73/74	14	6	2	D2
Glenrothes	74/75				
Stirling A	75/76	16	2	7	D2
	76/77	36	2	4	D2
	77/78	28	4	5	D1
	78/79	11		1	D1
Raith R	78/79	19		1	D1
	79/80	6	3	1	D1
East Fife	80/81	38		10	D2
	81/82	18		1	D2
	82/83	38		14	D2
Cowdenbeath	83/84	1			D2
East Stirlingshire	83/84	1			D2

THOMSON W

Club	Season				Div
Falkirk	46/47	4			D1

THORBURN James Hope Forrest
b. Lanark 10.3.1938
Douglasdale

Raith R	57/58	6			D1
	58/59	7			D1
	59/60	15			D1
	60/61	31			D1
	61/62	22			D1
	62/63	31			D1
Ipswich T	63/64	10			FL
	64/65	14			FL
St Mirren	65/66	18			D1
	66/67	11			D1
	67/68				D2
	68/69	13			D1
	69/70	11			D1
Albion R	70/71				D2

THORNTON William
b. Winchburgh 3.3.1920 Caps: S - 7
Winchburgh A

Rangers	46/47	25		18	D1
	47/48	30		17	D1
	48/49	29		23	D1
	49/50	19		11	D1
	50/51	21		12	D1
	51/52	28		18	D1
	52/53	4		4	D1
	53/54	8		7	D1

THORUP Borge
b. Denmark 4.10.1943 Caps: Den - 1
Bronshoj

Morton	66/67	18		2	D2
	67/68	5	1		D1
	68/69	12	2		D1
Crystal Palace	69/70		1		FL
	70/71				FL
Morton	71/72	8	8	2	D1
Clydebank	72/73	2			D2

THYNE Robert Brown
b. Glasgow 9.1.1920 d. 16.9.1986
Neilston V
Clydebank Jnrs

Darlington	46/47	7			FL
Kilmarnock	46/47	20			D1
	47/48	27			D2
	48/49	23			D2
	49/50	29			D2
	50/51	24		1	D2
Ayr U	L 50/51				D2
Kilmarnock	51/52	27		3	D2
	52/53	29		4	D2
	53/54	27			D2
	54/55	12			D1

TIERNEY James
b. 2.5.1940

St Mirren	59/60	12			D1
	60/61	5			D1
	61/62	1			D1
Worcester C	62/63				
	63/64				

TIGHE Terence William
b. Edinburgh 12.8.1934
Newtongrange Star

Hibernian	53/54				D1
	54/55				D1
	55/56				D1
Dunfermline A	56/57	9		3	D1
Accrington S	57/58	20			FL
	58/59	42		9	FL
	59/60	45		11	FL
	60/61	10			FL
Crewe Alex.	60/61	20		1	FL
	61/62	35		2	FL
	62/63	23		2	FL
Southport	63/64	36		3	FL
Runcorn					
Great Harwood					

TILL Ernest

Raith R	49/50	29		1	D1
	50/51	5			D1
	51/52	2			D1

TIMMINS William
b. Glasgow
Renfrew Jnrs

Stirling A	55/56	13		1	D1

TINNEY Hugh Joseph
b. Glasgow 14.5.1944
Bathgate St Marys

Partick T	63/64	28			D1
	64/65	15			D1
	65/66				D1
	66/67	21			D1
Bury	66/67	10			FL
	67/68	44			FL
	68/69	24	1	1	FL
	69/70	39	2	1	FL
	70/71	45			FL
	71/72	46			FL
	72/73	27		1	FL
Fleetwood T					

TODD Thomas Bell
b. Stonehouse 1.6.1926
Burnbank A
Motherwell

Airdrieonians	48/49				D2
Stonehouse Violet					
Hamilton A	50/51	10		6	D2
	51/52	20		5	D2
	52/53	11		4	D2
	53/54	18		5	D1
	54/55	6		5	D2
Crewe Alex.	55/56	13		3	FL
Derby Co	55/56	4		3	FL
Rochdale	56/57	5		1	FL

TODD William

Third Lanark	63/64	2			D1
	64/65	19		1	D1

TOLMIE

Airdrieonians	56/57	1			D1

TONER James
b. Glasgow 23.8.1924
Fauldhouse U

Dundee	49/50	10		3	D1
	50/51	8		3	D1
	51/52	11		2	D1
	52/53	16		2	D1
	53/54	6		4	D1
Leeds U	54/55	7		1	FL
Motherwell	55/56	1			D1
Forfar A					

TONER William
b. Glasgow 18.12.1929 d. 3.1999 Caps: S - 2
Shettleston St Pauls

Queen's Park	47/48				D1
Celtic	47/48				D1
	48/49				D1
	49/50	2			D1
	50/51				D1
Sheffield U	51/52	17			FL
	52/53	15			FL
	53/54	23		2	FL
Guildford C	54/55				
Kilmarnock	54/55	12		4	D1
	55/56	15			D1
	56/57	27			D1
	57/58	34			D1
	58/59	19			D1
	59/60	26			D1
	60/61	31			D1
	61/62	22			D1
Hibernian	62/63	8			D1
	63/64	1			D1
Ayr U	63/64	18			D2
Dumbarton					

TORLEY Robert
Blantyre Celtic

Hamilton A	46/47	6		1	D1

TOSH Gordon

Dundee	57/58	1			D1

TOTTEN Alexander
b. Dennyloanhead 12.2.1946
Liverpool

Dundee	64/65	9			D1
Dunfermline A	65/66	3			D1
	66/67	16			D1
	67/68	2	1		D1
	68/69	6	1		D1
Falkirk	69/70	13	1	1	D1
	70/71	7			D1
Queen of the South	71/72	28	3		D2
	72/73	31		6	D2
Alloa A	73/74	31		1	D2
	74/75	19		1	D2
	75/76				D2
	76/77		1		D2
	77/78		1		D1

TOWNSEND James Clabby
b. Greenock 2.2.1945
Port Glasgow R

St Johnstone	61/62	3			D1
	62/63	30		7	D2
	63/64	24		1	D1
Middlesbrough	63/64	13			FL
	64/65	37		5	FL
	65/66	15	2	1	FL
St Johnstone	66/67	31		4	D1
Heart of Midlothian	66/67	1			D1
	67/68	21		1	D1
	68/69	11			D1
	69/70	20	2	7	D1
	70/71	29		1	D1
	71/72	23		2	D1
	72/73				D1
Morton	72/73	20	2	1	D1
	73/74	21	1		D1
	74/75	20	1		D1
	75/76	4			D1
	76/77	20			D1
Ontario					

TRACEY Andrew
Lochore Welfare

Dunfermline A	70/71	2	1		D1
Hakoah (Aus)					

TRAILL Derek John Falconer
b. Leith 2.1.1946

Club	Season				Div
Rangers	63/64	3			D1
	64/65				
	65/66	1			D1
Falkirk	66/67	2			D1
Workington	67/68	19		1	FL
	68/69	20	5	4	FL
Hartlepool U	69/70	36	3	2	FL
South Sydney					
Meadowbank T	74/75	4			D2
Alloa A	75/76	1			D2

TRAIN George

Club	Season				Div
Airdrieonians	67/68	2			D1
	68/69	2			D1

TRAIN Leslie
Ayr U Boys Club

Club	Season				Div
Ayr U	74/75	1			D1

TRAVERS William
b. Dalmellington

Club	Season				Div
Morton	52/53	4			D2
Cumnock Jnrs	53/54				
Ayr U	54/55				D2
	55/56				D2
	56/57	15			D1
	57/58				D2
Stranraer					

TRAYNOR James
Petershill

Club	Season				Div
Dunfermline A	69/70	2		1	D1
St Mirren	70/71	6	1	2	D1
Stranraer	71/72	36		13	D2
	72/73	32	1	19	D2
	73/74	28	4	17	D2
	74/75	38		8	D2
	75/76	22	1	12	D2

TRAYNOR John
Hurlford U

Club	Season				Div
Ayr U	53/54	1			D2
	54/55				D2
	55/56				D2
	56/57	18			D1

TRAYNOR Thomas
b. Bonnybridge 27.9.1943
d. Melbourne 22.12.1992
Dunipace Jnrs

Club	Season				Div
Heart of Midlothian	62/63	1			D1
	63/64	29		1	D1
	64/65	17		3	D1
	65/66	30		9	D1
	66/67	24	1	1	D1
	67/68	24	2	6	D1
	68/69	28	1	6	D1
	69/70	16		4	D1
Dundee U	70/71	19	2	1	D1
	71/72	26		5	D1
	72/73	22	1	2	D1
	73/74	26	2	3	D1
	74/75	17	3	5	D1
	75/76	1	2		P
Morton	75/76	4			D1
Falkirk	76/77	5		8	D1

TRAYNOR William
Rutherglen Glencairn

Club	Season				Div
Stirling A	65/66	1			D1

TREACY Francis
b. Glasgow 14.7.1939
Johnstone Burgh

Club	Season				Div
Ipswch T	60/61				FL
	61/62				FL
	62/63				FL
	63/64	1			FL
	64/65	12		5	FL
	65/66	4	1		FL
	66/67				FL
St Mirren	66/67	9		4	D1

TULLOCH George
Dumbarton

Club	Season				Div
Falkirk	61/62	5			D1
Arbroath	62/63				D2
	63/64	23		6	D2
	64/65	24		8	D2
Stenhousemuir *	65/66	13		2	D2
Brechin C *	65/66	10		3	D2
	66/67	27	1	4	D2
	67/68	3	1		D2

TULLY Charles Patrick
b. Belfast 11.7.1924
d. Belfast 27.7.1971 Caps: NI - 10
Whiterock Jnrs
Belfast Celtic

Club	Season				Div
Cliftonville	L				
Ballyclare Comrad	L				
Celtic	48/49	30		4	D1
	49/50	25		2	D1
	50/51	27		3	D1
	51/52	23		4	D1
	52/53	25		7	D1
	53/54	11		1	D1
	54/55	21		4	D1
	55/56	17		4	D1
	56/57	21		1	D1
	57/58	10			D1
	58/59	5			D1
Stirling A	L 58/59				D1
Rangers	L 58/59				D1
Cork Hibernian	59/60				
	60/61				

TURNBULL Edward Hunter
b. Falkirk 12.4.1923 Caps: S - 8
Forth R

Club	Season				Div
Hibernian	46/47	20		13	D1
	47/48	23		11	D1
	48/49	27		8	D1
	49/50	27		18	D1
	50/51	25		15	D1
	51/52	29		7	D1
	52/53	29		17	D1
	53/54	27		14	D1
	54/55	25		4	D1
	55/56	33		17	D1
	56/57	30		14	D1
	57/58	30		9	D1
	58/59	23		2	D1

TURNBULL John Mackay
b. Kilmarnock ?.?.1916
Glenafton A

Club	Season				Div
Kilmarnock	37/38	2			D1
	38/39	26		3	D1
	46/47	27		7	D1
	47/48	26		11	D2
Queen of the South	48/49	6		1	D1
Ayr U	T 49/50				D2
Dumbarton	49/50	13			D2
Stirling A	T 50/51				D2

TURNBULL Ronald William
b. Ashington 18.7.1922
RAF

Club	Season				Div
Dundee	47/48	11		9	D1
Sunderland	47/48	16		8	FL
	48/49	24		8	FL
Manchester C	49/50	29		4	FL
	50/51	1		1	FL
Swansea T	50/51	15		9	FL
	51/52	40		22	FL
	52/53	12		6	FL
Dundee	53/54	16		5	D1
Ashington					

TURNBULL Roy
b. Edinburgh 22.10.1948
Gorgie Hearts

Club	Season				Div
Heart of Midlothian	68/69	1			D1
Lincoln C	69/70	2			FL

TURNER Patrick
b. Dublin Caps: Ei - 2

Club	Season				Div
Shamrock R	58/59				
	59/60				
Shelbourne	60/61				
	61/62				
Morton	61/62				D2
	62/63				D2
Celtic	63/64	7		1	D1
Glentoran	64/65				
Dundalk	65/66				
	66/67				
	67/68				
	68/69				
	69/70				
	70/71				
	71/72				
Bohemians	72/73				

UGOLINI Rolando
b. Lucca 4.6.1924
Armadale Thistle
Heart of Midlothian T

Club	Season				Div
Celtic	46/47	1			D1
	47/48	3			D1
Middlesbrough	48/49	39			FL
	49/50	41			FL
	50/51	42			FL
	51/52	41			FL
	52/53	41			FL
	53/54	42			FL
	54/55	38			FL
	55/56	36			FL
	56/57				FL
Wrexham	57/58	35			FL
	58/59	31			FL
	59/60	17			FL
Dundee U	60/61	27			D1
	61/62	16			D1
Berwick R	T				
Cowdenbeath	T				

URE John Francombe
b. Ayr 7.12.1939 Caps: S - 11
Ayr Albion
Dalry Thistle

Club	Season				Div
Dundee	58/59	2			D1
	59/60	7			D1
	60/61	32			D1
	61/62	34			D1
	62/63	32			D1
Arsenal	63/64	41		1	FL
	64/65	22		1	FL
	65/66	21			FL
	66/67	37			FL
	67/68	21			FL
	68/69	23			FL
	69/70	3			FL
Manchester U	69/70	34		1	FL
	70/71	13			FL
	71/72				FL
St Mirren	72/73	3			D2
	73/74				D2

URQUHART George Stuart McWilliam
b. Glasgow 22.4.1950

Club	Season				Div
St Mirren	68/69	9			D1
	69/70	6	1		D1
Ross Co					
Wigan A	79/80	37	4	4	FL
	80/81	26	1	2	FL

URQUHART John
b. Kirkcaldy 3.2.1925

Club	Season				Div
Heart of Midlothian	46/47	11		3	D1
	47/48	17		3	D1
	48/49	3			D1
	49/50	1		1	D1
Raith R	L 49/50	4		3	D1
Heart of Midlothian	50/51	3		2	D1
	51/52	18		2	D1
	52/53	28		12	D1
	53/54	28		10	D1
	54/55	29		10	D1
	55/56	19		5	D1
Raith R	55/56	3			D1
	56/57	33		9	D1
	57/58	29		11	D1
	58/59	29		11	D1
	59/60	32		8	D1
	60/61	32		8	D1
	61/62	11		3	D1

VALENTINE John C
b. Buckie
Buckie Thistle

Club	Season			Div
Queen's Park	53/54	24		D2
	54/55	17		D2
	55/56	32		D2
	56/57	32		D1
Rangers	57/58	2		D1
St Johnstone	58/59	32		D2
	59/60	17		D2

VALENTINE Martin

Club	Season		Div
Airdrieonians	52/53	4	D1
Stirling A	53/54		

VANDERMOTTEN William
b. Glasgow 26.8.1930 d. ?.?.1979

Club	Season			Div
Cowdenbeath	52/53	3		D2
Third Lanark	52/53			D1
Bradford PA	52/53	1		FL
Renfrew Jnrs	53/54			
	54/55			
Stirling A	55/56	10	2	D1

VARGA Zoltan
b. Hungary Caps: Hun - 12
Ferencvaros
Hertha Berlin

Club	Season			Div
Aberdeen	72/73	26	10	D1
Ajax Amsterdam				

VEITCH R

Club	Season		Div
Clyde	62/63	2	D1

VEITCH Thomas
b. Edinburgh 16.10.1949 d. Edinburgh 16.10.1987
Elphinstone Primrose
Bonnyrigg Rose

Club	Season				Div
Heart of Midlothian	68/69	6	3	2	D1
	69/70	18	3		D1
	70/71	3	1		D1
	71/72	10	2		D1
Tranmere R	72/73	22	2	1	FL
	73/74	32		1	FL
	74/75	22	1	3	FL
Denver Dynamos	75	21		1	NA
Halifax T	75/76	20	2		FL
Hartlepool U	76/77	10			FL
Morton	76/77	15			D1
	77/78	36			D1
Airdrieonians	78/79	15			D1
	79/80	22			D1
Queen of the South	80/81	1	2		D2

VENTERS Alexander
b. Cowdenbeath 9.6.1913
d. 30.4.1959 Caps: S - 3
Southend R
St Andrews U

Club	Season			Div
Cowdenbeath	30/31	13	3	D1
	31/32	33	11	D1
	32/33	37	12	D1
	33/34	13	10	D1
Rangers	33/34	15	5	D1
	34/35	28	10	D1
	35/36	32	17	D1
	36/37	33	10	D1
	37/38	34	12	D1
	38/39	33	35	D1
Third Lanark	46/47	8	2	D1
Blackburn R	46/47	10	3	FL
	47/48	15	4	FL
Raith R	47/48			D2

VINCENT Stanley

Club	Season				Div
Cowdenbeath	61/62	1		1	D2
	62/63				D2
	63/64	23		13	D2
Hibernian	63/64	7		4	D1
	64/65	9		4	D1
	65/66	1			D1
Falkirk	66/67	23		6	D1
	67/68	3	1		D1
	68/69				D1
Raith R	69/70	2			D1
East Fife	70/71				D2

WADDELL Ian

Club	Season				Div
Queen's Park	64/65	7			D2
	65/66	4			D2
Airdrieonians	66/67	3			D1
Hamilton A	67/68	20	1	1	D2
Rutherglen Glencairn					

WADDELL Robert
b. Kirkcaldy 5.9.1939
St Andrews Swifts

Club	Season			Div
Dundee	59/60	3	2	D1
	60/61	8	4	D1
	61/62	4	1	D1
	62/63	9	4	D1
	63/64	28	14	D1
	64/65	8	2	D1
Blackpool	64/65	5	3	FL
	65/66	14	1	FL
	66/67	9	1	FL
Bradford PA	66/67	20	3	FL
East Fife	67/68	25	2	D2
	68/69		16	D2
	69/70	26	7	D2

WADDELL Robert B
Kilbirnie Ladeside

Club	Season			Div
Kilmarnock	68/69			D1
	69/70			D1
Arbroath	70/71			D2
	71/72	22	2	D2
	72/73	32		D1
	73/74	28		D1
Toronto Metros	74	15		NA
Brechin C	74/75	14		D2
Clyde	74/75			D1

WADDELL William
Renfrew Jnrs

Club	Season		Div
Aberdeen	38/39	3	D1
	46/47	12	D1
	47/48	23	D1
	48/49	25	D1
	49/50	11	D1

WADDELL William
b. Forth 7.3.1921
d. Glasgow 13.10.1992 Caps: S - 17
Forth W
Strathclyde

Club	Season			Div
Rangers	38/39			
	46/47	22	5	D1
	47/48	12	2	D1
	48/49	20	3	D1
	49/50	7	4	D1
	50/51	28	6	D1
	51/52	24	5	D1
	52/53	16	2	D1
	53/54	29	3	D1
	54/55	11		D1

WADDELL William
b. Denny 16.4.1950

Club	Season				Div
Leeds U	67/68				FL
Kilmarnock	69/70	10	3		D1
	70/71	9	2	2	D1
Barnsley	71/72	17	1	4	FL
Hartlepool U	71/72	13	1	7	FL
	72/73	25	4	2	FL
Workington	L 72/73	1	2		FL
Hartlepool U	73/74	5			FL

WALDIE Simon
Inverness Caley

Club	Season		Div
Hibernian	47/48	8	D1
	48/49	1	D1
Queen of the South	49/50	26	D1
	50/51		D2
	51/52	8	D1
Ross Co			

WALDRON Ernest
b. Birmingham 3.6.1913 d. ?.?.1994
Bromsgrove R

Club	Season			Div
Crystal Palace	34/35	2		FL
	35/36	18	5	FL
	36/37	21	7	FL
	37/38	23	14	FL
	38/39	12	3	FL
	46/47	4	1	FL
Aberdeen	46/47	7	3	D1
	47/48	1		D1

WALKER Andrew
Banks o'Dee

Club	Season		Div
Aberdeen	58/59	2	D1

WALKER Bert

Club	Season			Div
Dundee	52/53	1		D1
	53/54	1	1	D1
	54/55	7	2	D1

WALKER Christopher John
b. 20.8.1951
Methil Star

Club	Season				Div
East Fife	71/72	10	2	1	D1
	72/73				D1
	73/74	1			D1

WALKER David
b. Edinburgh
Hutcheson Vale

Club	Season		Div
Airdrieonians	52/53	6	D1
	53/54	3	D1
	54/55		D2
	55/56	24	D1
	56/57	26	D1
	57/58	7	D1
St Mirren	58/59	13	D1
	59/60	10	D1

WALKER Eric
b. Bathgate
Alloa A

Club	Season			Div
Dundee U	59/60	6	1	D2
	60/61	2	1	D1
Brechin C	61/62	13	1	D2

WALKER Hay

Club	Season	Apps	Sub	Goals	Div
St Johnstone	65/66	1			D1

WALKER James
b. Detroit
Renfrew Jnrs

Club	Season	Apps	Sub	Goals	Div
Heart of Midlothian	46/47	8		1	D1
Partick T	46/47	3		1	D1
	47/48	14		7	D1
	48/49	25		13	D1
	49/50	30		16	D1
	50/51	24		7	D1
	51/52	27		10	D1
	52/53	27		12	D1
	53/54	9		6	D1
	54/55				D1
	55/56	2			D1
	56/57	1			D1
Third Lanark	56/57				D2

WALKER James
b. Stenhousemuir
Clydebank Jnrs

Club	Season	Apps	Sub	Goals	Div
Rangers	56/57	2			D1
Southend U	57/58				FL
St Johnstone	58/59	24		10	D2
	59/60	33		3	D2
	60/61	33		5	D1
	61/62	8		1	D1
East Fife	62/63				D2
	63/64				D2
	64/65				D2
	65/66				D2
Forfar A	66/67	11			D2
	67/68				D2

WALKER James
b. Aberdeen 25.8.1933

Club	Season	Apps	Sub	Goals	Div
Aberdeen	57/58	11			D1
	58/59	7			D1
Bradford PA	59/60	39			FL
	60/61	20		1	FL
	61/62	46			FL
	62/63	24		1	FL
	63/64	15			FL

WALKER Robert
b. Airdrie
Larkhall Thistle
Wolverhampton W

Club	Season	Apps	Sub	Goals	Div
Hamilton A	53/54	11			D1
	54/55	28		9	D2
	55/56	19			D2
	56/57	20		1	D2
	57/58	27		8	D2
	58/59	22			D2
Heart of Midlothian	59/60				D1
Ayr U	60/61	22			D1

WALKER Robert
Armadale Thistle

Club	Season	Apps	Sub	Goals	Div
Stirling A	49/50	3			D1
	50/51				D2
Berwick R					

WALKER Thomas
b. Livingston Station 26.5.1915
d. Edinburgh 11.1.1993 Caps: S - 20
Berryburn R
Livingstone Violet
Broxburn R

Club	Season	Apps	Sub	Goals	Div
Heart of Midlothian	32/33	17		8	D1
	33/34	27		15	D1
	34/35	36		19	D1
	35/36	35		18	D1
	36/37	37		11	D1
	37/38	37		10	D1
	38/39	37		23	D1
	46/47	9		3	D1
Chelsea	46/47	39		9	FL
	47/48	37		7	FL
	48/49	21		7	FL
Heart of Midlothian	48/49	1			D1

WALKER Thomas
b. Arbroath 15.3.1952
Arbroath LC

Club	Season	Apps	Sub	Goals	Div
Arbroath	69/70	36		7	D2
	70/71	34		9	D2
	71/72	3	1	1	D2
Airdrieonians	71/72	25	2	5	D1
	72/73	24	5	5	D1
Arbroath	L 73/74	14		8	D1
Airdrieonians	74/75	23	2	4	D1
	75/76	10	2	1	D1
	76/77	26	2	1	D1
	77/78	37	1	2	D1
	78/79	31	2	1	D1
	79/80	36	2		D1
	80/81	34	1	2	P
	81/82	22	3	2	P
Stirling A	82/83	26		1	D2
	83/84	30			D2

WALKER William
Crosshill Amateurs

Club	Season	Apps	Sub	Goals	Div
Ayr U	67/68	28	1	3	D2
	68/69				D2
	69/70				D1
	70/71	6			D1

WALLACE Brian

Club	Season	Apps	Sub	Goals	Div
Raith R	55/56	4		1	D1
	56/57	1			D1
	57/58	4			D1
	58/59	2			D1

WALLACE Brian
Cardowan Amateurs
Kilsyth R

Club	Season	Apps	Sub	Goals	Div
Clyde	70/71	8			D1
St Rochs					
Hamilton A	T 71/72	2			D2
Albion R	72/73	1			D2

WALLACE Clive Low
b. Kirriemuir 6.1.1932
Kirrie Thistle

Club	Season	Apps	Sub	Goals	Div
Dundee	57/58	1			D1
	58/59				D1
Bury	58/59				FL
Stockport Co	59/60	13		4	FL

WALLACE Douglas
b. South Africa

Club	Season	Apps	Sub	Goals	Div
Clyde	46/47	2			D1
Dunfermline A	47/48				D2
Albion R	47/48				D2
	48/49	14		6	D1

WALLACE Gordon
b. Dundee 20.6.1943
Lawside R
Dundee N E
Alyth U

Club	Season	Apps	Sub	Goals	Div
Montrose	62/63				D2
	63/64	36		20	D2
	64/65	33		19	D2
	65/66	36		17	D2
	66/67	7		6	D2
Raith R	66/67	30		17	D2
	67/68	34		27	D1
	68/69	34		13	D1
	69/70	4		1	D1
Dundee	69/70	30		21	D1
	70/71	33		11	D1
	71/72	30	2	16	D1
	72/73	31	1	9	D1
	73/74	23	1	14	D1
Toronto Metros	74	3		1	NA
Dundee	74/75	13	1	6	D1
	75/76	29	2	12	P
Seattle Sounders	76	21		12	NA
Dundee U	76/77	24	1	13	P
	77/78	14	1	3	P
Raith R	77/78	14		6	D2
Seattle Sounders	78	24		4	NA
Raith R	78/79	34	3	14	D1
	79/80	13	1	5	D1

WALLACE Ian Andrew
b. Glasgow 23.5.1956 Caps: S - 3
Yoker A

Club	Season	Apps	Sub	Goals	Div
Dumbarton	74/75	7	1	2	D1
	75/76	25	1	9	D1
Coventry C	76/77	24	2	9	FL
	77/78	41		20	FL
	78/79	38		15	FL
	79/80	25		13	FL
Nottingham F	80/81	37		11	FL
	81/82	28	1	9	FL
	82/83	41		13	FL
	83/84	22	5	3	FL
Brest	84/85				
Sunderland	84/85	14	1	3	FL
	85/86	14	5	3	FL
Maritimo					
Sydney Croatia					

WALLACE James
b. Kirkintilloch 17.2.1933

Club	Season	Apps	Sub	Goals	Div
Aberdeen	52/53	4			D1
	53/54	.			D1
	54/55	5		1	D1
	55/56				D1
Northampton T	L 55/56				FL
Aberdeen	56/57	6			D1
	57/58	5		1	D1
Dundee U	58/59	20		3	D2

WALLACE James
b. Stirling 9.6.1954
Sauchie

Club	Season	Apps	Sub	Goals	Div
Dunfermline A	70/71				D1
	71/72				D1
	72/73				D2
	73/74	29		3	D1
	74/75	9			D1
Aldershot	75/76	31		3	FL
	76/77	22			FL
Alloa A	77/78	19	6	2	D1
	78/79	23	4	1	D2

WALLACE John Martin Bokas
b. Musselburgh 6.9.1935 d. ?.?.1996
Wallyford BC
Blackpool

Workington	52/53	5		FL
Ashton under Lyme	53/54			
	54/55			
Berwick R	55/56			D2
Airdrieonians	56/57			D1
	57/58	14		D1
	58/59	34		D1
	59/60	6		D1
West Bromwich A	59/60	30		FL
	60/61	22		FL
	61/62	17		FL
Bedford T	62/63			
	63/64			
Hereford U	64/65			
	65/66			
Berwick R	66/67	21		D2
	67/68	31		D2
	68/69			D2

WALLACE William

Lugar Boswell				
Motherwell	62/63	2	1	D1
Clydebank	63/64			D2
Stranraer *	63/64	12	4	D2
	64/65	10	4	D2

WALLACE William Semple Brown
b. Kirkintilloch 23.6.1941 Caps: S - 7
Kilsyth R

Stenhousemuir	58/59				D2
Raith R	59/60	26		12	D1
	60/61	30		11	D1
Heart of Midlothian	60/61	2		1	D1
	61/62	26		6	D1
	62/63	34		17	D1
	63/64	34		23	D1
	64/65	34		21	D1
	65/66	33		19	D1
	66/67	10		4	D1
Celtic	66/67	21		14	D1
	67/68	29		21	D1
	68/69	29	2	18	D1
	69/70	29	1	16	D1
	70/71	25	1	19	D1
	71/72	2	2		D1
Crystal Palace	71/72	27	2	3	FL
	72/73	9	1	1	FL
Dumbarton	72/73	24	2	6	D1
	73/74	32		3	D1
	74/75	26		12	D1
Apia					
Partick T	T 76/77				P
Ross Co	76/77				

WALLER Thomas

Raith R	50/51	1		D1

WALLS Arthur Joseph
b. Glasgow 15.1.1931

Airdrieonians	53/54	7		D1
Tranmere R	54/55	14	3	FL
	55/56	8	3	FL
Macclesfield T				

WALMSLEY William
b. Kilmarnock d. 3.9.2001
Clydebank

Rangers	48/49	1		D1

WALSH Arthur

Oakley U				
Dunfermline A	70/71	4		D1

WALSH Francis
b. Wishaw 15.9.1923
Ardeer Recreation

Kilmarnock	46/47	13	3	D1
Celtic	47/48	10	3	D1
	48/49			D1
Torquay U	T 49/50			FL
Southport	49/50	5	3	FL
Stranraer	L 49/50			D3
Hamilton A	50/51			D2
	51/52			D2
Limerick	51/52			
Ards	52/53			
East Stirlingshire	53/54			D2
	54/55			D2
	55/56			D2

WALSH James
b. Bellshill 3.12.1930
Valleyfield Colliery
Bo'ness U

Celtic	50/51	1		D1
	51/52	21	7	D1
	52/53	22	7	D1
	53/54	19	5	D1
	54/55	28	19	D1
	55/56	16	8	D1
	56/57	2		D1
Leicester C	56/57	1		FL
	57/58	19	13	FL
	58/59	38	20	FL
	59/60	22	4	FL
	60/61	37	22	FL
	61/62	33	14	FL
	62/63	26	6	FL
Rugby T				

WALSH W

Falkirk	55/56	1	1	D1

WALTERS Gavin

Airdrieonians	66/67	3	1	1	D1
Partick T	67/68	2			D1
	68/69	1			D1

WALTERS Joseph

Clyde	55/56	4		D1
	56/57			D2
	57/58	32	1	D1
	58/59	29		D1
	59/60	28		D1
	60/61	4		D1
	61/62			D1
Albion R	62/63			D2
	63/64	21		D2

WARD

Raith R	58/59	6	1	D1

WARD

Arbroath	68/69	1	1	D1
	69/70	10	3	3	D2

WARD James
b. Glasgow 26.7.1929 d. ?.?.1985

Queen's Park	52/53	24	19	D2
	53/54	13	10	D2
	54/55	20	10	D2
	55/56	18	8	D2
	56/57	2		D1
Crewe A	56/57	5		FL
	57/58			FL
St Johnstone	T 58/59	2		D2

WARD John

Baillieston				
Aberdeen	56/57	6		D1
	57/58	6	1	D1

WARD Joseph
b. Glasgow 25.11.1954
St Rochs

Clyde	74/75	27	4	3	D1
	75/76	13	11	3	D1
	76/77	19	4	8	D2
	77/78	30	5	15	D2
	78/79	14	1	10	D1
Aston Villa	78/79	1			FL
	79/80	1	1		FL
Dundee U	80/81	4	2		P
Ayr U	81/82	12	4	2	D1
	82/83	16	6	1	D1
	83/84		1		D1
Stirling A	83/84	5	3	1	D2
Berwick R	84/85	1	2		D2
St Johnstone	85/86	18	9	7	D2
	86/87	5	7	1	D2

WARD Noel Gerard
b. Strabane 8.12.1952
Portadown

Aberdeen	74/75	2		D1
	75/76	4	1	P
Wigan A	76/77	42	2	NL
	77/78	44	5	NL
	78/79	44	4	FL
	79/80	3	1	FL

WARD Patrick
b. Dumbarton 28.12.1926
Renton Guild
Glasgow Perthshire

Hibernian	50/51	1		D1
	51/52	3		D1
	52/53	3		D1
	53/54	24		D1
	54/55	15	1	D1
Leicester C	55/56	27		FL
	56/57	27		FL
	57/58	3		FL
Crewe Alex.	58/59	31	1	FL
Rugby T				

WARDHAUGH James
b. Marshall Meadows 21.3.1929
d. Edinburgh 2.1.1978 Caps: S - 2
Shaftesbury Park

Heart of Midlothian	46/47	11	2	D1
	47/48	1		D1
	48/49	22	10	D1
	49/50	30	20	D1
	50/51	29	15	D1
	51/52	19	14	D1
	52/53	26	12	D1
	53/54	28	27	D1
	54/55	30	15	D1
	55/56	32	30	D1
	56/57	31	22	D1
	57/58	30	28	D1
	58/59	14	11	D1
Dunfermline A	59/60	10	4	D1
	60/61	2		D1

WARDLAW James

Falkirk	46/47	14	9	D1

WARDLAW John

Morton	48/49	7		D1
	49/50			D2
Falkirk	50/51	10		D1

WARK Alexander

St Mirren	69/70	1		D1

WARK Joseph
b. Glasgow 9.10.1947
Irvine V

Club	Season				Div
Motherwell	68/69	36		8	D2
	69/70	34		1	D1
	70/71	34		1	D1
	71/72	25			D1
	72/73	33		1	D1
	73/74	34			D1
	74/75	32			D1
	75/76	36			P
	76/77	35		2	P
	77/78	34			P
	78/79	33			P
	79/80	27	1	1	D1
	80/81	29			D1
	81/82	25		3	D1
	82/83	5		1	P
	83/84	7			P

WATKINS Charles
b. Glasgow 14.1.1921

Club	Season			Div
Rangers	46/47	6		D1
	47/48	3		D1
Luton T	48/49	27	1	FL
	49/50	39	4	FL
	50/51	35	1	FL
	51/52	41	1	FL
	52/53	35	4	FL
	53/54	30	2	FL
	54/55	11	3	FL

WATSON

Club	Season		Div
Airdrieonians	59/60	5	D1

WATSON Brian
b. c1940

Club	Season			Div
Raith R	61/62	20	5	D1
Worcester C	62/63			

WATSON David Craig
b. c1942 d. Glasgow 7.11.2001
Arthurlie

Club	Season				Div
Rangers	60/61				D1
	61/62				D1
	62/63	6			D1
	63/64	7		4	D1
	64/65	1			D1
Morton	65/66	34		8	D1
Kilmarnock	66/67	26	2	8	D1
	67/68	2			D1
Falkirk	67/68	27		5	D1
	68/69	29	1	3	D1
Arcadia Shepherds	69/70				
	70/71				
	71/72				
Morton	72/73	7		3	D1

WATSON Frank
Peebles R

Club	Season		Div
Aberdeen	46/47	4	D1
	47/48		D1
	48/49	1	D1
	49/50	18	D1
	50/51	3	D1
	51/52	7	D1

WATSON George
St Johnstone

Club	Season			Div
Airdrieonians	46/47			D2
	47/48	14	3	D1
St Johnstone	48/49	21	2	D2

WATSON Hugh

Club	Season			Div
Airdrieonians	47/48	8	2	D1

WATSON James
b. Stirling 16.1.1924 Caps: S - 2
Armadale Thistle

Club	Season			Div
Motherwell	46/47	23	4	D1
	47/48	19	10	D1
	48/49	28	9	D1
	49/50	27	9	D1
	50/51	29	10	D1
	51/52	21	6	D1
Huddersfield T	52/53	28	6	FL
	53/54	30	6	FL
	54/55	42	11	FL
	55/56	23	5	FL
	56/57	17	1	FL
Dunfermline A	57/58			D2
	58/59	24	5	D1

WATSON Joseph
d. Sydney ?.9.2000 Caps: Aus - 17
Nottingham F

Club	Season			Div
Dundee U	70/71	5		D1
	71/72	3		D1
	72/73			D1
Forfar A	72/73	35	4	D2
Sydney City				

WATSON Kenneth
Salvesen BC

Club	Season		Div
Rangers	69/70	2	D1
	70/71	1	D1

WATSON Kenneth
Dunfermline U

Club	Season				Div
Dunfermline A	73/74	1	2		D1
	74/75	23	2	7	D1
	75/76	24	1		D1
	76/77	26	5	3	D2
	77/78	5	12		D2

WATSON Matthew McLuskie
b. Paisley 3.5.1936
Glen A
Kilmarnock Amateurs
Kilwinning R

Club	Season			Div
Kilmarnock	54/55	5		D1
	55/56	32		D1
	56/57	21		D1
	57/58	9		D1
	58/59	34		D1
	59/60	34	1	D1
	60/61	32		D1
	61/62	32	1	D1
	62/63	34		D1
	63/64	30		D1
	64/65	29	1	D1
	65/66	19		D1
	66/67	3	1	D1
	67/68	7	1	D1
Queen of the South	68/69			D2
	69/70			D2
	70/71			D2
Cumnock Jnrs				

WATSON Michael

Club	Season		Div
Clyde	53/54	3	D1
	54/55		D1
	55/56	19	D1
	56/57		D2
	57/58	6	D1
Dundee	58/59	2	D1

WATSON R

Club	Season		Div
Morton	46/47	1	D1

WATSON Robert
b. Airdrie 1.5.1946 Caps: S - 1
Airdrie Academy

Club	Season				Div
Rangers	65/66	21		2	D1
	66/67	4			D1
	67/68	7	2	1	D1
	68/69	10		1	D1
	69/70	5	3		D1
Motherwell	69/70	7			D1
	70/71	29			D1
	71/72	20		1	D1
	72/73	27		1	D1
	73/74	33			D1
	74/75	33			D1
	75/76	30	3		P

WATSON William
b. New Stevenston 4.12.1949

Club	Season				Div
Manchester U	65/66				FL
	66/67				FL
	67/68				FL
	68/69				FL
	69/70				FL
Huddersfield T	L 69/70				FL
Manchester U	70/71	8			FL
	71/72				FL
	72/73	3			FL
Miami Toros	73	18			NA
Burnley	T 73/74				FL
Motherwell	73/74	22		1	D1
	74/75	32		1	D1
	75/76	17	2		P
	76/77	18	1		P
	77/78	33	2		P
Dundee	78/79	34			D1
	79/80	4	1		P

WATT Donald

Club	Season			Div
Dundee U	56/57	17	8	D2
Dundee	57/58	1		D1

WATT Donald
b. 23.7.1953
Shettleston

Club	Season			Div
Celtic	70/71			D1
	71/72			D1
	72/73			D1
Dumbarton	73/74	11	1	D1
	74/75	34		D1
	75/76	25		D1
	76/77	29		D1
	77/78	9	3	D1
	78/79			D1
East Stirlingshire	79/80	22	3	D2
	80/81	34	1	D1
	81/82	32	1	D1

WATT James
Berwick R

Club	Season			Div
Dundee	55/56	1		D1
	56/57	12	7	D1
Queen of the South	57/58			D2

WATT William Douglas
b. Aberdeen 6.6.1946

Club	Season				Div
Preston NE	62/63				FL
	63/64				FL
	64/65	4			FL
	65/66	3	1		FL
Aberdeen	66/67	4	1	5	D1
	67/68	10	1	3	D1
	68/69	1			D1
Raith R	68/69	6			D1
	69/70	3	3		D1

WATTERS James
b. Buckhaven 12.8.1927
d. Dunfermline 10.10.1999
Buckhaven

Club	Season	Apps	Gls	Div
Heart of Midlothian	47/48			D1
	48/49			D1
	49/50	6		D1
	50/51	3		D1
	51/52	1		D1
	52/53	30		D1
	53/54	30		D1
	54/55	4		D1
	55/56	1		D1
East Fife	56/57	1		D1

WATTERS Patrick

Club	Season	Apps	Gls	Div
Stirling A	59/60	2		D1
Portadown				
Stranraer *	61/62	6		D2
Stenhousemuir *	62/63			D2
	63/64	25	7	D2
	64/65	22	1	D2
East Stirlingshire	65/66	29	5	D2

WATTERS William
Bonnyrigg A

Club	Season	Apps	Gls	Div
Motherwell	47/48	28	5	D1
	48/49	1		D1
	49/50	16	5	D1
	50/51	16	2	D1
Dunfermline A				

WEAMES Thomas
Maybole Jnrs

Club	Season	Apps	Gls	Div
Ayr U	67/68	13	1	D2
	68/69			D2
	69/70	1		D1

WEIR Andrew Best
b. Paisley ?.?.1937 d. 11.5.1992 Caps: S - 6
Arthurlie Jnrs

Club	Season	Apps	Gls	Div
Motherwell	57/58	17	1	D1
	58/59	34	14	D1
	59/60	27	7	D1
	60/61	20	9	D1
	61/62	8	1	D1
	62/63	23	2	D1
	63/64	27	5	D1
	64/65	30	5	D1
	65/66	2		D1
	66/67	9	1	D1
	67/68	2	1	D1

WEIR David
b. Glasgow
Manchester U

Club	Season	Apps	Gls	Div
Raith R	68/69	4		D1
	69/70	12		D1

WEIR Donald
b. Cadder East ?.?.1930
d. Aughengeish 18.9.1959
Kilwinning R

Club		Season	Apps	Gls	Div
Celtic		48/49	1		D1
		49/50			D1
		50/51	4	1	D1
		51/52	1		D1
Portadown		52/53			
Ards	T				
Canterbury C					
Forfar A		56/57			D2

WEIR Ian

Club	Season	Apps	Gls	Div
Clyde	57/58	1		D1
Motherwell	60/61	21		D1
	61/62	1		D1
Stirling A	61/62	23		D1
	62/63			D2
Waterford				

WEIR John Britton
b. Fauldhouse 20.10.1923 d. 7.1.2003
Leith Renton

Club	Season	Apps	Gls	Div
Hibernian	46/47	19	14	D1
Blackburn R	46/47	13	6	FL
	47/48	10	1	FL
Celtic	47/48	5	4	D1
	48/49	27	9	D1
	49/50	13	4	D1
	50/51	24	7	D1
	51/52	11	3	D1
Falkirk	52/53	15	2	D1
Llanelly	53/54			
Dumbarton	53/54	16	5	D2

WEIR S Hastie
b. Glasgow ?.?.1930 d. Glasgow 21.12.1999
Baillieston

Club	Season	Apps	Gls	Div
Queen's Park	49/50			D2
	50/51	28		D2
	51/52	3		D2
	52/53	29		D2
	53/54	28		D2
Motherwell	54/55	12		D1
	55/56	34		D1
	56/57	34		D1
	57/58	22		D1
	58/59	31		D1
	59/60	14		D1
	60/61	29		D1
	61/62	20		D1
Partick T	64/65	2		D1

WEIR Thomas
Bayview YC

Club	Season	Apps	Gls	Div
East Fife	49/50	7		D1
	50/51	6		D1
	51/52	12		D1
	52/53	1		D1
	53/54	1		D1
Raith R	54/55	3		D1
	55/56	13		D1

WEIR Thomas
Shotts Bon Accord
Dundee

Club		Season	Apps	Gls	Div
St Johnstone		66/67	1	1	D1
Hamilton A	T	67/68	1		D2

WELLS David
b. New Cumnock 19.9.1951
Netherthird Colliery
Auchinleck Talbot

Club	Season	Apps	Sub	Gls	Div
Ayr U	70/71	1		1	D1
	71/72	1			D1
	72/73	22	1	1	D1
	73/74	19			D1
	74/75	19		1	D1
	75/76	17	1	2	P
	76/77	25			P
	77/78	12			P
	78/79	33	1	2	D1
	79/80	3		1	D1
Glenafton A					

WELLS William J
b. 18.8.1952
Blairgowrie

Club	Season	Apps	Sub	Gls	Div
Arbroath	74/75	13		1	D1
	75/76	6			D1
	76/77	8		2	D1
	77/78	19		1	D1
	78/79	15		3	D1
	79/80	16	1	1	D1
	80/81	1			D2
Clyde	80/81	2			D2

WELSH Francis
b. Glasgow 14.5.1954
Avoca Amateurs
Celtic
Shettleston L

Club		Season	Apps	Sub	Gls	Div
Celtic		71/72				D1
		72/73				D1
		73/74	3			D1
		74/75	1	1		D1
Coventry C	T	75/76				FL
Hamilton A	T	75/76	1			D1
Kilmarnock		75/76				D1
		76/77	24			P
		77/78	20		3	D1
		78/79	9		4	D1
		79/80	17		1	P
Partick T		80/81	26		1	P
		81/82				P
		82/83	5		1	D1
Morton		83/84	38		1	D1
Hamilton A		84/85				D1
Morton		84/85	7		1	P
Hamilton A	T	85/86	1			D1
Morton		85/86	3			D1

WELSH James
b. Longriggend
Coltness U

Club	Season	Apps	Gls	Div
St Johnstone	48/49	7	1	D2
	49/50	7	5	D2
	50/51	3	1	D2
Airdrieonians	50/51	26	8	D1
	51/52	19	6	D1
	52/53	9	3	D1
	53/54	14	4	D1
Stirling A	53/54			D1
Airdrieonians	54/55			D2
	55/56	25	6	D1
	56/57	20	6	D1
	57/58	6		D1
Third Lanark	57/58	8	2	D1
	58/59	2	1	D1
Airdrieonians	58/59	4		D1
	59/60	5		D1

WELSH William

Club	Season	Apps	Gls	Div
Airdrieonians	56/57	1		D1

WENTZEL Vernon James
b. Bulawayo ?.?.1938
Queens Club

Club	Season	Apps	Gls	Div
Kilmarnock	57/58	3	1	D1
	58/59	18	13	D1
	59/60	22	9	D1
	60/61	1	1	D1
Queens Club				
Apia				
Addington				

WEST Charles
Clydebank Strollers

Club		Season	Apps	Gls	Div
Partick T		65/66	4		D1
		66/67	1		D1
		67/68	7		D1
Lincoln C	T				
Chelmsford C					

WESTLAND Douglas George
b. Aberdeen ?.?.1909
Banks o'Dee

Club	Season	Apps	Gls	Div
Aberdeen	34/35	2		D1
	35/36	8		D1
Stoke C	36/37			FL
	37/38	1		FL
	38/39	3		FL
Barlaston St Giles				
Raith R	48/49			D2
	49/50	2		D1

WESTWATER George Alan
Caps: Aus - 15
Bankstown

Club	Season	Apps	Sub	Gls	Div
Stirling A	63/64	14		2	D2
	64/65	10		4	D2
	65/66	13		2	D1
Pan Hellenic					

WESTWATER William
b. c1921 d. 18.7.1985

Club	Season	Apps	Sub	Gls	Div
Morton	46/47	12		1	D1
	47/48	4			D1
	48/49	16			D1
	49/50	24			D2
	50/51	3			D1
	51/52	10			D1
Dundee	52/53				D1
Dundee U	53/54	3			D2

WHEATLEY Stewart
Oakley U

Club	Season	Apps	Sub	Gls	Div
Falkirk	70/71	1			D1
	71/72	3			D1
	72/73	1			D1
	73/74	24	3	2	D1
	74/75	26	3	3	D2
	75/76	22	1	3	D1
Raith R	76/77	6	8		D1
Berwick R	77/78	36		1	D2
	78/79	28	2	3	D2
	79/80	23	2	2	D1

WHIGHAM John E

Club	Season	Apps	Sub	Gls	Div
Queen's Park	46/47	30		3	D1
Morton	47/48	17			D1
	48/49	18			D1
	49/50	30			D2
	50/51	28			D1
	51/52	19			D1

WHIGHAM William Murdoch Morrison
b. Airdrie 9.10.1939
Shotts Bon Accord

Club	Season	Apps	Sub	Gls	Div
Falkirk	60/61	27			D2
	61/62	30			D1
	62/63	30			D1
	63/64	33			D1
	64/65	32			D1
	65/66	30			D1
	66/67	4			D1
Middlesbrough	66/67	35			FL
	67/68	32			FL
	68/69	41			FL
	69/70	28			FL
	70/71	42			FL
	71/72	9			FL
Dumbarton	72/73	7			D1
	73/74				D1
Darlington	74/75	4			FL

WHITE Alexander
b. Joes twin
Glenrothes

Club	Season	Apps	Sub	Gls	Div
Dundee U	71/72	6	6	4	D1
	72/73	17	4	5	D1
	73/74	6	6	2	D1
	74/75		2		D1
Forfar A	75/76	25	1	10	D2
	76/77	31	3	10	D2
	77/78	1		1	D2
Glenrothes					

WHITE David
Royal Albert

Club	Season	Apps	Sub	Gls	Div
Clyde	57/58	3			D1
	58/59	18		2	D1
	59/60	31		8	D1
	60/61	19		5	D1
	61/62				D2
	62/63	29		3	D1
	63/64	30		7	D2
	64/65	34		2	D1
	65/66	27		2	D1

WHITE Edward Richard
b. Musselburgh 13.4.1935

Club	Season	Apps	Sub	Gls	Div
Falkirk	57/58	12		6	D1
	58/59	8		6	D1
Bradford C	59/60	4		1	FL
Arbroath					

WHITE John Anderson
b. Musselburgh 28.4.1937
d. Crews Hill 21.7.1964 Caps: S - 22
Musselburgh Union
Bonnyrigg Rose A

Club	Season	Apps	Sub	Gls	Div
Alloa A	56/57				D2
	57/58				D2
Falkirk	58/59	25		8	D1
	59/60	5		3	D2
Tottenham H	59/60	28		5	FL
	60/61	42		13	FL
	61/62	36		8	FL
	62/63	37		8	FL
	63/64	40		6	FL

WHITE Joseph
b. Alex's twin
Glenrothes

Club	Season	Apps	Sub	Gls	Div
Dundee U	71/72	4			D1
	72/73	1			D1
Cowdenbeath	73/74		2		D2
Stirling A	74/75				D2

WHITE Thomas
b. Musselburgh 12.8.1939
Bonnyrigg Rose

Club	Season	Apps	Sub	Gls	Div
Raith R	59/60	5		2	D1
	60/61	2		1	D1
	61/62	20		9	D1
	62/63	3			D1
St Mirren	62/63	28		17	D1
	63/64	7		1	D1
Heart of Midlothian	63/64	19		17	D1
	64/65	18		13	D1
Aberdeen	65/66	14		4	D1
Crystal Palace	66/67	19		6	FL
	67/68	18	2	7	FL
Blackpool	67/68	11		4	FL
	68/69	22		5	FL
	69/70	1			FL
Bury	70/71	33	2	11	FL
	71/72	13		2	FL
Crewe Alex.	71/72	4			FL
Fleetwood					

WHITE William
Alloa BC

Club	Season	Apps	Sub	Gls	Div
Rangers	69/70	1			D1

WHITEFORD David
Jordanhill TC

Club	Season	Apps	Sub	Gls	Div
Motherwell	65/66				D1
	66/67	27			D1
	67/68	34		3	D1
	68/69	34		6	D2
	69/70	10			D1
	70/71	34		3	D1
	71/72	23			D1
	72/73	34		1	D1
	73/74	1			D1
Falkirk	73/74	23			D1
	74/75	28		1	D2
	75/76	10	4		D1
East Stirlingshire	76/77	38	1	1	D2
	77/78	32	1		D2
	78/79	10	1		D2

WHITEFORD Derek
b. Salsburgh 13.5.1947 d. Shotts 12.1.2002

Club	Season	Apps	Sub	Gls	Div
Hibernian	64/65	1			D1
	65/66				D1
	66/67				D1
Airdrieonians	67/68	31		3	D1
	68/69	34		6	D1
	69/70	34			D1
	70/71	27		6	D1
	71/72	34		10	D1
	72/73	30		4	D1
	73/74	35		19	D2
	74/75	32		8	D1
	75/76	32		8	D1
	76/77	35	2	15	D1
Dumbarton	77/78	39		15	D1
	78/79	22	5	7	D1
	79/80	11		2	D1
Falkirk	79/80	12		2	D2
Ayr U	80/81				

WHITEFORD John
Ayr U

Club	Season	Apps	Sub	Gls	Div
Stirling A	45/46				
	46/47				D3
	47/48				D2
	48/49				D2
	49/50	20			D1
	50/51				D2
	51/52	1			D1

WHITEFORD John
b. Airdrie

Club	Season	Apps	Sub	Gls	Div
Airdrieonians	68/69	3	2	1	D1
	69/70	7	2	2	D1
	70/71	14	1	2	D1
	71/72	9	3	1	D1
	72/73				D1
Falkirk	73/74	12	9	2	D1
	74/75	36	1	23	D2
	75/76	24		17	D1
	76/77	4			D1
Dumbarton	76/77	19		14	D1
	77/78	27		15	D1
	78/79	13	3	4	D1

WHITEHEAD Ian

Club	Season	Apps	Sub	Gls	Div
Queen's Park	68/69	3		2	D2
	69/70	20		12	D2
Ayr U	70/71	20		10	D1
	71/72	4		1	D1
Berwick R	72/73	17	5	4	D2

WHITEHEAD Richard
b. Newtongrange 1.1.1928
d. Vancouver 4.8.1996
Inveresk Thistle

Club	Season				
Heart of Midlothian	46/47	7		2	D1
	47/48				D1
	48/49	2			D1
	49/50	1			D1
	50/51	8		1	D1
	51/52				D1
	52/53	1			D1
Stirling A	53/54	30		1	D1
	54/55	16		1	D1
Queen of the South	54/55	10			D1
	55/56	22			D1
	56/57	25		2	D1
	57/58	28		2	D1
	58/59	10			D1

WHITEHEAD William
b. Edinburgh
Musselburgh A

Club	Season			
Dunfermline A	63/64	4		D1

WHITELAW Gordon
Army

Club	Season				
Partick T	60/61	1			D1
	61/62	3		2	D1
	62/63	24		10	D1
Airdrieonians	63/64	13		1	D1
St Johnstone	64/65	18		8	D1
	65/66	18		5	D1
	66/67	34		19	D1
	67/68	27	4	6	D1
	68/69	19	1	5	D1
	69/70	13	3	5	D1
	70/71	7	1		D1
	71/72	15	2	1	D1
	72/73	1			D1
Raith R	72/73	3			D2

WHITELAW Jack

Club	Season			
Falkirk	47/48	26		D1
	48/49	12		D1
	49/50	17	1	D1
	50/51	23	2	D1
Morton	51/52	6		D1

WHITESIDE William
b. Glasgow ?.?.1948
Campsie Black Watch
Ashfield

Club	Season		
Raith R	68/69	3	D1
	69/70	5	D1
Ashfield			
Barrow			
Stranraer	70/71		D2
	71/72	36	D2
	72/73	36	D2
Hamilton A	73/74	8	D2

WHITTAKER Brian
b. Glasgow 23.9.1956 d. Edinburgh 7.9.1997
Sighthill Amateurs
Crystal Palace T

Club	Season				
Partick T	74/75			1	D1
	75/76	1			D1
	76/77	36		1	P
	77/78	34	1		P
	78/79	36			P
	79/80	35		1	P
Borussia Dortmund T	80/81				
Hertha Berlin T	80/81				
Partick T	80/81	34		1	P
	81/82	28			P
	82/83	36		1	D1
Celtic	83/84	10		2	P
Heart of Midlothian	84/85	25	3	1	P
	85/86	24	1		P
	86/87	37			P
	87/88	42			P
	88/89	24			P
	89/90	6			P
Falkirk	90/91	26		1	D1
	91/92	6			P

WHITTLE James Archibald
b. Hamilton 5.9.1929 d. 23.7.2001
Cambuslang R

Club	Season				
Heart of Midlothian	47/48				D1
	48/49				D1
	49/50				D1
	50/51	1			D1
	51/52	16		9	D1
	52/53	12		4	D1
	53/54				D1
Southampton L	53/54	2			FL
Heart of Midlothian	54/55	5		1	D1
	55/56			2	D1
	56/57	1			D1
Ayr U	56/57	20		5	D1
	57/58				D2

WHYTE Andrew

Club	Season			
Dunfermline A	50/51	26		D2
	51/52			D2
East Fife	51/52	11		D1
	52/53	20	1	D1
	53/54	5		D1
	54/55	3		D1

WHYTE Francis
b. Govanhill 18.4.1935
St Pauls Whiteinch BG

Club	Season		
Celtic	51/52		D1
Maryhill Harp L	51/52		
Celtic	52/53		D1
	53/54		D1
	54/55		D1
	55/56	7	D1
Swindon T	56/57	7	FL

WHYTE Hugh
b. Kilmarnock 24.7.1955
Hurlford U

Club	Season		
Hibernian	74/75	4	D1
	75/76	1	P
Dunfermline A	76/77	39	D2
	77/78	39	D2
	78/79	38	D2
	79/80	39	D1
	80/81	39	D1
	81/82	19	D1
	82/83	27	D1
	83/84	39	D2
	84/85	30	D2
	85/86		D2
	86/87	2	D1

WHYTE James

Club	Season			
Morton	46/47	19		D1
Airdrieonians	47/48	1		D1
Morton	47/48	22	2	D1
	48/49	13		D1
	49/50	3		D2
	50/51	29		D1
	51/52	3		D1

WHYTE James Boslem
b. Kilsyth ?.?.1941
Kilsyth R

Club	Season			
Aberdeen	62/63			D1
	63/64			D1
	64/65			D1
	65/66	25	2	D1
	66/67	30	3	D1
	67/68	28		D1
	68/69	19	1	D1
	69/70	3		D1
Kilmarnock	70/71	18		D1
	71/72	22		D1
	72/73	33	1	D1
	73/74	29		D2
	74/75	1	1	D1
Kirkintilloch Rob Roy				

WHYTE James McCreadie
b. Glasgow 19.1.1930

Club	Season			
Third Lanark	51/52	5	2	D1
	52/53	2		D1
	53/54	1		D2
Southend U	54/55	20	4	FL
	55/56	12	4	FL
	56/57	1		FL
Sittingbourne				

WHYTE John Nimmo
b. West Calder 7.5.1921 d. Bradford 17.10.1998
Lugar Home Guard
Kilmarnock
Bedlay Jnrs
Forth R

Club	Season			
Falkirk	46/47	24		D1
	47/48	23		D1
	48/49	30		D1
	49/50	20		D1
Bradford C	50/51	42	1	FL
	51/52	29		FL
	52/53	43	1	FL
	53/54	45		FL
	54/55	29		FL
	55/56	42		FL
	56/57	6		FL
Wigan A	57/58	26		LC

WILKIE Alexander

Club	Season		
Raith R	50/51	1	D1
	51/52	13	D1
	52/53	1	D1
Berwick R	53/54		D3
	54/55		D3
	55/56		D2
East Fife	56/57	16	D1
	57/58	13	D1

WILKIE John Carlin
b. Dundee 1.7.1947
Lochee U

Club	Season				
Arbroath	65/66	27		1	D2
	66/67	15	4	6	D2
	67/68	7	1	1	D2
	68/69	26	1	3	D1
	69/70	19	1	5	D2
	70/71				D2
Morton	71/72	1			D1
Ross Co					
Halifax T	72/73	15	1	3	FL
	73/74	14	7	5	FL
Elgin C	74/75				
	75/76				
Wigan A	76/77	36	1	13	NL
	77/78	46		20	NL
	78/79	3	1		FL

WILKINSON Ian

Club	Season			Div
Hibernian	68/69	3		D1
	69/70	1		D1
Raith R	70/71			D2
Hamilton A	71/72	19	1	D2

WILKINSON William

St Anthonys

Club	Season			Div
Dumbarton	67/68	4	1	D2
	68/69			D2
	69/70	4		D2
	70/71	4		D2
	71/72	23		D2
	72/73	30		D1
	73/74	21		D1
Alloa A	74/75	38	5	D2
	75/76	26	1	D2
	76/77	35	3	D2
	77/78	21	2	D1

WILLIAMS Alfred Stanley
b. South Africa c1928 Caps: S Afr

Club	Season			Div
Aberdeen	37/38	1		D1
	38/39	5		D1
	46/47	23	5	D1
	47/48	17	6	D1
	48/49	26	6	D1
Plymouth A	49/50	35	4	FL
Dundee	50/51	21	3	D1
	51/52	7	1	D1

WILLIAMS Archibald
b. Edinburgh 13.5.1927 d. Edinburgh 29.9.1985
Loanhead Braeside

Club	Season			Div
Heart of Midlothian	47/48	19	1	D1
	48/49	8		D1
	49/50	1		D1
	50/51	15		D1
	51/52	2		D1
Motherwell	52/53	3	1	D1
	53/54	6	5	D2
	54/55	23	5	D1
	55/56	4		D1

WILLIAMS Evan Samuel
b. Dumbarton 15.7.1943
Duntochter Juveniles
Vale of Leven

Club	Season			Div
East Fife	T 63/64	2		D2
Third Lanark	64/65	26		D1
	65/66	24		D2
Wolverhampton W	66/67			FL
	67/68	13		FL
	68/69			FL
Aston Villa	L 69/70	12		FL
Celtic	69/70	16		D1
	70/71	31		D1
	71/72	20		D1
	72/73	15		D1
Clyde	74/75	21		D1
Arbroath	T 75/76			D1
Falkirk	75/76			D1

WILLIAMS Lawrence
b. Johnstone 16.11.1947
Port Glasgow

Club	Season			Div
Dumbarton	68/69			D2
	69/70	5		D2
	70/71	36		D2
	71/72	34		D2
	72/73	26		D1
	73/74	25		D1
	74/75	16		D1
	75/76	26		D1
	76/77	38		D1
	77/78	36		D1
	78/79	24		D1
	79/80	30		D1
	80/81			
Motherwell	L 80/81	4		D1
Dundee	L 80/81	4		D1

WILLIAMSON Arthur Hamilton
b. Stanley 26.7.1930

Club	Season			Div
Clyde	54/55	1		D1
Southend U	55/56	40		FL
	56/57	46	1	FL
	57/58	46		FL
	58/59	46		FL
	59/60	46		FL
	60/61	34	1	FL
	61/62	11		FL

WILLIAMSON James
b. Stanley
Blairgowrie

Club	Season			Div
Dunfermline A	55/56	10		D1

WILLIAMSON James

Club	Season			Div
Arbroath	65/66	1		D2
	66/67	36		D2
	67/68	33		D2
	68/69	17		D1

WILLIAMSON John

Club	Season			Div
Raith R	51/52	1		D1
	52/53	24		D1
	53/54	16		D1
	54/55	1		D1
	55/56	3		D1
	56/57	26	13	D1
	57/58	32	12	D1
	58/59	11		D1
Dunfermline A	58/59	7	2	D1
	59/60	19		D1
	60/61	26		D1
	61/62	27		D1
	62/63	3		D1

WILLIAMSON Richard
Armadale Thistle

Club	Season			Div
Partick T	61/62	11	2	D1
	62/63	2	1	D1
Berwick R	63/64	32	5	D2
	64/65	4		D2
Stenhousemuir *	64/65	13	2	D2
	65/66	24	3	D2

WILLIAMSON Robert
b. Edinburgh 6.12.1933

Club	Season			Div
Arbroath	59/60	33		D1
St Mirren	60/61	10		D1
	61/62	13		D1
	62/63	20		D1
Barnsley	63/64	15		FL
	64/65	31		FL
Leeds U	65/66			FL
Rochdale	66/67	34		FL
	67/68	2		FL
Chorley				

WILLIAMSON T

Club	Season			Div
Raith R	57/58	2		D1

WILLIAMSON William
b. Glasgow

Club	Season			Div
Rangers	46/47	5	6	D1
	47/48	7	3	D1
	48/49	6	2	D1
	49/50	19	11	D1
	50/51	6	2	D1
St Mirren	51/52	4	1	D1
	52/53	2	1	D1
Stirling A	53/54	25	2	D1
	54/55	13	1	D1
	55/56	15	3	D1

WILLIAMSON William
b. Dumfries 29.9.1952
Kirkconnel Amateurs

Club	Season				Div
Aberdeen	70/71	1			D1
	71/72				D1
	72/73	12			D1
	73/74	2	2		D1
	74/75	27	4	9	D1
	75/76	35	1	8	P
Dundee U	76/77	7	4	1	P
Dundee	77/78	37		17	D1
	78/79	20	3	4	D1
	79/80	3	4		P
	80/81	15	5	1	D1
Brisbane Lions					

WILLOUGHBY Alexander Brown
b. Glasgow 17.9.1944

Club	Season				Div
Rangers	62/63	3		2	D1
	63/64	6		3	D1
	64/65	5		2	D1
	65/66	23		6	D1
	66/67	11	1	16	D1
	67/68	20	3	10	D1
	68/69	2	1		D1
Aberdeen	69/70	18	1		D1
	70/71	10	9	2	D1
	71/72	26	3	7	D1
	72/73	22	4	1	D1
	73/74	8	3		D1
Hong Kong R					

WILSON Alexander
b. Stenhousemuir 13.7.1938

Club	Season			Div
Clyde	59/60	29	10	D1
	60/61	11		D1
Rotherham U	61/62	5		FL
Falkirk	61/62	5	1	D1

WILSON Alexander
Shotts Bon Accord

Club	Season			Div
Aberdeen	62/63	5	1	D1
	63/64	4		D1
	64/65	2		D1
Albion R				

WILSON Andrew

Club	Season			Div
Partick T	46/47	3		D1
	47/48	2		D1
	48/49	5	1	D1
	49/50	3		D1
Kilmarnock	50/51	5		D2
Montrose	51/52			D3

WILSON Brian
Arbroath Victoria

Club	Season			Div
Arbroath	73/74	2		D1
	74/75	13		D1
	75/76	10		D1
Heart of Midlothian	76/77	9		P
Nairn Co				
Stenhousemuir	77/78	34		D2
	78/79	34		D2
	79/80	20		D2

WILSON David B
b. Glasgow 10.1.1939 Caps: S - 22
Baillieston Jnrs

Club	Season				Div
Rangers	56/57	6		1	D1
	57/58	12		2	D1
	58/59	15		2	D1
	59/60	27		8	D1
	60/61	34		19	D1
	61/62	29		15	D1
	62/63	32		23	D1
	63/64	16		6	D1
	64/65	25		10	D1
	65/66	12		6	D1
	66/67	17	2	6	D1
Dundee U	67/68	30		8	D1
	68/69	22	5	4	D1
	69/70	30	2	6	D1
	70/71	33	1	2	D1
	71/72	5	3		D1
Dumbarton	72/73	31	3		D1

WILSON George

Stranraer

Club	Season	Apps	Sub	Goals	Div
St Mirren	46/47	3		3	D1
	47/48				D1
	48/49	2			D1
Hamilton A	48/49	1			D2

WILSON Harry
b. c1935
Worcester C 54/55

Club	Season	Apps	Sub	Goals	Div
Clyde	55/56	1			D1

WILSON Hugh
b. c1934 d. ?.9.1992
Hibernian
Lochore Welfare

Club	Season	Apps	Sub	Goals	Div
East Fife	54/55	7		1	D1
	55/56	3		1	D1
	56/57	6			D1

Lochore Welfare

WILSON James

Club	Season	Apps	Sub	Goals	Div
Third Lanark	52/53	4			D1

WILSON James
b. Newmains 20.4.1942
Shotts Bon Accord

Club	Season	Apps	Sub	Goals	Div
Newcastle U	59/60				FL
	60/61	2			FL
	61/62	10		2	FL
Morton	62/63				D2
	63/64	28		17	D2
	64/65	26		2	D1
Aberdeen	65/66	34		8	D1
	66/67	31		13	D1
	67/68	10		3	D1
Motherwell	67/68	20		4	D1
	68/69	31		6	D2
	69/70	33		1	D1
Dundee	70/71	19	2		D1
	71/72	15	4	1	D1
	72/73	20	1	3	D1
	73/74	22	1	4	D1
	74/75	3	2		D1
Falkirk	74/75	10		1	D2
	75/76	17	1	3	D1
	76/77	9	1	3	D1
	77/78	7		3	D2
	78/79	4			D2

Elgin C

WILSON James

Club	Season	Apps	Sub	Goals	Div
Dundee U	61/62	1			D1

WILSON James

Club	Season	Apps	Sub	Goals	Div
Raith R	69/70	2			D1

WILSON James Murray
b. Saltcoats 19.3.1923

Club	Season	Apps	Sub	Goals	Div
Queen of the South	47/48	1			D1
Dundalk	48/49				
Accrington S	49/50	4			FL

WILSON John

Club	Season	Apps	Sub	Goals	Div
Falkirk	50/51	13			D1
	51/52	29		4	D2
	52/53	4			D1

WILSON John
Ardeer Recreation

Club	Season	Apps	Sub	Goals	Div
St Mirren	55/56				D1
	56/57	11			D1
	57/58	32		7	D1
	58/59	25		5	D1
	59/60	28			D1
	60/61	31			D1
	61/62	34			D1
	62/63	17			D1
	63/64	22		4	D1
	64/65	29		2	D1
	65/66	1			D1
	66/67	2			D1

WILSON John

Club	Season	Apps	Sub	Goals	Div
Partick T	56/57	1			D1
	57/58	2			D1
	58/59	20		6	D1
	59/60	4		1	D1
Stirling A	60/61				D2
	61/62	2			D1

WILSON Kenneth Malcolm
b. Dumbarton 15.9.1946
Beith

Club	Season	Apps	Sub	Goals	Div
St Johnstone	68/69	4		2	D1
	69/70	7	2	3	D1
Dumbarton	70/71	36		28	D2
	71/72	35	1	38	D2
	72/73	4			D2
Carlisle U	72/73	14	6	1	FL
York C	L 73/74	2			FL
Workington	L 74/74	4	1		FL
Hamilton A	73/74	8	2	2	D2

WILSON Patrick
b. High Valleyfield c1946
Blairhall Jnrs

Club	Season	Apps	Sub	Goals	Div
Dunfermline A	63/64				D1
	64/65	1			D1
	65/66	5		2	D1
Aberdeen	66/67	5			D1
	67/68		1		D1
Raith R	67/68	9		1	D1
	68/69	31		4	D1
	69/70	13	2	2	D1
	70/71			5	D2
Berwick R	71/72	29		4	D2
	72/73	15	3	1	D2
	73/74	11	4	2	D2
	74/75	10	4	2	D2
Cowdenbeath	75/76	1	3		D2

WILSON Paul
b. Milngavie 23.11.1950 Caps: S - 1
Maryhill Jnrs

Club	Season	Apps	Sub	Goals	Div
Celtic	66/67				D1
	67/68				D1
	68/69				D1
	69/70				D1
	70/71	1			D1
	71/72	2	2	1	D1
	72/73	2	2	1	D1
	73/74	10	9	5	D1
	74/75	31	2	13	D1
	75/76	18	8	4	P
	76/77	19	5	5	P
	77/78	14	6	1	P
	78/79		1		P
Motherwell	78/79	18	3	1	P
Partick T	79/80	1	9		P

Blantyre Celtic

WILSON Robert
b. Motherwell

Club	Season	Apps	Sub	Goals	Div
Airdrieonians	47/48	1			D1
Stirling A	47/48				D2
	48/49				D2
	49/50	13			D1
	50/51				D2
	51/52	6			D1
	52/53				D2
Workington	52/53	2			FL
Stenhousemuir	53/54	22			D2

WILSON Robert
Newarthill Hearts

Club	Season	Apps	Sub	Goals	Div
Hamilton A	51/52	14			D2
	52/53	14		1	D2
	53/54	20			D1
Stranraer	54/55				D3

Albion R

WILSON Robert
b. Kirkcaldy
Dundonald Bluebell

Club	Season	Apps	Sub	Goals	Div
Cowdenbeath	61/62	8		2	D2
	62/63				D2
	63/64	36			D2
	64/65	36			D2
Dundee	65/66	11			D1
	66/67	15			D1
	67/68	34		1	D1
	68/69	34		1	D1
	69/70	22		1	D1
	70/71	32		3	D1
	71/72	32			D1
	72/73	32	1		D1
	73/74	31	2	1	D1
	74/75	33		1	D1
	75/76	17			P

Lossiemouth

WILSON Robert Smail Whitelaw
b. Musselburgh 29.6.1934
Musselburgh

Club	Season	Apps	Sub	Goals	Div
Aberdeen	54/55				D1
	55/56	13		1	D1
	56/57	7			D1
Norwich C	57/58	45			FL
	58/59	17			FL
	59/60				FL
Gillingham	60/61	35			FL
Accrington S	61/62				FL
Chester	62/63	15			FL

GKN Sankey

WILSON Samuel
b. Glasgow 16.12.1931
Uddingston BC
Renfrew Jnrs

Club	Season	Apps	Sub	Goals	Div
St Mirren	51/52	6		4	D1
	52/53	5			D1
	53/54	10		2	D1
	54/55	8		3	D1
	55/56	7		1	D1
	56/57	16			D1
Celtic	57/58	33		23	D1
	58/59	14		3	D1
Millwall	59/60	23		11	FL
Northampton T	60/61				FL

Ross Co

WILSON Samuel J
b. Dromore c1937 Caps: NI - 12
Downshire YM
Crusaders

Team	Season				
Glenavon	55/56				
	56/57				
	57/58				
	58/59				
	59/60				
	60/61				
	61/62				
	62/63				
Falkirk	63/64	25		17	D1
	64/65	21		5	D1
	65/66	14		5	D1
Dundee	65/66	7		3	D1
	66/67	18	1	9	D1
	67/68	24		6	D1
	68/69				D1
Coleraine	68/69				
	69/70				
	70/71				
Glenavon	71/72				

WILSON Thomas

Team	Season			
Clyde	59/60	12		D1
	60/61	4		D1

WILSON Thomas
Largs Thistle

Team	Season				
St Johnstone	66/67	10		3	D1
	67/68	18	2	3	D1
	68/69	1			D1

WILSON Thomas
b. Glasgow 10.11.1950
Sandyhills YC

Team	Season				
Aberdeen	69/70	9	2	1	D1
	70/71				D1
	71/72	7			D1
	72/73	9			D1
Elgin C					

WILSON William
b. Dumfries

Team	Season			
Queen of the South	46/47	16		D1
	47/48	7		D1
	48/49			D1
	49/50	1		D1
Clyde	50/51	1		D1
	51/52			D2
	52/53	28		D1
	53/54	27		D1
	54/55	15		D1
	55/56	11		D1

WILSON William
Sauchie

Team	Season			
Raith R	60/61	10		D1
	61/62	18		D1
	62/63	28	1	D1
	63/64	30		D2
	64/65	17	1	D2

WILSON William
b. Wallyford c1943 d. ?.11.2001
Musselburgh Windsor

Team	Season			
Hibernian	59/60	13		D1
	60/61			D1
	61/62			D1
	62/63	4		D1
	63/64	3		D1
	64/65	33		D1
	65/66	21		D1
	66/67	3		D1
	67/68	20		D1
	68/69	18		D1
Berwick R	69/70	30		D2
	70/71			D2
	71/72	33		D2
	72/73	35		D2
	73/74			D2
Cowdenbeath	74/75	27		D2
	75/76	23		D2
	76/77	21		D2

WILSON William
Kilsyth R

Team	Season				
Airdrieonians	67/68	10	1		D1
	68/69	27	1	2	D1
	69/70	22		5	D1
	70/71	33		8	D1
	71/72	32	1	3	D1
	72/73	24		1	D1
	73/74	28	4	11	D2
	74/75	23	1	5	D1
	75/76	25		6	D1
	76/77	30	1	3	D1
	77/78	10	2	2	D1
	78/79	1	3		D1

WINCHESTER Ernest T
b. Aberdeen 18.5.1944
Torry FPs

Team	Season				
Aberdeen	61/62	2			D1
	62/63	25		17	D1
	63/64	27		16	D1
	64/65	21		13	D1
	65/66	30		16	D1
	66/67	15	3	10	D1
Chicago Spurs	67	13		13	NA
Kansas City Spurs	68	27		10	NA
Heart of Midlothian	68/69	1			D1
	69/70	13	2	3	D1
	70/71	5	4	1	D1
	71/72	21	1	2	D1
Arbroath	72/73	33			D1

WING Lennart
b. c1935 Caps: Swe - 36
Orgryte

Team	Season			
Dundee U	64/65	13		D1
	65/66	24	7	D1
	66/67	31	2	D1
Kingsbacka BI				
Orgryte				

WISHART Robert
b. Edinburgh c1941
Merchiston Thistle

Team	Season			
Aberdeen	52/53			
Portadown	L 52/53			
Aberdeen	53/54	8	2	D1
	54/55	23	7	D1
	55/56	32	8	D1
	56/57	29	9	D1
	57/58	27	7	D1
	58/59	32	8	D1
	59/60	24	4	D1
	60/61	3		D1
Dundee	60/61	15		D1
	61/62	29	6	D1
	62/63	29	1	D1
	63/64	3		D1
Airdrieonians	64/65	6		D1
Raith R *	64/65	9	3	D2

WOOD

Team	Season		
Raith R	69/70	1	D1

WOOD A

Team	Season		
Raith R	60/61	1	D1

WOOD Albert

Team	Season			
Raith R	51/52	9	2	D1
	52/53	6		D1

WOOD Robert
b. Elphinstone 15.2.1930

Team	Season			
Hibernian	50/51	5	2	D1
Barnsley	51/52	20	4	FL
	52/53	6		FL
	53/54	4		FL
	54/55	35	12	FL
	55/56	38	8	FL
	56/57	14	1	FL
	57/58	35	6	FL
	58/59	23	5	FL
	59/60			FL
	60/61	12		FL
	61/62	38	3	FL
	62/63	29		FL
	63/64	40		FL
	64/65	24		FL

WOOD Wilson
b. Whitburn 25.1.1943
Lothian U
Shotts Bon Accord

Team	Season				
Newcastle U	61/62				FL
Rangers	61/62				D1
	62/63				D1
	63/64	4			D1
	64/65	26		3	D1
	65/66	5		1	D1
Dundee U	67/68	32	1	2	D1
	68/69	34		3	D1
	69/70				D1
Heart of Midlothain	70/71	15			D1
	71/72	10			D1
	72/73	7		1	D1
Raith R	73/74	23		1	D2
	74/75	17	4		D2

WOODBURN William Alexander
b. Edinburgh 8.8.1919
d. Edinburgh 2.12.2001 Caps: S - 24
Edinburgh Ashton
Musselburgh A
Queens Park Victoria

Team	Season			
Rangers	46/47	18		D1
	47/48	23		D1
	48/49	30		D1
	49/50	29		D1
	50/51	28	1	D1
	51/52	27		D1
	52/53	27		D1
	53/54	21		D1
	54/55	1		D1

WOODCOCK James
b. Aberdeen

Team	Season		
Raith R	49/50	11	D1
	50/51	2	D1
St Johnstone	51/52	11	D2
	52/53	27	D2
	53/54	27	D2
	54/55	26	D2
	55/56	25	D2
	56/57	28	D2
Keith			

WOODS John
b. Glasgow

Team	Season			
Rangers	54/55	1		D1
	55/56			D1
Hamilton A	L 55/56	17	11	D2
	56/57	30	8	D2

WOODS Norman

Club	Season	Apps	Goals	Div
Dunfermline A	56/57	3		D1

WOOTTON Leonard
b. Stoke 13.6.1925 d. Hartshill 9.9.1990
Everton

Club	Season	Apps	Goals	Div
Port Vale	46/47	10	1	FL
Northwich V	47/48			
	48/49			
	49/50			
Queen of the South	49/50	11	1	D1
	50/51			D2
Wrexham	51/52	20	2	FL

WREN John Mackie
b. Bonnybridge 26.4.1936

Club	Season	Apps	Goals	Div
Hibernian	56/57	21		D1
	57/58	1		D1
	58/59	3		D1
	59/60	6		D1
Rotherham U	60/61	1		FL
Stirling A	61/62	11		D1
Dundee U	62/63			D1

WRIGHT Alexander
b. Glasgow c1930 d. Linwood 12.1.2000
Dalry Thistle

Club	Season	Apps	Goals	Div
Partick T	48/49	7		D1
	49/50	6	1	D1
	50/51			
	51/52	5	3	D1
	52/53	9	1	D1
	53/54	28	12	D1
	54/55	28	1	D1
	55/56	25	10	D1
	56/57	22	7	D1
	57/58	22	7	D1
	58/59	25	6	D1
	59/60	22	1	D1
	60/61	30	3	D1
	61/62	2		D1
	62/63			D1
East Fife	63/64	32	5	D2

WRIGHT Alexander Mason
b. Kirkcaldy 18.10.1925
Bowhill R

Club	Season	Apps	Goals	Div
Hibernian	46/47	2		D1
Barnsley	47/48	20	5	FL
	48/49	16	5	FL
	49/50	41	17	FL
	50/51	7	4	FL
Tottenham H	50/51	2	1	FL
Bradford PA	51/52	37	12	FL
	52/53	36	9	FL
	53/54	34	1	FL
	54/55	25	3	FL
Falkirk	55/56	31	11	D1
	56/57	22	3	D1
	57/58	17	1	D1
	58/59	23	5	D1
Arbroath	59/60	23		D1
Stenhousemuir				

WRIGHT Archibald Watson
b. Glasgow 23.11.1924 d. ?.?.1990
Rutherglen Glencairn

Club	Season	Apps	Goals	Div
Hamilton A	47/48	28	13	D2
Clyde	48/49	30	13	D1
	49/50	2		D1
Falkirk	49/50	14	3	D1
	50/51	20	4	D1
Blackburn R	51/52	13	5	FL
	52/53	9	5	FL
Grimsby T	53/54	39	9	FL
Accrington S	54/55	46	15	FL
	55/56	31	12	FL
	56/57	3		FL
Netherfield				

WRIGHT Douglas
Blantyre Celtic

Club	Season	Apps	Goals	Div
Partick T	60/61	1	1	D1
	61/62	1		D1
	62/63			D1
	63/64	2		D1
Pan Hellenic (Aus)				

WRIGHT Ian
Auchtermuchty Jnrs

Club	Season	Apps	Goals	Div
East Fife	52/53	4	2	D1

WRIGHT John
Petershill

Club	Season	Apps	Goals	Div
Clyde	63/64			D2
	64/65			D1
	65/66	18		D1
	66/67	11		D1
	67/68	26		D1
	68/69	20		D1
	69/70	11		D1

WRIGHT R

Club	Season	Apps	Goals	Div
Queen of the South	62/63	1		D1

WRIGHT Ronald William
b. Falkirk 6.12.1940
Shettleston

Club	Season	Apps	Goals	Div
Leeds U	59/60			FL
	60/61	1		FL
St Johnstone	60/61	5	1	D1
	61/62	10	2	D1
	62/63	1		D2
Guildford C				

WRIGHT Thomas
b. Clackmannan 20.1.1928 Caps: S - 3
Blairhall Colliery

Club	Season	Apps	Goals	Div
Partick T	47/48	25	15	D1
	48/49	8	5	D1
Sunderland	48/49	12	1	FL
	49/50	42	13	FL
	50/51	34	10	FL
	51/52	4	1	FL
	52/53	35	9	FL
	53/54	38	18	FL
	54/55	5		FL
East Fife	54/55	10	6	D1
	55/56	24	10	D1
	56/57	2	2	D1
Oldham A	56/57	7	2	FL

WYLES William
Windygates Thistle
Brechin C

Club	Season	Apps	Goals	Div
Falkirk	61/62	5	1	D1
East Fife	62/63			D2
	63/64			D2
Brechin C	63/64	14	1	D2

WYLIE Alan
b. c1837 d. ?.?.1973
Penicuik A

Club	Season	Apps	Goals	Div
Motherwell	57/58	12		D1
	58/59	3		D1
	59/60	1		D1
	60/61	5		D1
	61/62	13		D1
	62/63	34		D1
	63/64	31		D1
	64/65	29		D1
	65/66	2		D1
	66/67	2		D1
	67/68			D1
Cowdenbeath	68/69			D2
	69/70	33		D2
	70/71	19		D1

WYLIE Charles
Tannochside

Club	Season	Apps	Goals	Div
Airdrieonians	69/70	1		D1
	70/71			D1
	71/72			D1
Albion R	72/73	30	3	D2
	73/74		3	D2

WYLIE Gordon
Bellfield BC
Darvel Jnrs

Club	Season	Apps	Goals	Div
Kilmarnock	70/71	1		D1

YARD Ernest John
b. Stranraer 3.5.1941

Club	Season	Apps	Goals	Div
Stranraer	58/59			D2
	59/60			D2
	60/61			D2
Kilmarnock	60/61			D1
	61/62	15	9	D1
	62/63	9	7	D1
	63/64	1		D1
Partick T	63/64	15	5	D1
Bury	63/64	20	4	FL
	64/65	25	9	FL
Crystal Palace	65/66	33	1 3	FL
	66/67	2	1	FL
Reading	66/67	29		FL
	67/68	38	1 3	FL
	68/69	34	2 3	FL
Cape Town C				

YEATS Ronald
b. Aberdeen 15.11.1937 Caps: S - 2
Aberdeen Lads Club

Club	Season	Apps	Goals	Div
Dundee U	57/58	15		D2
	58/59	19		D2
	59/60	33	1	D2
	60/61	28		D1
Liverpool	61/62	41		FL
	62/63	38		FL
	63/64	36	1	FL
	64/65	35		FL
	65/66	42	2	FL
	66/67	40	2	FL
	67/68	38	2	FL
	68/69	39	2	FL
	69/70	37	3	FL
	70/71	11 1	1	FL
Tranmere R	71/72	19	2	FL
	72/73	42	1	FL
	73/74	35 1	2	FL
Stalybridge C	74/75			
Barrow	75/76			
	76/77			

YORSTON Henry
b. Aberdeen 9.6.1929
d. Aberdeen 16.5.1992 Caps: S - 1
Aberdeen St Clements

Club	Season	Apps	Goals	Div
Aberdeen	47/48	6	6	D1
	48/49			D1
	49/50	26	10	D1
	50/51	29	18	D1
	51/52	27	19	D1
	52/53	19	6	D1
	53/54	16	7	D1
	54/55	28	12	D1
	55/56	30	12	D1
	56/57	20	8	D1
Buckie Thistle				
Fraserburgh				
Deveronvale				
Lossiemouth				

YOUNG Alexander
b. Glasgow
Blantyre Victoria

Club	Season				Div
Aberdeen	50/51	26			D1
	51/52	19			D1
	52/53	23			D1
	53/54	27		1	D1
	54/55	30			D1
	55/56	12			D1
	56/57	26			D1
	57/58	5			D1

YOUNG Alexander
b. Loanhead 3.2.1937 Caps: S - 8
Broughton Star
Musselburgh Union
Newtongrange Star

Club	Season				Div
Heart of Midlothian	55/56	27		15	D1
	56/57	27		6	D1
	57/58	34		24	D1
	58/59	27		7	D1
	59/60	28		23	D1
	60/61	10		2	D1
Everton	60/61	13		6	FL
	61/62	40		14	FL
	62/63	42		22	FL
	63/64	27		12	FL
	64/65	20		3	FL
	65/66	26		7	FL
	66/67	35		8	FL
	67/68	24	1	5	FL
Glentoran	68/69				
Stockport Co	68/69	23		5	FL

YOUNG Andrew
b. Oakley 21.6.1925
Steelend Victoria
Dunfermline A   T
Celtic

Club	Season				Div
Raith R	46/47				D2
	47/48				D2
	48/49				D2
	49/50	13			D1
	50/51	30		18	D1
	51/52	29		6	D1
	52/53	30		7	D1
	53/54	29		10	D1
	54/55	30		10	D1
	55/56	28		6	D1
	56/57	33		1	D1
	57/58	31		1	D1
	58/59	28		7	D1
	59/60	27		5	D1

YOUNG Andrew
b. Milton of Campsie 15.3.1950
Glasgow U

Club	Season				Div
Heart of Midlothian	67/68				D1
	68/69				D1
	69/70				D1
	70/71	9	5		D1
Airdrieonians	71/72	7	4	1	D1
Hamilton A	72/73	34		7	D2
	73/74	36		4	D2
	74/75	16	1		D2
	75/76	23	2	1	D1
	76/77	24	2	3	D1
	77/78	29	1		D1
	78/79	9	1		D1
	79/80	7	1		D1
	80/81	1	1		D1
Montrose	81/82	25	4		D2

YOUNG David

Club	Season				Div
St Mirren	66/67	9			D1
	67/68	1			D2

YOUNG George Lewis
b. Grangemouth 27.10.1922
d. 10.1.1997 Caps: S - 53
Kirkintilloch Rob Roy

Club	Season				Div
Rangers	46/47	28		4	D1
	47/48	15		1	D1
	48/49	28		3	D1
	49/50	30		3	D1
	50/51	30		1	D1
	51/52	28		3	D1
	52/53	29		5	D1
	53/54	20			D1
	54/55	28		1	D1
	55/56	29			D1
	56/57	28		1	D1

YOUNG Harry
Cowdenbeath

Club	Season				Div
Dunfermline A	55/56	3		1	D1

YOUNG Ian
b. 21.5.1943
Neilston Waverley

Club	Season				Div
Celtic	62/63	5			D1
	63/64	29			D1
	64/65	33			D1
	65/66	16		2	D1
	66/67	1			D1
	67/68				D1
St Mirren	68/69	13			D1
	69/70	8	1		D1

YOUNG Ian Robert
St Rochs

Club	Season				Div
Airdrieonians	74/75		2		D1
	75/76	2			D1
Clydebank	76/77	1			D1

YOUNG James

Club	Season				Div
Third Lanark	47/48	18			D1

YOUNG James

Club	Season				Div
Forfar A	67/68	13	1	10	D2
	68/69			22	D2
St Mirren	69/70	11	2	3	D1
Montrose	70/71			23	D2
	71/72	26	3	14	D2
Forfar A	72/73	30		8	D2
	73/74	9		5	D2
Brechin C	73/74	18	2	2	D2
	74/75	34		12	D2
	75/76	9	2	2	D2

YOUNG John
Carnoustie Panmure

Club	Season				Div
Dundee	54/55	1			D1
	55/56				D1
	56/57	1			D1
Arbroath	57/58				D2
	58/59				D2
	59/60	29			D1
East Fife	60/61				D2
	61/62	36			D2
	62/63				D2
	63/64	36			D2
	64/65	35			D2
St Mirren	65/66	4			D1
Keith					
Forfar A	66/67	1			D2
	67/68	22		1	D2
	68/69				D2
	69/70	4			D2

YOUNG John

Club	Season				Div
Hibernian	58/59	2			D1
	59/60	28		2	D1
	60/61	7			D1
	61/62	4			D1
Toronto C	62				
St Johnstone	62/63	7			D2
Toronto C	63				
	64				
	65				

YOUNG John
b. Edinburgh 22.10.1951
Edinburgh A

Club	Season				Div
Hibernian	70/71			1	D1
Broxburn A					
Falkirk	72/73	15	2	3	D1
	73/74	6	9	3	D1
St Mirren	74/75	38		1	D2
	75/76	24	2	1	D1
	76/77	31	7		D1
	77/78	17	8		P
	78/79	25	2	1	P
	79/80	25	2		P
	80/81	28			P
	81/82	5			P
Hong Kong R					
Queen of the South	82/83	3			D2
Morton	82/83				
Brechin C	83/84	38			D1
	84/85	27			D1
Arbroath	85/86	27			D2
	86/87	10			D2

YOUNG Joseph
Burnbank Swifts
Blantyre Celtic
Airdrieonians
Burnbank A

Club	Season				Div
Hamilton A	53/54	11			D1
	54/55	3			D2
	55/56	18			D2
	56/57	26			D2
	57/58	36			D2
	58/59	24		1	D2
	59/60	3			D2

YOUNG Quintin
b. Irvine 19.9.1947
Kello R

Club	Season				Div
Ayr U	68/69	2			D2
	69/70	32		5	D1
	70/71	33	1	4	D1
Coventry C	71/72	21		2	FL
	72/73	4	1		FL
Rangers	72/73	26		13	D1
	73/74	19	1	7	D1
	74/75	22	6	6	D1
	75/76	7	1	2	P
East Fife	76/77	30	1	3	D1
	77/78	22	1	5	D1
	78/79	10			D2
	79/80	3		1	D2
Whitletts Victoria					

YOUNG Robert
Neilston V

Club	Season				Div
Motherwell	59/60	4		1	D1
	60/61	6		2	D1
	61/62	16		4	D1
St Johnstone	62/63	35		15	D2
Celtic	63/64				D1
Dundee U	63/64	7		3	D1
	64/65				D1
Airdrieonians					
Berwick R	65/66	33		18	D2
Dumbarton	66/67	25	2	4	D2
Saltcoats V					

YOUNG T

Club	Season				Div
Falkirk	61/62	5		1	D1

YOUNG Thomas McIlwaine
b. Glasgow 24.12.1947
Stephens Juveniles

Falkirk	67/68	1	1		D1
	68/69	22	1	4	D1
	69/70	23	1	19	D2
	70/71	15	2	8	D1
	71/72	17	4	2	D1
Tranmere R	72/73	43		9	FL
	73/74	40		8	FL
	74/75	41		4	FL
	75/76	25	2	2	FL
	76/77	21		4	FL
Rotherham U	77/78	3	4		FL
	78/79	8		1	FL

YOUNG William

Clyde
Alloa A

Hamilton A	52/53	29	12	D2
	53/54	12	2	D1

Stenhousemuir

YOUNG William David
b. Edinburgh 25.11.1951
Seton A

Falkirk	T			
Aberdeen	69/70			D1
	70/71	9		D1
	71/72	26	3	D1
	72/73	30	2	D1
	73/74	34	2	D1
	74/75	31	3	D1
	75/76	3		P
Tottenham H	75/76	35	2	FL
	76/77	19	1	FL
Arsenal	76/77	14	1	FL
	77/78	35	3	FL
	78/79	33		FL
	79/80	38	3	FL
	80/81	40	4	FL
	81/82	10		FL
Nottingham F	81/82	25	1	FL
	82/83	34	4	FL
Norwich C	83/84	5	1	FL
Brighton & HA	L 83/84	4		FL
Darlington	84/85	4		FL

YOUNGER Thomas
b. Edinburgh 10.4.1930
d. Edinburgh 13.1.1984 Caps: S - 24
Hutcheson Vale

Hibernian	48/49	4	D1
	49/50	29	D1
	50/51	29	D1
	51/52	24	D1
	52/53	27	D1
	53/54	11	D1
	54/55	24	D1
	55/56	33	D1
Liverpool	56/57	40	FL
	57/58	39	FL
	58/59	41	FL
Falkirk	59/60	6	D2
Stoke C	59/60	10	FL
	60/61		FL
Toronto C	61		
Leeds U	61/62	31	FL
	62/63	6	FL

YULE John

Aberdeen EE

Aberdeen	59/60	1	D1

YULE Thomas E
b. Glasgow 27.1.1953
Beith

Arbroath	73/74		7		D1
	74/75	17	4	4	D1
	75/76	20	4	7	D1
	76/77	30	3	13	D1
	77/78	26	10	4	D1
	78/79	33	6	9	D1
	79/80	36	3	10	D1
	80/81	19	8	3	D2
	81/82	19	8	9	D2
	82/83	8			D2

ZIESING Kenneth
b. South Africa c1927 Caps: SAf

Dundee	50/51	3	3	D1
	51/52	12	3	D1
	52/53	23	1	D1
	53/54	7		D1

THE FIRST DIVISION PLAYING RECORD 1946/47 to 1974/75

	No. of Seasons	Champs	Home:						Away:						Totals			
			P	W	D	L	F	A	W	D	L	F	A	TF	TA	Points	% won
Aberdeen	29	1	950	253	105	117	1064	627	165	94	216	742	850	1806	1477	1035	44.00
Airdrieonians	23		762	157	73	151	740	759	82	78	221	495	963	1235	1722	629	31.36
Albion Rovers	1		30	3	1	11	18	44	0	1	14	12	61	30	105	8	10.00
Arbroath	5		170	25	18	42	128	157	8	17	60	76	229	204	386	101	19.41
Ayr United	10		340	71	43	56	251	242	31	35	104	191	403	442	645	282	30.00
Celtic	29	10	950	306	92	77	1204	515	234	93	148	963	665	2167	1180	1265	56.84
Clyde	24		784	161	87	144	703	653	106	83	203	574	875	1277	1528	704	34.06
Cowdenbeath	1		34	1	2	14	13	39	6	1	10	20	38	33	77	17	20.59
Dumbarton	3		102	13	17	21	68	77	11	11	29	62	108	130	185	76	23.53
Dundee	28	1	920	270	84	106	1004	586	139	121	200	681	804	1685	1390	1023	44.46
Dundee Utd.	15		510	136	56	63	567	390	86	56	113	368	458	935	848	556	43.53
Dunfermline Athletic	18		612	151	64	91	666	477	84	69	153	411	564	1077	1041	603	38.40
East Fife	13		414	99	36	72	413	329	55	49	103	277	435	690	764	393	37.20
East Stirlingshire	1		34	4	2	11	19	36	1	0	16	18	55	37	91	12	14.71
Falkirk	24		784	147	97	148	667	652	80	81	231	483	942	1150	1594	632	28.95
Hamilton Academical	3		94	8	8	31	58	131	1	4	42	36	165	94	296	30	9.57
Heart of Midlothian	29	2	950	265	108	102	1072	604	197	107	171	858	770	1930	1374	1139	48.63
Hibernian	29	3	950	284	88	103	1180	608	202	85	188	900	849	2080	1457	1145	51.16
Kilmarnock	21	1	706	189	89	75	710	468	120	84	149	543	615	1253	1083	791	43.77
Morton	15		490	97	63	85	408	352	58	49	138	300	473	708	825	422	31.63
Motherwell	27		886	197	95	151	840	696	122	97	224	633	884	1473	1580	830	36.00
Partick Thistle	28		916	218	97	143	854	684	131	95	232	674	957	1528	1641	890	38.10
Queen of the South	14		444	98	45	79	429	416	39	41	142	243	587	672	1003	360	30.86
Queen's Park	4		128	18	9	37	98	136	14	7	43	90	172	188	308	80	25.00
Raith Rovers	17		554	112	60	105	509	451	63	49	165	382	666	891	1117	459	31.59
Rangers	29	11	950	338	74	63	1210	444	276	99	100	1022	562	2232	1006	1401	64.63
St Johnstone	14		476	99	53	86	401	383	57	59	122	307	473	708	856	424	32.77
St Mirren	24		780	167	78	145	682	634	79	80	231	489	909	1171	1543	650	31.54
Stirling Albion	11		358	51	33	95	237	360	18	29	132	171	535	408	895	200	19.27
Third Lanark	15		482	102	36	103	474	454	62	39	140	383	620	857	1074	403	34.02

SCOTTISH LEAGUE PLAYERS' RECORDS 1975/76 to 1999/2000

by Derek Gray and Steve Emms

Available by mail order from the publisher, price £12 including post and packing.

This was the first volume of what we expect to be a three-part set of Scottish Players' Records. It includes all players with at least one appearance in the Scottish Premier Division from 1975/76 to 1997/98 and in the first two seasons of the Scottish Premier League.

As with the volume in your hands, details of a player's career in other Leagues and with other clubs are given when known.

An "Abbott to Zetterlund" of Scottish football.